3 95

# The Major Poets:

## ENGLISH AND AMERICAN

*Edited by* CHARLES M. COFFIN, *Kenyon College*

*Harcourt, Brace & World, Inc.*
*New York and Burlingame*

## COPYRIGHTS AND ACKNOWLEDGMENTS

*The author thanks the following publishers and copyright holders for their
permission to use the selections reprinted in this book:*

FABER AND FABER, LIMITED, for Canadian rights to "Musée des Beaux Arts,"
"In Memory of W. B. Yeats," "Lay your sleeping head, my love,"
"September 1, 1939," "Fish in the unruffled lakes," and "Look, stranger,
on this island now" from W. H. Auden's *Collected Shorter Poems;* "In
Praise of Limestone" and "A Walk after Dark" from *Nones* by Auden;
T. S. Eliot's "The Love Song of J. Alfred Prufrock," "Gerontion,"
"Mr. Eliot's Sunday Morning Service," "Sweeney Among the Nightin-
gales," "Journey of the Magi" from *Collected Poems 1908-1935* and "The
Dry Salvages" from *Four Quartets.*

HARCOURT, BRACE AND COMPANY, INC., for "The Love Song of J. Alfred
Prufrock," "Gerontion," "Mr. Eliot's Sunday Morning Service," "Sweeney
Among the Nightingales," "Journey of the Magi," from *Collected Poems
1909-1935* by T. S. Eliot, copyright, 1936, by Harcourt, Brace and Com-
pany, Inc.; "The Dry Salvages" from *Four Quartets,* copyright, 1943, by
T. S. Eliot. Reprinted by permission of Harcourt, Brace and Company,
Inc.

HARPER AND BROTHERS for "Tell all the truth but tell it slant," "There is a
strength in knowing that it can be borne," and "Until the desert knows"
from *Bolts of Melody, New Poems of Emily Dickinson,* copyright, 1945,
by Millicent Todd Bingham. Reprinted by permission of the publishers.

HARVARD UNIVERSITY PRESS, whose *Collected Poems of Sir Thomas Wyatt,*
edited by Kenneth Muir, served as a basis for the text of "Is it possible?" and "Forget not yet the tried intent."

HENRY HOLT AND COMPANY for "The Vantage Point," "October," "Home
Burial," "Meeting and Passing," "The Oven Bird," "Range-Finding,"
"Stopping by Woods on a Snowy Evening," "Acquainted with the Night,"
"Come In," "The Most of It," "The Gift Outright," and "Directive"
from *Complete Poems of Robert Frost,* copyright 1930, 1947, 1949, by
Henry Holt and Company, Inc.; copyright 1936, 1942, by Robert Frost;
used by the permission of the publishers. For "To an Athlete Dying
Young," "Is my team ploughing," "On Wenlock Edge the wood's in
trouble," "Terence, this is stupid stuff," "Tell me not here, it needs not
saying," "Stars, I have seen them fall," "The farms of home lie lost in
even," "How clear, how lovely bright," "I did not lose my heart in summer's even," "Smooth between sea and land," and "The Olive" from
*The Collected Poems of A. E. Housman,* copyright 1922, 1940, by Henry
Holt and Company, Inc.; copyright 1936, 1950, by Barclays Bank, Ltd.
Reprinted by the permission of the publishers.

HOUGHTON MIFFLIN COMPANY for "Truth" and "Gentilesse" which are re-
printed from *The Complete Works of Geoffrey Chaucer,* edited by F. N.
Robinson, copyright by Houghton Mifflin Company, Boston (Student's
Cambridge Edition). Used by the courtesy of the publishers.

LITTLE, BROWN AND COMPANY for "I asked no other thing," "The soul
selects her own society," "Some things that fly there be," "I taste a liquor
never brewed," "A bird came down the walk," "The gentian weaves her
fringes," "Of all the souls that stand create," "The bustle in a house,"
"Because I could not stop for Death," "This world is not conclusion," "A
clock stopped—not the mantel's" from *Poems by Emily Dickinson,* edited

TO THE MEN OF KENYON COLLEGE WHO HAVE
READ POETRY WITH ME FOR MANY YEARS

*"Such pierlesse pleasures have we in these places."*

# Contents

v

# EDMUND SPENSER

# WILLIAM SHAKESPEARE

# BEN JONSON

vii

# To the Reader

THIS BOOK is an "anthology" of poets rather than of poems. As the Table of Contents shows, it represents poetry in English from Chaucer to the present with a generous selection from a limited number of our best poets. What it is and how it is that poetry contributes to the improvement and precision of our knowledge about the human situation and to the refinement of our sensibility, in my judgment, are better learned at first from a concentration upon the work of a few authors, such as we have here, rather than from scattering our attention over many isolated texts. My term "major poets" possibly needs definition. It assumes a poet who has a considerable production to his credit. Furthermore, if the work belongs to an earlier period, it must continue to discharge its duty as poetry even when subjected to hard study and criticism, or, for reasons which may never have been put down, it must persist for us as some inevitably right and satisfactory expression. If the work is of our own age, while standing up to the rigor of similar, close inspection, it must be felt to possess the present with a peculiar power and freshness at the same time that it admits comparison with traditional work. In this sense all of my thirty-four poets, I believe, can be said to enjoy a majority like that accorded Gerard Manley Hopkins by his critic who remarked that he was "a great or at least a major poet."

In assembling the particular titles, I have simply tried to include typical and important poems, representative so far as possible of different phases of a poet's career and of the different conditions of his art. At no time, however, have I wished to sacrifice quality merely for the sake of full illustration. Poets who perform best for us in their longer pieces obviously permit the choice of fewer titles. For instance, justice is hardly done to Chaucer's scope and mastery by a couple of lyrics and only one of the famous Tales; nor, to take a poet of our own time, is it entirely satisfactory to omit Eliot's *The Waste Land*, which has come to be a fixture in some collections. Nevertheless, we cannot be disappointed if what we do have is of Chaucer's best, or, if we have not allowed *The Waste Land*, with all of its power and novelty, to pre-empt the attention which the later and *positive* statement of *Four Quartets* deserves. That would have been to deny both to the poet and to ourselves the importance of the vision which Eliot's sustained devotions to his art and to its spiritual objects have earned. Moreover, the "waste land" tone is suggested—though not, of course, in the structured symbolic of the great poem—in shorter pieces which are included, notably in "Gerontion." Nor is it entirely suppressed in my selection, "The Dry Salvages," the one *Quartet* in which is mingled most evidently Eliot's sense of the substantial, inadequate world and his need to transcend it through assertion of what is seen by the spirit's eye.

A further example of the kind of situation which called for close decision has to do with W. B. Yeats, whose later work shows a complication and intensification of language clearly setting it off from the earlier poems. Yet, there remains the intrinsic merit of Yeats in the handling of the simpler, often more immediate things, and this aspect of the poet should be shown. Then, too, the transformation itself is a matter of literary concern. We should like to see the documents which report the young poet's exchange of the "linnet's wings" for the bird of "hammered gold and gold enamelling" some thirty years later, or those which trace the early romantic longing for the "bee-loud glade" of Innisfree into the old man's desire for something "out of nature" in Byzantium.

The reader will not expect to encounter the whole of big poems like *Don Juan, Paradise Lost,* or *The Faerie Queene* in this book. There are, however, large pieces from such works, for I found, contrary to earlier prejudice, that important excerpts could be made, particularly where the narrative permitted isolation of the coherent episode, or where there was a concentrated statement of the argument. Tennyson's "wild and wandering cries" in *In Memoriam,* it will be agreed, will tolerate abridgment without grossly ill effect; and the "characters" and incidents of Pope's *Epistles* actually invite independent presentation.

I have spoken as the "editor," I trust with modest justification, for with the exception of the poems which copyright has fixed, I have tried to exercise some judgment in establishing every text. A disappointing feature of so many collections of verse is the reticence of their compilers to name the original of their texts, or to account for the readings which they seem to endorse. I have consulted the early printed editions of the authors and have based my texts upon those which in my opinion give the most satisfactory reading of their poems. The principal "sources" are indicated (see page 540). I have not felt bound to a slavish reproduction of the "basic" text, however, if another occasionally provided a better version, or if the scholarly editions which had reconsidered existing manuscripts had made some reading unacceptable. It was not practical to note the detail of every departure from my chosen text, though I believe that all the noteworthy variations have been recorded.

I have taken but few liberties with original spellings and punctuation, having meant only to eliminate obvious errors and such typographical matters peculiar to a poet or his printers as would now be downright troublesome. The general principle followed here is simply this: poems were printed to be read—and reading poetry, as we are relearning to advantage, means also *reading aloud* —and spelling and punctuation directly affect the way we speak the poet's words. Hence, I have avoided revisions in spelling which would affect the sound of a word when spoken, or the metrical quantity of the line, and, in punctuation, changes which would influence the movement or cadence of the poet's language. There is, for example, from the sixteenth century onwards into the nineteenth century, as Tennyson makes clear—an almost universal respect for the final syllable of the imperfect tense in *ed*, and the similar participial ending. Remarking Shakespeare's ". . . well turned, and true filed lines," Ben Jonson means for *turned* and *filed* to receive their full syllabic value, just as he intends his spelling of "brandish't" a moment later to show the suppression of the suffix vowel. Usually then the reader will pronounce the *ed* when it appears in the earlier verse, or at least be aware of the possibility. There are exceptions, to be sure, but it is astonishing to note how habitually the poets mark this one distinction in their spelling. Our practice of marking the pronounced *ed* with the sign of the grave or acute accent has been avoided except where the poet himself has authorized its use.

Our present rules for punctuation are suited to the needs of prose, not verse. We officially punctuate according to the sentence-logic rather than the rhetoric, which would oblige us to respect the way the phrasing sounds and moves as well as what it openly intends to say. The poets will usually point their sentences to mark the emphatic period or the pace and motion of the language, on the ground that these considerations also contribute to the "sense," or affect the meaning; and I have generally tried to respect their intentions. In practice, it means that the common punctuation marks, from comma to period, are more likely to signify the different degrees of pause appropriate to the rhythm of the line or strophe, than a division of the grammatical elements to show their logical relations. Thus, the colon, particularly among the earlier poets, does not appear according to our usage, but as the sign of an emphatic pause just short of what the period itself commands; and the semicolon likewise indicates an interruption in the rhythm, though it does serve also on occasion as we use it to mark the separation of long co-ordinate elements. The comma is used variously, and more frequently or less, to dictate the rhythmical effect.

The poet may use it to separate independent constructions (our "comma fault"), or he may disregard what is our current practice of setting off the nonrestrictive or general sentence modifiers.

Nowhere, I dare say, among our texts, has the matter of punctuation been more debatable than in Shakespeare's sonnets. The poet presumably had nothing to do with their first publication in 1609, and sometimes the printer is obviously careless. Before concluding, however, that the text exists merely according to a printer's whim or some convention which the printer had more to do with than the author, we should reckon as I have done with the possibility that the punctuation as it stands contributes something to the movement of the poet's lines. This is a possibility to which modern editors have not always been sensitive enough. After all, "modernization"—unless we mean adherence to our academic rules—is a relative thing in verse; and rather than revise the texts according to the "secretary's handbook," we should try to conform our reading to the texts. Moreover, our efforts at bringing verse punctuation into agreement with that of prose appear to be posited too firmly upon silent reading; and, as remarked, we know now that a value is added to poetry by the voice. Although much of our reading will in fact be silent, we may nevertheless read aloud with the imagination, as if poetry were in truth a language in the mouths of men.

In the main, I have eliminated excessive capitalization and the use of italics, as they less directly influence the reading of the text. Even so, I have been more tolerant of the capitals than adequate respect for my authors really would have prescribed. It was my policy to retain them where they clearly signified personification of the abstract nouns; or where I had some sense that upper case conferred a special honor upon the word that reduction would have subdued. I freely admit the play of personal taste in this matter, as, in fact, it also must be granted to the poet in the first place—or the printer—for there is no strict consistency among the poets in this matter, nor none intended by the editor.

Regarding consistency in the mechanics of the text throughout, I have not thought it a virtue of sufficient weight to insist upon it, as the poets themselves were not fearful of this "hobgoblin." On the other hand, I have not indulged them in plain eccentricity. If my texts do not always "look" like those we are accustomed to find in similar collections, the observation is no doubt correct, for apart from the possible error that can get into a book like this, I have intended that the texts should rather closely reflect their "original" condition—and yet be eminently readable. Here a word on Chaucer is in order, for in the preparation of the text of his poems I have been necessarily obligated to his modern editors, as

I have elsewhere indicated. The text of "The Nun's Priest's Tale," however, does not reproduce the work of any one editor. It compromises several legitimate readings, often bringing the Middle English somewhat closer to us than any one of the "best" editions does. Where a permissible spelling, for example, approximated the modern spelling, or was the same, I have preferred it to another, equally authoritative but more obviously "archaic" to our eyes, and, at the same time, less likely to permit a ready adaptation to Chaucer's basic iambic metre. Such eclecticism may not recommend itself to orthodox Chaucerians, but there is much to be said for it here where the editor's first responsibility is to enlist the reader's interest in a great poem.

The poets appear in chronological order, and roughly their poems as well, so far as such an arrangement was either possible or practical. We simply do not know the date of every poem of every author; nor does every poet presumably wish his works to be read in the order of their composition. The 1645 volume of Milton's "minor poems" was carefully prepared for publication—by Milton himself—and yet *Lycidas* (1637) appears before the earlier *Comus;* and among recent poets, Dylan Thomas, for example, in his *Collected Poems* (1953) scrambles the order of his verses. Wordsworth's and Browning's "arrangements" are familiar to us; and Eliot, it will be remembered, regularly sets "Gerontion" before earlier pieces like "Mr. Eliot's Sunday Morning Service" and "Sweeney Among the Nightingales."

An approximation of chronology has, on the whole, seemed to me to be the best principle of arrangement. It suits the historical interest, obviously; and it permits the poems to appear free from manipulation into arbitrary categories. Formality in verse structure or kind is the only other principle which could be so readily justified; but if it could be applied convincingly, the result, I am sure, would obscure many of the interests which my arrangement allows us to discover. Schemes of classification, according to subjects or themes, the "serious lyric," the "religious poem," "symbolic poetry," etc., seem to me to be so generally private and capricious as—at least in my experience—to require the reader at once to set about resorting the titles to suit his own concerns.

The purpose of a note should be to help the reader to possess the text. Few periods, I dare say, have sought that possession more energetically than ours, and my notes mean to assist that effort. What one reader needs, another, it is true, may find superfluous; but it has seemed altogether reasonable to assume that our needs are rather large and that, accordingly, the help should be abundant —and near at hand, on the page with the text.

In the main, I have meant to inform rather than to explain; but as explanation is admittedly one method of informing, I have occasionally found it the only proper way of putting what I thought needed to be said. This is particularly true of notes on words and phrases, which although clear enough in their plain meaning, because of context, a condition of the syntax, or metaphorical function called for some comment. The moment, of course, one goes beyond the simple, formal gloss to attempt paraphrase or exposition he enters upon interpretation and so invites query and disagreement. The risk—if it is that—has seemed to be worth taking, in fact advisable. The only occasions for interpretation are precisely those where the meaning is closely packed and probably uncertain; and it has seemed the better part of honesty for me to give a definite opinion than to trust to an innocently phrased evasion, or to say nothing at all. Economy has obliged me often to be more positive than I should probably appear if opportunity were given for full argument. No single word, for instance, has its exact, inevitable equivalent in another. There are always several choices, each showing possibly only one facet of the poet's dense original term; but I have generally restricted myself to one or two alternatives of no more than central reference. My summary identification of Milton's "two-handed engine" (page 159) would be another example of such "risk" as I have taken, or my remarks on Marvell's "The Garden," or the commentary on Thomas's "In the beginning."

The frequent cross references will help to give the reader some sense of the large community of English and American poetry and also suggest specimens for comparative study or matter for the enlargement of illustration.

No one independently annotates so many poems; nor should one wish to conceal the help that many scholars and critics have given him. I have gladly made use of their work, directly—where acknowledgment is shown—and indirectly in the many ways that one comes to appropriate learning through long acquaintance with it. Whenever the notes or discussion in some book have given me a clue to the meaning or probable source of a phrase or an allusion, I have attempted to check the reference, rather more to satisfy curiosity and conscience than to verify its accuracy, though the latter interest has occasionally been profitable. More useful than the scholars, however, have been the authors whom the poets themselves read, so it is not surprising that the works of Homer, Plato, Virgil, and Ovid, and the English Bible have been the staple of my library. And it would be ungracious to pass over the dictionaries simply because of their usual air of anonymity. The *Oxford English Dictionary* has literally been indispensable, our *American Century Dictionary* constantly useful, and other "standard reference books" as well. I trust that my practice will invite their further use.

Few persons, I am bound to think, have been more generously assisted in the preparation of a book of this sort than I have been —in truth, I should be embarrassingly in debt if the help and suggestion had not been so freely given. While naming these friends and colleagues is a courtesy I owe to the reader, such brief process ought not to be taken as a measure of my gratitude. There are Hallet Smith and his colleagues, Paul Bowerman, Kent Clarke, Beach Langston, and Dan Piper of the California Institute of Technology; Paul McLane of Notre Dame University; F. P. Wilson, Merton College, Oxford; James and Aurelia Hallam of the Colorado A. and M.; Ernest Strathmann, Charles Holmes, and Ray Frazer of the Claremont Colleges; Marvin Felheim, the University of Michigan; Margaret Duckett, the University of Washington; John Moore and Nan Carpenter of Montana State University; William Ringler, Washington University (St. Louis); Frank Sullivan, Loyola University (Los Angeles); James Phillips and Philip Durham of UCLA; Mary Knapp, The Western College (Oxford, Ohio); Howard Babb, Ohio State University; Alexander Kern, the State University of Iowa; Elizabeth Boyd, the New Jersey College for Women; William Templeman, the University of Southern California; and the officers and members of the staff of the Henry E. Huntington Library, to whom I am grateful in a particular way for putting the books I needed so freely at my use and for other handsome cordialities and services. I reluctantly single out anyone from the Huntington community, but I would even more reluctantly refrain from mentioning especially French Fogle, Carey Bliss, and Mary Isabel Fry. The book was begun under the supervision of William Borst of Harcourt, Brace and Company. He died tragically soon afterwards, but not before his scholarship and imagination had made their impression upon me. I remember him affectionately and gratefully.

Nearer at home, of course, one meets the persons who somehow are always responsible for one's enterprise and interests, and I cordially acknowledge an enviable debt to my Kenyon colleagues, especially Philip Timberlake, Denham Sutcliffe, and John Crowe Ransom, with whom long conversation about "the poetry of earth"—and men I readily account the "fair guerdon" of my teaching years. And lastly there are the young men who have listened while I read poems to them, and have made the everlastingly right response—and to them I have modestly assigned the book.

C. M. C

## NOTE ON READING CHAUCER'S ENGLISH:

Chaucer's language (late Middle English), like our own, is not a fixed and uniform phenomenon; hence, a simple, unqualified description of its operations is impossible. The following generalizations are offered merely as preliminary helps to a first reading. Pronounce all the syllables in a word. (Final *e,* silent in Modern English, is ordinarily pronounced.) *Vowels* are short and long. Length, commonly though not consistently, is indicated by doubling the vowel. Pronounce the vowels according to their so-called Continental value (e.g., as in Modern French).

| Chaucer's spelling | Example | Sound | Pronounce like |
|---|---|---|---|
| a, aa | *bathed* | ā | *a* in *father* |
| a | *whan* | ă | *a* in German *Mann* |
| e, ee | *swe(e)te* | ē (close) | *e* in *they* |
| e, ee | *eek* | ē (open) | *e* in *where* |
| e | *tendre* | ĕ | *e* in *let* |
| e | *soote* | e | *a* in *about* |
| i, y | *ryde* | ī | *i* in *machine* |
| i, y | *his* | ĭ | *i* in *sit* |
| o, oo | *roote* | ō (close) | *o* in *vote* |
| o, oo | *holt* | ō (open) | *oa* in *broad* |
| o | *on* | ŏ | *o* in *hot* |
| ou, ow, ogh | *fowles* | ū | *oo* in *toot* |
| u, o | *yonge* | ŭ | *u* in *full* |
| u, eu, ew | *vertu* | iū | *u* in *mute* |
| au, aw | *straunge* | au | *ou* in *mouse* |

*Consonants.* Pronunciation according to Modern English in general is a safe guide. But: there are no silent consonants except *h* in French words like *honour; g* in French *gn* (*resigne*). Pronounce *g, k, w* in native English *gn, kn* (*cn*), *wr*. Pronounce *gh* like *ch* in German *ich, doch.* Pronounce *ch* normally as in *chirp.* Pronounce *ng* as in *finger.* Pronounce *l* before *f, k, m.* Pronounce *r* with a trill.

*Meter.* Variations from the iambic pattern (Chaucer's normal measure) occur. Downright irregularities, however, are exceptional if all syllables are pronounced and if the regular *elision* (of final lightly stressed vowel with the initial vowel, or silent *h,* of a word immediately following) is respected.

# GEOFFREY CHAUCER  *c.* 1340–1400

## *Truth*

BALADE DE BON CONSEYL

Flee fro the prees, and dwelle with sothfastnesse,
Suffyce unto thy good, though it be smal;
For hord hath hate, and climbing tikelnesse,
Prees hath envye, and wele blent overal;
Savour no more than thee bihove shal;      5
Reule wel thyself, that other folk canst rede;
And trouthe thee shal delivere, it is no drede.

Tempeste thee noght al croked to redresse,
In trust of hir that turneth as a bal:
Gret reste stant in litel besinesse;      10
Be war also to sporne ayeyns an al;
Stryve not, as doth the crokke with the wal.
Daunte thyself, that dauntest otheres dede;
And trouthe thee shal delivere, it is no drede.

TRUTH. *Bal(l)ade:* a French poetic form, which "Truth" well illus-
trates, usually of three stanzas, each with identical rhymes recurring in
the same order. Each stanza closes with a refrain, and the entire poem,
with an additional stanza, the *envoy.*
See note on opposite page on reading Chaucer's English.
 1 *prees:* crowd, busy world. *sothfastnesse:* truth. 2 *Suffyce . . .
smal:* Let your goods, though small, suffice. 3 *hord . . . hate:* hoard-
ing, avarice, invites hatred. *climbing tikelnesse:* ambition is precarious.
4 *wele . . . overal:* success blinds completely. 5 *Savour . . . shal:*
Enjoy only what will be to your profit. 6 *Reule:* Rule. *rede:* take
counsel. 7 *And trouthe . . . drede:* And truth shall make you free,
no doubt about it. 8 *Tempeste . . . redresse:* Do not distress yourself
in trying to set straight all crookedness. 9 *hir:* her (Fortune). 10 *reste
. . . besinesse:* doing little to remedy the whole world's wrongs gives
peace of mind. 11 *Be war:* Beware. *to sporne . . . al:* to spurn
against an owl, "English equivalent of the Greek phrase which our bibles
render by 'to kick against the pricks' (Acts, 9:5)."—Walter W. Skeat,
ed., *The Complete Works . . . Minor Poems,* Oxford, 1894. 12 *crokke*
[crock] *. . . wal:* which breaks when dashed against the wall. Possibly
adapted from Aesop's fable of the earthen and the bronze pots. 13
*Daunte . . . dede:* Conquer yourself if you would control the actions
of others.

That thee is sent, receyve in buxumnesse,    15
The wrastling for this world axeth a fal.
Her is non hoom, her nis but wildernesse:
Forth, pilgrim, forth! Forthe, beste, out of thy stal!
Know thy contree, look up, thank God of al;
Hold the heye wey, and lat thy gost thee lede;    20
And trouthe thee shal delivere, it is no drede.

### Envoy

Therfore, thou Vache, leve thyn old wrecchednesse
Unto the world; leve now to be thral;
Crye him mercy, that of his hy goodnesse
Made thee of noght, and in especial    25
Draw unto him, and pray in general
For thee, and eek for other, hevenlich mede;
And trouthe thee shal delivere, it is no drede.

*Explicit Le bon counseill de G. Chaucer.*

## Gentilesse

#### MORAL BALADE OF CHAUCIER

The firste stok, fader of gentilesse—
What man that claymeth gentil for to be
Must folowe his trace, and alle his wittes dresse
Vertu to sewe, and vyces for to flee.
For unto vertu longeth dignitee,    5
And noght the revers, saufly dar I deme
Al were he mytre, croune, or diademe.

15 *in buxumnesse:* obediently. 16 *axeth:* asks for. 17 *Her:* Here, in this world. *hoom:* home. *nis:* is not, nothing. 18 *beste:* beast. 19 *contree:* native land; heaven. 20 *heye wey:* main, sure way. *gost:* spirit. Cf. Rom. 8:4. 22 *Vache:* literally, cow. Cf. *beste,* l. 18. It has been suggested, however, that Chaucer had in mind Sir Philip (de) la Vache, a gentleman in disfavor at Court, 1386-89. See note in F. N. Robinson, ed., *The . . . Works of Chaucer,* Boston, 1933. 23 *leve . . . thral:* cease being a slave to the world. 25 *Made . . . noght:* i.e., according to the orthodox account of Creation. 27 *eek:* also. *hevenlich mede:* heavenly reward.

GENTILESSE. 1 *stok:* origin. *fader of gentilesse:* "The general idea of the poem is that Christ was the true pattern of 'gentleness' or gentility, i.e., of noble authority."—Skeat, *op. cit.* 3 *trace:* course, footsteps. 3-4 *alle . . . sewe:* prepare all of his wits (faculties) to pursue virtue. 5 *longeth:* belongeth. 6 *saufly . . . deme:* I dare safely suppose. 7 *Al were . . . diademe:* Although he wear mitre, crown, or diadem (i.e., be "bishop," "king," "emperor"—Skeat, *op. cit.*).

This firste stok was ful of rightwisnesse,
Trewe of his word, sobre, pitous, and free,
Clene of his gost, and loved besinesse,                    10
Ayeinst the vyce of slouthe, in honestee;
And, but his heir love vertu, as dide he,
He is noght gentil, thogh he riche seme,
Al were he mytre, croune, or diademe.

Vyce may wel be to heir to old richesse;                   15
But ther may no man, as men may wel see,
Bequethe his heir his vertuous noblesse,
That is appropred unto no degree,
But to the firste fader in magestee,
That maketh his heir him that can him queme,               20
Al were he mytre, croune, or diademe.


*from* THE CANTERBURY TALES

## from *The General Prologue*

Whan that Aprille with his shoures soote
The droghte of March hath perced to the roote
And bathed every veyne in swich licour
Of which vertu engendred is the flour;
Whan Zephirus eek with his sweete breeth            5
Inspired hath in every holt and heeth
The tendre croppes, and the yonge sonne
Hath in the Ram his halve cours y-ronne,
And smale fowles maken melodye
That slepen al the nyght with open ye,               10
So priketh hem Nature in hir corages;

8 *rightwisnesse:* righteousness.   9 *pitous:* merciful.   10 *Clene* . . .
*besinesse:* Pure of spirit, and loved diligence.   11 *Ayeinst:* Against.
*slouthe:* sloth.   12 *his heir:* if the "first stok" is Christ, then *his heir* is
mankind in general.   15 *Vyce . . . richesse:* Vice may inherit riches.
18 *appropred unto:* made the property of.   *degree:* rank.   20 *queme:*
please.
THE CANTERBURY TALES: PROLOGUE.   1 *Whan that:* When.   *soote:*
sweet.   3 *veyne:* vein, sap-vessel.   *swich licour:* such liquid.   4 *Of
vertu:* By power of which   5 *eek:* also.   6 *holt:* wood.   7 *croppes:*
sprouts.   8 *Hath . . . y-ronne:* Has run his half-course approximately
the second half—in the Ram (first of the twelve constellations through
which the sun—actually, the earth—passes in its annual revolution).
The date is approximately April 11.   9 *fowles:* birds.   11 *priketh hem:*
stirs them.   *hir corages:* their hearts.

4

Than longen folk to goon on pilgrimages,
And palmers for to seken straunge strondes,
To ferne halwes kouthe in sondry londes.
And specially, from every shires ende                    15
Of Engelond, to Caunterbury they wende,
The holy, blisful martir for to seke
That hem hath holpen whan that they were seeke.
    Bifel that in that seson on a day
In Southwerk at the Tabard, as I lay                     20
Redy to wenden on my pilgrimage
To Caunterbury with ful devout corage,
At nyght was come into that hostelrye
Wel nyne-and-twenty in a compaignye
Of sondry folk by aventure y-falle                       25
In felaweshipe, and pilgrims were they alle
That toward Caunterbury wolden ryde.
The chambres and the stables weren wyde,
And wel we weren esed atte beste.
And shortly, whan the sonne was to reste,                30
So hadde I spoken with hem everichon
That I was of hir felawshipe anon;
And made forward erly for to ryse
To take our wey ther as I yow devyse.*

12 *Than longen:* Then long.  *goon:* go.  13 *palmers:* pilgrims.  *seken:*
seek.  *strondes:* shores.  14 *ferne . . . kouthe:* distant shrines known.
17 *martir: Thomas à Becket,* Archbishop of Canterbury, whose martyrdom occurred in 1170.  18 *holpen:* helped.  *seeke:* sick.  19 *Bifel:* It
befell.  25 *by . . . y-falle:* fallen by chance.  27 *wolden:* intended to.
28 *wyde:* spacious.  29 *esed . . . beste:* entertained in the best way.
31 *everichon:* every one.  32 *That:* So that.  *hir:* their.  33 *made
forward:* (we) agreed.  34 *devyse:* tell.

* The Prologue continues with a description of many of the Pilgrims.
At the end of the Prologue, Harry Bailly, the "merry" Host of the
Tabard Inn, offers a plan for the entertainment of the Pilgrims on their
way to and from Canterbury. After supper, reminding his guests that

        . . . trewely confort ne myrthe is noon
        To ryde by the weye domb as a stoon,

he proposes that each member of the company tell two stories "to
Canterburyward" and two on the homeward journey. The one whose
stories are of ". . . best sentence [meaning] and most solas [delight]"
will be rewarded with a supper at the general expense when all return
to the Tabard. Furthermore, he will ride along with them as their self-
appointed guide. They heartily approve the whole program and beg the
Host to serve also as judge and critic of the tales and to take charge
of arrangements for the prospective supper celebration. Wine is fetched
at once, the agreement pledged, and looking forward to the morning, the
Pilgrims retire "withouten any lenger taryinge." (The ambitious plan
was not fully carried out.)

## The Nun's Priest's Tale *

A poure widwe, somdel stape in age,
Was whilom dwellyng in a narwe cotage
Biside a grove, stondyng in a dale.
This widwe of which I telle yow my tale,
Syn thilke day that she was last a wyf,                          5
In pacience ladde a ful symple lyf,
For litel was hir catel and hir rente.
By houshondrye of swich as God hir sente
She foond hirself and eek hir doghtren two.
Thre large sowes hadde she and namo,                            10
Thre kyn, and eek a sheep that highte Malle.
Ful sooty was hir bour and eek hir halle,
In which she eet ful many a sklendre meel.
Of poynaunt sauce hir neded never a deel.
No deyntee morsel passed thurgh hir throte;                     15
Hir diete was acordant to hir cote.
Repleccioun ne made hir never syk;
Attempree diete was al hir phisyk,
And excercise, and hertes suffisaunce.
The goute lette hir no thyng for to daunce,                     20
N'apoplexie shente nat hir heed.
No wyn ne drank she, neither whit ne reed.

* THE NUN'S PRIEST'S TALE : The story-telling is well under way by
the time Sir John, the Nun's priest, is called upon for his story. The
Host has been an expert master of ceremonies. Some of the best and
merriest tales have been told ; and, in the main, the program has run on
in the spirit of "confort" and "solas." But, disappointingly, the Monk
has turned the "note to tragic" with his heavy and prolonged narration
of the "sudden fall" of men from high and agreeable estate. Even the
Knight's patience has been strained, and he interrupts the Monk, as if
hauling up his horse, with "Whoa! Good Sir, no more of this!" The
Host concurring—"such talk isn't worth a butterfly, for there's no fun
or game in it"—invites the Monk to revise his style ; but he declines.
Sir John is then brought forward to counterpoint the depression with
"something such as may cheer our hearts." And the Tale of Chauntecleer
and Pertelote begins.

1 widwe : widow.  somdel stape : somewhat advanced.  2 whilom : once.
narwe : small.  3 stondyng : standing.  5 Syn thilke : Since that same.
6 ladde : led.  7 catel : goods.  rente : income.  8 swich : such.  9 foond :
supported.  eek : also.  doghtren : daughters.  10 namo : no more.  11
kyn : cows.  highte : was called.  12 bour : bedroom.  13 sklendre :
slender.  14 poynaunt : pungent.  hir neded : she needed.  deel : bit.  16
cote : means.  17 Repleccioun : Over-eating.  18 Attempree : Temperate.
19 suffisaunce : sufficiency.  20 lette : hindered.  no thyng : in no way.
21 N'apoplexie . . . heed : Nor did apoplexy trouble her head.  22 whit :
white.  reed : red.

6

Hir bord was served moost with whit and blak,
Milk and broun breed, in which she foond no lak,
Seynd bacoun, and som tyme an ey or tweye,              25
For she was, as it were, a maner deye.
   A yeerd she hadde, enclosed al aboute
With stikkes, and a drye dych withoute,
In which she hadde a cok hight Chauntecleer.
In al the land of crowyng nas his peer.                30
His voys was murier than the murie orgon
On massedayes that in the chirche gon.
Wel sikerer was his crowyng in his logge
Than is a clokke or an abbey orlogge.
By nature he knew ech ascensioun                       35
Of the equinoxial in thilke toun,
For whan degrees fiftene were ascended,
Thanne crew he that it myghte nat ben amended.
His comb was redder than the fyn coral
And batailled as it were a castel wal.                 40
His byle was blak, and as the jeet it shoon.
Lyk asure were his legges and his toon,
Hise nayles whitter than the lylye flour,
And lyk the burned gold was his colour.
This gentil cok hadde in his governaunce               45
Sevene hennes for to doon al his plesaunce,
Whiche were his sustres and his paramours,
And wonder lyk to hym as of colours,
Of whiche the faireste hewed on hir throte
Was cleped faire damoysele Pertelote.                  50
Curteys she was, discreet, and debonaire,
And compaignable, and bar hirself so faire
Syn thilke day that she was seven nyght oold
That, trewely, she hath the herte in hoold
Of Chauntecleer, loken in every lith.                  55

23 bord: table.  25 Seynd: Broiled.  ey or tweye: egg or two.  26 maner
deye: sort of dairy-woman.  28 dych: ditch.  30 nas: (there) was not.
31 murier: merrier.  32 gon: go, i.e., play; orgon (l. 31) is regularly
plural.  33 Wel sikerer: Much more accurate.  logge: lodge.  34 orlogge: clock.  35-36 ascensioun . . . equinoxial: In the old astronomy,
the heavens were thought to make a complete revolution around the
equator—through a counterclockwise motion, called "ascension"—every
twenty-four hours. When fifteen degrees were "ascended," an hour had
passed.  38 that . . . amended: that the accuracy of his crowing
couldn't be improved upon.  40 batailled as: battlemented as if.  41
byle: bill.  jeet: jet.  42 toon: toes.  44 burned: burnished.  46 doon:
do.  47 sustres: sisters.  paramours: mistresses.  48 wonder: wonder-
fully.  50 cleped: called.  52 bar: carried.  55 loken: locked.  lith:
limb.

He loved hir so that wel was hym therwith.
But swich a joye was it to here hem synge,
Whan that the brighte sonne gan to sprynge,
In swete acord "My leef is faren in londe."
For thilke tyme, as I have understonde,                                60
Beestes and briddes koude speke and synge.
  And so bifel that in a dawenynge,
As Chauntecleer among his wyves alle
Sat on his perche, that was in the halle,
And next hym sat this faire Pertelote,                                65
This Chauntecleer gan gronen in his throte
As man that in his dreem is drecched soore.
  And whan that Pertelote thus herde hym rore,
She was agast and seyde, "Herte deere,
What eyleth yow to grone in this manere?                                70
Ye ben a verray sleper. Fy, for shame!"
  And he answerde and seyde thus: "Madame,
I pray yow that ye take it nat agrief.
By God, me mette I was in swich meschief
Right now, that yet myn herte is soore afright.                                75
Now God," quod he, "my swevene recche aright,
And keep my body out of foul prisoun!
Me mette how that I romed up and doun
Withinne our yeerd, where as I saugh a beest,
Was lyk an hound and wolde han maad areest                                80
Upon my body and wolde han had me deed.
His colour was bitwixe yelow and reed,
And tipped was his tayl and bothe his erys
With blak, unlik the remenaunt of his herys,
His snowte smal, with glowyng eyen tweye.                                85
Yet of his look for fere almoost I deye.
This caused me my gronyng, doutelees."
  "Avoy!" quod she. "Fy on yow, hertelees!
Allas," quod she, "for, by that God above,
Now han ye lost myn herte and al my love.                                90
I kan nat love a coward, by my feith!
For, certes, what so any womman seith,
We alle desiren, if it myghte be,

56 *wel . . . therwith:* he was well-contented.   57 *hem:* them.   58
*sprynge:* rise.   59 *My . . . londe:* cf. "My bonnie lies over the ocean."
61 *briddes:* birds.   62 *in . . . dawenynge:* one early morning.   67
*drecched:* tormented.   71 *verray:* sound.   73 *agrief:* ill.   74 *me mette:*
I dreamed.   76 *quod:* said.   *my . . . aright:* (God) interpret my dream
favorably.   79 *saugh:* saw.   80 *han . . . areest:* have seized.   81 *han
. . . deed:* have killed me.   83 *erys:* ears.   84 *remenaunt:* rest.   *herys:*
hair.   88 *Avoy:* Shame.   92 *certes:* certainly.   *what so:* whatever.

8

To han housbondes hardy, wise, and free,
And secree, and no nygard, ne no fool,                    95
Ne hym that is agast of every tool,
Ne noon avauntour, by that God above.
How dorste ye seyn, for shame, unto youre love
That any thyng myghte make yow aferd?
Have ye no mannes herte, and han a berd?             100
    "Allas, and konne ye ben agast of swevenys.
No thyng, God woot, but vanytee in sweven is.
Swevenes engendren of replexions,
And ofte of fume and of complexions,
Whan humours ben to habundant in a wight.          105
    "Certes, this dreem which ye han met to-nyght
Cometh of the grete superfluytee
Of youre rede colera, pardee,
Which causeth folk to dreden in hir dremes
Of arwes, and of fyr with rede lemes,                  110
Of rede bestes that they wol hem byte,
Of contek, and of whelpes grete and lyte;
Right as the humour of malencolie
Causeth ful many a man in sleep to crie
For fere of blake beres, or boles blake,               115
Or elles blake develes, wol hem take.
Of othere humours koude I telle also
That werken many a man in sleep ful wo,
But I wol passe as lightly as I kan.
    "Lo Catoun, which that was so wys a man,         120
Seyde he nat thus: 'Ne do no fors of dremes'?

94 *free*: generous.   95 *secree*: trustworthy.   96 *tool*: weapon.   97 *avauntour*: boaster.   98 *dorste*: dared.   101 *ben* . . . *swevenys*: be afraid of dreams.   102 ff. *No thyng, etc.*: It is folly to attach significance to dreams. Pertelote claims that they are simply the result of natural causes, such as over-eating (l. 103), or of a superfluity of one of the bodily humors (l. 105) : yellow bile (productive of choler, i.e., hot-headedness, anger), black bile (of melancholy), phlegm (of a "phlegmatic" temper), blood (of a sanguine disposition). From the colors associated with Chauntecleer's dream, she quickly diagnoses it as coming from an excess of choler, and prescribes a "digestive" of worms to absorb the bile (and to allay any accompanying bad effects, ll. 139-40), to be followed by a laxative.   102 *woot*: knows.   104 *fume*: vapor.   *complexions*: temperaments.   105 *ben to*: are too.   *wight*: person.   108 *colera*: choler. *pardee*: certainly.   109 *to dreden*: be frightened.   *hir*: their.   110 *arwes*: arrows.   *lemes*: flames.   112 *contek*: strife.   113 *Right*: Just.   115 *beres*: bears.   *boles*: bulls.   116 *hem*: them.   118 *werken*: make.   *ful wo*: woeful.   120 *Catoun*: (Dionysius) Cato. In causing Pertelote to cite Cato, and Chauntecleer to refute her out of Macrobius and Scipio (ll. 303-04), the Bible, classical story, etc. (ll. 308 ff.), Chaucer pokes fun at excessive citation of authority by medieval scholars.   121 *Ne* . . . *of*: Pay no attention to.

"Now sire," quod she, "whan we fle fro the bemes,
For Goddes love, as taak som laxatif.
Up peril of my soule and of my lif,
I conseille yow the beste, I wol nat lye,                    125
That bothe of colere and of malencolye
Ye purge yow. And, for ye shal nat tarye,
Thogh in this toun is noon apothecarye,
I shal myself to herbes techen yow
That shul ben for youre heele and for your prow.            130
And in oure yerd tho herbes shal I fynde
The whiche han of hir propretee by kynde
To purge yow byrnethe and eek above.
Foryet nat this, for Goddes owene love!
Ye ben ful colerik of complexioun.                          135
Ware the sonne in his ascensioun
Ne fynde yow nat repleet of humours hote,
And, if it do, I dar wel leye a grote
That ye shul have a fevere terciane
Or an agu that may be youre bane.                           140
A day or two ye shul have digestyves
Of wormes er ye take your laxatyves
Of lauriol, centaure, and fumetere,
Or elles of ellebor that groweth there,
Of katapuce, or of gaitrys beryis,                          145
Of herbe yve growyng in oure yerd, ther merye is.
Pekke hem up right as they growe, and ete hem in.
Be myrie, housbond, for your fader kyn!
Dredeth no dreem. I kan sey yow namoore."

"Madame," quod he, "graunt mercy of your loore.           150
But nathelees, as touchyng daun Catoun,
That hath of wisdom swich a gret renoun,
Thogh that he bad no dremes for to drede,
By God, men may in olde bokes rede
Of many a man moore of auctoritee                          155
Than ever Catoun was, so mote I thee,

---

122 *fle fro:* fly down from.  123 *as taak:* take.  124 *Up:* Upon.  127
*for:* in order that.  129 *techen:* direct.  130 *heele:* cure.  *prow:* bene-
fit.  131 *tho:* those.  132 *kynde:* nature.  134 *Foryet:* Forget.  136
*Ware:* Beware that.  138 *grote:* groat (fourpence).  139 *fevere
terciane:* tertian fever (a fever every third day).  142 *er:* before.  143 ff.
*lauriol, centaure, etc.:* medicinal herbs (see l. 131), and presumably
nauseous. Cf. pleasant (*merye*) garden, l. 146.  144 *elles:* else.  148
*fader kyn:* literally, father's kin; family honor. See l. 475.  150
*graunt . . . loore:* thanks for your instruction.  151 *daun:* sir.  156
*so . . . thee:* so may I thrive. Cf. "As I live."

That al the revers seyn of his sentence
And han wel founden by experience
That dremes ben significaciouns
As wel of joye as of tribulaciouns                      160
That folk enduren in this lyf present.
Ther nedeth make of this noon argument;
The verray preeve sheweth it in dede.

   "Oon of the gretteste auctor that men rede
Seith thus, that whilom two felawes wente          165
On pilgrimage in a ful good entente,
And happed so they coomen in a toun
Where as ther was swich congregacioun
Of peple, and eek so streit of herbergage
That they ne founde as muche as a cotage          170
In which they bothe myghte y-logged be.
Wherfore they mosten of necessitee,
As for that nyght, departen compaignye,
And ech of hem gooth to his hostelrye
And took his loggyng as it wolde falle.              175
That oon of hem was logged in a stalle,
Fer in a yeerd, with oxen of the plow.
That oother man was logged wel ynow
As was his aventure or his fortune,
That us governeth alle as in commune.              180

   "And so bifel that, longe er it were day,
This man mette in his bed ther as he lay
How that his felawe gan upon hym calle
And seyde, 'Allas, for in an oxes stalle
This nyght I shal be mordred ther I lye.             185
Now help me, deere brother, or I dye.
In alle haste com to me,' he sayde.

   "This man out of his sleep for feere abrayde,
But whan that he was wakned of his sleep,
He turned hym and took of this no keep.           190
Hym thoughte his dreem nas but a vanytee.
Thus twies in his slepyng dremed he,
And atte thridde tyme yet his felawe

157 *revers:* contrary.  *sentence:* opinion.  159 *ben:* are.  162 *Ther
nedeth:* There is (no) need to.  163 *preeve:* proof.  164 *Oon:* One.
*auctor:* author(s).  165 *felawes:* companions.  167 *happed:* it happened.  *so:* as.  169 *streit of herbergage:* short of lodgings.  171
*y-logged:* lodged.  172 *mosten:* must.  173 *As for:* For.  *departen:*
part.  177 *Fer . . . yeerd:* Far off in a courtyard.  178 *ynow:* enough.
179 *aventure:* lot.  180 *commune:* common.  182 *ther as:* where.  185
*mordred ther:* murdered where.  188 *abrayde:* started up.  190 *keep:*
heed.  191 *nas but:* was only.  193 *thridde:* third.

Cam, as hym thoughte, and seyde, 'I am now slawe.
Bihoold my blody woundes, depe and wyde.                   195
Arys up erly in the morwe tyde,
And at the west gate of the toun,' quod he,
'A carte ful of dong ther shaltow se,
In which my body is hid ful prively.
Do thilke carte aresten boldely.                           200
My gold caused my mordre, sooth to seyn';
And tolde hym every point how he was slayn
With a ful pitous face pale of hewe.
And wroote wel his dreem he fond ful trewe,
For on the morwe, as soone as it was day,                  205
To his felawes in he took the way,
And whan that he cam to this oxes stalle,
After his felawe he bigan to calle.

    "The hostiler answerde hym anon
And seyde, 'Sire, your felawe is agon.                      210
As soone as day he wente out of the toun.'

    "This man gan fallen in suspecioun,
Remembrynge on his dremes that he mette,
And forth he gooth, no lenger wolde he lette,
Unto the west gate of the toun and fond                    215
A dong carte, wente as it were to donge lond,
That was arrayed in the same wise
As ye han herd the dede man devyse,
And with an hardy herte he gan to crye
Vengeaunce and justice of this felonye.                     220
'My felawe mordred is this same nyght,
And in this carte he lyth gapyng upright.
I crye out on the ministres,' quod he,
'That sholden kepe and reulen this citee.
Harrow, allas! Heer lyth my felawe slayn!'                 225
What sholde I moore unto this tale sayn?
The peple out sterte and caste the cart to grounde,
And in the myddel of the dong they founde
The dede man, that mordred was al newe.

    "O blisful God, that art so just and trewe,           230
Lo, how that thow biwreyest mordre alway!
Mordre wol out, that se we day by day.

194 *slawe*: slain. 196 *Arys*: Rise. *morwe tyde*: morning. 198 *dong*: dung. *shaltow se*: you will see. 199 *ful prively*: very secretly. 200 *aresten*: stop. 201 *sooth to seyn*: truth to tell. 206 *in*: inn. 214 *lette*: stay. 216 *to donge*: to manure. 218 *devyse*: describe, tell. 222 *lyth*: lies. *upright*: face-upward. 225 *Harrow*: Help. 229 *al newe*: just recently. 231 *biwreyest*: make known. 232 *se*: see.

Mordre is so wlatsom and abhomynable
To God, that is so just and resonable,
That he ne wol nat suffre it heled be,                    235
Thogh it abyde a yeer, or two, or thre.
Mordre wol out, this is my conclusioun.
And right anon ministres of that toun
Han hent the cartere and so soore hym pyned
And eek the hostiler so soore engyned                    240
That they biknewe hir wikkednesse anon
And were an-hanged by the nekke bon.
   "Heere may men seen that dremes ben to drede.
And, certes, in the same book I rede,
Right in the nexte chapitre after this—                  245
I gabbe nat, so have I joye or blys—
Two men that wolde han passed over see
For certeyn cause into a fer contree,
If that the wynd ne hadde ben contrarie,
That made hem in a citee for to tarie,                   250
That stood ful myrie upon an haven syde.
But on a day, agayn the even tyde,
The wynd gan chaunge and blew right as hem leste.
Jolif and glad they wente unto hir reste
And casten hem ful erly for to saille.                   255
   "But herkneth! To that o man fil a greet mervaille,
That oon of hem, in slepyng as he lay,
Hym mette a wonder dreem agayn the day.
Hym thoughte a man stood by his beddes syde,
And hym comanded that he sholde abyde,                   260
And seyde hym thus: 'If thow tomorwe wende,
Thow shalt be dreynt. My tale is at an ende.'
He wook, and tolde his felawe what he mette,
And preyde hym his viage for to lette.
As for that day, he preyde hym to abyde.                 265
His felawe, that lay by his beddes syde,
Gan for to laughe, and scorned hym ful faste.
'No dreem,' quod he, 'may so myn herte agaste

233 *wlatsom:* foul. 235 *ne . . . be:* will not let it be hidden. 239
*hent:* seized. *pyned:* examined (him) by torture. 240 *engyned:*
racked. 241 *biknewe hir:* confessed their. 242 *bon:* bone. 244 *book:*
see l. 164. 246 *gabbe:* jest. *so have I:* may I have. 247 *han . . . see:*
have crossed the sea. 251 *myrie:* pleasant. *haven:* harbor. 252 *agayn*
*. . . tyde:* towards evening. 253 *hem leste:* they wished. 254 *Jolif:*
Jolly. 255 *casten hem:* they decided. 256 *o:* one. *fil:* befell. 258
*wonder:* wonderful. 262 *dreynt.* drowned. 263 *wook:* awoke. 264
*viage . . . lette:* to delay his voyage. 268 *agaste:* frighten.

That I wol lette for to do my thynges.
I sette nat a straw by thy dremynges,                           270
For swevenes ben but vanytees and japes.
Men dreme alday of owles and of apes
And eek of many a maze therwithal;
Men dreme of thyng that never was ne shal.
But, sith I see that thow wolt here abyde,                      275
And thus forslewthen wilfully thy tyde,
God woot, it reweth me, and have good day!'
And thus he took his leve and wente his way.
But er that he hadde half his cours y-seyled,
Noot I that why ne what mischaunce it eyled,                    280
But casuelly the shippes botme rente,
And ship and man under the water wente
In sighte of othere shippes it bisyde
That with hem seyled at the same tyde.

And therfor, faire Pertelote so deere,                          285
By swiche ensamples olde maystow leere
That no man sholde been to recchelees
Of dremes, for I sey thee, doutelees,
That many a dreem ful soore is for to drede.

    "Lo, in the lyf of Seint Kenelm I rede,                     290
That was Kenulphus sone, the noble kyng
Of Mercenrike, how Kenelm mette a thyng.
A lite er he was mordred on a day,
His mordre in his avysioun he say.
His norice hym expowned every del                               295
His swevene, and bad hym for to kepe hym wel
For traisoun, but he nas but seven yeer old,
And therfore litel tale hath he told
Of any dreem, so holy was his herte.
By God, I hadde levere than my sherte                           300
That ye had rad his legende as have I.
Dame Pertelote, I sey yow trewely,

269 *lette . . . thynges:* stop my activities.   271 *japes:* tricks.   272
*alday:* every day.   273 *maze:* wonder.   274 *shal:* shall (be).   275 *sith:*
since.   276 *forslewthen:* waste.   *tyde:* time.   277 *it . . . me:* I rue it.
279 *y-seyled:* sailed.   280 *Noot I:* I don't know.   *ne:* nor.   *eyled:*
ailed (it).   281 *casuelly:* by chance.   283 *bisyde:* beside.   286 *maystow
leere:* you may learn   287 *to recchelees:* too reckless.   288 *sey:* tell.
289 *for to drede:* to be dreaded.   291 *Kenulphus, Ccnwulf'o.*   292 *Mercenrike:* Mercia.   293 *lite:* little.   294 *avysioun:* vision.   *say:* saw.
295 *norice:* nurse.   *expowned . . . del:* expounded fully.   296 *for . . .
hym:* to take care of himself.   297 *For:* For fear of.   *nas but:* was
only.   298 *tale:* heed.   *told:* paid.   300-01 *I . . . rad:* I'd have given
my shirt if you had read.

Macrobeus, that writ the avysioun
In Affrike of the worthy Cipioun,
Affermeth dremes and seith that they been          305
Warnynge of thynges that men after seen.
And forthermoore, I pray yow, looketh wel
In the Olde Testament, of Daniel,
If he heeld dremes any vanytee.
Rede eek of Joseph, and there shul ye see          310
Wher dremes be somtyme, I sey nat alle,
Warnynge of thynges that shul after falle.
Looke of Egipt the kyng, daun Pharao,
His bakere, and his butiller also,
Wher they ne felte noon effect in dremes.          315
Who-so wol seken actes of sondry remes
May rede of dremes many a wonder thyng.
Lo Cresus, which that was of Lyde kyng,
Mette he nat that he sat upon a tree,
Which signified he sholde an-hanged be?          320
Lo heere Andromacha, Ectores wyf,
That day that Ector sholde lese his lyf,
She dremed on the same nyght biforn
How that the lyf of Ector sholde be lorn
If thilke day he wente in to bataille.          325
She warned hym, but it myghte nat availle;
He wente for to fighte, nathelees.
But he was slayn anon of Achilles.
But thilke tale is al to long to telle,
And eek it is ny day, I may nat dwelle.          330
    "Shortly I seye, as for conclusioun,
That I shal han of this avysioun
Adversitee, and I seye forthermoor,
That I ne telle of laxatyves no stoor,
For they ben venymes, I woot it wel.          335
I hem deffye! I love hem never a del.
    "Now lat us speke of myrthe and stynte al this.
Madame Pertelote, so have I blis,
Of o thyng God hath sent me large grace,

303 *Macrobe*[or *i*]*us:* Cicero's *Somnium Scipionis* (Scipio Africanus
Minor; see l. 304) with the Latin commentary of Macrobius was a
popular dream-book of the Middle Ages.  308 *Olde Testament:* see Dan.
7; Gen. 37, 40, 41.  311 *Wher:* Whether.  316 *remes:* realms.  318
*Lyde:* Lydia.  321 *Andromacha:* Andromache, Hector's wife.  322
*lese:* lose.  324 *lorn:* lost.  327 *nathelees:* nevertheless.  328 *of:* by.
330 *ny:* near.  334 *ne . . . stoor:* set no store by laxatives.  335
*venymes:* venomous.  336 *never a del:* not at all.  337 *stynte:* stop.
338 *so . . . I:* may I have.  339 *o:* one.

For whan I se the beautee of youre face,    340
Ye ben so scarlet reed aboute youre eyen,
It maketh al my drede for to dyen,
For, also siker as *In principio*,
'*Mulier est hominis confusio.*'
   "Madame, the sentence of this Latyn is,    345
'Womman is mannes joye and al his blis.'
For whan I feele a-nyght your softe syde,
Al be it that I may nat on yow ryde
For that our perche is maad so narwe, allas,
I am so ful of joye and of solas    350
That I deffye bothe swevene and dreem."
   And with that word he fley doun fro the beem,
For it was day, and eek hise hennes alle.
And with a chuk he gan hem for to calle,
For he had founde a corn, lay in the yerd.    355
Real he was; he was na moore aferd.
He fethered Pertelote twenty tyme
And trad as ofte, er that it was pryme.
He looketh as it were a grym leoun,
And on his toos he rometh up and doun.    360
Hym deyned nat to sette his foot to grounde.
He chukketh whan he hath a corn y-founde,
And to hym rennen thanne his wyves alle.
Thus real as a prince is in his halle
Leve I this Chauntecleer in his pasture,    365
And after wol I telle his aventure.
   Whan that the monthe in which the world bigan,
That highte March, whan God first maked man,
Was complet, and passed were also,
Syn March bigan, thritty dayes and two,    370
Bifel that Chauntecleer in al his pryde,
His seven wyves walkyng hym bisyde,
Caste up hise eyen to the brighte sonne,
That in the signe of Taurus hadde y-ronne
Twenty degrees and oon, and somwhat moore,    375
And knew by kynde and by noon oother loore

---

341 *reed:* red.  343 *also . . . In principio:* as surely as "in the beginning" (John 1:1) ; i.e., "as surely as Gospel truth."  344 *Mulier est
hominis confusio:* Woman is man's ruin.  345 *sentence:* meaning.  349
*For that:* Because.  351 *swevene:* vision.  355 *corn:* grain (of corn).
*lay:* (which) lay.  356 *Real:* Regal.  *aferd:* afraid.  358 *trad:* trod, covered (her).  *pryme:* prime; period from 6 to 9 A.M.  359 *leoun:* lion.  361
*Hym deyned:* He deigned.  363 *rennen thanne:* then run.  367 *Whan
. . . bigan:* i.e., according to medieval opinion.  370 *Syn:* Since.  371
*Bifel:* It befell.  376 *kynde:* nature. Cf. l. 35.

That it was pryme, and crew with blisful stevene.
"The sonne," he seyde, "is clomben up on hevene
Fourty degrees and oon, and moore ywis.
Madame Pertelote, my worldes blis,                          380
Herkneth thise blisful briddes, how they synge,
And se the fresshe floures how they sprynge.
Ful is myn herte of revel and solas."
But sodeynly hym fil a sorweful cas,
For ever the latter ende of joye is wo.                      385
God woot that worldly joye is soone ago,
And if a rethor koude faire endite,
He in a cronycle saufly myghte it write
As for a sovereyn notabilitee.
Now every wys man, lat hym herkne me;                       390
This storie is also trewe, I undertake,
As is the book of *Launcelot de Lake*,
That wommen holde in ful gret reverence.
Now wol I torne agayn to my sentence.

  A colfox ful of sly iniquitee,                            395
That in the grove hadde woned yeres three,
By heigh ymaginacioun forncast,
The same nyght thurgh-out the hegges brast
Into the yerd ther Chauntecleer the faire
Was wont, and eek his wyves, to repaire,                    400
And in a bed of wortes stille he lay
Til it was passed undren of the day,
Waitynge his tyme on Chauntecleer to falle,
As gladly doon thise homycides alle
That in await liggen to mordre men.                         405
O false mordrour, lurkynge in thy den,
O newe Scariot, newe Genyloun,
False dissimilour, O Greek Synoun,

377 *stevene:* voice. 378 *is clomben:* has climbed. 379 *ywis:* indeed.
381 *Herkneth:* Listen to. 384 *hym fil:* befell him. *cas:* mishap. 386
*ago:* gone. 387 *rethor:* rhetorician. *endite:* compose. 388 *saufly:*
safely. 389 *As . . . notabilitee:* As a most notable fact. 391 *also:* as.
*undertake:* vow. 392 *Launcelot de Lake:* A romance relating the love
of Lancelot for Guinevere, King Arthur's Queen; not *trewe* (l. 391),
but entirely fictitious. 394 *sentence:* subject. 395 *colfox:* fox with
much black hair. 396 *woned:* lived. 397 *By . . . forncast:* By divine
knowledge foreordained. 398 *hegges:* hedges. *brast:* burst. 401
*wortes:* plants. 402 *undren:* midmorning. 404 *gladly:* habitually.
*homycides:* murderers. 405 *liggen:* lie. 407 *Scariot:* (Judas) Iscariot.
*Genyloun:* Ganelon, officer of Charlemagne, whose treachery caused
Roland's death and the defeat at Roncesvalles. Synonym for traitor. 408
*dissimilour:* deceiver. *Synoun:* Sinon, conspirator, who persuaded the
Trojans to admit the Greeks' Wooden Horse into their city.

That broghtest Troye al outrely to sorwe!
O Chauntecleer, acursed be that morwe                    410
That thou into the yerd flaugh fro the bemes.
Thou were ful wel y-warned by thy dremes
That thilke day was perilous to thee.
But what that God forwoot moot nedes be
After the opynyoun of certeyn clerkis.                   415
Witnesse on hym that any parfit clerk is,
That in scole is greet altercacioun
In this matere, and greet disputisoun,
And hath ben of an hundred thousand men.
But I ne kan nat bulte it to the bren                    420
As kan the holy doctour Augustyn
Or Boece, or the Bisshop Bradwardyn,
Wheither that Goddes worthy forewityng
Streyneth me nedely for to doon a thyng—
"Nedely" clepe I symple necessitee—                      425
Or ellis, if free choys be graunted me
To do that same thyng, or do it noght,
Though God forwoot it er that it was wroght;
Or if his wityng streyneth nevei a del
But by necessitee condicionel.                           430
I wol nat han to do of swich matere.
My tale is of a cok, as ye may heere,
That took his conseil of his wyf, with sorwe,
To walken in the yerd upon that morwe
That he had met the dreem that I yow tolde.              435

409 *al outrely:* utterly. *sorwe:* grief.    410 *morwe:* morning.    411
*flaugh:* flew.    414 *forwoot . . . be:* foreknows must needs be. Cf. l.
397.    415 *clerkis:* scholars.    418 *matere . . . disputisoun* (disputation
—in the schools) : The "matter" is one of the perennial difficulties of
theology : Inasmuch as God is omniscient, he correctly knows in advance ("foreknows") every human choice; is man's will, then, entirely
free? if not, is man responsible for his actions? Boethius (l. 422 and
note) distinguished between "simple" (l. 425) and "conditional" (l. 430)
necessity. The former, contrasted with "free choice," applies to situa-
tions in which Providence takes a direct hand; the latter, to those
which left to man's discretion, nevertheless, are not contradictory to the
Divine Will. Bishop Bradwardine (l. 422) lectured on the subject at
Oxford. See Robinson, *op. cit.,* pp. 860-61. Cf. "if I [God] foreknew,
/ Foreknowledge had no influence on their [Adam and Eve's] fault."—
*Paradise Lost,* III, 118-19.    420 *bulte:* sift.    *bren:* bran.    421 *Au-
gustyn:* (Saint) Augustine, Bishop of Hippo (354-430).    422 *Boece:*
Boethius, 6th century philosopher, whose *Cynsolution of Philosophy*
Chaucer translated. He was also an authority on music. See l. 474.
*Bradwardyn:* (Thomas) Bradwardine (Archbishop of Canterbury, d.
1349).    423 *forewityng:* foreknowing.    424 *Streyneth:* Constrains.
*nedely:* necessarily.    425 *clepe:* call.    429 *wityng . . . del:* knowing
constrains not at all.    431 *han:* have (anything).    *of:* with.

Wommennes conseils ben ful ofte colde.
Wommannes conseil broghte us first to wo
And made Adam fro Paradys to go,
Ther as he was ful myrie and wel at ese.
But, for I noot to whom it myghte displese          440
If I conseil of wommen wolde blame,
Passe over, for I seyde it in my game.
Rede auctours wher they trete of swich matere,
And what they seyn of wommen ye may heere.
Thise ben the cokkes wordes and nat myne;          445
I kan noon harm of no womman divyne.
    Faire in the sond to bathe hir myrily
Lith Pertelote, and alle hir sustres by,
Agayn the sonne; and Chauntecleer so free
Song myrier than the mermayde in the see,          450
For Phisiologus seith sikerly
How that they syngen wel and myrily.
    And so bifel that, as he caste his eye
Among the wortes on a boterflye,
He was war of this fox that lay ful lowe.          455
No thyng ne liste hym thanne for to crowe,
But cryde anon "Cok! cok!" and up he sterte
As man that was affrayed in his herte,
For naturelly a beest desireth flee
Fro his contrarie, if he may it see,              460
Though he never erst had syn it with his eye.
    This Chauntecleer, whan he gan hym espye,
He wolde han fled but that the fox anon
Seyde, "Gentil sire, allas! Wher wol ye gon?
Be ye affrayed of me that am your freend?          465
Now, certes, I were worse than a feend
If I to yow wolde harm or vileynye.
I am nat come your conseil for t'espye,
But trewely the cause of my comynge
Was oonly for to herkne how that ye synge,          470

436 *colde:* fatal.  437 *first:* cf. *In principio,* l. 343.  440 *for I noot:*
since I don't know.  442 *game:* jest.  444 *seyn:* say.  446 *divyne:* imagine.  447 *sond:* sand.  448 *Lith:* Lies.  449 *Agayn:* In.  450 *Song:*
Sang.  451 *Phisiologus:* Reputed author of a Greek work on natural
history (2nd century), which inspired many later imitations known as
Bestiaries. They were extremely popular in the Middle Ages for their
fictitious, pseudoscientific, and allegorical interpretation of animal lore.
*seith sikerly:* says truly.  455 *war:* aware.  456 *No . . . thanne:* He
did not at all then wish.  458 *As man:* Like someone.  459 *flee:* to flee.
460 *contrarie:* opposite; i.e., enemy.  461 *erst:* before.  *syn:* seen.
462 *gan . . . espye:* noticed him.  467 *wolde:* intended.  468 *conseil:*
secret; i.e., private affairs.

For trewely ye have as myrie a stevene
As any aungel hath that is in hevene.
Therwith ye han in musyk moore feelynge
Than hadde Boece, or any that kan synge.
My lord, your fader—God his soule blesse!—          475
And eek your moder, of hir gentillesse,
Han in myn hous y-ben to my greet ese.
And, certes, sire, ful fayn wolde I yow plese.
    "But, for men speke of syngynge, I wol seye—
So mote I brouke wel myne cyen tweye!—          480
Save yow, I herde never man so synge
As dide your fader in the morwenynge
Certes, it was of herte, al that he song.
And for to make his voys the moore strong,
He wolde so peyne hym that with bothe his eyen          485
He moste wynke, so loude he wolde cryen,
And stonden on his tiptoon ther-with-al,
And strecche forth his nekke long and smal.
And eek he was of swich discrecioun
That ther nas no man in no regioun          490
That hym in song or wisdom myghte passe.
I have wel rad in Daun Burnel the Asse,
Among his vers, how that ther was a cok,
For a preestes sone yaf hym a knok
Upon his leg, whil he was yong and nyce,          495
He made hym for to lese his benefice.
But, certeyn, ther nys no comparisoun
Bitwix the wisdom and discrecioun
Of youre fader and of his subtiltee.
Now syngeth, sire, for seinte charitee!          500
Lat se, konne ye your fader countrefete?"
    This Chauntecleer his wynges gan to bete
As man that koude his traysoun nat espie,
So was he ravysshed with his flaterie.
    Allas, ye lordes, many a fals flatour          505

474 *Boece:* see l. 422 and note.   475 *fader:* cf. l. 148.   477 *y-ben:*
been.   *ese:* satisfaction.   478 *fayn:* gladly.   479 *for:* in spite of what.
480 *So . . . tweye:* So may I enjoy (the use of) my two eyes. Mild
oath Cf. "As I live."   482 *morwenynge:* morning.   483 *of herte:* hearty.
485 *peyne hym:* strive.   486 *moste wynke:* must shut (his eyes).   492
*Burnel[lus] the Asse:* 12th century Latin poem by Nigel Wireker.   495
*he:* the priest's son.   *nyce:* foolish.   496 *lese:* lose his benefice, according to the story, because the cock failed to crow to awaken Gundulf
(the priest's son) in time for him to attend his ordination and receive
appointment to his living.   500 *seinte:* holy.   501 *Lat se:* Let's see (if).
*countrefete:* imitate.   503 *As man:* Like one.   505 *flatour:* flatterer.

Is in your courtes, and many a losengeour,
That plesen yow wel moore, by my feith,
Than he that soothfastnesse unto yow seith.
Redeth Ecclesiaste of flaterye.
Beth war, ye lordes, of hir trecherye.                    510
This Chauntecleer stood hye upon his toos,
Strecchynge his nekke, and heeld his eyen cloos,
And gan to crowe loude for the nones.
And daun Russell the fox stirte up atones,
And by the gargat hente Chauntecleer,                     515
And on his bak toward the wode hym beer,
For yet ne was ther no man that hym sewed.

O destynee, that mayst nat ben eschewed!
Allas, that Chauntecleer fleigh fro the bemes!
Allas, his wif ne roghte nat of dremes!                   520
And on a Friday fil al this meschaunce.

O Venus, that art goddesse of plesaunce,
Syn that thy servant was this Chauntecleer,
And in thy servyce dide al his power
Moore for delit than world to multiplie,                  525
Why woldestow suffre hym on thy day to dye?

O Gaufred, deere maister soverayn,
That whan thy worthy kyng Richard was slayn
With shot, compleynedest his deth so soore,
Why ne hadde I now thy sentence and thy loore             530
The Friday for to chide, as diden ye?
For on a Friday, soothly, slayn was he.
Than wolde I shewe yow how that I koude pleyne
For Chauntecleres drede and for his peyne.

Certes, swich cry ne lamentacioun                         535
Was nevere of ladyes maad whan Ylioun
Was wonne, and Pirrus with his streite swerd
Whan he hadde hent kyng Priam by the berd
And slayn hym, as seith us *Eneydos,*

506 *losengeour:* deceiver.  507 *plesen:* please.  508 *soothfastnesse:*
truth.  509 *Ecclesiaste of:* Ecclesiasticus, a book in the Apocrypha.
See 12:10 ff. Cf. Prov. 29:5.  510 *Beth war:* Beware.  512 *cloos:*
closed.  513 *nones:* occasion.  514 *stirte up atones:* sprang up at once.
515 *gargat hente:* throat seized.  516 *beer:* carried.  517 *sewed:* pursued.  520 *ne . . . nat:* took no heed.  521 *Friday: vendredi,* day of
Venus. See ll. 522 ff.  525 *delit:* delight.  526 *woldestow:* would you.
527 *Gaufred:* Geoffrey de Vin Sauf, 12th-century author of a Latin
treatise on poetics. Chaucer alludes to his "lamentation" on Richard I,
slain on a Friday (1199). See ll. 528, 532.  529 *compleynedest:* lamented.  530 *sentence:* erudition.  *loore:* learning.  535 *ne:* nor.  536
*Ylioun:* Ilium (Troy).  537 *Pirrus:* Pyrrhus, Achilles' son.  *streite
swerd:* drawn sword.  539 *seith us Eneydos:* (the) *Aeneid* tells us.

As maden alle the hennes in the cloos 540
Whan they had seyn of Chauntecleer the sighte.
But sovereynly dame Pertelote shrighte
Ful louder than dide Hasdrubales wyf
Whan that hir housbonde hadde lost his lyf
And that the Romayns hadden brend Cartage. 545
She was so ful of torment and of rage
That wilfully into the fyr she sterte
And brende hirselven with a stedefast herte.
    O woful hennes, right so cryden ye
As, whan that Nero brende the citee 550
Of Rome, cryden senatours wyves
For that hir housbondes losten alle hir lyves.
Withouten gilt this Nero hath hem slayn.
Now wol I turne to my tale agayn.
    The sely widwe and eek hir doghtres two 555
Herden thise hennes crye and maken wo,
And out at dores stirten they anon,
And syen the fox toward the grove gon,
And bar upon his bak the cok away,
And criden "Out! Harrow!" and "Weilaway! 560
Ha, ha, the fox!" And after hym they ran,
And eek with staves many another man.
Ran Colle our dogge, and Talbot, and Gerland,
And Malkyn, with a distaf in hir hand.
Ran cow, and calf, and eek the verray hogges, 565
So fered for the berkyng of the dogges
And shoutyng of the men and wommen eek.
They ronne so, hem thoughte hir herte breek.
They yelleden as fendes doon in helle.
The dokes cryden as men wolde hem quelle. 570
The gees for feere flowen over the trees.
Out of the hyve cam the swarm of bees.
So hydous was the noyse, A, *benedicitee!*

540 *cloos:* enclosure. 542 *sovereynly:* especially. *shrighte:* shrieked.
543 *Hasdrubal(es):* General, and defender of Carthage against the
Romans under Scipio (146 B.C.). Forced to surrender, he made terms
with the enemy permitting him to live in honorable captivity (Chaucer
is mistaken, l. 544). But his wife regarded him as a coward and killed
herself (ll. 547-48). 545 *brend:* burned. 547 *wilfully:* voluntarily.
*sterte,* leapt. 553 *Withouten gilt:* modifies (t)*hem.* 555 *sely:* poor.
558 *syen:* saw. 559 *bar:* carried. 560 *Harrow:* Help. *"Weilaway":*
Alas. 564 *Malkyn:* name for a country girl. 566 *fered for:* frightened
by. 567 *shoutyng:* shouting. 568 *They . . . breek:* They ran so (hard)
they thought their heart(s) would break. 569 *fendes doon:* fiends do.
570 *dokes:* ducks. *as:* as if. *quelle:* kill. 573 *hydous:* hideous.
*A:* Ah. *benedicitee:* bless ye (three syllables).

Certes, he Jakke Straw and his meynee
Ne made never shoutes half so shrille 575
Whan that they wolden any Flemyng kille
As thilke day was maad upon the fox.
Of bras they broghten bemes, and of box,
Of horn, of boon, in whiche they blewe and powped,
And ther-with-al they skryked, and they howped. 580
It semed as that heven sholde falle.
Now goode men, I pray yow, herkneth alle.
    Lo, how Fortune turneth sodeynly
The hope and pryde eek of hire enemy.
This cok that lay upon the foxes bak 585
In al his drede unto the fox he spak
And seyde, "Sire, if that I were as ye,
Yet sholde I seyn, as wys God helpe me,
'Turneth agayn, ye proude cherles alle.
A verray pestilence upon yow falle! 590
Now I am come unto this wodes syde,
Maugree youre heed, the cok shal here abyde.
I wol hym ete, in feith, and that anon.'"
    The fox answerde, "In feith, it shal be don."
And as he spak that word, al sodeynly 595
This cok brak from his mouth delyverly,
And hye upon a tree he fley anon.
And whan the fox say that he was gon,
"Allas," quod he, "O Chauntecleer, allas!
I have to yow," quod he, "y-doon trespas 600
In as muche as I maked yow aferd
Whan I yow hente and broghte out of the yerd.
But, sire, I dide it in no wikke entente.
Com doun, and I shal telle yow what I mente.
I shal seye sooth to yow, God help me so." 605
    "Nay thanne," quod he, "I shrewe us bothe two.
And first I shrewe myself, bothe blood and bones,
If thou bigile me ofter than ones.

574 *Jakke . . . meynee:* During the Peasants' Revolt (1381), Jack
Straw led a company (*meynee*) of Kentish rebels into London. He was
later executed. 576 *Flemyng kille:* Hostility was shown to Flemish
clothmakers coming into England because of their competition in labor
and reputed unwillingness to disclose the secrets of their craft to the
native workmen. 578 *broghten bemes:* brought trumpets (made of brass,
box[wood], horn, and bone). 579 *powped:* puffed. 580 *skryked:*
shrieked. *howped:* whooped. 588 *seyn:* say. *wys:* wise. 589 *agayn:*
back. *cherles:* churls. 591 *wodes:* wood's. 592 *Maugree . . . heed:*
Despite all you can do. 596 *delyverly:* nimbly. 598 *say:* saw. 600
*trespas:* offense. 603 *wikke:* evil. 606 *shrewe:* curse. 608 *bigile:*
beguile. *ofter:* more often.

Thou shalt namoore thurgh thy flaterye
Do me to synge and wynke with myn eye, 610
For he that wynketh, whan he sholde see,
Al wilfully, God lat hym never thee."
"Nay," quod the fox, "but God yeve hym meschaunce
That is so undiscreet of governaunce
That jangleth whan he sholde holde his pees." 615
Lo, swich it is for to be recchelees,
And necligent, and truste on flaterye.
But ye that holden this tale a folye
As of a fox, or of a cok and hen,
Taketh the moralitee, good men. 620
For seint Paul seith that al that writen is,
To oure doctryne it is y-write, ywis.
Taketh the fruyt, and lat the chaf be stille.
Now goode God, if that it be thy wille,
As seith my lord, so make us alle good men, 625
And brynge us to his heye blisse. Amen.

609 *thurgh:* through. 610 *Do:* Persuade. *wynke with:* close. 612 *God . . . thee:* God, let him never prosper. 613 *yeve:* give. 614 *governaunce:* self-control. 615 *jangleth:* chatters. *pees:* peace. 618 *a folye:* foolishness. 621-22 *al . . . ywis:* all that is written is surely written for our instruction. See I Cor. 10:11. 626 *heye:* high.

# SIR THOMAS WYATT   1503–1542

## *Whoso list to hunt, I know where is an hind*

Whoso list to hunt, I know where is an hind,
  But as for me, alas, I may no more:
  The vain travail hath wearied me so sore.
I am of them that farthest cometh behind;
Yet may I by no means my wearied mind            5
  Draw from the deer: but as she fleeth afore,
Fainting I follow. I leave off therefore,
  Since in a net I seek to hold the wind.
Who list her hunt, I put him out of doubt,
  As well as I may spend his time in vain:       10
  And, graven with diamonds, in letters plain
There is written her fair neck round about:
  *Noli me tangere*, for Caesar's I am;
  And wylde for to hold, though I seem tame.

## *My galley charged with forgetfulness*

My galley charged with forgetfulness
  Thorough sharp seas in winter nights doth pass
'Tween rock and rock; and eke mine enemy, alas,
  That is my lord, steereth with cruelness;
And every oar a thought in readiness,            5
  As though that death were light in such a case.

WHOSO LIST TO HUNT. *Whoso . . . hind:* Adapted from the Italian of Petrarch's sonnet, *In vita,* CLVII (Bohn tr.).
  1 *list to hunt:* wishes to go hunting. Read as *t'hunt.*   4 *cometh:* read as *com'th.*   9-10 *I . . . vain:* I assure him that he, too, will be wasting his time.   11 *graven:* engraved, cut with. Her necklace is the sign—as distinct as if incised by a diamond—that she is Caesar's.   13 *Noli me tangere* [*Caesaris enim sum*]: "Touch me not for I am Caesar's."   14 *wylde:* wild; pronounce final *e,* but Wyatt is not consistent in this practice.

MY GALLEY. *My galley . . . forgetfulness:* Adapted from Petrarch's sonnet, *In vita,* CLVI (Bohn tr.).
  1 *charged . . . forgetfulness:* overloaded with forgetfulness: the "lover" is so heavily burdened by love that he "forgets" everything but his troubled state.   3 *eke:* also.   3, 4 *enemy, lord:* love.   5-6 *every . . . case:* the peril is so great that the possibility of death comes to mind at every stroke of the oar.

24

An endless wind doth tear the sail apace
   Of forced sighs and trusty fearfulness.
A rain of tears, a cloud of dark disdain,
   Hath done the wearied cords great hinderance:    10
   Wreathed with error and eke with ignorance.
The stars be hid that led me to this pain;
   Drowned is reason that should me consort,
   And I remain despairing of the port.

## *They flee from me that sometime did me seek*

They flee from me that sometime did me seek
   With naked foot stalking in my chamber.
I have seen them gentle tame and meek
   That now are wild and do not remember
   That sometime they put themselves in danger    5
To take bread at my hand; and now they range
Busily seeking with a continual change.

Thank'd be fortune, it hath been otherwise
   Twenty times better; but once in special,
In thin array after a pleasant guise,    10
   When her loose gown from her shoulders did fall,
   And she me caught in her arms long and small,
Therewith all sweetly did me kiss,
And softly said, *Dear heart, how like you this?*

It was no dream: I lay broad waking.    15
   But all is turned thorough my gentleness
Into a strange fashion of forsaking;
   And I have leave to go of her goodness,
   And she also to use new-fangleness.
But since that I so kindely am served,    20
I would fain know what she hath deserved.

10 *hinderance:* damage. 11 *Wreathed:* Entangled, fouled. 13 *me consort:* (should) attend me as a guide and governor and not let me be exposed to the peril (of love, which "steereth with cruelness"). Some read *consort* in the MS as *comfort.*
THEY FLEE FROM ME. 5 *put . . . danger:* put themselves in his power; or, risked the scandal attached to the relation   7 *seeking:* paying court to others.   8 *it:* fortune.   9 *in special:* especially.   10 *guise:* (according to) fashion, style; or (after a) masquerade.   15 *broad waking:* wide awake.   16 *thorough:* a monosyllable (?).   18 *goodness:* sarcastic. Cf. *kindely am served,* l. 20.   19 *new-fangleness:* new fashions; fickleness. Cf. ll. 16-17.   20 *kindely:* is it trisyllabic?

### *Patience, though I have not*

Patience, though I have not
  The thing that I require,
I must of force, God wot,
  Forbear my most desire;
For no ways can I find          5
To sail against the wind.

Patience, do what they will
  To work me woe or spite,
I shall content me still
  To think both day and night,     10
To think and hold my peace,
Since there is no redress.

Patience, withouten blame
  For I offended nought;
I know they know the same,     15
  Though they have chang'd their thought.
Was ever thought so moved
To hate that it hath loved?

Patience of all my harm,
  For fortune is my foe;     20
Patience must be the charm
  To heal me of my woe.
Patience without offence
Is a painful patience.

### *My lute awake!*

My lute awake! perform the last
Labor that thou and I shall waste,
  And end that I have now begun;
For when this song is sung and past,
  My lute be still, for I have done.     5

PATIENCE. 3 *wot:* knows. 16 *thought:* way of thinking (about me),
contrasted with what they *know* to be true (l. 15). 18 *that:* what. 19
*my harm:* evil done to me. 24 *patience:* read as a trisyllable.
MY LUTE AWAKE! 3 *that:* what. Cf. l. 38.

As to be heard where ear is none,
As lead to grave in marble stone,
  My song may pierce her heart as soon;
Should we then sigh, or sing, or moan?
  No, no, my lute, for I have done.         10


The rocks do not so cruelly
Repulse the waves continually,
  As she my suit and affection,
So that I am past remedy:
  Whereby my lute and I have done,      15


Proud of the spoil that thou hast got
Of simple hearts thorough love's shot,
  By whom, unkind, thou hast them won,
Think not he hath his bow forgot,
  Although my lute and I have done.      20


Vengeance shall fall on thy disdain,
That mak'st but game on earnest pain;
  Think not alone under the sun
Unquit to cause thy lovers plain,
  Although my lute and I have done.      25


Perchance thee lie weathered and old,
The winter nights that are so cold,
  Plaining in vain unto the moon;
Thy wishes then dare not be told;
  Care then who list, for I have done.      30


And then may chance thee to repent
The time that thou hast lost and spent
  To cause thy lovers sigh and swoon;
Then shalt thou know beauty but lent,
  And wish and want as I have done.      35

7 *As lead . . . marble:* As lead, which is soft, to cut into marble.  17
*love's shot:* Cupid's arrow.  18 *unkind:* cruel lady.  19 *Think . . . forgot:* i.e., Cupid will desert her to serve another lady.  22 *mak'st . . .
pain:* jests at a lover's suffering.  24 *Unquit to cause:* Acquitted for
having caused.  *plain:* (to) suffer.  26 *weathered:* cf. "withered,"
Tottel's *Miscellany* (1557).  30 *list:* wishes to care.

Now cease, my lute: this is the last
Labor that thou and I shall waste,
And ended is that we begun;
Now is this song both sung and past:
My lute be still, for I have done.                    40


### *In eternum I was once determed*

In eternum I was once determed
For to have loved, and my mind affirmed
That with my heart it should be confirmed,
            In eternum.

Forthwith I found the thing that I might like          5
And sought with love to warm her heart alike,
For, as methought, I should not see the like
            In eternum.

To trace this dance I put myself in press;
Vain hope did lead and bade I should not cease        10
To serve, to suffer, and still to hold my peace
            In eternum.

With this first rule I ford'red me apace,
That, as methought, my truth had taken place
With full assurance to stand in her grace             15
            In eternum.

It was not long or I by proof had found
That feeble building is on feeble ground;
For in her heart this word did never sound,
            "In eternum."                              20

*In eternum* then from my heart I kest
That I had first determin'd for the best;
Now in the place another thought doth rest,
            In eternum.

IN ETERNUM. 1 *In eternum:* Everlastingly. 2-3 *mind . . . confirmed:* mind and heart were in accord; what the mind asserted to be
true (*affirmed*) was ratified (*confirmed*) by the heart. 9 *To . . . press:*
To follow this course I exerted myself. 13 *ford'red . . . apace:* got
on so well. 14 *truth . . . place:* faithfulness had won a place (in her
favor). 17 *or:* ere. 18 *feeble . . . is:* one builds feebly. 21 *kest:*
cast (out).

### To cause accord or to agree

To cause accord or to agree
Two contraries in one degree
And in one point, as seemeth me,
To all man's wit it cannot be:
    It is impossible.          5

Of heat and cold when I complain
And say that heat doth cause my pain,
When cold doth shake me every vein,
And both at once—I say again,
    It is impossible.         10

That man that hath his heart away,
If life liveth there, as men do say,
That he heartless should last one day
Alive, and not to turn to clay,
    It is impossible.         15

'Twixt life and death, say what who saith,
There liveth no life that draweth breath,
They join so near; and eke, i' faith,
To seek for life by wish of death,
    It is impossible.         20

Yet love, that all thing doth subdue,
Whose power there may no life eschew,
Hath wrought in me that I may rue
These miracles to be so true,
    That are impossible.       25

---

To cause accord. 1-3 *To . . . point:* To bring two contraries into accord; to make one of two. 3 *as . . . me:* as it seems to me. 4 *To . . . wit:* (It is plain) to every man's intelligence (that). 8 *me:* my. 11 *hath . . . away:* hath lost—with sense of actual loss—his heart (because of love). 12 *there:* in the heart, as the seat of life. Some editors enclose this line in parentheses, as also "They join so near" (l. 18) and "that I may rue" (l. 23). 16 *say . . . saith:* say what one will. 17 *There . . . breath:* i.e., because a man who has lost his heart (l. 11) is dead.

### *You that in love find luck and abundance*

You that in love find luck and abundance
   And live in lust and joyful jollity,
   Arise for shame! Do away your sluggardy!
Arise, I say, do May some observance!
Let me in bed lie dreaming in mischance;     5
   Let me remember the haps most unhappy
   That me betide in May most commonly,
As one whom love list little to advance.
Sephame said true that my nativity
   Mischanc'd was with the ruler of the May:     10
   He guessed, I prove, of that the verity.
In May my wealth and eke my life, I say,
   Have stood so oft in such perplexity:
   Rejoice! Let me dream of your felicity.


### *Is it possible?*

   Is it possible
  That so high debate,
So sharp, so sore, and of such rate,
Should end so soon and was begun so late?
   Is it possible?     5

   Is it possible
  So cruel intent,
So hasty heat and so soon spent,
From love to hate, and thence for to relent?
   Is it possible?     10

   Is it possible
  That any may find
Within one heart so diverse mind,
To change or turn as weather and wind?
   Is it possible?     15

YOU THAT IN LOVE. 2 *lust:* pleasure. 4 *do . . . observance:* cf.
Herrick, p. 126, l. 14 and note. 5 *mischance:* unlucky state. 7 *me . . .
May:* May, in fact, was Wyatt's unlucky month. 9 *Sephame:* Some
astrologer who cast the poet's horoscope. 10 *ruler:* dominant planetary
influence. 11 *I prove:* i.e., by the misfortunes which have befallen me.
IS IT POSSIBLE? 3 *rate:* cost.

Is it possible
To spy it in an eye
That turns as oft as chance on die?
The truth whereof can any try?
Is it possible?                                    20

It is possible
For to turn so oft,
To bring that lowest that was most aloft,
And to fall highest yet to light soft:
It is possible.                                    25

All is possible,
Whoso list believe;
Trust therefore first, and after preve:
As men wed ladies by license and leave,
All is possible.                                   30

## Forget not yet the tried intent

Forget not yet the tried intent
Of such a truth as I have meant,
My great travail so gladly spent,
    Forget not yet.

Forget not yet when first began            5
The weary life ye know, since whan
The suit, the service none tell can,
    Forget not yet.

Forget not yet the great assays,
The cruel wrong, the scornful ways,        10
The painful patience in denays,
    Forget not yet.

17 *it*: i.e., anything certain and steady.   18 *die*: throw of the dice.   19
*The truth . . . try?*: can anyone distinguish the truth in such a situation?   27 *list*: wishes to.   28 *preve*: prove.   29 *As . . . leave*: Troilcal;
As men wed only at the ladies' pleasure and permission.

FORGET NOT YET.   2 *truth*: faithfulness.   6 *whan*: when.   7 *suit, service*: solicitation for his lady's hand, and devotion to her.   9 *assays*:
trials testing his worthiness to be her suitor.   11 *denays*: denials.

Forget not yet, forget not this,
How long ago hath been and is
The mind that never meant amiss,
    Forget not yet.

Forget not then thine own approved,
The which so long hath thee so loved,
Whose steadfast faith yet never moved,
    Forget not this.

15

20

14 *How . . . is:* How long since and (still) is; i.e., how constant.

---

ASTROPHEL AND STELLA. A "sonnet sequence" celebrating the love of the "star lover" (Astrophel) and his "star" (Stella).

ASTROPHEL AND STELLA [I] 1 *fain:* desirous. 6 *inventions fine:* fine ways other poets had devised for entertaining their ladies. *Invention* is a rhetorical term: originality, the natural creative faculty (or its work). See l. 10. 8 *sun-burn'd brain: burn'd* by the hot beams of love from his lady's eyes. Cf. p. 42, ll. 12, 16. Cf. Shakespeare's jesting, "My mistress' eyes are nothing like the sun" (Sonnet 130). 9 *stay:* support. 10 *stepdame . . . blows:* Study (the real mother of learning and art [skill], but only the *stepdame* of Invention), conceived as a hard schoolmistress. 13 *truant:* wayward.

# SIR PHILIP SIDNEY 1554–1586

*from* ASTROPHEL AND STELLA

## I

Loving in truth, and fain in verse my love to show,
  That she, dear she, might take some pleasure of my pain:
  Pleasure might cause her read, reading might make her
    know,
  Knowledge might pity win, and pity grace obtain,
I sought fit words to paint the blackest face of woe,       5
  Studying inventions fine, her wits to entertain:
  Oft turning others' leaves, to see if thence would flow
  Some fresh and fruitful showers upon my sun-burn'd brain.
But words came halting forth, wanting Invention's stay,
  Invention, Nature's child, fled stepdame Study's blows,    10
  And others' feet still seem'd but strangers in my way.
Thus great with child to speak, and helpless in my throes,
  Biting my truant pen, beating myself for spite,
  Fool, said my Muse to me, look in thy heart and write.

## II

Not at the first sight, nor with a dribbed shot
  Love gave the wound, which while I breathe will bleed:
  But known worth did in mine of time proceed,
  Till by degrees it had full conquest got.
I saw and liked, I liked but loved not,             5
  I loved, but straight did not what Love decreed:
  At length to Love's decrees, I forc'd, agreed,
  Yet with repining at so partial lot.
Now even that footstep of lost liberty
  Is gone, and now like slave-born Muscovite,      10
  I call it praise to suffer tyranny;
And now employ the remnant of my wit,
  To make myself believe that all is well,
  While with a feeling skill I paint my hell.

[I] See opposite page (p. 32) for notes on this sonnet.
  [II] 1 *dribbed:* in archery, a shot that is short or wide of the
mark. 3 *mine:* a very long (time). 10 *Muscovite:* generally, a Russian.

34

## IV

Virtue, alas, now let me take some rest,
 Thou set'st a bate between my will and wit,
 If vain love have my simple soul opprest:
 Leave what thou lik'st not, deal not thou with it.
Thy sceptre use in some old Cato's breast;　　　　5
 Churches or schools are for thy seat more fit:
 I do confess, pardon a fault confest—
 My mouth too tender is for thy hard bit.
But if that needs thou wilt usurping be
 The little reason that is left in me,　　　　10
 And still th' effect of thy persuasion prove:
I swear, my heart such one shall show to thee,
 That shrines in flesh so true a deity,
 That, Virtue, thou thyself shalt be in love.


## V

It is most true, that eyes are form'd to serve
 The inward light: and that the heavenly part
 Ought to be king, from whose rules who do swerve,
 Rebels to Nature, strive for their own smart.
It is most true, what we call Cupid's dart,　　　　5
 An image is, which for ourselves we carve;
 And, fools, adore in temple of our heart,
 Till that good God make Church and Churchman starve.
True, that true Beauty Virtue is indeed,
 Whereof this Beauty can be but a shade,　　　　10
 Which elements with mortal mixture breed:
True, that on earth we are but pilgrims made,
 And should in soul up to our country move:
 True, and yet true that I must Stella love.

[IV] 2 *bate . . . wit*: debate between my desire and reason. 4 *deal
not*: have nothing to do with. 5 *Cato* (the Younger, 95 B.C.–46 B.C):
Roman patriot and Stoic, who took his life with his sword (cf. *sceptre*)
when his political views were discredited by Caesar's victory at Thapsus.
9 *needs . . . wilt*: you must.

[V] 2 *inward light*: i.e., of the soul, reflected in the eyes. 3-4 *from
. . . smart*: those who disobey the king's rules are rebels against Nature

## X

Reason, in faith thou art well serv'd, that still
  Wouldst brabbling be with sense and love in me:
  I rather wisht thee climb the Muses' hill,
  Or reach the fruit of Nature's choicest tree,
Or seek heav'n's course, or heav'n's inside to see:    5
  Why shouldst thou toil our thorny soil to till?
  Leave sense, and those which sense's objects be:
  Deal thou with powers of thoughts, leave love to will.
But thou wouldst needs fight both with love and sense,
  With sword of wit, giving wounds of dispraise,    10
  Till downright blows did soil thy cunning fence:
For soon as they strake thee with Stella's rays,
  Reason, thou kneel'dst, and offerdst straight to prove
  By reason good, good reason her to love.

and do injury to themselves. 6 *carve:* and thus create for ourselves an artificial and false notion of what love is. 7-8 *fools . . . starve:* in worshipping the image, fools put the false god before the true God, who then punishes the idolatry by "starving" both the heart (Church) and the lover (Churchman). Cf. ll. 3-4. 9-11 *True . . . breed:* The Platonic notion that *this* (earthly) Beauty is *but a shade* of the *true* (heavenly) Beauty, which is Virtue. The reference of *which* (l. 11) is uncertain; but the poet may be simply acknowledging that it is from the mysterious union of heavenly Beauty with matter that the earthly Beauty is produced.

[X] 2 *brabbling:* quibbling. 3-5 *I . . . see:* The poet remarks the proper occupations of Reason: to direct him to the Muses, whose inspiration he may then receive; to the study of Nature and the acquisition of natural knowledge; to the study of the heavens (astronomy) or the contemplation of heavenly things (religion). 7 *those:* those things. 10 *sword of wit:* sword of intellect. Reason is like a fencer (l. 11) using his favorite weapon. 11 *downright blows:* i.e., of love and sense. Cf. *Stella's rays,* l. 12. *soil . . . fence:* spoil Reason's deft fencing, i.e., love and sense will refute (an old use of *soil*) Reason. 12 *strake:* struck.

## XX

Fly, fly, my friends, I have my death wound; fly,
   See there that boy, that murth'ring boy, I say,
   Who like a thief, hid in dark bush doth lie,
   Till bloody bullet get him wrongful prey.
So tyrant he no fitter place could spy,          5
   Nor so fair level in so secret stay,
   As that sweet black which veils the heav'nly eye:
   There himself with his shot he close doth lay.
Poor passenger, pass now thereby I did,
   And stay'd pleas'd with the prospect of the place,    10
   While that black hue from me the bad guest hid:
But straight I saw motions of lightning grace,
   And then descried the glist'ring of his dart:
   But ere I could fly thence, it pierc'd my heart.

## XXXI

With how sad steps, O Moon, thou climb'st the skies,
   How silently, and with how wan a face!
   What may it be, that even in heav'nly place
   That busy archer his sharp arrows tries?
Sure if that long-with-love-acquainted eyes      5
   Can judge of love, thou feel'st a lover's case;
   I read it in thy looks; thy languisht grace
   To me that feel the like, thy state descries.
Then ev'n of fellowship, O Moon, tell me
   Is constant love deem'd there but want of wit?    10
   Are beauties there as proud as here they be?
Do they above love to be lov'd, and yet
   Those lovers scorn whom that love doth possess?
   Do they call Virtue there ungratefulness?

[XX] 2 *murth'ring boy:* Cupid. 3 *bush:* ambush, Stella's *dark* eyes.
6 *Nor . . . stay:* Nor be able to take such good aim from such a good
ambush. 7 *As . . . eye:* As in Stella's eye, which veils her "heavenly
part." See No. V, p. 34, ll. 1-2, 9-11 and note. 9 *passenger:* passer-by.
11 *While . . . hid:* cf. l. 3.
   [XXXI] 4 *busy archer:* Cupid. 10 *want of wit:* madness.

## XLVIII

Soul's joy, bend not those morning stars from me,
   Where Virtue is made strong by Beauty's might,
   Where Love is Chasteness, Pain doth learn delight,
   And Humbleness grows one with Majesty.
Whatever may ensue, O let me be            5
   Copartner of the riches of that sight:
   Let not mine eyes be hell-driv'n from that light:
   O look, O shine, O let me die and see.
For though I oft myself of them bemoan,
   That through my heart their beamy darts be gone,   10
   Whose cureless wounds even now most freshly bleed:
Yet since my death-wound is already got,
   Dear killer, spare not thy sweet cruel shot:
   A kind of grace it is to slay with speed.


## LXIX

O joy, too high for my low style to show:
   O bliss, fit for a nobler state than me:
   Envy, put out thine eyes, lest thou do see
   What oceans of delight in me do flow.
My friend, that oft saw through all masks my woe,   5
   Come, come, and let me pour myself on thee;
   Gone is the winter of my misery,
   My spring appears, O see what here doth grow.
For Stella hath with words where faith doth shine,
   Of her high heart giv'n me the monarchy:       10
   I, I, O I may say, that she is mine.
And though she give but thus conditionly
   This realm of bliss, while virtuous course I take,
   No kings be crown'd but they some covenants make.


[XLVIII] 1 *morning stars:* Stella's eyes, which communicate her
grace and favor.  4 *grows:* becomes.  10 *beamy darts:* the rays from
the "morning stars" (l. 1) are now like the "darts" from Cupid's bow.

## LXXI

Who will in fairest book of Nature know,
  How Virtue may best lodg'd in beauty be,
  Let him but learn of Love to read in thee,
  Stella, those fair lines, which true goodness show.
There shall he find all vices' overthrow      5
  Not by rude force, but sweetest sovereignty
  Of reason, from whose light those night-birds fly;
  That inward sun in thine eyes shineth so.
And not content to be Perfection's heir
  Thyself, dost strive all minds that way to move,   10
  Who mark in thee what is in thee most fair.
So while thy beauty draws the heart to love,
  As fast thy virtue bends that love to good:
  But, ah, Desire still cries, Give me some food.

## XCIX

When far-spent night persuades each mortal eye,
  To whom nor art nor nature granteth light,
  To lay his then mark-wanting shafts of sight,
  Clos'd with their quivers in sleep's armory;
With windows ope then most my mind doth lie,    5
  Viewing the shape of darkness and delight,
  Takes in that sad hue, which with th' inward night
  Of his 'maz'd powers keeps perfit harmony:
But when birds charm, and that sweet air, which is
  Morn's messenger, with rose-enamel'd skies     10
  Calls each wight to salute the flow'r of bliss;
In tomb of lids then buried are mine eyes,
  Forc'd by their Lord, who is asham'd to find
  Such light in sense, with such a darken'd mind.

[LXXI] 1 *book of Nature:* the whole of created nature, including the moral character of man. 7 *night-birds:* vices, as in l. 5. 8 *inward . . . so:* cf. No. V, p. 34, l. 2; No. XLVIII, p. 37, l. 1 and note. 9 *Perfection's heir:* cf. No. V, p. 34, ll. 9-11 and note. 10 *that . . . move:* i.e., towards Virtue; cf. No. V, p. 34, l. 13.

[XCIX] 3 *mark- . . . sight:* in sleep the eye has no object against which to aim its shafts. 7-8 *Takes . . . harmony:* The mind receives into itself the *sad hue* of night, which perfectly matches the dark state of its own perplexed and stupefied (amaz'd) powers. 11 *wight:* person. *flow'r of bliss:* object which gives him joy. 13 *Forc'd:* i.e., to remain buried. *Lord:* the "lover" who is speaking. 14 *light:* delight.

## CVII

Stella, since thou so right a princess art
  Of all the powers which life bestows on me,
  That ere by them ought undertaken be,
  They first resort unto that sovereign part;
Sweet, for a while give respite to my heart,      5
  Which pants as though it still should leap to thee:
  And on my thoughts give thy lieutenancy
  To this great cause, which needs both use and art.
And as a queen, who from her presence sends
  Whom she employs, dismiss from thee my wit,    10
  Till it have wrought what thy own will attends.
On servants' shame oft masters' blame doth sit;
  O let not fools in me thy works reprove,
  And scorning say, See what it is to love!


*from* CERTAINE SONETS


*Leave me, O Love, which reachest but to dust*

Leave me, O Love, which reachest but to dust,
And thou, my mind, aspire to higher things:
Grow rich in that which never taketh rust:
Whatever fades, but fading pleasure brings.


Draw in thy beams, and humble all thy might,    5
To that sweet yoke, where lasting freedoms be:
Which breaks the clouds and opens forth the light,
That doth both shine and give us sight to see.


  [CVII] 3 *ought:* anything. 4 *resort , , , part:* go to his Love for
approval and authorization as a subject would go to his sovereign. 7
*lieutenancy:* commission. 8 *use and art:* practice and skill. 11 *attends:*
directs to be done.
  LEAVE ME, O LOVE. 3 *that . . . rust:* ". . . treasures in heaven,
where neither moth nor rust doth corrupt."—Matt. 6:20. 4 *but:* only.

O take fast hold, let that light be thy guide,
In this small course which birth draws out to death,    10
And think how evil becometh him to slide,
Who seeketh heav'n, and comes of heav'nly breath.
   Then farewell world, thy uttermost I see,
   Eternal Love maintain thy life in me.

*Splendidis longum valedico nugis.*

### *The nightingale as soon as April bringeth*

The nightingale as soon as April bringeth
Unto her rested sense a perfect waking,
While late bare earth, proud of new clothing springeth,
Sings out her woes, a thorn her song-book making:
   And mournfully bewailing,                         5
   Her throat in tunes expresseth
   What grief her breast oppresseth,
For Tereus' force on her chaste will prevailing.
   O Philomela fair, O take some gladness,
   That here is juster cause of plaintful sadness:   10
   Thine earth now springs, mine fadeth,
   Thy thorn without, my thorn my heart invadeth.

11 *evil:* ill.  *slide:* err, lapse morally.  12 *comes . . . breath:* "And the Lord God formed man . . . and breathed into his nostrils the breath of life, etc."—Gen. 2:7.  *Splendidis . . . nugis:* I bid farewell forever to the splendid trifles (of the world).

THE NIGHTINGALE. 2 *rested sense:* i.e., after her winter's silence. 4 *thorn:* ambiguously, the hawthorn tree (in which the bird is singing), and presumably some remembered sorrow, which pricks the bird to plaintive song.  8-9 *For . . . fair:* Tereus, a Thracian king (according to Ovid's account of the legend) who ravished Philomela, the sister of Procne his wife, and then cut out her tongue to keep her from telling of his brutality and infidelity. Philomela managed, however, to weave her story into a web which was taken to Procne, and the sisters joined in a horrible revenge: Itys, Tereus' son by Procne, was slain and served to the father. When he discovered what had taken place, he tried to kill the sisters, but they were saved from his hand by being transformed into birds, Philomela into a nightingale, Procne into a swallow. See "Philomela," p. 394.

Alas, she hath no other cause of anguish
But Tereus' love, on her by strong hand wroken,
Wherein she suff'ring all her spirits languish, 15
Full womanlike complains her will was broken.
But I who daily craving,
Cannot have to content me,
Have more cause to lament me,
Since wanting is more woe than too much having. 20
O Philomela fair, O take some gladness,
That here is juster cause of plaintful sadness:
Thine earth now springs, mine fadeth;
Thy thorn without, my thorn my heart invadeth.

## In wonted walks, since wonted fancies change

In wonted walks, since wonted fancies change,
Some cause there is, which of strange cause doth rise:
For in each thing whereto mine eye doth range,
Part of my pain meseems engraved lies.

The rocks which were of constant mind, the mark 5
In climbing steep, now hard refusal show:
The shading woods seem now my sun to dark,
And stately hills disdain to look so low.

The restful caves now restless visions give,
In dales I see each way a hard ascent: 10
Like late mown meads, late cut from joy I live.
Alas sweet brooks do in my tears augment:
Rocks, woods, hills, caves, dales, meads, brooks, answer
me,
Infected minds infect each thing they see.

14 wroken. inflicted. 15 languish. (to) languish. 16 have. have anything.
    IN WONTED WALKS. 1 wonted: familiar. 4 meseems: it seems to me.
5-6 the mark . . . show: what once pointed out the way to the climber
now appears as an obstacle.

## When to my deadly pleasure

When to my deadly pleasure,
When to my lively torment,
Lady mine eyes remained,
Joined alas to your beams.

With violence of heav'nly                    5
Beauty tied, to virtue,
Reason abasht retired,
Gladly my sense yielded.

Gladly my senses yielding,
Thus to betray my heart's fort,              10
Left me devoid of all life.

They to the beamy suns went,
Where by the death of all deaths,
Find to what harm they hast'n'd.

Like to the silly sylvan,                    15
Burn'd by the light he best liked,
When with a fire he first met.

Yet, yet, a life to their death,
Lady you have reserved,
Lady the life of all love.                   20

For though my sense be from me,
And I be dead who want sense,
Yet do we both live in you.

Turned anew by your means,
Unto the flow'r that, ay, turns,             25
As you, alas, my sun bends.

WHEN TO MY DEADLY PLEASURE. 1 *When . . . pleasure:* On the
paradoxical state of the lover's mind and the imagery mingling the sensuous and spiritual manifestations of love, see the sonnets from *Astrophel
and Stella.* 7 *abasht:* confounded. 12 *beamy . . . went:* cf. ll. 4, 16;
and No. I, p. 33, l. 8. 15 *silly sylvan:* simple country fellow. 21 *be
. . . me:* is lost ("to the beamy suns," l. 12). 24-26 *Turned . . .
bends:* As the sunflower follows the sun, so the lover, his lady.

Thus do I fall to rise thus,
Thus do I die to live thus,
Changed to a change, I change not.

Thus may I not be from you:                    30
Thus be my senses on you:
Thus what I think is of you:
Thus what I seek is in you:
    All what I am, it is you.


*from* ARCADIA (THIRD BOOK)


*My true love hath my heart, and I have his*

[Charita's Song to Dametas]

My true love hath my heart, and I have his,
By just exchange, one for the other giv'n.
I hold his dear, and mine he cannot miss:
There never was a better bargain driv'n.


His heart in me, keeps me and him in one,     5
My heart in him, his thoughts and senses guides:
He loves my heart, for once it was his own:
I cherish his, because in me it bides.


His heart his wound received from my sight:
My heart was wounded with his wounded heart,   10
For as from me, on him his hurt did light,
So still methought in me his hurt did smart:
    Both equal hurt, in this change sought our bliss:
    My true love hath my heart and I have his.


CHARITA'S SONG. 9 *his . . . sight:* cf. No. II, p. 33, ll. 1-2.

## *O words which fall like summer dew on me*

[Dametas' Reply]

O words which fall like summer dew on me,
O breath more sweet than is the growing bean,
O tongue in which all honied liquors be,
O voice that doth the thrush in shrillness stain,
    Do you say still, this is her promise due,         5
    That she is mine, as I to her am true.


Gay hair, more gay than straw when harvest lies,
Lips red and plum, as cherries' ruddy side,
Eyes fair and great, like fair great oxes' eyes,
O breast in which two white sheep swell in pride:    10
    Join you with me, to seal this promise due,
    That she be mine, as I to her am true.


But thou white skin, as white as cruddes well prest,
So smooth, as sleekstone-like, it smooths each part,
And thou dear flesh, as soft as wool new drest,     15
And yet as hard, as brawn made hard by art:
    First four but say, next four their saying seal,
    But you must pay, the gage of promist weal.

---

DAMETAS' REPLY. 4 *shrillness stain*: obscures the brightness (of the
thrush's song by excelling it). 13 *cruddes*: curds. 14 *sleekstone-like*:
like a stone used for polishing a surface. 16 *hard by art*: by muscular
exercise (or some athletic "art"). 17 *First four*: words, breath, tongue,
voice (ll. 1-4). *next four*: hair, Lips, Eyes, breast (ll. 7-10). See *say*,
l. 5; *seal*, l. 11. 18 *gage*: pledge. *weal*: well-being.

# EDMUND SPENSER  *c.* 1552–1599

*from* THE SHEPHEARDES CALENDER

## November

### AEGLOGA UNDECIMA

#### Argument

*In this xi. Aeglogue he bewayleth the death of some mayden of greate bloud, whom he calleth Dido. The personage is secrete, and to me altogether unknowne, albe of him selfe I often required the same. This Aeglogue is made in imitation of Marot his song, which he made upon the death of Loys the frenche Queene. But farre passing his reache, and in myne opinion all other the Eglogues of this booke.*

#### THENOT

Colin my deare, when shall it please thee sing,
As thou were wont songs of some jouisaunce?
Thy Muse to long slombreth in sorrowing,
Lulled a sleepe through loves misgovernaunce.

---

THE SHEPHEARDES CALENDER. With the composition of this poem, Spenser naturalized in English a kind of verse which had enjoyed distinction for nearly two thousand years: from Theocritus (3rd cent. B.C.), who wrote in Greek, and Latin Virgil, through Spenser's more immediate French and Italian predecessors. In the pastoral poems shepherds simply "behave like human beings," or human beings masking as shepherds go about their singing, playing, grieving, debating in ways which fit their rural masks. Nothing is "natural," or "realistic," as we commonly take those terms, for a multitude of "conventions"—habits of expression, matters of reference—suitable to the shepherd life had come through long and able usage to pre-empt direct and vulgar statement. And yet, from this world which pastoralism evokes, truth is not excluded: it is rather revealed through its masks, or sustained in its allegories.

In giving his pastoral a native location, Spenser resorts to a language which is often old, colloquial, and dialectal. Ben Jonson remarked that he "writ no language," but today we are likely to respect the power of "old and unwonted words" not only to excite attention, but also to enrich the music and meaning of verse.

*Aeglogue:* A term of *Eclogue*, meaning simply *a selection,* appropriate to whatever kind of poetry it is applied; by long usage associated with Pastoral.

NOVEMBER. Much of the gloss is that of "E.K.," the original editor.
2 *wont:* used to do.  *jouisaunce:* myrth (E.K.).  4 *misgovernaunce:* misgovernment.

Now somewhat sing, whose endles sovenaunce,                    5
Emong the shepeheards swaines may aye remaine,
Whether thee list thy loved lasse advaunce,
Or honor *Pan* with hymnes of higher vaine.


### COLIN

*Thenot*, now nis the time of merimake.
Nor *Pan* to herye, nor with love to playe:                   10
Sike myrth in May is meetest for to make,
Or summer shade under the cocked haye.
But nowe sadde Winter welked hath the day,
And *Phoebus* weary of his yerely taske,
Ystabled hath his steedes in lowlye laye,                     15
And taken up his ynne in *Fishes* haske.
Thilke sollein season sadder plight doth aske:
And loatheth sike delightes, as thou doest prayse:
The mornefull Muse in myrth now list ne maske,
As shee was wont in youngth and sommer dayes.                 20
But if thou algate lust light virelayes,
And looser songs of love to underfong
Who but thy selfe deserves sike Poetes prayse?
Relieve thy Oaten pypes, that sleepen long.


### THENOT

The Nightingale is sovereigne of song,                        25
Before him sits the Titmose silent bee:
And I unfitte to thrust in skilfull thronge,
Should *Colin* make judge of my fooleree.
Nay, better learne of hem, that learned bee,

5. *sovenaunce:* remembrance (E.K.). 7 *list:* wish. *advaunce:* extol.
8 *Pan:* god of the fields, of shepherds. *vaine:* vein. 9 *nis:* is not. 10
*herye:* praise. 11 *Sike:* Such. *meetest:* most suitable. *make:* write
verses. 13 *welked:* "shortned or empayred."—E.K. 14 *Phoebus:* the
sun god, who drives his chariot across the heavens; the sun. *yerely
taske:* annual revolution. 15 *laye:* stall ( ?) ; field. 16 *ynne:* inn, abode.
*Fishes haske:* "a wicker pad, wherein they use to carry fish."—E.K. The
sign of Pisces corresponds, however, to the position of the sun in February, not November. 17 *Thilke sollein:* This gloomy. 19 *mornefull
Muse:* Melpomene, Muse of Tragedy. See l. 53 and note. *list ne:* is
not inclined to. *maske:* take part in a "pageant, disguising, or other
dramatic or semi-dramatic performance."—*Variorum* (The Johns Hopkins Spenser), III, 355. 20 *youngth:* youth. 21 *algate:* nevertheless.
*lust:* desire. *virelayes:* "A light kind of song."—E.K. 22 *underfong:*
undertake. 24 *Relieve:* Take up again. *Oaten pypes:* shepherds' pipes.
Cf. Milton, p. 56, l. 33. 27 *thronge:* i.e., of singers. 29 *hem:* them.

And han be watered at the Muses well: 30
The kindlye dewe drops from the higher tree,
And wets the little plants that lowly dwell.
But if sadde winters wrathe and season chill,
Accorde not with thy Muses meriment:
To sadder times thou mayst attune thy quill, 35
And sing of sorrowe and deathes dreeriment.
For deade is Dido, dead alas and drent,
Dido the greate shepehearde his daughter sheene:
The fayrest may she was that ever went,
Her like she has not left behinde I weene. 40
And if thou wilt bewayle my wofull tene,
I shall thee give yond cosset for thy payne:
And if thy rymes as rownd and rufull bene,
As those that did thy *Rosalind* complayne,
Much greater gyfts for guerdon thou shalt gayne, 45
Then kidde or cosset, which I thee bynempt:
Then up I say, thou jolly shepeheard swayne,
Let not my small demaund be so contempt.


#### COLIN

*Thenot* to that I choose, thou doest me tempt,
But ah to well I wote my humble vaine, 50
And howe my rymes bene rugged and unkempt:
Yet as I conne, my conning I will strayne.

Up then *Melpomene* thou mournefulst Muse of nyne,
Such cause of mourning never hadst afore:
Up grieslie ghostes and up my rufull ryme, 55
Matter of myrth now shalt thou have no more.
For dead shee is, that myrth thee made of yore.
  *Dido* my deare alas is dead,
  Dead and lyeth wrapt in lead:
    O heavie herse, 60
Let streaming teares be poured out in store:
    O carefull verse.

30 *han . . . well:* have drunk of the waters of Helicon, over which
the Muses preside.  35 *quill:* shepherd's pipe.  36 *dreeriment:* anguish.
37 *Dido:* see p. 45, Argument.  *dront:* drowned.  38 *sheene:* fair.  39
*may:* maid (E.K.).  40 *weene:* think.  41 *tene:* sorrow.  42 *cosset:* lamb.
43 *rownd:* perfect.  *bene:* be.  44 *complayne:* lament.  45 *guerdon:*
reward.  46 *bynempt:* promised.  48 *contempt:* viewed with contempt.
50 *wote:* know.  51 *bene:* are.  52 *conne:* am able.  53 *nyne:* There
are nine Muses.  59 *lead:* her lead coffin.  60 *herse:* "the solemn obsequy (burial rites) in funerals."—E.K.  62 *carefull:* full of care.

48

Shepheards, that by your flocks on Kentish downes abyde,
Waile ye this wofull waste of natures warke:
Waile we the wight, whose presence was our pryde:    65
Waile we the wight, whose absence is our carke.
The sonne of all the world is dimme and darke:
   The earth now lacks her wonted light,
   And all we dwell in deadly night,
      O heavie herse.    70
Breake we our pypes, that shrild as lowde as larke,
      O carefull verse.


Why doe we longer live (ah why live we so long)
Whose better dayes death hath shut up in woe?
The fayrest floure our gyrlond all emong,    75
Is faded quite and into dust ygoe.
Sing now ye shepheards daughters, sing no moe
   The songs that *Colin* made in her prayse,
   But into weeping turne your wanton layes,
      O heavie herse,    80
Now is time to dye. Nay time was long ygoe,
      O carefull verse.


Whence is it, that the flouret of the field doth fade,
And lyeth buryed long in Winters bale:
Yet soone as spring his mantle hath displayd,    85
It floureth fresh, as it should never fayle?
But thing on earth that is of most availe,
   As vertues braunch and beauties budde,
   Reliven not for any good.
      O heavie herse,    90
The braunch once dead, the budde eke needes must quaile,
      O carefull verse.


She while she was (that was, a woful word to sayne)
For beauties prayse and plesaunce had no pere:
So well she couth the shepherds entertayne,    95
With cakes and cracknells and such country chere.

64 *warke:* work.  65 *wight:* person.  66 *carke:* care.  75 *gyrlond:*
garland.  76 *ygoe:* gone.  77 *moe:* more.  79 *wanton:* merry.  *layes:*
songs.  84 *bale:* misery.  89 *Reliven not:* Come not to life again.  91
*eke:* also.  *quaile:* perish.  93 *sayne:* say.  95 *couth:* could; knew
how (to).

Ne would she scorne the simple shepheards swaine,
　　For she would cal hem often heame
　　And give hem curds and clouted creame.
　　　　O heavie herse,
Als *Colin Cloute* she would not once disdayne.　　　　100
　　　　O carefull verse.


But nowe sike happy cheere is turnd to heavie chaunce,
Such pleasaunce now displast by dolors dint:
All musick sleepes, where death doth leade the daunce,　　105
And shepherds wonted solace is extinct.
The blew in black, the greene in gray is tincte,
　　The gaudie girlonds deck her grave,
　　The faded flowres her corse embrave.
　　　　O heavie herse,　　　　110
Morne nowe my Muse, now morne with teares besprint.
　　　　O carefull verse.


O thou greate shepheard *Lobbin*, how great is thy griefe,
Where bene the nosegayes that she dight for thee:
The colourd chaplets wrought with a chiefe,
The knotted rushrings, and gilte rosemaree?　　　　115
For shee deemed nothing too deere for thee.
　　Ah they bene all yclad in clay,
　　One bitter blast blewe all away.
　　　　O heavie herse,
Thereof nought remaynes but the memoree.　　　　120
　　　　O carefull verse.


Ay me that dreerie death should strike so mortall stroke,
That can undoe Dame natures kindly course:
The faded lockes fall from the loftie oke,
The flouds do gaspe, for dryed is theyr sourse,　　　　125
And flouds of teares flowe in theyr stead perforse.
　　The mantled medowes mourne,
　　Theyr sondry colours tourne.
　　　　O heavie herse,
The heavens doe melt in teares without remorse.　　　　130
　　　　O carefull verse.

98 *heame:* home. 99 *clouted:* clotted. 103 *chaunce:* misfortune. 104 *dint:* stroke. 107 *The blew . . . tincte;* The blue is stained black; the green, gray. 109 *corse:* corpse. *embrave:* beautify. 111 *besprint:* sprinkled. 113 *Lobbin:* a favorite of Dido's. 114 *dight:* made. 115 *chaplets . . . chiefe:* probably, garlands woven to make a special feature of some flower. 116 *gilte:* golden. 118 *yclad . . . clay:* clad in clay—dead. 126 *flouds:* rivers.

The feeble flocks in field refuse their former foode,
And hang theyr heads, as they would learne to weepe:
The beastes in forest wayle as they were woode,          135
Except the wolves, that chase the wandring sheepe:
Now she is gon that safely did hem keepe.
 The turtle on the bared braunch,
 Laments the wound, that death did launch.
  O heavie herse,          140
And *Philomele* her song with teares doth steepe.
  O carefull verse.

The water Nymphs, that wont with her to sing and daunce,
And for her girlond olive braunches beare,
Now balefull boughes of cypres doen advaunce:          145
The Muses, that were wont greene bayes to weare,
Now bringen bitter eldre braunches seare:
 The fatall sisters eke repent,
 Her vitall threde so soone was spent.
  O heavie herse,          150
Morne now my Muse, now morne with heavie cheare.
  O carefull verse.

O trustlesse state of earthly things, and slipper hope
Of mortal men, that swincke and sweate for nought,
And shooting wide, doe misse the marked scope:          155
Now have I learnd (a lesson derely bought)
That nys on earth assuraunce to be sought:
 For what might be in earthlie mould,
 That did her buried body hould.
  O heavie herse,          160
Yet saw I on the beare when it was brought,
  O carefull verse.

But maugre death, and dreaded sisters deadly spight,
And gates of hel, and fyrie furies forse:
She hath the bonds broke of eternall night,          165
Her soule unbodied of the burdenous corpse.

135 *woode:* mad. 138 *turtle:* turtledove. 141 *Philomele:* nightingale.
Cf. Sidney, p. 40; Arnold, p. 394. 145 *cypres:* "sign of all sorrow"—
E.K. 148 *fatall sisters:* the Fates. 149 *vitall threde:* i.e., of life,
as spun, measured, and cut by the Fates. Cf. Milton, pp. 157-58, ll. 75-
76. 151 *cheare:* countenance. 153 *slipper:* slippery. 154 *swincke:* toil.
155 *scope:* target. 161 *beare:* bier. 163 *maugre:* in spite of. *dreaded
sisters:* see l. 148.

Why then weepes Lobbin so without remorse?
  O Lobb, thy losse no longer lament,
  Dido nis dead, but into heaven hent.
     O happye herse,                  170
Cease now my Muse, now cease thy sorrowes sourse,
     O joyfull verse.

Why wayle we then? why weary we the Gods with playnts,
As if some evill were to her betight?
She raignes a goddesse now emong the saintes,    175
That whilome was the saynt of shepheards light:
And is enstalled nowe in heavens hight
  I see thee blessed soule, I see,
  Walke in *Elisian* fieldes so free.
     O happy herse,                 180
Might I once come to thee (O that I might)
     O joyfull verse.

Unwise and wretched men to weete whats good or ill,
We deeme of Death as doome of ill desert:
But knewe we fooles, what it us bringes until,    185
Dye would we dayly, once it to expert.
No daunger there the shepheard can astert:
  Fayre fieldes and pleasaunt layes there bene,
  The fieldes ay fresh, the grasse ay greene:
     O happy herse,                 190
Make hast ye shepheards, thether to revert,
     O joyfull verse.

*Dido* is gone afore (whose turne shall be the next?)
There lives shee with the blessed Gods in blisse,
There drincks she *Nectar* with *Ambrosia* mixt,    195
And joyes enjoyes, that mortall men doe misse.
The honor now of highest gods she is,
  That whilome was poore shepheards pryde,
  While here on earth she did abyde.
     O happy herse,                 200
Ceasse now my song, my woe now wasted is.
     O joyfull verse.

---

169 *hent:* caught (up).  173 *playnts:* lamentations.  174 *betight:* betide.  176 *whilome:* once.  183 *weete:* know.  184 *deeme:* think.  186 *expert:* experience.  187 *astert:* disturb.  189 *ay:* always.  191 *revert:* return.  201 *wasted:* spent.

## THENOT

Ay francke shepheard, how bene thy verses meint
With doolful pleasaunce, so as I ne wotte,
Whether rejoyce or weepe for great constrainte?          205
Thyne be the cossette, well hast thow it gotte.
Up *Colin* up, ynough thou morned hast,
Now gynnes to mizzle, hye we homeward fast.

### COLINS EMBLEME

*La mort ny mord.*

### *from* THE FAERIE QUEENE (BOOK III, CANTOS IX, X)

### [*Malbecco and Hellenore*]

I

Redoubted knights, and honorable Dames,
  To whom I levell all my labours end,
  Right sore I feare, least with unworthy blames
  This odious argument my rimes should shend,
  Or ought your goodly patience offend,          5
  Whiles of a wanton Lady I do write,
  Which with her loose incontinence doth blend
  The shyning glory of your soveraigne light,
And knighthood fowle defaced by a faithlesse knight.

2

But never let th' ensample of the bad          10
  Offend the good: for good by paragone
  Of evill, may more notably be rad,
  As white seemes fairer, macht with blacke attone;

203 *francke:* honest. *meint:* mingled. 204 *wotte:* know. 206 *cossette:*
see l. 42. 208 *gynnes to mizzle:* begins to drizzle. *La mort ny mord:*
". . . death biteth not."—E.K.
  THE FAERIE QUEENE. 1 *Redoubted:* Renowned. 3 *least:* lest.
*blames:* blemishes. 4 *shend:* disgrace. 7 *blend:* stain. 10 *ensample:*
example. 11 *paragone:* comparison. 12 *rad:* made known. 13 *macht:*
matched. *attone:* together.

Ne all are shamed by the fault of one:
For lo in heaven, whereas all goodnesse is,                    15
Emongst the Angels, a whole legione
Of wicked Sprights did fall from happy blis;
What wonder then, if one of women all did mis?

### 3

Then listen Lordings, if ye list to weet
The cause, why Satyrane and Paridell                          20
Mote not be entertaynd, as seemed meet,
Into that Castle (as that Squire does tell).
Therein a cancred crabbed Carle does dwell,
That has no skill of Court nor courtesie,
Ne cares, what men say of him ill or well;                    25
For all his dayes he drownes in privitie,
Yet has full large to live, and spend at libertie.

### 4

But all his mind is set on mucky pelfe,
To hoord up heapes of evill gotten masse,
For which he others wrongs, and wreckes himselfe;            30
Yet is he lincked to a lovely lasse,
Whose beauty doth her bounty far surpasse,
The which to him both far unequall yeares,
And also far unlike conditions has;
For she does joy to play emongst her peares,                 35
And to be free from hard restraint and gealous feares.

### 5

But he is old, and withered like hay,
Unfit faire Ladies service to supply;
The privie guilt whereof makes him alway
Suspect her truth, and keepe continuall spy                  40
Upon her with his other blincked eye;
Ne suffreth he resort of living wight
Approch to her, ne keepe her company,

14 *Ne:* Nor.   15 *whereas:* where.   17 *wicked Sprights:* the rebel
angels.   18 *if . . . mis:* if one woman should err.   19 *Lordings:* Sirs.
*list:* please.   *weet:* learn.   21 *Mote:* May.   *entertaynd:* received.
*meet:* fit.   22 *Squire:* Squire of Dames, with whom Paridell and
Satyrane were riding.   23 *Carle:* a rude man.   26 *privitie:* seclusion.
27 *has . . . live:* has an abundance upon which to live   28 *mucky
pelfe:* filthy lucre.   29 *masse:* stuff.   32 *bounty:* virtue.   35 *peares:* companions.   39 *privie:* secret.   41 *his . . . eye:* he is blind in one eye
(see l. 136) and can't see well out of the other—it is blinking.   42-43
*Ne . . . her:* Nor does he allow any living person to visit her.

But in close bowre her mewes from all men's sight,
Depriv'd of kindly joy and naturall delight.                           45

### 6

Malbecco he, and Hellenore she hight,
  Unfitly yokt together in one teeme,
  That is the cause, why never any knight
  Is suffred here to enter, but he seeme
  Such, as no doubt of him he neede misdeeme.                          5ᴦ
  Thereat Sir Satyrane gan smile, and say;
  Extremely mad the man I surely deeme,
  That weenes with watch and hard restraint to stay
A woman's will, which is disposd to go astray.

### 7

In vaine he feares that, which he cannot shonne:                       55
  For who wotes not, that woman's subtiltyes
  Can guilen Argus, when she list misdonne?
  It is not yron bandes, nor hundred eyes,
  Nor brasen walls, nor many wakefull spyes,
  That can withhold her wilfull wandring feet;                         60
  But fast good will with gentle courtesyes,
  And timely service to her pleasures meet
May her perhaps containe, that else would algates fleet.

### 8

Then is he not more mad (said Paridell)
  That hath himselfe unto such service sold,                           65
  In dolefull thraldome all his dayes to dwell?
  For sure a foole I do him firmely hold,
  That loves his fetters, though they were of gold.
  But why do we devise of others ill,
  Whiles thus we suffer this same dotard old                           70
  To keepe us out, in scorne of his owne will,
And rather do not ransack all, and him selfe kill?

### 9

Nay let us first (said Satyrane) entreat
  The man by gentle meanes, to let us in,

44 *bowre:* lodgings.  *her mewes:* shuts her up.  46 *Malbecco:* "The
cuckold."  *hight:* called.  49 *but:* unless.  50 *as . . . misdeeme:* as
one he need not suspect.  53 *weenes:* imagines.  55 *shonne:* avoid.  56
*wotes:* knows.  57 *guilen:* beguile.  *Argus:* who had a hundred
eyes.  *list misdonne:* is pleased to do evil.  62 *meet:* suitable.  63
*algates fleet:* run away anyhow.  69 *devise:* converse.  71 *in . . . will:*
(but) in contempt of his wishes.

And afterwardes affray with cruell threat,                    75
Ere that we to efforce it do begin:
Then if all fayle, we will by force it win,
And eke reward the wretch for his mesprise,
As may be worthy of his haynous sin.
That counsell pleasd: then Paridell did rise,                 80
And to the Castle gate approcht in quiet wise.

### 10

Whereat soft knocking, entrance he desyrd.
The good man selfe, which then the Porter playd,
Him answered, that all were now retyrd
Unto their rest, and all the keyes convayd                    85
Unto their maister, who in bed was layd,
That none him durst awake out of his dreme;
And therefore them of patience gently prayd.
Then Paridell began to chaunge his theme,
And threatned him with force and punishment extreme.   90

### 11

But all in vaine; for nought mote him relent,
And now so long before the wicket fast
They wayted, that the night was forward spent,
And the faire welkin fowly overcast,
Gan blowen up a bitter stormy blast,                          95
With shoure and hayle so horrible and dred,
That this faire many were compeld at last,
To fly for succour to a little shed,
The which beside the gate for swine was ordered.

.   .   .*

75 *affray:* scare (him).   76 *efforce:* carry by force.   78 *mesprise:* contempt.   91 *mote . . . relent:* might soften him.   92 *wicket:* gate.   94
*welkin:* sky.   97 *many:* company.   99 *ordered:* prepared.

\* While Paridell and the others are in the shed out of the storm, another knight comes up to the castle. He, too, is refused admission, and
seeks refuge in the shed but is told that it is full. Indignant, he swears
that he will go in even if he has to "dislodge" the present occupants.
Paridell accepts this as a challenge. The two fight; both are unhorsed at
the first encounter, Paridell receiving a very heavy blow. He is revived
by the Squire, and the fight resumes afoot with swords. Satyrane then
intervenes to halt the senseless quarrel and succeeds in pacifying both.
They all resolve to assault the castle and to burn its gates.

Although no hint is given of the fact, it turns out that the stranger is
Britomart, the invincible and virtuous Lady Knight of *The Faerie
Queene.* (See ll. 134, 198.)

### 18

Malbecco seeing them resolv'd in deed       100
  To flame the gates, and hearing them to call
  For fire in earnest, ran with fearfull speed,
  And to them calling from the castle wall,
  Besought them humbly, him to beare with all,
  As ignoraunt of servants bad abuse,       105
  And slacke attendaunce unto straungers call.
  The knights were willing all things to excuse,
Though nought belev'd, and entraunce late did not refuse.

### 19

They bene ybrought into a comely bowre,
  And serv'd of all things that mote needfull bee;       110
  Yet secretly their hoste did on them lowre,
  And welcomde more for feare, then charitee;
  But they dissembled, what they did not see,
  And welcomed themselves. Each gan undight
  Their garments wet, and weary armour free,       115
  To dry them selves by Vulcanes flaming light,
And eke their lately bruzed parts to bring in plight.

.  .  *

### 25

  . . . Supper was dight;
  Then they Malbecco prayd of curtesy,
  That of his Lady they might have the sight,       120
And company at meat, to do them more delight.

### 26

But he to shift their curious request,
  Gan causen, why she could not come in place;
  Her crased health, her late recourse to rest,
  And humid evening, ill for sicke folkes cace:       125
  But none of those excuses could take place;

112 *then:* than.  113 *dissembled . . . see:* pretended not to notice his inhospitality.  114 *undight:* to take off.  116 *Vulcanes . . . light:* the open fire.  117 *in plight:* into good condition.

  \* While the members of the company are composing themselves, the feminine identity of the Lady Knight is revealed, though who she is remains unknown.

  118 *dight:* prepared.  123 *causen:* to give reasons.  *come in place:* take her place, as would befit a Lady.  124 *crased:* infirm.  *late . . . rest:* recent retirement.  126 *take place:* stand.

Ne would they eate, till she in presence came.
　She came in presence with right comely grace,
　And fairely them saluted, as became,
And shewd her selfe in all a gentle curteous Dame.　　130

### 27

They sate to meat, and Satyrane his chaunce
　Was her before, and Paridell besyde;
　But he him selfe sate looking still askaunce,
　Gainst Britomart, and ever closely eyde
　Sir Satyrane, that glaunces might not glyde:　　135
　But his blind eye, that syded Paridell,
　All his demeasnure from his sight did hyde:
　On her faire face so did he feede his fill,
And sent close messages of love to her at will.

### 28

And ever and anone, when none was ware,　　140
　With speaking lookes, that close embassage bore,
　He rov'd at her, and told his secret care:
　For all that art he learned had of yore.
　Ne was she ignoraunt of that lewd lore,
　But in his eye his meaning wisely red,　　145
　And with the like him answerd evermore:
　She sent at him one firie dart, whose hed
Empoisned was with privy lust, and gealous dred.

### 29

He from that deadly throw made no defence,
　But to the wound his weake hart opened wyde;　　150
　The wicked engine through false influence,
　Past through his eyes, and secretly did glyde
　Into his hart, which it did sorely gryde.
　But nothing new to him was that same paine,
　Ne paine at all; for he so oft had tryde　　155
　The powre thereof, and lov'd so oft in vaine,
That thing of course he counted, love to entertaine.

### 30

Thenceforth to her he sought to intimate
His inward griefe, by meanes to him well knowne,
Now Bacchus fruit out of the silver plate                    160
He on the table dasht, as overthrowne,
Or of the fruitfull liquor overflowne,
And by the dauncing bubbles did divine,
Or therein write to let his love be showne;
Which well she red out of the learned line,                  165
A sacrament prophane in mistery of wine.

### 31

And when so of his hand the pledge she raught,
The guilty cup she fained to mistake,
And in her lap did shed her idle draught,
Shewing desire her inward flame to slake:                    170
By such close signes they secret way did make
Unto their wils, and one eyes watch escape;
Two eyes him needeth, for to watch and wake,
Who lovers will deceive. Thus was the ape,
By their faire handling, put into Malbeccoes cape.           175

### 32

Now when of meats and drinks they had their fill,
Purpose was moved by that gentle Dame,
Unto those knights adventurous, to tell
Of deeds of armes, which unto them became,
And every one his kindred, and his name.                     180
Then Paridell, in whom a kindly pryde
Of gracious speach, and skill his words to frame
Abounded, being glad of so fit tyde
Him to commend to her, thus spake, of all well eyde.

· · ·

160-70 *Now . . . slake:* Apparently based on an old "guessing game"
among lovers, in which wine "accidentally" spilled upon the table was
taken to make a pattern wherein the lady could "read" her lover's intentions. *A sacrament . . . wine:* ". . . wine being used in a sacred
ceremony, as an outward sign or symbol containing a divine mystery.
Sir Paridell here abuses wine prophanely, as a sign or symbol of his
unlawful love."—*Variorum,* III, 280.   167 *raught:* snatched.   168 *fained
to mistake:* pretended not to get good hold of.   172 *one* [eye's] : Malbecco's.   174-75 *the . . . cape:* Court fools often carried apes, and to
put the ape on another's shoulder (over which he wore his "cape") was
to make a fool of him—*loc. cit.*   179 *became:* (were) fitting; happened.
183 *tyde:* occasion.

52

But all the while, that he these speaches spent,                    185
  Upon his lips hong faire Dame Hellenore,
  With vigilant regard, and dew attent,
  Fashioning worlds of fancies evermore
  In her fraile wit, that now her quite forlore:
  The whiles unwares away her wondring eye,        190
  And greedy eares her weake hart from her bore:
  Which he perceiving, ever privily
In speaking, many false belgardes at her let fly.

1

The morow next, so soone as Phoebus Lamp
  Bewrayed had the world with early light,        195
  And fresh Aurora had the shady damp
  Out of the goodly heaven amoved quight,
  Faire Britomart and that same Faerie knight
  Uprose, forth on their journey for to wend:
  But Paridell complaynd, that his late fight      200
  With Britomart, so sore did him offend,
That ryde he could not, till his hurts he did amend.

2

So forth they far'd, but he behind them stayd,
  Maulgre his host, who grudged grievously,
  To house a guest, that would be needes obayd,    205
  And of his owne him left not liberty:
  Might wanting measure moveth surquedry.
  Two things he feared, but the third was death;
  That fierce youngmans unruly maistery;
  His money, which he lov'd as living breath;       210
And his faire wife, whom honest long he kept uneath.

3

But patience perforce he must abie,
  What fortune and his fate on him will lay,
  Fond is the feare, that findes no remedie;

189 *forlore:* abandoned.   193 *belgardes:* amorous looks.
  * After long "discourse" they all "go to rest."
  195 *Bewrayed:* Revealed.   196 *Aurora:* dawn.   197 *quight:* quite.
198 *Faerie knight:* Sir Satyrane.   201 *offend:* assail.   204 *Maulgre:*
In spite of.   207 *Might . . . surquedry:* The intemperate use of power
is arrogance.   211 *honest:* virtuous.   *uneath:* with difficulty.   212 *abie:*
abide.   214 *Fond:* Foolish.

Yet warily he watcheth every way,　　　　　　　　215
By which he feareth evill happen may:
So th' evill thinkes by watching to prevent;
Ne doth he suffer her, nor night, nor day,
Out of his sight her selfe once to absent.
So doth he punish her and eke himselfe torment.　　　220

### 4

But Paridell kept better watch, then hee,
　A fit occasion for his turne to find:
False love, why do men say, thou canst not see,
　And in their foolish fancy feigne thee blind,
That with thy charmes the sharpest sight doest bind,　225
　And to thy will abuse? Thou walkest free,
　And seest every secret of the mind;
　Thou seest all, yet none at all sees thee;
All that is by the working of thy Deitee.

### 5

So perfect in that art was Paridell,　　　　　　　230
　That he Malbeccoes halfen eye did wyle,
His halfen eye he wiled wondrous well,
　And Hellenors both eyes did eke beguyle,
Both eyes and hart attonce, during the whyle
That he there sojourned his wounds to heale;　　　235
　That Cupid selfe it seeing, close did smyle,
　To weet how he her love away did steale,
And bad, that none their joyous treason should reveale.

### 6

The learned lover lost no time nor tyde,
　That least avantage mote to him afford,　　　　240
Yet bore so faire a saile, that none espyde
　His secret drift, till he her layd abord.
When so in open place, and commune bord,
　He fortun'd her to meet, with commune speach
He courted her, yet bayted every word,　　　　　245
　That his ungentle hoste n'ote him appeach
Of vile ungentlenesse, or hospitages breach.

222 *turne:* opportunity.　226 *abuse:* deceive.　231 *halfen:* imperfect. *wyle:* beguile.　237 *weet:* learn.　238 *bad:* forbade.　241 *bore
. . . saile:* put on such a good face.　242 *layd abord:* literally, brought
his ship along side of.　243 *commune bord:* common table.　246 *n'ote:*
might not. *appeach:* accuse.　247 *hospitages:* hospitalities.

### 7

But when apart (if ever her apart)
  He found, then his false engins fast he plyde,
  And all the sleights unbosomd in his hart;         250
  He sigh'd, he sobd, he swownd, he perdy dyde,
  And cast himselfe on ground her fast besyde:
  Tho when againe he him bethought to live,
  He wept, and wayld, and false laments belyde,
  Saying, but if she Mercie would him give,       255
That he mote algates dye, yet did his death forgive.

### 8

And otherwhiles with amorous delights,
  And pleasing toyes he would her entertaine,
  Now singing sweetly, to surprise her sprights,
  Now making layes of love and lovers paine,      260
  Bransles, ballads, virelayes, and verses vaine;
  Oft purposes, oft riddles he devysd,
  And thousands like, which flowed in his braine,
  With which he fed her fancie, and entysd
To take to his new love, and leave her old despysd.   265

### 9

And every where he might, and every while
  He did her service dewtifull, and sewed
  At hand with humble pride, and pleasing guile,
  So closely yet, that none but she it vewed,
  Who well perceived all, and all indewed.      270
  Thus finely did he his false nets dispred,
  With which he many weake harts had subdewd
  Of yore, and many had ylike misled:
What wonder then, if she were likewise carried?

### 10

No fort so fensible, no wals so strong,      275
  But that continuall battery will rive,
  Or daily siege through dispurvayance long,
  And lacke of reskewes will to parley drive;

249 *engins:* wiles.  251 *swownd:* swooned.  *perdy:* verily.  252 *fast:* close.  254 *belyde:* pretended.  255 *but if:* unless.  256 *he . . . for-give:* he might indeed die, and yet forgive her for killing him.  259 *sprights:* spirits.  261 *Bransles:* Dance songs.  *ballad[e]s, virelayes:* Old French verse forms. See p. 46, l. 21 and note.  262 *purposes:* a game of questions and answers.  264 *entysd:* enticed.  267 *sewed:* pursued.  270 *indewed:* took in.  271 *dispred:* spread out.  273 *ylike:* alike.  276 *rive:* destroy.  277 *dispurvayance:* lack of provisions.

And Peace, that unto parley eare will give,
Will shortly yeeld it selfe, and will be made     280
The vassall of the victors will bylive:
That stratageme had oftentimes assayd
This crafty paramoure, and now it plaine displayd.


### 11

For through his traines he her intrapped hath,
That she her love and hart hath wholy sold     285
To him, without regard of gaine, or scath,
Or care of credite, or of husband old,
Whom she hath vow'd to dub a faire cucquold.
Nought wants but time and place, which shortly shee
Devized hath, and to her lover told.     290
It pleased well. So well they both agree;
So readie rype to ill, ill wemens counsels bee.


### 12

Darke was the evening, fit for lovers stealth,
When chaunst Malbecco busie be elsewhere,
She to his closet went, where all his wealth     295
Lay hid: thereof she countlesse summes did reare,
The which she meant away with her to beare;
The rest she fyr'd for sport, or for despight;
As Hellene, when she saw aloft appeare
The Trojane flames, and reach to heavens hight,     300
Did clap her hands, and joyed at that dolefull sight.


### 13

This second Hellene, faire Dame Hellenore,
The whiles her husband ran with sory haste,
To quench the flames which she had tyn'd before,
Laught at his foolish labour spent in waste;     305
And ran into her lovers armes right fast;
Where streight embraced, she to him did cry
And call aloud for helpe, ere helpe were past;
For loe that guest would beare her forcibly,
And meant to ravish her, that rather had to dy.     310

281 *bylive:* quickly. 282 *assayd:* tried. 284 *traines:* nets. See *nets,*
l. 271. 286 *scath:* injury. 287 *credite:* reputation. 288 *cucquold:*
see l. 46 and note. 296 *reare:* take. 298 *fyr'd:* set fire to. 299-301
*As . . . sight:* Alludes to Helen's conduct at the siege of Troy. Just
how did Helen behave on that occasion? See *Variorum,* III, 285. 304
*tyn'd:* kindled. 310 *rather . . . dy:* preferred (in pretense) to die.

14

The wretched man hearing her call for ayd,
  And readie seeing him with her to fly,
  In his disquiet mind was much dismayd:
  But when againe he backward cast his eye,
  And saw the wicked fire so furiously                         315
  Consume his hart, and scorch his Idoles face,
  He was therewith distressed diversly,
  Ne wist he how to turne, nor to what place;
Was never wretched man in such a wofull cace.

15

Ay when to him she cryde, to her he turnd,                       320
  And left the fire; love money overcame:
  But when he marked, how his money burnd,
  He left his wife; money did love disclame:
  Both was he loth to loose his loved Dame,
  And loth to leave his liefest pelfe behind,                  325
  Yet sith he n'ote save both, he sav'd that same,
  Which was the dearest to his donghill mind,
The God of his desire, the joy of misers blind.

16

Thus whilest all things in troublous uprore were,
  And all men busie to suppresse the flame,                   330
  The loving couple neede no reskew feare,
  But leasure had, and libertie to frame
  Their purpost flight, free from all mens reclame;
  And Night, the patronesse of love-stealth faire,
  Gave them safe conduct, till to end they came:                335
  So bene they gone yfeare, a wanton paire
Of lovers loosely knit, where list them to repaire.

17

Soone as the cruell flames yslaked were,
  Malbecco seeing, how his losse did lye,
  Out of the flames, which he had quencht whylere                340
  Into huge waves of griefe and gealosye
  Full deepe emplonged was, and drowned nye,
  Twixt inward doole and felonous despight;

316 *hart, Idoles face:* gold, Mammon.   325 *liefest:* dearest.   *pelfe:*
lucre.   326 *sith he n'ote:* since he might not.   336 *yfeare:* together.
337 *list them:* they please.   340 *whylere:* some time ago.   342 *emplonged:* plunged.   *nye:* nearly.   343 *doole:* pain.   *despight:* anger.

He rav'd, he wept, he stampt, he lowd did cry,
  And all the passions, that in man may light,      345
Did him attonce oppresse, and vex his caytive spright.

### 18

Long thus he chawd the cud of inward griefe,
  And did consume his gall with anguish sore,
  Still when he mused on his late mischiefe,
  Then still the smart thereof increased more,      350
  And seem'd more grievous, then it was before:
  At last when sorrow he saw booted nought,
  Ne griefe might not his love to him restore,
  He gan devise, how her he reskew mought,
Ten thousand wayes he cast in his confused thought.     355

### 19

At last resolving, like a pilgrim pore,
  To search her forth, where so she might be fond,
  And bearing with him treasure in close store,
  The rest he leaves in ground: So takes in hond
  To seeke her endlong, both by sea and lond.     360
  Long he her sought, he sought her farre and nere,
  And every where that he mote understond,
  Of knights and ladies any meetings were,
And of eachone he met, he tydings did inquere.

### 20

But all in vaine, his woman was too wise,     365
  Ever to come into his clouch againe,
  And he too simple ever to surprise
  The jolly Paridell, for all his paine.
  One day, as he forpassed by the plaine
  With weary pace, he farre away espide     370
  A couple, seeming well to be his twaine,
  Which hoved close under a forrest side,
As if they lay in wait, or else themselves did hide.

### 21

Well weened he, that those the same mote bee,
  And as he better did their shape avize,     375
  Him seemed more their manner did agree;

---

349 *mischiefe*: injury.   352 *booted*: profited.   354 *mought*: might.   355
*cast*: considered.   356 *pore*: poor.   359 *takes in hond*: undertakes.
360 *endlong*: continuously.   362 *understond*: learn.   366 *clouch*: clutch.
369 *forpassed*: went.   372 *hoved*: waited.   375 *avize*: observe.

For th' one was armed all in warlike wize,
    Whom, to be Paridell he did devize;
    And th' other all yclad in garments light,
    Discolour'd like to womanish disguise,                       380
    He did resemble to his Ladie bright;
And ever his faint hart much earned at the sight.

### 22

And ever faine he towards them would goe,
    But yet durst not for dread approchen nie,
    But stood aloofe, unweeting what to doe;                     385
    Till that prickt forth with loves extremitie,
    That is the father of foule gealosy,
    He closely nearer crept, the truth to weet:
    But, as he nigher drew, he easily
    Might scerne, that it was not his sweetest sweet,            390
Ne yet her belamour, the partner of his sheet.

### 23

But it was scornefull Braggadochio,
    That with his servant Trompart hoverd there,
    Sith late he fled from his too earnest foe:
    Whom such when as Malbecco spyed clere,                      395
    He turned backe, and would have fled arere;
    Till Trompart ronning hastily, him did stay,
    And bad before his soveraine Lord appere:
    That was him loth, yet durst he not gainesay,
And comming him before, low louted on the lay.                   400

### 24

The Boaster at him sternely bent his browe,
    As if he could have kild him with his looke,
    That to the ground him meekely made to bowe,
    And awfull terror deepe into him strooke,
    That every member of his bodie quooke.                       405
    Said he, Thou man of nought, what doest thou here,
    Unfitly furnisht with thy bag and booke,
    Where I expected one with shield and spere,
To prove some deedes of armes upon an equall pere.

381 *resemble:* liken to.   382 *earned:* yearned.   385 *unweeting:* not
knowing   386 *prickt:* goaded.   390 *scerne:* discern.   391 *belamour:*
lover.   *his:* Malbecco's.   392 *Braggadochio:* the Braggart (see l. 401).
393 *Trompart:* "Vainglorious man," *F.Q.,* II, iii.   400 *low . . . lay:*
bent low on the ground.   405 *quooke:* quaked.   407 *booke:* account
book (?).

### 25

The wretched man at his imperious speach,     410
  Was all abasht, and low prostrating, said;
  Good Sir, let not my rudenesse be no breach
  Unto your patience, ne be ill ypaid;
  For I unwares this way by fortune straid,
  A silly Pilgrim driven to distresse,     415
  That seeke a Lady, There he suddein staid,
  And did the rest with grievous sighes suppresse,
While teares stood in his eies, few drops of bitternesse.

### 26

What Ladie, man? (said Trompart) take good hart,
  And tell thy griefe, if any hidden lye;     420
  Was never better time to shew thy smart,
  Then now, that noble succor is thee by,
  That is the whole worlds commune remedy.
  That chearefull word his weake hart much did cheare,
  And with vaine hope his spirits faint supply,     425
  That bold he said; O most redoubted Pere,
Vouchsafe with mild regard a wretches cace to heare.

### 27

Then sighing sore, It is not long (said hee)
  Sith I enjoyd the gentlest Dame alive;
  Of whom a knight, no knight at all perdee,     430
  But shame of all, that doe for honor strive,
  By treacherous deceipt did me deprive;
  Through open outrage he her bore away,
  And with fowle force unto his will did drive,
  Which all good knights, that armes do beare this day,  435
Are bound for to revenge, and punish if they may.

### 28

And you most noble Lord, that can and dare
  Redresse the wrong of miserable wight,
  Cannot employ your most victorious speare
  In better quarrell, then defence of right,     440
  And for a Ladie gainst a faithlesse knight;
  So shall your glory be advaunced much,
  And all faire Ladies magnifie your might,

412 *breach:* wound.   416 *staid:* checked himself.   426 *Pere:* champion.
430 *perdee:* surely.

And eke my selfe, albe I simple such,
Your worthy paine shall well reward with guerdon rich.    445


### 29

With that out of his bouget forth he drew
    Great store of treasure, therewith him to tempt;
    But he on it lookt scornefully askew,
    As much disdeigning to be so misdempt,
    Or a war-monger to be basely nempt;    450
    And said; Thy offers base I greatly loth,
    And eke thy words uncourteous and unkempt;
    I tread in dust thee and thy money both,
That, were it not for shame, So turned from him wroth.


### 30

But Trompart, that his maisters humor knew,    455
    In lofty lookes to hide an humble mind,
    Was inly tickled with that golden vew,
    And in his eare him rounded close behind:
    Yet stoupt he not, but lay still in the wind,
    Waiting advauntage on the pray to sease;    460
    Till Trompart lowly to the ground inclind,
    Besought him his great courage to appease,
And pardon simple man, that rash did him displease.


### 31

Bigge looking like a doughtie Doucepere,
    At last he thus; Thou clod of vilest clay,    465
    I pardon yield, and with thy rudenesse beare;
    But weete henceforth, that all that golden pray,
    And all that else the vaine world vaunten may,
    I loath as doung, ne deeme my dew reward:
    Fame is my meed, and glory vertues pray.    470
    But minds of mortall men are muchell mard,
And mov'd amisse with massie mucks unmeet regard.

444 *albe:* albeit. *I . . . such:* I am such a simple person. 445 *guerdon:* reward. 446 *bouget:* bag. 449 *misdempt:* misjudged. 450 *warmonger:* mercenary soldier. *nempt:* named. 458 *rounded:* whispered. 459 *Yet . . . wind:* from falconry: He did not swoop down, but remained poised above. 460 *pray to sease:* to seize the prey. 462 *courage to appease:* to calm his temper. 464 *Doucepere:* champion, one of the twelve Peers of Charlemagne. 467 *pray:* plunder. 468 *vaunten:* boast. 470 *meed:* reward. 471 *muchell mard:* greatly damaged. 472 *with . . . regard:* by unsuitable regard for piles of filth, i.e., gold.

### 32

And more, I graunt to thy great miserie
  Gratious respect, thy wife shall backe be sent,
  And that vile knight, who ever that he bee,        475
  Which hath thy Lady reft, and knighthood shent,
  By Sanglamort my sword, whose deadly dent
  The bloud hath of so many thousands shed,
  I sweare, ere long shall dearely it repent;
  Ne he twixt heaven and earth shall hide his hed,    480
But soone he shall be found, and shortly doen be ded.

### 33

The foolish man thereat woxe wondrous blith,
  As if the word so spoken, were halfe donne,
  And humbly thanked him a thousand sith,
  That had from death to life him newly wonne.    485
  Tho forth the Boaster marching, brave begonne
  His stolen steed to thunder furiously,
  As if he heaven and hell would overronne,
  And all the world confound with cruelty,
That much Malbecco joyed in his jollity.    490

### 34

Thus long they three together traveiled,
  Through many a wood, and many an uncouth way,
  To seeke his wife, that was farre wandered:
  But those two sought nought, but the present pray,
  To weete the treasure, which he did bewray,    495
  On which their eies and harts were wholly set,
  With purpose, how they might it best betray;
  For sith the houre, that first he did them let
The same behold, therewith their keene desires were whet.

### 35

It fortuned as they together far'd,    500
  They spide, where Paridell came pricking fast
  Upon the plaine, the which himselfe prepar'd
  To giust with that brave straunger knight a cast,

---

476 *reft:* seized.  *shent:* disgraced.  477 *dent:* stroke.  481 *doen be ded:* killed.  482 *woxe:* waxed.  484 *sith:* times.  486 *Tho:* Then.  487 *stolen steed:* Braggadochio had stolen the great Sir Guyon's horse. II, iii, 4.  *thunder:* thunder at.  490 *jollity:* gallant appearance.  492 *uncouth:* unfamiliar.  494 *pray:* see l. 467.  495 *To weete:* To wit.  *bewray:* reveal.  497 *betray:* steal.  501 *pricking:* riding.  503 *To . . . cast:* To tilt a bout with, etc.

As on adventure by the way he past:
  Alone he rode without his Paragone;        505
  For having filcht her bels, her up he cast
  To the wide world, and let her fly alone,
He nould be clogd. So had he served many one.


### 36

The gentle Lady, loose at randon left,
  The greene-wood long did walke, and wander wide   510
  At wilde adventure, like a forlorne weft,
  Till on a day the Satyres her espide
  Straying alone withouten groome or guide;
  Her up they tooke, and with them home her led,
  With them as housewife ever to abide,        515
  To milk their gotes, and make them cheese and bred,
And every one as commune good her handeled.


### 37

That shortly she Malbecco has forgot,
  And eke Sir Paridell, all were he deare;
  Who from her went to seeke another lot,      520
  And now by fortune was arrived here,
  Where those two guilers with Malbecco were:
  Soone as the oldman saw Sir Paridell,
  He fainted, and was almost dead with feare,
  Ne word he had to speake, his griefe to tell,   525
But to him louted low, and greeted goodly well.


### 38

And after asked him for Hellenore:
  I take no keepe of her (said Paridell)
  She wonneth in the forrest there before.
  So forth he rode, as his adventure fell;    530
  The whiles the Boaster from his loftie sell
  Faynd to alight, something amisse to mend;
  But the fresh Swayne would not his leasure dwell,

---

505 *Paragone:* mistress (Hellenore).   506 *filcht her bels:* In falconry the bells attached to the hawk's legs are not removed when the
bird is released; but he has robbed Hellenore of what he wanted before he let her go.   508 *He . . . clogd:* He would not be hampered.
509 *randon:* random.   511 *weft:* waif.   517 *as . . . handeled:* used
her as common property.   519 *all:* although.   522 *guilers:* deceivers.
526 *louted:* bowed.   528 *I . . . her:* I do not concern myself with her.
529 *wonneth:* dwells.   531 *sell:* saddle.   532 *Faynd:* Pretended.   533
*Swayne:* Paridell.   *dwell:* abide.

But went his way; whom when he passed kend,
He up remounted light, and after faind to wend.          535

### 39

Perdy nay (said Malbecco) shall ye not:
  But let him passe as lightly, as he came;
  For litle good of him is to be got,
  And mickle perill to be put to shame.
  But let us go to seeke my dearest Dame,          540
  Whom he hath left in yonder forrest wyld:
  For of her safety in great doubt I am,
  Least salvage beastes her person have despoyld:
Then all the world is lost, and we in vaine have toyld.

### 40

They all agree, and forward them addrest:          545
  Ah but (said craftie Trompart) weete ye well,
  That yonder in that wastefull wildernesse
  Huge monsters haunt, and many dangers dwell;
  Dragons, and Minotaures, and feendes of hell,
  And many wilde woodmen, which robbe and rend          550
  All travellers; therefore advise ye well,
  Before ye enterprise that way to wend:
One may his journey bring too soone to evill end.

### 41

Malbecco stopt in great astonishment,
  And with pale eyes fast fixed on the rest,          555
  Their counsell crav'd, in daunger imminent.
  Said Trompart, You that are the most opprest
  With burden of great treasure, I thinke best
  Here for to stay in safetie behind;
  My Lord and I will search the wide forrest.          560
  That counsell pleased not Malbeccoes mind;
For he was much affraid, himselfe alone to find.

### 42

Then is it best (said he) that ye doe leave
  Your treasure here in some securitie,
  Either fast closed in some hollow greave,          565

534 *whom . . . kend:* when Braggadochio saw that Paridell had gone
on.   539 *mickle:* much.   543 *salvage:* savage.   545 *them addrest:* be-
took themselves.   547 *wastefull:* desolate.   549 *Minotaures:* the Mino-
taur, a fabulous monster, half man, half bull. There was only one, but
Braggadochio multiplies the number to frighten Malbecco.   551 *advise:*
take counsel.   552 *enterpise:* undertake.   565 *greave:* thicket.

Or buried in the ground from jeopardie,
Till we returne againe in safetie:
As for us two, least doubt of us ye have,
Hence farre away we will blindfolded lie,
Ne privie be unto your treasures grave.                    570
It pleased: so he did. Then they march forward brave.

### 43

Now when amid the thickest woods they were,
    They heard a noyse of many bagpipes shrill,
    And shrieking Hububs them approching nere,
    Which all the forrest fild with horror fill;           575
    That dreadfull sound the boasters hart did thrill,
    With such amazement, that in haste he fled,
    Ne ever looked backe for good or ill,
    And after him eke fearefull Trompart sped;
The old man could not fly, but fell to ground halfe ded.   580

### 44

Yet afterwards close creeping, as he might,
    He in a bush did hide his fearefull hed,
    The jolly Satyres full of fresh delight,
    Came dauncing forth, and with them nimbly led
    Faire Hellenore, with girlonds all bespred,            585
    Whom their May-lady they had newly made:
    She proud of that new honour, which they red,
    And of their lovely fellowship full glade,
Daunst lively, and her face did with a lawrell shade.

### 45

The silly man that in the thicket lay                      590
    Saw all this goodly sport, and grieved sore,
    Yet durst he not against it doe or say,
    But did his hart with bitter thoughts engore,
    To see th'unkindnesse of his Hellenore.
    All day they daunced with great lustihed,              595
    And with their horned feet the greene grasse wore,
    The whiles their gotes upon the brouzes fed,
Till drouping Phoebus gan to hide his golden hed.

570 *privie*: cognizant.  576 *thrill*: pierce.  586 *May-lady*: Queen of
the May.  587 *red*: bestowed.  588 *glade*: glad.  590 *silly*: simple.
592 *not*: nothing.  593 *engore*: pierce.  595 *lustihed*: pleasure.  597
*brouzes*: young shoots.

### 46

Tho up they gan their merry pypes to trusse,
  And all their goodly heards did gather round,          600
  But every Satyre first did give a busse
  To Hellenore: so busses did abound.
  Now gan the humid vapour shed the ground
  With perly deaw, and th' Earthes gloomy shade
  Did dim the brightnesse of the welkin round,          605
  That every bird and beast awarned made,
To shrowd themselves, whiles sleepe their senses did invade.

### 47

Which when Malbecco saw, out of his bush
  Upon his hands and feete he crept full light,
  And like a gote emongst the gotes did rush,          610
  That through the helpe of his faire hornes on hight,
  And misty dampe of misconceiving night,
  And eke through likenesse of his gotish beard,
  He did the better counterfeite aright:
  So home he marcht emongst the horned heard,          615
That none of all the Satyres him espyde or heard.

### 48

At night, when all they went to sleepe, he vewd,
  Whereas his lovely wife emongst them lay,
  Embraced of a Satyre rough and rude,
  Who all the night did minde his joyous play:          620
  Nine times he heard him come aloft ere day,
  That all his hart with gealosie did swell;
  But yet that nights ensample did bewray,
  That not for nought his wife them loved so well,
When one so oft a night did ring his matins bell.          625

### 49

So closely as he could, he to them crept,
  When wearie of their sport to sleepe they fell,
  And to his wife, that now full soundly slept,
  He whispered in her eare, and did her tell,

599 *Tho:* Then. *trusse:* bundle up. 601 *busse:* kiss. 603 *shed:* sprinkle. 606 *awarned made:* was warned. 607 *shrowd:* shelter. 611 *hornes:* the sign of the cuckold is his horns. 612 *misconceiving:* i.e., permitting the misconception that Malbecco is a goat. 623 *bewray:* reveal.

That it was he, which by her side did dwell,            630
  And therefore prayd her wake, to heare him plaine.
As one out of a dreame not waked well,
  She turned her, and returned backe againe:
Yet her for to awake he did the more constraine.


### 50

At last with irkesome trouble she abrayd;              635
  And then perceiving, that it was indeed
Her old Malbecco, which did her upbrayd,
With loosenesse of her love, and loathly deed,
She was astonisht with exceeding dreed,                640
  And would have wakt the Satyre by her syde;
But he her prayd, for mercy, or for meed,
  To save his life, ne let him be descryde,
But hearken to his lore, and all his counsell hyde.


### 51

Tho gan he her perswade, to leave that lewd
  And loathsome life, of God and man abhord,          645
And home returne, where all should be renewd
With perfect peace, and bandes of fresh accord,
And she receiv'd againe to bed and bord,
  As if no trespasse ever had bene donne:
But she it all refused at one word,                    650
  And by no meanes would to his will be wonne,
But chose emongst the jolly Satyres still to wonne.


### 52

He wooed her, till day spring he espyde;
  But all in vaine: and then turnd to the heard,
Who butted him with hornes on every syde,             655
And trode downe in the durt, where his hore beard
Was fowly dight, and he of death afeard.
Early before the heavens fairest light
  Out of the ruddy East was fully reard,
The heardes out of their foldes were loosed quight,    660
And he emongst the rest crept forth in sory plight.

---

634 *constraine*: force.  635 *abrayd*: roused.  637 *upbrayd*: chide.  641
*meed*: a bribe.  642 *descryde*: discovered.  647 *bandes*: (in) bonds.
653 *day spring*: dawn.  656 *hore*: hoary.  657 *fowly dight*: defiled.
659 *reard*: risen.  660 *loosed quight*: freed.

### 53

So soone as he the Prison dore did pas,
 He ran as fast, as both his feete could beare,
 And never looked, who behind him was,
 Ne scarsely who before: like as a beare    665
 That creeping close, amongst the hives to reare
 An hony combe, the wakefull dogs espy,
 And him assayling, sore his carkasse teare,
 That hardly he with life away does fly,
Ne stayes, till safe himselfe he see from jeopardy.   670

### 54

Ne stayd he, till he came unto the place,
 Where late his treasure he entombed had,
 Where when he found it not (for Trompart bace
 Had it purloyned for his maister bad):
 With extreme fury he became quite mad,    675
 And ran away, ran with himselfe away:
 That who so straungely had him seene bestad,
 With upstart haire, and staring eyes dismay,
From Limbo lake him late escaped sure would say.

### 55

High over hilles and over dales he fled,     680
 As if the wind him on his winges had borne,
 Ne banck nor bush could stay him, when he sped
 His nimble feet, as treading still on thorne:
 Griefe, and despight, and gealosie, and scorne
 Did all the way him follow hard behind,    685
 And he himselfe himselfe loath'd so forlorne,
 So shamefully forlorne of womankind;
That as a snake, still lurked in his wounded mind.

### 56

Still fled he forward, looking backward still,
 Ne stayd his flight, nor fearefull agony,    690
 Till that he came unto a rockie hill,
 Over the sea, suspended dreadfully,

666 *reare*: carry off.   673 *bace*: base.   677 *bestad*: hard put to it.   678
*upstart*: (hair) on end.   *staring . . . dismay*: eyes staring in dismay.
679 *Limbo lake*: pit of hell.   686 *forlorne*: undone; also l. 687.   688
*snake*: image of woman in his mind, identifying her with Eve, by
whom Adam was "undone."

That living creature it would terrify,
To looke adowne, or upward to the hight:
From thence he threw himselfe dispiteously,                    695
All desperate of his fore-damned spright,
That seem'd no helpe for him was left in living sight.


### 57

But through long anguish, and selfe-murdring thought
  He was so wasted and forpined quight,
  That all his substance was consum'd to nought,          700
  And nothing left, but like an aery Spright,
  That on the rockes he fell so flit and light,
  That he thereby receiv'd no hurt at all;
  But chaunced on a craggy cliff to light;
  Whence he with crooked clawes so long did crall,          705
That at the last he found a cave with entrance small.


### 58

Into the same he creepes, and thenceforth there
  Resolv'd to build his balefull mansion,
  In drery darkenesse, and continuall feare
  Of that rockes fall, which ever and anon                  710
  Threates with huge ruine him to fall upon,
  That he dare never sleepe, but that one eye
  Still ope he keepes for that occasion;
  Ne ever rests he in tranquillity,
The roring billowes beat his bowre so boystrously.            715


### 59

Ne ever is he wont on ought to feed,
  But toades and frogs, his pasture poysonous,
  Which in his cold complexion do breed
  A filthy bloud, or humour rancorous,
  Matter of doubt and dread suspitious,                     720
  That doth with curelesse care consume the hart,
  Corrupts the stomacke with gall vitious,
  Croscuts the liver with internall smart,
And doth transfixe the soule with deathes eternall dart.

---

695 *dispiteously:* pitilessly.  696 *fore-damned spright:* already damned
spirit.  697 *That:* (So) that (it).  699 *forpined:* wasted away.  702
*flit:* unsubstantial.  705 *crall:* crawl.  713 *occasion:* occurrence, i.e., the
falling of the rock.  717 *pasture:* diet.  718 *complexion:* temperament.
719 *humour rancorous:* malignant fluid, matching his complexion.

## 60

Yet can he never dye, but dying lives,          725
   And doth himselfe with sorrow new sustaine,
   That death and life attonce unto him gives,
   And painefull pleasure turnes to pleasing paine.
   There dwels he ever, miserable swaine,
   Hatefull both to him selfe and every wight;     730
   Where he through privy griefe, and horrour vaine,
   Is woxen so deform'd, that he has quight
Forgot he was a man, and Gealosie is hight.


## *Prothalamion*

### 1

Calm was the day, and through the trembling air,
Sweet breathing Zephyrus did softly play
A gentle spirit, that lightly did delay
Hot Titan's beams, which then did glister fair:
When I whom sullen care,          5
Through discontent of my long fruitless stay
In Princes' Court, and expectation vain
Of idle hopes, which still do fly away,
Like empty shadows, did afflict my brain,
Walk'd forth to ease my pain          10
Along the shore of silver streaming Thames,
Whose rutty bank, the which his river hems,
Was painted all with variable flowers,
And all the meads adorn'd with dainty gems,
Fit to deck maidens' bow'rs,          15
And crown their paramours,
Against the bridal day, which is not long:
   Sweet Thames run softly, till I end my song.


### 2

There, in a meadow, by the river's side,
A flock of Nymphs I chanced to espy,          20
All lovely Daughters of the Flood thereby,

732 *woxen:* grown.   733 *hight:* named.
   PROTHALAMION : A "marriage song," honoring the "double marriage" of the Ladies Elizabeth and Katherine Somerset.  2 *Zephyrus:* the West Wind.  12 *rutty:* rooty.  21 *Flood:* River (Thames).

With goodly greenish locks all loose untied,
As each had been a bride,
And each one had a little wicker basket,
Made of fine twigs entrailed curiously,                    25
In which they gathered flowers to fill their flasket:
And with fine fingers, cropp'd full feateously
The tender stalks on high.
Of every sort, which in that meadow grew,
They gathered some; the violet pallid blue,                30
The little daisy, that at evening closes,
The virgin lily, and the primrose true,
With store of vermeil roses,
To deck their bridegrooms' posies,
Against the bridal day, which was not long:                35
    Sweet Thames run softly, till I end my song.


3

With that I saw two Swans of goodly hue,
Come softly swimming down along the lee;
Two fairer birds I yet did never see:
The snow which doth the top of Pindus strew,               40
Did never whiter shew,
Nor Jove himself when he a swan would be
For love of Leda, whiter did appear:
Yet Leda was they say as white as he,
Yet not so white as these, nor nothing near;              45
So purely white they were,
That even the gentle stream, the which them bare,
Seem'd foul to them, and bade his billows spare
To wet their silken feathers, least they might
Soil their fair plumes with water not so fair,             50
And mar their beauties bright,
That shone as heaven's light,
Against their bridal day, which was not long:
    Sweet Thames run softly, till I end my song.


23 *As:* As if.   25 *entrailed:* entwined.   26 *flasket:* shallow basket.
27 *feateously:* deftly.   33 *vermeil:* bright red.   38 *lee:* Lee (1596
edn.) : the stream(?). See *Variorum, Minor Poems*, II, 498.   40 *Pindus:*
mountain in Thessaly.   42-43 *Jove . . . Leda:* Leda, a mortal beloved
by Jove (Zeus), who visited her in the shape of a swan. Among their
offspring were Castor and Pollux (l. 173) and Helen of Troy. See
Yeats, p. 479.

## 4

Eftsoons the Nymphs, which now had flowers their fill,  55
Ran all in haste, to see that silver brood,
As they came floating on the crystal flood,
Whom when they saw, they stood amazed still,
Their wond'ring eyes to fill.
Them seem'd they never saw a sight so fair,  60
Of fowls so lovely, that they sure did deem
Them heavenly born, or to be that same pair
Which through the sky draw Venus silver team,
For sure they did not seem
To be begot of any earthly seed,  65
But rather angels or of angels' breed:
Yet were they bred of Somers-heat they say,
In sweetest season, when each flower and weed
The earth did fresh array,
So fresh they seem'd as day,  70
Even as their bridal day, which was not long:
  Sweet Thames run softly, till I end my song.

## 5

Then forth they all out of their baskets drew,
Great store of flowers, the honor of the field,
That to the sense did fragrant odors yield,  75
All which upon those goodly Birds they threw,
And all the waves did strew,
That like old Peneus' waters they did seem,
When down along by pleasant Tempe's shore
Scatt'red with flow'rs, through Thessaly they stream,  80
That they appear through lilies' plenteous store,
Like a bride's chamber floor:
Two of those Nymphs, meanwhile, two garlands bound,
Of freshest flow'rs which in that mead they found,
The which presenting all in trim array,  85

55 *Eftsoons:* At once.  63 *Venus . . . team:* local "mythology"; a
poem by an obscure contemporary also fits the Thames' swans to Venus's
chariot. See *Variorum, M.P.,* II, 498.  67 *Somers-heat:* Pun on Somerset, surname of the two brides whose marriages are being celebrated.
78 *Peneus:* river in Thessaly, rising in Mt. Pindus (l. 40) and flowing
through the Vale of Tempe (l. 79). See Keats, p. 347, l. 7.

Their snowy foreheads therewithal they crown'd,
Whilst one did sing this lay,
Prepar'd against that day,
Against their bridal day, which was not long:
  Sweet Thames run softly, till I end my song.      90

6

Ye gentle Birds, the world's fair ornament,
And heaven's glory, whom this happy hour
Doth lead unto your lovers' blissful bower,
Joy may you have and gentle hearts' content
Of your loves' couplement:      95
And let fair Venus, that is Queen of love,
With her heart-quelling Son upon you smile,
Whose smile they say, hath virtue to remove
All Love's dislike, and friendship's faulty guile
For ever to assoil.      100
Let endless Peace your steadfast hearts accord,
And blessed Plenty wait upon your board,
And let your bed with pleasures chaste abound,
That fruitful issue may to you afford,
Which may your foes confound,      105
And make your joys redound,
Upon your bridal day, which is not long:
  Sweet Thames run softly, till I end my song.

7

So ended she; and all the rest around
To her redoubled that her undersong,      110
Which said, their bridal day should not be long.
And gentle Echo from the neighbor ground,
Their accents did resound.
So forth those joyous Birds did pass along,
Adown the lee, that to them murmur'd low,      115
As he would speak, but that he lack'd a tongue
Yet did by signs his glad affection show,
Making his stream run slow.

97 Son: Child, 100 assoil: absolve 110 redoubled . . . undersong:
repeated the refrain of the lay. See l. 87. 112 Echo: nymph of woods
and hills. See p. 327, l. 127 and note.

And all the fowl which in his flood did dwell
'Gan flock about these twain, that did excel          120
The rest, so far, as Cynthia doth shend
The lesser stars. So they enranged well,
Did on those two attend,
And their best service lend,
Against their wedding day, which was not long:          125
  Sweet Thames run softly, till I end my song.


### 8

At length they all to merry London came,
To merry London, my most kindly nurse,
That to me gave this life's first native source:
Though from another place I take my name,          130
An house of ancient fame.
There when they came, whereas those bricky tow'rs,
The which on Thames' broad aged back do ride,
Where now the studious lawyers have their bowers,
There whilom wont the Templar Knights to bide,          135
Till they decay'd through pride:
Next whereunto there stands a stately place,
Where oft I gained gifts and goodly grace
Of that great Lord, which therein wont to dwell,
Whose want too well, now feels my friendless case:          140
But Ah, here fits not well
Old woes but joys to tell
Against the bridal day, which is not long:
  Sweet Thames run softly, till I end my song.


### 9

Yet therein now doth lodge a noble Peer,          145
Great England's glory and the world's wide wonder,
Whose dreadful name, late through all Spain did thunder,

121 *Cynthia:* the moon goddess (probably an allusion to Queen Elizabeth). *shend:* outshine. 122 *enranged:* arranged. 128 *my:* the poet's, Spenser's. 130 *place . . . name:* possibly from the "Spencers of Althorpe" (Northamptonshire). 132-35 *bricky . . . bide:* The Temple (Inner Temple, Middle Temple); from former occupation by the Knights Templars. Upon the suppression of their Order (14th century) their house in course of time was turned over for the use of law students and became known as the Inns of Court. 136 *they:* the Knights Templars. 137 *stately place:* probably the house of the Earl of Essex (see l. 145 and note), formerly the home of the Earl of Leicester (cf. *great Lord,* l. 139), at one time Spenser's patron. 145 *Peer:* Earl of Essex, who had just returned (1596) from the successful Cadiz Expedition.

And Hercules' two pillars standing near,
Did make to quake and fear:
Fair branch of honor, flower of chivalry,                    150
That fillest England with thy triumph's fame,
Joy have thou of thy noble victory,
And endless happiness of thine own name
That promiseth the same:
That through thy prowess and victorious arms,               155
Thy country may be freed from foreign harms:
And great Elisa's glorious name may ring
Through all the world, fill'd with thy wide alarms,
Which some brave muse may sing
To ages following,                                          160
Upon the bridal day, which is not long:
  Sweet Thames run softly, till I end my song.


### 10

From those high towers, this noble Lord issuing,
Like radiant Hesper when his golden hair
In th' ocean billows he hath bathed fair,                    165
Descended to the river's open viewing,
With a great train ensuing.
Above the rest were goodly to be seen
Two gentle knights of lovely face and feature
Beseeming well the bower of any queen,                       170
With gifts of wit and ornaments of nature,
Fit for so goodly stature:
That like the twins of Jove they seem'd in sight,
Which deck the baldric of the heavens bright,
They two forth pacing to the river's side,                   175
Received those two fair brides, their loves' delight,
Which at th' appointed tide,
Each one did make his bride,
Against their bridal day, which is not long:
  Sweet Thames run softly, till I end my song.        180

148 *Hercules' two pillars:* as the Strait of Gibraltar was anciently called.
157 *Elisa's:* Queen Elizabeth's.  164 *Hesper:* Evening Star.  173 *twins:*
Castor and Pollux, the constellation Gemini. See ll. 42-43 and note.

# WILLIAM SHAKESPEARE 1564–1616

*from* SONNETS

## 18

Shall I compare thee to a summer's day?
Thou art more lovely and more temperate:
Rough winds do shake the darling buds of May,
And summer's lease hath all too short a date:
Sometime too hot the eye of heaven shines,                    5
And often is his gold complexion dimm'd;
And every fair from fair sometime declines,
By chance, or nature's changing course untrimm'd:
But thy eternal summer shall not fade,
Nor lose possession of that fair thou ow'st;                  10
Nor shall Death brag thou wand'rest in his shade,
When in eternal lines to time thou grow'st:
　　So long as men can breathe or eyes can see,
　　So long lives this, and this gives life to thee.

## 29

When in disgrace with Fortune and men's eyes,
I all alone beweep my outcast state,
And trouble deaf heaven with my bootless cries,
And look upon myself and curse my fate,
Wishing me like to one more rich in hope,                    5
Featur'd like him, like him with friends possess'd,
Desiring this man's art, and that man's scope,
With what I most enjoy contented least;
Yet in these thoughts myself almost despising,
Haply I think on thee, and then my state,                    10
Like to the lark at break of day arising
From sullen earth, sings hymns at heaven's gate;
　　For thy sweet love rememb'red such wealth brings,
　　That then I scorn to change my state with Kings.

[*18*] 4 *lease:* term (as of a lease).  7 *every fair:* every beautiful
thing (woman).  8 *untrimm'd:* stripped (of beauty).  10 *fair thou
ow'st:* beauty you own.  12 *to time:* for all time.
　[*29*] 3 *bootless:* profitless.  6 *Featur'd:* (well)-formed.  7 *art:* skill
*scope:* range of mind.  12 *sullen:* gloomy.

## 30

When to the sessions of sweet silent thought,
I summon up remembrance of things past,
I sigh the lack of many a thing I sought,
And with old woes new wail my dear time's waste:
Then can I drown an eye, unus'd to flow,          5
For precious friends hid in death's dateless night,
And weep afresh love's long since cancell'd woe,
And moan th' expense of many a vanish'd sight.
Then can I grieve at grievances foregone,
And heavily from woe to woe tell o'er          10
The sad account of fore-bemoaned moan,
Which I new pay as if not paid before.
    But if the while I think on thee, dear friend,
    All losses are restor'd, and sorrows end.

## 65

Since brass, nor stone, nor earth, nor boundless sea,
But sad mortality o'ersways their power,
How with this rage shall beauty hold a plea,
Whose action is no stronger than a flower?
O how shall summer's honey breath hold out          5
Against the wrackful siege of batt'ring days,
When rocks impregnable are not so stout,
Nor gates of steel so strong but time decays?
O fearful meditation, where alack,
Shall time's best jewel from time's chest lie hid?          10
Or what strong hand can hold his swift foot back,
Or how his spoil of beauty can forbid?
    O none, unless this miracle have might,
    That in black ink my love may still shine bright.

[30] 1 *sessions:* cf. "court sessions."   8 *expense:* loss.   9 *foregone:*
past.   10 *tell:* count.
    [65] 2 *o'ersways:* overrules.   *power,* property, quality.   8 *rage:* i.e.,
of "mortality."   *hold a plea:* put its case to trial.   4 *action:* cf. *power*
(1. 2); legal action (cf. *plea,* l. 3).   10 *Shall . . . hid:* Will Beauty
escape the "rage" of time? A pun on *chest:* a jewel box (casket); a
coffin.   12 *of: or* (1609 edn.).

## 73

That time of year thou mayst in me behold,
When yellow leaves, or none, or few, do hang
Upon those boughs which shake against the cold,
Bare ruin'd choirs, where late the sweet birds sang.
In me thou see'st the twilight of such day,    5
As after sunset fadeth in the west,
Which by and by black night doth take away,
Death's second self, that seals up all in rest.
In me thou see'st the glowing of such fire,
That on the ashes of his youth doth lie,    10
As the death-bed whereon it must expire,
Consum'd with that which it was nourish'd by.
  This thou perceiv'st, which makes thy love more strong,
  To love that well, which thou must leave ere long.

## 90

Then hate me when thou wilt; if ever, now,
Now while the world is bent my deeds to cross,
Join with the spite of fortune, make me bow,
And do not drop in for an after-loss:
Ah, do not, when my heart hath 'scap'd this sorrow,    5
Come in the rearward of a conquer'd woe;
Give not a windy night a rainy morrow,
To linger out a purpos'd overthrow.
If thou wilt leave me, do not leave me last,
When other petty griefs have done their spite,    10
But in the onset come: so shall I taste
At first the very worst of fortune's might,
  And other strains of woe, which now seem woe,
  Compar'd with loss of thee will not seem so.

[73]  12 *that*: the ashes.
[90]  2 *cross*: thwart.  4 *for an after-loss*: as a further misfortune.  5
[*'*]*scap'd*.  8 *linger out*: prolong.  13 *strains*: kinds.

## 94

They that have power to hurt, and will do none,
That do not do the thing they most do show,
Who, moving others, are themselves as stone,
Unmoved, cold, and to temptation slow,
They rightly do inherit heaven's graces,          5
And husband nature's riches from expense;
They are the lords and owners of their faces,
Others but stewards of their excellence.
The summer's flower is to the summer sweet,
Though to itself it only live and die,            10
But if that flower with base infection meet,
The basest weed outbraves his dignity:
    For sweetest things turn sourest by their deeds;
    Lilies that fester smell far worse than weeds.

## 106

When in the chronicle of wasted time,
I see descriptions of the fairest wights,
And beauty making beautiful old rhyme,
In praise of ladies dead and lovely knights,
Then, in the blazon of sweet beauty's best,       5
Of hand, of foot, of lip, of eye, of brow,
I see their antique pen would have express'd
Even such a beauty as you master now.
So all their praises are but prophecies
Of this our time, all you prefiguring;            10
And, for they look'd but with divining eyes,
They had not skill enough your worth to sing:
    For we which now behold these present days,
    Have eyes to wonder, but lack tongues to praise.

[94] 2 *show:* appear (able to do).   6 *expense:* waste.   12 *outbraves his dignity:* surpasses its worth.

[106] 2 *wights:* persons.   5 *blazon:* heraldic description.   11 *for:* because.   12 *skill:* still (1609 edn.).

## *107*

Not mine own fears, nor the prophetic soul
Of the wide world dreaming on things to come,
Can yet the lease of my true love control,
Suppos'd as forfeit to a confin'd doom.
The mortal moon hath her eclipse endur'd,     5
And the sad augurs mock their own presage;
Incertainties now crown themselves assur'd,
And peace proclaims olives of endless age.
Now with the drops of this most balmy time,
My love looks fresh, and Death to me subscribes,    10
Since, spite of him, I'll live in this poor rhyme,
While he insults o'er dull and speechless tribes:
   And thou in this shalt find thy monument,
   When tyrants' crests and tombs of brass are spent.

## *110*

Alas, 'tis true, I have gone here and there,
And made myself a motley to the view,
Gor'd mine own thoughts, sold cheap what is most dear,
Made old offences of affections new.
Most true it is, that I have look'd on truth    5
Askance and strangely: but, by all above,
These blenches gave my heart another youth,
And worse essays prov'd thee my best of love.
Now all is done, have what shall have no end:
Mine appetite I never more will grind    10
On newer proof, to try an older friend,
A god in love, to whom I am confin'd.
   Then give me welcome, next my heaven the best,
   Even to thy pure and most most loving breast.

[*107*] 3 *lease:* duration. Cf. No. 18, p. 82, l. 4.  4 *Suppos'd . . . doom:* Assumed (wrongly) to be doomed to forfeiture.  5 *mortal:* i.e., as subject to decay and change.  6 *sad augurs:* prophets of doom. *presage:* predictions.  7-8 *Incertainties . . . age:* Uncertainties give way to certainties, and a lasting peace appears prospective.  10 *subscribes:* yields.  12 *insults:* triumphs.

[*110*] 2 *motley . . . view:* public fool.  3 *Gor'd:* Wounded.  4 *Made . . . new:* Offended new friends as he had his old ones; or, made new friends and neglected old.  7 *blenches:* side glances.  8 *essays:* trials. 10 *grind:* sharpen.  12 *A . . . love:* his friend.

### 116

Let me not to the marriage of true minds
Admit impediments. Love is not love
Which alters when it alteration finds,
Or bends with the remover to remove.
O, no! it is an ever-fixed mark                                    5
That looks on tempests and is never shaken;
It is the star to every wand'ring bark,
Whose worth's unknown, although his height be taken.
Love's not Time's fool, though rosy lips and cheeks
Within his bending sickle's compass come;                          10
Love alters not with his brief hours and weeks,
But bears it out even to the edge of doom.
   If this be error and upon me proved,
   I never writ, nor no man ever loved.


### 121

'Tis better to be vile than vile esteemed,
When not to be, receives reproach of being,
And the just pleasure lost, which is so deemed,
Not by our feeling, but by others' seeing.
For why should others' false adulterate eyes                       5
Give salutation to my sportive blood?
Or on my frailties why are frailer spies,
Which in their wills count bad what I think good?
No, I am that I am, and they that level
At my abuses, reckon up their own:                                 10
I may be straight though they themselves be bevel;
By their rank thoughts my deeds must not be shown;
   Unless this general evil they maintain,
   All men are bad, and in their badness reign.

---

[*116*] 4 *remover:* a person of shifting affections.  8 *Whose . . .
taken:* Although the "elevation" of a star is reckoned (for navigational
purpose), its real worth remains (like that of love) unknowable.
   [*121*] 7 *on . . . spies:* spies frailer than I am, spying on my frailties.
11 *bevel:* oblique.

## 129

Th' expense of spirit in a waste of shame
Is lust in action; and till action, lust
Is perjur'd, murd'rous, bloody, full of blame,
Savage, extreme, rude, cruel, not to trust,
Enjoy'd no sooner but despised straight,                    5
Past reason hunted, and no sooner had,
Past reason hated as a swallowed bait,
On purpose laid to make the taker mad:
Mad in pursuit, and in possession so,
Had, having, and in quest to have, extreme,                 10
A bliss in proof, and prov'd, a very woe,
Before, a joy propos'd, behind, a dream.
   All this the world well knows; yet none knows well
   To shun the heaven that leads men to this hell.

## 141

In faith, I do not love thee with mine eyes,
For they in thee a thousand errors note,
But 'tis my heart that loves what they despise,
Who in despite of view is pleas'd to dote.
Nor are mine ears with thy tongue's tune delighted,       5
Nor tender feeling to base touches prone,
Nor taste, nor smell, desire to be invited
To any sensual feast with thee alone:
But my five wits, nor my five senses can
Dissuade one foolish heart from serving thee,             10
Who leaves unsway'd the likeness of a man,
Thy proud heart's slave and vassal wretch to be:
   Only my plague thus far I count my gain,
   That she that makes me sin awards my pain.

[*129*] *Th' expense of spirit, etc.:* An "anatomy of lust," exposing
this vice *before, during,* and *after* its satisfactions.
1 *expense:* expenditure.   9 *Mad:* mistakenly *Made* (1609).   11
*prov'd: proud and* (1609).
   [*141*] 4 *of view:* of what the eyes see.   6 *base:* sensual.   9 *five wits:*
common sense, imagination, memory, judgment, fancy.

*146*

Poor soul, the center of my sinful earth,
[Rebuke] these rebel pow'rs that thee array!
Why dost thou pine within and suffer dearth,
Painting thy outward walls so costly gay?
Why so large cost, having so short a lease,                    5
Dost thou upon thy fading mansion spend?
Shall worms, inheritors of this excess,
Eat up thy charge? Is this thy body's end?
Then, soul, live thou upon thy servant's loss,
And let that pine to aggravate thy store;                     10
Buy terms divine in selling hours of dross;
Within be fed, without be rich no more:
  So shalt thou feed on Death, that feeds on men,
  And Death once dead, there's no more dying then.


*The Phoenix and Turtle*

Let the bird of loudest lay,
On the sole Arabian tree,
Herald sad and trumpet be,
To whose sound chaste wings obey.

[*146*]  2 [*Rebuke*]: conjectural; through a typographical blunder the
last phrase of the first line is repeated in the 1609 edition.  8 *charge:*
the body.  11 *terms divine:* i.e., eternity (in heaven).

THE PHOENIX AND TURTLE. According to fable, the Phoenix was a
wonderful bird, possessing special powers of regeneration: periodically,
the Phoenix, consumed by fire, was reborn from its own ashes. Widely
accepted as a symbol of immortality and readily drawn into the context of Christianity. See Donne, p. 108, ll. 23-24.

In "Love's Martyr," the poem by Robert Chester, from which the
collection including "The Phoenix and Turtle" receives its title, the
chaste love and mating of the Phoenix and the Turtledove are emblematic of chastity and fidelity in marriage. Shakespeare follows Chester in associating these birds in a relation of constancy and high mystical
rapport.

2 *sole . . . tree:* cf. ". . . in Arabia / There is one tree  the phoenix
throne, one phoenix / At this hour reigning there."—*The Tempest,* III,
iii, 22-24.  4 *chaste wings:* other than birds of prey.

But thou shriking harbinger,         5
Foul precurrer of the fiend,
Augur of the fever's end,
To this troop come thou not near.

From this session interdict
Every fowl of tyrant wing,         10
Save the Eagle, feath'red king:
Keep the obsequy so strict.

Let the priest in surplice white,
That defunctive music can,
Be the death-divining Swan,         15
Lest the requiem lack his right.

And thou treble-dated Crow,
That thy sable gender mak'st,
With the breath thou giv'st and tak'st,
'Mongst our mourners shalt thou go.         20

Here the anthem doth commence:
Love and Constancy is dead,
Phoenix and the Turtle fled,
In a mutual flame from hence.

So they lov'd as love in twain,         25
Had the essence but in one;
Two distincts, division none:
Number there in love was slain.

Hearts remote, yet not asunder;
Distance and no space was seen,         30
'Twixt this Turtle and his Queen;
But in them it were a wonder.

---

5 *shriking harbinger:* shrieking foreteller of disaster; the screech owl.
6 *precurrer:* forerunner. 7 *Augur . . . end:* foreteller of death. 9
*interdict:* forbid. 14 *defunctive:* funeral. *can:* has skill in. 16 *right:*
rite. 17 *treble-dated Crow:* The crow was reputed to live "nine times as
long as we" live. 18-19 *thy sable . . . tak'st:* reference to tradition
that crows conceive by an exchange of breath between hen and cock.
Delicate as such relations are, Shakespeare improves upon them by
permitting the chaste phoenix and turtle to enjoy only the intercourse
of eyes (ll. 33-36). 27 *distincts:* individual persons. 28 *Number:*
Two is one, and "one is no number." 32 *But:* Except.

So between them Love did shine,
That the Turtle saw his right
Flaming in the Phoenix sight,                    35
Either was the Other's mine.


Property was thus appalled,
That the self was not the same;
Single Nature's double name,
Neither two nor one was called.                  40


Reason, in itself confounded,
Saw division grow together,
To themselves yet either neither,
Simple were so well compounded,


That it cried, How true a twain,                 45
Seemeth this concordant one!
Love hath Reason, Reason none,
If what parts, can so remain.


Whereupon it made this *threne*,
To the Phoenix and the Dove,                     50
Co-Supremes and stars of Love,
A chorus to their tragic scene.


### THRENOS

Beauty, Truth, and Rarity,
Grace in all simplicity,
Here enclos'd, in cinders lie.                   55


Death is now the Phoenix nest,
And the Turtle's loyal breast,
To eternity doth rest,

34 *right:* what was rightfully his; i.e., himself.   36 *Either . . . mine:*
Either was claimed by the other as *mine.*   37-38 *Property . . . same:*
Property in logic, meaning the quality, or characteristic, predicated of
something. In the union of the lovers logic also is *appalled,* for *self,* as
a distinct entity, no longer applies to either the Phoenix or the Turtle.
See ll. 41-44.   44 *Simple:* Pure unmixed elements.   47-48 *Love . . .
remain:* Love here is reasonable in uniting the two; but reason is un-
reasonable *If what parts* [divides] *remains* divided, or, becomes *one.*
Either way reason is *confounded.*   49 *threne:* a dirge. Cf. Threnos, ll.
53 ff.

Leaving no posterity:
'Twas not their infirmity,                                    60
But was married Chastity.

Truth may seem, but cannot be,
Beauty brag, but 'tis not she:
Truth and Beauty buried be.

To this urn let those repair,                                 65
That are either true or fair,
For those dead birds, sigh a prayer.

SONGS FROM THE PLAYS

*Spring: When daisies pied and violets blue*

[By Holofernes, Moth, Costard, and Others]

When daisies pied and violets blue,
And lady-smocks of silver white,
And cuckoo-buds of yellow hue,
Do paint the meadows with delight,
The cuckoo then on every tree,                                5
Mocks married men, for thus sings he,
Cuckoo.
Cuckoo, cuckoo: O word of fear,
Unpleasing to a married ear.

When shepherds pipe on oaten straws,                          10
And merry larks are ploughmen's clocks,
When turtles tread, and rooks and daws,
And maidens bleach their summer smocks,
The cuckoo then on every tree,
Mocks married men, for thus sings he,                         15
Cuckoo.
Cuckoo, cuckoo: O word of fear,
Unpleasing to a married ear.

[*Love's Labor's Lost,* V, ii]

WHEN DAISIES PIED. 1 *pied:* many-colored. 2-3 *And lady-* . . . *hue:*
The order of these lines is reversed in both the Quarto of 1598 and
the Folio (1623). 6 *Mocks:* The name of the bird and its call suggest
cuckold(ry). 10 *shepherds* . . . *straws:* cf. Spenser, p. 46, l. 24 and
note. 12 *turtles:* turtledoves. *tread:* copulate. 13 *maidens* . . .
*smocks:* cf. Herrick, p. 128, l. 51.

## Winter: When icicles hang by the wall

[By Holofernes, Moth, Costard, and Others]

When icicles hang by the wall,
And Dick the shepherd blows his nail,
And Tom bears logs into the hall,
And milk comes frozen home in pail;
When blood is nipp'd, and ways be foul,        5
Then nightly sings the staring owl,
Tu-whit, to-who:
   A merry note,
   While greasy Joan doth keel the pot.

When all aloud the wind doth blow,        10
And coughing drowns the parson's saw,
And birds sit brooding in the snow,
And Marian's nose looks red and raw;
When roasted crabs hiss in the bowl,
Then nightly sings the staring owl,        15
Tu-whit, to-who:
   A merry note,
   While greasy Joan doth keel the pot.

[*Love's Labor's Lost,* V, ii]

## Blow, blow, thou winter wind

[Amiens' Song]

Blow, blow, thou winter wind,
Thou art not so unkind,
   As man's ingratitude:
Thy tooth is not so keen,
Because thou art not seen,        5
   Although thy breath be rude.
Heigh-ho! sing heigh-ho, unto the green holly,
Most friendship is feigning, most loving mere folly:
   Then, heigh-ho, the holly,
   This life is most jolly.        10

WINTER: WHEN ICICLES. 9 *keel:* cools. 11 *saw:* maxim. 12 *brooding:* warming (themselves). 14 *crabs:* crab apples.

Freeze, freeze, thou bitter sky,
That dost not bite so nigh,
   As benefits forgot:
Though thou the waters warp,
Thy sting is not so sharp,           15
   As friend rememb'red not.
Heigh-ho! sing heigh-ho, unto the green holly,
Most friendship is feigning, most loving mere folly:
   Then, heigh-ho, the holly,
   This life is most jolly.         20
                    [*As You Like It,* II, vii]

## Come away, come away, death

[Feste's Song]

Come away, come away, death,
And in sad cypress let me be laid.
Fly away, fly away, breath,
I am slain by a fair cruel maid:
   My shroud of white, stuck all with yew, O prepare it,   5
   My part of death, no one so true did share it.

Not a flower, not a flower sweet,
On my black coffin, let there be strown;
Not a friend, not a friend greet
My poor corpse, where my bones shall be thrown:     10
   A thousand thousand sighs to save, lay me O where
   Sad true lover never find my grave, to weep there.

                    [*Twelfth Night,* II, iv]

## Fear no more the heat o' th' sun

[Dirge: Sung by Guiderius and Arviragus]

GUI.   Fear no more the heat o' th' sun,
       Nor the furious winter's rages,
       Thou thy worldly task hast done,
       Home art gone, and ta'en thy wages.
       Golden lads, and girls all must,     5
       As chimney-sweepers, come to dust.

COME AWAY. 2, 5 *cypress, yew:* symbols of mourning.

ARV.    Fear no more the frown o' th' great,
       Thou art past the tyrant's stroke;
       Care no more to clothe and eat;
       To thee the reed is as the oak:     10
          The scepter, learning, physic, must,
          All follow this and come to dust.

GUI.    Fear no more the lightning flash.
ARV.    Nor th' all-dreaded thunderstone.
GUI.    Fear not slander, censure rash.    15
ARV.    Thou hast finish'd joy and moan.
BOTH.    All lovers young, all lovers must,
       Consign to thee, and come to dust.

GUI.    No exorciser harm thee,
ARV.    Nor no witchcraft charm thee.    20
GUI.    Ghost unlaid forbear thee.
ARV.    Nothing ill come near thee,
BOTH.    Quiet consummation have,
       And renowned be thy grave.

                       [*Cymbeline,* IV, ii]


### Full fadom five thy father lies

[Ariel's Song]

Full fadom five thy father lies.
Of his bones are coral made;
Those are pearls that were his eyes:
Nothing of him that doth fade,
But doth suffer a sea-change    5
Into something rich and strange.
Sea nymphs hourly ring his knell.
             *Burthen:* Ding dong.
Hark! now I hear them, ding-dong bell.

                 [*The Tempest,* I, ii]

FEAR NO MORE. 11 *physic:* art of healing.   14 *thunderstone:* thunder-bolt.   18 *Consign:* Submit to the same condition as yours.

# BEN JONSON 1573?–1637

*from* EPIGRAMS

## To the Reader

Pray thee, take care, that tak'st my book in hand,
To read it well: that is, to understand.

## To My Book

It will be look'd for, book, when some but see
    Thy title, *Epigrams,* and nam'd of me,
Thou shouldst be bold, licentious, full of gall,
    Wormwood, and sulphur, sharp, and tooth'd withal;
Become a petulant thing, hurl ink, and wit,      5
    As mad-men stones: not caring whom they hit.
Deceive their malice, who could wish it so.
    And by thy wiser temper, let men know
Thou art not covetous of least self-fame,
    Made from the hazard of another's shame:      10
Much less with lewd, profane, and beastly phrase,
    To catch the world's loose laughter, or vain gaze.
He that departs with his own honesty
    For vulgar praise, doth it too dearly buy.

## To John Donne

Donne, the delight of Phoebus, and each Muse,
    Who, to thy one, all other brains refuse;
Whose every work, of thy most early wit,
    Came forth example, and remains so, yet:
Longer a knowing, than most wits do live.      5
    And which no' affection praise enough can give!

To My Book. 10 *the hazard:* exposing.

To John Donne. 1 *Phoebus:* God of poetry. 2 *to thy:* in preference
to your (brain). 3 *wit:* activity of mind. 6 The " ! " points the line,
but does not *stop* the thought.

To it, thy language, letters, arts, best life,
　Which might with half mankind maintain a strife.
All which I meant to praise, and, yet, I would;
　But leave, because I cannot as I should!    10


## On My First Son

Farewell, thou child of my right hand, and joy;
　My sin was too much hope of thee, lov'd boy,
Seven years tho' wert lent to me, and I thee pay,
　Exacted by thy fate, on the just day.
O, could I lose all father, now. For why    5
　Will man lament the state he should envy?
To have so soon scap'd world's, and flesh's rage,
　And, if no other misery, yet age?
Rest in soft peace, and, ask'd, say here doth lie
　BEN. JONSON his best piece of *poetry*.    10
For whose sake, henceforth, all his vows be such,
　As what he loves may never like too much.


## To John Donne

Who shall doubt, Donne, where I a Poet be,
　When I dare send my *Epigrams* to thee?
That so alone canst judge, so' alone dost make:
　And, in thy censures, evenly, dost take
As free simplicity, to disavow,    5
　As thou hast best authority, t' allow.
Read all I send: and, if I find but one
　Mark'd by thy hand, and with the better stone,

---

7-8 *To . . . strife:* You have given the best of your life "to it" ("knowing," etc.), which might rival the like accomplishment of half mankind.  9 *yet:* still.

ON MY FIRST SON. 1 *child:* who died of the plague in 1603.  *right hand:* cf. "son of my right hand," the Hebrew signification of Benjamin, the name given by Jacob to his youngest son.—Gen. 35:18.  5 *lose all father:* lose all sense of being a father and cease grieving, since the child has attained the state men should envy, not lament (l. 6)  10 *poetry:* something *made;* as for Jonson, following the ancients, the poet is a *maker.*

TO JOHN DONNE. 1 *where:* whether.  3 *make:* write poetry.  8 *better stone:* stamp of approval.

My title's seal'd. Those that for claps do write,
   Let pui'nes', porters', players' praise delight,      10
And, till they burst, their backs, like asses' load:
   A man should seek great glory, and not broad.


## Inviting a Friend to Supper

To night, grave sir, both my poor house, and I
   Do equally desire your company:
Not that we think us worthy such a guest,
   But that your worth will dignify our feast,
With those that come; whose grace may make that seem  5
   Something, which, else, could hope for no esteem.
It is the fair acceptance, Sir, creates
   The entertainment perfect: not the cates.
Yet shall you have, to rectify your palate,
   An olive, capers, or some better salad       10
Ush'ring the mutton; with a short legg'd hen,
   If we can get her, full of eggs, and then,
Lemons, and wine for sauce: to these, a cony
   Is not to be despair'd of, for our money;
And, though fowl, now, be scarce, yet there are clarks,   15
   The sky not falling, think we may have larks.
I'll tell you of more, and lie, so you will come:
   Of partrich, pheasant, wood-cock, of which some
May yet be there; and godwit, if we can:
   Knat, rail, and ruffe too. How so' ere, my man    20
Shall read a piece of Virgil, Tacitus,
   Livy, or of some better book to us,
Of which we'll speak our minds, amidst our meat;
   And I'll profess no verses to repeat:
To this, if ought appear, which I know not of,      25
   That will the pastry, not my paper, show of.
Digestive cheese, and fruit there sure will be;
   But that, which most doth take my Muse, and me,

---

9 *claps:* popular approval.  10 *pui'nes:* phonetically, *punies:* inferiors.
   INVITING. 8 *cates:* delicacies.  10 *salad:* rhymes with *palate.*  13
*cony:* coney, rabbit; rhymes with *money.*  15 *clarks:* clerks.  19 *god-wit:* a marsh-bird.  20 *Knat . . . ruffe:* two other birds, and a fish.
21-22 *Virgil, Tacitus, Livy:* Indicative of Jonson's taste for the classical
authors. Cf. *Horace, Anacreon,* l. 31.  25 *To this:* In addition to what
already has been listed. *appear:* on the table.  26 *That . . . of* [f]:
The pastry will show off that, not this letter.  27 *Digestive:* Aiding
digestion.

Is a pure cup of rich Canary wine,
   Which is the Mermaid's, now, but shall be mine:    30
Of which had Horace, or Anacreon tasted,
   Their lives, as do their lines, till now had lasted.
Tobacco, Nectar, or the Thespian spring,
   Are all but Luther's beer, to this I sing.
Of this we will sup free, but moderately,    35
   And we will have no Pooly', or Parrot by;
Nor shall our cups make any guilty men:
   But, at our parting we will be, as when
We innocently met. No simple word,
   That shall be utter'd at our mirthful board,    40
Shall make us sad next morning: or affright
   The liberty, that we'll enjoy tonight.

### Epitaph on S[alomon] P[avy]
### A Child of Q[ueen] El[izabeth's] Chapel

Weep with me all you that read
   This little story:
And know, for whom a tear you shed,
   Death's self is sorry.
'Twas a child, that so did thrive    5
   In grace, and feature,
As Heaven and Nature seem'd to strive
   Which own'd the creature.
Years he numb'red scarce thirteen
   When Fates turn'd cruel,    10
Yet three fill'd zodiacs had he been
   The stage's jewel;
And did act (what now we moan)
   Old men so duly,
As, sooth, the Parcae thought him one,    15
   He play'd so truly.

---

30 *Mermaid* (*Tavern*): a rendezvous of Jonson and his admirers ("Sons of Ben"). 33-34 *Tobacco . . . sing: Tobacco,* etc., are little better than Luther's beer compared to *Canary wine* (1. 29) whose praises I sing. *Nectar* is the drink of the gods; *Thespian spring,* the waters of the spring sacred to Thespis, reputed founder of Greek drama. 36 *Pooly', or Parrot:* Conjectured to be "two damn'd villains" who once attacked Jonson.

EPITAPH. *S[alomon] P[avy]:* A child actor (d. 1602), who had taken part in Jonson's *Cynthia's Revels* (1600) and *Poetaster* (1601).

11 *three . . . zodiacs:* three years. 15 *Parcae:* the Three Fates. Cf. Spenser, p. 50, ll. 148-49 and notes.

So, by error, to his fate
    They all consented:
But viewing him since (alas, too late)
    They have repented.         20
And have sought (to give new birth)
    In baths to steep him;
But, being so much too good for earth,
    Heaven vows to keep him.

### *from* THE FOREST *and* UNDERWOODS

## To Celia

#### SONG

Drink to me, only, with thine eyes,
    And I will pledge with mine;
Or leave a kiss but in the cup,
    And I'll not look for wine.
The thirst, that from the soul doth rise,       5
    Doth ask a drink divine:
But might I of Jove's nectar sup,
    I would not change for thine.
I sent thee, late, a rosy wreath,
    Not so much honoring thee,       10
As giving it a hope, that there
    It could not withered be.
But thou thereon didst only breathe,
    And sent'st it back to me:
Since when it grows, and smells, I swear,       15
    Not of itself, but thee.

## Her Triumph

See the chariot at hand here of Love
    Wherein my lady rideth!
Each that draws, is a swan, or a dove
    And well the car Love guideth.

*22 baths . . . him:* to bathe him in restorative waters.

THE FOREST, UNDERWOODS. *The Forest, Underwoods:* Picturesque titles which Jonson gave to collections of his "lesser Poems."

HER TRIUMPH. *Triumph:* Ceremonial; celebration (of Charis).

As she goes, all hearts do duty 5
            Unto her beauty;
And enamor'd, do wish, so they might
            But enjoy such a sight,
That they still were, to run by her side,
Thorough swords, thorough seas, whether she would ride. 10

Do but look on her eyes, they do light
   All that Love's world compriseth!
Do but look on her hair, it is bright
   As Love's star when it riseth!
Do but mark her forehead's smoother 15
            Than words that soothe her!
And from her arch'd brows, such a grace
            Sheds itself through the face,
As alone there triumphs to the life
All the gain, all the good, of the elements' strife. 20

Have you seen but a bright lily grow,
   Before rude hands have touch'd it?
Ha' you mark'd but the fall o' the snow
   Before the soil hath smutch'd it?
Ha' you felt the wool of beaver? 25
            Or swan's down ever?
Or have smelt o' the bud o' the briar?
            Or the nard in the fire?
Or have tasted the bag of the bee?
O so white! O so soft! O so sweet is she! 30

                 [from *A Celebration of Charis*]


SONGS FROM THE PLAYS

### *Come, my Celia, let us prove*

[Volpone's Song]

Come, my Celia, let us prove,
While we can, the sports of love;
Time will not be ours, forever,
He, at length, our good will sever;

---

10 *Thorough:* Through. *whether:* wherever. 28 *nard:* an aromatic
plant, spikenard.
     COME, MY CELIA. *Song:* cf. Catullus, fifth ode; Herrick, p. 128, esp.
ll. 57-58 and note; l. 68.
     1 *prove:* experience.

Spend not then his gifts, in vain.　　　　5
Suns, that set, may rise again:
But if, once, we lose this light,
'Tis with us perpetual night.
Why should we defer our joys?
Fame, and rumor are but toys.　　　　10
Cannot we delude the eyes
Of a few poor household spies?
Or his easier ears beguile,
Thus removed, by our wile?
'Tis no sin, love's fruit to steal,　　　　15
But the sweet thefts to reveal:
To be taken, to be seen,
These have crimes accounted been.

[*Volpone, or the Fox*, III, vii]


## Still to be neat, still to be drest

[Clerimont's Song]

Still to be neat, still to be drest,
As, you were going to a feast;
Still to be powd'red, still perfum'd:
Lady, it is to be presum'd,
Though art's hid causes are not found,　　　　5
All is not sweet, all is not sound.

Give me a look, give me a face,
That makes simplicity a grace;
Robes loosely flowing, hair as free:
Such sweet neglect more taketh me,　　　　10
Than all th' adulteries of art.
They strike mine eye, but not my heart.

[*Epicoene, or the Silent Woman*, I, i]


## To the Memory of . . . William Shakespeare

To draw no envy (Shakespeare) on thy name,
　　Am I thus ample to thy Book, and Fame:
While I confess thy writings to be such,
　　As neither Man, nor Muse, can praise too much.

STILL TO BE NEAT. 1 *neat:* in approved taste. *drest:* i.e., in fashion.
To SHAKESPEARE. 2 *ample:* liberal. *Book:* The First Folio, 1623;
his total accomplishment as a writer.

'Tis true, and all men's suffrage. But these ways          5
   Were not the paths I meant unto thy praise:
For seeliest Ignorance on these may light,
   Which, when it sounds at best, but echoes right;
Or blind Affection, which doth ne'er advance
   The truth, but gropes, and urgeth all by chance;          10
Or crafty Malice, might pretend this praise,
   And think to ruin, where it seem'd to raise.
These are, as some infamous bawd, or whore,
   Should praise a matron. What could hurt her more?
But thou art proof against them, and indeed          15
   Above th' ill fortune of them, or the need.
I, therefore will begin. Soul of the Age!
   The applause! delight! the wonder of our Stage!
My Shakespeare, rise; I will not lodge thee by
   Chaucer, or Spenser, or bid Beaumont lie          20
A little further, to make thee a room:
   Thou art a moniment, without a tomb,
And art alive still, while thy Book doth live,
   And we have wits to read, and praise to give.
That I not mix thee so, my brain excuses;          25
   I mean with great, but disproportion'd Muses:
For, if I thought my judgment were of years,
   I should commit thee surely with thy peers,
And tell, how far thou didst our Lyly out-shine,
   Or sporting Kyd, or Marlowe's mighty line.          30
And though thou hadst small Latin, and less Greek,
   From thence to honour thee, I would not seek
For names; but call forth thund'ring Aeschylus,
   Euripides, and Sophocles to us,
Pacuvius, Accius, him of Cordova dead,          35
   To life again, to hear thy buskin tread,
And shake a stage: or, when thy socks were on,
   Leave thee alone, for the comparison

5 *suffrage*: opinion of all men.    7 *seeliest*: most wretched.    19 *lodge thee*: that is, in Westminster Abbey, where the poets named were buried. Further, Jonson would probably avoid comparison of Shakespeare with these authors.    20 (Francis) *Beaumont* (1584-1616): a fellow-dramatist and friend of Jonson and Shakespeare.    22 *moniment*: monument.    26 *disproportion'd Muses*: poets of uneven accomplishment.    29-30 *Lyly, Kyd, Marlowe*: Shakespeare's predecessors in drama who especially influenced his work.    33-35 *Aeschylus . . . dead*: The principal Greek and Roman writers of tragedy.    *him of Cordova*: Seneca.    36 *buskin*: the high, thick-soled boot (*cothurnus*) worn by actors in ancient Athenian tragedy; hence, here tragedy.    37 *socks*: comedy, from the low light shoe (*soccus*) worn by the comic actors on the Greek and Roman stage.

Of all, that insolent Greece, or haughty Rome
    Sent forth, or since did from their ashes come.     40
Triumph, my Britain, thou hast one to show,
    To whom all scenes of Europe homage owe.
He was not of an age, but for all time!
    And all the Muses still were in their prime,
When like Apollo he came forth to warm     45
    Our ears, or like a Mercury to charm!
Nature herself was proud of his designs,
    And joy'd to wear the dressing of his lines!
Which were so richly spun, and woven so fit,
    As, since, she will vouchsafe no other wit.     50
The merry Greek, tart Aristophanes,
    Neat Terence, witty Plautus, now not please;
But antiquated, and deserted lie
    As they were not of Nature's family.
Yet must I not give Nature all: thy Art,     55
    My gentle Shakespeare, must enjoy a part.
For though the poet's matter, Nature be,
    His Art doth give the fashion. And, that he,
Who casts to write a living line, must sweat,
    (Such as thine are) and strike the second heat     60
Upon the Muse's anvil: turn the same,
    (And himself with it) that he thinks to frame;
Or for the laurel, he may gain a scorn,
    For a good poet's made, as well as born.
And such wert thou. Look how the father's face     65
    Lives in his issue, even so, the race
Of Shakespeare's mind, and manners brightly shines
    In his well-turned, and true-filed lines:
In each of which, he seems to shake a lance,
    As brandisht at the eyes of Ignorance.     70
Sweet Swan of Avon! what a sight it were
    To see thee in our waters yet appear,
And make those flights upon the banks of Thames,
    That so did take Eliza, and our James!

---

41 *Triumph:* Rejoice.   42 *scenes:* theatres, stages.   45-46 *Apollo . . . charm:* like Apollo (Phoebus), the god of poetry, and here also the sun god, he came forth to *warm* (please), and like Mercury, the god of eloquence, to *charm.*   51-52 *Aristophanes* (Greek); *Terence, Plautus* (Romans): writers of comedy.   59 *casts:* contrives.   68 *true-filed:* polished.   74 *Eliza[beth], James [I]*: The monarchs reigning during Shakespeare's life.

But stay, I see thee in the hemisphere                          75
   Advanc'd, and made a constellation there!
Shine forth, thou Star of Poets, and with rage,
   Or influence, chide, or cheer the drooping Stage;
Which, since thy flight from hence, hath mourn'd like night,
   And despairs day, but for thy Volume's light.                80

80 *Volume:* cf. *Book,* ll. 2, 23.

# JOHN DONNE  1572–1631

*from* SONGS AND SONNETS

## The Good-Morrow

I wonder by my troth, what thou, and I
Did, till we lov'd? were we not wean'd till then?
But suck'd on country pleasures, childishly?
Or snorted we in the seven sleepers' den?
'Twas so; but this, all pleasures fancies be.                    5
If ever any beauty I did see,
Which I desir'd, and got, 'twas but a dream of thee.

And now good morrow to our waking souls,
Which watch not one another out of fear;
For love, all love of other sights controls,                    10
And makes one little room, an every where.
Let sea-discoverers to new worlds have gone,
Let maps to other, worlds on worlds have shown,
Let us possess one world, each hath one, and is one.

My face in thine eye, thine in mine appears,                    15
And true plain hearts do in the faces rest,
Where can we find two better hemispheres
Without sharp North, without declining West?
Whatever dies, was not mixt equally;
If our two loves be one, or, thou and I                         20
Love so alike, that none do slacken, none can die.


## Song

Go, and catch a falling star,
    Get with child a mandrake root,
Tell me, where all past years are,
    Or who cleft the Devil's foot,

---

THE GOOD-MORROW. 4 *seven sleepers:* seven Christian youths, who
escaped persecution (*c.* A.D. 150) by hiding in a cave, where they slept
for two centuries.  13 *other:* others.  17-18 *hemispheres . . . West:*
from which are absent the coldness of the north, and the *declining* of
the west (emblematic of decay and death; see p. 124, l. 9 and note).
    SONG. 2 *mandrake:* whose fruit, or root, when eaten, was supposed
to aid conception.

Teach me to hear mermaids singing,                5
  Or to keep off envy's stinging,
      And find
      What wind
Serves to advance an honest mind.

If thou beest born to strange sights,             10
  Things invisible to see,
Ride ten thousand days and nights,
  Till age snow white hairs on thee,
Thou, when thou return'st, wilt tell me
  All strange wonders that befell thee,           15
      And swear
      No where
Lives a woman true, and fair.

If thou find'st one, let me know,
  Such a pilgrimage were sweet;                   20
Yet do not, I would not go,
  Though at next door we might meet,
Though she were true, when you met her,
  And last, till you write your letter,
      Yet she                                     25
      Will be
False, ere I come, to two, or three.


## The Canonization

For Godsake hold your tongue, and let me love,
  Or chide my palsy, or my gout,
My five gray hairs, or ruin'd fortune flout,
  With wealth your state, your mind with arts improve,
      Take you a course, get you a place,         5
      Observe his Honor, or his Grace,
Or the King's real, or his stamped face
  Contemplate, what you will, approve,
  So you will let me love.

18 *born . . . sights:* gifted with powers of clairvoyance.

THE CANONIZATION. *Canonization:* the official process by which a person (after death) is made a saint.

4 *state:* estate.   *arts:* learning.   5 *course:* of action.   *place:* position, at Court.   7 *stamped:* i.e., on coins.

Alas, alas, who's injur'd by my love?        10
  What merchants' ships have my sighs drown'd?
Who says my tears have overflow'd his ground?
  When did my colds a forward spring remove?
    When did the heats which my veins fill
    Add one more to the plaguy bill?        15
Soldiers find wars, and lawyers find out still
  Litigious men, which quarrels move,
  Though she and I do love.

Call us what you will, we are made such by love;
  Call her one, me another fly,        20
We're tapers too, and at our own cost die,
  And we in us find th' Eagle and the Dove.
    The Phoenix riddle hath more wit
    By us, we two being one, are it.
So, to one neutral thing both sexes fit.        25
  We die and rise the same, and prove
  Mysterious by this love.

We can die by it, if not live by love,
  And if unfit for tombs and hearse
Our legend be, it will be fit for verse;        30
  And if no piece of Chronicle we prove,
    We'll build in sonnets pretty rooms;
    As well a well-wrought urn becomes
The greatest ashes, as half-acre tombs,
  And by these hymns, all shall approve        35
  Us *canoniz'd* for Love:

And thus invoke us: You whom reverend love
  Made one another's hermitage;
You, to whom love was peace, that now is rage;
  Who did the whole world's soul contract, and drove 40
    Into the glasses of your eyes
    (So made such mirrors, and such spies,

13 *colds:* low spirits.  *forward . . . remove:* delay an early spring.  15
*plaguy bill:* official report of deaths caused by the Plague.  17 *move:*
stir up.  22 *Eagle, Dove:* strength, mildness; with important ecclesiastical associations.  23 *Phoenix riddle:* see Shakespeare, p. 89, title
and note.  25 *So . . . fit:* In their accord both *sexes* become *one* (which
is *neutral*) and indistinguishable. Cf. p. 115, ll. 31-36; Shakespeare, pp.
90-91.  30 *Our legend:* Their life story, as saints.  39 *You . . . rage:*
cf. p. 116, ll. 15-18.  40-41 *world's . . . eyes:* cf. p. 106, ll. 10-11.

That they did all to you epitomize),
 Countries, towns, courts: Beg from above
 A pattern of your love.      45

## Lovers' Infiniteness

If yet I have not all thy love,
Dear, I shall never have it all,
I cannot breathe one other sigh, to move,
Nor can entreat one other tear to fall,
And all my treasure, which should purchase thee,  5
Sighs, tears, and oaths, and letters I have spent.
Yet no more can be due to me,
Than at the bargain made was meant,
If then thy gift of love were partial,
That some to me, some should to others fall,  10
 Dear, I shall never have thee all.

Or if then thou gavest me all,
All was but all, which thou hadst then;
But if in thy heart, since, there be or shall,
New love created be, by other men,    15
Which have their stocks entire, and can in tears,
In sighs, in oaths, and letters outbid me,
This new love may beget new fears,
For, this love was not vow'd by thee.
And yet it was, thy gift being general,   20
The ground, thy heart is mine, what ever shall
 Grow there, dear, I should have it all.

Yet I would not have all yet,
He that hath all can have no more,
And since my love doth every day admit  25
New growth, thou shouldst have new rewards in store;
Thou canst not every day give me thy heart,
If thou canst give it, then thou never gavest it:
Love's riddles are, that though thy heart depart,
It stays at home, and thou with losing savest it: 30
But we will have a way more liberal,
Than changing hearts, to join them, so we shall
 Be one, and one another's All.

45 *your:* or possibly "our."

## Song

Sweetest love, I do not go,
   For weariness of thee,
Nor in hope the world can show
   A fitter love for me;
     But since that I     5
Must die at last, 'tis best,
To use myself in jest
     Thus by feign'd deaths to die;

Yesternight the sun went hence,
   And yet is here today,     10
He hath no desire nor sense,
   Nor half so short a way:
     Then fear not me,
But believe that I shall make
Speedier journeys, since I take     15
     More wings and spurs than he.

O how feeble is man's power,
   That if good fortune fall,
Cannot add another hour,
   Nor a lost hour recall!     20
     But come bad chance,
And we join to' it our strength,
And we teach it art and length,
     Itself o'er us t' advance.

When thou sigh'st, thou sigh'st not wind,     25
   But sigh'st my soul away,
When thou weep'st, unkindly kind,
   My life's blood doth decay.
     It cannot be
That thou lov'st me, as thou say'st,     30
If in thine my life thou waste,
     That art the best of me.

SONG. 23 *art*: skill.  25-26 *When . . . away*: based on the notion that a sigh is literally the expiration of the soul.

Let not thy divining heart
  Forethink me any ill,
Destiny may take thy part,                         35
  And may thy fears fulfill;
    But think that we
Are but turn'd aside to sleep;
They who one another keep
  Alive, ne'er parted be.                          40

## *A Nocturnal upon Saint Lucy's Day,*
### *Being the Shortest Day*

'Tis the year's midnight, and it is the day's,
*Lucy's,* who scarce seven hours herself unmasks,
  The sun is spent, and now his flasks
  Send forth light squibs, no constant rays;
    The world's whole sap is sunk:              5
The general balm th' hydroptic earth hath drunk,
Whither, as to the bed's-feet life is shrunk,
Dead and interr'd; yet all these seem to laugh,
Compar'd with me, who am their epitaph.


Study me then, you who shall lovers be          10
At the next world, that is, at the next spring:
  For I am every dead thing,
  In whom love wrought new alchemy.
    For his art did express
A quintessence even from nothingness,           15
From dull privations, and lean emptiness:
He ruin'd me, and I am re-begot
Of absence, darkness, death; things which are not.

A Nocturnal. 1-2 *day's, Lucy's:* December 13.    3 *flasks:* as in *powder flasks.*    4 *light squibs:* slight explosive rays.    5-6 *world's . . . drunk:* no life is left in the world, because its vital sap (medicinally, preservative balm) has been *drunk* by the thirsty, *hydroptic,* earth.    12-15 *For . . . nothingness:* Alchemy ordinarily tries to discover the elixir or quintessence for transmuting base metals into gold, and for prolonging life. Here, in ironical reversal the lover, already every dead thing, is reduced even further by love to a superlative degree of annihilation: the *quintessence* of nothingness.    17 *ruin'd:* probably an alchemical term, broken down into elements.

All others, from all things, draw all that's good,
Life, soul, form, spirit, whence they being have;                    20
  I, by love's limbec, am the grave
  Of all, that's nothing. Oft a flood
    Have we two wept, and so
Drown'd the whole world, us two; oft did we grow
To be two chaoses, when we did show                                  25
Care to ought else; and often absences
Withdrew our souls, and made us carcasses.

But I am by her death (which word wrongs her),
Of the first nothing, the elixir grown;
  Were I a man, that I were one,                               30
  I needs must know; I should prefer,
    If I were any beast,
Some ends, some means; yea plants, yea stones detest,
And love; all, all some properties invest;
If I an ordinary nothing were,                                       35
As shadow, a light, and body must be here.

But I am none; nor will my sun renew.
You lovers, for whose sake, the lesser sun
  At this time to the Goat is run
  To fetch new lust, and give it you,                          40
    Enjoy your summer all;
Since she enjoys her long night's festival,
Let me prepare towards her, and let me call
This hour her vigil, and her eve, since this
Both the year's, and the day's deep midnight is.                    45

## A Valediction: Forbidding Mourning

As virtuous men pass mildly away,
  And whisper to their souls, to go,
Whilst some of their sad friends do say,
  The breath goes now, and some say, no:

21 *limbec*: alembic; apparatus used in alchemical distillation.  29 *elixir*:
see note on ll. 12-15.  34 *properties invest*: are endued with powers, etc.
39 *Goat*: Capricorn (cf. *goat's horn*), the constellation into which the
sun *runs* at the winter solstice, about December 22.  42 *festival*: the
feast of the Saint.  43 *prepare*: make ready for my devotions.

So let us melt, and make no noise,                    5
    No tear-floods, nor sigh-tempests move,
'Twere profanation of our joys
    To tell the laity our love.


Moving of th' earth brings harms and fears,
    Men reckon what it did and meant,          10
But trepidation of the spheres,
    Though greater far, is innocent.


Dull sublunary lovers' love
    (Whose soul is sense) cannot admit
Absence, because it doth remove                       15
    Those things which elemented it.


But we by a love, so much refin'd,
    That our selves know not what it is,
Inter-assured of the mind,
    Care less, eyes, lips, and hands to miss.        20


Our two souls therefore, which are one,
    Though I must go, endure not yet
A breach, but an expansion,
    Like gold to airy thinness beat.


If they be two, they are two so                       25
    As stiff twin compasses are two,
Thy soul the fixt foot, makes no show
    To move, but doth, if th' other do.


And though it in the center sit,
    Yet when the other far doth roam,          30
It leans, and hearkens after it,
    And grows erect, as that comes home.

A VALEDICTION. 5 *melt*: melting is a separation, like the *mild* passing away of *virtuous men*. It also suggests a fusion or blending, implying that the moment of separation of lovers is also a moment of secret communion. 8 *laity*: those who are not lovers like us. 9 *Moving . . . earth*: probably earthquakes. 11 *trepidation*: "trembling," a condition observed in the inconstant positions of the equinoctial points ("precession"); in the old astronomy it was referred to an oscillating motion in the eighth sphere. 13 *sublunary*: earthly. 16 *elemented*: constituted. 21 *Our . . . one*: see p. 108, ll. 24 ff.; p. 115, l. 36; Shakespeare, pp. 90-91.

Such wilt thou be to me, who must
  Like th' other foot, obliquely run;
Thy firmness makes my circle just,                    35
  And makes me end, where I begun.


## The Ecstasy

Where, like a pillow on a bed,
  A pregnant bank swell'd up, to rest
The violet's reclining head,
  Sat we two, one another's best.
Our hands were firmly cemented                        5
  With a fast balm, which thence did spring,
Our eye-beams twisted, and did thread
  Our eyes, upon one double string:
So to' intergraft our hands, as yet
  Was all the means to make us one,                   10
And pictures in our eyes to get
  Was all our propagation.
As 'twixt two equal armies, Fate
  Suspends uncertain victory,
Our souls (which to advance their state,              15
  Were gone out), hung 'twixt her, and me.
And whilst our souls negotiate there,
  We like sepulchral statues lay;
All day, the same our postures were,
  And we said nothing, all the day.                   20
If any, so by love refin'd,
  That he souls' language understood,
And by good love were grown all mind,
  Within convenient distance stood,
He (though he knew not which soul spake,              25
  Because both meant, both spake the same)
Might thence a new concoction take,
  And part far purer than he came.
This ecstasy doth unperplex
  (We said) and tell us what we love,                 30

THE ECSTASY. 18 *sepulchral statues:* sculptured figures decorating burial vaults and tombs. 21-23 *If . . . mind:* the Platonist whose intellectual devotion to the ideal excludes regard for the operation of sense in love. 27-28 *concoction . . . came:* the Platonic lover, paradoxically, would leave improved, having seen a new kind of love relation, better than a love which is "all mind."

We see by this, it was not sex,
   We see, we saw not what did move:
But as all several souls contain
   Mixture of things, they know not what,
Love, these mixt souls, doth mix again,          35
   And makes both one, each this and that.
A single violet transplant,
   The strength, the color, and the size
(All which before was poor, and scant),
   Redoubles still, and multiplies.               40
When love, with one another so
   Interinanimates two souls,
That abler soul, which thence doth flow,
   Defects of loneliness controls.
We then, who are this new soul, know,            45
   Of what we are compos'd, and made,
For, th' atomies of which we grow,
   Are souls, whom no change can invade.
But O alas, so long, so far
   Our bodies why do we forbear?                  50
They are ours, though they are not we, we are
   The intelligences, they the spheres.
We owe them thanks, because they thus,
   Did us, to us, at first convey,
Yielded their forces, sense, to us,              55
   Nor are dross to us, but allay.
On man heaven's influence works not so,
   But that it first imprints the air,
So soul into the soul may flow,
   Though it to body first repair.               60
As our blood labors to beget
   Spirits, as like souls as it can,
Because such fingers need to knit
   That subtle knot, which makes us man:

36 *And . . . that:* again, cf. Shakespeare, p. 90, ll. 25-28.   47 *atomies:*
atoms.   52 *intelligences . . . spheres:* in medieval cosmology each of
the heavenly bodies was supposed to be moved by an angel, or intelligence.   54 *Did . . . convey:* Their bodies first brought their souls
together.   55 *forces, sense:* some texts read *senses' force.*   56 *allay:*
alloy.   57-60 *heaven's . . . repair:* as the stars, according to astrology,
transmit their influence through the medium of air, and, in a sense, connect heaven and earth; so the body serves as a medium through which
the souls of the lovers effect their union.   61-68 *As . . . lies:* As the blood
(in a bodily process) begets vital spirits—"the active part of the blood"
—which are the subtle agents (*like souls*) effecting the unity of body
and soul proper to man, so the souls of pure lovers must *descend* to the

So must pure lovers' souls descend     65
    T' affections, and to faculties,
Which sense may reach and apprehend,
    Else a great Prince in prison lies.
To' our bodies turn we then, that so
    Weak men on love reveal'd may look;     70
Love's mysteries in souls do grow,
    But yet the body is his book.
And if some lover, such as we,
    Have heard this dialogue of one,
Let him still mark us, he shall see     75
    Small change when we' are to bodies gone.


## Love's Deity

I long to talk with some old lover's ghost,
    Who died before the God of Love was born:
I cannot think that he, who then lov'd most,
    Sunk so low, as to love one which did scorn.
But since this god produc'd a destiny,     5
And that vice-nature, custom, lets it be;
    I must love her, that loves not me.


Sure, they which made him god, meant not so much,
    Nor he, in his young godhead practis'd it.
But when an even flame two hearts did touch,     10
    His office was indulgently to fit
Actives to passives. Correspondency
Only his subject was; it cannot be
    Love, till I love her, that loves me.


But every modern god will now extend     15
    His vast prerogative, as far as Jove.
To rage, to lust, to write to, to commend,
    All is the purlieu of the God of Love.

---

affections, etc. (of sense), which promote a union of bodies proper to the completion and perfection of the love relation. If there is no bodily union, Love (the *Prince*) *in prison lies*. Cf. ll. 27-28 and note.

Love's Deity. 5 *destiny:* course of events certain to come about. 12 *Actives, passives:* subjects capable of acting (here, loving); objects (of love) capable of receiving the effects of the action. Such matching subjects and objects are in *correspondence* (l. 12). 18 *purlieu:* domain.

Oh were we waken'd by this tyranny
To ungod this child again, it could not be          20
    I should love her, who loves not me.

Rebel and atheist too, why murmur I,
    As though I felt the worst that love could do?
Love might make me leave loving, or might try
    A deeper plague, to make her love me too,          25
Which, since she loves before, I' am loth to see;
Falsehood is worse than hate; and that must be,
    If she whom I love, should love me.


## The Relic

When my grave is broke up again
Some second guest to entertain,
(For graves have learn'd that woman-head
To be to more than one a bed)
    And he that digs it, spies          5
A bracelet of bright hair about the bone,
    Will he not let' us alone,
And think that there a loving couple lies,
Who thought that this device might be some way
To make their souls, at the last busy day,          10
Meet at this grave, and make a little stay?

If this fall in a time, or land,
· Where mis-devotion doth command,
Then, he that digs us up, will bring
Us, to the Bishop, and the King,          15
    To make us relics; then
Thou shalt be a Mary Magdalen, and I
    A something else thereby;
All women shall adore us, and some men;
And since at such time, miracles are sought,          20
I would have that age by this paper taught
What miracles we harmless lovers wrought.

THE RELIC. 1-2 *When . . . entertain:* Allusion to a common practice of conserving burial space by re-using the graves. 6 *bracelet . . .
bone:* a bracelet of his lady's hair about his arm, worn in respect to the
custom of lovers carrying some intimate token of their devotion    13
*mis-devotion:* probably a pun: devotion to the wrong object; or, mass-
devotion, "popery." 17 *Mary Magdalen:* a reformed sinner (Luke
7 :37) ; afterwards canonized. 20 *miracles are sought:* i.e., to establish
the worthiness of the relics for veneration.

First, we lov'd well and faithfully,
Yet knew not what we lov'd, nor why,
Difference of sex no more we knew,                    25
Than our guardian angels do;
       Coming and going, we
Perchance might kiss, but not between those meals;
       Our hands ne'er touch'd the seals,
Which nature, injur'd by late law, sets free:          30
These miracles we did; but now alas,
All measure, and all language, I should pass,
Should I tell what a miracle she was.


## Satire III

Kind pity chokes my spleen; brave scorn forbids
Those tears to issue which swell my eye-lids;
I must not laugh, nor weep sins, and be wise,
Can railing then cure these worn maladies?
Is not our Mistress fair Religion,                     5
As worthy of all our soul's devotion,
As virtue was to the first blinded age?
Are not heaven's joys as valiant to assuage
Lusts, as earth's honor was to them? Alas,
As we do them in means, shall they surpass             10
Us in the end, and shall thy father's spirit
Meet blind philosophers in heaven, whose merit
Of strict life may be imputed faith, and hear
Thee, whom he taught so easy ways and near
To follow, damn'd? O if thou dar'st, fear this:        15
This fear great courage, and high valor is,
Dar'st thou aid mutinous Dutch, and dar'st thou lay
Thee in ships' wooden sepulchers, a prey

25 *Difference of sex:* Angels (l. 26) were thought to be asexual. But cf.
p. 115, ll. 31-36; p. 108, l. 25.  28 *meals:* joyful occasions.  29-30 *Our
. . . free:* We never engaged in sexual intimacies, which, though nat-
urally innocent, are now forbidden by *late law:* the seventh command-
ment, or *vice-nature custom* (cf. p. 116, l. 6).  32 *measure:* moderation.
  SATIRE III. 7-9 *As . . . them:* The pre-Christian pagan world had
*virtue* inasmuch as it was instructed by reason and the "light of Nature";
yet it was *blinded* in being without Christian revelation. For the pagans
the greatest good was *earth's honor;* for Christians, *heaven's joy.*  10
*means:* our religion.  12 *blind philosophers:* Plato, Socrates, *et al.,* who
did not know Christianity.  14 *so . . . ways:* cf. "my yoke is easy, and
my burden is light."—Matt. 11 :30.  17-28 *Dar'st . . . straw:* the haz-
ards man endures for gain require *courage of straw* compared to the

To leaders' rage, to storms, to shot, to dearth?
Dar'st thou dive seas, and dungeons of the earth?                    20
Hast thou courageous fire to thaw the ice
Of frozen North discoveries? and thrice
Colder than salamanders, like divine
Children in th' oven, fires of Spain, and the line,
Whose countries limbecs to our bodies be,                           25
Canst thou for gain bear? and must every he
Which cries not, goddess, to thy mistress, draw,
Or eat thy poisonous words? courage of straw!
O desperate coward, wilt thou seem bold, and
To thy foes and his (who made thee to stand                         30
Sentinel in his world's garrison) thus yield,
And for forbidden wars, leave th' appointed field?
Know thy foes: the foul Devil h' is (whom thou
Striv'st to please), for hate, not love, would allow
Thee fain, his whole realm to be quit; and as                       35
The world's all parts wither away and pass,
So the world's self, thy other lov'd foe, is
In her decrepit wane, and thou loving this
Dost love a withered and worn strumpet; last,
Flesh (it self's death) and joys which flesh can taste,             40
Thou lovest; and thy fair goodly soul, which doth
Give this flesh power to taste joy, thou dost loathe.
Seek true religion. O where? Mirreus
Thinking her unhous'd here, and fled from us,
Seeks her at Rome; there, because he doth know                      45
That she was there a thousand years ago,
He loves her rags so, as we here obey
The statecloth where the Prince sat yesterday.
Crantz to such brave loves will not be inthrall'd,
But loves her only, who at Geneva is call'd                         50
Religion, plain, simple, sullen, young,
Contemptuous, yet unhandsome; as among
Lecherous humors, there is one that judges
No wenches wholesome, but coarse country drudges.

---

*high valor* required for living a Christian life. Note the paradoxical
relation to *easy ways,* l. 14. Cf. Hopkins, p. 433, ll. 9-11.  *23-24 colder
. . . line:* as if they were salamanders (supposed to be able to live in
fire); like Meshach, Shadrach, and Abednego, who survived the fiery
furnace (Dan. 3:19-27), men will endure for gain the torments of the
Spanish climate and equatorial heat. Cf. Hardy, p. 446, l. 5.  *25 limbecs:*
see p. 112, l. 21.  *33 thy foes:* the Devil, the world, and the flesh.  *48
statecloth:* which is spread over a throne.  *53 Lecherous humors:*
Lecherous men.

Graius stays still at home here, and because                55
Some preachers, vile ambitious bawds, and laws
Still new like fashions, bid him think that she
Which dwells with us, is only perfect, he
Embraceth her, whom his godfathers will
Tender to him, being tender, as wards still              60
Take such wives as their guardians offer, or
Pay values. Careless Phrygius doth abhor
All, because all cannot be good, as one
Knowing some women whores, daies marry none.
Graccus loves all as one, and thinks that so            65
As women do in divers countries go
In divers habits, yet are still one kind;
So doth, so is Religion; and this blind-
ness too much light breeds; but unmoved thou
Of force must one, and forc'd but one allow;            70
And the right; ask thy father which is she,
Let him ask his; though truth and falsehood be
Near twins, yet truth a little elder is;
Be busy to seek her, believe me this,
He's not of none, nor worst, that seeks the best.       75
To adore, or scorn an image, or protest,
May all be bad; doubt wisely; in strange way
To stand inquiring right, is not to stray;
To sleep, or run wrong, is. On a huge hill,
Cragged, and steep, Truth stands, and he that will      80
Reach her, about must, and about must go;
And what the hill's suddenness resists, win so;
Yet strive so, that before age, death's twilight,
Thy soul rest, for none can work in that night.
To will, implies delay, therefore now do:               85
Hard deeds, the body's pains; hard knowledge too
The mind's endeavors reach, and mysteries
Are like the sun, dazzling, yet plain to all eyes.
Keep the truth which thou hast found; men do not stand
In so ill case here, that God hath with his hand        90
Sign'd kings' blank-charters to kill whom they hate,

62, 65 *Phrygius, Graccus:* symbols, respectively, of the extremes of
fastidiousness and stupid indifference, by the inclusion of which the
possible unsatisfactory "religious attitudes" open to the inquirer are
practically exhausted.  77-78 *in . . . right:* to stand firm seeking right.
82 *suddenness:* steepness.  83-84 *death's . . . night:* cf. John 9 :4. 86-
88 *Hard . . . eyes:* Hard deeds are achieved by toil; hard knowledge,
by the mind's effort; but mysteries, *dazzling* like the sun, blind the
understanding, and yet their truth is plain to all.  90 *case:* condition.
91 *blank-charters: carte blanche* authority.

Nor are they vicars, but hangmen to Fate.
Fool and wretch, wilt thou let thy soul be tied
To man's laws, by which she shall not be tried
At the last day? Oh, will it then boot thee                    95
To say a Philip, or a Gregory,
A Harry, or a Martin taught thee this?
Is not this excuse for mere contraries,
Equally strong? cannot both sides say so?
That thou mayest rightly obey power, her bounds know;  100
Those past, her nature, and name is chang'd; to be
Then humble to her is idolatry.
As streams are, power is; those blest flowers that dwell
At the rough stream's calm head, thrive and do well,
But having left their roots, and themselves given       105
To the stream's tyrannous rage, alas are driven
Through mills, and rocks, and woods, and at last, almost
Consum'd in going, in the sea are lost:
So perish souls, which more choose men's unjust
Power from God claim'd, than God himself to trust.      110


*from* HOLY SONNETS


I


Thou hast made me, and shall thy work decay?
Repair me now, for now mine end doth haste,
I run to death, and death meets me as fast,
And all my pleasures are like yesterday;
I dare not move my dim eyes any way,                     5
Despair behind, and death before doth cast
Such terror, and my feeble flesh doth waste
By sin in it, which it t'wards hell doth weigh;
Only thou art above, and when towards thee
By thy leave I can look, I rise again;                   10
But our old subtle foe so tempteth me,
That not one hour myself I can sustain;
Thy Grace may wing me to prevent his art,
And thou like adamant draw mine iron heart.

92 *hangmen to Fate. Executors of Fate's orders.*  95 *boot:* profit.  96-
97 *Philip . . . Martin:* Symbolic of various recognized churches; Philip
II of Spain, or Philipp Melanchthon; Pope Gregory (XIII, XIV);
Henry VIII; Luther.  101 *Those past:* (Once) past the bounds.

[II] 8 *weigh:* carry.  11 *subtle foe:* Satan.  13 *wing:* give me wings
to escape hell and to *sustain* me.  14 *adamant:* the loadstone.

## VII

At the round earth's imagin'd corners, blow
Your trumpets, Angels, and arise, arise
From death, you numberless infinities
Of souls, and to your scatter'd bodies go,
All whom the flood did, and fire shall o'erthrow,          5
All whom war, dearth, age, agues, tyrannies,
Despair, law, chance, hath slain, and you whose eyes,
Shall behold God, and never taste death's woe.
But let them sleep, Lord, and me mourn a space,
For, if above all these, my sins abound,          10
'Tis late to ask abundance of thy grace,
When we are there; here on this lowly ground,
Teach me how to repent; for that's as good
As if thou' hadst seal'd my pardon, with thy blood.

## IX

If poisonous minerals, and if that tree,
Whose fruit threw death on else immortal us,
If lecherous goats, if serpents envious
Cannot be damn'd; Alas; why should I be?
Why should intent or reason, born in me,          5
Make sins, else equal, in me more heinous?
And mercy being easy, and glorious
To God; in his stern wrath, why threatens he?
But who am I, that dare dispute with thee
O God? Oh! of thine only worthy blood,          10
And my tears, make a heavenly Lethean flood,
And drown in it my sins' black memory;
That thou remember them, some claim as debt,
I think it mercy, if thou wilt forget.

[VII] 1-2 *blow . . . trumpets:* i.e., at the Resurrection.  6 *dearth:*
mistakenly *death* in early printed texts.

[IX] 1 *tree:* "forbidden tree" in Eden.  2 *else:* otherwise.  5 *intent:*
will.  11 *Lethean flood:* Lethe, river in Hades, whose waters caused
forgetfulness.

## X

Death be not proud, though some have called thee
Mighty and dreadful, for, thou art not so,
For, those, whom thou think'st thou dost overthrow,
Die not, poor death, nor yet canst thou kill me.
From rest and sleep, which but thy pictures be,          5
Much pleasure, then from thee, much more must flow,
And soonest our best men with thee do go,
Rest of their bones, and souls' delivery.
Thou art slave to Fate, Chance, kings, and desperate men,
And dost with poison, war, and sickness dwell,          10
And poppy, or charms can make us sleep as well,
And better than thy stroke; why swell'st thou then?
One short sleep past, we wake eternally,
And death shall be no more; death, thou shalt die.


## XII

Why are we by all creatures waited on?
Why do the prodigal elements supply
Life and food to me, being more pure than I,
Simple, and further from corruption?
Why brook'st thou, ignorant horse, subjection?          5
Why dost thou bull, and boar so seelily
Dissemble weakness, and by one man's stroke die,
Whose whole kind, you might swallow and feed upon?
Weaker I am, woe is me, and worse than you,
You have not sinn'd, nor need be timorous.          10
But wonder at a greater wonder, for to us
Created nature doth these things subdue,
But their Creator, whom sin, nor nature tied,
For us, his Creatures, and his foes, hath died.


[XII]  6 *seelily:* feebly.

XIV

Batter my heart, three person'd God; for, you
As yet but knock, breathe, shine, and seek to mend;
That I may rise, and stand, o'rthrow me,' and bend
Your force, to break, blow, burn and make me new.
I, like an usurpt town, to' another due,                    5
Labor to' admit you, but Oh, to no end,
Reason your viceroy in me, me should defend,
But is captiv'd, and proves weak or untrue.
Yet dearly' I love you,' and would be loved fain,
But am betroth'd unto your enemy:                          10
Divorce me, untie, or break that knot again,
Take me to you, imprison me, for I
Except you' enthrall me, never shall be free,
Nor ever chaste, except you ravish me.


### Hymn to God My God, in My Sickness

Since I am coming to that holy room,
    Where, with thy quire of saints for evermore,
I shall be made thy music; as I come
    I tune the instrument here at the door,
    And what I must do then, think here before.            5

Whilst my physicians by their love are grown
    Cosmographers, and I their map, who lie
Flat on this bed, that by them may be shown
    That this is my south-west discovery
    Per fretum febris, by these straits to die,             10

I joy, that in these straits, I see my West;
    For, though their currents yield return to none,
What shall my West hurt me? As West and East
    In all flat maps (and I am one) are one,
    So death doth touch the Resurrection.                   15

[XIV] 9 *fain:* gladly.
HYMN. 7 *Cosmographers:* Geographers of the universe. 9 *south-west
discovery:* south accords with fever; west, with death. 10 *Per fretum
febris:* through the strait of fever.

Is the Pacific Sea my home? Or are
  The Eastern riches? Is Jerusalem?
Anyan, and Magellan, and Gibraltar,
  All straits, and none but straits, are ways to them,
  Whether where Japhet dwelt, or Cham, or Sem.   20

We think that Paradise and Calvary,
  Christ's Cross, and Adam's tree, stood in one place;
Look Lord, and find both Adams met in me;
  As the first Adam's sweat surrounds my face,
  May the last Adam's blood my soul embrace.   25

So, in his purple wrapp'd receive me Lord,
  By these his thorns give me his other Crown;
And as to others' souls I preach'd thy word,
  Be this my text, my sermon to mine own,
  Therefore that he may raise the Lord throws down.   30

18 *Anyan:* Be(h)ring Strait.   20 *where . . . Sem:* sons of Noah,
whose descendants populated the earth.   21-22 *We . . . place:* illustra-
tive of the practice of finding correspondences between the Old and the
New Testaments.   23 *both Adams:* cf. Adam, "who is the figure of him
that was to come [Christ]."—Rom. 5 :14.

# ROBERT HERRICK  1591-1674

*from* HESPERIDES

## Delight in Disorder

A sweet disorder in the dress
Kindles in clothes a wantonness:
A lawn about the shoulders thrown
Into a fine distraction:
An erring lace, which here and there          5
Enthralls the crimson stomacher:
A cuff neglectful, and thereby
Ribbands to flow confusedly:
A winning wave (deserving note)
In the tempestuous petticoat:               10
A careless shoe-string, in whose tie
I see a wild civility:
Do more bewitch me, than when art
Is too precise in every part.

## Corinna's Going a Maying

Get up, get up for shame, the blooming morn
Upon her wings presents the god unshorn.
   See how Aurora throws her fair
   Fresh-quilted colors through the air:
   Get up, sweet-slug-a-bed, and see        5
   The dew-bespangling herb and tree.
Each flower has wept, and bow'd toward the east,
Above an hour since; yet you not drest,
   Nay! not so much as out of bed?
   When all the birds have matins said,       10
   And sung their thankful hymns: 'tis sin,
   Nay, profanation to keep in,
When as a thousand virgins on this day,
Spring, sooner than the lark, to fetch in May.

DELIGHT IN DISORDER. 2 *wantonness:* "glamor." 3 *lawn:* fine linen
scarf. 6 *stomacher:* ornamental part of the dress worn over the front.
8 *Ribbands:* Ribbons.

CORINNA'S. 2 *god unshorn:* Apollo, the sun god, often represented
with hair flowing down upon his neck. 3 *Aurora:* the Dawn. 10
*matins:* morning prayers. 14 *fetch in May:* the folk custom of bringing
in flowers on May Day, particularly, the white hawthorn (often called

Rise; and put on your foliage, and be seen                    15
To come forth, like the springtime, fresh and green;
    And sweet as Flora. Take no care
    For jewels for your gown, or hair:
    Fear not; the leaves will strew
    Gems in abundance upon you:                             20
Besides, the childhood of the day has kept,
Against you come, some orient pearls unwept:
    Come, and receive them while the light
    Hangs on the dew-locks of the night:
    And Titan on the eastern hill                          25
    Retires himself, or else stands still
Till you come forth. Wash, dress, be brief in praying:
Few beads are best, when once we go a Maying.


Come, my Corinna, come; and coming, mark
How each field turns a street; each street a park       30
    Made green, and trimm'd with trees: see how
    Devotion gives each house a bough,
    Or branch: each porch, each door, ere this,
    An ark a tabernacle is
Made up of white-thorn neatly interwove;                35
As if here were those cooler shades of love.
    Can such delights be in the street,
    And open fields, and we not see 't?
    Come, we'll abroad; and let's obey
    The proclamation made for May:                         40
And sin no more, as we have done, by staying;
But my Corinna, come, let's go a Maying.

---

"May"). Observance of May Day is rooted in the ancient pagan celebra-
tions of spring as the season emblematic of fertility. Herrick mixes
Christian and pagan imagery, not so much to Christianize the folk
"ritual" as to restore to it something of its primitive religious meaning.
17 *Flora:* flower goddess.   22 *Against:* For the time when.   *orient . . .
unwept:* dewdrops, still on the grass.   24 *dew-locks . . . night:* night
personified, as with dew-laden locks.   25 *Titan:* The sun god Helios (son
of Hyperion), representing the sun in its annual and daily course, i.e.,
in its physical rather than, as Apollo (with whom Hyperion is later identified), in its spiritual manifestation.   28 *beads:* of the rosary; prayers.
30-31 *each . . . trees:* field and town are indistinguishable: each field
is like the *green, trimm'd street,* as each street is like a park.   32 *Devotion:* Observance of May, in its "religious" sense. See l. 14 and note.
34 *An . . . is:* A place of worship, like the Biblical "ark" and "tabernacle."

There's not a budding boy, or girl, this day,
But is got up, and gone to bring in May.
    A deal of youth, ere this, is come          45
    Back, and with white-thorn laden home.
    Some have dispatcht their cakes and cream,
    Before that we have left to dream:
And some have wept, and woo'd, and plighted troth,
And chose their priest, ere we can cast off sloth:    50
    Many a green gown has been given;
    Many a kiss, both odd and even:
    Many a glance too has been sent
    From out the eye, Love's firmament:
Many a jest told of the keys betraying        55
This night, and locks pickt, yet w' are not a Maying.

Come, let us go, while we are in our prime;
And take the harmless folly of the time.
    We shall grow old apace, and die
    Before we know our liberty.          60
    Our life is short; and our days run
    As fast away as does the sun:
And as a vapor, or a drop of rain
Once lost, can ne'er be found again:
    So when or you or I are made          65
    A fable, song, or fleeting shade;
    All love, all liking, all delight
    Lies drown'd with us in endless night.
Then while time serves, and we are but decaying;
Come, my Corinna, come, let's go a Maying.    70


### To the Virgins, to Make Much of Time

    Gather ye rose-buds while ye may,
        Old Time is still a flying:
    And this same flower that smiles today,
        Tomorrow will be dying.

48 *left to dream:* left (off) dreaming.  51 *Many . . . given:* Many a
gown stained by the grass.  57-58 *Come . . . time:* These lines begin
the summary statement of the theme of the entire poem: *carpe diem,*
"seize the day," or the moment. Cf. "To the Virgins," below; "Come,
my Celia," p. 101; Marvell, p. 175. There are echoes of the theme in
many places, but in "Corinna's Going A-Maying" it receives its most
distinguished treatment in English.

The glorious lamp of heaven, the sun,    5
    The higher he's a getting;
The sooner will his race be run,
    And nearer he's to setting.


That age is best, which is the first,
    When youth and blood are warmer;    10
But being spent, the worse, and worst
    Times, still succeed the former.


Then be not coy, but use your time,
    And while ye may, go marry:
For having lost but once your prime,    15
    You may forever tarry.


## To Daffodils

Fair daffodils, we weep to see
    You haste away so soon:
As yet the early-rising sun
    Has not attain'd his noon.
        Stay, stay,    5
      Until the hasting day
        Has run
      But to the Even-song;
And, having pray'd together, we
      Will go with you along.    10


We have short time to stay, as you,
    We have as short a spring;
As quick a growth to meet decay,
    As you, or any thing.
        We die,    15
      As your hours do, and dry
        Away,
      Like to the summer's rain;
Or as the pearls of morning's dew
      Ne'er to be found again.    20

To Daffodils. 8 *Even-song:* Vespers, the service of Evening Prayer.
19 *pearls . . . dew:* cf. p. 127, l. 22.

## The Night-Piece, to Julia

Her eyes the glow-worm lend thee,
The shooting stars attend thee,
    And the elves also,
    Whose little eyes glow,
Like the sparks of fire, befriend thee.     5

No will-o'-th'-wisp mis-light thee;
Nor snake, or slow-worm bite thee;
    But on, on thy way
    Not making a stay,
Since ghost there's none to affright thee.     10

Let not the dark thee cumber;
What though the moon does slumber?
    The stars of the night
    Will lend thee their light,
Like tapers clear without number.     15

Then Julia let me woo thee,
Thus, thus to come unto me:
    And when I shall meet
    Thy silv'ry feet,
My soul I'll pour into thee.     20

## A Ternary of Littles, upon a Pipkin of Jelly Sent to a Lady

A little saint best fits a little shrine,
A little prop best fits a little vine,
As my small cruse best fits my little wine.

A little seed best fits a little soil,
A little trade best fits a little toil:
As my small jar best fits my little oil.

A little bin best fits a little bread,
A little garland fits a little head:
As my small stuff best fits my little shed.

THE NIGHT-PIECE. 11 *cumber*: trouble.
    A TERNARY: *Ternary*: A grouping or arrangement in threes. *Pipkin*
"small jar." See l. 6. 3 *cruse*: jar.

A little hearth best fits a little fire,                    10
A little chapel fits a little quire,
As my small bell best fits my little spire.

A little stream best fits a little boat;
A little lead best fits a little float;
As my small pipe best fits my little note.                 15

A little meat best fits a little belly,
As sweetly Lady, give me leave to tell ye,
This little pipkin fits this little jelly.

## Upon Julia's Clothes

Whenas in silks my Julia goes,
Then, then (methinks) how sweetly flows
That liquefaction of her clothes.

Next, when I cast mine eyes and see
That brave vibration each way free;
O how that glittering taketh me!

## An Ode for Him [Ben Jonson]

Ah Ben!
Say how, or when
Shall we thy guests
Meet at those lyric feasts,
Made at the Sun,                                            5
The Dog, the Triple Tun?
Where we such clusters had,
As made us nobly wild, not mad;
And yet each verse of thine
Outdid the meat, outdid the frolic wine.                   10

---

AN ODE FOR HIM. 5-6 *Sun, Dog, Triple Tun:* London taverns where
the "Sons of Ben" met. See Jonson, p. 99, l. 30 and note.   7 *clusters:*
gatherings.

My Ben
Or come again:
Or send to us,
Thy wit's great overplus;
But teach us yet                                    15
Wisely to husband it;
Lest we that talent spend:
And having once brought to an end
That precious stock, the store
Of such a wit the world should have no more.      20

*from* HIS NOBLE NUMBERS

### *His Litany, to the Holy Spirit*

In the hour of my distress,
When temptations me oppress,
And when I my sins confess,
    Sweet Spirit comfort me!

When I lie within my bed,                            5
Sick in heart, and sick in head,
And with doubts discomforted,
    Sweet Spirit comfort me!

When the house doth sigh and weep,
And the world is drown'd in sleep,                  10
Yet mine eyes the watch do keep;
    Sweet Spirit comfort me!

When the artless doctor sees
No one hope, but of his fees,
And his skill runs on the lees;                     15
    Sweet Spirit comfort me!

HIS LITANY. *Litany:* A formal prayer in which priest and congregation alternately respond in a series of invocations and supplications, particularly, *The Litany, Or General Supplication* in *The Book of Common Prayer.*
15 *runs . . . lees:* is "down to the dregs."

When his potion and his pill,
His, or none, or little skill,
Meet for nothing, but to kill;
  Sweet Spirit comfort me!   20

When the passing-bell doth toll,
And the Furies in a shoal
Come to fright a parting soul;
  Sweet Spirit comfort me!

When the tapers now burn blue,   25
And the comforters are few,
And that number more than true;
  Sweet Spirit comfort me!

When the priest his last hath prayed,
And I nod to what is said,   30
'Cause my speech is now decayed;
  Sweet Spirit comfort me!

When (God knows) I'm tost about,
Either with despair, or doubt;
Yet before the glass be out,   35
  Sweet Spirit comfort me!

When the Tempter me pursu'th
With the sins of all my youth,
And half damns me with untruth;
  Sweet Spirit comfort me!   40

When the flames and hellish cries
Fright mine ears, and fright mine eyes,
And all terrors me surprise;
  Sweet Spirit comfort me!

When the Judgment is reveal'd,   45
And that open'd which was seal'd,
When to Thee I have appeal'd;
  Sweet Spirit comfort me!

**22** *shoal:* crowd. **27** *more:* (is) larger. **35** *glass . . . out:* the hour-glass has run out.

## To His Conscience

Can I not sin, but thou wilt be
My private protonotary?
Can I not woo thee to pass by
A short and sweet iniquity?
I'll cast a mist and cloud, upon                          5
My delicate transgression,
So utter dark, as that no eye
Shall see the hug'd impiety:
*Gifts blind the wise,* and bribes do please,
And wind all other witnesses:                            10
And wilt not thou, with gold, be tied
To lay thy pen and ink aside?
That in the murk and tongueless night,
Wanton I may, and thou not write?
It will not be: And, therefore, now,                     15
For times to come, I'll make this vow,
From aberrations to live free;
So I'll not fear the Judge, or thee.

To His Conscience. 2 *protonotary:* chief clerk. 8 *hug'd:* hugged, cherished. 10 *wind:* to twist or corrupt. 11 *tied:* bound (by bribes). 13 *murk:* dark. 14 *Wanton:* sport (a verb).

# GEORGE HERBERT   1593–1633

*from* THE TEMPLE

## *Affliction (I)*

When first thou didst entice to thee my heart,
  I thought the service brave:
So many joys I writ down for my part,
  Besides what I might have
Out of my stock of natural delights,
Augmented with thy gracious benefits.

I looked on thy furniture so fine,
  And made it fine to me:
Thy glorious household-stuff did me entwine,
  And 'tice me unto thee.    10
Such stars I counted mine: both heav'n and earth
Paid me my wages in a world of mirth.

What pleasures could I want, whose King I served,
  Where joys my fellows were?
Thus argu'd into hopes, my thoughts reserved  15
  No place for grief or fear.
Therefore my sudden soul caught at the place,
And made her youth and fierceness seek thy face.

At first thou gav'st me milk and sweetnesses;
  I had my wish and way:    20
My days were straw'd with flow'rs and happiness;
  There was no month but May.
But with my years sorrow did twist and grow,
And made a party unawares for woe.

My flesh began unto my soul in pain,  25
  Sicknesses cleave my bones;

AFFLICTION. 2 *brave:* fine.   11 *Such stars:* thy furniture (l. 7),
glorious household stuff (l. 9).   17 *sudden:* rash, *caught at:* snatched
at.   *place:* i.e., "Where joys my fellows were," l. 14.   21 *straw'd:*
strewed.   23 *twist:* coil round (in growing).   24 *made . . . woe:* without warning, sorrow joined with sorrow in organized effort to keep me
miserable.   25 *began unto:* began to address.

Consuming agues dwell in ev'ry vein,
     And tune my breath to groans.
Sorrow was all my soul; I scarce believed,
Till grief did tell me roundly, that I lived.     30

When I got health, thou took'st away my life,
     And more; for my friends die:
My mirth and edge was lost; a blunted knife
     Was of more use than I.
Thus thin and lean without a fence or friend,     35
I was blown through with ev'ry storm and wind.

Whereas my birth and spirit rather took
     The way that takes the town;
Thou didst betray me to a ling'ring book,
     And wrap me in a gown.     40
I was entangled in the world of strife,
Before I had the power to change my life.

Yet, for I threat'ned oft the siege to raise,
     Not simp'ring all mine age,
Thou often didst with academic praise     45
     Melt and dissolve my rage.
I took thy sweet'ned pill, till I came where
I could not go away, nor persevere.

Yet lest perchance I should too happy be
     In my unhappiness,     50
Turning my purge to food, thou throwest me
     Into more sicknesses.
Thus doth thy power cross-bias me, not making
Thine own gift good, yet me from my ways taking.

Now I am here, what thou wilt do with me     55
     None of my books will show:
I read, and sigh, and wish I were a tree;
     For sure then I should grow
To fruit or shade: at least some bird would trust
Her household to me, and I should be just.     60

35 *fence:* defense.   37-38 *my . . . town:* my birth and disposition inclined me towards the pleasures of the town.   39-40 *to . . . gown:* at
Cambridge, 1609-1627.   44 *Not . . . age:* Not smirking all my years;
e.g., when he got up courage to resist his condition.   45 *academic praise:*
e.g., that received when Herbert was University Orator (1619/20-
1627/28).   47 *where:* near (1633 edn.).   51 *purge: sweet'ned pill,* l.
47.   53 *cross-bias:* cause me to go against my natural disposition.

Yet, though thou troublest me, I must be meek;
  In weakness must be stout.
Well, I will change the service, and go seek
  Some other master out.
Ah my dear God! though I am clean forgot,          65
Let me not love thee, if I love thee not.


## Prayer (I)

Prayer the Church's banquet, angels' age,
  God's breath in man returning to his birth,
The soul in paraphrase, heart in pilgrimage,
The Christian plummet sounding heav'n and earth;
Engine against th' Almighty, sinner's tower,          5
  Reversed thunder, Christ-side-piercing spear,
  The six-days-world transposing in an hour,
A kind of tune, which all things hear and fear;
Softness, and peace, and joy, and love, and bliss,
  Exalted manna, gladness of the best,          10
  Heaven in ordinary, man well drest,
The milky way, the bird of paradise,
  Church-bells beyond the stars heard, the soul's blood,
  The land of spices; something understood.


## Church-Monuments

While that my soul repairs to her devotion,
Here I entomb my flesh, that it betimes
May take acquaintance of this heap of dust;
To which the blast of death's incessant motion,
Fed with the exhalation of our crimes,          5
Drives all at last. Therefore I gladly trust

PRAYER. 1 *angels' age:* a long age, appropriate to angels, rather than
to men. See Ps. 90:9-10.    4 *plummet:* device for measuring depths.
*sounding:* "getting to the bottom of" (all that earth and heaven mean).
5 *Engine . . . tower:* Prayer is like an *engine* or a *tower* (ancient military machines) used to lay siege to a city—namely, God. Cf. Donne,
XIV n. 124.    7 *six-days-world:* it took God six days to make the world.
11 *in ordinary:* in regular, permanent service.
    CHURCH-MONUMENTS. 1 *repairs:* goes.    2 *Here:* in the church,
among the monuments.    3 *dust:* into which the dead have turned and his
body will turn; and whence his body came.    5 *Fed . . . crimes:* the
withering wind of death is *fed* by sin.

My body to this school, that it may learn
To spell his elements, and find his birth
Written in dusty heraldry and lines;
Which dissolution sure doth best discern,                    10
Comparing dust with dust, and earth with earth.
These laugh at jet and marble put for signs,


To sever the good fellowship of dust,
And spoil the meeting. What shall point out them,
When they shall bow, and kneel, and fall down flat   15
To kiss those heaps, which now they have in trust?
Dear flesh, while I do pray, learn here thy stem
And true descent; that when thou shalt grow fat,


And wanton in thy cravings, thou mayst know,
That flesh is but the glass, which holds the dust     20
That measures all our time; which also shall
Be crumbled into dust. Mark here below
How tame these ashes are, how free from lust,
That thou mayst fit thyself against thy fall.


## The Windows

Lord, how can man preach thy eternal word?
    He is a brittle crazy glass:
Yet in thy temple thou dost him afford
      This glorious and transcendent place,
      To be a window, through thy grace.            5


But when thou dost anneal in glass thy story,
    Making thy life to shine within
The holy Preachers; then the light and glory
      More rev'rend grows, and more doth win:
      Which else shows wat'rish, bleak, and thin.   10

8 *spell:* name.  *birth:* beginning, from dust. Gen. 2:7.  9 *dusty . . . lines:* the inscriptions on the monuments signify that death is but a returning to the original dust.  10 *Which:* refers to "birth."  12-14 *These laugh . . . meeting:* The indistinguishable dusts mock the monuments which, by identifying the dead, would keep the dusts from mingling.  24 *fit:* prepare.

THE WINDOWS. 2 *crazy:* cracked.  6 *anneal:* fix by heat the colors applied to glass.

Doctrine and life, colors and light, in one
      When they combine and mingle, bring
A strong regard and awe: but speech alone
      Doth vanish like a flaring thing,
      And in the ear, not conscience ring.      15

## Man

      My God, I heard this day,
That none doth build a stately habitation,
      But he that means to dwell therein.
      What house more stately hath there been,
Or can be, than is Man? to whose creation      5
      All things are in decay.

      For Man is ev'ry thing,
And more: He is a tree, yet bears [more] fruit;
      A beast, yet is, or should be more:
      Reason and speech we only bring,      10
Parrots may thank us, if they are not mute,
      They go upon the score.

      Man is all symmetry,
Full of proportions, one limb to another,
      And all to all the world besides:      15
      Each part may call the furthest, brother:
For head with foot hath private amity,
      And both with moons and tides.

      Nothing hath got so far,
But Man hath caught and kept it, as his prey.      20
      His eyes dismount the highest star:
      He is in little all the sphere.

MAN. 5-6 *to . . . decay:* cf. Donne, XII, p. 123, ll. 11-14. 7 *ev'ry thing:* a microcosm, little world. 8 [*more*]: a manuscript reading: *no.* (1633 edn.). 10 *we . . . bring:* man alone has. 12 *They . . . score:* they are in debt to man. 13-18 *Man . . . tides:* The universe is a system of correspondences comprising a harmonious whole. As man's parts are symmetrical, so they are analogously proportional to universal structures and operations, which, in turn, enjoy special relations with one another. Here (ll. 17-18), as the head is to the foot, and as the moon is to the tides, so are the head and foot to the moon and tides. 21 *dismount:* bring down, by using the telescope. 22 *all . . . sphere:* a microcosm. See Milton, p. 171, ll. 14-15 and note.

Herbs gladly cure our flesh, because that they
    Find their acquaintance there.

For us the winds do blow,               25
The earth doth rest, heav'n move, and fountains flow.
    Nothing we see, but means our good,
    As our delight, or as our treasure:
The whole is, either our cupboard of food,
    Or cabinet of pleasure.           30

The stars have us to bed;
Night draws the curtain, which the sun withdraws;
    Music and light attend our head.
    All things unto our flesh are kind
In their descent and being; to our mind     35
    In their ascent and cause.

Each thing is full of duty:
Waters united are our navigation;
    Distinguished, our habitation;
    Below, our drink; above, our meat;     40
Both are our cleanliness. Hath one such beauty?
    Then how are all things neat?

More servants wait on Man,
Than he'll take notice of: in ev'ry path
    He treads down that which doth befriend him,     45
    When sickness makes him pale and wan.
Oh mighty love! Man is one world, and hath
    Another to attend him.

Since then, my God, thou hast
So brave a palace built; O dwell in it,     50
    That it may dwell with thee at last!
    Till then, afford us so much wit;
That, as the world serves us, we may serve thee,
    And both thy servants be.

---

24 *acquaintance:* cf. ll. 13-18 and note.   31 *have:* lead.   34 (*unto*) *are
kind:* i.e., serve.   35 *In . . . being:* As put down here by the Creator.
36 *In . . . cause:* i.e., as they refer to their Creator who ordained their
usefulness.   38-39 *Waters . . . habitation:* cf. "And God called the dry
land Earth [*our habitation*]; and the gathering together of the waters
called he Seas [*our navigation*]."—Gen. 1:10.   40 *above, our meat:* i.e.,
as the rains make the earth productive.   41 *cleanliness:* bodily, and
spiritual (as baptismal water).   *one:* element, water.   *beauty:* good use.
42 *neat:* apt for use.   52 *wit:* understanding.

## The Quip

The merry World did on a day
With his train-bands and mates agree
To meet together, where I lay,
And all in sport to jeer at me.

First, Beauty crept into a rose,                    5
Which when I pluckt not, Sir, said she,
Tell me, I pray, whose hands are those?
*But thou shalt answer, Lord, for me.*

Then Money came, and chinking still,
What tune is this, poor man? said he:            10
I heard in music you had skill.
*But thou shalt answer, Lord, for me.*

Then came brave Glory puffing by
In silks that whistled, who but he?
He scarce allow'd me half an eye.                 15
*But thou shalt answer, Lord, for me.*

Then came quick Wit and Conversation,
And he would needs a comfort be,
And to be short, make an oration.
*But thou shalt answer, Lord, for me.*            20

Yet when the hour of thy design
To answer these fine things shall come;
Speak not at large; say, I am thine:
And then they have their answer home.

## Artillery

As I one ev'ning sat before my cell,
Methought a star did shoot into my lap.
I rose, and shook my clothes, as knowing well,
That from small fires comes oft no small mishap.

THE QUIP. 2 *train-bands:* the London citizen soldiery.   23 *at large:*
indecisively.

When suddenly I heard one say,                    5
*Do as thou usest, disobey,*
*Expel good motions from thy breast,*
*Which have the face of fire, but end in rest.*


I, who had heard of music in the spheres,
But not of speech in stars, began to muse:        10
But turning to my God, whose ministers
The stars and all things are; if I refuse,
    Dread Lord, said I, so oft my good;
    Then I refuse not ev'n with blood
    To wash away my stubborn thought:      15
For I will do, or suffer what I ought.


But I have also stars and shooters too,
Born where thy servants both artilleries use.
My tears and prayers night and day do woo,
And work up to thee; yet thou dost refuse.        20
    Not but I am (I must say still)
    Much more oblig'd to do thy will,
    Than thou to grant mine: but because
Thy promise now hath ev'n set thee thy laws.


Then we are shooters both, and thou dost deign    25
To enter combat with us, and contest
With thine own clay. But I would parley fain:
Shun not my arrows, and behold my breast.
    Yet if thou shunnest, I am thine:
    I must be so, if I am mine.            30
    There is no articling with thee:
I am but finite, yet thine infinitely.

---

ARTILLERY. 6 *usest:* are accustomed to do. 7-8 *good motions . . .
rest:* good impulses, like the star, resemble fire and, therefore, seem
dangerous; but actually they bring peace. 14 *blood:* Christ's cleansing
blood. 17 *shooters:* shooting stars. 23-24 *because . . . laws:* because
you are obliged to receive my prayers and tears (l. 19) as you promised
through Christ. 27 *fain:* gladly. 28 *arrows:* tears and prayers. *breast:*
i.e., exposed to God's artillery. 31 *articling:* bargaining. It is combat
to the end, the "unconditional surrender" of the poet to God. Cf. p. 143,
ll. 33-36; p. 144, ll. 17-18.

## The Collar

I struck the board, and cried, No more.
       I will abroad.
What? shall I ever sigh and pine?
My lines and life are free; free as the road,
    Loose as the wind, as large as store.         5
      Shall I be still in suit?
Have I no harvest but a thorn
To let me blood, and not restore
What I have lost with cordial fruit?
      Sure there was wine           10
Before my sighs did dry it: there was corn
    Before my tears did drown it.
    Is the year only lost to me?
    Have I no bays to crown it?
No flowers, no garlands gay? all blasted?     15
    All wasted?
Not so, my heart: but there is fruit,
    And thou hast hands.
Recover all thy sigh-blown age
On double pleasures: leave thy cold dispute     20
Of what is fit, and not: forsake thy cage,
    Thy rope of sands,
Which petty thoughts have made, and made to thee
    Good cable, to enforce and draw,
      And be thy law,           25
While thou didst wink and wouldst not see.
    Away! take heed.
    I will abroad.
Call in thy death's-head there: tie up thy fears.
    He that forbears          30
    To suit and serve his need,
    Deserves his load.
But as I rav'd and grew more fierce and wild
    At every word,
Methought I heard one calling, *Child!*     35
    And I replied, *My Lord*.

---

THE COLLAR. 4 *lines:* lot. 5 *as . . . store:* abundant. 6 *suit:* (in)
service to another. 9 *cordial:* restorative. 14 *bays:* symbols of success. Cf. Marvell, p. 178, l. 2. 18 *hands:* i.e., for picking the fruit.
29 *death's-head:* skull, symbolizing his *fears* which keep him from going "abroad." 31 *To suit:* To satisfy (his need) by pursuing its interest.

## *Love (III)*

Love bade me welcome: yet my soul drew back,
      Guilty of dust and sin.
But quick-ey'd Love, observing me grow slack
      From my first entrance in,
Drew nearer to me, sweetly questioning,      5
      If I lack'd any thing.

A guest, I answer'd, worthy to be here:
      Love said, You shall be he.
I the unkind, ungrateful? Ah my dear,
      I cannot look on thee.      10
Love took my hand, and smiling did reply,
      Who made the eyes but I?

Truth Lord, but I have marr'd them: let my shame
      Go where it doth deserve.
And know you not, says Love, who bore the blame?      15
      My dear, then I will serve.
You must sit down, says Love, and taste my meat:
      So I did sit and eat.

LOVE. 7 *A guest:* (I lack) being a guest. 15 *who:* Christ. 17 *my meat:* Christ's body of the Eucharist.

# JOHN MILTON 1608-1674

## On Time

Fly envious *Time*, till thou run out thy race,
Call on the lazy leaden-stepping hours,
Whose speed is but the heavy plummet's pace;
And glut thy self with what thy womb devours,
Which is no more than what is false and vain,        5
And merely mortal dross;
So little is our loss,
So little is thy gain.
For when as each thing bad thou hast entomb'd,
And last of all, thy greedy self consum'd,          10
Then long Eternity shall greet our bliss
With an individual kiss;
And Joy shall overtake us as a flood,
When every thing that is sincerely good
And perfectly divine,                               15
With Truth, and Peace, and Love shall ever shine
About the supreme Throne
Of him, t' whose happy-making sight alone,
When once our heav'nly-guided soul shall climb,
Then all this earthy grossness quit,                20
Attir'd with stars, we shall for ever sit,
   Triumphing over Death, and Chance, and thee O Time.


## L'Allegro

Hence, loathed Melancholy,
   Of Cerberus, and blackest midnight born,
In Stygian cave forlorn.
   'Mongst horrid shapes, and shrieks, and sights unholy,

ON TIME. 2-3 *lazy . . . pace:* reference to the passing of time as
shown by a clock operated by falling weights. 4 *womb:* belly. 12 *individual:* indivisible. 20 *quit:* discarded.

L'ALLEGRO. 1 *Melancholy:* a word with important status in the seventeenth century, denominating not only low spirits generally and the so-
briety accompanying study and reflection (as in "Il Penseroso"), but
also the various pathological conditions, physical as well as psychic, and
even social, which indicate depression and morbid inclinations of the
mind. 2 *Cerberus:* the three-headed watchdog of Hades. 3 *Stygian
cave:* on the Styx, the principal river of the underworld.

145

Find out some uncouth cell, 5
　　Where brooding darkness spreads his jealous wings,
And the night-raven sings;
　　There, under ebon shades, and low-brow'd rocks,
As ragged as thy locks,
　　In dark Cimmerian desert ever dwell. 10
But come thou goddess fair and free,
In Heav'n yclep'd Euphrosyne,
And by men, heart-easing Mirth,
Whom lovely Venus at a birth
With two sister Graces more 15
To ivy-crowned Bacchus bore;
Or whether (as some sager sing)
The frolic Wind that breathes the Spring,
Zephyr with Aurora playing,
As he met her once a-Maying, 20
There on beds of violets blue,
And fresh-blown roses washt in dew,
Fill'd her with thee a daughter fair,
So buxom, blithe, and debonair.
Haste thee nymph, and bring with thee 25
Jest and youthful Jollity,
Quips and Cranks, and wanton Wiles,
Nods, and Becks, and wreathed Smiles,
Such as hang on Hebe's cheek,
And love to live in dimple sleek; 30
Sport that wrinkled Care derides,
And Laughter holding both his sides.
Come, and trip it as you go,
On the light fantastic toe,
And in thy right hand lead with thee, 35
The Mountain Nymph, sweet Liberty;
And if I give thee honor due,
Mirth, admit me of thy crew
To live with her, and live with thee,
In unreproved pleasures free; 40
To hear the lark begin his flight,
And singing startle the dull night,

---

5 *uncouth:* unknown. 10 *Cimmerian desert:* a place of mist and darkness, like the land of Homer's Cimmerians (*Odyssey,* XI, 14-18). 12
*yclep'd:* named. *Euphrosyne:* one of the three Graces, as l. 15 makes
clear. 16 *Bacchus:* God of wine. 17 *sager:* wiser person(s). 19
*Zephyr; Aurora:* West Wind; Dawn. 24 *buxom:* comely. 27 *Cranks
. . . Wiles:* witty turns of speech and playful tricks. 29 *Hebe:* Goddess
of youth. 39 *her:* Liberty, l. 36. 40 *unreproved:* unreprovable, innocent.

From his watch-tow'r in the skies,
Till the dappled dawn doth rise;
Then to come in spite of sorrow,                45
And at my window bid good-morrow,
Through the sweet-briar, or the vine,
Or the twisted eglantine.
While the cock with lively din,
Scatters the rear of darkness thin,             50
And to the stack, or the barn door,
Stoutly struts his dames before,
Oft list'ning how the hounds and horn
Cheerly rouse the slumb'ring morn,
From the side of some hoar hill,                55
Through the high wood echoing shrill.
Sometime walking not unseen
By hedge-row elms, on hillocks green,
Right against the eastern gate,
Where the great sun begins his state,           60
Rob'd in flames, and amber light,
The clouds in thousand liveries dight,
While the plowman near at hand,
Whistles o'er the furrow'd land,
And the milkmaid singeth blithe,                65
And the mower whets his scythe,
And every shepherd tells his tale
Under the hawthorn in the dale.
Straight mine eye hath caught new pleasures
Whilst the lantskip round it measures,          70
Russet lawns, and fallows gray,
Where the nibbling flocks do stray,
Mountains on whose barren breast
The laboring clouds do often rest:
Meadows trim with daisies pied,                 75
Shallow brooks, and rivers wide.
Towers, and battlements it sees
Bosom'd high in tufted trees,
Where perhaps some beauty lies,
The cynosure of neighboring eyes.               80

45 *to come:* in parallel construction with *To live* (l. 39), *To hear* (l. 41).
The subject is *me,* l. 38.  60 *state:* stately progress.  62 *dight:* dressed.
67 *tells his tale:* either, counts his sheep; or, tells his (love) story, in
song, like the poet shepherds in pastoral verse. Cf. Spenser, p. 46, ll.
21-22; p. 47, ll. 43-44.  70 *lantskip:* landscape.  71 *fallows:* unplanted
fields.  74 *laboring:* rolling.  75 *pied:* parti-colored.  80 *cynosure:*
center of attraction.

Hard by, a cottage chimney smokes,
From betwixt two aged oaks,
Where Corydon and Thyrsis met,
Are at their savory dinner set
Of herbs, and other country messes,                     85
Which the neat-handed Phillis dresses;
And then in haste her bow'r she leaves,
With Thestylis to bind the sheaves;
Or if the earlier season lead
To the tann'd haycock in the mead,                      90
Sometimes with secure delight
The upland hamlets will invite,
When the merry bells ring round,
And the jocund rebecks sound
To many a youth, and many a maid,                       95
Dancing in the checker'd shade;
And young and old come forth to play
On a sunshine holiday,
Till the live-long daylight fail,
Then to the spicy nut-brown ale,                       100
With stories told of many a feat,
How Fairy Mab the junkets eat,
She was pincht, and pull'd she said,
And he by Friar's Lanthorn led,
Tells how the drudging Goblin sweat,                   105
To earn his cream-bowl duly set,
When in one night, ere glimpse of morn,
His shadowy flail hath thresh'd the corn,
That ten day-laborers could not end,
Then lies him down the lubber fend,                    110
And stretch'd out all the chimney's length,
Basks at the fire his hairy strength;
And crop-full out of doors he flings,
Ere the first cock his matin rings.
Thus done the tales, to bed they creep,                115
By whispering winds soon lull'd asleep.
Tower'd cities please us then,
And the busy hum of men,

83 *Corydon, Thyrsis* (and *Phillis,* l. 86, *Thestylis,* l. 88) : names of shepherds and shepherdesses in pastoral poetry. 87 *bow'r:* cottage. 91 *secure:*
carefree. 94 *rebeck(s)* : stringed instrument, ancestor of the violin. 102
*Fairy Mab:* Queen of the fairies. *junkets:* sweetened curds. 103 *she:*
the one reporting the feats of Mab. 104 *he . . . led:* another one of
the story tellers, who, by his own report or according to gossip, had been
led by the mysterious will-o'-the-wisp (i.e., *Friar's Lanthorn*). 105
*drudging Goblin:* a beneficent goblin, Hobgoblin. 110 *lubber f[i]end:*
Hobgoblin, a Lob-lie-by-the-fire. 113 *crop-full:* stomach-full.

Where throngs of knights and barons bold,
In weeds of peace high triumphs hold,                          120
With store of ladies, whose bright eyes
Rain influence, and judge the prize,
Of wit, or arms, while both contend
To win her grace, whom all commend.
There let Hymen oft appear                                     125
In saffron robe, with taper clear,
And pomp, and feast, and revelry,
With masque, and antique pageantry,
Such sights as youthful poets dream
On summer eves by haunted stream.                             130
Then to the well-trod stage anon,
If Jonson's learned sock be on,
Or sweetest Shakespeare, Fancy's child,
Warble his native woodnotes wild,
And ever against eating Cares,                                 135
Lap me in soft Lydian airs,
Married to immortal verse
Such as the meeting soul may pierce
In notes, with many a winding bout
Of linked sweetness long drawn out,                           140
With wanton heed, and giddy cunning,
The melting voice through mazes running;
Untwisting all the chains that tie
The hidden soul of harmony;
That Orpheus' self may heave his head                         145

120 *weeds:* garments.   *triumphs:* festivities.   122 *Rain influence:* i.e., upon the men.   125-26 *Hymen . . . clear:* The god of marriage in his customary *saffron robe,* with his *taper* to light the bride and bridegroom to the marriage chamber.   128 *masque:* courtly entertainment (combining drama, music, dance and song into an elaborate pageantry).   132 *Jonson's . . . sock:* Jonson's *learned* comedy, as distinct from Shakespeare's romantic comedy. See Jonson, p. 103, l. 37 and note.   133 *Fancy's:* of the imagination, the creative faculty.   136 *Lydian:* One of the "modes" of ancient music, characterized by delicacy and softness.   138 *meeting:* responsive.   139 *winding bout:* intricate turn.   141 *wanton:* playful.   *giddy:* bewilderingly rapid.   145 *Orpheus:* Thracian poet, musician; son of Apollo and Calliope (Muse of heroic poetry). After the death of his wife Eurydice, he went to Hades in search of her. There, he played his lyre so well that Pluto was persuaded to grant her release on condition, however, that as she followed him he would not look back until they reached the upper air. Orpheus looked back; hence, Milton's *half-regain'd Eurydice* (l. 150). Orpheus was a demigod because of the command over man and nature which his lyre gave him. His visit to the underworld and return were viewed as a figure of the seasonal cycle of nature's decay and regeneration; and his death at the hands of the Thracian women, who tore him to pieces and threw his head into the Hebrus, was taken as the death necessarily suffered by the god in order to assure regeneration. See p. 157, ll. 58-63.

From golden slumber on a bed
Of heapt Elysian flow'rs, and hear
Such strains as would have won the ear
Of Pluto, to have quite set free
His half-regain'd Eurydice.                    150
These delights, if thou canst give,
Mirth, with thee, I mean to live.


## Il Penseroso

Hence vain deluding joys,
   The brood of folly without father bred,
How little you bestead,
   Or fill the fixed mind with all your toys;
Dwell in some idle brain,                       5
   And fancies fond with gaudy shapes possess,
As thick and numberless
   As the gay motes that people the sunbeams,
Or likest hovering dreams
   The fickle pensioners of Morpheus' train.    10
But hail thou Goddess, sage and holy,
Hail divinest Melancholy,
Whose saintly visage is too bright
To hit the sense of human sight;
And therefore to our weaker view,              15
O'erlaid with black, staid Wisdom's hue.
Black, but such as in esteem,
Prince Memnon's sister might beseem,
Or that starr'd Ethiope Queen that strove
To set her beauty's praise above               20
The Sea Nymphs, and their powers offended.
Yet thou art higher far descended;
Thee, bright-hair'd Vesta long of yore,

IL PENSEROSO. 3 *bestead:* avail. 6 *fond:* foolish. 8 *gay motes:*
bright (dust) particles. 9-10 *hovering . . . train:* dreams, which come
and go (hence, *hovering, fickle*), in the service and retinue (hence,
*pensioners, train*) of Morpheus, god of dreams. 12 *Melancholy:* Unlike
*loathed Melancholy* of "L'Allegro," Melancholy is now deified. 18
*Prince Memnon's sister:* black is made an estimable color (cf. *Wisdom's
hue*) such as might become Hemera, sister of Memnon, the dark-fea-
tured, glowing Ethiopian Prince and hero of Troy. 19 *starr'd . . .
Queen:* Cassiopea, who became a constellation. 20 *her beauty('s)* :
Andromeda, Cassiopea's daughter. Cassiopea's pride in her daughter's
beauty aroused the envy of the Sea Nymphs. 23 *Vesta:* Melancholy's
mother, chaste goddess of the hearth and household ; daughter of Saturn.

To solitary Saturn bore;
His daughter she (in Saturn's reign,                    25
Such mixture was not held a stain).
Oft in glimmering bow'rs and glades
He met her, and in secret shades
Of woody Ida's inmost grove,
While yet there was no fear of Jove.                    30
Come pensive Nun, devout and pure,
Sober, steadfast, and demure,
All in a robe of darkest grain,
Flowing with majestic train,
And sable stole of cypress lawn,                         35
Over thy decent shoulders drawn.
Come, but keep thy wonted state,
With ev'n step, and musing gait,
And looks commercing with the skies,
Thy rapt soul sitting in thine eyes:                    40
There held in holy passion still,
Forget thyself to marble, till
With a sad leaden downward cast,
Thou fix them on the earth as fast.
And join with thee calm Peace, and Quiet,               45
Spare Fast, that oft with gods doth diet,
And hears the Muses in a ring,
Aye round about Jove's altar sing.
And add to these retired Leisure,
That in trim gardens takes his pleasure;                50
But first, and chiefest, with thee bring,
Him that yon soars on golden wing,
Guiding the fiery-wheeled throne,
The Cherub Contemplation,
And the mute Silence hist along,                        55
'Less Philomel will deign a song,
In her sweetest, saddest plight,
Smoothing the rugged brow of night,

---

24 *Saturn:* the god who ruled in the ancient Golden Age.   29 *Ida:* mountain in Crete, where Saturn reigned and Jove was nurtured.   30 *Jove* (Jupiter): who dethroned Saturn.   35 *stole:* a long, loose garment, falling from the shoulders.   *cypress lawn:* fine black fabric.   37 *wonted state:* customary dignity.   39 *commercing:* in communion with.   42 *Forget . . . marble: rapt, held in holy passion* (ll. 40, 41), lose all sense of yourself and become as motionless as marble. Cf. Donne, p. 114, l. 18.   54 *Cherub Contemplation:* one of the Cherubim, an order of angels next to the highest, the Seraphim.   56-57 *Philomel:* see "The nightingale," p. 40; "Philomela," p. 394.   58 *rugged:* wrinkled.

While Cynthia checks her dragon yoke,
Gently o'er th' accustom'd oak;                          60
Sweet bird that shunn'st the noise of folly,
Most musical, most melancholy!
Thee, chauntress, oft the woods among,
I woo to hear thy even-song;
And missing thee, I walk unseen                          65
On the dry smooth-shaven green,
To behold the wand'ring moon,
Riding near her highest noon,
Like one that had been led astray
Through the heav'ns wide pathless way;                   70
And oft, as if her head she bow'd,
Stooping through a fleecy cloud.
Oft on a plat of rising ground,
I hear the far-off curfew sound,
Over some wide-water'd shore,                            75
Swinging slow with sullen roar;
Or if the air will not permit,
Some still removed place will fit,
Where glowing embers through the room
Teach light to counterfeit a gloom,                      80
Far from all resort of mirth,
Save the cricket on the hearth,
Or the bellman's drowsy charm,
To bless the doors from nightly harm:
Or let my lamp at midnight hour,                         85
Be seen in some high lonely tow'r,
Where I may oft out-watch the Bear,
With thrice great Hermes, or unsphere
The spirit of Plato to unfold
What worlds, or what vast regions hold                   90
The immortal mind that hath forsook
Her mansion in this fleshly nook:
And of those demons that are found
In fire, air, flood, or under ground,
Whose power hath a true consent                          95

59 *Cynthia:* the moon goddess. *dragon yoke:* which draws her chariot. 73
*plat:* plot. 78 *fit:* suit. 83 *bellman:* night watchman, who cries the
hours. *charm:* song. 87 *Bear:* constellation Ursa Major. 88 *thrice
great Hermes:* Hermes Trismegistus, a legendary Egyptian philosopher
and scientist, esteemed with Moses as one of the first men of learning
and wisdom. 88-92 *unsphere . . . nook:* to call down from its heavenly sphere the spirit of Plato to disclose what becomes of the soul
after death. 95 *consent:* accord.

With planet, or with element.
Sometime let gorgeous Tragedy
In sceptr'd pall come sweeping by,
Presenting Thebes, or Pelops' line,
Or the tale of Troy divine.                                    100
Or what (though rare) of later age,
Ennobled hath the buskin'd stage.
But, O sad Virgin, that thy power
Might raise Musaeus from his bower,
Or bid the soul of Orpheus sing                                105
Such notes as warbled to the string,
Drew iron tears down Pluto's cheek,
And made Hell grant what Love did seek.
Or call up him that left half told
The story of Cambuscan bold,                                   110
Of Camball, and of Algarsife,
And who had Canace to wife,
That own'd the virtuous ring and glass,
And of the wondrous horse of brass,
On which the Tartar king did ride;                             115
And if ought else, great bards beside,
In sage and solemn tunes have sung,
Of tourneys and of trophies hung;
Of forests, and enchantments drear,
Where more is meant than meets the ear.                        120
Thus Night, oft see me in thy pale career,
Till civil-suited Morn appear,
Not trickt and frounct as she was wont,
With the Attic Boy to hunt,
But kerchieft in a comely cloud,                               125

97-98 *Tragedy . . . pall:* The Greek Tragedy (which is in Milton's mind) is royally clad (*In sceptr'd pall*) because its subjects were of the royal houses of Thebes and Troy, and descendants of Pelops (Agamemnon, etc.). 99-100 See note above. Cf. Robinson, p. 466, ll. 11-12. 102 *buskin'd stage:* tragedy; see Jonson, p. 103, l. 36 and note. 104 *Musaeus:* probably the poet-son of Orpheus. 108 *And . . . seek:* see pp. 149-50, ll. 145-50. 109-15 *him . . . ride:* Chaucer, whose *story of Cambuscan* exists as a fragmentary narrative and is assigned to the Squire in *The Canterbury Tales*. In the tale, a mysterious Indian knight gives Cambuscan, the Tartar King, a magic horse and sword and mirror, and to Canace, his daughter, a ring by which she can understand the language of the birds. The King's adventures are left untold, but we do have the sad romantic tale of unregulated love which Canace gets from a wounded falcon. 122 *civil-suited:* modestly dressed. *she:* Morn (Aurora, Eos). 124 *Attic Boy:* Cephalus; the eventual complication of his romance unintentionally led him to kill his wife Procris.

While rocking winds are piping loud,
Or usher'd with a shower still,
When the gust hath blown his fill,
Ending on the rustling leaves,
With minute drops from off the eaves.            130
And when the sun begins to fling
His flaring beams, me Goddess bring
To arched walks of twilight groves,
And shadows brown that Sylvan loves
Of pine, or monumental oak,                     135
Where the rude axe with heaved stroke,
Was never heard the Nymphs to daunt,
Or fright them from their hallow'd haunt,
There in close covert by some brook,
Where no profaner eye may look,                 140
Hide me from Day's garish eye,
While the bee with honied thigh,
That at her flow'ry work doth sing,
And the waters murmuring
With such consort as they keep,                 145
Entice the dewy-feather'd Sleep;
And let some strange mysterious dream,
Wave at his wings in airy stream,
Of lively portraiture display'd,
Softly on my eye-lids laid.                     150
And as I wake, sweet music breathe
Above, about, or underneath,
Sent by some spirit to mortals good,
Or th' unseen Genius of the Wood.
But let my due feet never fail,                 155
To walk the studious cloister's pale.
And love the high embowed roof,
With antic pillars massy proof,
And storied windows richly dight,
Casting a dim religious light.                  160
There let the pealing organ blow,
To the full voic'd quire below,
In service high, and anthems clear,

---

134 *Sylvan*[*us*] : God of the woodland.  145 *consort* : company.  147-50
*And . . . laid* : Let me dream something *strange* and *mysterious,* such
as comes to one in airy streams of lively pictures, which ruffle the
wings of sleep as they lie *softly* upon one's eyelids.  154 *Genius* :
Guardian spirit. Cf. l. 134.  155 *due* : as would be fitting or proper.  156
*pale* : enclosure.  157 *embowed* : vaulted.  158 *antic* : ancient.  159
*storied* : depicting in stained glass (*richly dight*) the Bible stories.

As may with sweetness, through mine ear,
Dissolve me into ecstasies,                                   165
And bring all Heav'n before mine eyes.
And may at last my weary age
Find out the peaceful hermitage,
The hairy gown and mossy cell,
Where I may sit and rightly spell            170
Of every star that heav'n doth shew,
And every herb that sips the dew;
Till old experience do attain
To something like prophetic strain.
These pleasures Melancholy, give,           175
And I with thee will choose to live.

## Lycidas

Yet once more, O ye laurels, and once more
Ye myrtles brown, with ivy never sere,
I come to pluck your berries harsh and crude,
And with forc'd fingers rude,
Shatter your leaves before the mellowing year.    5
Bitter constraint, and sad occasion dear,
Compels me to disturb your season due:
For Lycidas is dead, dead ere his prime,
Young Lycidas, and hath not left his peer:
Who would not sing for Lycidas? he knew            10
Himself to sing, and build the lofty rhyme.
He must not float upon his wat'ry bier
Unwept, and welter to the parching wind,
Without the meed of some melodious tear.

---

170 *spell*: speculate upon.

LYCIDAS. *Lycidas*: Milton adds: *In this Monody the author bewails
a learned friend* [Edward King, whom Milton knew at Cambridge], *un-
fortunately drown'd in his passage from* Chester *on the* Irish *Seas,* 1637.
*And by occasion foretells the ruin of our corrupted Clergy then in their
height.* (Last sentence added in 1645.) See "Shepheardes Calender," p.
45, note. *Lycidas*: the name of one of Virgil's shepherds.

1-7 *Yet . . . due;* Reluctantly, and before he is fully ready for the
effort which the occasion requires, the poet again puts his hand to the
writing of verses. The laurels, etc., are evergreens with which the ancient poets were crowned, and the symbols of poetry itself. *2 brown*:
dark, but not dead.  13 *welter*: toss about.  14 *meed . . . tear*: the
reward of some mourning song.

Begin then, Sisters of the sacred well,                     15
That from beneath the seat of Jove doth spring,
Begin, and somewhat loudly sweep the string.
Hence with denial vain, and coy excuse,
So may some gentle Muse
With lucky words favor my destin'd urn,                      20
And as he passes turn,
And bid fair peace be to my sable shroud.
For we were nurst upon the self-same hill,
Fed the same flock; by fountain, shade, and rill.

Together both, ere the high lawns appear'd                  25
Under the opening eye-lids of the morn,
We drove afield, and both together heard
What time the gray-fly winds her sultry horn,
Batt'ning our flocks with the fresh dews of night,
Oft till the star that rose, at ev'ning, bright,            30
Toward Heav'ns descent had slop'd his westering wheel.
Meanwhile the rural ditties were not mute,
Temper'd to th' oaten flute,
Rough Satyrs danc'd, and Fauns with clov'n heel,
From the glad sound would not be absent long,              35
And old Damætas lov'd to hear our song.

But O the heavy change, now thou art gone,
Now thou art gone, and never must return!
Thee Shepherd, thee the woods, and desert caves,
With wild thyme and the gadding vine o'ergrown,            40
And all their echoes mourn.
The willows, and the hazel copses green,
Shall now no more be seen,
Fanning their joyous leaves to thy soft lays.
As killing as the canker to the rose,                      45
Or taint-worm to the weanling herds that graze,

---

15 *Sisters:* the Muses. *sacred well:* Pierian Spring, at the foot of Mount Olympus; source of poetic inspiration. 18 *coy:* modest. 19-22 *So . . . shroud:* So, as I am doing now, may some poet inspired by the Muses *favor* my burial urn with verses appropriate to my death, and then bid me rest in peace. 24 *Fed . . . flock:* The pastoral strain begins. 25 *lawns:* meadows. 28 *What . . . horn:* in the heat of the day, noon, when the insects are humming. *winds:* blows. 29 *Batt'ning:* Feeding. 32 *ditties:* their own student verse making. 33 *oaten flute:* see Spenser, p. 46, l. 24 and note. 36 *Damætas:* Possibly a tutor; named for one of Virgil's "shepherds." 40 *gadding:* straggling. 45 *canker:* cankerworm. 46 *weanling:* recently weaned.

Or frost to flowers, that their gay wardrop wear,
When first the white thorn blows;
Such, Lycidas, thy loss to shepherd's ear.
   Where were ye Nymphs when the remorseless deep   50
Clos'd o'er the head of your lov'd Lycidas?
For neither were ye playing on the steep,
Where your old Bards, the famous Druids, lie,
Nor on the shaggy top of Mona high,
Nor yet where Deva spreads her wizard stream:   55
Ay me, I fondly dream!
Had ye been there—for what could that have done?
What could the Muse herself that Orpheus bore,
The Muse herself for her enchanting son
Whom universal nature did lament,   60
When by the rout that made the hideous roar,
His gory visage down the stream was sent,
Down the swift Hebrus to the Lesbian shore.
   Alas! What boots it with uncessant care
To tend the homely slighted shepherd's trade,   65
And strictly meditate the thankless Muse?
Were it not better done as others use,
To sport with Amaryllis in the shade,
Or with the tangles of Neæra's hair?
Fame is the spur that the clear spirit doth raise   70
(That last infirmity of noble mind)
To scorn delights, and live laborious days;
But the fair guerdon when we hope to find,
And think to burst out into sudden blaze,
Comes the blind Fury with th' abhorred shears,   75

---

48 *white thorn:* May. See Herrick, p. 126, l. 14 and note.   53-55
*Bards, Druids, Mona, Deva:* Allusions which serve to identify the place
where King met his death, and to naturalize the pastoral by bringing
its traditional, classical symbols into association with local Celtic folklore and religion. The *Druids* were an order of priests, poets, and con-
jurers in the ancient Celtic religion; *Mona* is the Isle of Anglesey,
actually the northwestern county of Wales; and *Deva* is the river Dee,
emptying into the Irish Sea just above Chester, the port from which
King embarked on his fatal voyage. Cf. Thomas, p. 534, ll. 20-21.   56
*fondly:* foolishly.   58-63 *Muse . . . shore:* see p. 149, l. 145 and note.
59 *enchanting:* able to enchant, charm.   64 *boots:* profits.   *uncessant:*
unceasing.   65 *shepherd's trade:* poet's craft.   67 *use:* do.   68, 69
*Amaryllis, Neæra:* playful shepherdesses.   72 *sleep:* pure.   73 *guerdon:*
reward.   75 *blind Fury:* Atropos, the blind Fate, who cuts the threads
of life. Cf. Spenser, p. 50, l. 149 and note.

And slits the thin spun life. But not the praise,
Phoebus repli'd, and touch'd my trembling ears;
Fame is no plant that grows on mortal soil,
Nor in the glistering foil
Set off to th' world, nor in broad rumor lies,                    80
But lives and spreads aloft by those pure eyes,
And perfet witness of all-judging Jove;
As he pronounces lastly on each deed,
Of so much fame in Heav'n expect thy meed.

O Fountain Arethuse, and thou honor'd flood,                 85
Smooth-sliding Mincius, crown'd with vocal reeds,
That strain I heard was of a higher mood:
But now my oat proceeds,
And listens to the Herald of the Sea
That came in Neptune's plea.                                        90
He ask'd the waves, and ask'd the felon winds,
What hard mishap hath doom'd this gentle swain?
And question'd every gust of rugged wings
That blows from off each beaked promontory;
They knew not of his story,                                         95
And sage Hippotades their answer brings,
That not a blast was from his dungeon stray'd,
The air was calm, and on the level brine,
Sleek Panope with all her sisters play'd.
It was that fatal and perfidious bark                              100
Built in th' eclipse, and rigg'd with curses dark,
That sunk so low that sacred head of thine.
Next Camus, reverend Sire, went footing slow,
His mantle hairy, and his bonnet sedge,

76 *slits:* ends. *But . . . praise:* But (destroys) not the praise.  77
*Phoebus:* Apollo, god of wisdom, poetic inspiration.  79 *glistering foil:*
glittering gold or silver leaf under a gem to show it off.  82 *perfet:* perfect.
*Jove:* Jove (Jupiter) is the supreme deity of the pagan classical religion. His testimony accords closely with a Christian sense of value
(see I Sam. 16:7), but it is not peculiarly Christian, nor here to be
taken as such. Cf. Donne, p. 118, ll. 7-9.  85-86 *O Fountain . . .
Mincius:* After the "digression," the poet readdresses the pastoral Muse
by referring to the Sicilian fountain of the Greek pastoralist Theocritus
and the river near the place of Latin Virgil's birth.  88 *oat proceeds:*
the poet continues in the pastoral vein as if he were playing upon an
oaten flute.  89 *listens:* gives ear to.  89-90 *Herald . . . plea:* Triton,
son of Neptune (god of the sea), the calmer of storms and tempest,
who came in behalf of his father's plea.  96 *Hippotades:* Aeolus, god
of the winds.  99 *Panope:* Nereid (sea nymph).  100-02 Presumably
the poet here speaks to Lycidas.  103 *Camus:* Personification of the
Cambridge river, Cam, and thus symbol of the University.

Inwrought with figures dim, and on the edge                    105
Like to that sanguine flower inscrib'd with woe.
Ah! Who hath reft (quoth he) my dearest pledge?
Last came, and last did go,
The Pilot of the Galilean lake.
Two massy keys he bore of metals twain,                        110
(The golden opes, the iron shuts amain).
He shook his miter'd locks, and stern bespake:
How well could I have spar'd for thee, young swain,
Anow of such as for their bellies' sake,
Creep and intrude, and climb into the fold?                    115
Of other care they little reck'ning make,
Than how to scramble at the shearer's feast,
And shove away the worthy bidden guest;
Blind mouths! that scarce themselves know how to hold
A sheep-hook, or have learn'd ought else the least             120
That to the faithful herdman's art belongs!
What recks it them? What need they? They are sped;
And when they list, their lean and flashy songs
Grate on their scrannel pipes of wretched straw,
The hungry sheep look up, and are not fed,                     125
But swoln with wind, and the rank mist they draw,
Rot inwardly, and foul contagion spread:
Besides what the grim Wolf with privy paw
Daily devours apace, and nothing said,
But that two-handed engine at the door,                        130
Stands ready to smite once, and smite no more.
    Return Alpheus, the dread voice is past,
That shrunk thy streams; return Sicilian Muse,

106 *sanguine . . . woe:* the purple hyacinth, whose markings (made by
the blood of young Hyacinth whom Apollo slew) were thought to spell
in Greek the words for *Woe! Woe!* 107 *pledge:* child.  109-12 *Pilot
. . . locks:* St. Peter the fisherman, keeper of the keys to heaven and
the apostolic founder and first bishop (*pastor*) of the Church, as symbolized by his *miter'd locks.*  114-27 *Anow . . . spread:* cf. comment
on the *corrupted Clergy* in subtitle.  122 *What . . , sped:* Why should
they worry, they are getting what they want.  124 *scrannel:* harsh.  128-
29 *Wolf . . . said:* Customarily said to refer to the "secret proselytiz-
ing" of the Roman Church; but also, perhaps, Satan himself, "a prowl-
ing Wolf, / Whom hunger drives to seek new haunt for prey," in
*Paradise Lost.*  130 *two-handed engine:* Instrument of Divine Justice
in a Christian sense (cf. l. 82 and note), particularly, the sword of the
Archangel Michael, which he wields "with huge two-handed sway"
(*Paradise Lost*, VI, 251).  132-33 *Return . . . Muse:* After another
"digression," Milton readdresses the pastoral Muse, again by reference
to the Sicilian Muse of Theocritus, and to the river Alpheus, who was
linked in love with Arethusa. See ll. 85-86.

And call the vales, and bid them hither cast
Their bells, and flowrets of a thousand hues.                    135
Ye valleys low where the mild whispers use,
Of shades and wanton winds, and gushing brooks,
On whose fresh lap the swart star sparely looks,
Throw hither all your quaint enamel'd eyes,
That on the green turf suck the honied show'rs,             140
And purple all the ground with vernal flow'rs.
Bring the rathe primrose that forsaken dies,
The tufted crow-toe, and pale jessamine,
The white pink, and the pansy freakt with jet,
The glowing violet,                                                         145
The musk-rose, and the well attir'd woodbine,
With cowslips wan that hang the pensive head,
And every flower that sad embroidery wears:
Bid Amaranthus all his beauty shed,
And daffadillies fill their cups with tears,                    150
To strew the laureate hearse where Lycid lies.
For so to interpose a little ease,
Let our frail thoughts dally with false surmise.
Ay me! Whilst thee the shores, and sounding seas
Wash far away, where ere thy bones are hurl'd,           155
Whether beyond the stormy Hebrides
Where thou perhaps under the whelming tide
Visit'st the bottom of the monstrous world;
Or whether thou to our moist vows denied,
Sleep'st by the fable of Bellerus old,                            160
Where the great vision of the guarded Mount
Looks toward Namancos and Bayona's hold;
Look homeward Angel now, and melt with ruth.
And, O ye dolphins, waft the hapless youth.

136 *use:* frequent. 138 *swart star:* the Dog Star, Sirius, whose malign influence blights the flowers (turns them black, *swart*). *sparely:* very seldom. 142 *rathe:* early. 144 *freakt:* striped. 149 *Amaranthus:* the "unfading flower." 151 *hearse:* bier. 156-62 *Hebrides, Bellerus, guarded Mount, Namancos, Bayona's hold:* Again (as in ll. 53-55), the geographical and historical allusions are connected with the place—its scope now enlarged—where Lycidas was drowned: the Hebrides (islands), west of northern Scotland, suggest a northern limit; Bellerus (Land's End), a southern. St. Michael's Mount, the tip of Land's End, according to *fable,* was *guarded* by the archangel, whose vigilant eye looked southward to Namancos and Bayona's (strong)hold in north-western Spain. 158 *monstrous:* filled with monsters. 163-64 *Look . . . ruth:* The lines addressed to the Archangel Michael (of the *guarded Mount*)—the same hitherto associated with the avenging sword of Justice (see note on l. 130)—significantly close the passage wherein the poet has *returned* to the gentle, pastoral vein. By imploring the Angel

Weep no more, woeful shepherds, weep no more,     165
For Lycidas your sorrow is not dead,
Sunk though he be beneath the wat'ry floor,
So sinks the day-star in the ocean bed,
And yet anon repairs his drooping head,
And tricks his beams, and with new-spangled ore,     170
Flames in the forehead of the morning sky:
So Lycidas sunk low, but mounted high,
Through the dear might of him that walk'd the waves
Where other groves, and other streams along,
With nectar pure his oozy locks he laves,     175
And hears the unexpressive nuptial song,
In the blest kingdoms meek of joy and love.
There entertain him all the Saints above,
In solemn troops, and sweet societies
That sing, and singing in their glory move,     180
And wipe the tears forever from his eyes.
Now Lycidas the shepherds weep no more;
Henceforth thou art the Genius of the shore,
In thy large recompense, and shalt be good
To all that wander in that perilous flood.     185

   Thus sang the uncouth swain to th' oaks and rills,
While the still morn went out with sandals gray,
He touch'd the tender stops of various quills,
With eager thought warbling his Doric lay:
And now the sun had stretch'd out all the hills,     190
And now was dropt into the western bay;
At last he rose, and twitch'd his mantle blue:
To-morrow to fresh woods, and pastures new.

---

to *melt with ruth,* Milton signifies that Mercy should and will succeed Justice.   168 *day-star:* the sun.   170 *tricks:* dresses.   *ore:* gold, radiance.   171 *Flames . . . sky:* cf. the resurrected Christ, "the bright and morning star." Cf. *him,* Christ, l. 173.   175 *his, he:* Lycidas.   176 *unexpressive:* inexpressible.   *nuptial song:* cf. "Let us be glad and rejoice, . . . for the marriage of the Lamb is come. . . . Blessed are they which are called unto the marriage supper of the Lamb."—Rev. 19:7.   181 *And . . . eyes:* cf. ", . . God shall wipe away all tears from their eyes."—Rev. 7:17; cf. Rev. 21:4; Isa. 25:8.   183 *Genius: Guardian* spirit.   186 *uncouth swain:* unknown, rustic poet, like the Virgil and Spenser of their pastoral verses. Cf. ll. 1-7 and note.   189 *Doric:* the dialect of the Greek pastoralists, Theocritus, Bion, Moschus; hence, "pastoral."   192 *twitch'd:* threw about him.

162

## On the Detraction Which Follow'd upon My Writing Certain Treatises

I did but prompt the age to quit their clogs
  By the known rules of ancient liberty,
  When straight a barbarous noise environs me
Of owls and cuckoos, asses, apes and dogs.
As when those hinds that were transform'd to frogs   5
  Rail'd at Latona's twin-born progeny
  Which after held the sun and moon in fee.
But this is got by casting pearl to hogs,
That bawl for freedom in their senseless mood,
  And still revolt when truth would set them free.   10
  Licence they mean when they cry liberty;
For who loves that, must first be wise and good:
  But from that mark how far they rove we see,
  For all this waste of wealth, and loss of blood.

                      [1646?]

## Fairfax, whose name in arms through Europe rings

Fairfax, whose name in arms through Europe rings
  Filling each mouth with envy, or with praise,
  And all her jealous monarchs with amaze,
  And rumors loud, that daunt remotest kings,

On the Detraction. *On the Detraction, etc.:* The title given to the
sonnet in the Cambridge Manuscript; probably written in reply to the
attacks upon one of his pamphlets favoring divorce. *Detraction:* Defamation. 1 *prompt:* urge. *quit . . . clogs:* throw off their restraints.
4 *owls, etc.:* reputed by old natural historians to typify aspects of bad
character 5-7 *those . . . fee:* Latona was the mother of twins by
Jupiter—Diana, destined goddess of the moon, and Apollo, god of the
sun. While carrying the children, she was forced by Juno, Jupiter's
jealous wife, to quit the country. Arriving at Lycia, tired and thirsty,
she knelt at a pool to quench her thirst, but peasants working nearby
*rail'd* at her and would not let her drink, nor would they listen to her
plea. At last aroused, she prayed to Jupiter, who answered by turning
the *hinds* into frogs. 7 *in fee:* in possession. 8 *this:* the detraction.
*casting . . . hogs:* see Matt. 7:6. 12 *that:* liberty.
Fairfax. *Fairfax, whose name, etc.:* Sometimes entitled: *On the Lord
General Fairfax at the Siege of Colchester.* (Sir Thomas) Fairfax
(1612-1671), for a time Commander-in-Chief of the Parliamentary
Forces during the English Civil Wars. Upon his refusal to launch an
aggressive campaign against the Scots without the provocation of their
invasion of England, his military career closed and Cromwell became
head of the Parliamentary Army. See Marvell, p. 180.

Thy firm unshak'n virtue ever brings                                5
   Victory home, though new rebellions raise
   Their Hydra heads, and the false North displays
   Her brok'n league, to imp their serpent wings,
O yet a nobler task awaits thy hand;
   For what can war, but endless war still breed,       10
   Till Truth and Right from Violence be freed,
And Public Faith clear'd from the shameful brand
   Of Public Fraud. In vain doth Valor bleed
   While Avarice and Rapine share the land.

                               [1648]

## *Cromwell, our chief of men, who through a cloud*

Cromwell, our chief of men, who through a cloud
   Not of war only, but detractions rude,
   Guided by faith and matchless fortitude
   To peace and truth thy glorious way hast plough'd,
And on the neck of crowned Fortune proud               5
   Hast rear'd God's trophies and his work pursu'd,
   While Darwen stream with blood of Scots imbru'd,
   And Dunbar field resounds thy praises loud,
And Worster's laureate wreath; yet much remains
   To conquer still; peace hath her victories            10
   No less renown'd than war, new foes arise
Threat'ning to bind our souls with secular chains:
   Help us to save free Conscience from the paw
   Of hireling wolves whose Gospel is their maw.

                               [1652]

5 *virtue:* valour.   7 *Hydra:* the many-headed monster that gen-
erated two new heads whenever one was cut off.   7-8 *false . . .
league:* Scotland, although having entered the Solemn League and
Covenant with the English Parliament (1645), sent help to Charles the
First's armies in 1648. See Marvell, p. 183, l. 106.   8 *imp . . . wings:*
graft new feathers upon the damaged wings of rebellion; so that an
uprising is no sooner put down than it flares up again. Cf. l. 10.

CROMWELL. *Cromwell . . . men:* By May, 1652, the date of this sonnet, Cromwell was at a height. The year following he expelled the Long
Parliament and declared himself Lord Protector.

5 *on the neck, etc.:* cf. Josh. 10:24.   6 *rear'd:* set up.   7, 8, 9 *Darwen
stream, Dunbar, Worster* [Worcester]: Battles in which Cromwell de-
feated the Scots.   9 *laureate wreath;* Cromwell is said to have called
the victory at Worster a "crowning mercy." 11-14 *new . . . maw:* In
the spring of 1652 a Parliamentary committee proposed the establish-
ment of a state-supported Presbyterian Church. Milton feared a state-
supported church would bind *our souls with secular chains,* and put *free
Conscience* into the charge of a clergy become *hirelings* of the state.
14 *maw:* belly.

## When I consider how my light is spent

When I consider how my light is spent,
  Ere half my days, in this dark world and wide,
  And that one talent which is death to hide,
  Lodg'd with me useless, though my soul more bent
To serve therewith my Maker, and present     5
  My true account, lest he returning chide;
  Doth God exact day labor, light denied,
  I fondly ask; But Patience to prevent
That murmur, soon replies, God doth not need
  Either man's work or his own gifts, who best     10
  Bear his mild yoke, they serve him best; his state
Is kingly. Thousands at his bidding speed
  And post o'er land and ocean without rest:
  They also serve who only stand and wait.

                     [1652?]

## On the Late Massacre in Piemont

Avenge O Lord thy slaughter'd Saints, whose bones
  Lie scatter'd on the Alpine mountains cold,
  Ev'n them who kept thy truth so pure of old
  When all our fathers worship't stocks and stones,
Forget not: in thy book record their groans     5
  Who were thy sheep and in their ancient fold
  Slain by the bloody Piemontese that roll'd
  Mother with infant down the rocks. Their moans
The vales redoubl'd to the hills, and they
  To Heav'n. Their martyr'd blood and ashes sow     10
  O'er all th' Italian fields where still doth sway
The triple Tyrant: that from these may grow
  A hunderd-fold, who having learnt thy way
  Early may fly the Babylonian woe.

                     *[1655]

WHEN I CONSIDER (*On His Blindness*). *2 Ere . . . days:* Milton was 42 when he became totally blind, soon after the publication of *The Defence of the English People,* March, 1651. *3 one talent:* see Matt. 25: 24-30. *8 fondly:* foolishly. *12 Thousands:* the heavenly angels—and perhaps human beings. *14 They also:* Angels other than the *Thousands.*

ON THE LATE MASSACRE. *1 slaughter'd Saints:* the Waldenses, a pre-Reformation Protestant sect (twelfth century) living in northwestern Italy, in the realm of the Duke of Savoy, under whose authority the massacre was carried out, April 24, 1655—"Piedmontese Easter." Protestant indignation ran high. In England, Cromwell made an official protest to the Duke of Savoy (written by Milton as Secretary for Foreign Tongues). *12 triple Tyrant:* the Pope. *14 Babylonian woe:* probably an allusion to Petrarch's comparison of the Papal Court to Babylon (*In vita,* CVII [Bohn tr.]).

## Lawrence, of virtuous father virtuous son

Lawrence, of virtuous father virtuous son,
  Now that the fields are dank, and ways are mire,
  Where shall we sometimes meet, and by the fire
  Help waste a sullen day; what may be won
From the hard season gaining: time will run          5
  On smoother, till Favonius re-inspire
  The frozen earth; and clothe in fresh attire
  The lily and the rose, that neither sow'd nor spun.
What neat repast shall feast us, light and choice,
  Of Attic taste, with wine, whence we may rise       10
  To hear the lute well toucht, or artful voice
Warble immortal notes and Tuscan air?
  He who of those delights can judge, and spare
  To interpose them oft, is not unwise.

[1655]


## Methought I saw my late espoused Saint

Methought I saw my late espoused Saint
  Brought to me like Alcestis from the grave,
  Whom Jove's great Son to her glad husband gave,
  Rescu'd from death by force though pale and faint.
Mine as whom wash'd from spot of child-bed taint,    5
  Purification in the old Law did save,
  And such, as yet once more I trust to have
  Full sight of her in Heaven without restraint,
Came vested all in white, pure as her mind:

LAWRENCE. 1 *Lawrence . . . son:* The father was Henry Lawrence, the "President of Oliver's [Cromwell's] Council, and Commonwealth statesman." According to Edward Phillips, Milton's biographer, young Lawrence (Edward) was among the intimates who visited Milton's home. He died at twenty-four. 6 *Favonius* [Zephyrus]: cf. Chaucer, p. 3, ll. 5-6. 8 *The lily . . . spun:* cf. Matt. 6:28. 10, 12 *Attic, Tuscan:* Greek, Italian (Florentine); cf. Jonson, p. 98, ll. 21-22.
  METHOUGHT I SAW. 1 *Saint:* Katherine Woodcock, Milton's second wife, who died in childbirth (1658), fifteen months after their marriage. 2 *Alcestis:* the wife of Admetus. She offered herself in place of her husband, who, about to die, was told by Apollo that he might live if a substitute for him could be found. In Euripides' version of the story (*Alcestis*), Alcestis was rescued by Hercules (*Jove's great Son*) and brought back to the upper world. 5-6 *Mine . . . save:* In his vision, Milton sees his wife as saved or purified according to the old Levitical law regarding the ritualistic cleansing of women after childbirth (see Lev. 12).

Her face was veil'd, yet to my fancied sight, 10
Love, sweetness, goodness, in her person shin'd
So clear, as in no face with more delight.
But O as to embrace me she inclin'd
I wak'd, she fled, and day brought back my night.

[1658]

*from* PARADISE LOST

[*The Superior Fiend*]

He scarce had ceas't when the superior Fiend
Was moving toward the shore; his ponderous shield
Etherial temper, massy, large and round,
Behind him cast; the broad circumference
Hung on his shoulders like the moon, whose orb 5
Through optic glass the Tuscan artist views
At ev'ning from the top of Fesole,
Or in Valdarno, to descry new lands,
Rivers or mountains in her spotty globe.
His spear, to equal which the tallest pine 10
Hewn on Norwegian hills, to be the mast
Of some great ammiral, were but a wand,
He walkt with to support uneasy steps
Over the burning marl, not like those steps
On Heaven's azure, and the torrid clime 15
Smote on him sore besides, vaulted with fire;
Nathless he so endur'd, till on the beach
Of that inflamed sea, he stood and call'd
His legions, angel forms, who lay intrans't
Thick as autumnal leaves that strow the brooks 20
In Vallombrosa, where th' Etrurian shades
High overarch't imbow'r; or scatter'd sedge

10 *veil'd:* as was Alcestis' face.  14 *night:* blindness.
THE SUPERIOR FIEND. 1 *He:* Beelzebub, among the Fallen Angels,
Satan's chief lieutenant.  2 *shore:* that is, of the burning lake in Hell.
3 *Etherial:* heavenly.  *temper:* substance.  6-9 *Through . . . globe:*
Reference to Galileo's observations with his telescope of the irregularities of the moon's surface.  6 *Tuscan[y]:* Region in west-central Italy.
7 *F[i]esole:* small town near Florence (in Tuscany). Florence is in the
valley of the Arno (*Valdarno*, 1. 8).  8 *descry:* discover.  12 *ammiral:*
flag ship.  14 *marl:* soil.  17 *Nathless:* Nevertheless.  19 *intrans't:* en-
tranced (as a result of their fall from Heaven).  21 *Vallombrosa:*
"Valley of Shadows."  *Etrurian:* Tuscan.  22-29 *scatter'd . . . wheels:*
On the miraculous crossing of the Red Sea by the Israelites (*Sojourners of Goshen*) in their flight from Egypt, and the destruction of their
pursuers (*Busiris and his Memphian Chivalry*), see Exod. 14:21-30.

Afloat, when with fierce winds Orion arm'd
Hath vext the Red-Sea Coast, whose waves o'erthrew
Busiris and his Memphian Chivalry,                        25
While with perfidious hatred they pursu'd
The Sojourners of Goshen, who beheld
From the safe shore their floating carcasses
And broken chariot wheels, so thick bestrown
Abject and lost lay these, covering the flood,           30
Under amazement of their hideous change.
He call'd so loud, that all the hollow deep
Of Hell resounded. Princes, Potentates,
Warriors, the Flow'r of Heav'n, once yours, now lost,
If such astonishment as this can seize                   35
Eternal spirits; or have ye chos'n this place
After the toil of battle to repose
Your wearied virtue, for the ease you find
To slumber here, as in the vales of Heav'n?
Or in this abject posture have ye sworn                  40
To adore the Conqueror? who now beholds
Cherub and Seraph rolling in the flood
With scatter'd arms and ensigns, till anon
His swift pursuers from Heav'n Gates discern
Th' advantage, and descending tread us down             45
Thus drooping, or with linked thunderbolts
Transfix us to the bottom of this gulf.
Awake, arise, or be for ever fall'n.

                                        [Book I, ll. 283-330]


[*The Creation of the World*]

                    . . . Meanwhile the Son
On his great expedition now appear'd,
Girt with Omnipotence, with Radiance crown'd
Of Majesty Divine, Sapience and Love
Immense, and all his Father in him shone.                5
About his chariot numberless were pour'd

23 *Orion:* the constellation, at whose rising and setting storms were
said often to occur.    25 *Chivalry:* Cavalry.    30 *Abject:* Cast down
(from Heaven).    31 *change:* from what they had been in Heaven.    35
*astonishment:* literally, having been "thundered out" (of Heaven), as,
in fact, they were, by God's thunder.    38 *virtue:* strength.    42 *Cherub,
Seraph:* see p. 151, l. 54 and note.

    THE CREATION. 1 *the Son:* The Son of God, the divinely active, crea-
tive agent.

Cherub and Seraph, Potentates and Thrones,
And Virtues, winged Spirits, and chariots wing'd,
From the armory of God, where stand of old
Myriads between two brazen mountains lodg'd          10
Against a solemn day, harnest at hand,
Celestial equipage; and now came forth
Spontaneous, for within them Spirit liv'd,
Attendant on their Lord: Heav'n op'nd wide
Her ever during gates, harmonious sound              15
On golden hinges moving, to let forth
The King of Glory in his powerful Word
And Spirit coming to create new worlds.
On heav'nly ground they stood, and from the shore
They view'd the vast immeasurable abyss              20
Outrageous as a sea, dark, wasteful, wild,
Up from the bottom turn'd by furious winds
And surging waves, as mountains to assault
Heav'ns highth, and with the center mix the pole.
    Silence, ye troubl'd waves, and thou deep, peace,   25
Said then th' Omnific Word, your discord end:
    Nor stay'd, but on the wings of Cherubim
Uplifted, in Paternal Glory rode
Far into Chaos, and the world unborn;
For Chaos heard his voice: him all his train         30
Follow'd in bright procession to behold
Creation, and the wonders of his might.
Then stay'd the fervid wheels, and in his hand
He took the golden compasses, prepar'd
In God's eternal store, to circumscribe              35
This universe, and all created things:
One foot he center'd, and the other turn'd
Round through the vast profundity obscure,
And said, thus far extend, thus far thy bounds,
This be thy just circumference, O World.             40
Thus God the Heav'n created, thus the Earth,
Matter unform'd and void: Darkness profound
Cover'd the abyss: but on the wat'ry calm
His brooding wings the Spirit of God outspread,
And vital virtue infus'd, and vital warmth           45

7-8 *Cherub . . . Spirits:* angelic and spiritual orders. See p. 167, l.
42 and note. 20 *abyss:* creation, as the account proceeds to show, is
the imposition by the Divine Spirit of order and form upon Chaos, which
is elementary matter already existent, but in confusion and discord. 26
*Omnific:* All-creating. 38 *obscure:* dark; literally, destitute of light.
See l. 21.

Throughout the fluid mass, but downward purg'd
The black tartareous cold infernal dregs
Adverse to life: then founded, then conglob'd
Like things to like, the rest to several place
Disparted, and between spun out the air,                    50
And earth self-balanc't on her center hung.

[Book VII, ll. 192-242]

## [Adam, First Man of Men]

For man to tell how human life began
Is hard; for who himself beginning knew?
Desire with thee still longer to converse
Induc'd me. As new wak't from soundest sleep
Soft on the flow'ry herb I found me laid              5
In balmy sweat, which with his beams the sun
Soon dri'd, and on the reeking moisture fed.
Straight toward Heav'n my wond'ring eyes I turn'd,
And gaz'd a while the ample sky, till rais'd
By quick instinctive motion up I sprung,              10
As thitherward endeavoring, and upright
Stood on my feet; about me round I saw
Hill, dale, and shady woods, and sunny plains,
And liquid lapse of murmuring streams; by these,
Creatures that liv'd, and mov'd, and walk'd, or flew,   15
Birds on the branches warbling; all things smil'd,
With fragrance and with joy my heart o'erflow'd.
Myself I then perus'd, and limb by limb
Survey'd, and sometimes went, and sometimes ran
With supple joints, as lively vigor led:              20
But who I was, or where, or from what cause,
Knew not; to speak I tri'd, and forthwith spake,
My tongue obey'd and readily could name
Whate'er I saw. Thou sun, said I, fair light,
And thou enlight'n'd earth, so fresh and gay,         25

46 *purg'd:* expelled.   47 *tartareous:* infernal, hellish; from Tartarus
(infernal regions).   48 *conglob'd:* collected into the form of a globe.   50
*Disparted:* Separated.

ADAM. 3 *thee:* the Archangel Raphael, the hospitable angel, sent by
God to Eden to warn Adam and Eve of Satan's evil intentions towards
them. Having listened to Raphael's account of the War in Heaven, the
Creation, etc., Adam now wishes to tell "his story."   11 *thitherward:*
heavenward.   14 *lapse:* falling.

Ye hills and dales, ye rivers, woods, and plains,
And ye that live and move, fair creatures, tell,
Tell, if ye saw, how came I thus, how here?
Not of myself; by some great Maker then,
In goodness and in power preeminent;                    30
Tell me, how may I know him, how adore,
From whom I have that thus I move and live,
And feel that I am happier than I know.
While thus I call'd, and stray'd I knew not whither,
From where I first drew air, and first beheld           35
This happy light, when answer none return'd,
On a green shady bank profuse of flow'rs
Pensive I sat me down; there gentle sleep
First found me, and with soft oppression seiz'd
My drowsed sense, untroubl'd, though I thought          40
I then was passing to my former state
Insensible, and forthwith to dissolve:
When suddenly stood at my head a dream,
Whose inward apparition gently mov'd
My fancy to believe I yet had being,                    45
And liv'd: One came, methought, of shape divine,
And said, Thy mansion wants thee, Adam, rise,
First Man, of men innumerable ordain'd
First Father, call'd by thee I come thy Guide
To the Garden of bliss, thy seat prepar'd.              50

[Book VIII, ll. 250-99]


## [O Earth, how like to Heav'n]

### [SATAN'S SOLILOQUY]

O Earth, how like to Heav'n, if not preferr'd
More justly, seat worthier of gods, as built
With second thoughts, reforming what was old!
For what God after better worse would build?

47 *mansion:* dwelling place, that is, the Garden of Eden. *wants:* lacks.

O EARTH. On his first attempt to *seduce* Adam and Eve, Satan was detected by the angelic guard placed over Eden and driven away. He returns unseen, "involv'd in rising mist," still "Bent on man's destruction." Resolved to enter into the Serpent—"Fit vessel, fittest imp of fraud"—in order to carry out his deception, he "first from inward grief / His bursting passion into plaints thus pour'd."

3 *what was old:* namely, Heaven, the scene of Satan's rebellion, in his judgment, an imperfect place.

Terrestrial Heav'n, danc't round by other Heav'ns      5
That shine, yet bear their bright officious lamps,
Light above light, for thee alone, as seems,
In thee concentring all their precious beams
Of sacred influence: As God in Heav'n
Is Center, yet extends to all, so thou      10
Centring receiv'st from all those orbs; in thee,
Not in themselves, all their known virtue appears
Productive in herb, plant, and nobler birth
Of creatures animate with gradual life
Of Growth, Sense, Reason, all summ'd up in Man.      15
With what delight could I have walkt thee round,
If I could joy in aught, sweet interchange
Of hill, and valley, rivers, woods and plains,
Now land, now sea, and shores with forest crown'd,
Rocks, dens, and caves; but I in none of these      20
Find place or refuge; and the more I see
Pleasures about me, so much more I feel
Torment within me, as from the hateful siege
Of contraries; all good to me becomes
Bane, and in Heav'n much worse would be my state.      25
But neither here seek I, no nor in Heav'n
To dwell, unless by mast'ring Heav'n's Supreme;
Nor hope to be myself less miserable
By what I seek, but others to make such
As I, though thereby worse to me redound:      30
For only in destroying I find ease
To my relentless thoughts; and him destroy'd,
Or won to what may work his utter loss,
For whom all this was made, all this will soon
Follow, as to him linkt in weal or woe,      35
In woe then; that destruction wide may range:

5 *danc't . . . Heav'ns:* the celestial planetary spheres, whose harmonious, ordered motions were frequently likened to the movements of the
dance.  6 *officious lamps:* serving as lamps.  7 *thee alone:* the earth.
14-15 *Of . . . Man:* Satan draws upon two Renaissance ideas: man as
microcosm, and the "great chain of being." In the microcosm idea, man
is a little world, "summing up" the whole of his external world. God
the Creator is outside. (See Herbert, p. 139, l. 7 and note; Marvell,
p. 179, ll. 43-48.) According to the "chain of being," creation rises
through a hierarchy of forms from lowest to highest, God the Creator,
who is pure being. Satan, as God's enemy, will not acknowledge God as
the divine perfection, preferring rather to view man the microcosm as
the final stage of being, exhibiting, moreover, a perfection beyond anything heaven could show—and *what God after better worse would build?*
23 *siege:* seat, abode.  25 *Bane:* Evil.  27 *Heav'n's Supreme:* God.

To me shall be the glory sole among
The infernal Powers, in one day to have marr'd
What he *Almighty* styl'd, six nights and days
Continu'd making, and who knows how long               40
Before had been contriving, though perhaps
Not longer than since I in one night freed
From servitude inglorious well-nigh half
Th' Angelic Name, and thinner left the throng
Of his adorers: he to be aveng'd,                      45
And to repair his numbers thus impair'd,
Whether such virtue spent of old now fail'd
More Angels to create, if they at least
Are his created, or to spite us more,
Determin'd to advance into our room                    50
A creature form'd of earth, and him endow,
Exalted from so base original,
With heav'nly spoils, our spoils: what he decreed
He effected; Man he made, and for him built
Magnificent this World, and Earth his seat,            55
Him Lord pronounc'd, and, O indignity!
Subjected to his service angel wings,
And flaming ministers to watch and tend
Their earthy charge: Of these the vigilance
I dread, and to elude, thus wrapt in mist              60
Of midnight vapor glide obscure, and pry
In every bush and brake, where hap may find
The Serpent sleeping, in whose mazy folds
To hide me, and the dark intent I bring.
O foul descent! that I who erst contended              65
With gods to sit the highest, am now constrain'd
Into a beast, and mixt with bestial slime,
This essence to incarnate and imbrute,
That to the highth of Deity aspir'd;
But what will not Ambition and Revenge                 70
Descend to? who aspires must down as low
As high he soar'd, obnoxious first or last
To basest things. Revenge, at first though sweet,

42 *one night:* when Satan plotted his rebellion against God (Book V).
42-45 *freed . . . adorers:* falsehood and exaggeration. 44 *Name:* Race,
stock. 52 *base original:* base origin: "dust of the ground" (Gen. 2:7).
53 *spoils:* literally, the arms stripped from the vanquished angels; their
angelic endowment. 57-59 *Subjected . . . charge:* cf. p. 169, l. 3 and
note; p. 164, ll. 12-13. 68 *This essence:* Angelic essence. *incarnate:*
become flesh. 72 *obnoxious:* subject to harm by (*basest things,* l. 73).

Bitter ere long back on itself recoils;
Let it; I reck not, so it light well aim'd,                    75
Since higher I fall short, on him who next
Provokes my envy, this new favorite
Of Heav'n, this Man of Clay, Son of despite,
Whom us the more to spite his Maker rais'd
From dust: spite then with spite is best repaid.              80

[Book IX, ll. 99-178]


## [*The Sum of Wisdom*]

Greatly instructed I shall hence depart,
Greatly in peace of thought, and have my fill
Of knowledge, what this vessel can contain;
Beyond which was my folly to aspire.
Henceforth I learn, that to obey is best,                     5
And love with fear the only God, to walk
As in his presence, ever to observe
His providence, and on him sole depend,
Merciful over all his works, with good
Still overcoming evil, and by small                           10
Accomplishing great things, by things deem'd weak
Subverting worldly strong, and worldly wise
By simply meek; that suffering for Truth's sake
Is fortitude to highest victory,
And to the faithful Death the Gate of Life;                   15
Taught this by his example whom I now
Acknowledge my Redeemer ever blest.
   To whom thus also th' Angel last repli'd:
This having learnt, thou hast attain'd the sum
Of wisdom; hope no higher, though all the stars              20
Thou knew'st by name, and all th' ethereal Powers,
All secrets of the deep, all Nature's works,
Or works of God in heav'n, air, earth, or sea,

75 *reck not:* care not.  78 *despite:* the spite towards him which Satan
ascribes to God.
   THE SUM. 1 *instructed . . . depart:* fallen Adam will depart from
Eden instructed by the Archangel Michael in the course of human history, which has shown him how God will bring Good out of Evil (ll.
9-11) by sending the promised Redeemer in the *fulness of time, born of*
Woman, to crush the Serpent.  3 *vessel:* the human mind.  4 *Beyond
. . . aspire:* As signified by his eating of the fruit of the Tree of the
Knowledge of Good and Evil.  18 *Angel:* Michael.

And all the riches of this world enjoy'dst,
And all the rule, one empire; only add          25
Deeds to thy knowledge answerable, add Faith,
Add Virtue, Patience, Temperance, add Love,
By name to come call'd Charity, the soul
Of all the rest: then wilt thou not be loath
To leave this Paradise, but shalt possess          30
A Paradise within thee, happier far.

[Book XII, ll. 557-87]

# ANDREW MARVELL  1621–1678

## To His Coy Mistress

Had we but world enough, and time,
This coyness lady were no crime.
We would sit down, and think which way
To walk, and pass our long love's day.
Thou by the Indian Ganges' side          5
Should'st rubies find: I by the tide
Of Humber would complain. I would
Love you ten years before the Flood:
And you should if you please refuse
Till the conversion of the Jews.          10
My vegetable love should grow
Vaster than empires, and more slow.
An hundred years should go to praise
Thine eyes, and on thy forehead gaze.
Two hundred to adore each breast:          15
But thirty thousand to the rest.
An age at least to every part,
And the last age should show your heart.
For lady you deserve this state;
Nor would I love at lower rate.          20
  But at my back I always hear
Time's winged chariot hurrying near:
And yonder all before us lie
Deserts of vast eternity.
Thy beauty shall no more be found;          25
Nor, in thy marble vault, shall sound
My echoing song: then worms shall try
That long preserv'd virginity:
And your quaint honor turn to dust;
And into ashes all my lust.          30
The grave's a fine and private place,
But none I think do there embrace.

To His Coy Mistress. 7 *Humber:* River flowing between Lincoln-
shire and Marvell's native Yorkshire. *complain:* sing sadly of love.
11 *vegetable love:* i.e., with proclivity for growth. Cf. "souls" of
growth, sense, intellect, in old psychology. 29 *quaint:* fastidious.

Now therefore, while the youthful hue
Sits on thy skin like morning lew,
And while thy willing soul transpires          35
At every pore with instant fires,
Now let us sport us while we may;
And now, like am'rous birds of prey,
Rather at once our time devour,
Than languish in his slow-chapt pow'r.          40
Let us roll all our strength, and all
Our sweetness, up into one ball:
And tear our pleasures with rough strife,
Thorough the iron gates of life.
Thus, though we cannot make our sun          45
Stand still, yet we will make him run.


## The Definition of Love

### I

My love is of a birth as rare
As 'tis for object strange and high:
It was begotten by despair
Upon impossibility.


### II

Magnanimous Despair alone          5
Could show me so divine a thing,
Where feeble Hope could ne'er have flown
But vainly flapt its tinsel wing.


### III

And yet I quickly might arrive
Where my extended soul is fixt,          10
But Fate does iron wedges drive,
And always crowds itself betwixt.

---

34 *lew:* warmth, according to H. M. Margoliouth, ed. *The Poems and Letters of Andrew Marvell,* Oxford, 1927.  35 *transpires:* breathes out.
40 *slow-chapt:* slowly devouring.  44 *Thorough:* Through.
    THE DEFINITION OF LOVE. 10 *extended:* outstretched, to join the soul of his beloved. Cf. Donne, p. 113, ll. 21-23.  12 *betwixt:* between him and his lady.

### IV

For Fate with jealous eye does see
Two perfect loves; nor lets them close:
Their union would her ruin be,                          15
And her tyrannic pow'r depose.


### V

And therefore her decrees of steel
Us as the distant poles have plac'd,
(Though Love's whole world on us doth wheel)
Not by themselves to be embrac'd.                       20


### VI

Unless the giddy heaven fall,
And earth some new convulsion tear;
And, us to join, the world should all
Be cramp'd into a planisphere.


### VII

As lines so loves *oblique* may well                    25
Themselves in every angle greet:
But ours so truly *parallel*,
Though infinite can never meet.


### VIII

Therefore the love which us doth bind,
But Fate so enviously debars,                           30
Is the conjunction of the mind,
And opposition of the stars.


17 *decrees of steel:* cf. *iron wedges,* l. 11.   19 *Love's . . . wheel:* We
are the axis on which Love's world turns.   20 *Not . . . embrac'd:* The
poles, at opposite ends of the same axis, cannot touch one another,   24
*planisphere:* the representation of the sphere on a plane.   31-32 *conjunction . . . stars:* the lovers' minds are in accord, but Fate keeps
them poles apart, i.e., as far apart as planets in *opposition* (whose
longitude differs by 180 degrees).

# The Garden

### I

How vainly men themselves amaze
To win the palm, the oak, or bays;
And their uncessant labors see
Crown'd from some single herb or tree,
Whose short and narrow verged shade          5
Does prudently their toils upbraid;
While all flow'rs and all trees do close
To weave the garlands of repose.

### II

Fair quiet, have I found thee here,
And Innocence thy sister dear!          10
Mistaken long, I sought you then
In busy companies of men.
Your sacred plants, if here below,
Only among the plants will grow.
Society is all but rude,          15
To this delicious solitude.

### III

No white nor red was ever seen
So am'rous as this lovely green.
Fond lovers, cruel as their flame,
Cut in these trees their mistress' name.          20
Little, alas, they know, or heed,
How far these beauties hers exceed!
Fair trees! wheres'e'er your barks I wound,
No name shall but your own be found.

### IV

When we have run our passions' heat,          25
Love hither makes his best retreat.
The gods, that mortal beauty chase,
Still in a tree did end their race.

THE GARDEN. 1 *amaze:* perplex. 2 *palm . . . bays:* symbols of earthly reward. 3 *uncessant:* unceasing. 4-8 *Crown'd . . . repose:* The branches, etc., cut to crown the success of worldly striving soon wither to become symbols of its vanity; meanwhile, all nature offers true peace of mind. 15 *rude:* barbarous. 18 *am'rous:* lovable. 27-32 *The . . . reed:* The fable of the futile pursuit of Daphne and of Syrinx by their lovers is well summarized. See Ovid, *Metamorphoses,* I.

Apollo hunted Daphne so,
Only that she might laurel grow.                    30
And Pan did after Syrinx speed,
Not as a nymph, but for a reed.


v

What wond'rous life in this I lead!
Ripe apples drop about my head;
The luscious clusters of the vine                   35
Upon my mouth do crush their wine;
The nectarine, and curious peach,
Into my hands themselves do reach;
Stumbling on melons, as I pass,
Insnar'd with flow'rs, I fall on grass.             40


VI

Meanwhile the mind, from pleasure less,
Withdraws into its happiness:
The mind, that ocean where each kind
Does straight its own resemblance find;
Yet it creates, transcending these,                 45
Far other worlds, and other seas;
Annihilating all that's made
To a green thought in a green shade.


VII

Here at the fountain's sliding foot,
Or at some fruit-tree's mossy root,                 50
Casting the body's vest aside,
My soul into the boughs does glide:
There like a bird it sits, and sings,
Then whets, and combs its silver wings;
And, till prepar'd for longer flight,               55
Waves in its plumes the various light.

41 *pleasure less:* the inferior pleasure of society (II) ; and, also, of the
body (V).  42 *its happiness:* contemplation.  43-44 *The . . . find:* The
mind is a microcosm. Cf. Milton, p. 171, ll. 14-15 and note ; Herbert,
p. 130, l. 7.  47-48 *Annihilating . . . shade:* In creating (*other worlds,*
etc.), the mind transcends Nature (*all that's made*), leaving it as nothing
but a thought, possessing, however, the quality (*green*) originally ex-
hibited by Nature in its choicest state (*green shade*). Cf. p. 479, ll. 25,
27 and notes ; p. 482, ll. 9, 11-12 and notes.  51 *body's vest:* the flesh.
54 *whets:* preens.  56 *various:* as filtered through the trees.

### VIII

Such was that happy garden-state,
While man there walk'd without a mate:
After a place so pure, and sweet,
What other help could yet be meet!          60
But 'twas beyond a mortal's share
To wander solitary there:
Two paradises 'twere in one
To live in Paradise alone.

### IX

How well the skilful gardner drew          65
Of flow'rs and herbs this dial new;
Where from above the milder sun
Does through a fragrant zodiac run;
And, as it works, th' industrious bee
Computes its time as well as we.          70
How could such sweet and wholesome hours
Be reckon'd but with herbs and flow'rs!


## An Horatian Ode upon Cromwell's Return from Ireland

The forward Youth that would appear
Must now forsake his Muses dear,
    Nor in the shadows sing
    His numbers languishing.
'Tis time to leave the books in dust,          5
And oil th' unused armor's rust:
    Removing from the wall
    The corslet of the hall.
So restless Cromwell could not cease
In the inglorious arts of peace,          10
    But through adventrous war

57 *happy . . . state:* Eden. 58 *without a mate:* that is, before Eve
was created. 60 *help . . . meet:* help suitable, a pun on *helpmeet,* as
Eve was called (Gen. 2:18, 20). 66, 68 *dial, zodiac:* flowers and herbs
planted to resemble a sun dial with the signs of the zodiac.

AN HORATIAN ODE. *Cromwell's . . . Ireland:* At the end of May,
1650, to direct the Scottish campaign. See ll. 105-12. Cf. "Fairfax,
whose name," p. 162, and "Cromwell, our chief of men," p. 163.

2-4 *now forsake . . . languishing:* because a public occasion requires
the poet's service. 8 *corslet:* body armor.

Urged his active star.
And, like the three-fork'd lightning, first
Breaking the clouds where it was nurst,
   Did thorough his own side                    15
   His fiery way divide.
For 'tis all one to courage high
The emulous or enemy;
   And with such, to inclose
   Is more than to oppose.                        20
Then burning through the air he went,
And palaces and temples rent:
   And Caesar's head at last
   Did through his laurels blast.
'Tis madness to resist or blame                     25
The force of angry Heaven's flame:
   And, if we would speak true,
   Much to the Man is due.
Who, from his private gardens, where
He liv'd reserved and austere,                      30
   As if his highest plot
   To plant the bergamot,
Could by industrious valor climb
To ruin the great work of Time,
   And cast the kingdom old                    35
   Into another mold.
Though Justice against Fate complain,
And plead the ancient rights in vain:
   But those do hold or break
   As men are strong or weak.                 40
Nature that hateth emptiness,
Allows of penetration less:
   And therefore must make room
   Where greater spirits come.
What field of all the Civil Wars,                   45
Where his were not the deepest scars?
   And Hampton shows what part
   He had of wiser art.

12 *Urged . . . star:* Encouraged his own destiny.  15 *side:* party: with
reference to Cromwell's emergence as the leader of the Parliamentary
forces.  18 *emulous:* rival.  19 *inclose:* restrain.  23 *Caesar('s):*
Charles I, whom Cromwell dethroned.  30 *bergamot:* pear tree.  41
*hateth emptiness:* abhors a vacuum.  42 *Allows . . . less:* much less,
permits two bodies to occupy the same space simultaneously.  47 *Hampton:* Hampton Court, from which Charles I fled, 11 November 1647,
to Carisbrooke Castle (l. 52).  48, 50 *He:* Cromwell.

Where, twining subtle fears with hope,
He wove a net of such a scope,                                    50
   That Charles himself might chase
   To Carisbrook's narrow case.
That thence the Royal Actor born
The tragic scaffold might adorn:
   While round the armed bands                       55
   Did clap their bloody hands.
*He* nothing common did or mean
Upon that memorable scene:
   But with his keener eye
   The axe's edge did try:                             60
Nor call'd the gods with vulgar spite
To vindicate his helpless right,
   But bow'd his comely head,
   Down as upon a bed.
This was that memorable hour                                      65
Which first assur'd the forced pow'r.
   So when they did design
   The Capitol's first line,
A bleeding head where they begun,
Did fright the architects to run;                                70
   And yet in that the State
   Foresaw its happy fate.
And now the Irish are asham'd
To see themselves in one year tam'd:
   So much one Man can do,                             75
   That does both act and know.
They can affirm his praises best,
And have, though overcome, confest
   How good he is, how just,
   And fit for highest trust:                          80
Nor yet grown stiffer with command,
But still in the Republic's hand:
   How fit he is to sway
   That can so well obey.
He to the Commons' feet presents                                 85
A kingdom, for his first year's rents:

52 *case:* plight.  54 *tragic scaffold:* Charles was executed, January 30, 1649.  57 *He:* Charles I.  66 *forced:* gained.  68 *Capitol's:* Rome's. *line:* plan.  69 *bleeding . . . begun:* found when they were laying the foundation of the Temple of Jupiter.  74 *one year:* Cromwell had landed at Dublin, August 15, 1649, less than a year before his return. 82 *in . . . hand:* acting under Commonwealth authority; Cromwell had not yet become Lord Protector.  85 *Commons':* common (1681 edn.).

And, what he may, forbears
His fame to make it theirs:
And has his sword and spoils ungirt,
To lay them at the Public's skirt.                    90
So when the falcon high
Falls heavy from the sky,
She, having kill'd, no more does search,
But on the next green bough to perch;
Where, when he first does lure,                       95
The falconer has her sure.
What may not then our Isle presume
While victory his crest does plume!
What may not others fear
If thus he crown each year!                            100
A Caesar he ere long to Gaul,
To Italy an Hannibal,
And to all States not free
Shall climacteric be.
The Pict no shelter now shall find                    105
Within his party-color'd mind;
But from this valor sad
Shrink underneath the plad:
Happy if in the tufted brake
The English Hunter him mistake;                       110
Nor lay his hounds in near
The Caledonian Deer.
But thou the Wars' and Fortune's Son
March indefatigably on;
And for the last effect                               115
Still keep thy sword erect:
Besides the force it has to fright
The spirits of the shady night,
The same arts that did gain
A Pow'r must it maintain.                             120

90 *skirt*: cf. *to the Commons' feet*, l. 85.  104 *climacteric*: the marker of an epoch.  105 *The Pict*: The Scot(s), who were divided between loyalty to the Crown and zeal for their own national and religious interests; hence, *his party-color'd mind*, l. 106.  107 *sad*: steadfast.  108 *plad*: plaid, often of checkered pattern.  110 *English . . . mistake*: (If) Cromwell fail to identify him because of this protective coloring. Cf. *party-color'd, plad*.  111 *hounds*: troops.  112 *Caledonian Deer*: Scots.  117 *it*: the raised sword-hilt as the sign of the cross, which will fright the spirits of the shady night.

# HENRY VAUGHAN 1621–1693

*from* SILEX SCINTILLANS

## The Retreat

Happy those early days! when I
Shin'd in my Angel-infancy.
Before I understood this place
Appointed for my second race,
Or taught my soul to fancy ought           5
But a white, celestial thought,
When yet I had not walkt above
A mile, or two, from my first love,
And looking back (at that short space),
Could see a glimpse of his bright-face;     10
When on some gilded cloud, or flow'r
My gazing soul would dwell an hour,
And in those weaker glories spy
Some shadows of eternity;
Before I taught my tongue to wound          15
My conscience with a sinful sound,
Or had the black art to dispense
A sev'ral sin to ev'ry sense,
But felt through all this fleshly dress
Bright shoots of everlastingness.           20

O how I long to travel back
And tread again that ancient track!
That I might once more reach that plain,
Where first I left my glorious train,
From whence th' enlightened spirit sees     25
That shady City of Palm Trees;
But (ah!) my soul with too much stay
Is drunk, and staggers in the way.

THE RETREAT. Cf. Wordsworth, pp. 261-66.
17 *black art:* the devil's magic, evil. 20 *Bright shoots:* Cf. Thomas,
p. 528. 24 *train:* retinue (of angels). Cf. above, l. 2. 25-26 *From
. . . Trees:* As Moses on Mt. Pisgah was permitted a vision of the
land of Gilead and ". . . the plain of the valley of Jericho, the city of
palm trees, etc." (Deut. 34:1, 3). 27 *stay:* delaying in "this fleshly
dress" (l. 19).

Some men a forward motion love,
But I by backward steps would move,                    30
And when this dust falls to the urn
In that state I came return.


### The Morning-Watch

O joys! infinite sweetness! with what flow'rs,
And shoots of glory, my soul breaks, and buds!
  All the long hours
   Of night, and rest,
  Through the still shrouds                    5
  Of sleep, and clouds,
 This dew fell on my breast;
   O how it bloods,
And spirits all my earth! hark! In what rings,
And hymning circulations the quick world              10
  Awakes, and sings;
   The rising winds,
   And falling springs,
  Birds, beasts, all things
 Adore him in their kinds.                         15
  Thus all is hurl'd
In sacred hymns, and order, the great chime
And symphony of nature. Prayer is
  The world in tune,
   A spirit-voice,                         20
   And vocal joys
 Whose echo is heav'n's bliss.
  O let me climb
When I lie down! The pious soul by night
Is like a clouded star, whose beams though said       25
  To shed their light
  Under some cloud
   Yet are above,
  And shine, and move
 Beyond that misty shroud.                         30
  So in my bed
That curtain'd grave, though sleep, like ashes, hide
My lamp, and life, both shall in thee abide.

THE MORNING-WATCH. 2 *breaks*: bursts forth.  5-6 *shrouds* . . .
*sleep*: cf. ll. 31-33.  8 *bloods*: makes alive.  16 *hurl'd*: driven.

# The World

### 1

I saw Eternity the other night
Like a great ring of pure and endless light,
    All calm, as it was bright,
And round beneath it, Time in hours, days, years
      Driv'n by the spheres     5
Like a vast shadow mov'd, in which the world
    And all her train were hurl'd;
The doting Lover in his quaintest strain
    Did there complain,
Near him, his lute, his fancy, and his flights,     10
    Wit's sour delights,
With gloves, and knots the silly snares of pleasure
    Yet his dear treasure
All scatter'd lay, while he his eyes did pour
    Upon a flow'r.     15

### 2

The darksome Statesman hung with weights and woe
Like a thick midnight-fog mov'd there so slow
    He did nor stay, nor go;
Condemning thoughts (like sad eclipses) scowl
    Upon his soul,     20
And clouds of crying witnesses without
    Pursued him with one shout.
Yet digg'd the Mole, and lest his ways be found
    Workt under ground,
Where he did clutch his prey, but one did see     25
    That policy,
Churches and altars fed him, perjuries
    Were gnats and flies,
It rain'd about him blood and tears, but he
    Drank them as free.     30

THE WORLD. 4-6 *Time . . . mov'd:* cf. "Time is the moving image of eternity." 7 *train:* retinue. 8-12 *his quaintest . . . knots:* the behavior and dress befitting the "doting lover." 10 *flights:* that is, of passion or fancy. 11 *Wit's:* the mind's. 12 *knots:* love knots. 14 *eyes did pour:* that is, in weeping. 16 *darksome:* sinister. 21 *clouds . . . witnesses:* see Heb. 12:1. 23 *Mole:* the *darksome Statesman.* 26 *policy:* stratagem. 27-28 *Churches . . . flies:* He exploited good institutions, and perjuries were as inconsequential to him as *gnats and flies.* 30 *as free:* freely.

3

The fearful Miser on a heap of rust
Sat pining all his life there, did scarce trust
    His own hands with the dust,
Yet would not place one piece above, but lives
    In fear of thieves.               35
Thousands there were as frantic as himself
    And hugg'd each one his pelf,
The downright Epicure plac'd heav'n in sense
    And scorn'd pretense
While others slipt into a wide excess      40
    Said little less,
The weaker sort slight, trivial wares enslave
    Who think them brave,
And poor, despised Truth sat counting by
    Their victory.               45

4

Yet some, who all this while did weep and sing,
And sing, and weep, soar'd up into the ring,
    But most would use no wing.
O fools (said I), thus to prefer dark night
    Before true light,           50
To live in grots, and caves, and hate the day
    Because it shows the way,
The way which from this dead and dark abode
    Leads up to God,
A way where you might tread the sun, and be    55
    More bright than he.
But as I did their madness so discuss
    One whisper'd thus,
*This ring the Bridegroom did for none provide*
    *But for his Bride.*        60

*All that is in the world, the lust of the flesh, the lust of the Eyes,
and the pride of life, is not of the father, but is of the world.*
    *And the world passeth away, and the lusts thereof, but he that doth
the will of God abideth for ever.*

                    [I John 2:16-17]

31 *Miser:* cf. Malbecco, p. 53, ll. 28-30.    34 *place . . . above:* cf. "lay
up for yourselves treasures in heaven."—Matt. 6:20.    37 *pelf:* filthy
lucre.    38 *Epicure.* Epicureum, who "plac'd heav'n" in sensuous enjoy-
ment.    42 *wares:* goods.    43 *brave:* fine, beautiful.    44 *counting by:*
reckoning.    45 *Their:* All the worldly ones named above.    48 *use . . .
wing:* not soar *up into the ring* because they were "of the world." See
"Postscript."    57-58 *But . . . thus:* cf. Herbert, p. 143, ll. 33-35.    59-
60 *This . . . Bride:* Reference to Christ and the Church, the bride of
the Lamb. See Rev. 21:9.

### *They are all gone into the world of light*

They are all gone into the world of light!
    And I alone sit ling'ring here;
Their very memory is fair and bright,
    And my sad thoughts doth clear.


It glows and glitters in my cloudy breast      5
    Like stars upon some gloomy grove,
Or those faint beams in which this hill is drest,
    After the Sun's remove.


I see them walking in an air of glory,
    Whose light doth trample on my days:     10
My days, which are at best but dull and hoary,
    Mere glimmering and decays.


O holy hope! and high humility,
    High as the Heavens above!
These are your walks, and you have shew'd them me     15
    To kindle my cold love,


Dear, beauteous death! the Jewel of the Just,
    Shining no where, but in the dark;
What mysteries do lie beyond thy dust;
    Could man outlook that mark!     20


He that hath found some fledg'd birds' nest, may know
    At first sight, if the bird be flown;
But what fair Well, or Grove he sings in now,
    That is to him unknown.


And yet, as Angels in some brighter dreams     25
    Call to the soul, when man doth sleep:
So some strange thoughts transcend our wonted themes,
    And into glory peep.


THEY ARE ALL GONE. 4 *clear:* brighten. 5 *It:* their very memory, l. 3.
20 *mark:* boundary. 27 *wonted:* accustomed.

If a star were confin'd into a Tomb
   Her captive flames must needs burn there;          30
But when the hand that lockt her up, gives room,
    She'll shine through all the sphere.

O Father of eternal life, and all
   Created glories under thee!
Resume thy spirit from this world of thrall          35
    Into true liberty.

Either disperse these mists, which blot and fill
   My perspective (still) as they pass,
Or else remove me hence unto that hill,
    Where I shall need no glass.          40

## Cock-Crowing

Father of lights! what sunny seed,
What glance of day hast thou confin'd
Into this bird? To all the breed
This busy ray thou hast assign'd;
        Their magnetism works all night,      5
        And dreams of paradise and light.

Their eyes watch for the morning hue,
Their little grain expelling night
So shines and sings, as if it knew
The path unto the house of light.          10
        It seems their candle, howe'er done,
        Was tinn'd and lighted at the sun.

If such a tincture, such a touch,
So firm a longing can impow'r
Shall thy own image think it much          15
To watch for thy appearing hour?
        If a mere blast so fill the sail,
        Shall not the breath of God prevail?

31 *gives room:* yielde   35 *Resume:* Take back.   *spirit:* the poet's, which belongs to God.   *thrall:* thraldom, bondage.   38 *perspective:* telescope; vision, as through it.   40 *Where . . . glass:* cf. I Cor. 13:12.
   COCK-CROWING. 5 *magnetism:* the mysterious power in birds which draws them to the "light."   8 *grain:* cf. *seed,* l. 1.   12 *tinn'd:* kindled.
13 *tincture:* spirit (*seed*) infused into the bird.   15 *thy own image:* man.

O thou immortal light and heat!
Whose hand so shines through all this frame,    20
That by the beauty of the seat,
We plainly see, who made the same.
       Seeing thy seed abides in me,
       Dwell thou in it, and I in thee.

To sleep without thee, is to die;    25
Yea, 'tis a death partakes of hell:
For where thou dost not close the eye
It never opens, I can tell.
       In such a dark, Egyptian border,
       The shades of death dwell and disorder.  30

If joys, and hopes, and earnest throws,
And hearts, whose pulse beats still for light,
Are given to birds; who, but thee, knows
A love-sick soul's exalted flight?
       Can souls be track'd by any eye    35
       But his, who gave them wings to fly?

Only this veil which thou hast broke,
And must be broken yet in me,
This veil, I say, is all the cloak
And cloud which shadows thee from me.    40
       This veil thy full-eyed love denies,
       And only gleams and fractions spies.

O take it off! make no delay,
But brush me with thy light, that I
May shine unto a perfect day,    45
And warm me at thy glorious eye!
       O take it off! or till it flee,
       Though with no lily, stay with me!

20 *frame:* universe. 21 *seat:* the earth. 29 *dark, Egyptian:* darkness is associated with Egypt because of the "plague" of darkness which God caused there. See Exod. 10:21-23. 31 *throws:* efforts. 41-42 *This . . . spies:* cf. I Cor. 13:12; p. 189, l. 40 and note. 48 *Though . . . me:* Apparently a recollection of the special significance attached to the beauty of the lily in the Scriptures. There the lily, "brushed" with Divine Light, is "arrayed" more handsomely than "Solomon in all his glory"; and, further, "my beloved" (Christ, the Bridegroom) "feedeth among the lilies." The poet is not to be compared with the lily, neither being "arrayed" with its significant beauty, nor in its immediate association with Christ; but the "seed abides" in him (l. 23) and it is his

## The Water-Fall

With what deep murmurs through time's silent stealth
Doth thy transparent, cool and wat'ry wealth
    Here flowing fall,
    And chide, and call,
As if his liquid, loose retinue staid        5
Ling'ring, and were of this steep place afraid,
    The common pass
    Where, clear as glass,
    All must descend
    Not to an end:        10
But quicken'd by this deep and rocky grave,
Rise to a longer course more bright and brave.


    Dear stream! dear bank, where often I
    Have sat, and pleas'd my pensive eye,
    Why, since each drop of thy quick store        15
    Runs thither, whence it flow'd before,
    Should poor souls fear a shade or night,
    Who came (sure) from a sea of light?
    Or since those drops are all sent back
    So sure to thee, that none doth lack,        20
    Why should frail flesh doubt any more
    That what God takes, he'll not restore?
    O useful element and clear!
    My sacred wash and cleanser here,
    My first consigner unto those        25
    Fountains of life, where the Lamb goes,
    What sublime truths, and wholesome themes,
    Lodge in thy mystical, deep streams!
    Such as dull man can never find
    Unless that Spirit lead his mind,        30
    Which first upon thy face did move,

---

connection with the Divine; hence, he can pray for it to "stay" with
him until his communion with God is full and permanent. See Matt.
6:28-29; Luke 12.27; Song of Sol. 6:3. Cf. p. 187, ll. 59-60.
    THE WATER-FALL. 2 *wat'ry wealth:* i.e., of the stream. 5 *his; its.*
*retinue:* the company of "living" elements. 24-26 *My sacred . . .
Lamb goes:* In Holy Baptism. 31-32 *first . . . love:* "And the Spirit
of God moved upon the face of the waters."—Gen. 1:2. Cf. Milton,

And hatch'd all with his quick'ning love.
As this loud brook's incessant fall
In streaming rings restagnates all,
Which reach by course the bank, and then          35
Are no more seen, just so pass men.
O my invisible estate,
My glorious liberty, still late!
Thou art the channel my soul seeks,
Not this with cataracts and creeks.               40


## Quickness

False life! a foil and no more, when
                    Wilt thou be gone?
Thou foul deception of all men
That would not have the true come on.

Thou art a moon-like toil; a blind                5
                    Self-posing state;
A dark contest of waves and wind;
A mere tempestuous debate.

Life is a fix'd, discerning light,
                    A knowing joy;                10
No chance, or fit: but ever bright,
And calm and full, yet doth not cloy.

'Tis such a blissful thing, that still
                    Doth vivify,
And shine and smile, and hath the skill           15
To please without eternity.

Thou art a toilsome mole, or less
                    A moving mist.
But life is, what none can express,
A quickness, which my God hath kist.              20

---

p. 168, ll. 43-45. Cf. ". . . from the first / Wast present, and . . .
Dove-like sat'st brooding on the vast Abyss / And mad'st it pregnant."
—*Paradise Lost,* I, ll. 19-22.  34 *restagnates:* overflows.

QUICKNESS. 1 *foil:* something which sets off the "true" life to advantage. 4 *true:* true life. 5 *moon-like toil:* ambiguously, turmoil,
harassing labor, because the moon is inconstant, and frequently in
eclipse; or a snare or trap, because of the moon's delusive beauty. Cf.
*fix'd . . . light,* l. 9.  6 *Self-posing:* Puzzling, self-deceptive.  14
*vivify:* impart life.  17 *Thou:* False life.

## The Queer

O tell me whence that joy doth spring
Whose diet is divine and fair,
Which wears heaven, like a bridal ring,
And tramples on doubts and despair?

Whose eastern traffic deals in bright                    5
And boundless empyrean themes,
Mountains of spice, day-stars and light,
Green trees of life, and living streams?

Tell me, O tell who did thee bring
And here, without my knowledge, plac'd,          10
Till thou didst grow and get a wing,
A wing with eyes, and eyes that taste?

Sure, holiness the magnet is,
And love the lure, that woos thee down;
Which makes the high transcendent bliss          15
Of knowing thee, so rarely known.

*from* THALIA REDIVIVA

## The Revival

Unfold, unfold! take in his light,
Who makes thy cares more short than night.
The joys, which with his Day-star rise,
He deals to all, but drowsy eyes:
And what the men of this world miss,                   5
Some drops and dews of future bliss.

THE QUEER. 3 *bridal ring:* cf. p. 187, ll. 59-60 and note.    5 *eastern:* rich, a connotation deriving from the legendary wealth of the "gorgeous East," and from the association of the East with Christ. Cf. Donne, p. 125, ll. 16-17.    6 *empyrean:* heavenly.    12 *wing with eyes:* see Rev. 4:8.

THE REVIVAL. 3 *Day-star:* cf. Christ, "the bright and morning star"— Rev. 22:16. See above, l. 7; Milton, p. 161, l. 168.    4 *drowsy eyes:* of the worldly man.

Hark! how his winds have chang'd their note,
And with warm whispers call thee out.
The frosts are past, the storms are gone:
And backward life at last comes on.                    10
The lofty groves in express joys
Reply unto the turtle's voice,
And here in dust and dirt, O here
The lilies of his love appear!

12 *turtle's:* turtledove's.   14 *lilies:* cf. p. 190, l. 48 and note.

# JOHN DRYDEN   1631–1700

## Mac Flecknoe

All human things are subject to decay,
And, when Fate summons, monarchs must obey:
This Fleckno found, who, like Augustus, young
Was call'd to empire, and had govern'd long:
In prose and verse, was own'd, without dispute          5
Through all the realms of Nonsense, absolute.
This aged prince now flourishing in peace,
And blest with issue of a large increase,
Worn out with business, did at length debate
To settle the succession of the state:          10
And pond'ring which of all his sons was fit
To reign, and wage immortal war with Wit,
Cried, 'Tis resolv'd; for Nature pleads that he
Should only rule, who most resembles me:
Shadwell alone my perfect image bears,          15
Mature in dullness from his tender years.
Shadwell alone, of all my sons, is he
Who stands confirm'd in full stupidity.
The rest to some faint meaning make pretense,
But Shadwell never deviates into sense.          20
Some beams of wit on other souls may fall,
Strike through and make a lucid interval;
But Shadwell's genuine night admits no ray,
His rising fogs prevail upon the day:
Besides his goodly fabric fills the eye,          25
And seems design'd for thoughtless majesty:

MAC FLECKNOE. *Mac Flecknoe:* The first edition (1682) adds: *Or A Satyr Upon The True-Blew-Protestant Poet, T[homas] S[hadwell].* Thomas Shadwell (1640-1692) was a fellow dramatist and at one time something of a friend of Dryden's. Precisely what moved Dryden to attack Shadwell is obscure—on the surface, at least, it is solely Shadwell's literary gifts and attainments that come in for abuse. *Mac Flecknoe,* meaning "the son of Flecknoe," derives from *Flecknoe,* the name of an Irish priest, who was something of a poet and musician. Dryden had no quarrel with this poor man, but his reputation as a witless poetaster of bulky accomplishment and dullard of the first order suited him exactly for the role of Prince of Nonsense.

3 *Augustus* (Caesar): First Roman Emperor, who came into power when he was thirty-two years old, and ruled for more than forty years. 12 *Wit:* intelligence.   25 *goodly fabric:* Shadwell was fat and awkward.

Thoughtless as monarch oaks, that shade the plain,
And, spread in solemn state, supinely reign.
Heywood and Shirley were but types of thee,
Thou last great Prophet of Tautology:                                    30
Even I, a dunce of more renown than they,
Was sent before but to prepare the way;
And coarsely clad in Norwich drugget came
To teach the nations in thy greater name.
My warbling lute, the lute I whilom strung                               35
When to King John of Portugal I sung,
Was but the prelude to that glorious day,
When thou on silver Thames didst cut thy way,
With well-tim'd oars before the royal barge,
Swell'd with the pride of thy celestial charge,                          40
And big with hymn, commander of an host,
The like was ne'er in Epsom blankets tost.
Methinks I see the new Arion sail,
The lute still trembling underneath thy nail.
At thy well-sharp'n'd thumb from shore to shore                          45
The treble squeaks for fear, the basses roar:
Echoes from Pissing-Alley, Shadwell call,
And Shadwell they resound from A[ston] Hall.
About thy boat the little fishes throng,
As at the morning toast, that floats along.                              50
Sometimes as prince of thy harmonious band
Thou wield'st thy papers in thy threshing hand.
St. André's feet ne'er kept more equal time,
Not ev'n the feet of thy own *Psyche's* rhyme:

29 (Thomas) *Heywood,* (James) *Shirley:* early seventeenth-century
dramatists. 33 *Norwich drugget:* coarse cloth of wool and cotton mixture. 36 *When . . . sung:* Fleckno visited the court at King John's
invitation and successfully made "some two or three hours tryall of my
skill" (in music). 42 *in . . . tost:* Blanket-tossing as a crude kind of
humiliation is well-known, and perhaps some reference to Shadwell's
comedy, *Epsom Wells,* is intended; but blanket-tossing is not one of its
comic diversions. 43 *Arion:* The "new Arion," Shadwell, like the
legendary Greek Arion, is a poet and musician, exhibiting his talents
while "under sail." Arion, thrown overboard from a ship, is reported to
have been saved from drowning by a dolphin which, charmed by Arion's
music, carried him ashore on his back. Shadwell's tunes receive the
tribute of echoes from possibly unseemly places, and the little fishes
thronging about the boat are rather less charmed by his playing than by
the "morning toast that floats along." 47 *Pissing-Alley:* Stow says:
"a very proper name for it."—*A Survey of . . . London,* ed. John
Strype, London, 1720, II, 4, 117. 48 *A[ston] Hall:* The reference is
obscure; cf. "dull Aston" (*Essay on Satire*). 53 *St. André('s)* : a well-
known dancing-master. 54 *Psyche's rhyme:* reference to Shadwell's
rhyming verse opera *Psyche* (1675).

Though they in number as in sense excel;                                55
So just, so like tautology they fell,
That, pale with envy, Singleton forswore
The lute and sword which he in triumph bore,
And vow'd he ne'er would act Villerius more.
Here stopt the good old sire, and wept for joy               60
In silent raptures of the hopeful boy.
All arguments, but most his plays, persuade,
That for anointed dullness he was made.
   Close to the walls which fair Augusta bind
(The fair Augusta much to fears inclin'd),                     65
An ancient fabric, rais'd t' inform the sight,
There stood of yore, and Barbican it hight:
A watch tower once, but now, so Fate ordains,
Of all the pile an empty name remains.
From its old ruins brothel houses rise,                        70
Scenes of lewd loves, and of polluted joys,
Where their vast courts the mother-strumpets keep,
And, undisturb'd by watch, in silence sleep.
Near these a nursery erects its head,
Where queens are form'd, and future heroes bred;      75
Where unfledg'd actors learn to laugh and cry,
Where infant punks their tender voices try,
And little Maximins the gods defy.
Great Fletcher never treads in buskins here,
Nor greater Jonson dares in socks appear.                     80
But gentle Simkin just reception finds
Amidst this monument of vanish'd minds:
Pure clinches, the suburban muse affords,
And Panton waging harmless war with words.
Here Fleckno, as a place to Fame well known,           85
Ambitiously design'd his Shadwell's throne.
For ancient Dekker prophesied long since,
That in this pile should reign a mighty prince,
Born for a scourge of Wit, and flail of Sense:

57 (John) *Singleton:* a musician of some note.   59 *Villerius:* a leading
role in William D'Avenant's dramatic opera *The Siege of Rhodes,* 1656.
64 *fair Augusta:* London.   65 *fears:* perhaps of political disturbances.
67 *Barbican it hight:* Called Barbican, from a tower which once stood
in North London.   74 *nursery:* a theater for the training of young actors.
77 *punks:* harlots.   78 *Maximins:* the protagonist in Dryden's *Tyrannic
Love.*   79 (John) *Fletcher:* early 17th-century dramatist.   79, 80
*buskins, socks:* cf. Jonson, p. 103, ll. 36, 37 and notes.   81 *Simkin:* a
clown.   83 *clinches:* puns.   84 (Thomas) *Panton:* a "wit."   87
(Thomas) *Dekker:* Elizabethan dramatist.

To whom true dullness should some *Psyches* owe,   90
But worlds of *Misers* from his pen should flow;
*Humorists* and hypocrites it should produce,
Whole Raymond families, and tribes of Bruce.
   Now Empress Fame had publish'd the renown
Of Shadwell's coronation through the Town.   95
Rous'd by report of Fame, the Nations meet,
From near Bun-Hill, and distant Watling Street.
No Persian carpets spread th' imperial way,
But scatter'd limbs of mangled poets lay:
From dusty shops neglected authors come,   100
Martyrs of pies, and relics of the bum.
Much Heywood, Shirley, Ogilby there lay,
But loads of Shadwell almost chok'd the way.
Bilk'd stationers for yeoman stood prepar'd,
And H[erringman] was Captain of the Guard.   105
The hoary prince in majesty appear'd,
High on a throne of his own labors rear'd.
At his right hand our young Ascanius sat
Rome's other hope, and pillar of the state.
His brows thick fogs, instead of glories, grace,   110
And lambent dullness played around his face.
As Hannibal did to the altars come,
Sworn by his sire a mortal foe to Rome,
So Shadwell swore, nor should his vow be vain,
That he till death true dullness would maintain;   115
And in his father's right, and realm's defence,
Ne'er to have peace with Wit, nor truce with Sense.
The king himself the sacred unction made,
As king by office, and as priest by trade:

90-93 *Psyches . . . Bruce:* Dryden is sarcastically sampling Shadwell's dramatic repertory: *Psyche* (see l. 54); *The Miser* is a comedy adapted from Molière's *L'Avare;* Raymond is "a gentleman of wit and honour" in *The Humourists;* Bruce, the same in *The Virtuoso.* 97 *Bun-Hill, Watling Street:* Bun-Hill Fields was a burial place for "dissenters from the Church of England"; Watling Street was "very well inhabited by great dealers, chiefly by wholesale." The places are "distant" from one another, as from the heart of the city to its furthest outskirts. 101 *Martyrs . . . bum:* Leaves torn from the books of "neglected authors" were placed under pies or used as toilet paper. 102 *Heywood . . . Ogilby:* see l. 29 and note; John Ogilby was a translator of classics. 104 *Bilk'd stationers:* booksellers with unsalable poetry. 105 (Henry) *Herringman:* Dryden's first publisher. 108 *Ascanius:* son of Aeneas (Virgil), as Shadwell is the son of Fleckno. 112 *Hannibal:* who was forced to swear eternal hatred to Rome. 118 *sacred . . . made:* the anointing.

In his sinister hand, instead of ball,                     120
He plac'd a mighty mug of potent ale;
Love's Kingdom to his right he did convey,
At once his scepter and his rule of sway,
Whose righteous lore the prince had practic'd young,
And from whose loins recorded *Psyche* sprung.             125
His temples last with poppies were o'erspread,
That nodding seem'd to consecrate his head:
Just at that point of time, if Fame not lie,
On his left hand twelve reverend owls did fly.
So Romulus, 'tis sung, by Tiber's brook,                   130
Presage of sway from twice six vultures took.
Th' admiring throng loud acclamations make,
And omens of the future empire take.
The sire then shook the honors of his head,
And from his brows damps of oblivion shed                  135
Full on the filial dullness: long he stood,
Repelling from his breast the raging god;
At length burst out in this prophetic mood:
    Heavens bless my son, from Ireland let him reign
To far Barbadoes on the western main;                      140
Of his dominion may no end be known,
And greater than his father's be his throne.
Beyond love's kingdom let him stretch his pen;
He paus'd, and all the people cried *Amen*.
Then thus, continu'd he, My son advance                    145
Still in new Impudence, new Ignorance.
Success let others teach, learn thou from me
Pangs without birth, and fruitless Industry.
Let *Virtuosos* in five years be writ;
Yet not one thought accuse thy toil of wit.                150
Let gentle George in triumph tread the stage,
Make Dorimant betray, and Loveit rage;
Let Cully, Cockwood, Fopling, charm the pit,
And in their folly show the writer's wit.
Yet still thy fools shall stand in thy defence,            155
And justify their author's want of sense.

---

120 *sinister:* left.  *ball:* a globe surmounted by a cross, symbolizing
God's sovereignty over the world.  122 *Love's Kingdom:* published,
1664.  130-31 *So Romulus . . . took:* The proposal of Romulus for a
site for Rome was preferred because he saw "twice-six vultures," and
Remus but a half-dozen.  151 *George* (Etherege): an eminent writer of
comedies.  *Dorimant, Loveit,* etc. (ll. 152-53), are characters in his plays.
153 *pit:* occupants of the cheap ground-floor seats in the theater.

Let 'em be all by thy own model made
Of dullness, and desire no foreign aid:
That they to future ages may be known,
Not copies drawn, but issue of thy own. 160
Nay let thy men of wit too be the same,
All full of thee, and diff'ring but in name;
But let no alien S[e]dl[e]y interpose
To lard with wit thy hungry Epsom prose.
And when false flowers of rhetoric thou wouldst cull, 165
Trust Nature, do not labor to be dull;
But write thy best, and top; and in each line,
Sir Formal's oratory will be thine.
Sir Formal, though unsought, attends thy quill,
And does thy *Northern Dedications* fill. 170
Nor let false friends seduce thy mind to fame,
By arrogating Jonson's hostile name.
Let Father Fleckno fire thy mind with praise,
And Uncle Ogilby thy envy raise.
Thou art my blood, where Jonson has no part; 175
What share have we in Nature or in Art?
Where did his wit on learning fix a brand,
And rail at arts he did not understand?
Where made he love in Prince Nicander's vein,
Or swept the dust in *Psyche's* humble strain? 180
Where sold he bargains, whip-stitch, kiss my arse,
Promis'd a play and dwindled to a farce?
When did his muse from Fletcher scenes purloin,
As thou whole Eth'rege dost transfuse to thine?
But so transfus'd as oil on waters' flow, 185
His always floats above, thine sinks below.
This is thy province, this thy wondrous way,
New humors to invent for each new play:
This is that boasted bias of thy mind,
By which one way, to dullness, 'tis inclin'd, 190
Which makes thy writings lean on one side still,
And in all changes that way bends thy will.
Nor let thy mountain belly make pretense
Of likeness; thine's a tympany of sense.

163-64 *Sedley, Epsom:* Charles Sedley, from whom Shadwell borrowed
in *Epsom Wells.* 168 *Sir Formal* (Trifle): a character in *The Virtuoso.*
170 *Northern Dedications:* to the Duke of Newcastle and members of
his family in the "north country." 172 *arrogating . . . name:* Shadwell
pretended to be a literary disciple of Ben Jonson and even affected Ben's
rough speech and manner. 174 *Ogilby:* see l. 102. 179 *Nicander's
vein:* Nicander's stilted addresses to Psyche, *Psyche,* Act I. 181 *whip-
stitch . . . arse:* samples the essential idiom of Sir Samuel Hearty (in
*The Virtuoso*). 183 *Fletcher:* see l. 79 and note. 194 *tympany:* "an
arrogant inflation."

A tun of man in thy large bulk is writ,                        195
But sure thou 'rt but a kilderkin of wit.
Like mine thy gentle numbers feebly creep,
Thy tragic muse gives smiles, thy comic sleep.
With whate'er gall thou sett'st thyself to write,
Thy inoffensive satires never bite.                           200
In thy felonious heart, though venom lies,
It does but touch thy Irish pen, and dies.
Thy genius calls thee not to purchase fame
In keen iambics, but mild anagram:
Leave writing plays, and choose for thy command               205
Some peaceful province in Acrostic Land
There thou mayst wings display and altars raise,
And torture one poor word ten thousand ways.
Or if thou wouldst thy diff'rent talents suit,
Set thy own songs, and sing them to thy lute.                 210
He said, but his last words were scarcely heard,
For Bruce and Longvil had a *trap* prepar'd,
And down they sent the yet declaiming bard.
Sinking he left his drugget robe behind,
Borne upwards by a subterranean wind.                         215
The mantle fell to the young prophet's part,
With double portion of his father's art.


## The Tears of Amynta, for the Death of Damon

### I

On a bank, beside a willow,
Heav'n her cov'ring, earth her pillow,
Sad Amynta sighed alone:
From the cheerless dawn of morning
Till the dews of night returning                              5
Singing thus she made her moan:
        Hope is banish'd
        Joys are vanish'd;
Damon, my belov'd is gone!

196 *kilderkin*: small barrel, contrasted with *tun*.  202 *Irish pen*: see
general note.  207 *wings . . . raise*: poems typographically shaped like
wings, altars, etc., as Herbert's "Easter Wings" and "The Altar" and
Dylan Thomas's "Vision and Prayer."  212 *For Bruce . . . prepar'd*:
In Act III, *The Virtuoso*, Sir Formal's (l. 168) speech-making is cut
short as he "sinks below" through a trapdoor prepared by Bruce and
Longvil.

THE TEARS (A Song).  3 *Amynta* (and *Damon*): popular names for
lovers found in pastoral poetry.  6 *moan*: lover's complaint.

### 2

Time, I dare thee to discover 10
Such a youth, and such a lover,
Oh so true, so kind was he!
Damon was the pride of Nature,
Charming in his every feature,
Damon liv'd alone for me: 15
Melting kisses
Murmuring blisses,
Who so liv'd and lov'd as we!

### 3

Never shall we curse the morning,
Never bless the night returning, 20
Sweet embraces to restore:
Never shall we both lie dying
Nature failing, Love supplying
All the joys he drain'd before:
Death, come end me 25
To befriend me;
Love and Damon are no more.


## A Song for St. Cecilia's Day

### NOVEMBER 22, 1687

### 1

From harmony, from heav'nly harmony
This universal frame began.
When Nature underneath a heap
Of jarring atoms lay,
And could not heave her head, 5
The tuneful voice was heard from high,
Arise ye more than dead.
Then cold, and hot, and moist, and dry,

10 *discover :* disclose.
A SONG. St. Cecilia is the patron of musicians, and of music, especially of church music; the legendary inventor of the organ.
1-2 *From . . . began :* Based upon the idea that the world is like a musical harmony, called from chaos by "the tuneful voice of heav'n."
8 *cold . . . dry :* the elementary properties of the "jarring atoms."

In order to their stations leap,
   And Music's pow'r obey.    **10**
From harmony, from heav'nly harmony
   This universal frame began:
   From harmony to harmony
Through all the compass of the notes it ran,
The diapason closing full in Man.    **15**

### 2

What passion cannot Music raise and quell!
   When Jubal struck his corded shell,
 His list'ning brethren stood around
 And wond'ring, on their faces fell
 To worship that celestial sound.   **20**
Less than a god they thought there could not dwell
   Within the hollow of that shell
   That spoke so sweetly and so well.
What passion cannot Music raise and quell!

### 3

 The trumpet's loud clangor   **25**
   Excites us to arms
 With shrill notes of anger
   And mortal alarms.
 The double double double beat
   Of the thund'ring drum   **30**
Cries, hark the foes come;
Charge, charge, 'tis too late to retreat.

### 4

 The soft complaining flute
 In dying notes discovers
 The woes of hopeless lovers,   **35**
Whose dirge is whisper'd by the warbling lute.

### 5

Sharp violins proclaim
Their jealous pangs, and desperation,
Fury, frantic indignation,
Depths of pains, and height of passion,   **40**
 For the fair, disdainful dame,

---

15 *diapason:* octave. *Man:* cf. Herbert, p. 139, l. 7 and note. 17
*Jubal:* a descendant of Cain, and "the father of all such as handle the
harp and organ"—Gen. 4:21.

## 6

But oh! what art can teach
    What human voice can reach
The sacred organ's praise?
Notes inspiring holy love,              45
Notes that wing their heav'nly ways
    To mend the choirs above.

## 7

Orpheus could lead the savage race;
And trees unrooted left their place,
        Sequacious of the lyre:        50
But bright Cecilia rais'd the wonder high'r;
When to her organ, vocal breath was giv'n
An angel heard, and straight appear'd
        Mistaking Earth for Heav'n.

### GRAND CHORUS

*As from the pow'r of sacred lays*    55
    *The spheres began to move,*
*And sung the great Creator's praise*
    *To all the bless'd above;*
*So when the last and dreadful hour*
*This crumbling pageant shall devour,*    60
*The trumpets shall be heard on high,*
*The dead shall live, the living die,*
*And music shall untune the sky.*

## Song to a Fair, Young Lady,
## Going Out of the Town in the Spring

### I

Ask not the cause, why sullen Spring
    So long delays her flow'rs to bear;
Why warbling birds forget to sing,
    And winter storms invert the year?
Chloris is gone; and Fate provides    5
To make it Spring, where she resides.

---

44 *sacred organ('s)* : the organ on which sacred music was played : sacred because of St. Cecilia's playing. 48 *Orpheus :* see Milton, p. 149, l. 145 and note. 50 *Sequacious :* inclined to follow. 63 *And music . . . sky :* as music called the world into being, so shall it preside at its destruction.

SONG TO A FAIR. *provides :* gets ready, arranges.

### 2

Chloris is gone, the Cruel Fair;
   She cast not back a pitying eye:
But left her lover in despair;
   To sigh, to languish, and to die.       10
Ah, how can those fair eyes endure
To give the wounds they will not cure!

### 3

Great God of Love, why hast thou made
   A face that can all hearts command,
That all religions can invade,       15
   And change the laws of ev'ry land?
Where thou hadst plac'd such pow'r before,
Thou shouldst have made her mercy more.

### 4

When Chloris to the Temple comes,
   Adoring crowds before her fall;      20
She can restore the dead from tombs,
   And ev'ry life but mine recall.
I only am by Love design'd
To be the victim for mankind.

## Rondelay

### 1

Chloe found Amyntas lying
   All in tears, upon the plain;
Sighing to himself, and crying,
   Wretched I, to love in vain!
Kiss me, Dear, before my dying;      5
   Kiss me once, and ease my pain!

### 2

Sighing to himself, and crying
   Wretched I, to love in vain:
Ever scorning and denying
   To reward your faithful swain:      10
Kiss me, Dear, before my dying;
   Kiss me once, and ease my pain!

RONDELAY. *Rondelay:* Roundelay, a song with a similar refrain recurring frequently or at fixed intervals.
  1 *Chloe, Amyntas:* see p. 201, l. 3 and note.

### 3

Ever scorning, and denying
  To reward your faithful swain,
Chloe, laughing at his crying,        15
  Told him that he lov'd in vain:
Kiss me, Dear, before my dying;
  Kiss me once, and ease my pain!

### 4

Chloe, laughing at his crying,
  Told him that he lov'd in vain:      20
But repenting, and complying,
  When he kiss'd, she kiss'd again:
Kiss'd him up, before his dying;
  Kiss'd him up, and eas'd his pain.

## The Secular Masque

*Enter* JANUS.

JANUS    Chronos, Chronos, mend thy pace,
           An hundred times the rolling sun
           Around the radiant belt has run
           In his revolving race.
           Behold, behold, the goal in sight,   5
           Spread thy fans, and wing thy flight.

*Enter* CHRONOS, *with a scythe in his hand, and a great globe on his back, which he sets down at his entrance.*

CHRONOS    Weary, weary of my weight,
           Let me, let me drop my freight,
             And leave the World behind.
           I could not bear          10
           Another year
           The load of human-kind.

THE SECULAR MASQUE. The masque of the century, of the age; cf. *sæcularis,* belonging to an age or a generation (*sæculum*). This masque is said to be "an allegory of the seventeenth century." See p. 149, l. 128 and note.

  1 *Janus:* the God of gates and doors; hence the patron of all beginnings. *Chronos:* the God of Time. Cf. *Old Time,* l. 23. 2 *hundred times:* a century. 3 *radiant belt:* the "belt" formed by the constellations of the zodiac.

*Enter* MOMUS *laughing.*

MOMUS   Ha! ha! ha! Ha! ha! ha! well hast thou
   done,
  To lay down thy pack,
  And lighten thy back,     15
The World was a fool, e'er since it
   begun,
And since neither Janus, nor Chronos,
   nor I,
  Can hinder the crimes,
  Or mend the bad times,
'Tis better to laugh than to cry.   20

CHORUS OF   *'Tis better to laugh than to cry.*
ALL THREE

JANUS   Since Momus comes to laugh below,
  Old Time begin the Show,
That he may see, in every Scene,
What changes in this age have been.  25
CHRONOS   Then Goddess of the Silver Bow begin.

*Horns, or Hunting-Music within. Enter* DIANA.

DIANA   With horns and with hounds I waken the
   day,
And hie to my woodland walks away;  28
I tuck up my robe, and am buskin'd soon,
And tie to my forehead a waxing moon.
I course the fleet stag, unkennel the fox,
And chase the wild goats o'er summits of
   rocks,
With shouting and hooting we pierce
   through the sky;
And Echo turns hunter, and doubles the
   cry.

CHORUS OF ALL   *With shouting and hooting, we pierce*
   *through the sky;*    35
  *And Echo turns hunter, and doubles the*
   *cry.*

13 *Momus:* Ridicule.   26 *Goddess . . . Bow: Diana,* the huntress and
moon goddess (see l. 30).   29 *buskin'd:* booted.

| | |
|---|---|
| JANUS | Then our age was in its prime, |
| CHRONOS | Free from rage. |
| DIANA | ——— And free from crime. |
| MOMUS | A very merry, dancing, drinking,    40 |
| | Laughing, quaffing, and unthinking time. |

CHORUS OF ALL    *Then our age was in its prime,*
   *Free from rage, and free from crime,*
   *A very merry, dancing, drinking,*    44
   *Laughing, quaffing, and unthinking time.*

   *Dance of* DIANA's *Attendants.*

   *Enter* MARS.

MARS    Inspire the vocal brass, inspire;
   The World is past its infant age:
     Arms and Honor,
     Arms and Honor,
   See the martial mind on fire,    50
   And kindle manly rage.
   Mars has look'd the sky to red;
   And Peace, the Lazy Good, is fled.
   Plenty, Peace, and Pleasure fly;
     The sprightly green    55
   In woodland-walks, no more is seen;
   The sprightly green has drunk the
       Tyrian dye.

CHORUS OF ALL    *Plenty, Peace,* &c.

MARS    Sound the trumpet, beat the drum,
   Through all the World around;    60
   Sound a reveille, sound, sound,
     The Warrior God is come.

CHORUS OF ALL    *Sound the trumpet,* &c.

MOMUS    Thy sword within the scabbard keep,
     And let Mankind agree;    65
   Better the World were fast asleep,
     Than kept awake by thee.

---

46 *Mars:* the God of War. *Inspire . . . inspire:* cf. p. 203, ll. 25 ff.
57 *Tyrian dye:* (purple) blood of war.

    The fools are only thinner,
     With all our cost and care;
    But neither side a winner,     70
     For things are as they were.

CHORUS OF ALL   *The fools are only, &c.*

     *Enter* VENUS.

   VENUS   Calms appear, when storms are past;
    Love will have his hour at last:
    Nature is my kindly care;     75
    Mars destroys, and I repair;
    Take me, take me, while you may,
    Venus comes not ev'ry day.

CHORUS OF ALL   *Take her, take her, &c.*

   CHRONOS  The World was then so light,    80
    I scarcely felt the weight;
    Joy ruled the day, and Love the night.
    But since the Queen of Pleasure left the
      ground,
     I faint, I lag,
     And feebly drag      85
    The pond'rous orb around.

   MOMUS   All, all, of a piece throughout;
*Pointing to* DIANA  Thy chase had a beast in view;
  *to* MARS  Thy wars brought nothing about;
  *to* VENUS  Thy lovers were all untrue.    90
   JANUS  'Tis well an Old Age is out,
   CHRONOS  And time to begin a New.

CHORUS OF ALL   *All, all, of a piece throughout;*
    *Thy chase had a beast in view;*
    *Thy wars brought nothing about;*   95
    *Thy lovers were all untrue.*
    *'Tis well an Old Age is out,*
    *And time to begin a New.*

*Dance of Huntsmen, Nymphs, Warriors and Lovers.*

83 *Queen . . . ground:* Queen Mary of Modena, in exile with James
II (?).

SONGS FROM THE PLAYS

### *Ah fading joy, how quickly art thou past?*

[Indian Woman's Song]

Ah fading joy, how quickly art thou past?
        Yet we thy ruin haste:
As if the cares of human life were few
        We seek out new:
And follow Fate that does too fast pursue.     5

See how on every bough the birds express
        In their sweet notes their happiness.
They all enjoy, and nothing spare;
        But on their Mother Nature lay their care:
Why then should Man, the Lord of all below     10
        Such troubles choose to know
As none of all his subjects undergo?

    Hark, hark, the waters fall, fall, fall;
    And with a murmuring sound
    Dash, dash, upon the ground,     15
        To gentle slumbers call.

[*The Indian Emperor,* 1667, IV, iii]

### *I feed a flame within which so torments me*

[Asteria's Song]

I feed a flame within which so torments me
That it both pains my heart, and yet contents me:
'Tis such a pleasing smart, and I so love it,
That I had rather die, than once remove it.

Yet he for whom I grieve shall never know it,     5
My tongue does not betray, nor my eyes show it:
Not a sigh nor a tear my pain discloses,
But they fall silently like dew on roses.

Thus to prevent my love from being cruel,
My heart's the sacrifice as 'tis the fuel:     10
And while I suffer this to give him quiet,
My faith rewards my love, though he deny it.

On his eyes will I gaze, and there delight me;
While I conceal my love, no frown can fright me:
To be more happy I dare not aspire;                     15
Nor can I fall more low, mounting no higher.

[*Secret Love,* 1668, IV, ii]


### *Ah how sweet it is to love*

[Damilcar's Song]

Ah how sweet it is to love,
Ah how gay is young desire!
And what pleasing pains we prove
When we first approach Love's fire!
   Pains of Love be sweeter far               5
   Than all other pleasures are.


Sighs which are from lovers blown,
Do but gently heave the heart:
Ev'n the tears they shed alone
Cure, like trickling balm their smart.                  10
   Lovers when they lose their breath,
   Bleed away in easy death.


Love and Time with reverence use,
Treat 'em like a parting friend:
Nor the golden gifts refuse                              15
Which in youth sincere they send:
   For each year their price is more,
   And they less simple than before.


Love, like spring-tides full and high,
Swells in every youthful vein:                          20
But each tide does less supply,
Till they quite shrink in again:
   If a flow in age appear,
   'Tis but rain, and runs not clear.

[*Tyrannick Love,* 1670, IV, i]

## *Calm was the even, and clear was the sky*

[Beatrix's Song]

### 1

Calm was the even, and clear was the sky,
  And the new budding flowers did spring,
When all alone went Amyntas and I
  To hear the sweet nightingale sing;
I sat, and he laid him down by me;                       5
  But scarcely his breath he could draw;
For when with a fear he began to draw near,
  He was dashed with A ha ha ha ha!

### 2

He blush'd to himself, and lay still for a while,
  And his modesty curb'd his desire;                    10
But straight I convinc'd all his fear with a smile,
  Which added new flames to his fire.
O Sylvia, said he, you are cruel,
  To keep your poor lover in awe;
Then once more he press'd with his hand to my breast,   15
  But was dashed with A ha ha ha ha.

### 3

I knew 'twas his passion that caus'd all his fear;
  And therefore I pitied his case:
I whisper'd him softly there's nobody near,
  And laid my cheek close to his face:                  20
But as he grew bolder and bolder,
  A shepherd came by us and saw;
And just as our bliss we began with a kiss,
  He laugh'd out with A ha ha ha ha.

[*An Evening's Love*—"In The Savoy," 1671— IV]

CALM WAS THE EVEN. 3, 13 *Amyntas, Sylvia:* see p. 201, l. 3 and
note.

## *Wherever I am, and whatever I do*

[Abdalla's Song]

I

Wherever I am, and whatever I do;
  My Phillis is still in my mind:
When angry I mean not to Phillis to go,
  My feet of themselves the way find:
Unknown to myself I am just at her door,                    5
And when I would rail, I can bring out no more,
  Than Phillis too fair and unkind!

2

When Phillis I see, my heart bounds in my breast,
  And the love I would stifle is shown:
But asleep, or awake, I am never at rest                   10
  When from my eyes Phillis is gone!
Sometimes a sad dream does delude my sad mind,
But, alas, when I wake and no Phillis I find
  How I sigh to myself all alone.

3

Should a king be my rival in her I adore                   15
  He should offer his treasure in vain:
O let me alone to be happy and poor,
  And give me my Phillis again:
Let Phillis be mine, and but ever be kind
I could to a desert with her be confin'd,                  20
  And envy no monarch his reign.

4

Alas, I discover too much of my love,
  And she too well knows her own power!
She makes me each day a new martyrdom prove,
  And makes me grow jealous each hour:                     25
But let her each minute torment my poor mind
I had rather love Phillis both false and unkind,
  Than ever be freed from her pow'r.

[*The Conquest of Granada*. I.—"In The Savoy," 1672— IV]

# ALEXANDER POPE 1688–1744

## The Rape of the Lock

### AN HEROIC-COMICAL POEM

*Nolueram, Belinda, tuos violare capillos;*
*Sed juvat, hoc precibus me tribuisse tuis.*

[Martial, *Epigrams* XII, 84]

### CANTO I

What dire offense from am'rous causes springs,
What mighty contests rise from trivial things,
I sing—This verse to Caryll, Muse! is due;
This ev'n Belinda may vouchsafe to view:
Slight is the subject, but not so the praise,     5
If She inspire, and He approve my lays.

    Say what strange motive, Goddess! could compel
A well-bred Lord t' assault a gentle Belle?
Oh say what stranger cause, yet unexplor'd,
Could make a gentle Belle reject a Lord?     10
In tasks so bold, can little men engage,
And in soft bosoms dwells such mighty rage?

    Sol through white curtains shot a tim'rous ray,
And op'd those eyes that must eclipse the day;
Now lap-dogs give themselves the rousing shake,     15
And sleepless lovers, just at twelve, awake:

THE RAPE OF THE LOCK: Celebrates an actual incident: Lord Petre (the "Baron") did cut off one of Miss Arabella Fermor's locks. At the suggestion of John Caryll (l. 3), a friend to all parties, that Pope write something to ease the tension which the incident had caused, he composed "The Rape" and sent it to Miss Fermor. She seems to have approved it well enough to "give about" copies to her friends. In 1712— possibly without Pope's knowledge—it was published anonymously in two cantos. Once in print, its earlier good effects were cancelled: a private matter had become public, and, embarrassingly, meanwhile, Lord Petre had married—not Arabella. The poem, nevertheless, had become a success, and Pope set about enlarging it for the edition of 1714. See *The Rape of the Lock*, ed., Geoffrey Tillotson (London, 1940), pp. 83 ff.

*Nolueram . . . tuis:* "I was loth, Belinda, to violate your locks; but I am pleased to have granted that much of your prayers." Adapted from Martial, Tillotson's translation.

CANTO I. 1-3 *What . . . Muse:* Pope affects the epic poet's address to the Muse to initiate his mock-heroic style. Throughout he parodies and burlesques such features of the epic as elegant diction, recurring epithets, the battle of heroes, the genealogy of weapons, and the involvement of supernatural agents (the "Machinery") in human affairs.

Thrice rung the bell, the slipper knock'd the ground,
And the press'd watch returned a silver sound.
Belinda still her downy pillow press'd,
Her guardian Sylph prolonged the balmy rest.                    20
'Twas He had summon'd to her silent bed
The morning-dream that hover'd o'er her head.
A youth more glitt'ring than a Birth-night Beau
(That ev'n in slumber caus'd her cheek to glow),
Seem'd to her ear his winning lips to lay,                       25
And thus in whispers said, or seem'd to say.
  Fairest of mortals, thou distinguish'd care
Of thousand bright Inhabitants of Air!
If e'er one vision touch'd thy infant thought,
Of all the nurse and all the priest have taught,                30
Of airy Elves by moonlight shadows seen,
The silver token, and the circled green,
Or virgins visited by Angel-pow'rs,
With golden crowns and wreaths of heav'nly flow'rs,
Hear and believe! thy own importance know,                      35
Nor bound thy narrow views to things below.
Some secret truths, from learned pride conceal'd,
To maids alone and children are reveal'd:
What though no credit doubting Wits may give?
The Fair and Innocent shall still believe.                      40
Know, then, unnumbered Spirits round thee fly,
The light Militia of the lower sky;
These, though unseen, are ever on the wing,
Hang o'er the Box, and hover round the Ring.
Think what an equipage thou hast in air,                         45
And view with scorn two pages and a Chair.

17 *slipper . . . ground:* to summon the maid.    18 *press'd . . . sound:* as
her "striking" watch sounded the hour.    20 *Sylph:* "The Machinery,
Madam, is a term invented by the Critics, to signify that part which the
Deities, Angels, or Demons are made to act in a Poem. . . . These
Machines I determin'd to raise on a very new and odd foundation, the
Rosicrucian doctrine of Spirits. . . . According to these gentlemen, the
four Elements are inhabited by Spirits, which they call Sylphs, Gnomes,
Nymphs, and Salamanders. The Gnomes or Demons of Earth delight
in mischief; but the Sylphs, whose habitation is in the Air, are the best-
condition'd creatures imaginable. For they say, any mortals may enjoy
the most intimate familiarities with these gentle Spirits, upon a condition very easy to all true Adepts, an inviolate preservation of chastity."
—From "To Mrs. [Miss] Arabella Fermor."    23 *Birth-night Beau:* a
suitor, particularly at a royal birthday party.    32 *silver token:* coin left
by the Elves as evidence of their visit.    *circled green:* print of the fairy
circle in the grass.    44 *Box:* at the theater.    *Ring:* a riding and carriage course in fashionable Hyde Park. Hyde Park Circus.    46 *Chair:*
Sedan chair.

As now your own, our beings were of old,
And once inclos'd in Woman's beauteous mold;
Thence, by a soft transition, we repair
From earthly vehicles to these of air.                          50
Think not, when Woman's transient breath is fled,
That all her vanities at once are dead;
Succeeding vanities she still regards,
And though she plays no more, o'erlooks the cards.
Her joy in gilded chariots, when alive,                         55
And love of ombre, after death survive.
For when the Fair in all their pride expire,
To their first elements their souls retire:
The Sprites of fiery Termagants in flame
Mount up, and take a Salamander's name.                         60
Soft yielding Minds to water glide away,
And sip, with Nymphs, their elemental tea.
The graver Prude sinks downward to a Gnome,
In search of mischief still on earth to roam.
The light Coquettes in Sylphs aloft repair,                     65
And sport and flutter in the fields of air.
    Know farther yet; whoever fair and chaste
Rejects mankind, is by some Sylph embrac'd:
For Spirits, freed from mortal law, with ease
Assume what sexes and what shapes they please.                  70
What guards the purity of melting maids,
In courtly balls, and midnight masquerades,
Safe from the treach'rous friend, the daring spark,
The glance by day, the whisper in the dark,
When kind occasion prompts their warm desires,                  75
When music softens, and when dancing fires?
'Tis but their Sylph, the wise Celestials know,
Though Honor is the word with Men below.
    Some Nymphs there are, too conscious of their face,
For life predestined to the Gnomes' embrace.                    80
These swell their prospects and exalt their pride,
When offers are disdain'd, and love denied.
Then gay Ideas crowd the vacant brain;
While Peers and Dukes, and all their sweeping train,

55 *chariots:* carriages.  56 *ombre:* (Spanish *hombre, man*), a popular
three-handed card game of Spanish origin; the name of the challenging
player. A standard deck minus the 8's, 9's, and 10's is used. Nine cards
are dealt to each player, in lots of three each; the remaining cards
make up the stock.  59 *Termagants:* scolding women; "imaginary beings," supposedly Mohammedan deities.  60 *Salamander's:* see l. 20 and
note.  62 *tea:* rhymes with (*a*)*way*.

And Garters, Stars, and Coronets appear,                              85
And in soft sounds, Your Grace salutes their ear.
'Tis these that early taint the female soul,
Instruct the eyes of young Coquettes to roll,
Teach Infant-Cheeks a bidden blush to know,
And little Hearts to flutter at a Beau.                               90
    Oft, when the world imagine women stray,
The Sylphs through mystic mazes guide their way,
Through all the giddy circle they pursue,
And old impertinence expel by new.
What tender maid but must a victim fall                               95
To one man's treat, but for another's ball?
When Florio speaks, what virgin could withstand,
If gentle Damon did not squeeze her hand?
With varying vanities, from ev'ry part,
They shift the moving toyshop of their heart;                        100
Where wigs with wigs, with sword-knots sword-knots strive,
Beaux banish beaux, and coaches coaches drive.
This erring mortals Levity may call,
Oh blind to truth! the Sylphs contrive it all.
    Of these am I, who thy protection claim,                         105
A watchful sprite, and Ariel is my name.
Late, as I rang'd the crystal wilds of air,
In the clear mirror of thy ruling star
I saw, alas! some dread event impend,
Ere to the main this morning sun descend,                            110
But heav'n reveals not what, or how, or where:
Warn'd by the Sylph, oh pious maid, beware!
This to disclose is all thy guardian can.
Beware of all, but most beware of Man!
    He said; when Shock, who thought she slept too long,            115
Leapt up, and wak'd his mistress with his tongue.
'Twas then, Belinda! if Report say true,
Thy eyes first open'd on a billet-doux;
Wounds, Charms, and Ardors were no sooner read,
But all the vision vanish'd from thy head.                           120
    And now, unveil'd, the Toilet stands display'd,
Each silver vase in mystic order laid.
First, rob'd in white, the Nymph intent adores
With head uncover'd, the Cosmetic Pow'rs.
A heav'nly image in the glass appears,                               125

85 Garters, etc.: Insignia of orders of honor and rank; here, wearers of.
94 impertinence: trifle.   97, 98 Florio, Damon: rival suitors.   101
wigs . . . sword-knots: attire of the beaux. A sword-knot is a ribbon
attached to the hilt.   115 Shock: Belinda's lap dog.   118 billet-doux:
love letter.

To that she bends, to that her eyes she rears;
Th' inferior Priestess, at her altar's side,
Trembling begins the sacred Rites of Pride.
Unnumber'd treasures ope at once, and here
The various off'rings of the world appear;                    130
From each she nicely culls with curious toil,
And decks the Goddess with the glitt'ring spoil.
This casket India's glowing gems unlocks,
And all Arabia breathes from yonder box.
The tortoise here and elephant unite,                         135
Transform'd to combs, the speckled, and the white.
Here Files of Pins extend their shining rows,
Puffs, Powders, Patches, Bibles, Billet-doux.
Now awful Beauty put on all its arms;
The fair each moment rises in her charms,                     140
Repairs her smiles, awakens ev'ry grace,
And calls forth all the wonders of her face;
Sees by degrees a purer blush arise,
And keener lightnings quicken in her eyes.
The busy Sylphs surround their darling Care,                  145
These set the head, and those divide the hair,
Some fold the sleeve, while others plait the gown;
And Betty's prais'd for labors not her own.

### CANTO II

Not with more glories, in th' ethereal plain,
The sun first rises o'er the purpled main,
Than issuing forth, the rival of his beams
Launch'd on the bosom of the silver Thames.
Fair Nymphs, and well-dress'd Youths around her shone,    5
But ev'ry eye was fix'd on her alone.
On her white breast a sparkling cross she wore,
Which Jews might kiss, and Infidels adore.
Her lively looks a sprightly mind disclose,
Quick as her eyes, and as unfix'd as those:                  10
Favors to none, to all she smiles extends;
Oft she rejects, but never once offends.
Bright as the sun, her eyes the gazers strike,
And, like the sun, they shine on all alike.
Yet graceful ease, and sweetness void of pride,              15
Might hide her faults, if belles had faults to hide:
If to her share some female errors fall,

127 *inferior Priestess:* Belinda's maid, Betty.
CANTO II. 3 *rival:* Belinda. 4 *Launch'd . . . Thames:* Embark'd for
Hampton Court, a royal palace about 12 miles upriver from London.

Look on her face, and you'll forget 'em all.
   This Nymph, to the destruction of Mankind,
Nourish'd two Locks which graceful hung behind     20
In equal curls, and well conspir'd to deck
With shining ringlets the smooth iv'ry neck.
Love in these labyrinths his slaves detains,
And mighty hearts are held in slender chains.
With hairy springes we the birds betray,     25
Slight lines of hair surprise the finny prey,
Fair tresses man's imperial race insnare,
And Beauty draws us with a single hair.
   Th' advent'rous Baron the bright locks admir'd,
He saw, he wish'd, and to the prize aspir'd.     30
Resolv'd to win, he meditates the way,
By force to ravish, or by fraud betray;
For when success a lover's toil attends,
Few ask, if fraud or force attain'd his ends.
   For this, ere Phoebus rose, he had implor'd     35
Propitious Heav'n, and every pow'r ador'd,
But chiefly Love—to Love an altar built,
Of twelve vast French Romances, neatly gilt.
There lay three garters, half a pair of gloves;
And all the trophies of his former loves;     40
With tender billet-doux he lights the pyre,
And breathes three am'rous sighs to raise the fire.
Then prostrate falls, and begs with ardent eyes
Soon to obtain, and long possess the prize:
The Pow'rs gave ear, and granted half his pray'r,     45
The rest, the winds dispers'd in empty air.
   But now secure the painted vessel glides,
The sun-beams trembling on the floating tides,
While melting music steals upon the sky,
And soften'd sounds along the waters die.     50
Smooth flow the waves, the Zephyrs gently play,
Belinda smiled, and all the world was gay.
All but the Sylph—with careful thoughts oppress'd,
Th' impending woe sat heavy on his breast.
He summons straight his Denizens of air;     55
The lucid squadrons round the sails repair:
Soft o'er the shrouds aerial whispers breathe,
That seem'd but Zephyrs to the train beneath.

25 *springes:* snares.  26 *finny prey:* fishes.  35 *Phoebus:* the sun.  45
*granted half his pray'r:* see IV, l. 80.  55 *Denizens:* inhabitants,
Sylphs.  56 *repair:* gather.

Some to the sun their insect-wings unfold,
Waft on the breeze, or sink in clouds of gold.                    60
Transparent forms, too fine for mortal sight,
Their fluid bodies half dissolv'd in light,
Loose to the wind their airy garments flew,
Thin glitt'ring textures of the filmy dew,
Dipp'd in the richest tincture of the skies,                      65
Where light disports in ever-mingling dyes,
While ev'ry beam new transient colors flings,
Colors that change whene'er they wave their wings.
Amid the circle, on the gilded mast,
Superior by the head, was Ariel plac'd;                           70
His purple pinions op'ning to the sun,
He rais'd his azure wand, and thus begun.
    Ye Sylphs and Sylphids, to your chief give ear,
Fays, Fairies, Genii, Elves, and Demons hear!
Ye know the spheres and various tasks assign'd                    75
By laws eternal to th' aerial kind.
Some in the fields of purest ether play,
And bask and whiten in the blaze of day.
Some guide the course of wand'ring orbs on high,
Or roll the planets through the boundless sky.                    80
Some less refin'd, beneath the moon's pale light
Pursue the stars that shoot athwart the night,
Or suck the mists in grosser air below,
Or dip their pinions in the painted bow,
Or brew fierce tempests on the wintry main,                       85
Or o'er the glebe distil the kindly rain.
Others on earth o'er human race preside,
Watch all their ways, and all their actions guide:
Of these the chief the care of nations own,
And guard with arms divine the British Throne.                    90
    Our humbler province is to tend the Fair,
Not a less pleasing, though less glorious care.
To save the powder from too rude a gale,
Nor let th' imprison'd essences exhale;
To draw fresh colors from the vernal flow'rs;                     95
To steal from rainbows e'er they drop in show'rs
A brighter wash; to curl their waving hairs,
Assist their blushes, and inspire their airs;
Nay oft, in dreams, invention we bestow,
To change a flounce, or add a furbelow.                          100

64 *textures . . . dew:* spider webs. 73 *Sylphids:* young Sylphs. 79-
80 *Some . . . sky:* cf. Donne, p. 115, l. 52 and note. 86 *glebe:* field.
100 *flounce . . . furbelow:* ornamental additions to a gown.

This day, black omens threat the brightest Fair,
That e'er deserv'd a watchful Spirit's care;
Some dire disaster, or by force, or slight;
But what, or where, the fates have wrapp'd in night.
Whether the Nymph shall break Diana's law,                    105
Or some frail China jar receive a flaw;
Or stain her honor, or her new brocade;
Forget her pray'rs, or miss a masquerade;
Or lose her heart, or necklace, at a ball;
Or whether Heav'n has doomed that Shock must fall.            110
Haste, then, ye spirits! to your charge repair:
The flutt'ring fan be Zephyretta's care;
The drops to thee, Brillante, we consign;
And, Momentilla, let the watch be thine;
Do thou, Crispissa, tend her fav'rite Lock;                   115
Ariel himself shall be the guard of Shock.

To fifty chosen Sylphs, of special note,
We trust th' important charge, the Petticoat:
Oft have we known that seven-fold fence to fail,
Though stiff with hoops, and arm'd with ribs of whale;        120
Form a strong line about the silver bound,
And guard the wide circumference around.

Whatever spirit, careless of his charge,
His post neglects, or leaves the Fair at large,
Shall feel sharp vengeance soon o'ertake his sins,           125
Be stopp'd in vials, or transfix'd with pins;
Or plung'd in lakes of bitter washes lie,
Or wedg'd whole ages in a bodkin's eye:
Gums and pomatums shall his flight restrain,
While clogg'd he beats his silken wings in vain;             130
Or alum styptics with contracting pow'r
Shrink his thin essence like a rivel'd flow'r:
Or as Ixion fix'd, the wretch shall feel
The giddy motion of the whirling mill,
In fumes of burning chocolate shall glow,                    135
And tremble at the sea that froths below!
He spoke; the Spirits from the sails descend;
Some, orb in orb, around the Nymph extend,

---

105 *Diana's law:* chastity.   113 *drops:* earrings.   118 *Petticoat:* cf. the
epic poet's attentions to the arms of his hero.   127 *bitter washes:* probably, medicinal lotions.   128 *bodkin's):* large-eyed, blunt needle. Cf.
IV, l. 98; V, ll. 55, 88, 95.   129 *Gums and pomatums:* perfumed oint-
ments.   132 *rivel'd:* shriveled.   133 *Ixion:* For insulting Juno, Ixion,
according to legend, in Hades, was lashed to an ever-turning wheel.
138 *orb in orb:* deployed in concentric circles, like the planetary spheres
around the sun. Belinda rivals the sun, II, ll. 2-3.

Some thrid the mazy ringlets of her hair,
Some hang upon the pendants of her ear;                    140
With beating hearts the dire event they wait,
Anxious, and trembling for the Birth of Fate.


CANTO III

Close by those meads, for ever crown'd with flow'rs,
Where Thames with pride surveys his rising tow'rs,
There stands a structure of majestic frame,
Which from the neighb'ring Hampton takes its name.
Here Britain's statesmen oft the fall foredoom            5
Of foreign tyrants, and of Nymphs at home;
Here Thou, Great Anna! whom three realms obey,
Dost sometimes counsel take—and sometimes tea.
  Hither the heroes and the nymphs resort,
To taste awhile the pleasures of a Court;                 10
In various talk th' instructive hours they pass'd,
Who gave the ball, or paid the visit last:
One speaks the glory of the British Queen,
And one describes a charming Indian screen;
A third interprets motions, looks, and eyes;              15
At ev'ry word a reputation dies.
Snuff, or the fan, supply each pause of chat,
With singing, laughing, ogling, and all that.
  Meanwhile declining from the noon of day,
The sun obliquely shoots his burning ray;                 20
The hungry judges soon the sentence sign,
And wretches hang that jurymen may dine;
The merchant from th' Exchange returns in peace,
And the long labors of the toilet cease.
Belinda now, whom thirst of fame invites,                 25
Burns to encounter two advent'rous Knights,
At ombre singly to decide their doom;
And swells her breast with conquests yet to come.
Straight the three bands prepare in arms to join,
Each band the number of the Sacred Nine.                  30

139 *thrid:* thread.   142 *of Fate:* by Fate.
  CANTO III. 3 *structure:* Hampton Court, see II, l. 4 and note.  7
*Great Anna:* Queen Anne, 1702-1714.   8 *tea:* rhymes with (*o*)*bey*.  18
*ogling:* flirtatious glancing.   23 *Exchange:* London "Stock Exchange."
29 *arms to join:* i.e., as the epic heroes join arms in combat.  30 *Sacred
Nine:* the nine cards dealt to each player.

Soon as she spreads her hand, th' aerial guard
Descend, and sit on each important card:
First Ariel perch'd upon a Matadore,
Then each, according to the rank they bore;
For Sylphs, yet mindful of their ancient race,    35
Are, as when women, wond'rous fond of place.

  Behold, four Kings in majesty rever'd,
With hoary whiskers and a forky beard;
And four fair Queens whose hands sustain a flow'r,
Th' expressive emblem of their softer pow'r;    40
Four Knaves in garbs succinct, a trusty band,
Caps on their heads, and halberds in their hand;
And particolor'd troops, a shining train,
Draw forth to combat on the velvet plain.

  The skilful Nymph reviews her force with care;    45
*Let Spades be trumps!* she said, and trumps they were.

  Now move to war her sable Matadores,
In show like leaders of the swarthy Moors.
Spadillio first, unconquerable Lord!
Led off two captive trumps, and swept the board.    50
As many more Manillio forc'd to yield,
And marched a victor from the verdant field.
Him Basto follow'd, but his fate more hard
Gain'd but one trump and one Plebeian card.
With his broad saber next, a chief in years,    55
The hoary Majesty of Spades appears;
Puts forth one manly leg, to sight reveal'd;
The rest, his many-color'd robe conceal'd.
The rebel Knave, who dares his prince engage,
Proves the just victim of his royal rage.    60
E'en mighty Pam, that Kings and Queens o'erthrew,
And mow'd down armies in the fights of Lu,
Sad chance of war! now, destitute of aid,
Falls undistinguish'd by the victor Spade!

  Thus far both armies to Belinda yield;    65
Now to the Baron fate inclines the field.

---

33 *Matadore:* card in ombre : either of the black aces, or Manillio (l. 51),
some other card designated as a Matadore after trump is declared.    36
*place*: distinction, high place.    41 *succinct:* close-fitting ; i.e., short tunics.
42 *halberd(s)* : a combination spear and battle-ax.    44 *velvet plain:* covering of the card table.    49 *Spadillio:* Ace of Spades, highest trump.
53 *Basto:* Ace of Clubs. See note on l. 33.    54 *Plebeian:* Common.
61 *Pam:* Jack of Clubs. In *Lu* (l. 62) it is "wild," superior to any card
in the trump suit.

His warlike Amazon her host invades,
Th' imperial consort of the crown of Spades.
The Club's black Tyrant first her victim died,
Spite of his haughty mien, and barb'rous pride:　　　　70
What boots the regal circle on his head,
His giant limbs, in state unwieldy spread?
That long behind he trails his pompous robe,
And, of all monarchs, only grasps the globe?
　　The Baron now his Diamonds pours apace;　　　　75
Th' embroidered King who shows but half his face,
And his refulgent Queen, with pow'rs combin'd
Of broken troops an easy conquest find.
Clubs, Diamonds, Hearts, in wild disorder seen,
With throngs promiscuous strow the level green.　　　　80
Thus when dispers'd a routed army runs,
Of Asia's troops, and Afric's sable sons,
With like confusion different nations fly,
Of various habit, and of various dye,
The pierc'd battalions dis-united fall,　　　　85
In heaps on heaps; one fate o'erwhelms them all.
　　The Knave of Diamonds tries his wily arts,
And wins (oh shameful chance!) the Queen of Hearts.
At this, the blood the Virgin's cheek forsook,
A livid paleness spreads o'er all her look;　　　　90
She sees, and trembles at th' approaching ill,
Just in the jaws of ruin, and Codille.
And now (as oft in some distemper'd state)
On one nice *trick* depends the gen'ral fate.
An Ace of Hearts steps forth: The King unseen　　　　95
Lurk'd in her hand, and mourn'd his captive Queen:
He springs to vengeance with an eager pace,
And falls like thunder on the prostrate Ace.
The Nymph exulting fills with shouts the sky;
The walls, the woods, and long canals reply.　　　　100
Oh thoughtless mortals! ever blind to fate,
Too soon dejected, and too soon elate!
Sudden, these honors shall be snatch'd away,
And curs'd for ever this victorious day.

---

67 *Amazon:* female warrior: Queen of Spades.　74 *globe:* the "orb,"
symbol of sovereignty, which only the King of Clubs is depicted as
holding.　80 *strow:* strew.　84 *habit:* dress.　*dye:* color.　92 *Codille:*
Codille, said to be given to the Ombre (challenger) if he loses the
game.　95 *King:* of hearts, which is better than the Ace of hearts
played by the Baron.

For lo! the board with cups and spoons is crown'd,    105
The berries crackle, and the mill turns round;
On shining altars of Japan they raise
The silver lamp; the fiery spirits blaze.
From silver spouts the grateful liquors glide,
While China's earth receives the smoking tide.    110
At once they gratify their scent and taste,
And frequent cups prolong the rich repast.
Straight hover round the Fair her Airy Band;
Some, as she sipp'd, the fuming liquor fann'd,
Some o'er her lap their careful plumes display'd,    115
Trembling, and conscious of the rich brocade.
Coffee (which makes the politician wise,
And see through all things with his half-shut eyes),
Sent up in vapors to the Baron's brain
New stratagems, the radiant Lock to gain.    120
Ah cease, rash youth! desist ere 'tis too late,
Fear the just Gods, and think of Scylla's fate!
Chang'd to a bird, and sent to flit in air,
She dearly pays for Nisus' injured hair!
    But when to mischief mortals bend their will,    125
How soon they find fit instruments of ill!
Just then, Clarissa drew with tempting grace
A two-edg'd weapon from her shining case;
So Ladies in Romance assist their Knight,
Present the spear, and arm him for the fight.    130
He takes the gift with rev'rence, and extends
The little engine on his fingers' ends;
This just behind Belinda's neck he spread,
As o'er the fragrant steams she bends her head.
Swift to the Lock a thousand Sprites repair,    135
A thousand wings, by turns, blow back the hair;
And thrice they twitch'd the diamond in her ear;
Thrice she looked back, and thrice the foe drew near.
Just in that instant, anxious Ariel sought
The close recesses of the Virgin's thought;    140
As on the nosegay in her breast reclin'd,
He watched th' Ideas rising in her mind,

---

106 *berries:* coffee beans: they crackle when roasted.   *mill:* coffee grinder.   107 *shining . . . Japan:* lacquered tables.   110 *China's earth:* china teapot.   122-24 *Scylla's fate . . . hair:* Scylla was changed into a bird and made the continual prey of the sea eagle as punishment for her treachery toward her father (King Nisus of Megara), whose purple lock—upon which depended his life—she plucked out and delivered to his enemy, Minos (II, King of Crete).

Sudden he view'd, in spite of all her art,
An earthly lover lurking at her heart.
Amaz'd, confus'd, he found his pow'r expir'd,      145
Resign'd to fate, and with a sigh retir'd.
　The Peer now spreads the glitt'ring Forfex wide,
T' enclose the Lock; now joins it, to divide.
E'en then, before the fatal engine clos'd,
A wretched Sylph too fondly interpos'd;      150
Fate urged the shears, and cut the Sylph in twain
(But airy substance soon unites again),
The meeting points the sacred hair dissever
From the fair head, for ever, and for ever!
　Then flash'd the living lightning from her eyes,      155
And screams of horror rend th' affrighted skies.
Not louder shrieks to pitying Heav'n are cast,
When husbands, or when lap-dogs breathe their last;
Or when rich China vessels fall'n from high,
In glitt'ring dust and painted fragments lie!      160
　Let wreaths of triumph now my temples twine
(The victor cried) the glorious Prize is mine!
While fish in streams, or birds delight in air,
Or in a coach and six the British Fair,
As long as *Atalantis* shall be read,      165
Or the small pillow grace a Lady's bed,
While visits shall be paid on solemn days,
When num'rous wax-lights in bright order blaze,
While nymphs take treats, or assignations give,
So long my honor, name, and praise shall live!      170
What Time would spare, from Steel receives its date,
And monuments, like men, submit to Fate!
Steel could the labor of the Gods destroy,
And strike to dust th' imperial tow'rs of Troy;
Steel could the works of mortal Pride confound,      175
And hew triumphal arches to the ground.
What wonder then, fair Nymph! thy hairs should feel,
The conqu'ring force of unresisted Steel?

---

147 *Forfex:* Scissors.　152 (*But airy . . . again*): cf. "The griding sword with discontinuous wound / Pass'd through him [Satan], but th' Eternal Substance clos'd / Not long divisible"—*Paradise Lost,* VI, 329-31.　165 *Atalantis: Secret Memoirs and Manners of several Persons of Quality of Both Sexes,* by [Mary Manley], London, 1709, which under thin allegorical disguise records the scandalous goings-on in the contemporary world of fashion.　168 *wax-lights:* carried by the lady's attendants on her visits.　171 *What . . . date:* What time spares, steel destroys.

## CANTO IV

But anxious cares the pensive Nymph oppress'd,
And secret passions labor'd in her breast.
Not youthful kings in battle seiz'd alive,
Not scornful virgins who their charms survive,
Not ardent lovers robb'd of all their bliss,                    5
Not ancient ladies when refus'd a kiss,
Not tyrants fierce that unrepenting die,
Not Cynthia when her manteau's pinn'd awry,
E'er felt such rage, resentment, and despair,
As Thou, sad Virgin! for thy ravish'd Hair.                     10

For, that sad moment, when the Sylphs withdrew
And Ariel weeping from Belinda flew,
Umbriel, a dusky, melancholy sprite,
As ever sullied the fair face of light,
Down to the central earth, his proper scene,                    15
Repaired to search the gloomy Cave of Spleen.

Swift on his sooty pinions flits the Gnome,
And in a vapor reached the dismal dome.
No cheerful breeze this sullen region knows,
The dreaded East is all the wind that blows.                    20
Here, in a grotto, shelter'd close from air,
And screen'd in shades from day's detested glare,
She sighs for ever on her pensive bed,
Pain at her side, and Megrim at her head.

Two handmaids wait the throne: alike in place,                  25
But diff'ring far in figure and in face.
Here stood Ill-nature like an ancient maid,
Her wrinkled form in black and white array'd;
With store of pray'rs, for mornings, nights, and noons,
Her hand is fill'd; her bosom with lampoons.                    30

There Affectation, with a sickly mien,
Shows in her cheek the roses of eighteen,
Practic'd to lisp, and hang the head aside,
Faints into airs, and languishes with pride;

CANTO IV. 8 *Cynthia:* Diana, goddess of chastity See II, 1. 105.
*manteau:* upper garment.  13 ff. A journey to the underworld is common in the epic.  16 *Spleen:* Low spirits; *vapors* (ll. 18, 59), a sickly
condition thought to be induced by exposure to a misty climate.  17
*Gnome:* see I, 1. 20 and note.  18 *vapor(s):* Pope plays with the meaning of the word. See 1. 16 and note.  20 *dreaded East* [wind]: supposed to encourage spleen.  24 *Megrim:* migraine, melancholy.  30
*lampoons:* malicious personal satires.

On the rich quilt sinks with becoming woe,                    35
Wrapp'd in a gown, for sickness, and for show.
The Fair-ones feel such maladies as these,
When each new night-dress gives a new disease.
   A constant Vapor o'er the palace flies;
Strange Phantoms rising as the mists arise;                   40
Dreadful, as hermit's dreams in haunted shades,
Or bright, as visions of expiring maids.
Now glaring fiends, and snakes on rolling spires,
Pale specters, gaping tombs, and purple fires:
Now lakes of liquid gold, Elysian scenes,                     45
And crystal domes, and angels in machines.
   Unnumber'd throngs on every side are seen,
Of bodies chang'd to various forms by Spleen.
Here living Tea-pots stand, one arm held out,
One bent; the handle this, and that the spout:                50
A Pipkin there, like Homer's Tripod walks;
Here sighs a Jar, and there a Goose-pie talks;
Men prove with child, as pow'rful Fancy works,
And Maids turn'd Bottles, call aloud for corks.
Safe pass'd the Gnome through this fantastic band,            55
A branch of healing spleenwort in his hand.
Then thus addressed the Pow'r: Hail, wayward Queen!
Who rule the sex to fifty from fifteen,
Parent of vapors and of female wit,
Who give th' hysteric, or poetic fit,                         60
On various tempers act by various ways,
Make some take physic, others scribble plays;
Who cause the proud their visits to delay,
And send the godly in a pet, to pray.
A Nymph there is, that all thy pow'r disdains,                65
And thousands more in equal mirth maintains.
But oh! if e'er thy Gnome could spoil a grace,
Or raise a pimple on a beauteous face,
Like citron-waters matrons' cheeks inflame,
Or change complexions at a losing game;                       70
If e'er with airy horns I planted heads,
Or rumpled petticoats, or tumbled beds,

43-46 *fiends . . . machines:* hallucinations symptomatic of spleen.   45-
46 allude satirically to the scenic effects and stage devices of opera and
pantomime.   51 *Pipkin:* small earthen vessel.   *Homer's Tripod:* see
*Iliad,* XVIII, "of Vulcan's walking tripods."   52 *a Goose-pie talks:*
". . . real fact, a Lady of distinction imagin'd herself in this condition."
—Pope.   64 *pet:* ill humor.   69 *citron-waters:* brandy flavored with
citron or lemon peel.

Or caused suspicion when no soul was rude,
Or discomposed the head-dress of a Prude,
Or e'er to costive lap-dog gave disease,     75
Which not the tears of brightest eyes could ease:
Hear me, and touch Belinda with chagrin;
That single act gives half the world the spleen.

   The Goddess with a discontented air
Seems to reject him, though she grants his pray'r.     80
A wondrous Bag with both her hands she binds,
Like that where once Ulysses held the winds;
There she collects the force of female lungs,
Sighs, sobs, and passions, and the war of tongues.
A Vial next she fills with fainting fears,     85
Soft sorrows, melting griefs, and flowing tears.
The Gnome rejoicing bears her gifts away,
Spreads his black wings, and slowly mounts to day.

   Sunk in Thalestris' arms the Nymph he found,
Her eyes dejected and her hair unbound.     90
Full o'er their heads the swelling Bag he rent,
And all the Furies issu'd at the vent.
Belinda burns with more than mortal ire,
And fierce Thalestris fans the rising fire.
O wretched maid! she spread her hands, and cried     95
(While Hampton's echoes, Wretched maid! replied),
Was it for this you took such constant care
The bodkin, comb, and essence to prepare?
For this your locks in paper durance bound,
For this with tort'ring irons wreath'd around?     100
For this with fillets strain'd your tender head,
And bravely bore the double loads of lead?
Gods! shall the ravisher display your hair,
While the Fops envy, and the Ladies stare!
Honor forbid! at whose unrival'd shrine     105
Ease, pleasure, virtue, all, our sex resign.
Methinks already I your tears survey,
Already hear the horrid things they say,
Already see you a degraded toast,
And all your honor in a whisper lost!     110
How shall I, then, your helpless fame defend?
'Twill then be infamy to seem your friend!

75 *costive:* constipated.   82 *Ulysses . . . winds:* see *Odyssey,* X, 19 ff.
85 *Vial:* Bottle. See l. 142.   89 *Thalestris':* a companion's.   99 *In
. . . durance:* i.e., in curl papers, said to have been fastened with strips
of lead (cf. *irons,* l. 100; l. 102).   101 *fillets:* bands.   109 *toast:* person
whose health is drunk.

And shall this prize, th' inestimable prize,
Expos'd through crystal to the gazing eyes,
And heighten'd by the diamond's circling rays,　　　　115
On that rapacious hand for ever blaze?
Sooner shall grass in Hyde-Park Circus grow,
And Wits take lodgings in the sound of Bow;
Sooner let earth, air, sea, to Chaos fall,
Men, monkeys, lap-dogs, parrots, perish all!　　　　120
　　She said; then raging to Sir Plume repairs,
And bids her Beau demand the precious hairs:
(Sir Plume of amber snuff-box justly vain,
And the nice conduct of a clouded cane)
With earnest eyes, and round unthinking face,　　　　125
He first the snuff-box open'd, then the case,
And thus broke out—My Lord, why, what the devil?
Z——ds! damn the lock! 'fore Gad, you must be civil!
Plague on 't! 'tis past a jest—nay prithee, Pox!
Give her the hair—he spoke, and rapped his box.　　　　130
　　It grieves me much (replied the Peer again)
Who speaks so well should ever speak in vain.
But by this Lock, this sacred Lock I swear
(Which never more shall join its parted hair;
Which never more its honors shall renew,　　　　135
Clipp'd from the lovely head where late it grew),
That while my nostrils draw the vital air,
This hand, which won it, shall for ever wear.
He spoke, and speaking, in proud triumph spread
The long-contended honors of her head.　　　　140
　　But Umbriel, hateful Gnome! forbears not so;
He breaks the vial whence the sorrows flow.
Then see! the Nymph in beauteous grief appears,
Her eyes half-languishing, half-drown'd in tears;
On her heav'd bosom hung her drooping head,　　　　145
Which, with a sigh, she raised; and thus she said:
　　Forever curs'd be this detested day,
Which snatch'd my best, my fav'rite curl away!
Happy! ah ten times happy, had I been,
If Hampton Court these eyes had never seen!　　　　150
Yet am not I the first mistaken maid,
By love of Courts to num'rous ills betray'd.

114 *crystal:* glass(?).　117 *Hyde-Park Circus:* see I, l. 44 and note.
118 *sound of Bow:* bell of St. Mary le Bow (Bowchurch), the commercial part of the City, distinct from the "polite" part.　124 *conduct:* manner of carrying.　138 *wear:* see l. 116.

Oh had I rather un-admired remain'd
In some lone isle, or distant Northern land;
Where the gilt Chariot never marks the way,                    155
Where none learn Ombre, none e'er taste bohea!
There kept my charms conceal'd from mortal eye,
Like roses that in deserts bloom and die.
What mov'd my mind with youthful Lords to roam?
O had I stayed, and said my pray'rs at home!                   160
'Twas this, the morning Omens seem'd to tell,
Thrice from my trembling hand the patch-box fell;
The tott'ring China shook without a wind,
Nay, Poll sat mute, and Shock was most unkind!
A Sylph too warned me of the threats of Fate,                  165
In mystic visions, now believed too late!
See the poor remnants of these slighted hairs!
My hands shall rend what ev'n thy rapine spares:
These, in two sable ringlets taught to break,
Once gave new beauties to the snowy neck;                      170
The sister-lock now sits uncouth, alone,
And in its fellow's fate foresees its own;
Uncurl'd it hangs, the fatal shears demands,
And tempts once more thy sacrilegious hands.
O hadst thou, Cruel! been content to seize                     175
Hairs less in sight, or any hairs but these!


CANTO V

She said: the pitying audience melt in tears.
But Fate and Jove had stopp'd the Baron's ears.
In vain Thalestris with reproach assails,
For who can move when fair Belinda fails?
Not half so fix'd the Trojan could remain,                       5
While Anna begg'd and Dido raged in vain.
Then grave Clarissa graceful waved her fan;
Silence ensu'd, and thus the Nymph began.
    Say, why are Beauties prais'd and honor'd most,
The wise man's passion, and the vain man's toast?              10
Why deck'd with all that land and sea afford,
Why Angels call'd, and Angel-like ador'd?

156 *bohea*: black tea; rhymes with *way*.   165 *warned me*: see I, ll.
109-12.   169 *break*: part.
    CANTO V. 5-6 *Not . . . vain*: Aeneas left Carthage deaf to Anna's
pleas for him to remain, made on behalf of her sister Dido.

Why round our coaches crowd the white-glov'd Beaus,
Why bows the side-box from its inmost rows?
How vain are all these glories, all our pains,                    15
Unless good Sense preserve what Beauty gains;
That men may say, when we the front-box grace,
Behold the first in virtue, as in face!
Oh! if to dance all night, and dress all day,
Charm'd the small-pox, or chas'd old age away;                   20
Who would not scorn what housewife's cares produce,
Or who would learn one earthly thing of use?
To patch, nay ogle, might become a Saint,
Nor could it sure be such a sin to paint.
But since, alas! frail Beauty must decay,                         25
Curl'd or uncurl'd, since locks will turn to gray,
Since painted, or not painted, all shall fade,
And she who scorns a man, must die a maid;
What then remains but well our pow'r to use,
And keep good-humor still whate'er we lose?                       30
And trust me, Dear! good-humor can prevail,
When airs, and flights, and screams, and scolding fail.
Beauties in vain their pretty eyes may roll;
Charms strike the sight, but merit wins the soul.
    So spoke the Dame, but no applause ensu'd;                    35
Belinda frowned, Thalestris call'd her Prude.
To arms, to arms! the fierce Virago cries,
And swift as lightning to the combat flies.
All side in parties, and begin th' attack;
Fans clap, silks rustle, and tough whalebones crack;             40
Heroes' and Heroines' shouts confus'dly rise,
And bass, and treble voices strike the skies.
No common weapons in their hands are found,
Like Gods they fight, nor dread a mortal wound.
    So when bold Homer makes the Gods engage,                     45
And heav'nly breasts with human passions rage;
'Gainst Pallas, Mars; Latona, Hermes arms;
And all Olympus rings with loud alarms:
Jove's thunder roars, Heav'n trembles all around,
Blue Neptune storms, the bellowing Deeps resound;                50
Earth shakes her nodding tow'rs, the ground gives way,
And the pale ghosts start at the flash of day!
    Triumphant Umbriel on a sconce's height
Clapp'd his glad wings, and sat to view the fight:

14, 17 *side-box, front-box:* theater boxes.  23 *patch:* wear decorative
patches on the face.  37 *Virago:* an Amazon, female warrior. Cf.
*Termagants,* I, l. 59.  44 *nor . . . wound:* see III, l. 152 and note.  45
*So when . . . engage:* as in the *Iliad,* XX.

Propp'd on the bodkin spears, the Sprites survey          55
The growing combat, or assist the fray.
    While through the press enrag'd Thalestris flies,
And scatters deaths around from both her eyes,
A Beau and Witling perished in the throng,
One died in metaphor, and one in song.          60
*O cruel Nymph! a living death I bear,*
Cried Dapperwit, and sunk beside his chair.
A mournful glance Sir Fopling upwards cast,
*Those eyes are made so killing*—was his last.
Thus on Mæander's flow'ry margin lies          65
Th' expiring swan, and as he sings he dies.
    When bold Sir Plume had drawn Clarissa down,
Chloe stepp'd in, and kill'd him with a frown;
She smil'd to see the doughty hero slain,
But at her smile, the Beau revived again.          70
    Now Jove suspends his golden scales in air,
Weighs the Men's wits against the Lady's Hair;
The doubtful beam long nods from side to side;
At length the Wits mount up, the Hairs subside.
    See fierce Belinda on the Baron flies,          75
With more than usual lightning in her eyes;
Nor fear'd the Chief th' unequal fight to try,
Who sought no more than on his foe to die.
But this bold Lord with manly strength indu'd,
She with one finger and a thumb subdu'd:          80
Just where the Breath of Life his nostrils drew,
A charge of snuff the wily virgin threw;
The Gnomes direct, to ev'ry atom just,
The pungent grains of titillating dust.
Sudden, with starting tears each eye o'erflows,          85
And the high dome re-echoes to his nose.
Now meet thy fate, incens'd Belinda cried,
And drew a deadly bodkin from her side.
(The same, his ancient personage to deck,
Her great great grandsire wore about his neck          90
In three seal-rings; which after, melted down,

---

62 *Dapperwit:* a fop in *Love in a Wood,* a comedy by William Wycherley (c. 1640-1715). 63 *Sir Fopling* (Flutter): principal character in *The Man of Mode,* a comedy by George Etherege (1635?-1691). 64 *Those . . . killing:* From a song in the popular opera *Camilla* by Buononcini. 65-66 *Thus . . . dies:* as the swan in Ovid's *Heroides* (VII) dies while singing the lament of "Dido to Aeneas" from the shallows of the river Menander. 71 *Now . . . scales:* symbol of Justice common in the epic. 91 *seal-rings:* rings used as seals, to signify the authenticity of anything upon which they were impressed.

Form'd a vast buckle for his widow's gown:
Her infant grandame's whistle next it grew,
The bells she jingled, and the whistle blew;
Then in a bodkin grac'd her mother's hairs,                    95
Which long she wore, and now Belinda wears).
  Boast not my fall (he cried) insulting foe!
Thou by some other shalt be laid as low.
Nor think, to die dejects my lofty mind;
All that I dread is leaving you behind!                        100
Rather than so, ah let me still survive,
And burn in Cupid's flames—but burn alive.
  *Restore the Lock!* she cries; and all around
*Restore the Lock!* the vaulted roofs rebound.
Not fierce Othello in so loud a strain                         105
Roar'd for the handkerchief that caus'd his pain.
But see how oft ambitious aims are cross'd,
And chiefs contend 'till all the prize is lost!
The Lock, obtained with guilt, and kept with pain,
In ev'ry place is sought, but sought in vain:                  110
With such a prize no mortal must be bless'd,
So Heav'n decrees! with Heav'n who can contest?
  Some thought it mounted to the lunar sphere,
Since all things lost on earth are treasur'd there.
There Heroes' wits are kept in pond'rous vases,                115
And beaus' in snuff-boxes and tweezer-cases.
There broken vows, and death-bed alms are found,
And lovers' hearts with ends of riband bound,
The courtier's promises, and sick man's pray'rs,
The smiles of harlots, and the tears of heirs,                 120
Cages for gnats, and chains to yoke a flea,
Dried butterflies, and tomes of casuistry.
  But trust the Muse—she saw it upward rise,
Though mark'd by none but quick, poetic eyes:
(So Rome's great founder to the Heav'ns withdrew,              125
To Proculus alone confess'd in view).

105-06 *Othello . . . handkerchief:* see *Othello,* IV, i, esp. ll. 38-46. Cf.
"So much ado, so much stress, so much passion, etc., about an handkerchief."—Thomas Rymer, *Short View of Tragedy,* 1693.   113 *lunar
sphere:* moon.   118 *riband:* ribbon.   122 *tomes of casuistry:* books
dealing with special problems of conscience, usually wordy, often evasive
and sophistical.   125-26 (*So Rome's . . . view*): According to Livy
(Book XVI), Romulus was "caught up on high" in the "blast" of a
thunderstorm and translated directly to heaven. To restore some order
and purpose to the citizens after this incident, Julius Proculus reported
that he had received a message directly from Romulus, that "Rome shall
be the capital of the world."

A sudden star, it shot through liquid air,
And drew behind a radiant trail of hair.
Not Berenice's Locks first rose so bright,
The Heav'ns bespangling with dishevel'd light.                    130
The Sylphs behold it kindling as it flies,
The pleas'd pursue its progress through the skies.
   This the beau-monde shall from the Mall survey,
And hail with music its propitious ray.
This the blest lover shall for Venus take,                         135
And send up vows from Rosamonda's Lake.
This Partridge soon shall view in cloudless skies,
When next he looks through Galileo's eyes;
And hence th' egregious wizard shall foredoom
The fate of Louis, and the fall of Rome.                          140
   Then cease, bright Nymph! to mourn thy ravish'd hair,
Which adds new glory to the shining sphere!
Not all the tresses that fair head can boast,
Shall draw such envy as the Lock you lost.
For, after all the murders of your eye,                           145
When, after millions slain, yourself shall die;
When those fair suns shall set, as set they must,
And all those tresses shall be laid in dust;
This Lock, the Muse shall consecrate to Fame,
And 'midst the stars inscribe Belinda's name.                     150


*from* OF TASTE

## [*Timon's Villa*]

   At Timon's Villa let us pass a day,
Where all cry out, "What sums are thrown away!"
So proud, so grand, of that stupendous air,
Soft and agreeable come never there.

129 *Berenice's Locks:* Berenice, an Egyptian Princess (3rd cent. B.C.),
according to legend, sacrificed a lock to the Gods as an offering for her
husband's safe return from war. The lock was transmitted to the heavens, to become a constellation.    133 *beau-monde:* world of fashion.
*Mall:* walk in St. James's Park.    136 *Rosamonda's Lake:* also in St.
James's Park.    137 *Partridge:* a London astrologer, well-known from
Swift's treatment of him in the Bickerstaff papers.    138 *Galileo's eyes:*
the telescope.    140 *fate of Louis:* allusion to Partridge's predictions of
the downfall of the King of France.

   TIMON'S VILLA. *Of Taste* (etc.) : In the half-title only : *An Epistle
To the Earl of Burlington. Occasion'd by his Publishing Palladio's Designs of the Baths, Arches, Theatres, &c. of Ancient Rome* (London,
1731).

Greatness, with Timon, dwells in such a draught          5
As brings all Brobdignag before your thought:
To compass this, his building is a Town,
His pond an ocean, his parterre a Down:
Who but must laugh, the master when he sees?
A puny insect, shiv'ring at a breeze!                    10
Lo! what huge Heaps of Littleness around!
The whole, a labored quarry above ground!
Two Cupids squirt before: a lake behind
Improves the keenness of the northern wind.
His gardens next your admiration call,                   15
On ev'ry side you look, behold the wall!
No pleasing intricacies intervene,
No artful wildness to perplex the scene;
Grove nods at grove, each alley has a brother,
And half the platform just reflects the other.          20
The suff'ring eye inverted Nature sees,
Trees cut to statues, statues thick as trees,
Where here a fountain, never to be played,
And there a summer-house, that knows no shade.
Here Amphitrite sails through myrtle bow'rs;            25
There Gladiators fight, or die, in flow'rs;
Unwater'd see the drooping sea-horse mourn,
And swallows roost in Nilus' dusty urn.

My Lord advances with majestic mien,
Smit with the mighty pleasure, to be seen:              30
But soft—by regular approach—not yet—
First through the length of yon hot terrace sweat,
And when up ten steep slopes you've dragg'd your thighs,
Just at his study door he'll bless your eyes.

His study! with what authors is it stor'd?              35
In books, not authors, curious is my Lord;
To all their dated backs he turns you round,

5 *draught:* a quantity.  6 *Brobdi[n]gnag:* Land of the giants, *Gulliver's Travels,* Book II.  7 *compass:* grasp with the mind.  8 *parterre a Down:* the level space in his garden is a great open expanse.  17-18 *No . . . scene:* None of the affected "wildness" which was fashionable in gardens.  19 *alley:* tree- or shrub-bordered walk.  20 *platform:* ground-plan(?).  22 *Trees . . . statues:* trees shaped to resemble human or animal forms.  25 *Amphitrite:* goddess of the sea, wife of Poseidon.  26 *Gladiators:* "The two famous statues of the Gladiator *pugnans* and *moriens.*"—Pope.  28 *Nilus:* God of the Nile.  29 *My . . . mien:* from 1751 edn.  34 *bless:* favor.

These Aldus printed, those Du Suëil has bound.
Lo some are vellum, and the rest as good
For all his Lordship knows, but they are wood.                    40
For Locke or Milton 'tis in vain to look,
These shelves admit not any modern book.

And now the chapel's silver bell you hear,
That summons you to all the Pride of Pray'r:
Light quirks of music, broken and uneven,                         45
Make the soul dance upon a jig to Heaven.
On painted ceilings you devoutly stare,
Where sprawls the Saints of Verrio, or Laguerre,
On gilded clouds in fair expansion lie,
And bring all Paradise before your eye.                           50
To rest, the cushion, and soft Dean invite,
Who never mentions Hell to ears polite.

But hark! the chiming clocks to dinner call;
A hundred footsteps scrape the marble hall:
The rich buffet well color'd Serpents grace,                      55
And gaping Tritons spew to wash your face.
Is this a dinner? this a genial room?
No, 'tis a temple, and a hecatomb;
A solemn sacrifice, perform'd in state,
You drink by measure, and to minutes eat.                         60
So quick retires each flying course, you'd swear
Sancho's dread Doctor and his wand were there:
Between each Act the trembling salvers ring,
From soup to sweet-wine, and God bless the King.
In plenty starving, tantaliz'd in state,                          65
And complaisantly help'd to all I hate,
Treated, caress'd, and tired, I take my leave,
Sick of his civil pride, from morn to eve;
I curse such lavish cost, and little skill,
And swear no day was ever pass'd so ill.                          70
[ll. 99-168]

38 *Aldus* (Minutius): sixteenth-century Italian printer.  (Abbe) *Du
Suëil* (Dusuil); a French bookbinder.  41 (John) *Locke* (1673-1746):
the English philosopher.  48 (Antonio) *Verrio*, (Louis) *Laguerre:* 17th-
century painters; the first helped decorate Windsor, Hampton Court;
the second, Blenheim Castle.  56 *Tritons:* sea gods.  58 *hecatomb:* literally, a sacrifice of a hundred oxen or cattle at once.  62 *Sancho's . . .
wand:* see *Don Quixote,* Ch. XLVII.  63 *salvers:* trays.

*from* OF THE USE OF RICHES

[*Sir Balaam*]

But you are tir'd—I'll tell a tale.—"Agreed."
  Where London's column, pointing at the skies
Like a tall bully, lifts the head, and lies;
There dwelt a citizen of sober fame,
A plain good man, and Balaam was his name;     5
Religious, punctual, frugal, and so forth;
His word would pass for more than he was worth.
One solid dish his week-day meal affords,
And added pudding solemniz'd the Lord's:
Constant at Church, and Change; his gains were sure,  10
His givings rare, save farthings to the poor.
  The Dev'l was piqu'd such saintship to behold,
And longed to tempt him like good Job of old:
But Satan now is wiser than of yore,
And tempts by making rich, not making poor.    15
  Rous'd by the Prince of Air, the whirlwinds sweep
The surge, and plunge his father in the deep;
Then full against his Cornish lands they roar,
And two rich shipwrecks bless the lucky shore.
  Sir Balaam now, he lives like other folks,    20
He takes his chirping pint, and cracks his jokes:
"Live like yourself," was soon my Lady's word;
And lo! two puddings smoked upon the board.
  Asleep and naked as an Indian lay,
An honest factor stole a gem away:    25
He pledged it to the knight; the knight had wit,
So kept the diamond, and the rogue was bit.
Some scruple rose, but thus he eas'd his thought,
"I'll now give six-pence where I gave a groat;
Where once I went to church, I'll now go twice—  30

SIR BALAAM. *Of . . . Riches: An Epistle To the Right Honorable Allen Lord Bathurst* (London, 1732).
*2-3 column . . . lies:* a monument to the Fire of London, 1666, bearing an inscription (according to Pope, a Roman Catholic) to the effect that the city was burned by the Papists.  *10 Change:* Stock Exchange.  *16-19 Rous'd . . . shore:* Satan, as the Prince of Air (Eph. 2:2) stirs up a "whirlwind" which drowns Balaam's father and wrecks two ships against his lands. Balaam receives his inheritance, appropriates the cargoes—and is *made rich.*  *21 chirping:* cheering.  *24-25 Asleep . . . away:* supposed to allude to the acquisition of the "Pitt Diamond" by Thomas Pitt, Governor of Madras, *c.* 1700 (the "honest factor").  *25 factor:* agent.  *26 pledged:* pawned.  *knight:* Sir Balaam.  *27 bit:* double-crossed.  *29 groat:* coin worth fourpence.

And am so clear too of all other vice."
   The Tempter saw his time; the work he plied;
Stocks and subscriptions pour on ev'ry side,
'Till all the Dæmon makes his full descent
In one abundant show'r of *Cent per Cent*,         35
Sinks deep within him, and possesses whole,
Then dubs *Director*, and secures his soul.
   Behold Sir Balaam, now a man of spirit,
Ascribes his gettings to his parts and merit,
What late he call'd a Blessing, now was Wit,     40
And God's good Providence, a lucky Hit.
Things change their titles, as our manners turn:
His compting-house employed the Sunday-morn:
Seldom at Church ('twas such a busy life),
But duly sent his family and wife.         45
There (so the Dev'l ordain'd) one Christmas-tide,
My good old Lady catch'd a cold, and died.
   A Nymph of Quality admires our knight;
He marries, bows at Court, and grows polite:
Leaves the dull Cits, and joins (to please the fair)   50
The well-bred cuckolds in St. James's air:
First, for his son a gay commission buys,
Who drinks, whores, fights, and in a duel dies:
His daughter flaunts a viscount's tawdry wife;
She bears a coronet and p—x for life.      55
In Britain's Senate he a seat obtains,
And one more Pensioner St. Stephen gains.
My Lady falls to play; so bad her chance,
He must repair it; takes a bribe from France;
The House impeach him; Co[nings]by harangues;   60
The Court forsakes him, and Sir Balaam hangs:
Wife, son, and daughter, Satan! are thy own,
His wealth, yet dearer, forfeit to the Crown:
The Devil and the King divide the prize,
And sad Sir Balaam curses God and dies.    65

                [ll. 338-402]

32 *Tempter:* Satan.   33 *subscriptions:* shares of stock.   35 *Cent:* abbr. *centum,* one hundred.   37 *dubs:* names him.   40 *Wit:* cleverness. Cf. l. 26.   43 *compting* (counting) *-house:* business office.   50 *Cits:* Citizens: "pert low townsmen"—Dr. Johnson.   51 *St. James's air:* "the polite end of town."   54 *flaunts . . . wife:* scorns marrying only a viscount. 55 *coronet:* crown which she wears as a peeress, evidently of the rank of countess.   56 *Senate:* Parliament.   57 *Pensioner . . . gains:* The House of Commons (which held its sessions in St. Stephen's Chapel, Westminster) "gains" another member ready to share in the spoils of office (politely, accept a pension).   58 *play:* gambling.   60 *Co[nings]by:* Thomas, Earl Coningsby, a strong Whig. Pope elsewhere satirizes him

*from* AN ESSAY ON MAN

EPISTLE II

Know then thyself, presume not God to scan;
The proper study of Mankind is Man.
Plac'd on this isthmus of a middle state,
A Being darkly wise, and rudely great:
With too much knowledge for the Skeptic side,        5
With too much weakness for the Stoic's pride,
He hangs between; in doubt to act, or rest;
In doubt to deem himself a God, or Beast;
In doubt his Mind or Body to prefer;
Born but to die, and reas'ning but to err;        10
Alike in ignorance, his reason such,
Whether he thinks too little, or too much:
Chaos of Thought and Passion, all confus'd;
Still by himself abus'd, or disabus'd;
Created half to rise, and half to fall;        15
Great lord of all things, yet a prey to all;
Sole judge of Truth, in endless Error hurl'd:
The glory, jest, and riddle of the world!
  Go, wond'rous creature! mount where Science guides,
Go, measure earth, weigh air, and state the tides;        20
Instruct the planets in what orbs to run,
Correct old Time, and regulate the Sun.

KNOW THEN. *An Essay, etc.:* To H. St. John, Lord Bolingbroke, in
four "epistles," which were published separately, between February 20,
1733, and January 24, 1734; and, together, in 1734.
  The four several parts of the poem comprehend Man's "nature" and
"state" with respect to (*a*) the universe, (*b*) himself, (*c*) society, and
(*d*) happiness. Perhaps the controlling idea of the poem is implied in
the familiar statement closing the first Epistle: "Whatever is, is right."
Superficially, this has been taken as a piece of unwarranted optimism,
but it is rather a summary phrasing of the poet's insight into the
totality of man's inescapable relationships—with himself, his fellow
men, and with the world of God and Nature—which constitute a divinely ordered system. Endowed with reason, if he will use it for knowing himself, he can understand his duties and his destiny, and, as a
consequence, achieve the virtue which will give him such happiness as
a creature of his "middle state" deserves.
  5 *Skeptic:* who distrusts the possibility of knowing anything for certain.  6 *Stoic('s)*: who is disciplined by reason to scorn human frailty.
19 *Science:* Knowledge gained from inquiry into nature, observation,
and experimentation.  22 *Correct old Time:* Probable allusion to Sir
Isaac Newton's proposals for chronological reform.

Go, soar with Plato to th' empyreal sphere,
To the first good, first perfect, and first fair;
Or tread the mazy round his follow'rs trod,                    25
And quitting sense call imitating God;
As Eastern priests in giddy circles run,
And turn their heads to imitate the Sun.
Go, teach Eternal Wisdom how to rule—
Then drop into thyself, and be a fool!                         30

[ll. 1-30]

*from* EPISTLE TO DR. ARBUTHNOT

## [*Atticus*]

Peace to all such! but were there One whose fires
True Genius kindles, and fair Fame inspires,
Blest with each talent and each art to please,
And born to write, converse, and live with ease:
Should such a man, too fond to rule alone,                     5
Bear, like the Turk, no brother near the throne,
View him with scornful, yet with jealous eyes,
And hate for Arts that caus'd himself to rise;
Damn with faint praise, assent with civil leer,
And without sneering, teach the rest to sneer;                 10
Willing to wound, and yet afraid to strike,
Just hint a fault, and hesitate dislike;
Alike reserv'd to blame, or to commend,
A tim'rous foe, and a suspicious friend,
Dreading ev'n fools, by flatterers besieg'd,                   15
And so obliging that he ne'er oblig'd;

23-24 *Go . . . fair:* Like Plato, contemplate the absolute and heavenly Goodness, Truth, and Beauty. 25 *mazy round:* fantastic dance of speculation. 26 *quitting sense:* either, abandoning common sense for fantasies; or abandoning sense (as an instrument of knowing) for useless abstraction. 27 *As . . . run:* As worshippers (not priests) imitate the ecstatic dance of the Gopis around the divine Krishna. The Gopis are Krishna's legendary female admirers.

ATTICUS. *Dr. (John) Arbuthnot:* the intimate of Pope, Gay, and Swift, was a mathematician, classical scholar, and physician, celebrated by his friends as a gentleman of great wit and humanity. *Atticus:* the name of a Roman scholar (1st cent. B.C.) and friend of Cicero, applied to Joseph Addison (1672-1719), the essayist and poet with whom Pope was once friendly. The "portrait" was written several years before Addison's death and before the *Epistle* as it now stands was completed.

1 *all such:* piddling authors, who were "raging" against Pope.

Like Cato, give his little Senate laws,
And sit attentive to his own applause;
While Wits and Templars ev'ry sentence raise,
And wonder with a foolish face of praise.                        20
Who but must laugh, if such a man there be?
Who would not weep, if Atticus were he!

[ll. 193-214]


## [*Sporus*]

Let Sporus tremble—"What? that Thing of silk,
Sporus, that mere white curd of ass's milk?
Satire, or sense alas! can Sporus feel?
Who breaks a butterfly upon a wheel?"
Yet let me flap this Bug with gilded wings,                      5
This painted Child of Dirt that stinks and stings;
Whose buzz the Witty and the Fair annoys,
Yet wit ne'er tastes, and beauty ne'er enjoys,
So well-bred spaniels civilly delight
In mumbling of the game they dare not bite.                      10
Eternal smiles his emptiness betray,
As shallow streams run dimpling all the way.
Whether in florid impotence he speaks,
And, as the prompter breathes, the puppet squeaks;
Or at the ear of Eve, familiar toad,                            15
Half froth, half venom, spits himself abroad,
In puns, or politics, or tales, or lies,
Or spite, or smut, or rhymes, or blasphemies.
His wit all see-saw between *that* and *this*,

17 *Cato:* see Sidney, p. 34, l. 5 and note. Addison wrote a tragedy,
*Cato,* 1713. *Senate:* The loyal Roman Senators who accepted Cato's
leadership after his retirement to Utica (Africa) upon Caesar's victory
at Pharsalia. The company of small authors who regarded Addison as
a literary dictator. 19 *Templars:* see Spenser, p. 80, ll. 132-35 and note.
Reference obscure. *raise:* applaud.

SPORUS. 1 *Sporus:* "Paris" originally. Sporus, a youth at the court of
Nero, was made the victim of the Emperor's homosexual perversion.
Here the name is applied to the author and courtier, Lord John Hervey,
a member of Walpole's Whig government and a counsellor to George
II's Queen, Caroline. 2 *ass's milk:* commonly prescribed to correct
dietary disorders. 5 *flap:* "slap"—Butt, ed., *Imitations of Horace*
(N.Y., 1942). 6 *painted:* His contemporaries report that Hervey
painted his face. 15 *ear . . . toad:* "[Satan sat] Squat like a Toad,
close at the ear of Eve [sleeping]"—*Paradise Lost,* IV, 800. 19 ff.: as
revised for edition of 1735.

Now high, now low, now Master up, now Miss,     20
And he himself one vile antithesis.
Amphibious Thing! that acting either part,
The trifling Head, or the corrupted Heart!
Fop at the toilet, flatt'rer at the board,
Now trips a Lady, and now struts a Lord.     25
Eve's Tempter thus the Rabbins have express'd,
A Cherub's face, a Reptile all the rest,
Beauty that shocks you, Parts that none will trust,
Wit that can creep, and Pride that licks the dust.

[ll. 305-33]

26 *Rabbins:* Jewish theologians.

# WILLIAM BLAKE 1757–1827

*from* POETICAL SKETCHES

## How sweet I roam'd from field to field

SONG

How sweet I roam'd from field to field,
And tasted all the summer's pride,
'Till I the prince of love beheld,
Who in the sunny beams did glide!

He show'd me lilies for my hair,  5
And blushing roses for my brow;
He led me through his gardens fair,
Where all his golden pleasures grow.

With sweet May dews my wings were wet,
And Phoebus fir'd my vocal rage;  10
He caught me in his silken net,
And shut me in his golden cage.

He loves to sit and hear me sing,
Then, laughing, sports and plays with me;
Then stretches out my golden wing,  15
And mocks my loss of liberty.

*from* SONGS OF INNOCENCE

## The Lamb

Little Lamb, who made thee?
Dost thou know who made thee?
Gave thee life and bid thee feed,
By the stream and o'er the mead;
Gave thee clothing of delight,  5
Softest clothing, wooly, bright;

HOW SWEET. 3 *prince of love:* Love; or, freely, Cupid, identified with *Phoebus,* l. 10. 9 *dews . . . wet:* so that his soaring soul is less fit for flight and the lover is made an easy victim of Phoebus. 10 *vocal rage:* passion for song. 11-12 *He . . . cage:* Love ensnares the lover.

Gave thee such a tender voice,
Making all the vales rejoice?
  Little Lamb who made thee?
  Dost thou know who made thee?       10


  Little Lamb, I'll tell thee,
  Little Lamb, I'll tell thee:
He is callèd by thy name,
For he calls himself a Lamb.
He is meek, and he is mild;       15
He became a little child.
I a child, and thou a lamb,
We are callèd by his name.
  Little Lamb, God bless thee!
  Little Lamb, God bless thee!       20


## The Divine Image

To Mercy, Pity, Peace, and Love
All pray in their distress:
And to these virtues of delight
Return their thankfulness.


For Mercy, Pity, Peace, and Love       5
Is God, our father dear:
And Mercy, Pity, Peace, and Love
Is Man, his child and care.


For Mercy has a human heart,
Pity, a human face,       10
And Love, the human form divine,
And Peace, the human dress.


Then every man of every clime,
That prays in his distress,
Prays to the human form divine,       15
Love, Mercy, Pity, Peace.


And all must love the human form,
In heathen, turk, or jew;
Where Mercy, Love, and Pity dwell,
There God is dwelling too.       20

## *Night*

The sun descending in the west,
The evening star does shine;
The birds are silent in their nest,
And I must seek for mine.
The moon, like a flower,                            5
In heaven's high bower,
With silent delight
Sits and smiles on the night.

Farewell green fields and happy groves,
Where flocks have took delight:                   10
Where lambs have nibbled, silent moves
The feet of angels bright:
Unseen they pour blessing,
And joy without ceasing,
On each bud and blossom,                          15
And each sleeping bosom.

They look in every thoughtless nest,
Where birds are cover'd warm:
They visit caves of every beast,
To keep them all from harm.                       20
If they see any weeping
That should have been sleeping,
They pour sleep on their head
And sit down by their bed.

When wolves and tigers howl for prey,             25
They pitying stand and weep,
Seeking to drive their thirst away,
And keep them from the sheep.
But if they rush dreadful,
The angels, most heedful,                          30
Receive each mild spirit,
New worlds to inherit.

And there the lion's ruddy eyes
Shall flow with tears of gold,
And pitying the tender cries,                      35
And walking round the fold,

Saying "Wrath, by his meekness,
And, by his health, sickness
Is driven away
From our immortal day.                          40

"And now beside thee, bleating lamb,
I can lie down and sleep;
Or think on him who bore thy name,
Graze after thee and weep.
For, wash'd in life's river,                     45
My bright mane for ever
Shall shine like the gold
As I guard o'er the fold."

## *from* SONGS OF EXPERIENCE

### The Sick Rose

O Rose, thou art sick!
The invisible worm,
That flies in the night
In the howling storm,

Has found out thy bed                            5
Of crimson joy;
And his dark secret love
Does thy life destroy.

### The Fly

Little Fly,
Thy summer's play
My thoughtless hand
Has brush'd away.

Am not I                                          5
A fly like thee?
Or art not thou
A man like me?

THE SICK ROSE. *2 invisible worm:* hidden guilt, jealous conscience, etc. (cf. Spenser, p. 76, ll. 725-33) ; also, the flesh, which corrupts love, a thing of the spirit.

For I dance,
And drink, and sing,                                  10
Till some blind hand
Shall brush my wing.

If thought is life
And strength and breath,
And the want                                          15
Of thought is death;

Then am I
A happy fly,
If I live
Or if I die.                                          20


## The Tiger

Tiger! Tiger! burning bright
In the forests of the night:
What immortal hand or eye,
Could frame thy fearful symmetry?

In what distant deeps or skies                        5
Burnt the fire of thine eyes?
On what wings dare he aspire?
What the hand dare seize the fire?

And what shoulder, and what art,
Could twist the sinews of thy heart?                  10
And when thy heart began to beat,
What dread hand? and what dread feet?

What the hammer? what the chain?
In what furnace was thy brain?
What the anvil? what dread grasp                      15
Dare its deadly terrors clasp?

When the stars threw down their spears,
And water'd heaven with their tears,
Did he smile his work to see?
Did he who made the Lamb make thee?                   20

THE TIGER. 7 *aspire*: soar. Cf. "Ah Sun-flower!" p. 249, l. 8.   17-18
*When . . . tears*: Allusion to the defeat of the rebel angels (*stars*) in
heaven. For Blake, *star* is a symbol of reason, and reason opposes the
good. Cf. *mind-forg'd manacles,* "London," p. 249, l. 8.

Tiger! Tiger! burning bright
In the forests of the night:
What immortal hand or eye,
Dare frame thy fearful symmetry?


## Ah Sun-flower!

Ah Sun-flower! weary of time,
Who countest the steps of the sun;
Seeking after that sweet golden clime
Where the traveller's journey is done;

Where the Youth pined away with desire,                    5
And the pale Virgin shrouded in snow,
Arise from their graves, and aspire
Where my Sun-flower wishes to go.


## London

I wander through each charter'd street,
Near where the charter'd Thames does flow,
And mark in every face I meet
Marks of weakness, marks of woe.

In every cry of every Man,                                 5
In every Infant's cry of fear,
In every voice, in every ban,
The mind-forg'd manacles I hear.

How the chimney-sweeper's cry
Every black'ning church appals;                            10
And the hapless soldier's sigh
Runs in blood down palace walls.

---

Ah Sun-flower! 7 *aspire:* soar.
London. 1 *charter'd:* mapped. 7 *ban:* curse. 8 *mind-* . . . *manacles:*
restrictions placed on life by reason, so that natural joy becomes
wretchedness. Cf. "The Tiger," p. 248, ll. 17-18 and note. 10 *appals:*
accuses. 12 *Runs . . . walls:* Stains the State.

But most through midnight streets I hear
How the youthful harlot's curse
Blasts the new-born infant's tear,                          15
And blights with plagues the marriage hearse.


## A Poison Tree

I was  angry with my friend:
I told my wrath, my wrath did end.
I was angry with my foe:
I told it not, my wrath did grow.

And I water'd it in fears,                                    5
Night and morning with my tears;
And I sunnèd it with smiles,
And with soft deceitful wiles.

And it grew both day and night,
Till it bore an apple bright;                                10
And my foe beheld it shine,
And he knew that it was mine,

And into my garden stole
When the night had veil'd the pole:
In the morning glad I see                                    15
My foe outstretch'd beneath the tree.


## The Human Abstract

Pity would be no more
If we did not make somebody poor;
And Mercy no more could be
If all were as happy as we.

And mutual fear brings peace,                                 5
Till the selfish loves increase;
Then Cruelty knits a snare,
And spreads his baits with care.

14 *curse:* cry of perverted love.  15 *Blasts:* Dries up.  16 *blights . . .
hearse:* love perverted turns the marriage-bed into a disease-ridden
hearse, productive of death not life.
    THE HUMAN ABSTRACT. 1-2 *Pity . . . poor, etc.:* How false virtues
rise from evils.

He sits down with holy fears,
And waters the ground with tears;                    10
Then Humility takes its root
Underneath his foot.

Soon spreads the dismal shade
Of Mystery over his head;
And the caterpillar and fly                          15
Feed on the Mystery.

And it bears the fruit of Deceit,
Ruddy and sweet to eat;
And the raven his nest has made
In its thickest shade.                               20

The Gods of the earth and sea
Sought through Nature to find this tree;
But their search was all in vain:
There grows one in the Human Brain.

14 (Tree of) *Mystery:* Established religion.    15 *caterpillar and fly:*
priests. Cf. "As the caterpillar chooses the fairest leaves to lay her eggs,
so the priest lays his curse on the fairest joys."—*Proverbs of Hell.*  20
*its:* Swinburne's emendation, from *the.*

# WILLIAM WORDSWORTH 1770–1850

## *Lines Composed a Few Miles Above Tintern Abbey*

Five years have past; five summers, with the length
Of five long winters! and again I hear
These waters, rolling from their mountain-springs
With a soft inland murmur.—Once again
Do I behold these steep and lofty cliffs,                              5
That on a wild secluded scene impress
Thoughts of more deep seclusion; and connect
The landscape with the quiet of the sky.
The day is come when I again repose
Here, under this dark sycamore, and view                              10
These plots of cottage-ground, these orchard-tufts,
Which at this season, with their unripe fruits,
Are clad in one green hue, and lose themselves
'Mid groves and copses. Once again I see
These hedge-rows, hardly hedge-rows, little lines                     15
Of sportive wood run wild: these pastoral farms,
Green to the very door; and wreaths of smoke
Sent up, in silence, from among the trees!
With some uncertain notice, as might seem
Of vagrant dwellers in the houseless woods,                          20
Or of some Hermit's cave, where by his fire
The Hermit sits alone.
                          These beauteous forms,
Through a long absence, have not been to me
As is a landscape to a blind man's eye:
But oft, in lonely rooms, and 'mid the din                            25
Of towns and cities, I have owed to them
In hours of weariness, sensations sweet,
Felt in the blood, and felt along the heart;
And passing even into my purer mind,
With tranquil restoration:—feelings too                               30
Of unremembered pleasure: such, perhaps,

LINES. *Lines . . . Abbey: On Revisiting The Banks Of The Wye,
Etc.,* first published, anonymously, in *Lyrical Ballads* (London, Bristol,
1798), which Wordsworth and Coleridge produced in collaboration.
14 *copses:* thickets.

As have no slight or trivial influence
On that best portion of a good man's life,
His little, nameless, unremembered acts
Of kindness and of love. Nor less, I trust,                    35
To them I may have owed another gift,
Of aspect more sublime; that blessed mood,
In which the burthen of the mystery,
In which the heavy and the weary weight
Of all this unintelligible world,                               40
Is lightened:—that serene and blessed mood,
In which the affections gently lead us on,—
Until, the breath of this corporeal frame
And even the motion of our human blood
Almost suspended, we are laid asleep                           45
In body, and become a living soul:
While with an eye made quiet by the power
Of harmony, and the deep power of joy,
We see into the life of things.
                                        If this
Be but a vain belief, yet, oh! how oft—                        50
In darkness and amid the many shapes
Of joyless daylight; when the fretful stir
Unprofitable, and the fever of the world,
Have hung upon the beatings of my heart—
How oft, in spirit, have I turned to thee,                     55
O sylvan Wye! thou wanderer through the woods,
How often has my spirit turned to thee!


    And now, with gleams of half-extinguished thought,
With many recognitions dim and faint,
And somewhat of a sad perplexity,                              60
The picture of the mind revives again:
While here I stand, not only with the sense
Of present pleasure, but with pleasing thoughts
That in this moment there is life and food
For future years. And so I dare to hope,                       65
Though changed, no doubt, from what I was when first
I came among these hills; when like a roe
I bounded o'er the mountains, by the sides
Of the deep rivers, and the lonely streams,
Wherever nature led: more like a man                           70
Flying from something that he dreads, than one
Who sought the thing he loved. For nature then

(The coarser pleasures of my boyish days,
And their glad animal movements all gone by)
To me was all in all.—I cannot paint                        75
What then I was. The sounding cataract
Haunted me like a passion: the tall rock,
The mountain, and the deep and gloomy wood,
Their colors and their forms, were then to me
An appetite; a feeling and a love,                          80
That had no need of a remoter charm,
By thought supplied, nor any interest
Unborrowed from the eye.—That time is past,
And all its aching joys are now no more,
And all its dizzy raptures. Not for this                    85
Faint I, nor mourn nor murmur; other gifts
Have followed; for such loss, I would believe,
Abundant recompense. For I have learned
To look on nature, not as in the hour
Of thoughtless youth; but hearing oftentimes               90
The still, sad music of humanity,
Nor harsh nor grating, though of ample power
To chasten and subdue. And I have felt
A presence that disturbs me with the joy
Of elevated thoughts; a sense sublime                      95
Of something far more deeply interfused,
Whose dwelling is the light of setting suns,
And the round ocean and the living air,
And the blue sky, and in the mind of man:
A motion and a spirit, that impels                         100
All thinking things, all objects of all thought,
And rolls through all things. Therefore am I still
A lover of the meadows and the woods,
And mountains; and of all that we behold
From this green earth; of all the mighty world             105
Of eye, and ear,—both what they half create,
And what perceive; well pleased to recognize
In nature and the language of the sense
The anchor of my purest thoughts, the nurse,
The guide, the guardian of my heart, and soul              110
Of all my moral being.
                            Nor perchance,
If I were not thus taught, should I the more
Suffer my genial spirits to decay:
For thou art with me here upon the banks

Of this fair river; thou my dearest Friend,                    115
My dear, dear Friend; and in thy voice I catch
The language of my former heart, and read
My former pleasures in the shooting lights
Of thy wild eyes. Oh! yet a little while
May I behold in thee what I was once,                          120
My dear, dear Sister! and this prayer I make,
Knowing that Nature never did betray
The heart that loved her; 'tis her privilege,
Through all the years of this our life, to lead
From joy to joy: for she can so inform                         125
The mind that is within us, so impress
With quietness and beauty, and so food
With lofty thoughts, that neither evil tongues,
Rash judgments, nor the sneers of selfish men,
Nor greetings where no kindness is, nor all                    130
The dreary intercourse of daily life,
Shall e'er prevail against us, or disturb
Our cheerful faith, that all which we behold
Is full of blessings. Therefore let the moon
Shine on thee in thy solitary walk;                            135
And let the misty mountain-winds be free
To blow against thee: and, in after years,
When these wild ecstasies shall be matured
Into a sober pleasure; when thy mind
Shall be a mansion for all lovely forms,                       140
Thy memory be as a dwelling-place
For all sweet sounds and harmonies; oh! then,
If solitude, or fear, or pain, or grief,
Should be thy portion, with what healing thoughts
Of tender joy wilt thou remember me,                           145
And these my exhortations! Nor, perchance—
If I should be where I no more can hear
Thy voice, nor catch from thy wild eyes these gleams
Of past existence—wilt thou then forget
That on the banks of this delightful stream                    150
We stood together; and that I, so long
A worshipper of Nature, hither came
Unwearied in that service: rather say
With warmer love—oh! with far deeper zeal
Of holier love. Nor wilt thou then forget,                     155

115 *Friend:* Wordsworth's sister, Dorothy. See l. 121.

That after many wanderings, many years
Of absence, these steep woods and lofty cliffs,
And this green pastoral landscape, were to me
More dear, both for themselves and for thy sake!


### She dwelt among the untrodden ways

She dwelt among the untrodden ways
    Beside the springs of Dove,
A Maid whom there were none to praise
    And very few to love:

A violet by a mossy stone         5
    Half hidden from the eye!
—Fair as a star, when only one
    Is shining in the sky.

She lived unknown, and few could know
    When Lucy ceased to be;      10
But she is in her grave, and, oh,
    The difference to me!


### A slumber did my spirit seal

A slumber did my spirit seal;
    I had no human fears:
She seemed a thing that could not feel
    The touch of earthly years.

No motion has she now, no force;     5
    She neither hears nor sees;
Rolled round in earth's diurnal course,
    With rocks, and stones, and trees.


A SLUMBER. 7 *diurnal:* daily.

SONNETS

## It is a beauteous evening, calm and free

It is a beauteous evening, calm and free,
The holy time is quiet as a Nun
Breathless with adoration; the broad sun
Is sinking down in its tranquillity;
The gentleness of heaven broods o'er the Sea:          5
Listen! the mighty Being is awake,
And doth with his eternal motion make
A sound like thunder—everlastingly.
Dear Child! dear Girl! that walkest with me here,
If thou appear untouched by solemn thought,          10
Thy nature is not therefore less divine:
Thou liest in Abraham's bosom all the year;
And worship'st at the Temple's inner shrine,
God being with thee when we know it not.

## The world is too much with us

The world is too much with us; late and soon,
Getting and spending, we lay waste our powers:
Little we see in Nature that is ours;
We have given our hearts away, a sordid boon!
This Sea that bares her bosom to the moon;          5
The winds that will be howling at all hours,
And are up-gathered now like sleeping flowers;
For this, for everything, we are out of tune,
It moves us not.—Great God! I'd rather be
A Pagan suckled in a creed outworn;          10
So might I, standing on this pleasant lea,
Have glimpses that would make me less forlorn;
Have sight of Proteus rising from the sea;
Or hear old Triton blow his wreathed horn.

IT IS A BEAUTEOUS. 9 *Child:* Wordsworth's daughter, Carolyn, by his French sweetheart, Annette Vallon.   12 *Abraham's bosom:* God's grace and protection. Cf. Luke 16:22-23.
THE WORLD. 10 *Proteus:* a sea god, able to change his form. 14 *Triton:* another sea god, son of Neptune, who roused or calmed the sea by blowing his conch-shell horn.

## Composed upon Westminster Bridge

SEPTEMBER 3, 1802

Earth has not anything to show more fair:
Dull would he be of soul who could pass by
A sight so touching in its majesty:
This City now doth, like a garment, wear
The beauty of the morning; silent, bare,　　5
Ships, towers, domes, theatres, and temples lie
Open unto the fields, and to the sky;
All bright and glittering in the smokeless air.
Never did sun more beautifully steep
In his first splendor, valley, rock, or hill;　　10
Ne'er saw I, never felt, a calm so deep!
The river glideth at his own sweet will:
Dear God! the very houses seem asleep;
And all that mighty heart is lying still!


## September, 1802

NEAR DOVER

Inland, within a hollow vale, I stood;
And saw, while sea was calm and air was clear,
The coast of France—the coast of France how near!
Drawn almost into frightful neighborhood.
I shrunk; for verily the barrier flood　　5
Was like a lake, or river bright and fair,
A span of waters; yet what power is there!
What mightiness for evil and for good!
Even so doth God protect us if we be
Virtuous and wise. Winds blow, and waters roll,　　10
Strength to the brave, and Power, and Deity;
Yet in themselves are nothing! One decree
Spake laws to *them*, and said that by the soul
Only, the Nations shall be great and free.

SEPTEMBER, 1802. 12-13 *One . . . them:* cf. Milton, p. 168, ll. 25-26.

### London, 1802

Milton! thou shouldst be living at this hour:
England hath need of thee: she is a fen
Of stagnant waters: altar, sword, and pen,
Fireside, the heroic wealth of hall and bower,
Have forfeited their ancient English dower         5
Of inward happiness. We are selfish men;
Oh! raise us up, return to us again;
And give us manners, virtue, freedom, power.
Thy soul was like a Star, and dwelt apart;
Thou hadst a voice whose sound was like the sea.    10
Pure as the naked heavens, majestic, free,
So didst thou travel on life's common way,
In cheerful godliness; and yet thy heart
The lowliest duties on herself did lay.

### When I have borne in memory what has tamed

When I have borne in memory what has tamed
Great Nations, how ennobling thoughts depart
When men change swords for ledgers, and desert
The student's bower for gold, some fears unnamed
I had, my Country!—am I to be blamed?              5
Now, when I think of thee, and what thou art,
Verily, in the bottom of my heart,
Of those unfilial fears I am ashamed.
For dearly must we prize thee; we who find
In thee a bulwark for the cause of men;            10
And I by my affection was beguiled:
What wonder if a Poet now and then,
Among the many movements of his mind,
Felt for thee as a lover or a child!

### I wandered lonely as a cloud

I wandered lonely as a cloud
That floats on high o'er vales and hills,
When all at once I saw a crowd,
A host, of golden daffodils;
Beside the lake, beneath the trees,                5
Fluttering and dancing in the breeze.

Continuous as the stars that shine
And twinkle on the milky way,
They stretched in never-ending line
Along the margin of a bay:                                    10
Ten thousand saw I at a glance,
Tossing their heads in sprightly dance.

The waves beside them danced; but they
Out-did the sparkling waves in glee:
A poet could not but be gay,                                  15
In such a jocund company:
I gazed—and gazed—but little thought
What wealth the show to me had brought:

For oft, when on my couch I lie
In vacant or in pensive mood,                                 20
They flash upon that inward eye
Which is the bliss of solitude;
And then my heart with pleasure fills,
And dances with the daffodils.

### The Solitary Reaper

Behold her, single in the field,
Yon solitary Highland Lass!
Reaping and singing by herself;
Stop here, or gently pass!
Alone she cuts and binds the grain,                            5
And sings a melancholy strain;
O listen! for the Vale profound
Is overflowing with the sound.

No Nightingale did ever chaunt
More welcome notes to weary bands                             10
Of travellers in some shady haunt,
Among Arabian sands:
A voice so thrilling ne'er was heard
In spring-time from the Cuckoo-bird,
Breaking the silence of the seas                              15
Among the farthest Hebrides.

THE SOLITARY REAPER. 16 *Hebrides:* cf. Milton, p. 160, l. 156 and
note.

Will no one tell me what she sings?—
Perhaps the plaintive numbers flow
For old, unhappy, far-off things,
And battles long ago:                                    20
Or is it some more humble lay,
Familiar matter of to-day?
Some natural sorrow, loss, or pain,
That has been, and may be again?

Whate'er the theme, the Maiden sang        25
As if her song could have no ending;
I saw her singing at her work,
And o'er the sickle bending;—
I listened, motionless and still;
And, as I mounted up the hill,                    30
The music in my heart I bore,
Long after it was heard no more.

# Ode

## INTIMATIONS OF IMMORTALITY FROM RECOLLECTIONS OF EARLY CHILDHOOD

*Pauló majora canamus.*

The Child is father of the Man;
And I could wish my days to be
Bound each to each by natural piety.

### I

There was a time when meadow, grove, and stream,
The earth, and every common sight,
        To me did seem
        Apparelled in celestial light,
The glory and the freshness of a dream.          5
It is not now as it hath been of yore;—
        Turn whereso'er I may,
            By night or day,
The things which I have seen I now can see no more.

21 *lay:* song.
    ODE. *Ode. Intimations, Etc.:* Composed 1802-1804. *Pauló majora canamus:* ". . . somewhat [more] loudly sweep the string."—*Lycidas.*
*The Child, etc.:* from *My heart leaps up* (The Rainbow).
    1-4 *There . . . light,* and ff.: cf. Vaughan, p. 184.

## II

The Rainbow comes and goes,　　　　　　　10
And lovely is the Rose,
The Moon doth with delight
Look round her when the heavens are bare;
Waters on a starry night
Are beautiful and fair;　　　　　　　15
The sunshine is a glorious birth;
But yet I know, where'er I go,
That there hath past away a glory from the earth.

## III

Now, while the birds thus sing a joyous song,
And while the young lambs bound　　　　　20
As to the tabor's sound,
To me alone there came a thought of grief:
A timely utterance gave that thought relief,
And I again am strong:
The cataracts blow their trumpets from the steep;　25
No more shall grief of mine the season wrong;
I hear the Echoes through the mountains throng,
The Winds come to me from the fields of sleep,
And all the earth is gay;
Land and sea　　　　　30
Give themselves up to jollity,
And with the heart of May
Doth every Beast keep holiday;—
Thou Child of Joy,
Shout round me, let me hear thy shouts, thou happy
Shepherd-boy!　　　　　35

## IV

Ye blessed Creatures, I have heard the call
Ye to each other make; I see
The heavens laugh with you in your jubilee;
My heart is at your festival,
My head hath its coronal,　　　　　40
The fulness of your bliss, I feel—I feel it all.
Oh evil day! if I were sullen
While Earth herself is adorning,
This sweet May-morning,

21 *tabor*('s) : a small drum, used as an accompaniment to a pipe.

And the Children are culling                                45
    On every side,
    In a thousand valleys far and wide,
    Fresh flowers; while the sun shines warm,
And the Babe leaps up on his Mother's arm:—
    I hear, I hear, with joy I hear!                     50
    —But there's a Tree, of many, one,
A single Field which I have looked upon,
Both of them speak of something that is gone:
    The Pansy at my feet
    Doth the same tale repeat:                          55
Whither is fled the visionary gleam?
Where is it now, the glory and the dream?


### V

Our birth is but a sleep and a forgetting:
The Soul that rises with us, our life's Star,
    Hath had elsewhere its setting,                      60
      And cometh from afar:
    Not in entire forgetfulness,
    And not in utter nakedness,
But trailing clouds of glory do we come
    From God, who is our home:                          65
Heaven lies about us in our infancy!
Shades of the prison-house begin to close
    Upon the growing Boy,
But He beholds the light, and whence it flows,
    He sees it in his joy;                               70
The Youth, who daily farther from the east
    Must travel, still is Nature's Priest,
    And by the vision splendid
    Is on his way attended;
At length the Man perceives it die away,                    75
And fade into the light of common day.


### VI

Earth fills her lap with pleasures of her own;
Yearnings she hath in her own natural kind,
And, even with something of a Mother's mind,
    And no unworthy aim,                                 80
    The homely Nurse doth all she can
To make her Foster-child, her Inmate Man,
    Forget the glories he hath known,
And that imperial palace whence he came.

## VII

Behold the Child among his new-born blisses,     85
A six years' Darling of a pigmy size!
See, where 'mid work of his own hand he lies,
Fretted by sallies of his mother's kisses,
With light upon him from his father's eyes!
See, at his feet, some little plan or chart,     90
Some fragment from his dream of human life,
Shaped by himself with newly-learned art;
    A wedding or a festival,
    A mourning or a funeral;
      And this hath now his heart,     95
    And unto this he frames his song:
      Then will he fit his tongue
To dialogues of business, love, or strife;
    But it will not be long
    Ere this be thrown aside,     100
    And with new joy and pride
The little Actor cons another part;
Filling from time to time his 'humorous stage'
With all the Persons, down to palsied Age,
That Life brings with her in her equipage;     105
    As if his whole vocation
    Were endless imitation.

## VIII

Thou, whose exterior semblance doth belie
    Thy Soul's immensity;
Thou best Philosopher, who yet dost keep     110
Thy heritage, thou Eye among the blind,
That, deaf and silent, read'st the eternal deep,
Haunted forever by the eternal mind,—
    Mighty Prophet! Seer blest!
    On whom those truths do rest,     115
Which we are toiling all our lives to find,
In darkness lost, the darkness of the grave;
Thou, over whom thy Immortality
Broods like the Day, a Master o'er a Slave,
A Presence which is not to be put by;     120
Thou little Child, yet glorious in the might
Of heaven-born freedom on thy being's height,

88 *Fretted:* Teased.  102 *cons:* studies.  103 *'humorous stage':* stage
exhibiting men of various inclinations, and temperaments.

Why with such earnest pains dost thou provoke
The years to bring the inevitable yoke,
Thus blindly with thy blessedness at strife?          125
Full soon thy Soul shall have her earthly freight,
And custom lie upon thee with a weight,
Heavy as frost, and deep almost as life!

### IX

O joy! that in our embers
Is something that doth live,                              130
That Nature yet remembers
What was so fugitive!
The thought of our past years in me doth breed
Perpetual benediction: not indeed
For that which is most worthy to be blest;               135
Delight and liberty, the simple creed
Of Childhood, whether busy or at rest,
With new-fledged hope still fluttering in his breast:—
    Not for these I raise
    The song of thanks and praise;                       140
    But for those obstinate questionings
    Of sense and outward things,
    Fallings from us, vanishings;
    Blank misgivings of a Creature
Moving about in worlds not realized,                     145
High instincts before which our mortal Nature
Did tremble like a guilty Thing surprised:
    But for those first affections,
    Those shadowy recollections,
    Which, be they what they may,                        150
Are yet the fountain light of all our day,
Are yet a master light of all our seeing;
    Uphold us, cherish, and have power to make
Our noisy years seem moments in the being
Of the eternal Silence: truths that wake,                155
        To perish never;
Which neither listlessness, nor mad endeavor,
        Nor Man nor Boy,
Nor all that is at enmity with joy,
Can utterly abolish or destroy!                          160
    Hence in a season of calm weather
        Though inland far we be,
Our Souls have sight of that immortal sea

141-47 *But . . . surprised:* A much debated passage. Cf. pp. 268-69,
ll. 72-83.

Which brought us hither,
Can in a moment travel thither, 165
And see the Children sport upon the shore,
And hear the mighty waters rolling evermore.

### X

Then sing, ye Birds, sing, sing a joyous song!
And let the young Lambs bound
As to the tabor's sound! 170
We in thought will join your throng,
Ye that pipe and ye that play,
Ye that through your hearts to-day
Feel the gladness of the May!
What though the radiance which was once so bright 175
Be now for ever taken from my sight,
Though nothing can bring back the hour
Of splendor in the grass, of glory in the flower;
We will grieve not, rather find
Strength in what remains behind; 180
In the primal sympathy
Which having been must ever be;
In the soothing thoughts that spring
Out of human suffering;
In the faith that looks through death, 185
In years that bring the philosophic mind.

### XI

And O, ye Fountains, Meadows, Hills, and Groves,
Forbode not any severing of our loves!
Yet in my heart of hearts I feel your might;
I only have relinquished one delight 190
To live beneath your more habitual sway.
I love the Brooks which down their channels fret,
Even more than when I tripped lightly as they;
The innocent brightness of a new-born Day
Is lovely yet; 195
The Clouds that gather round the setting sun
Do take a sober coloring from an eye
That hath kept watch o'er man's mortality;
Another race hath been, and other palms are won.
Thanks to the human heart by which we live, 200
Thanks to its tenderness, its joys, and fears,
To me the meanest flower that blows can give
Thoughts that do often lie too deep for tears.

181 *primal sympathy:* man's first attachment to Nature. Cf. pp. 253-54, ll. 66-83; p. 254, ll. 88-102. 192 *fret:* ripple.

*from* THE PRELUDE

OR GROWTH OF A POET'S MIND
AN AUTOBIOGRAPHICAL POEM

### [*Fair seed-time had my soul*]

Fair seed-time had my soul, and I grew up
Fostered alike by beauty and by fear:
Much favored in my birth-place, and no less
In that beloved Vale to which erelong
We were transplanted—there were we let loose    5
For sports of wider range. Ere I had told
Ten birth-days, when among the mountain slopes
Frost, and the breath of frosty wind, had snapped
The last autumnal crocus, 'twas my joy
With store of springes o'er my shoulder hung    10
To range the open heights where woodcocks run
Along the smooth green turf. Through half the night,
Scudding away from snare to snare, I plied
That anxious visitation;—moon and stars
Were shining o'er my head. I was alone,    15
And seemed to be a trouble to the peace
That dwelt among them. Sometimes it befell
In these night wanderings, that a strong desire
O'erpowered my better reason, and the bird
Which was the captive of another's toil    20
Became my prey; and when the deed was done
I heard among the solitary hills
Low breathings coming after me, and sounds
Of undistinguishable motion, steps
Almost as silent as the turf they trod.    25

Nor less when spring had warmed the cultured Vale,
Moved we as plunderers where the mother-bird
Had in high places built her lodge; though mean
Our object and inglorious, yet the end
Was not ignoble. Oh! when I have hung    30
Above the raven's nest, by knots of grass

THE PRELUDE. *The Prelude: Or Growth of a Poet's Mind; An Auto-biographical Poem,* written 1799-1805, and after much revision published, 1850, some parts having already appeared as independent poems.
FAIR SEED-TIME. 6 *told:* counted. 10 *springes:* traps.

And half-inch fissures in the slippery rock
But ill sustained, and almost (so it seemed)
Suspended by the blast that blew amain,
Shouldering the naked crag, oh, at that time          35
While on the perilous ridge I hung alone,
With what strange utterance did the loud dry wind
Blow through my ear! the sky seemed not a sky
Of earth—and with what motion moved the clouds!

. . .

One summer evening (led by her) I found          40
A little boat tied to a willow tree
Within a rocky cave, its usual home.
Straight I unloosed her chain, and stepping in
Pushed from the shore. It was an act of stealth
And troubled pleasure, nor without the voice          45
Of mountain-echoes did my boat move on;
Leaving behind her still, on either side,
Small circles glittering idly in the moon,
Until they melted all into one track
Of sparkling light. But now, like one who rows,          50
Proud of his skill, to reach a chosen point
With an unswerving line, I fixed my view
Upon the summit of a craggy ridge,
The horizon's utmost boundary; far above
Was nothing but the stars and the gray sky.          55
She was an elfin pinnace; lustily
I dipped my oars into the silent lake,
And, as I rose upon the stroke, my boat
Went heaving through the water like a swan;
When, from behind that craggy steep till then          60
The horizon's bound, a huge peak, black and huge,
As if with voluntary power instinct
Upreared its head. I struck and struck again,
And growing still in stature the grim shape
Towered up between me and the stars, and still,          65
For so it seemed, with purpose of its own
And measured motion like a living thing,
Strode after me. With trembling oars I turned,
And through the silent water stole my way
Back to the covert of the willow tree;          70
There in her mooring-place I left my bark,—
And through the meadows homeward went, in grave
And serious mood; but after I had seen
That spectacle, for many days, my brain

Worked with a dim and undetermined sense 75
Of unknown modes of being; o'er my thoughts
There hung a darkness, call it solitude
Or blank desertion. No familiar shapes
Remained, no pleasant images of trees,
Of sea or sky, no colors of green fields; 80
But huge and mighty forms, that do not live
Like living men, moved slowly through the mind
By day, and were a trouble to my dreams.

. . .

And in the frosty season, when the sun
Was set, and visible for many a mile 85
The cottage windows blazed through twilight gloom,
I heeded not their summons: happy time
It was indeed for all of us—for me
It was a time of rapture! Clear and loud
The village clock tolled six,—I wheeled about, 90
Proud and exulting like an untired horse
That cares not for his home. All shod with steel,
We hissed along the polished ice in games
Confederate, imitative of the chase
And woodland pleasures,—the resounding horn, 95
The pack loud chiming, and the hunted hare.
So through the darkness and the cold we flew,
And not a voice was idle; with the din
Smitten, the precipices rang aloud;
The leafless trees and every icy crag 100
Tinkled like iron; while far distant hills
Into the tumult sent an alien sound
Of melancholy not unnoticed, while the stars
Eastward were sparkling clear, and in the west
The orange sky of evening died away. 105
Not seldom from the uproar I retired
Into a silent bay, or sportively
Glanced sideway, leaving the tumultuous throng,
To cut across the reflex of a star
That fled, and, flying still before me, gleamed 110
Upon the glassy plain; and oftentimes,
When we had given our bodies to the wind,
And all the shadowy banks on either side
Came sweeping through the darkness, spinning still
The rapid line of motion, then at once 115

84-134 *And in . . . sea:* Earlier published in *Poetical Works,* 1849.
109 *reflex:* reflection.

Have I, reclining back upon my heels,
Stopped short; yet still the solitary cliffs
Wheeled by me—even as if the earth had rolled
With visible motion her diurnal round!
Behind me did they stretch in solemn train,                    120
Feebler and feebler, and I stood and watched
Till all was tranquil as a dreamless sleep.


   Ye Presences of Nature in the sky
And on the earth! Ye Visions of the hills!
And Souls of lonely places! can I think                         125
A vulgar hope was yours when ye employed
Such ministry, when ye through many a year
Haunting me thus among my boyish sports
On caves and trees, upon the woods and hills,
Impressed upon all forms the characters                         130
Of danger or desire; and thus did make
The surface of the universal earth
With triumph and delight, with hope and fear,
Work like a sea?

> [Book I. *Introduction—Childhood and School-Time,*
> ll. 301-39; 357-400; 425-75]


## [*There was a Boy*]

   There was a Boy: ye knew him well, ye cliffs
And islands of Winander!—many a time
At evening, when the earliest stars began
To move along the edges of the hills,
Rising or setting, would he stand alone                           5
Beneath the trees or by the glimmering lake,
And there, with fingers interwoven, both hands
Pressed closely palm to palm, and to his mouth
Uplifted, he, as through an instrument,
Blew mimic hootings to the silent owls,                          10
That they might answer him; and they would shout
Across the watery vale, and shout again,
Responsive to his call, with quivering peals,
And long halloos and screams, and echoes loud,
Redoubled and redoubled, concourse wild                          15
Of jocund din; and, when a lengthened pause

119 *diurnal:* daily.
   THERE WAS. Earlier published in *Lyrical Ballads,* 1800 (2nd ed.).
2 *Winander:* Winadermere, Windermere, one of the English Lakes.

Of silence came and baffled his best skill,
Then sometimes, in that silence while he hung
Listening, a gentle shock of mild surprise
Has carried far into his heart the voice                    20
Of mountain torrents; or the visible scene
Would enter unawares into his mind,
With all its solemn imagery, its rocks,
Its woods, and that uncertain heaven, received
Into the bosom of the steady lake.                         25

This Boy was taken from his mates, and died
In childhood, ere he was full twelve years old.
Fair is the spot, most beautiful the vale
Where he was born; the grassy churchyard hangs
Upon a slope above the village school,                     30
And through that churchyard when my way has led
On summer evenings, I believe that there
A long half hour together I have stood
Mute, looking at the grave in which he lies!

[Book V. *Books*, ll. 364-97]

## [*In one of those excursions*]

In one of those excursions (may they ne'er
Fade from remembrance!) through the Northern tracts
Of Cambria ranging with a youthful friend,
I left Bethgelert's huts at couching-time,
And westward took my way, to see the sun                    5
Rise from the top of Snowdon. To the door
Of a rude cottage at the mountain's base
We came, and roused the shepherd who attends
The adventurous stranger's steps, a trusty guide;
Then, cheered by short refreshment, sallied forth.          10

It was a close, warm, breezeless summer night,
Wan, dull, and glaring, with a dripping fog
Low-hung and thick that covered all the sky;
But, undiscouraged, we began to climb
The mountain-side. The mist soon girt us round,            15
And, after ordinary travellers' talk
With our conductor, pensively we sank
Each into commerce with his private thoughts:
Thus did we breast the ascent, and by myself

IN ONE. 3 *Cambria:* Wales (Latin).   4 *couching-time:* bed-time.

Was nothing either seen or heard that checked     20
Those musings or diverted, save that once
The shepherd's lurcher, who, among the crags,
Had to his joy unearthed a hedgehog, teased
His coiled-up prey with barkings turbulent.
This small adventure, for even such it seemed     25
In that wild place and at the dead of night,
Being over and forgotten, on we wound
In silence as before. With forehead bent
Earthward, as if in opposition set
Against an enemy, I panted up     30
With eager pace, and no less eager thoughts.
Thus might we wear a midnight hour away,
Ascending at loose distance each from each,
And I, as chanced, the foremost of the band;
When at my feet the ground appeared to brighten,     35
And with a step or two seemed brighter still;
Nor was time given to ask or learn the cause,
For instantly a light upon the turf
Fell like a flash, and lo! as I looked up,
The Moon hung naked in a firmament     40
Of azure without cloud, and at my feet
Rested a silent sea of hoary mist.
A hundred hills their dusky backs upheaved
All over this still ocean; and beyond,
Far, far beyond, the solid vapors stretched,     45
In headlands, tongues, and promontory shapes,
Into the main Atlantic, that appeared
To dwindle, and give up his majesty,
Usurped upon far as the sight could reach.
Not so the ethereal vault; encroachment none     50
Was there, nor loss; only the inferior stars
Had disappeared, or shed a fainter light
In the clear presence of the full-orbed Moon,
Who, from her sovereign elevation, gazed
Upon the billowy ocean, as it lay     55
All meek and silent, save that through a rift—
Not distant from the shore whereon we stood,
A fixed, abysmal, gloomy, breathing-place—
Mounted the roar of waters, torrents, streams
Innumerable, roaring with one voice!     60
Heard over earth and sea, and, in that hour,
For so it seemed, felt by the starry heavens.

22 *lurcher:* mongrel.   51 *inferior:* lower.

When into air had partially dissolved
That vision, given to spirits of the night
And three chance human wanderers, in calm thought     65
Reflected, it appeared to me the type
Of a majestic intellect, its acts
And its possessions, what it has and craves,
What in itself it is, and would become.
There I beheld the emblem of a mind                    70
That feeds upon infinity, that broods
Over the dark abyss, intent to hear
Its voices issuing forth to silent light
In one continuous stream; a mind sustained
By recognitions of transcendent power,                 75
In sense conducting to ideal form,
In soul of more than mortal privilege.
One function, above all, of such a mind
Had Nature shadowed there, by putting forth,
'Mid circumstances awful and sublime,                  80
That mutual domination which she loves
To exert upon the face of outward things,
So moulded, joined, abstracted, so endowed
With interchangeable supremacy,
That men, least sensitive, see, hear, perceive,        85
And cannot choose but feel.
                         [Book XIV. *Conclusion,* ll. 1-86]

76 *In . . . form:* cf. Milton, "Till body up to spirit work"—*Paradise
Lost,* V, 478. It is likely that the passage from which this phrase comes
was in Wordsworth's mind while he was composing the Conclusion of
*The Prelude.*

# SAMUEL TAYLOR COLERIDGE 1792–1834

## The Rime of the Ancient Mariner

IN SEVEN PARTS

ARGUMENT

*How a Ship, having first sailed to the Equator, was driven by Storms to the cold Country towards the South Pole; how the Ancient Mariner cruelly and in contempt of the laws of hospitality killed a Seabird and how he was followed by many and strange Judgements: and in what manner he came back to his own Country.*

PART I

An ancient Mariner meeteth three Gallants bidden to a wedding-feast, and detaineth one.

It is an ancient Mariner,
And he stoppeth one of three.
"By thy long gray beard and glittering eye,
Now wherefore stopp'st thou me?

"The Bridegroom's doors are opened wide,     5
And I am next of kin;
The guests are met, the feast is set:
May'st hear the merry din."

He holds him with his skinny hand,
"There was a ship," quoth he.                10
"Hold off! unhand me, gray-beard loon!"
Eftsoons his hand dropped he.

The Wedding-Guest is spellbound by the eye of the old seafaring man, and constrained to hear his tale.

He holds him with his glittering eye—
The Wedding-Guest stood still,
And listens like a three years' child:        15
The Mariner hath his will.

The Wedding-Guest sat on a stone:
He cannot choose but hear;
And thus spake on that ancient man,
The bright-eyed Mariner.                       20

THE ANCIENT MARINER. 12 *Eftsoons:* At once.

The ship was cheered, the harbor cleared,
Merrily did we drop
Below the kirk, below the hill,
Below the lighthouse top.

*The Mariner tells
how the ship
sailed southward
with a good wind
and fair weather,
till it reached the
Line.*

The sun came up upon the left,                    25
Out of the sea came he!
And he shone bright, and on the right
Went down into the sea.

Higher and higher every day,
Till over the mast at noon—                        30
The Wedding-Guest here beat his breast,
For he heard the loud bassoon.

*The Wedding-Guest
heareth the bridal
music; but the
Mariner continueth
his tale.*

The bride hath paced into the hall,
Red as a rose is she;
Nodding their heads before her goes               35
The merry minstrelsy.

The Wedding-Guest he beat his breast,
Yet he cannot choose but hear;
And thus spake on that ancient man,
The bright-eyed Mariner.                           40

*The ship driven
by a storm toward
the south pole.*

And now the Storm-blast came, and he
Was tyrannous and strong:
He struck with his o'ertaking wings,
And chased us south along.

With sloping masts and dipping prow,              45
As who pursued with yell and blow
Still treads the shadow of his foe,
And forward bends his head,
The ship drove fast, loud roared the blast,
And southward aye we fled.                         50

And now there came both mist and snow,
And it grew wondrous cold:
And ice, mast-high, came floating by,
As green as emerald.

36 *minstrelsy:* musicians.    41 *driven* (gloss): originally *drawn;*
emended, 1893.

276

The land of ice, and of fearful sounds where no living thing was to be seen.

And through the drifts the snowy clifts   55
Did send a dismal sheen:
Nor shapes of men nor beasts we ken—
The ice was all between.

The ice was here, the ice was there,
The ice was all around:   60
It cracked and growled, and roared and
      howled,
Like noises in a swound!

Till a great sea-bird, called the Albatross, came through the snow-fog, and was received with great joy and hospitality.

At length did cross an Albatross,
Thorough the fog it came;
As if it had been a Christian soul,   65
We hailed it in God's name.

It ate the food it ne'er had eat,
And round and round it flew.
The ice did split with a thunder-fit;
The helmsman steered us through!   70

And lo! the Albatross proveth a bird of good omen, and followeth the ship as it returned northward through fog and floating ice.

And a good south wind sprung up behind;
The Albatross did follow,
And every day, for food or play,
Came to the mariner's hollo!

In mist or cloud, on mast or shroud,   75
It perched for vespers nine;
Whiles all the night, through fog-smoke
      white,
Glimmered the white moon-shine.

The ancient Mariner inhospitably killeth the pious bird of good omen.

"God save thee, ancient Mariner!
From the fiends, that plague thee thus!—   80
Why look'st thou so?"—With my cross-bow
I shot the Albatross!

PART II

The Sun now rose upon the right:
Out of the sea came he,
Still hid in mist, and on the left   85
Went down into the sea.

55 *clifts:* cliffs.  57 *ken:* discern.  62 *swound:* swoon.  64 *Thorough:* Through.  76 *vespers:* evening; the time is reckoned according to the canonical hours.

And the good south wind still blew behind,
But no sweet bird did follow,
Nor any day for food or play
Came to the mariner's hollo!                                    90

His shipmates cry out against the ancient Mariner, for killing the bird of good luck.

And I had done a hellish thing,
And it would work 'em woe:
For all averred, I had killed the bird
That made the breeze to blow.
Ah wretch! said they, the bird to slay,        95
That made the breeze to blow!

But when the fog cleared off, they justify the same, and thus make themselves accomplices in the crime.

Nor dim nor red, like God's own head,
The glorious Sun uprist:
Then all averred, I had killed the bird
That brought the fog and mist.                           100
'Twas right, said they, such birds to slay,
That bring the fog and mist.

The fair breeze continues; the ship enters the Pacific Ocean, and sails northward, even till it reaches the Line.

The fair breeze blew, the white foam flew,
The furrow followed free;
We were the first that ever burst            105
Into that silent sea.

The ship hath been suddenly becalmed.

Down dropt the breeze, the sails dropt down,
'Twas sad as sad could be;
And we did speak only to break
The silence of the sea!                                        110

All in a hot and copper sky,
The bloody Sun, at noon,
Right up above the mast did stand,
No bigger than the Moon.

Day after day, day after day,                     115
We stuck, nor breath nor motion;
As idle as a painted ship
Upon a painted ocean.

And the Albatross begins to be avenged.

Water, water, every where,
And all the boards did shrink;                      120
Water, water, every where,
Nor any drop to drink.

278

The very deep did rot: O Christ!
That ever this should be!
Yea, slimy things did crawl with legs     125
Upon the slimy sea.

About, about, in reel and rout
The death-fires danced at night;
The water, like a witch's oils,
Burnt green, and blue and white.          130

A Spirit had fol-
lowed them; one of
the invisible inhabit-
ants of this planet,
neither departed
souls nor angels;
concerning whom
the learned Jew,
Josephus, and the Platonic Constantinopolitan, Michael Psellus, may be consulted.
They are very numerous, and there is no climate or element without one or more.

And some in dreams assured were
Of the Spirit that plagued us so;
Nine fathom deep he had followed us
From the land of mist and snow.

And every tongue, through utter
          drought,                        135
Was withered at the root;

The shipmates, in
their sore distress,
would fain throw
the whole guilt on
the ancient Mariner:
in sign whereof
they hang the dead
sea-bird round his
neck.

We could not speak, no more than if
We had been choked with soot.

Ah! well a-day! what evil looks
Had I from old and young!                 140
Instead of the cross, the Albatross
About my neck was hung.

PART III

There passed a weary time. Each throat
Was parched, and glazed each eye.
A weary time! a weary time!               145
How glazed each weary eye,

The ancient Mariner
beholdeth a sign in
the element afar
off.

When looking westward, I beheld
A something in the sky.

At first it seemed a little speck,
And then it seemed a mist;                150
It moved and moved, and took at last
A certain shape, I wist.

127 *reel and rout*: dance and uproar.  128 *death-fires*: luminous appear-
ances above dead bodies.  152 *wist*: knew.

A speck, a mist, a shape, I wist!
And still it neared and neared:
As if it dodged a water-sprite,                     155
It plunged and tacked and veered.

At its nearer ap-
proach, it seemeth
him to be a ship;
and at a dear ran-
som he freeth his
speech from the
bonds of thirst.

With throats unslaked, with black lips baked,
We could nor laugh nor wail;
Through utter drought all dumb we stood!
I bit my arm, I sucked the blood,                   160
And cried, A sail! a sail!

A flash of joy;

With throats unslaked, with black lips baked,
Agape they heard me call:
Gramercy! they for joy did grin,
And all at once their breath drew in,               165
As they were drinking all.

And horror follows.
For can it be a ship
that comes onward
without wind or
tide?

See! see! (I cried) she tacks no more!
Hither to work us weal;
Without a breeze, without a tide,
She steadies with upright keel!                     170

The western wave was all aflame,
The day was well nigh done!
Almost upon the western wave
Rested the broad bright Sun;
When that strange shape drove suddenly   175
Betwixt us and the Sun.

It seemeth him but
the skeleton of a
ship.

And straight the Sun was flecked with bars,
(Heaven's Mother send us grace!)
As if through a dungeon-grate he peered
With broad and burning face.                        180

Alas! (thought I, and my heart beat loud)
How fast she nears and nears!
Are those her sails that glance in the Sun,
Like restless gossameres?

And its ribs are seen
as bars on the face
of the setting Sun.
The Specter-Woman
and her Death-mate,
and no other on
board the skeleton-
ship.

Are those her ribs through which the Sun  185
Did peer, as through a grate?
And is that Woman all her crew?
Is that a Death? and are there two?
Is Death that woman's mate?

164 *Gramercy*: cf. *grand-merci*, "mercy on us."

Like vessel, like
crew!

Her lips were red, her looks were free, 190
Her locks were yellow as gold:
Her skin was as white as leprosy,
The Nightmare Life-in-Death was she,
Who thicks man's blood with cold.

Death and Life-in-
Death have diced
for the ship's crew,
and she (the latter)
winneth the ancient
Mariner.

The naked hulk alongside came, 195
And the twain were casting dice;
"The game is done! I've won, I've won!"
Quoth she, and whistles thrice.

No twilight within
the courts of the
Sun.

The Sun's rim dips; the stars rush out:
At one stride comes the dark; 200
With far-heard whisper, o'er the sea,
Off shot the specter-bark.

At the rising of the
Moon,

We listened and looked sideways up!
Fear at my heart, as at a cup,
My life-blood seemed to sip! 205
The stars were dim, and thick the night,
The steersman's face by his lamp gleamed
white;
From the sails the dew did drip–
Till clomb above the eastern bar
The horned Moon, with one bright star 210
Within the nether tip.

One after another,

One after one, by the star-dogged Moon,
Too quick for groan or sigh,
Each turned his face with a ghastly pang,
And cursed me with his eye. 215

His shipmates drop
down dead.

Four times fifty living men
(And I heard nor sigh nor groan),
With heavy thump, a lifeless lump,
They dropped down one by one.

But Life-in-Death
begins her work on
the ancient Mariner.

The souls did from their bodies fly,— 220
They fled to bliss or woe!
And every soul, it passed me by,
Like the whizz of my cross-bow!

209 *clomb:* climbed.

## PART IV

The Wedding-Guest
feareth that a spirit
is talking to him.

"I fear thee, ancient Mariner!
I fear thy skinny hand!                                    225
And thou art long, and lank, and brown,
As is the ribbed sea-sand.

"I fear thee and thy glittering eye,
And thy skinny hand, so brown."—
But the ancient
Mariner assureth
him of his bodily
life, and proceedeth
to relate his horrible
penance.
Fear not, fear not, thou Wedding-Guest!  230
This body dropt not down.

Alone, alone, all, all alone,
Alone on a wide wide sea!
And never a saint took pity on
My soul in agony.                                          235

He despiseth the
creatures of the
calm,
The many men, so beautiful!
And they all dead did lie:
And a thousand thousand slimy things
Lived on; and so did I.

And envieth that
they should live,
and so many lie
dead.
I looked upon the rotting sea,                             240
And drew my eyes away;
I looked upon the rotting deck,
And there the dead men lay.

I looked to heaven, and tried to pray;
But or ever a prayer had gusht,                            245
A wicked whisper came, and made
My heart as dry as dust.

I closed my lids, and kept them close,
And the balls like pulses beat;
For the sky and the sea, and the sea and the
        sky,                                               250
Lay like a load on my weary eye,
And the dead were at my feet.

But the curse liveth
for him in the eye
of the dead men.
The cold sweat melted from their limbs,
Nor rot nor reek did they:
The look with which they looked on me    255
Had never passed away.

An orphan's curse would drag to hell
A spirit from on high;
But oh! more horrible than that
Is the curse in a dead man's eye!          260
Seven days, seven nights, I saw that curse,
And yet I could not die.

In his loneliness
and fixedness he
yearneth towards
the journeying
Moon, and the stars
that still sojourn,
yet still move on-
ward; and every

The moving Moon went up the sky,
And nowhere did abide:
Softly she was going up,          265
And a star or two beside—

where the blue sky belongs to them, and is their appointed rest, and their native
country and their own natural homes, which they enter unannounced, as lords that
are certainly expected and yet there is a silent joy at their arrival.

Her beams bemocked the sultry main,
Like April hoar-frost spread;
But where the ship's huge shadow lay,
The charmed water burnt alway          270
A still and awful red.

By the light of the
Moon he beholdeth
God's creatures of
the great calm.

Beyond the shadow of the ship,
I watched the water-snakes:
They moved in tracks of shining white,
And when they reared, the elfish light          275
Fell off in hoary flakes.

Within the shadow of the ship
I watched their rich attire:
Blue, glossy green, and velvet black,
They coiled and swam; and every track          280
Was a flash of golden fire.

Their beauty and
their happiness.

O happy living things! no tongue
Their beauty might declare:
A spring of love gushed from my heart,

He blesseth them
in his heart.

And I blessed them unaware:          285
Sure my kind saint took pity on me,
And I blessed them unaware.

The spell begins to
break.

The selfsame moment I could pray;
And from my neck so free
The Albatross fell off, and sank          290
Like lead into the sea.

275 *elfish*: weird.

## PART V

Oh sleep! it is a gentle thing,
Beloved from pole to pole!
To Mary Queen the praise be given!
She sent the gentle sleep from Heaven,        295
That slid into my soul.

By grace of the holy
Mother, the ancient
Mariner is refreshed
with rain.

The silly buckets on the deck,
That had so long remained,
I dreamt that they were filled with dew;
And when I awoke, it rained.        300

My lips were wet, my throat was cold,
My garments all were dank;
Sure I had drunken in my dreams,
And still my body drank.

I moved, and could not feel my limbs:        305
I was so light—almost
I thought that I had died in sleep,
And was a blessed ghost.

He heareth sounds
and seeth strange
sights and commo-
tions in the sky and
the element.

And soon I heard a roaring wind:
It did not come anear;        310
But with its sound it shook the sails,
That were so thin and sere.

The upper air burst into life!
And a hundred fire-flags sheen,
To and fro they were hurried about!        315
And to and fro, and in and out,
The wan stars danced between.

And the coming wind did roar more loud,
And the sails did sigh like sedge;
And the rain poured down from one black
          cloud;        320
The Moon was at its edge.

The thick black cloud was cleft, and still
The Moon was at its side:

297 *silly*: probably, simple.    314 *fire-flags sheen*: meteor-like flames.

284

Like waters shot from some high crag,
The lightning fell with never a jag,       325
A river steep and wide.

The bodies of the ship's crew are inspired, and the ship moves on;

The loud wind never reached the ship,
Yet now the ship moved on!
Beneath the lightning and the Moon
The dead men gave a groan.       330

They groaned, they stirred, they all uprose,
Nor spake, nor moved their eyes;
It had been strange, even in a dream,
To have seen those dead men rise.

The helmsman steered, the ship moved on;
Yet never a breeze up blew;       336
The mariners all 'gan work the ropes,
Where they were wont to do;
They raised their limbs like lifeless tools—
We were a ghastly crew.       340

The body of my brother's son
Stood by me, knee to knee:
The body and I pulled at one rope,
But he said nought to me.

"I fear thee, ancient Mariner!"       345
Be calm, thou Wedding-Guest!

But not by the souls of the men, nor by demons of earth or middle air, but by a blessed troop of angelic spirits, sent down by the invocation of the guardian saint.

'Twas not those souls that fled in pain,
Which to their corses came again,
But a troop of spirits blest:

For when it dawned—they dropped their
       arms,       350
And clustered round the mast;
Sweet sounds rose slowly through their
       mouths,
And from their bodies passed.

Around, around, flew each sweet sound,
Then darted to the Sun;       355
Slowly the sounds come back again,
Now mixed, now one by one.

325 *jag*: fork.   348 *corses*: corpses.

Sometimes a-dropping from the sky
I heard the sky-lark sing;
Sometimes all little birds that are,      360
How they seemed to fill the sea and air
With their sweet jargoning!

And now 'twas like all instruments,
Now like a lonely flute;
And now it is an angel's song,      365
That makes the heavens be mute.

It ceased; yet still the sails made on
A pleasant noise till noon,
A noise like of a hidden brook
In the leafy month of June,      370
That to the sleeping woods all night
Singeth a quiet tune.

Till noon we quietly sailed on,
Yet never a breeze did breathe:
Slowly and smoothly went the ship,      375
Moved onward from beneath.

Under the keel nine fathom deep,
From the land of mist and snow,
The spirit slid: and it was he
That made the ship to go.      380
The sails at noon left off their tune,
And the ship stood still also.

The lonesome Spirit from the south-pole carries on the ship as far as the Line, in obedience to the angelic troop, but still requireth vengeance.

The Sun, right up above the mast,
Had fixed her to the ocean:
But in a minute she 'gan stir,      385
With a short uneasy motion—
Backwards and forwards half her length,
With a short uneasy motion.

Then like a pawing horse let go,
She made a sudden bound:      390
It flung the blood into my head,
And I fell down in a swound.

362 *jargoning*: twittering.

286

The Polar Spirit's
fellow-demons, the
invisible inhabitants
of the element, take
part in his wrong;
and two of them
relate, one to the
other, that penance
long and heavy for
the ancient Mariner
hath been accorded
to the Polar Spirit,
who returneth south-
ward.

How long in that same fit I lay,
I have not to declare;
But ere my living life returned,        395
I heard, and in my soul discerned
Two voices in the air.

"Is it he?" quoth one, "Is this the man?
By him who died on cross,
With his cruel bow he laid full low     400
The harmless Albatross.

"The spirit who bideth by himself
In the land of mist and snow,
He loved the bird that loved the man
Who shot him with his bow."              405

The other was a softer voice,
As soft as honey-dew:
Quoth he, "The man hath penance done,
And penance more will do."

### PART VI

#### First Voice

But tell me, tell me! speak again       410
Thy soft response renewing—
What makes that ship drive on so fast?
What is the ocean doing?

#### Second Voice

Still as a slave before his lord,
The ocean hath no blast;                 415
His great bright eye most silently
Up to the Moon is cast—

If he may know which way to go;
For she guides him smooth or grim.
See, brother, see! how graciously       420
She looketh down on him.

The Mariner hath
been cast into a
trance; for the an-
gelic power causeth
the vessel to drive
northward faster
than human life
could endure.

#### First Voice

But why drives on that ship so fast,
Without or wave or wind?

394 *have . . . declare:* cannot say.

### Second Voice

The air is cut away before,
And closes from behind.                                    425

Fly, brother, fly! more high, more high!
Or we shall be belated:
For slow and slow that ship will go,
When the Mariner's trance is abated.

The supernatural
motion is retarded;
the Mariner awakes,
and his penance
begins anew.

I woke, and we were sailing on            430
As in a gentle weather:
'Twas night, calm night, the moon was high;
The dead men stood together.

All stood together on the deck,
For a charnel-dungeon fitter:             435
All fixed on me their stony eyes,
That in the Moon did glitter.

The pang, the curse, with which they died,
Had never passed away:
I could not draw my eyes from theirs,     440
Nor turn them up to pray.

The curse is finally
expiated.

And now this spell was snapt: once more
I viewed the ocean green,
And looked far forth, yet little saw
Of what had else been seen—               445

Like one, that on a lonesome road
Doth walk in fear and dread,
And having once turned round walks on,
And turns no more his head;
Because he knows, a frightful fiend       450
Doth close behind him tread.

But soon there breathed a wind on me,
Nor sound nor motion made:
Its path was not upon the sea,
In ripple or in shade.                    455

It raised my hair, it fanned my cheek
Like a meadow-gale of spring—
It mingled strangely with my fears,
Yet it felt like a welcoming.

435 *charnel*: burial.

Swiftly, swiftly flew the ship,    460
Yet she sailed softly too:
Sweetly, sweetly blew the breeze—
On me alone it blew.

And the ancient
Mariner beholdeth
his native country.

Oh! dream of joy! is this indeed
The light-house top I see?    465
Is this the hill? is this the kirk?
Is this mine own countree?

We drifted o'er the harbor-bar,
And I with sobs did pray—
O let me be awake, my God!    470
Or let me sleep alway.

The harbor-bay was clear as glass,
So smoothly it was strewn!
And on the bay the moonlight lay,
And the shadow of the Moon.    475

The rock shone bright, the kirk no less,
That stands above the rock:
The moonlight steeped in silentness
The steady weathercock.

And the bay was white with silent light,    480
Till, rising from the same,
The angelic spirits
leave the dead
bodies,
Full many shapes, that shadows were,
In crimson colors came.

And appear in their
own forms of light.

A little distance from the prow
Those crimson shadows were:    485
I turned my eyes upon the deck—
Oh, Christ! what saw I there!

Each corse lay flat, lifeless and flat,
And, by the holy rood!
A man all light, a seraph-man,    490
On every corse there stood.

This seraph-band, each waved his hand:
It was a heavenly sight!
They stood as signals to the land,
Each one a lovely light;    495

489 *rood:* cross.   490 *seraph-:* angel, of the highest order.

This seraph-band, each waved his hand,
No voice did they impart –
No voice; but oh! the silence sank
Like music on my heart.

But soon I heard the dash of oars,          500
I heard the Pilot's cheer;
My head was turned perforce away,
And I saw a boat appear.

The Pilot and the Pilot's boy,
I heard them coming fast:                    505
Dear Lord in Heaven! it was a joy
The dead men could not blast.

I saw a third—I heard his voice:
It is the Hermit good!
He singeth loud his godly hymns              510
That he makes in the wood.
He'll shrieve my soul, he'll wash away
The Albatross's blood.

### PART VII

The Hermit of
the Wood,

This Hermit good lives in that wood
Which slopes down to the sea.              515
How loudly his sweet voice he rears!
He loves to talk with marineres
That come from a far countree.

He kneels at morn, and noon, and eve—
He hath a cushion plump:                    520
It is the moss that wholly hides
The rotted old oak-stump.

The skiff-boat neared: I heard them talk.
"Why, this is strange, I trow!
Where are those lights so many and fair,  525
That signal made but now?"

Approacheth the
ship with wonder.

"Strange, by my faith!" the Hermit said—
"And they answered not our cheer!
The planks looked warped! and see those
            sails,

512 *shrieve*: shrive; hear confession and give absolution.

How thin they are and sere!　　　　　530
I never saw aught like to them,
Unless perchance it were

"Brown skeletons of leaves that lag
My forest-brook along;
When the ivy-tod is heavy with snow,　　535
And the owlet whoops to the wolf below,
That eats the she-wolf's young."

"Dear Lord! it hath a fiendish look—
(The Pilot made reply)
I am a-feared"—"Push on, push on!"　　540
Said the Hermit cheerily.

The boat came closer to the ship,
But I nor spake nor stirred;
The boat came close beneath the ship,
And straight a sound was heard.　　　　545

The ship suddenly sinketh.

Under the water it rumbled on,
Still louder and more dread:
It reached the ship, it split the bay;
The ship went down like lead.

The ancient Mariner is saved in the Pilot's boat.

Stunned by that loud and dreadful sound,　550
Which sky and ocean smote,
Like one that hath been seven days drowned,
My body lay afloat;
But swift as dreams, myself I found
Within the Pilot's boat.　　　　　　　555

Upon the whirl, where sank the ship,
The boat spun round and round;
And all was still, save that the hill
Was telling of the sound.

I moved my lips—the Pilot shrieked,　　560
And fell down in a fit;
The holy Hermit raised his eyes,
And prayed where he did sit.

I took the oars: the Pilot's boy,
Who now doth crazy go,　　　　　　　565

535 *tod :* bush.

Laughed loud and long, and all the while
His eyes went to and fro.
"Ha! ha!" quoth he, "full plain I see,
The Devil knows how to row."

And now, all in my own countree, 570
I stood on the firm land!
The Hermit stepped forth from the boat,
And scarcely he could stand.

The ancient Mariner
earnestly entreateth
the Hermit to
shrieve him; and
the penance of life
falls on him.

"O shrieve me, shrieve me, holy man!"
The Hermit crossed his brow, 575
"Say quick," quoth he, "I bid thee say—
What manner of man art thou?"

Forthwith this frame of mine was wrenched
With a woeful agony,
Which forced me to begin my tale; 580
And then it left me free.

And ever and anon
throughout his fu-
ture life an agony
constraineth him
to travel from land
to land;

Since then, at an uncertain hour,
That agony returns;
And till my ghastly tale is told,
This heart within me burns. 585

I pass, like night, from land to land;
I have strange power of speech;
That moment that his face I see,
I know the man that must hear me:
To him my tale I teach. 590

What loud uproar bursts from that door!
The wedding-guests are there;
But in the garden-bower the bride
And bride-maids singing are:
And hark the little vesper bell, 595
Which biddeth me to prayer!

O Wedding-Guest! this soul hath been
Alone on a wide wide sea:
So lonely 'twas, that God himself
Scarce seemed there to be. 600

O sweeter than the marriage-feast,
'Tis sweeter far to me,

To walk together to the kirk
With a goodly company!—

To walk together to the kirk,                           605
And all together pray,
While each to his great Father bends,
Old men, and babes, and loving friends,
And youths and maidens gay!

And to teach, by
his own example,
love and reverence
to all things that
God made and lov-
eth.

Farewell, farewell! but this I tell                      610
To thee, thou Wedding-Guest!
He prayeth well, who loveth well
Both man and bird and beast.

He prayeth best, who loveth best
All things both great and small;                         615
For the dear God who loveth us,
He made and loveth all.

The Mariner, whose eye is bright,
Whose beard with age is hoar,
Is gone: and now the Wedding-Guest                       620
Turned from the bridegroom's door.

He went like one that hath been stunned,
And is of sense forlorn:
A sadder and a wiser man,
He rose the morrow morn.                                 625

## Dejection: An Ode

Late, late yestreen I saw the new Moon,
With the old Moon in her arms;
And I fear, I fear, my Master dear!
We shall have a deadly storm.

—*Ballad of Sir Patrick Spence*

### I

Well! If the Bard was weather-wise, who made
     The grand old ballad of Sir Patrick Spence,
     This night, so tranquil now, will not go hence
Unroused by winds, that ply a busier trade
Than those which mould yon cloud in lazy flakes,          5

623 *forlorn :* bereft.

Or the dull sobbing draft, that moans and rakes
    Upon the strings of this Eolian lute,
    Which better far were mute.
  For lo! the New-moon winter-bright!
  And overspread with phantom light,           10
  (With swimming phantom light o'erspread
  But rimmed and circled by a silver thread)
I see the old Moon in her lap, foretelling
  The coming on of rain and squally blast.
And oh! that even now the gust were swelling,     15
  And the slant night-shower driving loud and fast!
Those sounds which oft have raised me, whilst they awed
    And sent my soul abroad,
Might now perhaps their wonted impulse give,
Might startle this dull pain, and make it move and live!   20

II

A grief without a pang, void, dark, and drear,
  A stifled, drowsy, unimpassioned grief,
  Which finds no natural outlet, no relief,
    In word, or sigh, or tear—
O Lady! in this wan and heartless mood,       25
To other thoughts by yonder throstle woo'd,
  All this long eve, so balmy and serene,
Have I been gazing on the western sky,
  And its peculiar tint of yellow green:
And still I gaze—and with how blank an eye!     30
And those thin clouds above, in flakes and bars,
That give away their motion to the stars;
Those stars, that glide behind them or between,
Now sparkling, now bedimmed, but always seen:
Yon crescent Moon as fixed as if it grew     35
In its own cloudless, starless lake of blue;
I see them all so excellently fair,
I see, not feel how beautiful they are!

III

  My genial spirits fail;
  And what can these avail       40
To lift the smothering weight from off my breast?

DEJECTION. 7 *Eolian lute:* A frame fitted with strings which produce
musical tones when exposed to the wind. From *Aeolus,* the wind god.
19 *wonted:* accustomed.   25 *Lady:* originally, "Sara" (Hutchinson),
one of the poet's dearest friends. See ll. 47, 64, 67.   39 *genial spirits:*
native, inborn spirits; his genius. Cf. l. 85.

It were a vain endeavor,
Though I should gaze for ever
On that green light that lingers in the west:
I may not hope from outward forms to win          45
The passion and the life, whose fountains are within.


IV

O Lady! we receive but what we give,
And in our life alone does nature live:
Ours is her wedding-garment, ours her shroud!
    And would we aught behold, of higher worth,          50
Than that inanimate cold world allowed
To the poor loveless ever-anxious crowd,
    Ah! from the soul itself must issue forth,
A light, a glory, a fair luminous cloud
        Enveloping the Earth—          55
And from the soul itself must there be sent
    A sweet and potent voice, of its own birth,
Of all sweet sounds the life and element!


V

O pure of heart! thou need'st not ask of me
What this strong music in the soul may be!          60
What, and wherein it doth exist,
This light, this glory, this fair luminous mist,
This beautiful and beauty-making power.
    Joy, virtuous Lady! Joy that ne'er was given,
Save to the pure, and in their purest hour,          65
Life, and Life's effluence, cloud at once and shower,
Joy, Lady! is the spirit and the power,
Which wedding Nature to us gives in dower,
    A new Earth and new Heaven,
Undreamt of by the sensual and the proud—          70
Joy is the sweet voice, Joy the luminous cloud—
    We in ourselves rejoice!
And thence flows all that charms or ear or sight,
    All melodies the echoes of that voice,
All colors a suffusion from that light.          75

48-49 *in . . . shroud:* Nature *lives,* only in conjunction with man, particularly, in conjunction with the Imagination (the *shaping spirit,* l.
86) ; and, likewise, Nature dies in man (as the *shroud* signifies) when
the genius fails. Cf. ll. 39, 68.   68 *wedding . . . us:* see ll. 48-49 and
note.

## VI

There was a time when, though my path was rough,
  This joy within me dallied with distress,
And all misfortunes were but as the stuff
  Whence Fancy made me dreams of happiness:
For hope grew round me, like the twining vine,    80
And fruits and foliage, not my own, seemed mine.
But now afflictions bow me down to earth:
Nor care I that they rob me of my mirth;
  But oh! each visitation
Suspends what nature gave me at my birth,    85
  My shaping spirit of Imagination.
For not to think of what I needs must feel,
  But to be still and patient, all I can;
And haply by abstruse research to steal
  From my own nature all the natural man—    90
  This was my sole resource, my only plan:
Till that which suits a part infects the whole,
And now is almost grown the habit of my soul.

## VII

Hence, viper thoughts, that coil around my mind,
  Reality's dark dream!    95
I turn from you, and listen to the wind,
  Which long has raved, unnoticed. What a scream
Of agony by torture lengthened out
That lute sent forth! Thou Wind, that rav'st without,
  Bare craig, or mountain-tairn, or blasted tree,    100
Or pine-grove whither woodman never clomb,
Or lonely house, long held the witches' home,
  Methinks were fitter instruments for thee,
Mad Lutanist! who in this month of showers,
Of dark brown gardens, and of peeping flowers,    105
Mak'st Devils' yule, with worse than wintry song,
The blossoms, buds, and timorous leaves among.

79, 86 *Fancy, Imagination:* One way of distinguishing these terms is to
say that Fancy is the faculty which simply makes agreeable combina-
tions of dissimilar images (as ll, 78-79 assert), and that the Imagination, by combining images in a way to cause them to modify one
another, *creates* a reality more truthful than anything which ordinary
sense perceives.   84 *visitation:* that is, of afflictions (l. 82).   85 *nature
. . . birth:* cf. *genial spirits,* l. 39.   86 *Imagination:* cf. l. 79 and note.
99 *lute:* cf. l. 7.   100 *tairn:* tarn, mountain lake.   104 *Lutanist:* the
Storm-Wind.   106 *yule:* winter.

Thou Actor, perfect in all tragic sounds!
Thou mighty Poet, e'en to frenzy bold!
    What tell'st thou now about?                    110
    'Tis of the rushing of a host in rout,
With groans of trampled men, with smarting wounds—
At once they groan with pain, and shudder with the cold!
But hush! there is a pause of deepest silence!
    And all that noise, as of a rushing crowd,      115
With groans, and tremulous shudderings—all is over—
    It tells another tale, with sounds less deep and loud!
        A tale of less affright,
        And tempered with delight,
As Otway's self had framed the tender lay,          120
        'Tis of a little child
        Upon a lonesome wild,
Not far from home, but she hath lost her way:
And now moans low in bitter grief and fear,
And now screams loud, and hopes to make her mother
            hear.                                    125


                        VIII

'Tis midnight, but small thoughts have I of sleep:
Full seldom may my friend such vigils keep!
Visit her, gentle Sleep! with wings of healing,
    And may this storm be but a mountain-birth,
May all the stars hang bright above her dwelling,   130
    Silent as though they watched the sleeping Earth!
        With light heart may she rise,
        Gay fancy, cheerful eyes,
    Joy lift her spirit, joy attune her voice;
To her may all things live, from pole to pole,      135
Their life the eddying of her living soul!
    O simple spirit, guided from above,
Dear Lady! friend devoutest of my choice,
Thus mayest thou ever, evermore rejoice.


111 *host:* army.  120 (Thomas) *Otway:* a late-seventeenth-century
tragic dramatist.

# LORD BYRON
## (GEORGE NOEL GORDON) 1788–1824

### She walks in Beauty

#### I

She walks in Beauty, like the night
  Of cloudless climes and starry skies;
And all that's best of dark and bright
  Meet in her aspect and her eyes:
Thus mellow'd to that tender light      5
  Which Heaven to gaudy day denies.

#### II

One shade the more, one ray the less,
  Had half impair'd the nameless grace
Which waves in every raven tress,
  Or softly lightens o'er her face;      10
Where thoughts serenely sweet express
  How pure, how dear their dwelling-place.

#### III

And on that cheek, and o'er that brow,
  So soft, so calm, yet eloquent,
The smiles that win, the tints that glow,      15
  But tell of days in goodness spent,
A mind at peace with all below,
  A heart whose love is innocent!

### Stanzas for Music

#### THERE'S NOT A JOY

#### I

There's not a joy the world can give like that it takes away,
When the glow of early thought declines in feeling's dull
    decay;
'Tis not on youth's smooth cheek the blush alone, which fades
    so fast,
But the tender bloom of heart is gone, ere youth itself be past.

297

### 2

Then the few whose spirits float above the wreck of happiness
Are driven o'er the shoals of guilt or ocean of excess:      6
The magnet of their course is gone, or only points in vain
The shore to which their shiver'd sail shall never stretch again.

### 3

Then the mortal coldness of the soul like death itself comes
  down;
It cannot feel for others' woes, it dare not dream its own;   10
That heavy chill has frozen o'er the fountain of our tears,
And though the eye may sparkle still, 'tis where the ice
  appears.

### 4

Though wit may flash from fluent lips, and mirth distract the
  breast,
Through midnight hours that yield no more their former hope
  of rest;
'Tis but as ivy-leaves around the ruined turret wreath,      15
All green and wildly fresh without, but worn and gray
  beneath.

### 5

Oh could I feel as I have felt,—or be what I have been,
Or weep as I could once have wept, o'er many a vanish'd
  scene;
As springs in deserts found seem sweet, all brackish though
  they be,
So, midst the wither'd waste of life, those tears would flow to
  me.                                                         20

## So, we'll go no more a-roving

### 1

So, we'll go no more a-roving
  So late into the night,
Though the heart be still as loving,
  And the moon be still as bright.

So, we'll go no more. 1 *So,:* First edition, *So.*

II

For the sword outwears its sheath,                     5
  And the soul wears out the breast,
And the heart must pause to breathe,
  And love itself have rest.

III

Though the night was made for loving,
  And the day returns too soon,          10
Yet we'll go no more a-roving
  By the light of the moon.

## On This Day I Complete My Thirty-sixth Year

1

'Tis time this heart should be unmoved,
  Since others it hath ceased to move:
Yet, though I cannot be beloved,
    Still let me love!

2

My days are in the yellow leaf;                         5
  The flowers and fruits of love are gone;
The worm, the canker, and the grief
    Are mine alone!

3

The fire that on my bosom preys
  Is lone as some volcanic isle;          10
No torch is kindled at its blaze—
    A funeral pile.

4

The hope, the fear, the jealous care,
  The exalted portion of the pain
And power of love, I cannot share,                      15
    But wear the chain.

5

But 'tis not *thus*—and 'tis not *here*—
  Such thoughts should shake my soul, nor *now*,
Where glory decks the hero's bier,
    Or binds his brow.          20

### 6

The sword, the banner, and the field,
    Glory and Greece, around me see!
The Spartan, borne upon his shield,
    Was not more free.

### 7

Awake! (not Greece—she *is* awake!)    25
    Awake, my spirit! Think through *whom*
Thy life-blood tracks its parent lake,
    And then strike home!

### 8

Tread those reviving passions down,
    Unworthy manhood!—unto thee    30
Indifferent should the smile or frown
    Of beauty be.

### 9

If thou regret'st thy youth, *why live?*
    The land of honorable death
Is here:—up to the field, and give    35
    Away thy breath!

### 10

Seek out—less often sought than found—
    A soldier's grave, for thee the best;
Then look around, and choose thy ground,
    And take thy rest.    40
        [Missolonghi, Jan. 22, 1824]

*from* CHILDE HAROLD'S PILGRIMAGE

### [Lake Leman]

#### LXXXV

Clear, placid Leman! thy contrasted lake,
With the wide world I dwelt in, is a thing
Which warns me, with its stillness, to forsake
Earth's troubled waters for a purer spring.
This quiet sail is as a noiseless wing    5
To waft me from distraction; once I loved

Torn ocean's roar, but thy soft murmuring
Sounds sweet as if a sister's voice reproved,
That I with stern delights should e'er have been so moved.

### LXXXVI

It is the hush of night, and all between                    10
Thy margin and the mountains, dusk, yet clear,
Mellow'd and mingling, yet distinctly seen,
Save darken'd Jura, whose capt heights appear
Precipitously steep; and drawing near,
There breathes a living fragrance from the shore,          15
Of flowers yet fresh with childhood; on the ear
Drops the light drip of the suspended oar,
Or chirps the grasshopper one good-night carol more.

### LXXXVII

He is an evening reveller, who makes
His life an infancy, and sings his fill;                   20
At intervals, some bird from out the brakes
Starts into voice a moment, then is still.
There seems a floating whisper on the hill,
But that is fancy, for the starlight dews
All silently their tears of love instil,                   25
Weeping themselves away, till they infuse
Deep into Nature's breast the spirit of their hues.

### LXXXVIII

Ye stars! which are the poetry of heaven!
If in your bright leaves we would read the fate
Of men and empires,—'tis to be forgiven,                  30
That in our aspirations to be great,
Our destinies o'erleap their mortal state,
And claim a kindred with you; for ye are
A beauty and a mystery, and create
In us such love and reverence from afar,                  35
That Fortune, Fame, Power, Life, have named themselves a
    Star.

### LXXXIX

All heaven and earth are still—though not in sleep,
But breathless, as we grow when feeling most;
And silent, as we stand in thoughts too deep:—

LAKE LEMAN. 21 *brakes*: thickets.

All heaven and earth are still: From the high host     40
Of stars, to the lull'd lake and mountain-coast,
All is concenter'd in a life intense,
Where not a beam, nor air, nor leaf is lost,
But hath a part of being, and a sense
Of that which is of all Creator and defence.     45

### XC

Then stirs the feeling infinite, so felt
In solitude, where we are *least* alone;
A truth, which through our being then doth melt
And purifies from self: it is a tone,
The soul and source of music, which makes known     50
Eternal harmony, and sheds a charm
Like to the fabled Cytherea's zone,
Binding all things with beauty;—'twould disarm
The spectre Death, had he substantial power to harm.

### XCI

Not vainly did the early Persian make     55
His altar the high places and the peak
Of earth-o'ergazing mountains, and thus take
A fit and unwall'd temple, there to seek
The Spirit, in whose honor shrines are weak,
Uprear'd of human hands. Come, and compare     60
Columns and idol-dwellings, Goth or Greek,
With Nature's realms of worship, earth and air,
Nor fix on fond abodes to circumscribe thy pray'r!

[From *Canto III*]

## [*Rome*]

### LXXVIII

Oh Rome! my Country! City of the Soul!
The orphans of the heart must turn to thee,
Lone Mother of dead Empires! and control
In their shut breasts their petty misery.
What are our woes and sufferance? Come and see     5
The cypress, hear the owl, and plod your way
O'er steps of broken thrones and temples—Ye!
Whose agonies are evils of a day—
A world is at our feet as fragile as our clay.

42-45 *All . . . defence:* cf. Wordsworth, p. 254, ll. 93-102.    52 *Cytherea's zone:* The magic girdle of Venus which excites love.

### LXXIX

The Niobe of nations! there she stands,                    10
Childless and crownless, in her voiceless woe;
An empty urn within her wither'd hands,
Whose holy dust was scatter'd long ago;
The Scipios' Tomb contains no ashes now;
The very sepulchres lie tenantless                         15
Of their heroic dwellers: dost thou flow,
Old Tiber! through a marble wilderness?
Rise, with thy yellow waves, and mantle her distress!

### LXXX

The Goth, the Christian, Time, War, Flood, and Fire,
Have dealt upon the seven-hill'd city's pride;            20
She saw her glories star by star expire,
And up the steep barbarian monarchs ride,
Where the car climb'd the Capitol; far and wide
Temple and tower went down, nor left a site:—
Chaos of ruins! who shall trace the void,                 25
O'er the dim fragments cast a lunar light,
And say, "here was, or is," where all is doubly night?

### LXXXI

The double night of ages, and of her,
Night's daughter, Ignorance, hath wrapt and wrap
All round us; we but feel our way to err:                 30
The ocean hath his chart, the stars their map,
And Knowledge spreads them on her ample lap;
But Rome is as the desert, where we steer
Stumbling o'er recollections; now we clap
Our hands, and cry "Eureka!" "it is clear"—               35
When but some false mirage of ruin rises near.

. . .

ROME. 10 *Niobe of nations:* Niobe, the proud mother of many sons
and daughters, boasted of their superiority to the children of Latona,
Diana and Apollo. The vengeance of the gods was swift: all of her
children were slain by their arrows, and her husband, overwhelmed,
took his own life. Desolate and weeping, yet proud, Niobe was turned
to stone by Zeus, to become a monument of everlasting bereavement.
14 *The Scipios' Tomb:* The most important extant group of Roman
tombs, used by the Scipio family for nearly 400 years. This tomb and
many others are situated at the side of the Appian Way.

### CXLIII

A ruin—yet what ruin! from its mass
Walls, palaces, half-cities, have been rear'd;
Yet oft the enormous skeleton ye pass,
And marvel where the spoil could have appear'd.          40
Hath it indeed been plunder'd, or but clear'd?
Alas! developed, opens the decay,
When the colossal fabric's form is near'd:
It will not bear the brightness of the day,
Which streams too much on all, years, man, have reft away. 45

### CXLIV

But when the rising moon begins to climb
Its topmost arch, and gently pauses there;
When the stars twinkle through the loops of time,
And the low night-breeze waves along the air
The garland-forest, which the gray walls wear,          50
Like laurels on the bald first Caesar's head;
When the light shines serene but doth not glare,
Then in this magic circle raise the dead:
Heroes have trod this spot—'tis on their dust ye tread.

### CXLV

"While stands the Coliseum, Rome shall stand;          55
When falls the Coliseum, Rome shall fall;
And when Rome falls—the World." From our own land
Thus spake the pilgrims o'er this mighty wall
In Saxon times, which we are wont to call
Ancient; and these three mortal things are still          60
On their foundations, and unalter'd all;
Rome and her Ruin past Redemption's skill,
The World, the same wide den—of thieves, or what ye will.

[From *Canto IV*]

45 *reft:* robbed.   48 *loops of time:* apertures in the masonry.   51 *laurels*
. . . *head:* It is said that Caesar wore the laurel wreath on all occasions, not to show himself as the conqueror of the world, but to hide
his baldness.   55-57 *"While . . . World":* Quoted by Gibbon in *The*
*Decline and Fall of the Roman Empire* from the Venerable Bede.

## [*The Ocean*]

### CLXXVIII

There is a pleasure in the pathless woods,
There is a rapture on the lonely shore,
There is society, where none intrudes,
By the deep Sea, and music in its roar:
I love not Man the less, but Nature more,     5
From these our interviews, in which I steal
From all I may be, or have been before,
To mingle with the Universe, and feel
What I can ne'er express, yet can not all conceal.

### CLXXIX

Roll on, thou deep and dark blue ocean—roll!     10
Ten thousand fleets sweep over thee in vain;
Man marks the earth with ruin—his control
Stops with the shore;—upon the watery plain
The wrecks are all thy deed, nor doth remain
A shadow of man's ravage, save his own,     15
When, for a moment, like a drop of rain,
He sinks into thy depths with bubbling groan,
Without a grave, unknell'd, uncoffin'd, and unknown.

### CLXXX

His steps are not upon thy paths,—thy fields
Are not a spoil for him,—thou dost arise     20
And shake him from thee; the vile strength he wields
For earth's destruction thou dost all despise,
Spurning him from thy bosom to the skies,
And send'st him, shivering in thy playful spray
And howling, to his gods, where haply lies     25
His petty hope in some near port or bay,
And dashest him again to earth:—there let him lay.

.  .  .

### CLXXXIII

Thou glorious mirror, where the Almighty's form
Glasses itself in tempests; in all time,
Calm or convuls'd—in breeze, or gale, or storm,     30

Icing the pole, or in the torrid clime
Dark-heaving;—boundless, endless, and sublime—
The image of Eternity—the throne
Of the Invisible; even from out thy slime
The monsters of the deep are made; each zone          35
Obeys thee; thou goest forth, dread, fathomless, alone.


CLXXXIV

And I have loved thee, Ocean! and my joy
Of youthful sports was on thy breast to be
Borne, like thy bubbles, onward: from a boy
I wantoned with thy breakers—they to me          40
Were a delight; and if the freshening sea
Made them a terror—'twas a pleasing fear,
For I was as it were a child of thee,
And trusted to thy billows far and near,
And laid my hand upon thy mane—as I do here.          45

[From *Canto IV*]


*from* DON JUAN

['*Tis Sweet*]

CXXII

—'Tis sweet to hear
At midnight on the blue and moonlit deep
The song and oar of Adria's gondolier,
By distance mellow'd, o'er the waters sweep;
'Tis sweet to see the evening star appear;          5
'Tis sweet to listen as the night-winds creep
From leaf to leaf; 'tis sweet to view on high
The rainbow, based on ocean, span the sky.


CXXIII

'Tis sweet to hear the watch-dog's honest bark
Bay deep-mouth'd welcome as we draw near home;          10
'Tis sweet to know there is an eye will mark
Our coming, and look brighter when we come;
'Tis sweet to be awaken'd by the lark,
Or lull'd by falling waters; sweet the hum
Of bees, the voice of girls, the song of birds,          15
The lisp of children, and their earliest words.

THE OCEAN. 34-35 *out . . . made:* cf. Tennyson, p. 369, ll. 161-63.
40 *wantoned:* frolicked.

### CXXIV

Sweet is the vintage, when the showering grapes
   In Bacchanal profusion reel to earth,
Purple and gushing: sweet are our escapes
   From civic revelry to rural mirth;    20
Sweet to the miser are his glittering heaps,
   Sweet to the father is his first-born's birth,
Sweet is revenge—especially to women,
Pillage to soldiers, prize-money to seamen.

### CXXV

Sweet is a legacy, and passing sweet    25
   The unexpected death of some old lady
Or gentleman of seventy years complete,
   Who've made "us youth" wait too—too long already,
For an estate, or cash, or country-seat,
   Still breaking, but with stamina so steady,    30
That all the Israelites are fit to mob its
Next owner for their double-damn'd post-obits.

### CXXVI

'Tis sweet to win, no matter how, one's laurels,
   By blood or ink; 'tis sweet to put an end
To strife; 'tis sometimes sweet to have our quarrels,    35
   Particularly with a tiresome friend:
Sweet is old wine in bottles, ale in barrels;
   Dear is the helpless creature we defend
Against the world; and dear the schoolboy spot
We ne'er forget, though there we are forgot.    40

### CXXVII

But sweeter still than this, than these, than all,
   Is first and passionate love—it stands alone,
Like Adam's recollection of his fall;
   The Tree of Knowledge has been pluck'd—all's known—
And life yields nothing further to recall    45
   Worthy of this ambrosial sin, so shown,
No doubt in fable, as the unforgiven
Fire which Prometheus filch'd for us from Heaven.

[From Canto I]

'TIS SWEET. 18 *Bacchanal*: Riotous. 20 *civic*: city. 24 *prize-money*:
booty. 32 *post-obits*: legacies. 48 *Prometheus*: the Titan who stole
the fire from heaven after Zeus had denied its use to man. As a punishment Prometheus was chained by Zeus to a mountain (Caucasus) where
he was daily exposed to torture by vultures (or an eagle).

# [*Juan and Haidée*]

### CLXXIV

And thus a moon roll'd on, and fair Haidée
   Paid daily visits to her boy, and took
Such plentiful precautions, that still he
   Remain'd unknown within his craggy nook;
At last her father's prows put out to sea,      5
   For certain merchantmen upon the look,
Not as of yore to carry off an Io,
But three Ragusan vessels, bound for Scio.

### CLXXV

Then came her freedom, for she had no mother,
   So that, her father being at sea, she was      10
Free as a married woman, or such other
   Female, as where she likes may freely pass,
Without even the encumbrance of a brother,
   The freest she that ever gazed on glass:
I speak of Christian lands in this comparison,      15
Where wives, at least, are seldom kept in garrison.

### CLXXVI

Now she prolong'd her visits and her talk
   (For they must talk), and he had learnt to say
So much as to propose to take a walk,—
   For little had he wander'd since the day      20
On which, like a young flower snapped from the stalk,
   Drooping and dewy on the beach he lay,—
And thus they walk'd out in the afternoon,
And saw the sun set opposite the moon.

JUAN AND HAIDÉE. Shipwrecked, Juan is cast ashore upon an island—
"one of the wild and smaller Cyclades"—inhabited, as it turns out, only
by Lambro, a widowed pirate-smuggler, his lovely daughter Haidée, and
Zoe her nurse. Haidée and Zoe come upon Juan asleep, recovering from
his bout with the sea, and the young girl at once assumes responsibility
for his welfare.

7 *Io*: Byron is rhyming playfully, but his reference to Io, the maiden
whom Jupiter transformed into a cow to hide her identity from jealous
Juno, reminds us of the tricks Lambro played upon Haidée's mother.
8 *Ragusan*: of Ragusa, city in Sicily. *Scio*: isle in the Aegean Sea.

### CLXXVII

It was a wild and breaker-beaten coast,                    25
    With cliffs above, and a broad sandy shore,
Guarded by shoals and rocks as by an host,
    With here and there a creek, whose aspect wore
A better welcome to the tempest-tost;
    And rarely ceased the haughty billow's roar,      30
Save on the dead long summer days, which make
The outstretch'd ocean glitter like a lake.

### CLXXVIII

And the small ripple spilt upon the beach
    Scarcely o'erpass'd the cream of your champagne,
When o'er the brim the sparkling bumpers reach,          35
    That spring-dew of the spirit! the heart's rain!
Few things surpass old wine; and they may preach
    Who please,—the more because they preach in vain,—
Let us have Wine and Woman, Mirth and Laughter,
Sermons and soda-water the day after.                    40

### CLXXIX

Man, being reasonable, must get drunk;
    The best of life is but intoxication:
Glory, the Grape, Love, Gold, in these are sunk
    The hopes of all men, and of every nation;
Without their sap, how branchless were the trunk         45
    Of life's strange tree, so fruitful on occasion!
But to return,—Get very drunk; and when
You wake with headache, you shall see what then.

### CLXXX

Ring for your valet—bid him quickly bring
    Some hock and soda-water, then you'll know          50
A pleasure worthy Xerxes the great king;
    For not the blest sherbet, sublimed with snow,
Nor the first sparkle of the desert-spring,
    Nor Burgundy in all its sunset glow,
After long travel, Ennui, Love, or Slaughter,            55
Vie with that draught of hock and soda-water.

27 *host:* army.

### CLXXXI

The coast—I think it was the coast that I
　　Was just describing—Yes, it *was* the coast—
Lay at this period quiet as the sky,
　　The sands untumbled, the blue waves untost,　　　　60
And all was stillness, save the sea-bird's cry,
　　And dolphin's leap, and little billow crost
By some low rock or shelve, that made it fret
Against the boundary it scarcely wet.

### CLXXXII

And forth they wander'd, her sire being gone,　　　　6?
　　As I have said, upon an expedition;
And mother, brother, guardian, she had none,
　　Save Zoe, who, although with due precision
She waited on her lady with the Sun,
　　Thought daily service was her only mission,　　　　70
Bringing warm water, wreathing her long tresses,
And asking now and then for cast-off dresses.

### CLXXXIII

It was the cooling hour, just when the rounded
　　Red sun sinks down behind the azure hill,
Which then seems as if the whole earth it bounded,　　75
　　Circling all nature, hush'd, and dim, and still,
With the far mountain-crescent half surrounded
　　On one side, and the deep sea calm and chill
Upon the other, and the rosy sky,
With one star sparkling through it like an eye.　　　　80

### CLXXXIV

And thus they wander'd forth, and hand in hand,
　　Over the shining pebbles and the shells,
Glided along the smooth and harden'd sand,
　　And in the worn and wild receptacles
Work'd by the storms, yet work'd as it were plann'd,　　85
　　In hollow halls, with sparry roofs and cells,
They turn'd to rest; and, each clasp'd by an arm,
Yielded to the deep twilight's purple charm.

63 *fret :* ripple.

### CLXXXV

They look'd up to the sky, whose floating glow
   Spread like a rosy ocean, vast and bright;      90
They gazed upon the glittering sea below,
   Whence the broad moon rose circling into sight;
They heard the wave's splash, and the wind so low,
   And saw each other's dark eyes darting light
Into each other—and, beholding this,      95
Their lips drew near, and clung into a kiss;

### CLXXXVI

A long, long kiss, a kiss of youth, and love,
   And beauty, all concentrating like rays
Into one focus, kindled from above;
   Such kisses as belong to early days,      100
Where Heart, and Soul, and Sense, in concert move,
   And the blood's lava, and the pulse a blaze,
Each kiss a heart-quake,—for a kiss's strength,
I think, it must be reckon'd by its length.

### CLXXXVII

By length I mean duration; theirs endured      105
   Heaven knows how long—no doubt they never reckon'd;
And if they had, they could not have secured
   The sum of their sensations to a second:
They had not spoken; but they felt allured,
   As if their souls and lips each other beckon'd,      110
Which, being join'd, like swarming bees they clung—
Their hearts the flowers from whence the honey sprung.

### CLXXXVIII

They were alone, but not alone as they
   Who shut in chambers think it loneliness;
The silent ocean, and the starlight bay,      115
   The twilight glow, which momently grew less,
The voiceless sands, and dropping caves, that lay
   Around them, made them to each other press,
As if there were no life beneath the sky
Save theirs, and that their life could never die.      120

### CLXXXIX

They fear'd no eyes nor ears on that lone beach,
  They felt no terrors from the night; they were
All in all to each other: though their speech
  Was broken words, they *thought* a language there,—
And all the burning tongues the passions teach          125
  Found in one sigh the best interpreter
Of nature's oracle—first love,—that all
Which Eve has left her daughters since her fall.

### CXC

Haidée spoke not of scruples, ask'd no vows,
  Nor offer'd any; she had never heard          130
Of plight and promises to be a spouse,
  Or perils by a loving maid incurr'd;
She was all which pure ignorance allows,
  And flew to her young mate like a young bird;
And, never having dreamt of falsehood, she          135
Had not one word to say of constancy.

### CXCI

She loved, and was beloved—she adored,
  And she was worshipp'd; after nature's fashion,
Their intense souls, into each other pour'd,
  If souls could die, had perish'd in that passion,—          140
But by degrees their senses were restored,
  Again to be o'ercome, again to dash on;
And, beating 'gainst *his* bosom, Haidée's heart
Felt as if never more to beat apart.

### CXCII

Alas! they were so young, so beautiful,          145
  So lonely, loving, helpless, and the hour
Was that in which the heart is always full,
  And, having o'er itself no further power,
Prompts deeds eternity can not annul,
  But pays off moments in an endless shower          150
Of hell-fire—all prepared for people giving
Pleasure or pain to one another living.

### CXCIII

Alas! for Juan and Haidée! they were
  So loving and so lovely—till then never,

Excepting our first parents, such a pair                        155
   Had run the risk of being damn'd for ever;
And Haidée, being devout as well as fair,
   Had, doubtless, heard about the Stygian river,
And hell and purgatory—but forgot
Just in the very crisis she should not.                         160

### CXCIV

They look upon each other, and their eyes
   Gleam in the moonlight; and her white arm clasps
Round Juan's head, and his around hers lies
   Half buried in the tresses which it grasps;
She sits upon his knee, and drinks his sighs,                   165
   He hers, until they end in broken gasps;
And thus they form a group that's quite antique,
Half naked, loving, natural, and Greek.

### CXCV

And when those deep and burning moments pass'd,
   And Juan sunk to sleep within her arms,                 170
She slept not, but all tenderly, though fast,
   Sustain'd his head upon her bosom's charms;
And now and then her eye to heaven is cast,
   And then on the pale cheek her breast now warms,
Pillow'd on her o'erflowing heart, which pants                  175
With all it granted, and with all it grants.

### CXCVI

An infant when it gazes on a light,
   A child the moment when it drains the breast,
A devotee when soars the Host in sight,
   An Arab with a stranger for a guest,                     180
A sailor when the prize has struck in fight,
   A miser filling his most hoarded chest,
Feel rapture; but not such true joy are reaping
As they who watch o'er what they love while sleeping.

---

158 *Stygian river:* see Milton, p. 145, l. 3 and note.   179 *soars . . .
sight:* In the Mass, the elevation of the Host (the consecrated Bread)
by the priest for the worshippers to adore.   181 *struck:* lowered, to
indicate surrender.

### CXCVII

For there it lies so tranquil, so beloved,                    185
   All that it hath of life with us is living;
So gentle, stirless, helpless, and unmoved,
   And all unconscious of the joy 'tis giving;
All it hath felt, inflicted, pass'd, and proved,
   Hush'd into depths beyond the watcher's diving:    190
There lies the thing we love with all its errors
And all its charms, like death without its terrors.

### CXCVIII

The lady watch'd her lover—and that hour
   Of Love's, and Night's, and Ocean's solitude,
O'erflow'd her soul with their united power;                 195
   Amidst the barren sand and rocks so rude
She and her wave-worn love had made their bower,
   Where nought upon their passion could intrude,
And all the stars that crowded the blue space
Saw nothing happier than her glowing face.                   200

### CXCIX

Alas! the love of Women! it is known
   To be a lovely and a fearful thing;
For all of theirs upon that die is thrown,
   And if 'tis lost, life hath no more to bring
To them but mockeries of the past alone,                     205
   And their revenge is as the tiger's spring,
Deadly, and quick, and crushing; yet, as real
Torture is theirs, what they inflict they feel.

### CC

They are right; for Man, to man so oft unjust,
   Is always so to Women: one sole bond               210
Awaits them, treachery is all their trust;
   Taught to conceal, their bursting hearts despond
Over their idol, till some wealthier lust
   Buys them in marriage—and what rests beyond?
A thankless husband, next a faithless lover,                 215
Then dressing, nursing, praying, and all's over.

### CCI

Some take a lover, some take drams or prayers,
   Some mind their household, others dissipation,

217 *drams:* small drinks.

Some run away, and but exchange their cares,
   Losing the advantage of a virtuous station;     220
Few changes e'er can better their affairs,
   Theirs being an unnatural situation,
From the dull palace to the dirty hovel:
Some play the devil, and then write a novel.

### CCII

Haidée was Nature's bride, and knew not this;     225
   Haidée was Passion's child, born where the sun
Showers triple light, and scorches even the kiss
   Of his gazelle-eyed daughters; she was one
Made but to love, to feel that she was his
   Who was her chosen: what was said or done     230
Elsewhere was nothing.—She had nought to fear,
Hope, care, nor love beyond, her heart beat *here*.

### CCIII

And oh! that quickening of the heart, that beat!
   How much it costs us! yet each rising throb
Is in its cause as its effect so sweet,     235
   That Wisdom, ever on the watch to rob
Joy of its alchemy, and to repeat
   Fine truths; even Conscience, too, has a tough job
To make us understand each good old maxim,
So good—I wonder Castlereagh don't tax 'em.     240

### CCIV

And now 'twas done—on the lone shore were plighted
   Their hearts; the stars, their nuptial torches, shed
Beauty upon the beautiful they lighted:
   Ocean their witness, and the cave their bed,
By their own feelings hallow'd and united,     245
   Their priest was Solitude, and they were wed:
And they were happy, for to their young eyes
Each was an angel, and earth paradise.

[From *Canto II*]

240 (Viscount) *Castlereagh*: Robert Stewart, Foreign Secretary, whose
support of a tax program in peacetime to reduce the public debt was
opposed by the Whigs—Byron's party.

# PERCY BYSSHE SHELLEY 1792–1822

## Mont Blanc

### LINES WRITTEN IN THE VALE OF CHAMOUNI

#### I

The everlasting universe of things
Flows through the mind, and rolls its rapid waves,
Now dark—now glittering—now reflecting gloom—
Now lending splendor, where from secret springs
The source of human thought its tribute brings          5
Of waters,—with a sound but half its own,
Such as a feeble brook will oft assume
In the wild woods, among the mountains lone,
Where waterfalls around it leap for ever,
Where woods and winds contend, and a vast river          10
Over its rocks ceaselessly bursts and raves.

#### II

Thus thou, Ravine of Arve—dark, deep Ravine—
Thou many-colored, many-voicéd vale,
Over whose pines and crags and caverns sail
Fast clouds, shadows, and sunbeams; awful scene,          15
Where Power in likeness of the Arve comes down
From the ice-gulfs that gird his secret throne,
Bursting through these dark mountains like the flame
Of lightning through the tempest;—thou dost lie,
Thy giant brood of pines around thee clinging,          20
Children of elder time, in whose devotion
The chainless winds still come and ever came
To drink their odors, and their mighty swinging
To hear—an old and solemn harmony:
Thine earthly rainbows stretched across the sweep          25
Of the ethereal waterfall, whose veil
Robes some unsculptured image; the strange sleep
Which, when the voices of the desert fail,
Wraps all in its own deep eternity;—
Thy caverns echoing to the Arve's commotion,          30
A loud, lone sound, no other sound can tame;

Mont Blanc. 15 *clouds, shadows:* cloud shadows (1817 edn.). 20 *Thy:* from edition of 1824. 30-31 *Thy caverns . . . tame:* These lines have been variously punctuated.

Thou art pervaded with that ceaseless motion,
Thou art the path of that unresting sound—
Dizzy Ravine! and when I gaze on thee
I seem as in a trance sublime and strange                    35
To muse on my own separate fantasy,
My own, my human mind, which passively
Now renders and receives fast influencings,
Holding an unremitting interchange
With the clear universe of things around;                    40
One legion of wild thoughts, whose wandering wings
Now float above thy darkness, and now rest
Where that or thou art no unbidden guest,
In the still cave of the witch Poesy,
Seeking among the shadows that pass by                       45
Ghosts of all things that are, some shade of thee,
Some phantom, some faint image; till the breast
From which they fled recalls them, thou art there!

### III

Some say that gleams of a remoter world
Visit the soul in sleep,—that death is slumber,             50
And that its shapes the busy thoughts outnumber
Of those who wake and live.—I look on high;
Has some unknown omnipotence unfurled
The veil of life and death? or do I lie
In dream, and does the mightier world of sleep              55
Spread far around and inaccessibly
Its circles? For the very spirit fails,
Driven like a homeless cloud from steep to steep
That vanishes among the viewless gales!
Far, far above, piercing the infinite sky,                  60
Mont Blanc appears,—still, snowy, and serene—
Its subject mountains their unearthly forms
Pile around it, ice and rock; broad vales between
Of frozen floods, unfathomable deeps,
Blue as the overhanging heaven, that spread                 65
And wind among the accumulated steeps;
A desert peopled by the storms alone,
Save when the eagle brings some hunter's bone,

37-38 *passively . . . receives;* cf. Wordsworth, p. 254, ll. 105-07 and
elsewhere.  38 *just;* permanent.  44 40 cave . . . *that cave* of Plato's
"allegory of the cave," *The Republic,* Book VII.  54 *veil:* Shelley's use
of the veil is paradoxical: the veil does not hide but reveal. Cf. p. 331,
l. 259 and note. See also, Vaughan, p. 190, esp. ll. 37 ff.  56 *Spread:*
*Speed,* possibly an error (1839 edn.).  59 *viewless:* invisible.

And the wolf tracks her there—how hideously
Its shapes are heaped around! rude, bare, and high,                70
Ghastly, and scarred, and riven.—Is this the scene
Where the old Earthquake-demon taught her young
Ruin? Were these their toys? or did a sea
Of fire envelop once this silent snow?
None can reply—all seems eternal now.                             75
The wilderness has a mysterious tongue
Which teaches awful doubt, or faith so mild,
So solemn, so serene, that man may be
But for such faith with nature reconciled;
Thou hast a voice, great Mountain, to repeal                      80
Large codes of fraud and woe; not understood
By all, but which the wise, and great, and good,
Interpret, or make felt, or deeply feel.


IV

The fields, the lakes, the forests, and the streams,
Ocean, and all the living things that dwell                       85
Within the dædal earth; lightning, and rain,
Earthquake, and fiery flood, and hurricane,
The torpor of the year when feeble dreams
Visit the hidden buds, or dreamless sleep
Holds every future leaf and flower;—the bound                    90
With which from that detested trance they leap;
The works and ways of man, their death and birth,
And that of him and all that his may be;
All things that move and breathe with toil and sound
Are born and die, revolve, subside, and swell.                   95
Power dwells apart in its tranquillity
Remote, serene, and inaccessible:
And *this*, the naked countenance of earth,
On which I gaze, even these primeval mountains,
Teach the adverting mind. The glaciers creep                     100
Like snakes that watch their prey, from their far fountains,
Slow rolling on; there, many a precipice

86 *dædal*: ingeniously contrived or working, as if made by Daedalus,
the artificer, who built the Cretan Labyrinth, and later, after he and
his son Icarus were imprisoned in it, made wings wherewith they
escaped. Icarus flew too near the sun, and the wax which held on his
wings melted; he fell into the "Icarian" sea and was drowned. See
Auden, p. 514, l. 14. 88 *torpor . . . year*: winter. 102 *Slow*: Slowly
(1839 edn.).

Frost and the Sun in scorn of mortal power
Have piled—dome, pyramid, and pinnacle,
A city of death, distinct with many a tower      105
And wall impregnable of beaming ice.
Yet not a city, but a flood of ruin
Is there, that from the boundaries of the sky
Rolls its perpetual stream; vast pines are strewing
Its destined path, or in the mangled soil      110
Branchless and shattered stand; the rocks, drawn down
From yon remotest waste, have overthrown
The limits of the dead and living world,
Never to be reclaimed. The dwelling-place
Of insects, beasts, and birds, becomes its spoil;      115
Their food and their retreat forever gone,
So much of life and joy is lost. The race
Of man flies far in dread; his work and dwelling
Vanish, like smoke before the tempest's stream,
And their place is not known. Below, vast caves      120
Shine in the rushing torrent's restless gleam,
Which from those secret chasms in tumult welling
Meet in the vale, and one majestic River,
The breath and blood of distant lands, forever
Rolls its loud waters to the ocean waves,      125
Breathes its swift vapors to the circling air.

### v

Mont Blanc yet gleams on high:—the power is there,
The still and solemn power of many sights
And many sounds, and much of life and death.
In the calm darkness of the moonless nights,      130
In the lone glare of day, the snows descend
Upon that Mountain; none beholds them there,
Nor when the flakes burn in the sinking sun,
Or the star-beams dart through them:—Winds contend
Silently there, and heap the snow with breath      135
Rapid and strong, but silently! Its home
The voiceless lightning in these solitudes
Keeps innocently, and like vapor broods
Over the snow. The secret strength of things
Which governs thought, and to the infinite dome      140
Of heaven is as a law, inhabits thee!
And what were thou, and earth, and stars, and sea,
If to the human mind's imaginings
Silence and solitude were vacancy?

## Ozymandias

SONNET

I met a traveler from an antique land
Who said: Two vast and trunkless legs of stone
Stand in the desert. Near them, on the sand,
Half sunk, a shattered visage lies, whose frown,
And wrinkled lip, and sneer of cold command,          5
Tell that its sculptor well those passions read
Which yet survive, stamped on these lifeless things,
The hand that mocked them and the heart that fed;
And on the pedestal these words appear:
"My name is Ozymandias, king of kings:                10
Look on my works, ye Mighty, and despair!"
Nothing beside remains. Round the decay
Of that colossal wreck, boundless and bare
The lone and level sands stretch far away.


## Ode to the West Wind

I

O wild West Wind, thou breath of Autumn's being,
Thou, from whose unseen presence the leaves dead
Are driven, like ghosts from an enchanter fleeing,

Yellow, and black, and pale, and hectic red,
Pestilence-stricken multitudes: O thou,                5
Who chariotest to their dark wintry bed

The wingéd seeds, where they lie cold and low,
Each like a corpse within its grave, until
Thine azure sister of the Spring shall blow

Her clarion o'er the dreaming earth, and fill         10
(Driving sweet buds like flocks to feed in air)
With living hues and odors plain and hill:

Wild Spirit, which art moving everywhere;
Destroyer and preserver; hear, oh hear!

OZYMANDIAS. 7-8 *survive . . . fed:* outlast the sculptor and his subject.  10 *Ozymandias:* the Egyptian Pharaoh who oppressed the Children of Israel.

ODE TO THE WEST WIND. 4 *hectic:* feverish.

## II

Thou on whose stream, 'mid the steep sky's commotion,    15
Loose clouds like earth's decaying leaves are shed,
Shook from the tangled boughs of Heaven and Ocean,

Angels of rain and lightning: there are spread
On the blue surface of thine airy surge,
Like the bright hair uplifted from the head    20

Of some fierce Maenad, even from the dim verge
Of the horizon to the zenith's height
The locks of the approaching storm. Thou dirge

Of the dying year, to which this closing night
Will be the dome of a vast sepulcher,    25
Vaulted with all thy congregated might

Of vapors, from whose solid atmosphere
Black rain, and fire, and hail will burst: Oh hear!

## III

Thou who didst waken from his summer dreams
The blue Mediterranean, where he lay,    30
Lulled by the coil of his crystálline streams,

Beside a pumice isle in Baiae's bay,
And saw in sleep old palaces and towers
Quivering within the wave's intenser day,

All overgrown with azure moss and flowers    35
So sweet, the sense faints picturing them! Thou
For whose path the Atlantic's level powers

Cleave themselves into chasms, while far below
The sea-blooms and the oozy woods which wear
The sapless foliage of the ocean, know    40

Thy voice, and suddenly grow gray with fear,
And tremble and despoil themselves: Oh hear!

21 *Maenad:* a frenzied nymph participating in the rites of Bacchus
(Dionysus).  31 *coil:* din.  32 *Baiae's bay:* west of Naples.  39-42 *sea-
. . . themselves:* The vegetation at the bottom of the sea, etc., "sympa-
thizes with that of the land in the change of seasons, and is conse-
quently influenced by the winds which announce it."—Shelley's note.

### IV

If I were a dead leaf thou mightest bear;
If I were a swift cloud to fly with thee;
A wave to pant beneath thy power, and share          45

The impulse of thy strength, only less free
Than thou, O uncontrollable! If even
I were as in my boyhood, and could be

The comrade of thy wanderings over heaven,
As then, when to outstrip thy skyey speed          50
Scarce seemed a vision, I would ne'er have striven

As thus with thee in prayer in my sore need.
Oh! lift me as a wave, a leaf, a cloud!
I fall upon the thorns of life! I bleed!

A heavy weight of hours has chained and bowed          55
One too like thee: tameless, and swift, and proud.

### V

Make me thy lyre, even as the forest is:
What if my leaves are falling like its own!
The tumult of thy mighty harmonies

Will take from both a deep, autumnal tone,          60
Sweet though in sadness. Be thou, spirit fierce,
My spirit! Be thou me, impetuous one!

Drive my dead thoughts over the universe
Like withered leaves to quicken a new birth;
And, by the incantation of this verse,          65

Scatter, as from an unextinguished hearth
Ashes and sparks, my words among mankind!
Be through my lips to unawakened earth

The trumpet of a prophecy! O Wind,
If Winter comes, can Spring be far behind?          70

55 *hours . . . chained:* cf. p. 330, l. 234.

## *Adonais*

AN ELEGY ON THE DEATH OF JOHN KEATS, AUTHOR OF ENDYMION,
HYPERION, ETC.

I

I weep for Adonais—he is dead!
O, weep for Adonais! though our tears
Thaw not the frost which binds so dear a head!
And thou, sad Hour, selected from all years
To mourn our loss, rouse thy obscure compeers,      5
And teach them thine own sorrow, say: with me
Died Adonais; till the Future dares
Forget the Past, his fate and fame shall be
An echo and a light unto eternity!

II

Where wert thou, mighty Mother, when he lay,      10
When thy Son lay, pierced by the shaft which flies
In darkness? where was lorn Urania
When Adonais died? With veiled eyes,
'Mid listening Echoes, in her Paradise
She sate, while one, with soft enamored breath,      15
Rekindled all the fading melodies,
With which, like flowers that mock the corse beneath,
He had adorned and hid the coming bulk of death.

III

O, weep for Adonais—he is dead!
Wake, melancholy Mother, wake and weep!      20
Yet wherefore? Quench within their burning bed
Thy fiery tears, and let thy loud heart keep
Like his, a mute and uncomplaining sleep;
For he is gone, where all things wise and fair
Descend;—oh, dream not that the amorous Deep      25
Will yet restore him to the vital air;
Death feeds on his mute voice, and laughs at our despair.

ADONAIS. 10 *mighty Mother:* Urania (l. 12), the Heavenly Muse, and
highest source of poetic inspiration : also, the Uranian Aphrodite, or
Heavenly Venus, personifying Divine Love, the "mother" of all goodness, truth, and love.   12 *lorn:* bereft.

#### IV

Most musical of mourners, weep again!
Lament anew, Urania!—He died,
Who was the Sire of an immortal strain,        30
Blind, old, and lonely, when his country's pride,
The priest, the slave, and the liberticide,
Trampled and mocked with many a loathed rite
Of lust and blood; he went, unterrified,
Into the gulf of death; but his clear Sprite        35
Yet reigns o'er earth; the third among the sons of light.

#### V

Most musical of mourners, weep anew!
Not all to that bright station dared to climb;
And happier they their happiness who knew,
Whose tapers yet burn through that night of time    40
In which suns perished; others more sublime,
Struck by the envious wrath of man or God,
Have sunk, extinct in their refulgent prime;
And some yet live, treading the thorny road,      44
Which leads, through toil and hate, to Fame's serene abode.

#### VI

But now, thy youngest, dearest one, has perished,
The nursling of thy widowhood, who grew,
Like a pale flower by some sad maiden cherished,
And fed with true love tears, instead of dew;
Most musical of mourners, weep anew!        50
Thy extreme hope, the loveliest and the last,
The bloom, whose petals nipt before they blew,
Died on the promise of the fruit, is waste;
The broken lily lies—the storm is overpast.

#### VII

To that high Capital, where kingly Death        55
Keeps his pale court in beauty and decay,
He came; and bought, with price of purest breath,

29 *He*: Milton. Cf. "London, 1802," p. 259.  35 *Sprite*: cf. *spirit*, Milton,
p. 157, l. 70.  36 *third . . . light*: In *A Defence of Poetry*, Shelley suggests that the other two "sons of light" were Homer and Dante.  52 *blew*: bloomed.  55 *Capital*: Rome, where Keats died and was buried.

A grave among the eternal.—Come away!
Haste, while the vault of blue Italian day
Is yet his fitting charnel-roof! while still                    60
He lies, as if in dewy sleep he lay;
Awake him not! surely he takes his fill
Of deep and liquid rest, forgetful of all ill.


### VIII

He will awake no more, oh, never more!—
Within the twilight chamber spreads apace,                    65
The shadow of white Death, and at the door
Invisible Corruption waits to trace
His extreme way to her dim dwelling-place;
The eternal Hunger sits, but pity and awe
Soothe her pale rage, nor dares she to deface                  70
So fair a prey, till darkness, and the law
Of change, shall o'er his sleep the mortal curtain draw.


### IX

O, weep for Adonais!—The quick Dreams,
The passion-wingéd Ministers of thought,
Who were his flocks, whom near the living streams              75
Of his young spirit he fed, and whom he taught
The love which was its music, wander not,—
Wander no more, from kindling brain to brain,
But droop there, whence they sprung; and mourn their lot
Round the cold heart, where, after their sweet pain,           80
They ne'er will gather strength, or find a home again.


### X

And one with trembling hands clasps his cold head,
And fans him with her moonlight wings, and cries;
"Our love, our hope, our sorrow, is not dead;
See, on the silken fringe of his faint eyes,                   85
Like dew upon a sleeping flower, there lies
A tear some Dream has loosened from his brain."
Lost Angel of a ruined Paradise!
She knew not 'twas her own; as with no stain
She faded, like a cloud which had outwept its rain.            90

68 *extreme*: remote.   72 *Of . . . draw*: from 1839.   73 *quick*: living.
70 *droop*: linger bending downward.

### XI

One from a lucid urn of starry dew
Washed his light limbs as if embalming them;
Another clipt her profuse locks, and threw
The wreath upon him, like an anadem,
Which frozen tears instead of pearls begem;                    95
Another in her willful grief would break
Her bow and wingéd reeds, as if to stem
A greater loss with one which was more weak;
And dull the barbéd fire against his frozen cheek.

### XII

Another Splendor on his mouth alit,                            100
That mouth, whence it was wont to draw the breath
Which gave it strength to pierce the guarded wit,
And pass into the panting heart beneath
With lightning and with music: the damp death
Quenched its caress upon his icy lips;                         105
And, as a dying meteor stains a wreath
Of moonlight vapor, which the cold night clips,
It flushed through his pale limbs, and past to its eclipse.

### XIII

And others came . . . Desires and Adorations,
Wingéd Persuasions and veiled Destinies,                       110
Splendors, and Glooms, and glimmering Incarnations
Of hopes and fears, and twilight Phantasies;
And Sorrow, with her family of Sighs,
And Pleasure, blind with tears, led by the gleam
Of her own dying smile instead of eyes,                        115
Came in slow pomp;—the moving pomp might seem
Like pageantry of mist on an autumnal stream.

### XIV

All he had loved, and molded into thought,
From shape, and hue, and odor, and sweet sound,
Lamented Adonais. Morning sought                               120

94 *anadem:* garland.    107 *clips:* dissolves.    116 *pomp:* solemn procession.

Her eastern watchtower, and her hair unbound,
Wet with the tears which should adorn the ground,
Dimmed the aërial eyes that kindle day;
Afar the melancholy thunder moaned,
Pale Ocean in unquiet slumber lay,                               125
And the wild winds flew round, sobbing in their dismay.


XV

Lost Echo sits amid the voiceless mountains,
And feeds her grief with his remembered lay,
And will no more reply to winds or fountains,
Or amorous birds perched on the young green spray,    130
Or herdsman's horn, or bell at closing day;
Since she can mimic not his lips, more dear
Than those for whose disdain she pined away
Into a shadow of all sounds:—a drear
Murmur, between their songs, is all the woodmen hear.    135


XVI

Grief made the young Spring wild, and she threw down
Her kindling buds, as if she Autumn were,
Or they dead leaves; since her delight is flown,
For whom should she have waked the sullen year?
To Phoebus was not Hyacinth so dear,                            140
Nor to himself Narcissus, as to both
Thou Adonais: wan they stand and sere
Amid the faint companions of their youth,
With dew all turned to tears; odor, to sighing ruth.


127 *Echo:* Her chattering tongue caused Juno to deprive her of all use
of voice except for making reply. Hence, she could only "mimic" the
words Narcissus spoke to her. Her pursuit of him was without success.
See note on l. 141.    128 *lay:* song.    132 *his lips:* the dead poet's.    133
*those:* of Narcissus.    140 *Phoebus . . . Hyacinth:* Hyacinth, a youth
much loved by Phoebus (Apollo), was accidentally killed trying to retrieve the discus which Phoebus had thrown. To commemorate their
friendship and to honor the youth, Apollo signed the flower (Hyacinth), which sprang up on the spot where Hyacinth had died, with
*AI, AI,* expressive of his sorrow. Cf. Milton, p. 159, l. 106.    141 *Narcissus:* Moved by the prayers of a rejected maiden that Narcissus might
know the pain of unrequited love, the goddess Nemesis caused him to
fall in love with his own reflected image, for which he languished and
died.    143 *faint companions:* from 1839.

### XVII

Thy spirit's sister, the lorn nightingale    145
Mourns not her mate with such melodious pain;
Not so the eagle, who like thee could scale
Heaven, and could nourish in the sun's domain
Her mighty youth with morning, doth complain,
Soaring and screaming round her empty nest,  150
As Albion wails for thee: the curse of Cain
Light on his head who pierced thy innocent breast,
And scared the angel soul that was its earthly guest!

### XVIII

Ah woe is me! Winter is come and gone,
But grief returns with the revolving year;   155
The airs and streams renew their joyous tone;
The ants, the bees, the swallows reappear;
Fresh leaves and flowers deck the dead Seasons' bier;
The amorous birds now pair in every brake,
And build their mossy homes in field and brere;  160
And the green lizard, and the golden snake,
Like unimprisoned flames, out of their trance awake.

### XIX

Through wood and stream and field and hill and Ocean
A quickening life from the Earth's heart has burst
As it has ever done, with change and motion,  165
From the great morning of the world when first
God dawned on Chaos; in its stream immersed,
The lamps of Heaven flash with a softer light;
All baser things pant with life's sacred thirst;
Diffuse themselves; and spend in love's delight,  170
The beauty and the joy of their renewéd might.

### XX

The leprous corpse, touched by this spirit tender,
Exhales itself in flowers of gentle breath;
Like incarnations of the stars, when splendor
Is changed to fragrance, they illumine death  175

151 *Albion:* England. *curse of Cain:* God's mark upon Cain's fore-head to acquaint the world with his crime. See l. 306. 152 *his head:* of John Wilson Croker, author of the anonymous attack on Keats' *Endymion* in the *Quarterly Review* (April, 1818) thought by Shelley and others to have been instrumental in Keats' death. 160 *brere:* briar. 167 *stream:* from 1839. 173 *Exhales:* Transpires.

And mock the merry worm that wakes beneath;
Nought we know, dies. Shall that alone which knows
Be as a sword consumed before the sheath
By sightless lightning?—th' intense atom glows
A moment, then is quenched in a most cold repose.        180

#### XXI

Alas! that all we loved of him should be,
But for our grief, as if it had not been,
And grief itself be mortal! Woe is me!
Whence are we, and why are we? of what scene
The actors or spectators? Great and mean        185
Meet massed in death, who lends what life must borrow.
As long as skies are blue, and fields are green,
Evening must usher night, night urge the morrow,
Month follow month with woe, and year wake year to
        sorrow.

#### XXII

*He* will awake no more, oh, never more!        190
"Wake thou," cried Misery, "childless Mother, rise
Out of thy sleep, and slake, in thy heart's core,
A wound more fierce than his with tears and sighs."
And all the Dreams that watched Urania's eyes,
And all the Echoes whom their sister's song        195
Had held in holy silence, cried: "Arise!"
Swift as a Thought by the snake Memory stung,
From her ambrosial rest the fading Splendor sprung.

#### XXIII

She rose like an autumnal Night, that springs
Out of the East, and follows wild and drear        200
The golden Day, which, on eternal wings,
Even as a ghost abandoning a bier,
Had left the Earth a corpse. Sorrow and fear
So struck, so roused, so rapt Urania;
So saddened round her like an atmosphere        205
Of stormy mist; so swept her on her way
Even to the mournful place where Adonais lay.

177-79 *Shall . . . lightning:* Shall the mind die before the body, as a
sword destroyed by lightning before its sheath is consumed.   186 *lends
. . . borrow:* Possibly, life is nourished by death, by the plants and
creatures which lend themselves to that purpose.   204 *rapt:* lifted.

### XXIV

Out of her secret Paradise she sped,
Through camps and cities rough with stone, and steel,
And human hearts, which to her aery tread          210
Yielding not, wounded the invisible
Palms of her tender feet where'er they fell:
And barbéd tongues, and thoughts more sharp than they
Rent the soft Form they never could repel,
Whose sacred blood, like the young tears of May,          215
Paved with eternal flowers that undeserving way.


### XXV

In the death chamber for a moment Death,
Shamed by the presence of that living Might,
Blushed to annihilation, and the breath
Revisited those lips, and life's pale light          220
Flashed through those limbs, so late her dear delight.
"Leave me not wild and drear and comfortless,
As silent lightning leaves the starless night!
Leave me not!" cried Urania: her distress
Roused Death: Death rose and smiled, and met her vain
          caress.          225

### XXVI

"Stay yet awhile! speak to me once again;
Kiss me, so long but as a kiss may live;
And in my heartless breast and burning brain
That word, that kiss shall all thoughts else survive,
With food of saddest memory kept alive,          230
Now thou art dead, as if it were a part
Of thee, my Adonais! I would give
All that I am to be as thou now art!
But I am chained to Time, and cannot thence depart!

### XXVII

"O gentle child, beautiful as thou wert,          235
Why didst thou leave the trodden paths of men
Too soon, and with weak hands though mighty heart
Dare the unpastured dragon in his den?

219 *to annihilation*: as if Death had never been. Thus, Love overcomes
Death; but Distress brings Death back "to life" (l. 225). 234 *chained
to Time*: Time (cf. p. 322, ll. 55-56) enslaves the free spirit, and Love
is such a spirit; Death releases it. 238 *unpastured dragon*: the reviewer. See l. 152 and note.

Defenseless as thou wert, oh where was then
Wisdom the mirrored shield, or scorn the spear?     24t
Or hadst thou waited the full cycle, when
Thy spirit should have filled its crescent sphere,
The monsters of life's waste had fled from thee like deer.


XXVIII

"The herded wolves, bold only to pursue;
The obscene ravens, clamorous o'er the dead;     245
The vultures to the conqueror's banner true
Who feed where Desolation first has fed,
And whose wings rain contagion;—how they fled,
When like Apollo, from his golden bow,
The Pythian of the age one arrow sped     250
And smiled!—The spoilers tempt no second blow,
They fawn on the proud feet that spurn them lying low.


XXIX

"The sun comes forth, and many reptiles spawn;
He sets, and each ephemeral insect then
Is gathered into death without a dawn,     255
And the immortal stars awake again;
So is it in the world of living men:
A godlike mind soars forth, in its delight
Making earth bare and veiling heaven, and when
It sinks, the swarms that dimmed or shared its light     260
Leave to its kindred lamps the spirit's awful night."


XXX

Thus ceased she: and the mountain shepherds came,
Their garlands sere, their magic mantles rent;
The Pilgrim of Eternity, whose fame
Over his living head like Heaven is bent,     265
An early but enduring monument,

242 *filled . . . sphere:* as the full moon "fills" its "crescent sphere."
243 *monsters . . . waste:* e.g., the bad critics. See ll. 152, 238.   250
*Pythian . . . age:* Byron, for his earlier attack upon such critics as
Keats' detractors (in *English Bards and Scotch Reviewers,* 1809) is
given the name earned by Apollo for slaying the slime-born serpent
Python near Delphi.   252 *lying low:* from 1839.   259 *Making . . .
bare:* revealing the beauty of earth. Cf. *Nature's naked loveliness,* l. 275.
*veiling:* see p. 317, l. 54 and note.   260 *swarms . . . light:* cf. ll. 462-
63.   261 *kindred lamps:* poets like Adonais. Cf. *mountain shepherds,*
l. 262.   264 *Pilgrim:* Byron, because of *Childe Harold's Pilgrimage* (see
Canto III, stanza 70, ll. 7-8).

Came, veiling all the lightnings of his song
In sorrow; from her wilds Ierne sent
The sweetest lyrist of her saddest wrong,
And love taught grief to fall like music from his tongue.　270

### XXXI

Midst others of less note, came one frail Form,
A phantom among men; companionless
As the last cloud of an expiring storm
Whose thunder is its knell; he, as I guess,
Had gazed on Nature's naked loveliness,　275
Actaeon-like, and now he fled astray
With feeble steps o'er the world's wilderness,
And his own thoughts, along that rugged way,
Pursued, like raging hounds, their father and their prey.

### XXXII

A pardlike Spirit beautiful and swift—　280
A Love in desolation masked;—a Power
Girt round with weakness;—it can scarce uplift
The weight of the superincumbent hour;
It is a dying lamp, a falling shower,
A breaking billow;—even whilst we speak　285
Is it not broken? On the withering flower
The killing sun smiles brightly: on a cheek
The life can burn in blood, even while the heart may break.

### XXXIII

His head was bound with pansies overblown,
And faded violets, white, and pied, and blue;　290
And a light spear topped with a cypress cone,
Round whose rude shaft dark ivy-tresses grew
Yet dripping with the forest's noonday dew,
Vibrated, as the ever-beating heart
Shook the weak hand that grasped it; of that crew　295
He came the last, neglected and apart;
A herd-abandoned deer struck by the hunter's dart.

268 *Ierne* [Ireland] *sent:* i.e., sent Thomas Moore, the Irish lyrist. 271 *"one . . . Form:* Shelley himself. 276 *Actaeon-like:* Like Acteon, who, while hunting, came upon the chaste Diana at her bath. The goddess, incensed, dashed water into Acteon's face and turned him into a stag, which his own dogs pursued and tore to pieces. 280 *pardlike:* leopard-like. 290 *pied:* vari-colored. 295 *crew: mountain shepherds,* l. 262. Cf. *band,* l. 299.

#### XXXIV

All stood aloof, and at his partial moan
Smiled through their tears; well knew that gentle band
Who in another's fate now wept his own;                          300
As in the accents of an unknown land,
He sung new sorrow; sad Urania scanned
The Stranger's mien, and murmured: "Who art thou?"
He answered not, but with a sudden hand
Made bare his branded and ensanguined brow,                      305
Which was like Cain's or Christ's—Oh! that it should be so!

#### XXXV

What softer voice is hushed over the dead?
Athwart what brow is that dark mantle thrown?
What form leans sadly o'er the white death-bed,
In mockery of monumental stone,                                  310
The heavy heart heaving without a moan?
If it be He, who, gentlest of the wise,
Taught, soothed, loved, honored the departed one;
Let me not vex, with inharmonious sighs
The silence of that heart's accepted sacrifice.                  315

#### XXXVI

Our Adonais has drunk poison—oh!
What deaf and viperous murderer could crown
Life's early cup with such a draught of woe?
The nameless worm would now itself disown:
It felt, yet could escape the magic tone                         320
Whose prelude held all envy, hate, and wrong,
But what was howling in one breast alone,
Silent with expectation of the song,
Whose master's hand is cold, whose silver lyre unstrung.

---

298 *partial:* felt, with partiality.    306 *Cain's or Christ's:* Shelley does
not allude to Cain's crime, but to his suffering (*branded* brow, l. 305),
as the eternal, homeless wanderer, and to Christ's suffering (*ensanguined brow*, l. 305) as well. See Gen. 4.12-14;    316 *Adonais . . .
poison:* Shelley again attacks Croker—the *nameless worm,* l. 319—
whose "poison" killed Keats.    321-24 *Whose . . . unstrung:* Whose
first effort held back the envy, etc., of all but the reviewer, while they
anticipated the great poem Keats might have written had he lived.

334

Live thou, whose infamy is not thy fame!                           325
Live! fear no heavier chastisement from me,
Thou noteless blot on a remembered name!
But be thyself, and know thyself to be!
And ever at thy season be thou free
To spill the venom when thy fangs o'erflow:                        330
Remorse and Self-contempt shall cling to thee;
Hot Shame shall burn upon thy secret brow,
And like a beaten hound tremble thou shalt—as now.


XXXVIII

Nor let us weep that our delight is fled
Far from these carrion kites that scream below;                    335
He wakes or sleeps with the enduring dead;
Thou canst not soar where he is sitting now.—
Dust to the dust! but the pure spirit shall flow
Back to the burning fountain whence it came,
A portion of the Eternal, which must glow                          340
Through time and change, unquenchably the same,
Whilst thy cold embers choke the sordid hearth of shame.


XXXIX

Peace, peace! he is not dead, he doth not sleep—
He hath awakened from the dream of life—
'Tis we, who lost in stormy visions, keep                          345
With phantoms an unprofitable strife,
And in mad trance, strike with our spirit's knife
Invulnerable nothings.—*We* decay
Like corpses in a charnel; fear and grief
Convulse us and consume us day by day,                             350
And cold hopes swarm like worms within our living clay.


XL

He has outsoared the shadow of our night;
Envy and calumny and hate and pain,
And that unrest which men miscall delight,
Can touch him not and torture not again;                           355
From the contagion of the world's slow stain
He is secure, and now can never mourn
A heart grown cold, a head grown gray in vain;
Nor, when the spirit's self has ceased to burn,
With sparkless ashes load an unlamented urn.                       360

344 *dream of life:* or, death is an awakening. Cf. p. 317, ll. 49 ff.

### XLI

He lives, he wakes—'tis Death is dead, not he;
Mourn not for Adonais.—Thou young Dawn,
Turn all thy dew to splendor, for from thee
The spirit thou lamentest is not gone;
Ye caverns and ye forests, cease to moan!            365
Cease ye faint flowers and fountains, and thou Air,
Which like a mourning veil thy scarf hadst thrown
O'er the abandoned Earth, now leave it bare
Even to the joyous stars which smile on its despair!

### XLII

He is made one with Nature: there is heard         370
His voice in all her music, from the moan
Of thunder, to the song of night's sweet bird;
He is a presence to be felt and known
In darkness and in light, from herb and stone,
Spreading itself where'er that Power may move     375
Which has withdrawn his being to its own;
Which wields the world with never-wearied love,
Sustains it from beneath, and kindles it above.

### XLIII

He is a portion of the loveliness
Which once he made more lovely: he doth bear      380
His part, while the one Spirit's plastic stress
Sweeps through the dull dense world, compelling there,
All new successions to the forms they wear;
Torturing th' unwilling dross that checks its flight
To its own likeness, as each mass may bear;        385
And bursting in its beauty and its might
From trees and beasts and men into the Heaven's light.

### XLIV

The splendors of the firmament of time
May be eclipsed, but are extinguished not;
Like stars to their appointed height they climb,   390
And death is a low mist which cannot blot
The brightness it may veil. When lofty thought
Lifts a young heart above its mortal lair,
And love and life contend in it, for what
Shall be its earthly doom, the dead live there      395
And move like winds of light on dark and stormy air.

367 *veil*: cf. p. 317, l. 54 and note.   381 *plastic stress*: creative urgency.
Cf. Lycidas' reward, p. 161, ll. 172-81 ; Hallam's, p. 374, ll. 317-32.

### XLV

The inheritors of unfulfilled renown
Rose from their thrones, built beyond mortal thought,
Far in the Unapparent. Chatterton
Rose pale, his solemn agony had not                          400
Yet faded from him; Sidney, as he fought
And as he fell and as he lived and loved
Sublimely mild, a Spirit without spot,
Arose; and Lucan, by his death approved:
Oblivion as they rose shrank like a thing reproved.         405


### XLVI

And many more, whose names on Earth are dark
But whose transmitted effluence cannot die
So long as fire outlives the parent spark,
Rose, robed in dazzling immortality.
"Thou art become as one of us," they cry,                   410
"It was for thee yon kingless sphere has long
Swung blind in unascended majesty,
Silent alone amid an Heaven of song.
Assume thy wingéd throne, thou Vesper of our throng!"


### XLVII

Who mourns for Adonais? oh come forth                       415
Fond wretch! and know thyself and him aright.
Clasp with thy panting soul the pendulous Earth;
As from a center, dart thy spirit's light
Beyond all worlds, until its spacious might
Satiate the void circumference: then shrink                 420
Even to a point within our day and night;
And keep thy heart light lest it make thee sink
When hope has kindled hope, and lured thee to the brink.


### XLVIII

Or go to Rome, which is the sepulcher,
O, not of him, but of our joy: 'tis nought                  425
That ages, empires, and religions there
Lie buried in the ravage they have wrought;

399, 401, 404 (Thomas) *Chatterton* (1752-1771), (Sir Philip) *Sidney* (1554-1586), (Marcus Annaeus) *Lucan* (39-65): All poets who died young.  414 *Vesper*: Venus, as evening star, the brightest star.  416 *Fond*: Foolish.

For such as he can lend,—they borrow not
Glory from those who made the world their prey;
And he is gathered to the kings of thought                    430
Who waged contention with their time's decay,
And of the past are all that cannot pass away.


### XLIX

Go thou to Rome,—at once the Paradise,
The grave, the city, and the wilderness;
And where its wrecks like shattered mountains rise,          435
And flowering weeds, and fragrant copses dress
The bones of Desolation's nakedness
Pass, till the Spirit of the spot shall lead
Thy footsteps to a slope of green access
Where, like an infant's smile, over the dead,                440
A light of laughing flowers along the grass is spread;


### L

And gray walls molder round, on which dull Time
Feeds, like slow fire upon a hoary brand;
And one keen pyramid with wedge sublime,
Pavilioning the dust of him who planned                      445
This refuge for his memory, doth stand
Like flame transformed to marble; and beneath,
A field is spread, on which a newer band
Have pitched in Heaven's smile their camp of death,
Welcoming him we lose with scarce extinguished breath. 450


### LI

Here pause: these graves are all too young as yet
To have outgrown the sorrow which consigned
Its charge to each; and if the seal is set,
Here, on one fountain of a mourning mind,
Break it not thou! too surely shalt thou find               455
Thine own well full, if thou returnest home,
Of tears and gall. From the world's bitter wind
Seek shelter in the shadow of the tomb.
What Adonais is, why fear we to become?

444 *pyramid:* tomb of Caius Cestius (first cent. B.C.), in what is now
the Protestant Cemetery where Keats was buried.

### LII

The One remains, the many change and pass;  460
Heaven's light forever shines, Earth's shadows fly;
Life, like a dome of many-colored glass,
Stains the white radiance of Eternity,
Until Death tramples it to fragments.—Die,
If thou wouldst be with that which thou dost seek!  465
Follow where all is fled!—Rome's azure sky,
 Flowers, ruins, statues, music, words, are weak
The glory they transfuse with fitting truth to speak.

### LIII

Why linger, why turn back, why shrink, my Heart?
Thy hopes are gone before: from all things here  470
They have departed; thou shouldst now depart!
A light is past from the revolving year,
And man, and woman; and what still is dear
Attracts to crush, repels to make thee wither.
The soft sky smiles,—the low wind whispers near:  475
 'Tis Adonais calls! oh, hasten thither,
No more let Life divide what Death can join together.

### LIV

That Light whose smile kindles the Universe,
That Beauty in which all things work and move,
That Benediction which the eclipsing Curse  480
Of birth can quench not, that sustaining Love
Which through the web of being blindly wove
By man and beast and earth and air and sea,
Burns bright or dim, as each are mirrors of
 The fire for which all thirst; now beams on me,  485
Consuming the last clouds of cold mortality.

### LV

The breath whose might I have invoked in song
Descends on me; my spirit's bark is driven,
Far from the shore, far from the trembling throng
Whose sails were never to the tempest given;  490
The massy earth and spheréd skies are riven!
I am borne darkly, fearfully, afar;
 Whilst burning through the inmost veil of Heaven,
 The soul of Adonais, like a star,
Beacons from the abode where the Eternal are.  495

460-64 *The . . . fragments:* An epigrammatic summary of Shelley's
Platonism. 491 *riven:* split.

## To Night

Swiftly walk over the western wave,
  Spirit of Night!
Out of the misty eastern cave,
Where all the long and lone daylight,
Thou wovest dreams of joy and fear,    5
Which make thee terrible and dear,—
  Swift be thy flight!

Wrap thy form in a mantle gray,
  Star-inwrought!
Blind with thine hair the eyes of Day;   10
Kiss her until she be wearied out,
Then wander o'er city, and sea, and land,
Touching all with thine opiate wand—
  Come, long-sought!

When I arose and saw the dawn,    15
  I sighed for thee;
When light rode high, and the dew was gone,
And noon lay heavy on flower and tree,
And the weary Day turned to his rest,
Lingering like an unloved guest,    20
  I sighed for thee.

Thy brother Death came, and cried,
  Wouldst thou me?
Thy sweet child Sleep, the filmy-eyed,
Murmured like a noon-tide bee,    25
Shall I nestle near thy side?
Wouldst thou me?—And I replied,
  No, not thee!

Death will come when thou art dead,
  Soon, too soon—    30
Sleep will come when thou art fled;
Of neither would I ask the boon
I ask of thee, beloved Night—
Swift be thine approaching flight,
  Come soon, soon!    35

To Night. 1 over: o'er (Harvard MS).

## Lines: When the lamp is shattered

When the lamp is shattered,
The light in the dust lies dead—
  When the cloud is scattered,
The rainbow's glory is shed.
  When the lute is broken,          5
Sweet tones are remembered not;
  When the lips have spoken,
Loved accents are soon forgot.

  As music and splendor
Survive not the lamp and the lute,      10
  The heart's echoes render
No song when the spirit is mute:—
  No song but sad dirges,
Like the wind through a ruined cell,
  Or the mournful surges         15
That ring the dead seaman's knell.

  When hearts have once mingled,
Love first leaves the well-built nest;
  The weak one is singled
To endure what it once possest.       20
  O, Love! who bewailest
The frailty of all things here,
  Why choose you the frailest
For your cradle, your home, and your bier?

  Its passions will rock thee,      25
As the storms rock the ravens on high:
  Bright reason will mock thee,
Like the sun from a wintry sky.
  From thy nest every rafter
Will rot, and thine eagle home      30
  Leave thee naked to laughter,
When leaves fall and cold winds come.

LINES. *2 light in the dust:* light in the air disclosing dust particles.

# JOHN KEATS 1795–1821

## On First Looking into Chapman's Homer

Much have I travell'd in the realms of gold,
   And many goodly states and kingdoms seen;
   Round many western islands have I been
Which bards in fealty to Apollo hold.
Oft of one wide expanse had I been told      5
   That deep-brow'd Homer ruled as his demesne;
   Yet did I never breathe its pure serene
Till I heard Chapman speak out loud and bold:
Then felt I like some watcher of the skies
   When a new planet swims into his ken;      10
Or like stout Cortez when with eagle eyes
   He star'd at the Pacific—and all his men
Look'd at each other with a wild surmise—
   Silent, upon a peak in Darien.


## Keen, fitful gusts are whisp'ring here and there

Keen, fitful gusts are whisp'ring here and there
   Among the bushes half leafless, and dry;
   The stars look very cold about the sky,
And I have many miles on foot to fare.
Yet feel I little of the cool bleak air,      5
   Or of the dead leaves rustling drearily,
   Or of those silver lamps that burn on high,
Or of the distance from home's pleasant lair:
For I am brimfull of the friendliness
   That in a little cottage I have found;      10
Of fair-hair'd Milton's eloquent distress,
   And all his love for gentle Lycid drown'd;
Of lovely Laura in her light green dress,
   And faithful Petrarch gloriously crown'd.

ON FIRST LOOKING. 4 *in fealty:* by oath of fidelity. *Apollo:* patron
of music and poetry. 6 *demesne:* a lord's own domain. 8 (George)
*Chapman* (1559?-1634): Translator. 11 *Cortez:* in fact, Balboa.
   KEEN, FITFUL GUSTS. 11-12 *Milton's . . . drown'd:* see pp. 155-161.
13-14 *Laura . . . crown'd:* Laura, whom the Italian poet Petrarch
(1304-1374) celebrated in his sonnets. Petrarch was crowned poet
laureate at Rome in 1340.

## On the Sea

It keeps eternal whisperings around
    Desolate shores, and with its mighty swell
    Gluts twice ten thousand caverns, till the spell
Of Hecate leaves them their old shadowy sound.
Often 'tis in such gentle temper found,          5
      That scarcely will the very smallest shell
      Be moved for days from where it sometime fell,
When last the winds of heaven were unbound.
Oh ye, who have your eye-balls vex'd and tired,
      Feast them upon the wideness of the Sea;    10
        Oh, ye whose ears are dinn'd with uproar rude,
    Or fed too much with cloying melody,—
        Sit ye near some old cavern's mouth, and brood
Until ye start, as if the sea-nymphs quired.


## When I have fears that I may cease to be

When I have fears that I may cease to be
    Before my pen has glean'd my teeming brain,
Before high-piled books, in charact'ry,
    Hold like rich garners the full-ripen'd grain;
When I behold, upon the night's starr'd face,    5
    Huge cloudy symbols of a high romance,
And think that I may never live to trace
    Their shadows, with the magic hand of chance;
And when I feel, fair creature of an hour!
    That I shall never look upon thee more,    10
Never have relish in the faery power
    Of unreflecting love! then on the shore
Of the wide world I stand alone, and think
Till love and fame to nothingness do sink.

---

ON THE SEA. 4 *Hecate:* a goddess of the infernal regions; but earlier, as here, a Titan who ruled in the heaven, the earth, and the sea.

WHEN I HAVE FEARS. 3 *charact'ry:* words as symbols. Cf. *symbols,* l. 6. 4 *garners:* granaries. 8 *magic . . . chance:* the magic hand which chance has given him.

# *Bright star! would I were steadfast as thou art*

### LAST SONNET

Bright star! would I were steadfast as thou art—
   Not in lone splendor hung aloft the night
And watching, with eternal lids apart,
   Like nature's patient, sleepless Eremite,
The moving waters at their priestlike task     5
   Of pure ablution round earth's human shores,
Or gazing on the new soft-fallen mask
   Of snow upon the mountains and the moors—
No—yet still steadfast, still unchangeable,
   Pillow'd upon my fair love's ripening breast,   10
To feel for ever its soft fall and swell,
   Awake for ever in a sweet unrest,
Still, still to hear her tender-taken breath,
And so live ever—or else swoon to death.


### ODES

## *Ode on Melancholy*

### I

No, no, go not to Lethe, neither twist
   Wolf's-bane, tight-rooted, for its poisonous wine;
Nor suffer thy pale forehead to be kiss'd
   By nightshade, ruby grape of Proserpine;
Make not your rosary of yew-berries,     5
   Nor let the beetle, nor the death-moth be
     Your mournful Psyche, nor the downy owl
A partner in your sorrow's mysteries;
   For shade to shade will come too drowsily,
     And drown the wakeful anguish of the soul.   10

---

BRIGHT STAR! 4 *Eremite:* Hermit, or religious recluse. 6 *ablution:*
a cleansing, as a religious rite.

ODE ON MELANCHOLY. 1 *Lethe:* The river in Hades whose water
produces forgetfulness.

## 2

But when the melancholy fit shall fall
  Sudden from heaven like a weeping cloud,
That fosters the droop-headed flowers all,
  And hides the green hill in an April shroud;
Then glut thy sorrow on a morning rose,         15
  Or on the rainbow of the salt sand-wave,
    Or on the wealth of globéd peonies;
Or if thy mistress some rich anger shows,
  Emprison her soft hand, and let her rave,
    And feed deep, deep upon her peerless eyes.    20

## 3

She dwells with Beauty—Beauty that must die;
  And Joy, whose hand is ever at his lips
Bidding adieu; and aching Pleasure nigh,
  Turning to poison while the bee-mouth sips:
Ay, in the very temple of Delight          25
  Veil'd Melancholy has her sovran shrine,
    Though seen of none save him whose strenuous tongue
Can burst Joy's grape against his palate fine;
His soul shall taste the sadness of her might,
  And be among her cloudy trophies hung.     30

## Ode to a Nightingale

### 1

My heart aches, and a drowsy numbness pains
  My sense, as though of hemlock I had drunk,
Or emptied some dull opiate to the drains
  One minute past, and Lethe-wards had sunk:
'Tis not through envy of thy happy lot,        5
  But being too happy in thine happiness,—
    That thou, light-wingéd Dryad of the trees,
      In some melodious plot
  Of beechen green, and shadows numberless,
    Singest of summer in full-throated ease.     10

11 ff. Cf. Milton, p. 145, l. 1 and note, and p. 150, ll. 11 ff.
  ODE TO A NIGHTINGALE. 2 *hemlock :* a poisonous potion. 4 *Lethe-:*
see "Ode on Melancholy," p. 343, l. 1 and note. 7 *Dryad :* wood nymph.

2

O, for a draught of vintage! that hath been
  Cool'd a long age in the deep-delvéd earth,
Tasting of Flora and the country green,
  Dance, and Provençal song, and sunburnt mirth!
O for a beaker full of the warm South,        15
  Full of the true, the blushful Hippocrene,
    With beaded bubbles winking at the brim,
      And purple-stainéd mouth;
  That I might drink, and leave the world unseen,
  And with thee fade away into the forest dim    20

3

Fade far away, dissolve, and quite forget
  What thou among the leaves hast never known,
The weariness, the fever, and the fret
  Here, where men sit and hear each other groan;
Where palsy shakes a few, sad, last gray hairs,    25
  Where youth grows pale, and specter-thin, and dies;
    Where but to think is to be full of sorrow
      And leaden-eyed despairs,
  Where Beauty cannot keep her lustrous eyes,
    Or new Love pine at them beyond to-morrow.    30

4

Away! away! for I will fly to thee,
  Not charioted by Bacchus and his pards,
But on the viewless wings of Poesy,
  Though the dull brain perplexes and retards:
Already with thee! tender is the night,    35
  And haply the Queen-Moon is on her throne,
    Cluster'd around by all her starry Fays;
      But here there is no light,
  Save what from heaven is with the breezes blown    39
    Through verdurous glooms and winding mossy ways.

---

13 *Flora:* the Flower Goddess; here, flowers.  14 *Provençal song:* lyric
verses by twelfth-century Troubadours of Provence (SE France).  16
*Hippocrene:* the fountain of the Muses, on Mt. Helicon.  32 *Bacchus:*
the god of wine; his chariot here is drawn by leopards.  33 *viewless:*
invisible.  37 *Fays:* fairies.

### 5

I cannot see what flowers are at my feet,
   Nor what soft incense hangs upon the boughs,
But, in embalméd darkness, guess each sweet
   Wherewith the seasonable month endows
The grass, the thicket, and the fruit-tree wild;      45
   White hawthorn, and the pastoral eglantine;
      Fast fading violets cover'd up in leaves;
         And mid-May's eldest child,
The coming musk-rose, full of dewy wine,
      The murmurous haunt of flies on summer eves.   50

### 6

Darkling I listen; and, for many a time
   I have been half in love with easeful Death,
Call'd him soft names in many a muséd rhyme,
   To take into the air my quiet breath;
Now more than ever seems it rich to die,      55
   To cease upon the midnight with no pain,
      While thou art pouring forth thy soul abroad
         In such an ecstasy!
Still wouldst thou sing, and I have ears in vain—
      To thy high requiem become a sod.   60

### 7

Thou wast not born for death, immortal Bird!
   No hungry generations tread thee down;
The voice I hear this passing night was heard
   In ancient days by emperor and clown:
Perhaps the self-same song that found a path      65
   Through the sad heart of Ruth, when, sick for home,
      She stood in tears amid the alien corn;
         The same that oft-times hath
Charm'd magic casements, opening on the foam
      Of perilous seas, in faery lands forlorn.   70

---

43 *embalméd*: perfumed.  51 *Darkling*: In the dark.  59-60 *thou . . . sod*: Your song to me is like the music of the Mass for the Burial of the Dead.  66 *Ruth*: see Ruth 2.

### 8

Forlorn! the very word is like a bell
 To toll me back from thee to my sole self!
Adieu! the fancy cannot cheat so well
 As she is fam'd to do, deceiving elf.
Adieu! adieu! thy plaintive anthem fades   75
 Past the near meadows, over the still stream,
  Up the hill-side; and now 'tis buried deep
  In the next valley-glades:
 Was it a vision, or a waking dream?
  Fled is that music:—Do I wake or sleep?   80

## Ode on a Grecian Urn

### 1

Thou still unravish'd bride of quietness,
 Thou foster-child of silence and slow time,
Sylvan historian, who canst thus express
 A flowery tale more sweetly than our rhyme:
What leaf-fring'd legend haunts about thy shape  5
 Of deities or mortals, or of both,
  In Tempe or the dales of Arcady?
 What men or gods are these? What maidens loth?
What mad pursuit? What struggle to escape?
 What pipes and timbrels? What wild ecstasy?  10

### 2

Heard melodies are sweet, but those unheard
 Are sweeter; therefore, ye soft pipes, play on;
Not to the sensual ear, but, more endear'd,
 Pipe to the spirit ditties of no tone:
Fair youth, beneath the trees, thou canst not leave  15
 Thy song, nor ever can those trees be bare;
  Bold Lover, never, never canst thou kiss,
Though winning near the goal—yet, do not grieve;
 She cannot fade, though thou hast not thy bliss,
 For ever wilt thou love, and she be fair!  20

ODE ON A GRECIAN URN. 7 *Tempe, Arcady* [Arcadia]: places in
Greece of idyllic beauty and peacefulness; pastoral utopias. 10 *timbrels:*
tambourines.

### 3

Ah, happy, happy boughs! that cannot shed
  Your leaves, nor ever bid the Spring adieu;
And, happy melodist, unwearied,
  For ever piping songs for ever new;
More happy love! more happy, happy love!          25
  For ever warm and still to be enjoy'd,
    For ever panting, and for ever young;
All breathing human passion far above,
  That leaves a heart high-sorrowful and cloy'd,
    A burning forehead, and a parching tongue.     30

### 4

Who are these coming to the sacrifice?
  To what green altar, O mysterious priest,
Lead'st thou that heifer lowing at the skies,
  And all her silken flanks with garlands drest?
What little town by river or sea shore,          35
  Or mountain-built with peaceful citadel,
    Is emptied of this folk, this pious morn?
And, little town, thy streets for evermore
  Will silent be; and not a soul to tell
    Why thou art desolate, can e'er return.       40

### 5

O Attic shape! Fair attitude! with brede
  Of marble men and maidens overwrought,
With forest branches and the trodden weed;
  Thou, silent form, dost tease us out of thought
As doth eternity: Cold Pastoral!                 45
  When old age shall this generation waste,
    Thou shalt remain, in midst of other woe
Than ours, a friend to man, to whom thou say'st,
  Beauty is truth, truth beauty,—that is all
    Ye know on earth, and all ye need to know.    50

41 *Attic:* Greek, Athenian.  *brede:* possibly the ornamented band running around the urn.  49 *Beauty . . . beauty:* Enclosed in quotation marks, 1820.

## Ode to Psyche

O Goddess! hear these tuneless numbers, wrung
  By sweet enforcement and remembrance dear,
And pardon that thy secrets should be sung
  Even into thine own soft-conchéd ear:
Surely I dreamt to-day, or did I see            5
  The wingéd Psyche with awaken'd eyes?
I wander'd in a forest thoughtlessly,
  And, on the sudden, fainting with surprise,
Saw two fair creatures, couchéd side by side
  In deepest grass, beneath the whisp'ring roof     10
  Of leaves and trembled blossoms, where there ran
    A brooklet, scarce espied:

'Mid hush'd, cool-rooted flowers, fragrant-eyed,
  Blue, silver-white, and budded Tyrian,
They lay calm breathing, on the bedded grass;     15
  Their arms embracéd, and their pinions too;
  Their lips touch'd not, but had not bade adieu,
As if disjoinéd by soft-handed slumber,
And ready still past kisses to outnumber
  At tender eye-dawn of aurorean love:     20
    The wingéd boy I knew;
  But who wast thou, O happy, happy dove?
  His Psyche true!

O latest born and loveliest vision far
  Of all Olympus' faded hierarchy!     25
Fairer than Phoebe's sapphire-region'd star,
  Or Vesper, amorous glow-worm of the sky;

---

ODE TO PSYCHE. *Psyche:* A beautiful girl who fell in love with
Cupid. She was separated from him and subjected to hardship because
of her sisters' envy and Venus' jealousy. At last the two were reunited,
and Psyche was deified (cf. *latest born*, l. 24). The personification of the
soul.
4 *conchéd:* like a sea or conch shell.   9 *creatures:* Cupid and Psyche.
14 *Tyrian:* bluish-red.   20 *aurorean:* like Aurora, dawning.   24 *latest born:* Psyche, latecomer to Olympus, abode of the gods.   26 *Phoebe's*
[Cynthia's] . . . *star:* the moon.   27 *Vesper:* Venus, evening star

Fairer than these, though temple thou hast none,
    Nor altar heap'd with flowers;
Nor virgin-choir to make delicious moan         30
    Upon the midnight hours;
No voice, no lute, no pipe, no incense sweet
    From chain-swung censer teeming;
No shrine, no grove, no oracle, no heat
    Of pale-mouth'd prophet dreaming.         35

O brightest! though too late for antique vows,
    Too, too late for the fond believing lyre,
When holy were the haunted forest boughs,
    Holy the air, the water, and the fire;
Yet even in these days so far retir'd         40
    From happy pieties, thy lucent fans,
    Fluttering among the faint Olympians,
I see, and sing, by my own eyes inspired.
So let me be thy choir, and make a moan
    Upon the midnight hours;         45
Thy voice, thy lute, thy pipe, thy incense sweet
    From swingéd censer teeming;
Thy shrine, thy grove, thy oracle, thy heat
    Of pale-mouth'd prophet dreaming.

Yes, I will be thy priest, and build a fane         50
    In some untrodden region of my mind,
Where branchéd thoughts, new grown with pleasant pain,
    Instead of pines shall murmur in the wind:
Far, far around shall those dark-cluster'd trees
    Fledge the wild-ridged mountains steep by steep;     55
And there by zephyrs, streams, and birds, and bees,
    The moss-lain Dryads shall be lull'd to sleep;
And in the midst of this wide quietness
A rosy sanctuary will I dress
With the wreath'd trellis of a working brain,         60
    With buds, and bells, and stars without a name,
With all the gardener Fancy e'er could feign,
    Who breeding flowers, will never breed the same.
And there shall be for thee all soft delight
    That shadowy thought can win,         65
A bright torch, and a casement ope at night,
    To let the warm Love in!

44 *moan:* the lover's complaint.   50 *fane:* temple.   55 *Fledge:* Cover.
57 *Dryads:* wood nymphs.   62 *feign:* invent.

## To Autumn

### 1

Season of mists and mellow fruitfulness,
  Close bosom-friend of the maturing sun;
Conspiring with him how to load and bless
  With fruit the vines that round the thatch-eaves run;
To bend with apples the moss'd cottage-trees,    5
  And fill all fruit with ripeness to the core;
    To swell the gourd, and plump the hazel shells
With a sweet kernel; to set budding more,
And still more, later flowers for the bees,
Until they think warm days will never cease,    10
    For Summer has o'er-brimm'd their clammy cells.

### 2

Who hath not seen thee oft amid thy store?
  Sometimes whoever seeks abroad may find
Thee sitting careless on a granary floor,
  Thy hair soft-lifted by the winnowing wind;    15
Or on a half-reap'd furrow sound asleep,
  Drows'd with the fume of poppies, while thy hook
    Spares the next swath and all its twined flowers:
And sometimes like a gleaner thou dost keep
  Steady thy laden head across a brook;    20
  Or by a cider-press, with patient look,
    Thou watchest the last oozings hours by hours.

### 3

Where are the songs of Spring? Ay, where are they?
  Think not of them, thou hast thy music too,—
While barred clouds bloom the soft-dying day,    25
  And touch the stubble-plains with rosy hue;
Then in a wailful choir the small gnats mourn
  Among the river sallows, borne aloft
    Or sinking as the light wind lives or dies;
And full-grown lambs loud bleat from hilly bourn;    30
  Hedge-crickets sing; and now with treble soft
  The redbreast whistles from a garden-croft;
    And gathering swallows twitter in the skies.

To AUTUMN. 17 *hook:* reaping hook. 28 *sallows:* willows. 30 *bourn:* realm. 32 *-croft:* -plot.

# ALFRED, LORD TENNYSON 1809–1892

## *Mariana*

Mariana in the moated grange.
*Measure for Measure*

With blackest moss the flower-plots
　　Were thickly crusted, one and all:
The rusted nails fell from the knots
　　That held the pear to the gable-wall.
The broken sheds look'd sad and strange:　　　5
　　Unlifted was the clinking latch;
　　Weeded and worn the ancient thatch
Upon the lonely moated grange.
　　　　She only said, 'My life is dreary,
　　　　　He cometh not,' she said;　　　　10
　　　　She said, 'I am aweary, aweary,
　　　　　I would that I were dead!'


Her tears fell with the dews of even;
　　Her tears fell ere the dews were dried;
She could not look on the sweet heaven,　　　15
　　Either at morn or eventide.
After the flitting of the bats,
　　When thickest dark did trance the sky,
　　She drew her casement-curtain by,
And glanced athwart the glooming flats.　　　20
　　　　She only said, 'The night is dreary,
　　　　　He cometh not,' she said;
　　　　She said, 'I am aweary, aweary,
　　　　　I would that I were dead!'


Upon the middle of the night,　　　　　　　25
　　Waking she heard the night-fowl crow:
The cock sung out an hour ere light:
　　From the dark fen the oxen's low
Came to her: without hope of change,
　　In sleep she seem'd to walk forlorn,　　　30
　　Till cold winds woke the gray-eyed morn
About the lonely moated grange.

MARIANA. 4 *pear . . . -wall:* from the edition of 1860. 8 *grange:*
a house with farm buildings attached. 18 *trance:* entrance.

She only said, 'The day is dreary,
He cometh not,' she said;
She said, 'I am aweary, aweary,                    35
I would that I were dead!'

About a stone-cast from the wall
A sluice with blacken'd waters slept,
And o'er it many, round and small,
The cluster'd marish-mosses crept.              40
Hard by a poplar shook alway,
All silver-green with gnarled bark:
For leagues no other tree did mark
The level waste, the rounding gray.
She only said, 'My life is dreary,             45
He cometh not,' she said;
She said, 'I am aweary, aweary,
I would that I were dead!'

And ever when the moon was low,
And the shrill winds were up and away,         50
In the white curtain, to and fro,
She saw the gusty shadows sway.
But when the moon was very low,
And the wild winds bound within their cell,
The shadow of the poplar fell                  55
Upon her bed, across her brow.
She only said, 'The night is dreary,
He cometh not,' she said;
She said, 'I am aweary, aweary,
I would that I were dead!'                      60

All day within the dreamy house,
The doors upon their hinges creak'd;
The blue fly sung in the pane; the mouse
Behind the mouldering wainscot shriek'd,
Or from the crevice peer'd about.              65
Old faces glimmer'd through the doors,
Old footsteps trod the upper floors,
Old voices called her from without.
She only said, 'My life is dreary,
He cometh not,' she said;                       70
She said, 'I am aweary, aweary,
I would that I were dead!'

40 *marish*: marsh.

The sparrow's chirrup on the roof,
　　The slow clock ticking, and the sound
Which to the wooing wind aloof 　　　　　　75
　　The poplar made, did all confound
Her sense; but most she loathed the hour
　　When the thick-moted sunbeam lay
　　Athwart the chambers, and the day
Was sloping toward his western bower. 　　　80
　　　　　Then, said she, 'I am very dreary,
　　　　　　He will not come,' she said;
　　　　　She wept, 'I am aweary, aweary,
　　　　　　Oh God, that I were dead!'


## The Lotos-Eaters

"Courage!" he said, and pointed toward the land,
"This mounting wave will roll us shoreward soon."
In the afternoon they came unto a land,
In which it seemed always afternoon.
All round the coast the languid air did swoon, 　　5
Breathing like one that hath a weary dream.
Full-faced above the valley stood the moon;
And like a downward smoke, the slender stream
Along the cliff to fall and pause and fall did seem.

A land of streams! some, like a downward smoke, 　　10
Slow-dropping veils of thinnest lawn, did go;
And some through wavering lights and shadows broke,
Rolling a slumbrous sheet of foam below.
They saw the gleaming river seaward flow
From the inner land; far off, three mountain-tops, 　　15
Three silent pinnacles of aged snow,
Stood sunset-flush'd: and, dew'd with showery drops,
Up-clomb the shadowy pine above the woven copse.

The charmed sunset linger'd low adown
In the red West: through mountain clefts the dale 　　20
Was seen far inland, and the yellow down

THE LOTOS-EATERS. 1 *he:* Ulysses, or Odysseus, a king of Ithaca and
hero of the Trojan wars, whose famous ten years' homeward voyage
was celebrated by Homer in the *Odyssey.* The land of the lotos-eaters
was one of the places visited in his wanderings.

Border'd with palm, and many a winding vale
And meadow, set with slender galingale;
A land where all things always seem'd the same!
And round about the keel with faces pale,                    25
Dark faces pale against that rosy flame,
The mild-eyed melancholy Lotos-eaters came.

Branches they bore of that enchanted stem,
Laden with flower and fruit, whereof they gave
To each, but whoso did receive of them,                      30
And taste, to him the gushing of the wave
Far far away did seem to mourn and rave
On alien shores; and if his fellow spake,
His voice was thin, as voices from the grave;
And deep-asleep he seem'd, yet all awake,                    35
And music in his ears his beating heart did make.

They sat them down upon the yellow sand,
Between the sun and moon upon the shore;
And sweet it was to dream of Fatherland,
Of child, and wife, and slave; but evermore                  40
Most weary seem'd the sea, weary the oar,
Weary the wandering fields of barren foam.
Then some one said, "We will return no more";
And all at once they sang, "Our island home
Is far beyond the wave; we will no longer roam."             45

CHORIC SONG

I

There is sweet music here that softer falls
Than petals from blown roses on the grass,
Or night-dews on still waters between walls
Of shadowy granite, in a gleaming pass;
Music that gentlier on the spirit lies,                      50
Than tir'd eyelids upon tir'd eyes;
Music that brings sweet sleep down from the blissful skies.
Here are cool mosses deep,
And through the moss the ivies creep,
And in the stream the long-leaved flowers weep,             55
And from the craggy ledge the poppy hangs in sleep.

23 *galingale*: pungent-rooted plants related to the ginger.   44 *island home*: Ithaca.

### 2

Why are we weigh'd upon with heaviness,
And utterly consumed with sharp distress,
While all things else have rest from weariness?
All things have rest: why should we toil alone,     60
We only toil, who are the first of things,
And make perpetual moan,
Still from one sorrow to another thrown:
Nor ever fold our wings,
And cease from wanderings,     65
Nor steep our brows in slumber's holy balm;
Nor hearken what the inner spirit sings,
"There is no joy but calm!"
Why should we only toil, the roof and crown of things?

### 3

Lo! in the middle of the wood,     70
The folded leaf is woo'd from out the bud
With winds upon the branch, and there
Grows green and broad, and takes no care,
Sun-steep'd at noon, and in the moon
Nightly dew-fed; and turning yellow     75
Falls, and floats adown the air.
Lo! sweeten'd with the summer light,
The full-juiced apple, waxing over-mellow,
Drops in a silent autumn night.
All its allotted length of days     80
The flower ripens in its place,
Ripens and fades, and falls, and hath no toil,
Fast-rooted in the fruitful soil.

### 4

Hateful is the dark-blue sky,
Vaulted o'er the dark-blue sea.     85
Death is the end of life; ah, why
Should life all labor be?
Let us alone. Time driveth onward fast,
And in a little while our lips are dumb.
Let us alone. What is it that will last?     90

69 *roof :* the highest point.

All things are taken from us, and become
Portions and parcels of the dreadful Past.
Let us alone. What pleasure can we have
To war with evil? Is there any peace
In ever climbing up the climbing wave?                    95
All things have rest, and ripen toward the grave
In silence—ripen, fall, and cease:
Give us long rest or death, dark death, or dreamful ease.


                              5

How sweet It were, hearing the downward stream,
With half-shut eyes ever to seem                          100
Falling asleep in a half-dream!
To dream and dream, like yonder amber light,
Which will not leave the myrrh-bush on the height;
To hear each other's whisper'd speech;
Eating the Lotos day by day,                              105
To watch the crisping ripples on the beach,
And tender curving lines of creamy spray;
To lend our hearts and spirits wholly
To the influence of mild-minded melancholy;
To muse and brood and live again in memory,              110
With those old faces of our infancy
Heap'd over with a mound of grass,
Two handfuls of white dust, shut in an urn of brass!


                              6

Dear is the memory of our wedded lives,
And dear the last embraces of our wives                   115
And their warm tears: but all hath suffer'd change;
For surely now our household hearths are cold:
Our sons inherit us: our looks are strange:
And we should come like ghosts to trouble joy.
Or else the island princes over-bold                      120
Have eat our substance, and the minstrel sings
Before them of the ten years' war in Troy,
And our great deeds, as half-forgotten things.
Is there confusion in the little isle?
Let what is broken so remain.                             125
The Gods are hard to reconcile:
'Tis hard to settle order once again.

121 *eat:* eaten. *substance:* goods.

There *is* confusion worse than death,
Trouble on trouble, pain on pain,
Long labor unto aged breath,                                    130
Sore task to hearts worn out by many wars
And eyes grown dim with gazing on the pilot-stars.


7

But, propt on beds of amaranth and moly,
How sweet (while warm airs lull us, blowing lowly)
With half-dropt eyelid still,                                   135
Beneath a heaven dark and holy,
To watch the long bright river drawing slowly
His waters from the purple hill—
To hear the dewy echoes calling
From cave to cave through the thick-twined vine—               140
To watch the emerald-color'd water falling
Through many a woven acanthus-wreath divine!
Only to hear and see the far-off sparkling brine,
Only to hear were sweet, stretch'd out beneath the pine.


8

The Lotos blooms below the barren peak:                        145
The Lotos blows by every winding creek:
All day the wind breathes low with mellower tone:
Through every hollow cave and alley lone
Round and round the spicy downs the yellow Lotos-dust is
    blown.
We have had enough of action, and of motion we,               150
Roll'd to starboard, roll'd to larboard, when the surge was
    seething free,
Where the wallowing monster spouted his foam-fountains in
    the sea.
Let us swear an oath, and keep it with an equal mind,
In the hollow Lotos-land to live and lie reclined
On the hills like Gods together, careless of mankind.          155
For they lie beside their nectar, and the bolts are hurl'd
Far below them in the valleys, and the clouds are lightly
    curl'd
Round their golden houses, girdled with the gleaming world:

131 *by:* from 1893.  133 *amaranth:* an imaginary "unfading flower."
*moly:* the plant Hermes gave to Ulysses to protect him from Circe's
magic potion.

Where they smile in secret, looking over wasted lands,
Blight and famine, plague and earthquake, roaring deeps and
    fiery sands,         160
Clanging fights, and flaming towns, and sinking ships, and
    praying hands.
But they smile, they find a music centred in a doleful song
Steaming up, a lamentation and an ancient tale of wrong,
Like a tale of little meaning though the words are strong;
Chanted from an ill-used race of men that cleave the soil, 165
Sow the seed, and reap the harvest with enduring toil,
Storing yearly little dues of wheat, and wine and oil;
Till they perish and they suffer—some, 'tis whisper'd—down
    in hell
Suffer endless anguish, others in Elysian valleys dwell,
Resting weary limbs at last on beds of asphodel.     170
Surely, surely, slumber is more sweet than toil, the shore
Than labor in the deep mid-ocean, wind and wave and oar;
Oh rest ye, brother mariners, we will not wander more.


## Ulysses

It little profits that an idle king,
By this still hearth, among these barren crags,
Match'd with an aged wife, I mete and dole
Unequal laws unto a savage race,
That hoard, and sleep, and feed, and know not me.     5
I cannot rest from travel: I will drink
Life to the lees: all times I have enjoy'd
Greatly, have suffer'd greatly, both with those
That loved me, and alone; on shore, and when
Through scudding drifts the rainy Hyades     10
Vext the dim sea: I am become a name;
For always roaming with a hungry heart
Much have I seen and known;—cities of men
And manners, climates, councils, governments,
Myself not least, but honor'd of them all;—     15

167 *little dues:* only what was necessary.
  ULYSSES. See p. 354, l. 1 and note.
   3 *wife:* Penelope, famous for her devotion to her husband and the
ingenuity with which she put off her many suitors during Ulysses'
absence. *mete:* measure out. 10 *Hyades:* a cluster of stars supposed
to indicate rain when they rose with the sun.

And drunk delight of battle with my peers,
Far on the ringing plains of windy Troy.
I am a part of all that I have met;
Yet all experience is an arch wherethrough
Gleams that untravel'd world, whose margin fades      20
For ever and for ever when I move.
How dull it is to pause, to make an end,
To rust unburnish'd, not to shine in use!
As though to breathe were life! Life piled on life
Were all too little, and of one to me      25
Little remains; but every hour is saved
From that eternal silence, something more,
A bringer of new things; and vile it were
For some three suns to store and hoard myself,
And this gray spirit yearning in desire      30
To follow knowledge, like a sinking star,
Beyond the utmost bound of human thought.

    This is my son, mine own Telemachus,
To whom I leave the scepter and the isle—
Well-loved of me, discerning to fulfil      35
This labor, by slow prudence to make mild
A rugged people, and through soft degrees
Subdue them to the useful and the good.
Most blameless is he, centred in the sphere
Of common duties, decent not to fail      40
In offices of tenderness, and pay
Meet adoration to my household gods,
When I am gone. He works his work, I mine.

    There lies the port: the vessel puffs her sail:
There gloom the dark broad seas. My mariners,      45
Souls that have toil'd, and wrought, and thought with me—
That ever with a frolic welcome took
The thunder and the sunshine, and opposed
Free hearts, free foreheads—you and I are old;
Old age hath yet his honor and his toil.      50
Death closes all: but something ere the end,
Some work of noble note, may yet be done,
Not unbecoming men that strove with Gods.
The lights begin to twinkle from the rocks:
The long day wanes: the slow moon climbs: the deep      55
Moans round with many voices. Come, my friends,
'Tis not too late to seek a newer world.
Push off, and sitting well in order smite
The sounding furrows; for my purpose holds

To sail beyond the sunset, and the baths            60
Of all the western stars, until I die.
It may be that the gulfs will wash us down:
It may be we shall touch the Happy Isles,
And see the great Achilles, whom we knew.
Though much is taken, much abides; and though       65
We are not now that strength which in old days
Moved earth and heaven, that which we are, we are;—
One equal temper of heroic hearts,
Made weak by time and fate, but strong in will
To strive, to seek, to find, and not to yield.      70

*from* THE PRINCESS

### Tears, idle tears

[Sung by a "Maid"]

Tears, idle tears, I know not what they mean,
Tears from the depth of some divine despair
Rise in the heart, and gather to the eyes,
In looking on the happy autumn-fields,
And thinking of the days that are no more.          5

Fresh as the first beam glittering on a sail,
That brings our friends up from the underworld,
Sad as the last which reddens over one
That sinks with all we love below the verge;
So sad, so fresh, the days that are no more.        10

Ah, sad and strange as in dark summer dawns
The earliest pipe of half-awakened birds
To dying ears, when unto dying eyes
The casement slowly grows a glimmering square;
So sad, so strange, the days that are no more.      15

Dear as remember'd kisses after death,
And sweet as those by hopeless fancy feign'd
On lips that are for others; deep as love,
Deep as first love, and wild with all regret;
O Death in Life, the days that are no more.         20

60 *baths:* the seas into which they descend. 62 *gulfs:* whirlpools. 63
*Happy Isles:* Elysium. 64 *Achilles:* chiefest of the Greek heroes who
slew the Trojan Hector. He was himself slain by Paris, whose arrow,
directed by Apollo, struck his heel, his only vulnerable spot.

## *Ask me no more*

Ask me no more: the moon may draw the sea;
　The cloud may stoop from heaven and take the shape
　With fold to fold, of mountain or of cape;
But I too fond, when have I answer'd thee?
　　　Ask me no more.　　　　　　　　　5

Ask me no more: what answer should I give?
　I love not hollow cheek or faded eye:
　Yet, O my friend, I will not have thee die!
Ask me no more, lest I should bid thee live;
　　　Ask me no more.　　　　　　　　　10

Ask me no more: thy fate and mine are seal'd:
　I strove against the stream and all in vain:
　Let the great river take me to the main:
No more, dear love, for at a touch I yield;
　　　Ask me no more.　　　　　　　　　15

## *Now sleeps the crimson petal*

["Read" by Ida]

Now sleeps the crimson petal, now the white;
Nor waves the cypress in the palace walk;
Nor winks the gold fin in the porphyry font:
The fire-fly wakens: waken thou with me.

Now droops the milkwhite peacock like a ghost,　　5
And like a ghost she glimmers on to me.

Now lies the Earth all Danaë to the stars,
And all thy heart lies open unto me.

Now slides the silent meteor on, and leaves
A shining furrow, as thy thoughts in me.　　　10

Now folds the lily all her sweetness up,
And slips into the bosom of the lake:
So fold thyself, my dearest, thou, and slip
Into my bosom and be lost in me.

NOW SLEEPS. 7 *Danaë:* Mother of Perseus by Zeus who visited her
as a golden shower in her prison tower.

## Come down, O maid, from yonder mountain height

[A "Sweet Idyll" Read by Ida]

Come down, O maid, from yonder mountain height:
What pleasure lives in height (the shepherd sang)
In height and cold, the splendor of the hills?
But cease to move so near the Heavens, and cease
To glide a sunbeam by the blasted Pine,                    5
To sit a star upon the sparkling spire;
And come, for Love is of the valley, come,
For Love is of the valley, come thou down
And find him; by the happy threshold, he,
Or hand in hand with Plenty in the maize,                  10
Or red with spirted purple of the vats,
Or foxlike in the vine; nor cares to walk
With Death and Morning on the Silver Horns,
Nor wilt thou snare him in the white ravine,
Nor find him dropt upon the firths of ice,                 15
That huddling slant in furrow-cloven falls
To roll the torrent out of dusky doors:
But follow; let the torrent dance thee down
To find him in the valley; let the wild
Lean-headed Eagles yelp alone, and leave                   20
The monstrous ledges there to slope, and spill
Their thousand wreaths of dangling water-smoke,
That like a broken purpose waste in air:
So waste not thou; but come; for all the vales
Await thee; azure pillars of the hearth                    25
Arise to thee; the children call, and I
Thy shepherd pipe, and sweet is every sound,
Sweeter thy voice, but every sound is sweet;
Myriads of rivulets hurrying through the lawn,
The moan of doves in immemorial elms,                      30
And murmuring of innumerable bees.

COME DOWN. 11 *spirted:* spurted. 12 *foxlike . . . vine:* busy in the vineyard. But see Song of Sol. 2:15. 13 *Horns:* Probably the Silberhorn, a peak of the Jungfrau, whose forbidding, dangerous summit is beautiful in the morning light. 15 *firths of ice:* glaciers.

*from* IN MEMORIAM

## II

Old yew, which graspest at the stones
　　That name the under-lying dead,
　　Thy fibers net the dreamless head;
Thy roots are wrapt about the bones.

The seasons bring the flower again,　　　　　　5
　　And bring the firstling to the flock;
　　And in the dusk of thee, the clock
Beats out the little lives of men.

O not for thee the glow, the bloom,
　　Who changest not in any gale,　　　　　　10
　　Nor branding summer suns avail
To touch thy thousand years of gloom:

And gazing on thee, sullen tree,
　　Sick for thy stubborn hardihood,
　　I seem to fail from out my blood,　　　　　　15
And grow incorporate into thee.

## III

O Sorrow, cruel fellowship,
　　O Priestess in the vaults of Death,
　　O sweet and bitter in a breath,
What whispers from thy lying lip?　　　　　　20

'The stars,' she whispers, 'blindly run;
　　A web is wov'n across the sky;
　　From out waste places comes a cry,
And murmurs from the dying sun:

'And all the phantom, Nature, stands—　　　　　　25
　　With all the music in her tone,
　　A hollow echo of my own,—
A hollow form with empty hands.'

IN MEMORIAM. Addressed to the memory of Arthur Henry Hallam
(b. London, 1811, d. on the Continent, 1833), a dear friend of Tennyson's from their Cambridge days. At the time of his death Hallam
was engaged to Tennyson's sister Emily. First published, 1850.

And shall I take a thing so blind,
  Embrace her as my natural good;                    30
  Or crush her, like a vice of blood,
Upon the threshold of the mind?


### IV

To Sleep I give my powers away;
  My will is bondsman to the dark;
  I sit within a helmless bark,                       35
And with my heart I muse and say:


O heart, how fares it with thee now,
  That thou should'st fail from thy desire,
  Who scarcely darest to inquire,
'What is it makes me beat so low?'                    40


Something it is which thou hast lost,
  Some pleasure from thine early years.
  Break, thou deep vase of chilling tears,
That grief hath shaken into frost!


Such clouds of nameless trouble cross                45
  All night below the darken'd eyes;
  With morning wakes the will, and cries,
'Thou shalt not be the fool of loss.'


.    .    .


### VII

Dark house, by which once more I stand
  Here in the long unlovely street,                  50
  Doors, where my heart was used to beat
So quickly, waiting for a hand,


A hand that can be clasp'd no more—
  Behold me, for I cannot sleep,
  And like a guilty thing I creep                    55
At earliest morning to the door.

49-50 *Dark . . . street:* Hallam's father's house in Wimpole St., London.

He is not here; but far away
   The noise of life begins again,
   And ghastly thro' the drizzling rain
On the bald street breaks the blank day.     60

.   .   .

### XXXIV

My own dim life should teach me this,
   That life shall live for evermore,
   Else earth is darkness at the core,
And dust and ashes all that is;

This round of green, this orb of flame,     65
   Fantastic beauty; such as lurks
   In some wild Poet, when he works
Without a conscience or an aim.

What then were God to such as I?
   'Twere hardly worth my while to choose     70
   Of things all mortal, or to use
A little patience ere I die;

'Twere best at once to sink to peace,
   Like birds the charming serpent draws,
   To drop head-foremost in the jaws     75
Of vacant darkness and to cease.

.   .   .

### XXXV

Yet if some voice that man could trust
   Should murmur from the narrow house;
   'The cheeks drop in; the body bows;
Man dies: nor is there hope in dust':     80

Might I not say? 'Yet even here,
   But for one hour, O Love, I strive
   To keep so sweet a thing alive':
But I should turn mine ears and hear

78 *narrow house:* the grave.

The moanings of the homeless sea,                    85
   The sound of streams that swift or slow
   Draw down Aeonian hills, and sow
The dust of continents to be;

And Love would answer with a sigh,
   'The sound of that forgetful shore          90
   Will change my sweetness more and more,
Half-dead to know that I shall die.'

O me, what profits it to put
   An idle case? If Death were seen
   At first as Death, Love had not been,          95
Or been in narrowest working shut,

Mere fellowship of sluggish moods,
   Or in his coarsest Satyr-shape
   Had bruised the herb and crush'd the grape,
And bask'd and batten'd in the woods.                100

.   .   .

### LIV

Oh yet we trust that somehow good
   Will be the final goal of ill,
   To pangs of nature, sins of will,
Defects of doubt, and taints of blood:

That nothing walks with aimless feet;                105
   That not one life shall be destroy'd,
   Or cast as rubbish to the void,
When God hath made the pile complete;

That not a worm is cloven in vain;
   That not a moth with vain desire              110
   Is shrivel'd in a fruitless fire,
Or but subserves another's gain.

Behold, we know not anything;
   I can but trust that good shall fall
   At last—far off—at last, to all,              115
And every winter change to spring.

87 *Aeonian:* Everlasting.

So runs my dream: but what am I?
 An infant crying in the night:
 An infant crying for the light:
And with no language but a cry. 120

## LV

The wish, that of the living whole
 No life may fail beyond the grave,
 Derives it not from what we have
The likest God within the soul?

Are God and Nature then at strife, 125
 That Nature lends such evil dreams?
 So careful of the type she seems,
So careless of the single life;

That I, considering everywhere
 Her secret meaning in her deeds, 130
 And finding that of fifty seeds
She often brings but one to bear;

I falter where I firmly trod,
 And falling with my weight of cares
 Upon the great world's altar-stairs 135
That slope thro' darkness up to God;

I stretch lame hands of faith, and grope,
 And gather dust and chaff, and call
 To what I feel is Lord of all,
And faintly trust the larger hope. 140

## LVI

'So careful of the type?' but no.
 From scarped cliff and quarried stone
 She cries, 'A thousand types are gone:
I care for nothing, all shall go.

'Thou makest thine appeal to me: 145
 I bring to life, I bring to death:
 The spirit does but mean the breath:
I know no more.' And he, shall he,

127 *type*: genus, kind.  142 *scarped*: steep cut.

Man, her last work, who seem'd so fair,
   Such splendid purpose in his eyes,       150
   Who roll'd the psalm to wintry skies,
Who built him fanes of fruitless prayer,

Who trusted God was love indeed
   And love Creation's final law—
   Though Nature, red in tooth and claw      155
With ravine, shriek'd against his creed—

Who loved, who suffer'd countless ills,
   Who battled for the True, the Just,
   Be blown about the desert dust,
Or seal'd within the iron hills?      160

No more? A monster then, a dream,
   A discord. Dragons of the prime,
   That tare each other in their slime,
Were mellow music match'd with him.

O life as futile, then, as frail!      165
   O for thy voice to soothe and bless!
   What hope of answer, or redress?
Behind the veil, behind the veil.

.    .    .

## LXXXIII

Dip down upon the northern shore,
   O sweet new-year delaying long;      170
   Thou doest expectant Nature wrong;
Delaying long, delay no more.

What stays thee from the clouded noons,
   Thy sweetness from its proper place?
   Can trouble live with April days,      175
Or sadness in the summer moons?

Bring orchis, bring the foxglove spire,
   The little speedwell's darling blue,
   Deep tulips dash'd with fiery dew,
Laburnums, dropping-wells of fire.      180

152 *fanes:* churches.  156 *ravine:* rapine.  162 *Dragons of the prime:*
Prehistoric monsters.  163 *tare:* tore.  180 *Laburnums . . . fire:* The
dropping golden blossoms make a pool of fire on the ground.

O thou, new-year, delaying long,
   Delayest the sorrow in my blood,
   That longs to burst a frozen bud,
And flood a fresher throat with song.

.   .   .

## CVI

Ring out, wild bells, to the wild sky,       185
   The flying cloud, the frosty light:
   The year is dying in the night;
Ring out, wild bells, and let him die.

Ring out the old, ring in the new,
   Ring, happy bells, across the snow:       190
   The year is going, let him go;
Ring out the false, ring in the true.

Ring out the grief that saps the mind,
   For those that here we see no more;
   Ring out the feud of rich and poor,       195
Ring in redress to all mankind.

Ring out a slowly dying cause,
   And ancient forms of party strife;
   Ring in the nobler modes of life,
With sweeter manners, purer laws.       200

Ring out the want, the care, the sin,
   The faithless coldness of the times;
   Ring out, ring out my mournful rhymes,
But ring the fuller minstrel in.

Ring out false pride in place and blood,       205
   The civic slander and the spite;
   Ring in the love of truth and right,
Ring in the common love of good.

Ring out old shapes of foul disease,
   Ring out the narrowing lust of gold;       210
   Ring out the thousand wars of old,
Ring in the thousand years of peace.

Ring in the valiant man and free,
  The larger heart, the kindlier hand;
  Ring out the darkness of the land,  215
Ring in the Christ that is to be.

.   .   .

### CXV

Now fades the last long streak of snow,
  Now burgeons every maze of quick
    About the flowering squares, and thick
By ashen roots the violets blow.  220

Now rings the woodland loud and long,
  The distance takes a lovelier hue,
  And drown'd in yonder living blue
The lark becomes a sightless song.

Now dance the lights on lawn and lea,  225
  The flocks are whiter down the vale,
  And milkier every milky sail
On winding stream or distant sea;

Where now the seamew pipes, or dives
  In yonder greening gleam, and fly  230
  The happy birds, that change their sky
To build and brood; that live their lives

From land to land; and in my breast
  Spring wakens too; and my regret
  Becomes an April violet,  235
And buds and blossoms like the rest.

### CXVI

Is it, then, regret for buried time
  That keenlier in sweet April wakes,
  And meets the year, and gives and takes
The colors of the crescent prime?  240

218 *maze of quick:* hedgerows.   219 *flowering squares:* garden plots.
229 *seamew:* sea gull.   240 *crescent prime:* budding spring.

Not all: the songs, the stirring air,
   The life re-orient out of dust,
     Cry thro' the sense to hearten trust
In that which made the world so fair.

Not all regret: the face will shine         245
   Upon me, while I muse alone;
     And that dear voice, I once have known,
Still speak to me of me and mine:

Yet less of sorrow lives in me
   For days of happy commune dead;       250
     Less yearning for the friendship fled,
Than some strong bond which is to be.

### CXVII

O days and hours, your work is this,
   To hold me from my proper place,
     A little while from his embrace,       255
For fuller gain of after bliss:

That out of distance might ensue
   Desire of nearness doubly sweet;
     And unto meeting, when we meet,
Delight a hundredfold accrue,       260

For every grain of sand that runs,
   And every span of shade that steals,
     And every kiss of toothed wheels,
And all the courses of the suns.

### CXVIII

Contemplate all this work of Time,       265
   The giant laboring in his youth;
     Nor dream of human love and truth,
As dying Nature's earth and lime;

But trust that those we call the dead
   Are breathers of an ampler day      270

242 *re-orient:* rising again. 247-48 *And . . . Still:* From a late revision. 261 *sand . . . runs:* i.e., in the hourglass. 262 *span . . . steals:* shadows increasing as the day closes. 263 *kiss . . . wheels:* meshing of cog-wheels in clocks.

For ever nobler ends. They say,
The solid earth whereon we tread

In tracts of fluent heat began,
   And grew to seeming-random forms,
   The seeming prey of cyclic storms,    275
Till at the last arose the man;

Who throve and branch'd from clime to clime,
   The herald of a higher race,
   And of himself in higher place,
If so he type this work of thine    280

Within himself, from more to more;
   Or, crown'd with attributes of woe
   Like glories, move his course, and show
That life is not as idle ore,

But iron dug from central gloom,    285
   And heated hot with burning fears,
   And dipt in baths of hissing tears,
And batter'd with the shocks of doom

To shape and use. Arise and fly
   The reeling Faun, the sensual feast;    290
   Move upward, working out the beast,
And let the ape and tiger die.

.  .  .

## CXXIII

There rolls the deep where grew the tree.
   O earth, what changes hast thou seen!
   There where the long street roars, hath been    295
The stillness of the central sea.

The hills are shadows, and they flow
   From form to form, and nothing stands;
   They melt like mist, the solid lands,
Like clouds they shape themselves and go.    300

273 *tracts:* periods of time.  280 *type:* typify.  290 *Faun:* wood-god,
probably Pan himself, symbol of pagan sensuality and intemperance.
295 *street:* cf. l. 50.

But in my spirit will I dwell,
 And dream my dream, and hold it true;
 For tho' my lips may breathe adieu,
I cannot think the thing farewell.


### CXXIX

Dear friend, far off, my lost desire,     305
 So far, so near in woe and weal;
 O loved the most, when most I feel
There is a lower and a higher;


Known and unknown, human, divine;
 Sweet human hand and lips and eye;     310
 Dear heavenly friend that canst not die,
Mine, mine, for ever, ever mine;


Strange friend, past, present, and to be;
 Loved deeplier, darklier understood;
 Behold, I dream a dream of good,     315
And mingle all the world with thee.


### CXXX

Thy voice is on the rolling air;
 I hear thee where the waters run;
 Thou standest in the rising sun,
And in the setting thou art fair.     320


What art thou then? I cannot guess;
 But tho' I seem in star and flower
 To feel thee some diffusive power,
I do not therefore love thee less:


My love involves the love before;     325
 My love is vaster passion now;
 Tho' mix'd with God and Nature thou,
I seem to love thee more and more.


Far off thou art, but ever nigh;
 I have thee still, and I rejoice;
 I prosper, circled with thy voice;     330
I shall not lose thee tho' I die.

# ROBERT BROWNING 1812–1889

*from* DRAMATIC LYRICS

### Nay but you, who do not love her

#### SONG

Nay but you, who do not love her,
  Is she not pure gold, my mistress?
Holds earth aught—speak truth—above her?
  Aught like this tress, see, and this tress,
And this last fairest tress of all,        5
So fair, see, ere I let it fall?

Because you spend your lives in praising;
  To praise, you search the wide world over:
Then why not witness, calmly gazing,
  If earth holds aught—speak truth—above her?   10
Above this tress, and this, I touch
But cannot praise, I love so much!

### Evelyn Hope

#### 1

Beautiful Evelyn Hope is dead!
  Sit and watch by her side an hour.
That is her book-shelf, this her bed;
  She plucked that piece of geranium-flower,
Beginning to die too, in the glass.        5
  Little has yet been changed, I think:
The shutters are shut, no light may pass
  Save two long rays through the hinge's chink.

#### 2

Sixteen years old when she died!
  Perhaps she had scarcely heard my name;   10
It was not her time to love: beside,
  Her life had many a hope and aim,
Duties enough and little cares,
  And now was quiet, now astir,
Till God's hand beckoned unawares,—      15
  And the sweet white brow is all of her.

### 3

Is it too late then, Evelyn Hope?
   What, your soul was pure and true,
The good stars met in your horoscope,
   Made you of spirit, fire and dew—         20
And, just because I was thrice as old
   And our paths in the world diverged so wide,
Each was naught to each, must I be told?
   We were fellow mortals, naught beside?

### 4

No, indeed! for God above         25
   Is great to grant, as mighty to make,
And creates the love to reward the love:
   I claim you still, for my own love's sake!
Delayed it may be for more lives yet,
   Through worlds I shall traverse, not a few:     30
Much is to learn and much to forget
   Ere the time be come for taking you.

### 5

But the time will come,—at last it will,
   When, Evelyn Hope, what meant (I shall say)
In the lower earth, in the years long still,     35
   That body and soul so pure and gay?
Why your hair was amber, I shall divine,
   And your mouth of your own geranium's red—
And what you would do with me, in fine,
   In the new life come in the old one's stead.    40

### 6

I have lived (I shall say) so much since then,
   Given up myself so many times,
Gained me the gains of various men,
   Ransacked the ages, spoiled the climes;
Yet one thing, one, in my soul's full scope,     45
   Either I missed or itself missed me:
And I want and find you, Evelyn Hope!
   What is the issue? let us see!

7

I loved you, Evelyn, all the while!
    My heart seemed full as it could hold;                    50
There was place and to spare for the frank young smile,
    And the red young mouth, and the hair's young gold.
So, hush,—I will give you this leaf to keep—
    See, I shut it inside the sweet cold hand!
There, that is our secret: go to sleep;                       55
    You will wake, and remember, and understand.


## Love Among the Ruins

1

Where the quiet-colored end of evening smiles
    Miles and miles
On the solitary pastures where our sheep
    Half-asleep
Tinkle homeward through the twilight, stray or stop          5
    As they crop—
Was the site once of a city great and gay
    (So they say),
Of our country's very capital, its prince
    Ages since                                                10
Held his court in, gathered councils, wielding far
    Peace or war.


2

Now,—the country does not even boast a tree
    As you see,
To distinguish slopes of verdure, certain rills             15
    From the hills
Intersect and give a name to (else they run
    Into one),
Where the domed and daring palace shot its spires
    Up like fires                                             20
O'er the hundred-gated circuit of a wall
    Bounding all,
Made of marble, men might march on nor be prest,
    Twelve abreast.

LOVE AMONG THE RUINS. 11 *wielding:* determining.

### 3

And such plenty and perfection, see, of grass                    25
  Never was!
Such a carpet as, this summer-time, o'erspreads
  And embeds
Every vestige of the city, guessed alone,
  Stock or stone—                                       30
Where a multitude of men breathed joy and woe
  Long ago;
Lust of glory pricked their hearts up, dread of shame
  Struck them tame;
And that glory and that shame alike, the gold             35
  Bought and sold.

### 4

Now,—the single little turret that remains
  On the plains,
By the caper overrooted, by the gourd
  Overscored,                                             40
While the patching houseleek's head of blossom winks
  Through the chinks—
Marks the basement whence a tower in ancient time
  Sprang sublime,
And a burning ring all round, the chariots traced    45
  As they raced,
And the monarch and his minions and his dames
  Viewed the games.

### 5

And I know, while thus the quiet-colored eve
  Smiles to leave                                         50
To their folding, all our many-tinkling fleece
  In such peace,
And the slopes and rills in undistinguished gray
  Melt away—
That a girl with eager eyes and yellow hair            55
  Waits me there
In the turret whence the charioteers caught soul
  For the goal,
When the king looked, where she looks now, breathless, dumb
  Till I come.                                            60

39 *caper*: low-growing prickly Mediterranean shrub.   41 *patching*: growing in patches.   *houseleek*('s): a pink wallflower.

6

But he looked upon the city, every side,
    Far and wide,
All the mountains topped with temples, all the glades'
    Colonnades,
All the causeys, bridges, aqueducts,—and then,        65
    All the men!
When I do come, she will speak not, she will stand,
    Either hand
On my shoulder, give her eyes the first embrace
    Of my face,        70
Ere we rush, ere we extinguish sight and speech
    Each on each.

7

In one year they sent a million fighters forth
    South and North,
And they built their gods a brazen pillar high        75
    As the sky,
Yet reserved a thousand chariots in full force—
    Gold, of course.
Oh heart! oh blood that freezes, blood that burns!
    Earth's returns        80
For whole centuries of folly, noise and sin!
    Shut them in,
With their triumphs and their glories and the rest!
    Love is best.

*from* DRAMATIC ROMANCES

### Porphyria's Lover

The rain set early in to-night,
    The sullen wind was soon awake,
It tore the elm-tops down for spite,
    And did its worst to vex the lake:
I listened with heart fit to break;        5
When glided in Porphyria; straight
    She shut the cold out and the storm,
And kneeled and made the cheerless grate
    Blaze up, and all the cottage warm;

65 *causeys:* raised cobblestone roadways.

Which done, she rose, and from her form     10
Withdrew the dripping cloak and shawl,
    And laid her soiled gloves by, untied
Her hat, and let the damp hair fall,
    And, last, she sat down by my side
And called me. When no voice replied,     15
She put my arm about her waist,
    And made her smooth white shoulder bare,
And all her yellow hair displaced,
    And, stooping, made my cheek lie there,
And spread, o'er all, her yellow hair,     20
Murmuring how she loved me—she
    Too weak, for all her heart's endeavor,
To set its struggling passion free
    From pride, and vainer ties dissever,
And give herself to me forever.     25
But passion sometimes would prevail,
    Nor could to-night's gay feast restrain
A sudden thought of one so pale
    For love of her, and all in vain:
So, she was come through wind and rain.     30
Be sure I looked up at her eyes
    Happy and proud; at last I knew
Porphyria worshipped me; surprise
    Made my heart swell, and still it grew
While I debated what to do.     35
That moment she was mine, mine, fair,
    Perfectly pure and good: I found
A thing to do, and all her hair
    In one long yellow string I wound
Three times her little throat around,     40
And strangled her. No pain felt she;
    I am quite sure she felt no pain.
As a shut bud that holds a bee,
    I warily oped her lids: again
Laughed the blue eyes without a stain.     45
And I untightened next the tress
    About her neck; her cheek once more
Blushed bright beneath my burning kiss:
    I propped her head up as before,
Only, this time my shoulder bore     50
Her head, which droops upon it still:
    The smiling rosy little head,
So glad it has its utmost will,
    That all it scorned at once is fled,

And I, its love, am gained instead!                        55
Porphyria's love: she guessed not how
   Her darling one wish would be heard.
And thus we sit together now,
   And all night long we have not stirred,
And yet God has not said a word!                          60


*from* MEN AND WOMEN

## The Bishop Orders His Tomb at Saint Praxed's Church

ROME, 15—

Vanity, saith the preacher, vanity!
Draw round my bed: is Anselm keeping back?
Nephews—sons mine . . . ah God, I know not! Well—
She, men would have to be your mother once,
Old Gandolf envied me, so fair she was!                    5
What's done is done, and she is dead beside,
Dead long ago, and I am Bishop since,
And as she died so must we die ourselves,
And thence ye may perceive the world's a dream.
Life, how and what is it? As here I lie                   10
In this state-chamber, dying by degrees,
Hours and long hours in the dead night, I ask
"Do I live, am I dead?" Peace, peace seems all.
Saint Praxed's ever was the church for peace;
And so, about this tomb of mine. I fought                 15
With tooth and nail to save my niche, ye know:
—Old Gandolf cozened me, despite my care;
Shrewd was that snatch from out the corner South
He graced his carrion with, God curse the same!
Yet still my niche is not so cramped but thence           20
One sees the pulpit o' the epistle-side,
And somewhat of the choir, those silent seats,
And up into the aery dome where live
The angels, and a sunbeam's sure to lurk:
And I shall fill my slab of basalt there,                 25
And 'neath my tabernacle take my rest,

THE BISHOP. 1 *Vanity . . . vanity:* from Eccles. 1:2.   17 *cozened:*
cheated.   21 *epistle-side:* the right side, facing the altar.   25 *basalt:* a
dark, fine-grained igneous rock; a black marble.   26 *tabernacle:* canopy
above the coffin.

With those nine columns round me, two and two,
The odd one at my feet where Anselm stands:
Peach-blossom marble all, the rare, the ripe
As fresh-poured red wine of a mighty pulse. 30
—Old Gandolf with his paltry onion-stone,
Put me where I may look at him! True peach,
Rosy and flawless: how I earned the prize!
Draw close: that conflagration of my church
—What then? So much was saved if aught were missed! 35
My sons, ye would not be my death? Go dig
The white-grape vineyard where the oil-press stood,
Drop water gently till the surface sink,
And if ye find . . . Ah God, I know not, I! . . .
Bedded in store of rotten fig leaves soft, 40
And corded up in a tight olive-frail,
Some lump, ah God, of *lapis lazuli*,
Big as a Jew's head cut off at the nape,
Blue as a vein o'er the Madonna's breast . . .
Sons, all have I bequeathed you, villas, all, 45
That brave Frascati villa with its bath,
So, let the blue lump poise between my knees,
Like God the Father's globe on both his hands
Ye worship in the Jesu Church so gay,
For Gandolf shall not choose but see and burst! 50
Swift as a weaver's shuttle fleet our years:
Man goeth to the grave, and where is he?
Did I say basalt for my slab, sons? Black—
'Twas ever antique-black I meant! How else
Shall ye contrast my frieze to come beneath? 55
The bas-relief in bronze ye promised me,
Those Pans and Nymphs ye wot of, and perchance
Some tripod, thyrsus, with a vase or so,
The Savior at his sermon on the mount,
Saint Praxed in a glory, and one Pan 60
Ready to twitch the Nymph's last garment off,

---

31 *onion-stone:* inferior greenish marble. 41 *olive-frail:* basket made
of rushes. 42 *lapis lazuli:* a fine bright blue stone. 46 *Frascati:* a
town near Rome, famous for its handsome villas. 49 *Jesu:* Jesuit. 51
*Swift . . . years:* cf. Job 7 :6. 58 *tripod, thyrsus:* other pagan motifs
in the relief. The *tripod* is any altar vessel supported by three feet, but
in particular the cauldron before which the Delphic oracle sat when de-
livering revelations. The *thyrsus* is an attribute of Bacchus, the staff
surmounted by a pine cone, ivy leaves or grapes, used in the Bacchic
rites. See ll. 109-10. 59 *Savior . . . mount:* see Matt. 5. 60 *glory:*
halo.

And Moses with the tables . . . but I know
Ye mark me not! What do they whisper thee,
Child of my bowels, Anselm? Ah, ye hope
To revel down my villas while I gasp                            65
Bricked o'er with beggar's moldy travertine
Which Gandolf from his tomb-top chuckles at!
Nay, boys, ye love me—all of jasper, then!
'Tis jasper ye stand pledged to, lest I grieve
My bath must needs be left behind, alas!                       70
One block, pure green as a pistachio-nut,
There's plenty jasper somewhere in the world—
And have I not Saint Praxed's ear to pray
Horses for ye, and brown Greek manuscripts,
And mistresses with great smooth marbly limbs?                 75
—That's if ye carve my epitaph aright,
Choice Latin, picked phrase, Tully's every word,
No gaudy ware like Gandolf's second line—
Tully, my masters? Ulpian serves his need!
And then how I shall lie through centuries,                    80
And hear the blessed mutter of the mass,
And see God made and eaten all day long,
And feel the steady candle-flame, and taste
Good strong thick stupefying incense-smoke!
For as I lie here, hours of the dead night,                    85
Dying in state and by such slow degrees,
I fold my arms as if they clasped a crook,
And stretch my feet forth straight as stone can point,
And let the bedclothes, for a mortcloth, drop
Into great laps and folds of sculptor's-work:                  90
And as yon tapers dwindle, and strange thoughts
Grow, with a certain humming in my ears,
About the life before I lived this life,
And this life too, popes, cardinals and priests,
Saint Praxed at his sermon on the mount,                       95
Your tall pale mother with her talking eyes,
And new-found agate urns as fresh as day,

62 *Moses . . . tables:* see Exod. 24:12.  66 *travertine:* limestone.  68
*jasper:* opaque, vari-colored quartz.  74 *Greek manuscripts:* The poem
is set late in the period when the Greek writings fascinated Italian
scholars.  77 *Choice , , , Tully's:* The eloquent Latin of Cicero (Marcus Tullius) of the first century B.C.  79 *Ulpian:* Domitius Ulpianus, a
Roman jurist and legal writer who died 228 A.D. See l. 99 and note.  87
*crook:* pastoral staff, the bishop's symbol of office.  89 *mortcloth:* cloth
covering a corpse.  95 *Saint Praxed . . . mount:* The Bishop's mind
wanders: Saint Praxed was a female saint.

And marble's language, Latin pure, discreet,
—Aha, ELUCESCEBAT quoth our friend?
No Tully, said I, Ulpian at the best!　　　　　　100
Evil and brief hath been my pilgrimage.
All *lapis*, all, sons! Else I give the Pope
My villas! Will ye ever eat my heart?
Ever your eyes were as a lizard's quick,
They glitter like your mother's for my soul,　　105
Or ye would heighten my impoverished frieze,
Piece out its starved design, and fill my vase
With grapes, and add a visor and a term,
And to the tripod ye would tie a lynx
That in his struggle throws the thyrsus down,　110
To comfort me on my entablature
Whereon I am to lie till I must ask
"Do I live, am I dead?" There, leave me, there!
For ye have stabbed me with ingratitude
To death—ye wish it—God, ye wish it! Stone—　115
Gritstone, a-crumble! Clammy squares which sweat
As if the corpse they keep were oozing through—
And no more *lapis* to delight the world!
Well go! I bless ye. Fewer tapers there,
But in a row: and, going, turn your backs　　120
—Ay, like departing altar-ministrants,
And leave me in my church, the church for peace,
That I may watch at leisure if he leers—
Old Gandolf—at me, from his onion-stone,
As still he envied me, so fair she was!　　　　125


## Andrea Del Sarto

### (CALLED "THE FAULTLESS PAINTER")

But do not let us quarrel any more,
No, my Lucrezia; bear with me for once:
Sit down and all shall happen as you wish.
You turn your face, but does it bring your heart?

99 ELUCESCEBAT: "He Shone Forth." Cicero would have written *eluce-bat*.　108 *visor*: mask.　*term*: a pillar adorned on top with the head or upper part of the body.　116 *Gritstone*: Sandstone.

ANDREA DEL SARTO. *Andrea Del Sarto*: known as "Del Sarto" (because he was the son of a tailor). Andrea's proper name was d'Angelo (Agnolo) di Francisci di Luca (1486-1531). He was a painter of extraordinary technical proficiency and was called "the 'faultless' painter."

I'll work then for your friend's friend, never fear,     5
Treat his own subject after his own way,
Fix his own time, accept too his own price,
And shut the money into this small hand
When next it takes mine. Will it? tenderly?
Oh, I'll content him,—but to-morrow, Love!     10
I often am much wearier than you think,
This evening more than usual, and it seems
As if—forgive now—should you let me sit
Here by the window with your hand in mine
And look a half-hour forth on Fiesole,     15
Both of one mind, as married people use,
Quietly, quietly the evening through,
I might get up to-morrow to my work
Cheerful and fresh as ever. Let us try.
To-morrow, how you shall be glad for this!     20
Your soft hand is a woman of itself,
And mine the man's bared breast she curls inside.
Don't count the time lost, either; you must serve
For each of the five pictures we require:
It saves a model. So! keep looking so—     25
My serpentining beauty, rounds on rounds!
—How could you ever prick those perfect ears,
Even to put the pearl there! oh, so sweet—
My face, my moon, my everybody's moon,
Which everybody looks on and calls his,     30
And, I suppose, is looked on by in turn,
While she looks—no one's: very dear, no less.
You smile? why, there's my picture ready made,
There's what we painters call our harmony!
A common grayness silvers everything,—     35
All in a twilight, you and I alike
—You, at the point of your first pride in me
(That's gone you know),—but I, at every point;
My youth, my hope, my art, being all toned down
To yonder sober pleasant Fiesole.     40
There's the bell clinking from the chapel-top;
That length of convent-wall across the way
Holds the trees safer, huddled more inside;
The last monk leaves the garden; days decrease,
And autumn grows, autumn in everything.     45
Eh? the whole seems to fall into a shape
As if I saw alike my work and self

15 *Fiesole*: a suburb of Florence.   16 *use*: should be (?).

And all that I was born to be and do,
A twilight-piece. Love, we are in God's hand.
How strange now, looks the life he makes us lead;50
So free we seem, so fettered fast we are!
I feel he laid the fetter: let it lie!
This chamber for example—turn your head—
All that's behind us! You don't understand
Nor care to understand about my art,55
But you can hear at least when people speak:
And that cartoon, the second from the door
—It is the thing, Love! so such things should be—
Behold Madonna!—I am bold to say.
I can do with my pencil what I know,60
What I see, what at bottom of my heart
I wish for, if I ever wish so deep—
Do easily, too—when I say, perfectly,
I do not boast, perhaps: yourself are judge
Who listened to the Legate's talk last week,65
And just as much they used to say in France.
At any rate 'tis easy, all of it!
No sketches first, no studies, that's long past:
I do what many dream of all their lives
—Dream? strive to do, and agonize to do,70
And fail in doing. I could count twenty such
On twice your fingers, and not leave this town,
Who strive—you don't know how the others strive
To paint a little thing like that you smeared
Carelessly passing with your robes afloat,—75
Yet do much less, so much less, Someone says,
(I know his name, no matter)—so much less!
Well, less is more, Lucrezia: I am judged.
There burns a truer light of God in them,
In their vexed beating stuffed and stopped-up brain,80
Heart, or whate'er else, than goes on to prompt
This low-pulsed forthright craftsman's hand of mine.
Their works drop groundward, but themselves, I know,
Reach many a time a heaven that's shut to me,
Enter and take their place there sure enough,85
Though they come back and cannot tell the world.
My works are nearer heaven, but I sit here.
The sudden blood of these men! at a word—
Praise them, it boils, or blame them, it boils too.

57 *cartoon*: full-size study.  66 *used . . . France*: see ll. 149-50 and
note.

I, painting from myself and to myself,                                    90
Know what I do, am unmoved by men's blame
Or their praise either. Somebody remarks
Morello's outline there is wrongly traced,
His hue mistaken; what of that? or else,
Rightly traced and well ordered; what of that?     95
Speak as they please, what does the mountain care?
Ah, but a man's reach should exceed his grasp,
Or what's a heaven for? All is silver-gray
Placid and perfect with my art: the worse!
I know both what I want and what might gain;       100
And yet how profitless to know, to sigh
"Had I been two, another and myself,
Our head would have o'erlooked the world!" No doubt.
Yonder's a work now, of that famous youth
The Urbinate who died five years ago.              105
('Tis copied, George Vasari sent it me.)
Well, I can fancy how he did it all,
Pouring his soul, with kings and popes to see,
Reaching, that heaven might so replenish him,
Above and through his art—for it gives way;        110
That arm is wrongly put—and there again—
A fault to pardon in the drawing's lines,
Its body, so to speak: its soul is right,
He means right—that, a child may understand.
Still, what an arm! and I could alter it:          115
But all the play, the insight and the stretch—
Out of me, out of me! And wherefore out?
Had you enjoined them on me, given me soul,
We might have risen to Rafael, I and you!
Nay, Love, you did give all I asked, I think—      120
More than I merit, yes, by many times.
But had you—oh, with the same perfect brow,
And perfect eyes, and more than perfect mouth,
And the low voice my soul hears, as a bird
The fowler's pipe, and follows to the snare—       125
Had you, with these the same, but brought a mind!
Some women do so. Had the mouth there urged
"God and the glory! never care for gain.

93 *Morello('s)*: a peak in the Apennines.  105 *The Urbinate:* Rafael,
a famous contemporary painter, born at Urbino. His greatest work was
done in Rome, notably in the Vatican. See ll. 178, 186-88.  106 *George*
(Giorgio) *Vasari:* onetime student of Del Sarto, but best known as the
biographer and critic of artists.  118 *enjoined . . . me:* ordered me to
have them.  125 *fowler's pipe:* birdcall.

The present by the future, what is that?
Live for fame, side by side with Agnolo!                    130
Rafael is waiting: up to God, all three!"
I might have done it for you. So it seems:
Perhaps not. All is as God overrules.
Beside, incentives come from the soul's self;
The rest avail not. Why do I need you?                      135
What wife had Rafael, or has Agnolo?
In this world, who can do a thing, will not;
And who would do it, cannot, I perceive:
Yet the will's somewhat—somewhat, too, the power—
And thus we half-men struggle. At the end,                  140
God, I conclude, compensates, punishes.
'Tis safer for me, if the award be strict,
That I am something underrated here,
Poor this long while, despised, to speak the truth.
I dared not, do you know, leave home all day,              145
For fear of chancing on the Paris lords.
The best is when they pass and look aside;
But they speak sometimes; I must bear it all.
Well may they speak! That Francis, that first time,
And that long festal year at Fontainebleau!                 150
I surely then could sometimes leave the ground,
Put on the glory, Rafael's daily wear,
In that humane great monarch's golden look,—
One finger in his beard or twisted curl
Over his mouth's good mark that made the smile,             155
One arm about my shoulder, round my neck,
The jingle of his gold chain in my ear,
I painting proudly with his breath on me,
All his court round him, seeing with his eyes,
Such frank French eyes, and such a fire of souls           160
Profuse, my hand kept plying by those hearts,—
And, best of all, this, this, this face beyond,
This in the background, waiting on my work,
To crown the issue with a last reward!
A good time, was it not, my kingly days?                    165
And had you not grown restless . . . but I know—
'Tis done and past; 'twas right, my instinct said;

130 *Agnolo:* Michaelangelo.   149-50 *Francis . . . Fontainebleau:* In
1518 Andrea was invited to France to paint at the Court of Francis I.
Pressed by Lucrezia to return, he stayed but a year, leaving entrusted
with money to buy art works for Francis, which, instead, he spent for
the "melancholy little house," l. 212. See ll. 214, 247-49.

Too live the life grew, golden and not gray,
And I'm the weak-eyed bat no sun should tempt
Out of the grange whose four walls make his world. 170
How could it end in any other way?
You called me, and I came home to your heart.
The triumph was,—to reach and stay there; since
I reached it ere the triumph, what is lost?
Let my hands frame your face in your hair's gold, 175
You beautiful Lucrezia that are mine!
"Rafael did this, Andrea painted that;
The Roman's is the better when you pray,
But still the other's Virgin was his wife"—
Men will excuse me. I am glad to judge 180
Both pictures in your presence; clearer grows
My better fortune, I resolve to think.
For, do you know, Lucrezia, as God lives,
Said one day Agnolo, his very self,
To Rafael . . . I have known it all these years . . . 185
(When the young man was flaming out his thoughts
Upon a palace-wall for Rome to see,
Too lifted up in heart because of it),
"Friend, there's a certain sorry little scrub
Goes up and down our Florence, none cares how, 190
Who, were he set to plan and execute
As you are, pricked on by your popes and kings,
Would bring the sweat into that brow of yours!"
To Rafael's!—And indeed the arm is wrong.
I hardly dare . . . yet, only you to see, 195
Give the chalk here—quick, thus the line should go!
Ay, but the soul! he's Rafael! rub it out!
Still, all I care for, if he spoke the truth,
(What he? why, who but Michel Agnolo?
Do you forget already words like those?) 200
If really there was such a chance, so lost,—
Is, whether you're—not grateful—but more pleased.
Well, let me think so. And you smile indeed!
This hour has been an hour! Another smile?
If you would sit thus by me every night 205
I should work better, do you comprehend?
I mean that I should earn more, give you more.
See, it is settled dusk now; there's a star;
Morello's gone, the watch-lights show the wall,

173 *to reach . . . since:* from the latest edition.  178 *The Roman's:*
Rafael's. See l. 105 and note.

The cue-owls speak the name we call them by.                    210
Come from the window, love,—come in, at last,
Inside the melancholy little house
We built to be so gay with. God is just.
King Francis may forgive me: oft at nights
When I look up from painting, eyes tired out,        215
The walls become illumined, brick from brick
Distinct, instead of mortar, fierce bright gold,
That gold of his I did cement them with!
Let us but love each other. Must you go?
That Cousin here again? he waits outside?            220
Must see you—you, and not with me? Those loans?
More gaming debts to pay? you smiled for that?
Well, let smiles buy me! have you more to spend?
While hand and eye and something of a heart
Are left me, work's my ware, and what's it worth?    225
I'll pay my fancy. Only let me sit
The gray remainder of the evening out,
Idle, you call it, and muse perfectly
How I could paint, were I but back in France,
One picture, just one more—the Virgin's face,        230
Not yours this time! I want you at my side
To hear them—that is, Michel Agnolo—
Judge all I do and tell you of its worth.
Will you? To-morrow, satisfy your friend.
I take the subjects for his corridor,                235
Finish the portrait out of hand—there, there,
And throw him in another thing or two
If he demurs; the whole should prove enough
To pay for this same Cousin's freak. Beside,
What's better and what's all I care about,           240
Get you the thirteen scudi for the ruff!
Love, does that please you? Ah, but what does he,
The Cousin! what does he to please you more?

    I am grown peaceful as old age to-night.
I regret little, I would change still less.          245
Since there my past life lies, why alter it?
The very wrong to Francis!—it is true
I took his coin, was tempted and complied,
And built this house and sinned, and all is said.

210 *cue-owls:* little horned owls.   212 *house:* see ll. 149-50 and note.
220 *Cousin:* Lucrezia's lover.   238 *demurs:* hedges at paying.   239
*freak:* whim.   241 *scudi:* a *scudo* is worth about a dollar.

My father and my mother died of want.    250
Well, had I riches of my own? you see
How one gets rich! Let each one bear his lot.
They were born poor, lived poor, and poor they died:
And I have labored somewhat in my time
And not been paid profusely. Some good son    255
Paint my two hundred pictures—let him try!
No doubt, there's something strikes a balance. Yes,
You loved me quite enough, it seems to-night.
This must suffice me here. What would one have?
In heaven, perhaps, new chances, one more chance—    260
Four great walls in the New Jerusalem
Meted on each side by the angel's reed,
For Leonard, Rafael, Agnolo and me
To cover—the three first without a wife,
While I have mine! So—still they overcome    265
Because there's still Lucrezia,—as I choose.

Again the Cousin's whistle! Go, my Love.


*from* DRAMATIS PERSONAE

## Youth and Art

It once might have been, once only:
    We lodged in a street together,
You, a sparrow on the housetop lonely,
    I, a lone she-bird of his feather.

Your trade was with sticks and clay,    5
    You thumbed, thrust, patted and polished,
Then laughed "They will see some day
    Smith made, and Gibson demolished."

My business was song, song, song;
    I chirped, cheeped, trilled and twittered,    10
"Kate Brown's on the boards ere long,
    And Grisi's existence embittered!"

261-62 *Four . . . reed.* The "holy city" of Revelation (Ch. 21), whose
walls the angel measured (*meted*) with a "golden reed" (v. 15).    263
*Leonard:* Leonardo da Vinci.    265 *overcome:* excel.
    YOUTH AND ART. 8 (John) *Gibson* (1790-1866): Reckoned England's
greatest sculptor in the mid-nineteenth century.    12 (Giulia) *Grisi*
(1811-1869): an operatic soprano, famous in the 1850's and 1860's.

I earned no more by a warble
  Than you by a sketch in plaster;
You wanted a piece of marble,                    15
  I needed a music-master.


We studied hard in our styles,
  Chipped each at a crust like Hindoos,
For air, looked out on the tiles,
  For fun, watched each other's windows.          20


You lounged, like a boy of the South,
  Cap and blouse—nay, a bit of beard too;
Or you got it, rubbing your mouth
  With fingers the clay adhered to.


And I—soon managed to find                        25
  Weak points in the flower-fence facing,
Was forced to put up a blind
  And be safe in my corset-lacing.


No harm! It was not my fault
  If you never turned your eyes' tail up           30
As I shook upon E *in alt*,
  Or ran the chromatic scale up:


For spring bade the sparrows pair,
  And the boys and girls gave guesses,
And stalls in our street looked rare             35
  With bulrush and watercresses.


Why did not you pinch a flower
  In a pellet of clay and fling it?
Why did not I put a power
  Of thanks in a look, or sing it?                40


I did look, sharp as a lynx
  (And yet the memory rankles)
When models arrived, some minx
  Tripped up-stairs, she and her ankles.

31 *E in alt :* in the first octave above the treble staff.

But I think I gave you as good!                          45
  "That foreign fellow,—who can know
How she pays, in a playful mood,
  For his tuning her that piano?"

Could you say so, and never say
  "Suppose we join hands and fortunes,          50
And I fetch her from over the way,
  Her, piano, and long tunes and short tunes"?

No, no: you would not be rash,
  Nor I rasher and something over:
You've to settle yet Gibson's hash,                      55
  And Grisi yet lives in clover.

But you meet the Prince at the Board,
  I'm queen myself at *bals-paré*,
I've married a rich old lord,
  And you're dubbed knight and an R.A.             60

Each life unfulfilled, you see;
  It hangs still, patchy and scrappy:
We have not sighed deep, laughed free,
  Starved, feasted, despaired,—been happy.

And nobody calls you a dunce,                            65
  And people suppose me clever:
This could but have happened once,
  And we missed it, lost it forever.

57 *Prince:* Albert (?).   58 *bals-paré:* dress ball.   60 *an R.A.:* member
of the Royal Academy of Arts.

# MATTHEW ARNOLD 1822–1888

*from* SWITZERLAND

## To Marguerite

Yes: in the sea of life enisl'd,
With echoing straits between us thrown,
Dotting the shoreless watery wild,
We mortal millions live *alone*.
    The islands feel the enclasping flow,        5
And then their endless bounds they know.

But when the moon their hollows lights,
And they are swept by balms of spring,
And in their glens, on starry nights,
The nightingales divinely sing;          10
And lovely notes, from shore to shore,
Across the sounds and channels pour;

Oh then a longing like despair
Is to their farthest caverns sent;
For surely once, they feel, we were        15
Parts of a single continent.
Now round us spreads the watery plain—
Oh might our marges meet again!

Who order'd, that their longing's fire
Should be, as soon as kindled, cool'd?     20
Who renders vain their deep desire?—
    A God, a God their severance ruled;
And bade betwixt their shores to be
The unplumb'd, salt, estranging sea.

## Philomela

    Hark! ah, the Nightingale!
    The tawny-throated!
    Hark! from that moonlit cedar what a burst!
    What triumph! hark—what pain!

PHILOMELA. 1 *Nightingale :* Philomela. See Sidney, p. 40, ll. 8-9 and
note. Here Tereus cuts off Procne's tongue. See *dumb Sister,* l. 21.

394

O Wanderer from a Grecian shore,                          5
Still, after many years, in distant lands,
Still nourishing in thy bewilder'd brain
That wild, unquench'd, deep-sunken, old-world pain—
        Say, will it never heal?
And can this fragrant lawn                               10
With its cool trees, and night,
And the sweet, tranquil Thames,
And moonshine, and the dew,
To thy rack'd heart and brain
        Afford no balm?                                 15

        Dost thou to-night behold
Here, through the moonlight on this English grass,
The unfriendly palace in the Thracian wild?
        Dost thou again peruse
With hot cheeks and sear'd eyes                          20
The too clear web, and thy dumb Sister's shame?
        Dost thou once more assay
Thy flight, and feel come over thee,
Poor Fugitive, the feathery change
Once more, and once more seem to make resound            25
With love and hate, triumph and agony,
Lone Daulis, and the high Cephissian vale?
        Listen, Eugenia—
How thick the bursts come crowding through the leaves!
        Again—thou hearest!                             30
Eternal Passion!
Eternal Pain!

18 *unfriendly . . . wild:* where Tereus ravished Philomela.  21 *web:*
into which Philomela wove the "story of her wrongs."  27 *Daulis . . .
Cephissian vale:* the locale of Philomela's story.  28 *Eugenia:* person
addressed by the poet.

THE SCHOLAR GIPSY. (See following page.) The poem was originally
prefaced with the following condensed version of a passage in Joseph
Glanvill's *Vanity of Dogmatizing,* 1661.

"There was very lately a lad in the University of Oxford, who was
by his poverty forced to leave his studies there; and at last to join himself to a company of vagabond gipsies. Among these extravagant people,
by the insinuating subtilty of his carriage, he quickly got so much of
their love and esteem as that they discovered to him their mystery. After
he had been a pretty while well exercised in the trade, there chanced to
ride by a couple of scholars, who had formerly been of his acquaintance.
They quickly spied out their old friend among the gipsies; and he gave
them an account of the necessity which drove him to that kind of life,
and told them that the people he went with were not such impostors as
they were taken for, but that they had a traditional kind of learning

## The Scholar Gipsy

Go, for they call you, Shepherd, from the hill;
  Go, Shepherd, and untie the wattled cotes:
  No longer leave thy wistful flock unfed,
  Nor let thy bawling fellows rack their throats,
  Nor the cropp'd grasses shoot another head.      5
    But when the fields are still,
  And the tired men and dogs all gone to rest,
    And only the white sheep are sometimes seen
    Cross and recross the strips of moon-blanch'd green;
      Come, Shepherd, and again renew the quest.    10

Here, where the reaper was at work of late,
  In this high field's dark corner, where he leaves
    His coat, his basket, and his earthen cruise,
  And in the sun all morning binds the sheaves,
    Then here, at noon, comes back his stores to use;  15
      Here will I sit and wait,
  While to my ear from uplands far away
    The bleating of the folded flocks is borne;
    With distant cries of reapers in the corn—
      All the live murmur of a summer's day.         20

Screen'd is this nook o'er the high, half-reap'd field,
  And here till sun-down, Shepherd, will I be.
    Through the thick corn the scarlet poppies peep
  And round green roots and yellowing stalks I see
    Pale blue convolvulus in tendrils creep:          25
      And air-swept lindens yield
  Their scent, and rustle down their perfum'd showers
    Of bloom on the bent grass where I am laid,
    And bower me from the August sun with shade;
      And the eye travels down to Oxford's towers:     30

among them, and could do wonders by the power of the imagination,
their fancy binding that of others : that himself had learned much of
their art, and when he had compassed the whole secret, he intended, he
said, to leave their company, and give the world an account of what he
had learned.

1 *they:* the sheep. *Shepherd:* probably Arthur Clough, Arnold's
friend. 2 *untie . . . cotes:* loose the sheep from their folds. 4 *rack:*
strain. 7 *men . . . rest:* returned from the hunt. 9 *moon-blanch'd:*
white in the moonlight. 10 *quest:* of the Shepherd and his companion,
which becomes identified with the Scholar Gipsy's quest. 13 *cruise:*
water jar. 25 *convolvulus:* morning-glory. 29 *bower:* shelter. 30
*Oxford's towers:* the place names are of places around Oxford.

And near me on the grass lies Glanvil's book—
　Come, let me read the oft-read tale again,
　　The story of that Oxford scholar poor
Of pregnant parts and quick inventive brain,
　Who, tir'd of knocking at Preferment's door,      35
　　One summer morn forsook
His friends, and went to learn the Gipsy lore,
　And roam'd the world with that wild brotherhood,
　And came, as most men deem'd, to little good,
　　But came to Oxford and his friends no more.      40

But once, years after, in the country lanes,
　Two scholars whom at college erst he knew
　　Met him, and of his way of life inquir'd.
Whereat he answer'd, that the Gipsy crew,
　His mates, had arts to rule as they desir'd      45
　　The workings of men's brains;
And they can bind them to what thoughts they will:
　"And I," he said, "the secret of their art
　When fully learn'd, will to the world impart:
　　But it needs heaven-sent moments for this skill."      50

This said, he left them, and return'd no more,
　But rumors hung about the countryside
　　That the lost Scholar long was seen to stray,
Seen by rare glimpses, pensive and tongue-tied,
　In hat of antique shape, and cloak of gray,      55
　　The same the Gipsies wore.
Shepherds had met him on the Hurst in spring:
　At some lone alehouse in the Berkshire moors,
　On the warm ingle bench, the smock-frock'd boors
　　Had found him seated at their entering,      60

But, mid their drink and clatter, he would fly:
　And I myself seem half to know thy looks,
　　And put the shepherds, Wanderer, on thy trace;
And boys who in lone wheatfields scare the rooks
　I ask if thou hast pass'd their quiet place;      65
　　Or in my boat I lie

31 *Glanvil's book:* see general note, p. 395.   35 *Preferment's door:* advancement through ecclesiastical appointment.   50 *heaven-sent:* from 1857 edn.   57 *Hurst:* Hurst Hill, southwest of Oxford.   59 *ingle bench:* a bench in a nook by the fireside.   63 *trace:* path, course.

Moor'd to the cool bank in the summer heats,
  Mid wide grass meadows which the sunshine fills,
  And watch the warm, green-muffled Cumner hills,
    And wonder if thou haunt'st their shy retreats.      70

For most, I know, thou lov'st retired ground.
  Thee, at the ferry, Oxford riders blithe,
  Returning home on summer nights, have met
Crossing the stripling Thames at Bab-lock-hithe,
  Trailing in the cool stream thy fingers wet,        75
    As the slow punt swings round:
And leaning backwards in a pensive dream,
  And fostering in thy lap a heap of flowers
  Pluck'd in shy fields and distant woodland bowers,
    And thine eyes resting on the moonlit stream:      80

And then they land, and thou art seen no more.
  Maidens who from the distant hamlets come
    To dance around the Fyfield elm in May,
  Oft through the darkening fields have seen thee roam,
    Or cross a stile into the public way.             85
      Oft thou hast given them store
  Of flowers—the frail-leaf'd, white anemone—
    Dark bluebells drench'd with dews of summer eves—
    And purple orchises with spotted leaves—
      But none has words she can report of thee.       90

And, above Godstow Bridge, when hay-time's here
  In June, and many a scythe in sunshine flames,
  Men who through those wide fields of breezy grass
Where black-wing'd swallows haunt the glittering Thames,
    To bathe in the abandon'd lasher pass,             95
      Have often pass'd thee near
Sitting upon the river bank o'ergrown:
    Mark'd thy outlandish garb, thy figure spare,
    Thy dark vague eyes, and soft abstracted air;
      But, when they came from bathing, thou wert gone. 100

At some lone homestead in the Cumner hills,
  Where at her open door the housewife darns,
    Thou hast been seen, or hanging on a gate

78 *fostering*: cherishing.  79 *woodland*: *Wychwood* (1857, 1869).  95
*lasher*: pool below a dam.

To watch the threshers in the mossy barns.
   Children, who early range these slopes and late   105
     For cresses from the rills,
Have known thee watching, all an April day,
   The springing pastures and the feeding kine;
   And mark'd thee, when the stars come out and shine,
     Through the long dewy grass move slow away.   110


In autumn, on the skirts of Bagley wood,
   Where most the Gipsies by the turf-edg'd way
   Pitch their smok'd tents, and every bush you see
   With scarlet patches tagg'd and shreds of gray,
     Above the forest ground call'd Thessaly—   115
     The blackbird picking food
Sees thee, nor stops his meal, nor fears at all;
   So often has he known thee past him stray
   Rapt, twirling in thy hand a wither'd spray,
     And waiting for the spark from Heaven to fall.   120


And once, in winter, on the causeway chill
   Where home through flooded fields foot-travellers go,
   Have I not pass'd thee on the wooden bridge
   Wrapt in thy cloak and battling with the snow,
     Thy face towards Hinksey and its wintry ridge?   125
     And thou hast climb'd the hill
And gain'd the white brow of the Cumner range,
   Turn'd once to watch, while thick the snow-flakes fall,
   The line of festal light in Christ-Church hall—
     Then sought thy straw in some sequester'd grange. 130


But what—I dream! Two hundred years are flown
   Since first thy story ran through Oxford halls,
   And the grave Glanvil did the tale inscribe
That thou wert wander'd from the studious walls
     To learn strange arts, and join a Gipsy tribe:   135
     And thou from earth art gone
Long since, and in some quiet churchyard laid;
   Some country nook, where o'er thy unknown grave
   Tall grasses and white flowering nettles wave—
     Under a dark red-fruited yew-tree's shade.   140

120 *spark from Heaven*: cf. *mystery, secret* in general note, p. 395.
129 *Christ-Church*: an Oxford College.   130 *grange*: farm building.

No, no, thou hast not felt the lapse of hours.
  For what wears out the life of mortal men?
    'Tis that from change to change their being rolls:
  'Tis that repeated shocks, again, again,
    Exhaust the energy of strongest souls,          145
      And numb the elastic powers.
  Till having us'd our nerves with bliss and teen,
    And tir'd upon a thousand schemes our wit,
    To the just-pausing Genius we remit
      Our worn-out life, and are—what we have been.    150

Thou hast not liv'd, why shouldst thou perish, so?
  Thou hadst *one* aim, *one* business, *one* desire:
    Else wert thou long since number'd with the dead—
  Else hadst thou spent, like other men, thy fire.
    The generations of thy peers are fled,         155
      And we ourselves shall go;
  But thou possessest an immortal lot,
    And we imagine thee exempt from age
    And living as thou liv'st on Glanvil's page,
      Because thou hadst—what we, alas, have not!    160

For early didst thou leave the world, with powers
  Fresh, undiverted to the world without,
    Firm to their mark, not spent on other things;
  Free from the sick fatigue, the languid doubt,
    Which much to have tried, in much been baffled, brings.
    O Life unlike to ours!         166
  Who fluctuate idly without term or scope,
    Of whom each strives, nor knows for what he strives,
    And each half lives a hundred different lives;
      Who wait like thee, but not, like thee, in hope.    170

Thou waitest for the spark from Heaven: and we,
  Light half-believers of our casual creeds,
    Who never deeply felt, nor clearly will'd,
  Whose insight never has borne fruit in deeds,
    Whose vague resolves never have been fulfill'd:    175
      For whom each year we see
  Breeds new beginnings, disappointments new;

147 *us'd:* exhausted. *teen:* sorrow. 167 *term or scope:* cf. "end or aim." 172 *Light: Vague* (later editions). 175 *vague: weak* (later editions).

Who hesitate and falter life away,
And lose to-morrow the ground won to-day—
   Ah, do not we, Wanderer, await it too?        180


Yes, we await it, but it still delays,
   And then we suffer; and amongst us One,
   Who most has suffer'd, takes dejectedly
His seat upon the intellectual throne;
      And all his store of sad experience he        185
      Lays bare of wretched days;
Tells us his misery's birth and growth and signs,
   And how the dying spark of hope was fed,
   And how the breast was sooth'd, and how the head,
      And all his hourly varied anodynes.        190


This for our wisest: and we others pine,
   And wish the long unhappy dream would end,
   And waive all claim to bliss, and try to bear
With close-lipp'd Patience for our only friend,
      Sad Patience, too near neighbor to Despair:        195
      But none has hope like thine.
Thou through the fields and through the woods dost stray,
   Roaming the country side, a truant boy,
   Nursing thy project in unclouded joy,
      And every doubt long blown by time away.        200


O born in days when wits were fresh and clear,
   And life ran gaily as the sparkling Thames;
   Before this strange disease of modern life,
With its sick hurry, its divided aims,
      Its heads o'ertaxed, its palsied hearts, was rife—        205
      Fly hence, our contact fear!
Still fly, plunge deeper in the bowering wood!
   Averse, as Dido did with gesture stern
   From her false friend's approach in Hades turn,
      Wave us away, and keep thy solitude.        210

---

182-84 amongst . . . throne: possibly Tennyson, whose *In Memoriam*
was published in 1850, when also he succeeded Wordsworth to the
laureateship. The "intellectual throne" is from Tennyson's "Palace of
Art" (l. 216).    207 *bowering:* sheltering.    208-09 *Dido . . . turn:*
Dido spurned Aeneas' attempt to engage her attention when he saw her
during his visit to the underworld.

Still nursing the unconquerable hope,
  Still clutching the inviolable shade,
    With a free onward impulse brushing through,
  By night, the silver'd branches of the glade—
    Far on the forest skirts, where none pursue,      215
      On some mild pastoral slope
  Emerge, and resting on the moonlit pales,
    Freshen thy flowers, as in former years,
    With dew, or listen with enchanted ears,
      From the dark dingles, to the nightingales.    220

But fly our paths, our feverish contact fly!
  For strong the infection of our mental strife,
    Which, though it gives no bliss, yet spoils for rest;
  And we should win thee from thy own fair life,
    Like us distracted, and like us unblest.      225
      Soon, soon thy cheer would die,
  Thy hopes grow timorous, and unfix'd thy powers,
    And thy clear aims be cross and shifting made:
    And then thy glad perennial youth would fade,
      Fade, and grow old at last and die like ours.    230

Then fly our greetings, fly our speech and smiles!
  As some grave Tyrian trader, from the sea,
    Descried at sunrise an emerging prow
  Lifting the cool-hair'd creepers stealthily,
    The fringes of a southward-facing brow    235
      Among the Aegean isles;
  And saw the merry Grecian coaster come,
    Freighted with amber grapes, and Chian wine,
    Green bursting figs, and tunnies steep'd in brine;
      And knew the intruders on his ancient home,    240

The young light-hearted Masters of the waves;
  And snatch'd his rudder, and shook out more sail,
    And day and night held on indignantly
  O'er the blue Midland waters with the gale,
    Betwixt the Syrtes and soft Sicily,    245

211-12 *Still . . . shade:* cf. l. 120. 217 *pales:* fields. 218 *thy flowers:*
cf. l. 78. 220 *dingles:* valleys. 222 *infection:* cf. *contagion,* Shelley,
p. 334, l. 356. 232 *Tyrian:* Phoenician, from Tyre. 233 *prow:* of the
rival "Grecian coaster" (l. 237). 234 *creepers:* vines, overhanging the
anchorage. 239 *tunnies:* fish. 245 *Syrtes:* Syrtis Major and Minor,
sand banks off the coast of northern Africa.

To where the Atlantic raves
Outside the Western Straits, and unbent sails
    There, where down cloudy cliffs, through sheets of foam,
Shy traffickers, the dark Iberians come;
    And on the beach undid his corded bales.                250

## Dover Beach

The sea is calm to-night,
The tide is full, the moon lies fair
Upon the Straits;—on the French coast, the light
Gleams, and is gone; the cliffs of England stand,
Glimmering and vast, out in the tranquil bay.                5
Come to the window, sweet is the night air!
Only, from the long line of spray
Where the ebb meets the moon-blanch'd sand,
Listen! you hear the grating roar
Of pebbles which the waves suck back, and fling,          10
At their return, up the high strand,
Begin, and cease, and then again begin,
With tremulous cadence slow, and bring
The eternal note of sadness in.

    Sophocles long ago                                            15
Heard it on the Aegean, and it brought
Into his mind the turbid ebb and flow
Of human misery; we
Find also in the sound a thought,
Hearing it by this distant northern sea.                      20

The sea of faith
Was once, too, at the full, and round earth's shore
Lay like the folds of a bright girdle furl'd;
But now I only hear
Its melancholy, long, withdrawing roar,                      25
Retreating to the breath
Of the night-wind down the vast edges drear
And naked shingles of the world.

247 *Western Straits:* Gibraltar.
    DOVER BEACH. 8 *moon-blanch'd:* white in the moonlight.   15 *Sopho-cles . . . ago:* in his tragedy *Antigone,* where the sad fate which befell the house of Oedipus is said to pass "from life to life of the race."   28 *shingles:* gravelly beaches.

Ah, love, let us be true
To one another! for the world, which seems          30
To lie before us like a land of dreams,
So various, so beautiful, so new,
Hath really neither joy, nor love, nor light,
Nor certitude, nor peace, nor help for pain;
And we are here as on a darkling plain          35
Swept with confused alarms of struggle and flight,
Where ignorant armies clash by night.

35 *darkling :* dark.

# WALT WHITMAN 1819–1892

*from* SONG OF MYSELF

6

A child said *What is the grass?* fetching it to me with full
     hands;
How could I answer the child? I do not know what it is any
     more than he.

I guess it must be the flag of my disposition, out of hopeful
     green stuff woven.

Or I guess it is the handkerchief of the Lord,
A scented gift and remembrancer designedly dropt,      5
Bearing the owner's name someway in the corners, that we
     may see and remark, and say *Whose?*

Or I guess the grass is itself a child, the produced babe of the
     vegetation.

Or I guess it is a uniform hieroglyphic,
And it means, Sprouting alike in broad zones and narrow
     zones,
Growing among black folks as among white,      10
Kanuck, Tuckahoe, Congressman, Cuff, I give them the same,
     I receive them the same.

And now it seems to me the beautiful uncut hair of graves.

Tenderly will I use you curling grass,
It may be you transpire from the breasts of young men,
It may be if I had known them I would have loved them,    15
It may be you are from old people, or from offspring taken
     soon out of their mothers' laps.
And here you are the mothers' laps.

This grass is very dark to be from the white heads of old
     mothers,
Darker than the colorless beards of old men,
Dark to come from under the faint red roofs of mouths.    20

[6] 11 *Kanuck:* Canadian. *Tuckahoe:* a Virginian living east of the
Blue Ridge Mountains. *Cuff:* a Negro. 14 *transpire:* exhale.

O I perceive after all so many uttering tongues,
And I perceive they do not come from the roofs of mouths
for nothing.

I wish I could translate the hints about the dead young men
and women,
And the hints about old men and mothers, and the offspring
taken soon out of their laps.

What do you think has become of the young and old men? 25
And what do you think has become of the women and
children?

They are alive and well somewhere,
The smallest sprout shows there is really no death,
And if ever there was it led forward life, and does not wait at
the end to arrest it,
And ceas'd the moment life appear'd. 30

All goes onward and outward, nothing collapses,
And to die is different from what any one supposed, and
luckier.

### 8

The little one sleeps in its cradle,
I lift the gauze and look a long time, and silently brush away
flies with my hand.

The youngster and the red-faced girl turn aside up the bushy
hill,
I peeringly view them from the top.

The suicide sprawls on the bloody floor of the bedroom, 5
I witness the corpse with its dabbled hair, I note where the
pistol has fallen.

The blab of the pave, tires of carts, sluff of boot-soles, talk of
the promenaders,
The heavy omnibus, the driver with his interrogating thumb,
the clank of the shod horses on the granite floor,

[8] 7 *blab . . . pave:* the noise of the street. *sluff:* shuffle. 8
*granite floor:* cobblestone pavement.

The snow-sleighs, clinking, shouted jokes, pelts of snow-balls,
The hurrahs for popular favorites, the fury of rous'd mobs, 10
The flap of the curtain'd litter, a sick man inside borne to the
    hospital,
The meeting of enemies, the sudden oath, the blows and fall,
The excited crowd, the policeman with his star quickly
    working his passage to the centre of the crowd,
The impassive stones that receive and return so many echoes,
What groans of over-fed or half-starv'd who fall sunstruck or
    in fits, 15
What exclamations of women taken suddenly who hurry
    home and give birth to babes,
What living and buried speech is always vibrating here, what
    howls restrain'd by decorum,
Arrests of criminals, slights, adulterous offers made,
    acceptances, rejections with convex lips,
I mind them or the show or resonance of them—I come and
    I depart.

*11*

Twenty-eight young men bathe by the shore,
Twenty-eight young men and all so friendly;
Twenty-eight years of womanly life and all so lonesome.

She owns the fine house by the rise of the bank,
She hides handsome and richly drest aft the blinds of the
    window. 5

Which of the young men does she like the best?
Ah the homeliest of them is beautiful to her.

Where are you off to, lady? for I see you,
You splash in the water there, yet stay stock still in your
    room.

Dancing and laughing along the beach came the twenty-ninth
    bather, 10
The rest did not see her, but she saw them and loved them.

The beards of the young men glisten'd with wet, it ran from
    their long hair,
Little streams pass'd all over their bodies.

    [*11*] 5 *aft:* behind.

An unseen hand also pass'd over their bodies,
It descended tremblingly from their temples and ribs.     15


The young men float on their backs, their white bellies bulge
to the sun, they do not ask who seizes fast to them,
They do not know who puffs and declines with pendant and
bending arch,
They do not think whom they souse with spray.


### 15

The pure contralto sings in the organ loft,
The carpenter dresses his plank, the tongue of his foreplane
whistles its wild ascending lisp,
The married and unmarried children ride home to their
Thanksgiving dinner,
The pilot seizes the king-pin, he heaves down with a strong
arm,
The mate stands braced in the whale-boat, lance and harpoon
are ready,     5
The duck-shooter walks by silent and cautious stretches,
The deacons are ordain'd with cross'd hands at the altar,
The spinning-girl retreats and advances to the hum of the big
wheel,
The farmer stops by the bars as he walks on a First-day loafe
and looks at the oats and rye,
The lunatic is carried at last to the asylum a confirm'd case,  10
(He will never sleep any more as he did in the cot in his
mother's bed-room);
The jour printer with gray head and gaunt jaws works at his
case,
He turns his quid of tobacco while his eyes blur with the
manuscript;
The malform'd limbs are tied to the surgeon's table,
What is removed drops horribly in a pail;     15
The quadroon girl is sold at the auction-stand, the drunkard
nods by the bar-room stove,

[15] 2 *tongue:* the cutting edge. 4 *king-pin:* probably a big pin to
which a line is made fast. *heaves down:* draws the line fast. 9 *bars:*
gates. *First-day loafe:* idle Sunday. 12 *jour:* journeyman. *case:* tray
holding type. 16 *quadroon:* of one-quarter Negro blood.

The machinist rolls up his sleeves, the policeman travels his
      beat, the gate-keeper marks who pass,

The young fellow drives the express-wagon (I love him,
      though I do not know him);

The half-breed straps on his light boots to compete in the
      race,

The western turkey-shooting draws old and young, some lean
      on their rifles, some sit on logs,         20

Out from the crowd steps the marksman, takes his position,
      levels his piece;

The groups of newly-come immigrants cover the wharf or
      levee,

As the woolly-pates hoe in the sugar-field, the overseer views
      them from his saddle,

The bugle calls in the ball-room, the gentlemen run for their
      partners, the dancers bow to each other,

The youth lies awake in the cedar-roof'd garret and harks to
      the musical rain,         25

The Wolverine sets traps on the creek that helps fill the
      Huron,

The squaw wrapt in her yellow-hemm'd cloth is offering
      moccasins and bead-bags for sale,

The connoisseur peers along the exhibition-gallery with
      half-shut eyes bent sideways,

As the deck-hands make fast the steamboat the plank is
      thrown for the shore-going passengers,

The young sister holds out the skein while the elder sister
      winds it off in a ball, and stops now and then for
      the knots,         30

The one-year wife is recovering and happy having a week
      ago borne her first child,

The clean-hair'd Yankee girl works with her sewing-machine
      or in the factory or mill,

The paving-man leans on his two-handed rammer, the
      reporter's lead flies swiftly over the note-book,
      the sign-painter is lettering with blue and gold.

The canal boy trots on the tow-path, the book-keeper counts
      at his desk, the shoemaker waxes his thread,

The conductor beats time for the band and all the performers
      follow him,         35

The child is baptized, the convert is making his first
      professions,

26 *Wolverine:* native of Michigan.

The regatta is spread on the bay, the race is begun (how the
    white sails sparkle!),
The drover watching his drove sings out to them that would
    stray,
The pedler sweats with his pack on his back (the purchaser
    higgling about the odd cent);
The bride unrumples her white dress, the minute-hand of the
    clock moves slowly,                                    40
The opium-eater reclines with rigid head and just-open'd lips,
The prostitute draggles her shawl, her bonnet bobs on her
    tipsy and pimpled neck,
The crowd laugh at her blackguard oaths, the men jeer and
    wink to each other,
(Miserable! I do not laugh at your oaths nor jeer you);
The President holding a cabinet council is surrounded by the
    great Secretaries,                                     45
On the piazza walk three matrons stately and friendly with
    twined arms,
The crew of the fish-smack pack repeated layers of halibut in
    the hold,
The Missourian crosses the plains toting his wares and his
    cattle,
As the fare-collector goes through the train he gives notice by
    the jingling of loose change,
The floor-men are laying the floor, the tinners are tinning the
    roof, the masons are calling for mortar,              50
In single file each shouldering his hod pass onward the
    laborers;
Seasons pursuing each other the indescribable crowd is
    gather'd, it is the fourth of Seventh-month (what
    salutes of cannon and small arms!),
Seasons pursuing each other the plougher ploughs, the mower
    mows, and the winter-grain falls in the ground;
Off on the lakes the pike-fisher watches and waits by the hole
    in the frozen surface,
The stumps stand thick round the clearing, the squatter strikes
    deep with his axe,                                     55
Flatboatmen make fast towards dusk near the cotton-wood or
    pecan-trees,
Coon-seekers go through the regions of the Red river or
    through those drain'd by the Tennessee, or through
    those of the Arkansas,

38 *drover:* cattle- or sheep-driver.

Torches shine in the dark that hangs on the Chattahoochee
    or Altamahaw,
Patriarchs sit at supper with sons and grandsons and
    great-grandsons around them,
In walls of adobie, in canvas tents, rest hunters and trappers
    after their day's sport,      60
The city sleeps and the country sleeps,
The living sleep for their time, the dead sleep for their time,
The old husband sleeps by his wife and the young husband
    sleeps by his wife;
And these tend inward to me, and I tend outward to them,
And such as it is to be of these more or less I am,      65
And of these one and all I weave the song of myself.


### 26

Now I will do nothing but listen,
To accrue what I hear into this song, to let sounds contribute
    toward it.


I hear bravuras of birds, bustle of growing wheat, gossip of
    flames, clack of sticks cooking my meals,
I hear the sound I love, the sound of the human voice,
I hear all sounds running together, combined, fused or
    following,      5
Sounds of the city and sounds out of the city, sounds of the
    day and night,
Talkative young ones to those that like them, the loud laugh
    of work-people at their meals,
The angry bass of disjointed friendship, the faint tones of the
    sick,
The judge with hands tight to the desk, his pallid lips
    pronouncing a death-sentence,
The heave'e'yo of stevedores unlading ships by the wharves,
    the refrain of the anchor-lifters,      10
The ring of alarm-bells, the cry of fire, the whirr of
    swift-streaking engines and hose-carts with
    premonitory tinkles and color'd lights,
The steam-whistle, the solid roll of the train of approaching
    cars,

[26] 3 *bravuras:* brilliant songs.

The slow march play'd at the head of the association marching
    two and two,
(They go to guard some corpse, the flag-tops are draped with
    black muslin).        14

I hear the violoncello ('tis the young man's heart's complaint),
I hear the key'd cornet, it glides quickly in through my ears,
It shakes mad-sweet pangs through my belly and breast.

I hear the chorus, it is a grand opera,
Ah this indeed is music—this suits me.

A tenor large and fresh as the creation fills me,        20
The orbic flex of his mouth is pouring and filling me full.

I hear the train'd soprano (what work with hers is this?)
The orchestra whirls me wider than Uranus flies,
It wrenches such ardors from me I did not know I possess'd
    them,
It sails me, I dab with bare feet, they are lick'd by the indolent
    waves,        25
I am cut by bitter and angry hail, I lose my breath,
Steep'd amid honey'd morphine, my windpipe throttled in
    fakes of death,
At length let up again to feel the puzzle of puzzles,
And that we call Being.

## Give me the splendid silent sun

### I

Give me the splendid silent sun with all his beams
    full-dazzling,
Give me juicy autumnal fruit ripe and red from the orchard,
Give me a field where the unmow'd grass grows,
Give me an arbor, give me the trellis'd grape,
Give me fresh corn and wheat, give me serene-moving animals
    teaching content,        5
Give me nights perfectly quiet as on high plateaus west of the
    Mississippi, and I looking up at the stars,
Give me odorous at sunrise a garden of beautiful flowers
    where I can walk undisturb'd,

21 *orbic flex:* round movement.  23 *Uranus:* one of the remotest planets.

Give me for marriage a sweet-breath'd woman of whom I
    should never tire,
Give me a perfect child, give me away aside from the noise of
    the world a rural domestic life,
Give me to warble spontaneous songs recluse by myself, for
    my own ears only,          10
Give me solitude, give me Nature, give me again O nature
    your primal sanities!

These demanding to have them (tired with ceaseless
    excitement, and rack'd by the war-strife),
These to procure incessantly asking, rising in cries from my
    heart,
While yet incessantly asking still I adhere to my city,
Day upon day and year upon year O city, walking your
    streets,          15
Where you hold me enchain'd a certain time refusing to give
    me up,
Yet giving to make me glutted, enrich'd of soul, you give me
    forever faces;
(O I see what I sought to escape, confronting, reversing my
    cries,
I see my own soul trampling down what it ask'd for).

2

Keep your splendid silent sun,          20
Keep your woods, O Nature, and the quiet places by the
    woods,
Keep your fields of clover and timothy, and your corn-fields
    and orchards,
Keep the blossoming buckwheat fields where the
    Ninth-month bees hum;
Give me faces and streets—give me these phantoms incessant
    and endless along the trottoirs!
Give me interminable eyes—give me women—give me
    comrades and lovers by the thousand!          25
Let me see new ones every day—let me hold new ones by the
    hand every day!
Give me such shows—give me the streets of Manhattan!
Give me Broadway, with the soldiers marching—give me the
    sound of the trumpets and drums!

GIVE ME THE SPLENDID. 9 *away:* a way (?). Cf. ll. 18-19.   12 *war-strife:* the Civil War.   24 *trottoirs:* sidewalks.

(The soldiers in companies or regiments—some starting away,
    flush'd and reckless,
Some, their time up, returning with thinn'd ranks, young, yet
    very old, worn, marching, noticing nothing);    30
Give me the shores and wharves heavy-fring'd with black
    ships!
O such for me! O an intense life, full to repletion and varied!
The life of the theatre, bar-room, huge hotel, for me!
The saloon of the steamer! the crowded excursion for me!
    the torchlight procession!
The dense brigade bound for the war, with high piled military
    wagons following;    35
People, endless, streaming, with strong voices, passions,
    pageants,
Manhattan streets with their powerful throbs, with beating
    drums as now,
The endless and noisy chorus, the rustle and clank of muskets
    (even the sight of the wounded),
Manhattan crowds, with their turbulent musical chorus!
Manhattan faces and eyes forever for me.    40

## When lilacs last in the door-yard bloom'd

### 1

When lilacs last in the door-yard bloom'd,
And the great star early droop'd in the western sky in the
    night,
I mourn'd, and yet shall mourn with ever-returning spring.

Ever-returning spring, trinity sure to me you bring,
Lilac blooming perennial and drooping star in the west,    5
And thought of him I love.

### 2

O powerful western fallen star!
O shades of night—O moody, tearful night!
O great star disappear'd—O the black murk that hides the star!
O cruel hands that hold me powerless—O helpless soul of me!
O harsh surrounding cloud that will not free my soul.    11

35 *dense:* i.e., with its full complement. Cf. *thinn'd ranks,* l. 30.

WHEN LILACS LAST. 6 *him:* Abraham Lincoln. He died April 15, 1865,
the day after he was shot by John Wilkes Booth at Ford's Theatre,
Washington. Lincoln's body was taken to Springfield, Illinois, for burial.
See ll. 30 ff.

### 3

In the dooryard fronting an old farm-house near the
    white-wash'd palings,
Stands the lilac-bush tall-growing with heart-shaped leaves of
    rich green,
With many a pointed blossom rising delicate, with the
    perfume strong I love,
With every leaf a miracle—and from this bush in the
    dooryard,        15
With delicate color'd blossoms and heart-shaped leaves of
    rich green,
A sprig with its flower I break.

### 4

In the swamp in secluded recesses,
A shy and hidden bird is warbling a song.

Solitary the thrush,       20
The hermit withdrawn to himself, avoiding the settlements,
Sings by himself a song.

Song of the bleeding throat,
Death's outlet song of life (for well dear brother I know,
If thou wast not granted to sing thou would'st surely die).  25

### 5

Over the breast of the spring, the land, amid cities,
Amid lanes and through old woods, where lately the violets
    peep'd from the ground, spotting the gray debris,
Amid the grass in the fields each side of the lanes, passing the
    endless grass,
Passing the yellow-spear'd wheat, every grain from its shroud
    in the dark-brown fields uprisen,
Passing the apple-tree blows of white and pink in the
    orchards,        30
Carrying a corpse to where it shall rest in the grave,
Night and day journeys a coffin.

### 6

Coffin that passes through lanes and streets,
Through day and night with the great cloud darkening the
    land,

12 *palings* : fence pickets.   30 *blows :* blossoms.

With the pomp of the inloop'd flags with the cities draped in
    black,        35
With the show of the States themselves as of crape-veil'd
    women standing,
With processions long and winding and the flambeaus of the
    night,
With the countless torches lit, with the silent sea of faces and
    the unbared heads,
With the waiting depot, the arriving coffin, and the sombre
    faces,
With dirges through the night, with the thousand voices
    rising strong and solemn,    40
With all the mournful voices of the dirges pour'd around the
    coffin,
The dim-lit churches and the shuddering organs—where amid
    these you journey,
With the tolling tolling bells' perpetual clang,
Here, coffin that slowly passes,
I give you my sprig of lilac.    45

7

(Nor for you, for one alone,
Blossoms and branches green to coffins all I bring,
For fresh as the morning, thus would I chant a song for you
    O sane and sacred death.

All over bouquets of roses,
O death, I cover you over with roses and early lilies,    50
But mostly and now the lilac that blooms the first,
Copious I break, I break the sprigs from the bushes,
With loaded arms I come, pouring for you,
For you and the coffins all of you O death.)

8

O western orb sailing the heaven,    55
Now I know what you must have meant as a month since I
    walk'd,
As I walk'd in silence the transparent shadowy night,
As I saw you had something to tell as you bent to me night
    after night,
As you droop'd from the sky low down as if to my side
    (while the other stars all look'd on),

37 *flambeaus:* torches.

As we wander'd together the solemn night (for something I
  know not what kept me from sleep),    60
As the night advanced, and I saw on the rim of the west how
  full you were of woe,
As I stood on the rising ground in the breeze in the cool
  transparent night,
As I watch'd where you pass'd and was lost in the netherward
  black of the night,
As my soul in its trouble dissatisfied sank, as where you sad
  orb,
Concluded, dropt in the night, and was gone.    65

### 9

Sing on there in the swamp,
O singer bashful and tender, I hear your notes, I hear your
  call,
I hear, I come presently, I understand you,
But a moment I linger, for the lustrous star has detain'd me,
The star my departing comrade holds and detains me.    70

### 10

O how shall I warble myself for the dead one there I loved?
And how shall I deck my song for the large sweet soul that
  has gone?
And what shall my perfume be for the grave of him I love?

Sea-winds blown from east and west,
Blown from the Eastern sea and blown from the Western sea,
  till there on the prairies meeting,    75
These and with these and the breath of my chant,
I'll perfume the grave of him I love.

### 11

O what shall I hang on the chamber walls?
And what shall the pictures be that I hang on the walls,
To adorn the burial-house of him I love?    80

Pictures of growing spring and farms and homes,
With the Fourth-month eve at sundown, and the gray smoke
  lucid and bright,
With floods of the yellow gold of the gorgeous, indolent,
  sinking sun, burning, expanding the air,

63 *netherward :* hellish, the black of the netherworld (?).

With the fresh sweet herbage under foot, and the pale green
    leaves of the trees prolific,
In the distance the flowing glaze, the breast of the river, with
    a wind-dapple here and there,         85
With ranging hills on the banks, with many a line against the
    sky, and shadows,
And the city at hand with dwellings so dense, and stacks of
    chimneys,
And all the scenes of life and the workshops, and the
    workmen homeward returning.

12

Lo, body and soul—this land,
My own Manhattan with spires, and the sparkling and
    hurrying tides, and the ships,         90
The varied and ample land, the South and the North in the
    light, Ohio's shores and flashing Missouri,
And ever the far-spreading prairies cover'd with grass and
    corn.

Lo, the most excellent sun so calm and haughty,
The violet and purple morn with just-felt breezes,
The gentle soft-born measureless light,         95
The miracle spreading bathing all, the fulfill'd noon,
The coming eve delicious, the welcome night and the stars,
Over my cities shining all, enveloping man and land.

13

Sing on, sing on you gray-brown bird,
Sing from the swamps, the recesses, pour your chant from the
    bushes,         100
Limitless out of the dusk, out of the cedars and pines.

Sing on dearest brother, warble your reedy song,
Loud human song, with voice of uttermost woe.

O liquid and free and tender!
O wild and loose to my soul—O wondrous singer!     105
You only I hear—yet the star holds me (but will soon depart),
Yet the lilac with mastering odor holds me.

## 14

Now while I sat in the day and look'd forth,
In the close of the day with its light and the fields of spring,
  and the farmers preparing their crops,
In the large unconscious scenery of my land with its lakes and
  forests,                                                      110
In the heavenly aerial beauty (after the perturb'd winds and
  the storms),
Under the arching heavens of the afternoon swift passing,
  and the voices of children and women,
The many-moving sea-tides, and I saw the ships how they
  sail'd,
And the summer approaching with richness, and the fields all
  busy with labor,
And the infinite separate houses, how they all went on, each
  with its meals and minutia of daily usages,                  115
And the streets how their throbbings throbb'd, and the cities
  pent—lo, then and there,
Falling upon them all and among them all, enveloping me
  with the rest,
Appear'd the cloud, appear'd the long black trail,
And I knew death, its thought, and the sacred knowledge of
  death.                                                       119

Then with the knowledge of death as walking one side of me,
And the thought of death close-walking the other side of me,
And I in the middle as with companions, and as holding the
  hands of companions,
I fled forth to the hiding receiving night that talks not,
Down to the shores of the water, the path by the swamp in
  the dimness,
To the solemn shadowy cedars and ghostly pines so still.      125

And the singer so shy to the rest receiv'd me,
The gray-brown bird I know receiv'd us comrades three,
And he sang the carol of death, and a verse for him I love.

From deep secluded recesses,
From the fragrant cedars and the ghostly pines so still,      130
Came the carol of the bird.

115 *minutia:* probably a plural.

And the charm of the carol rapt me,
As I held as if by their hands my comrades in the night,
And the voice of my spirit tallied the song of the bird.

*Come lovely and soothing death,*      135
*Undulate round the world, serenely arriving, arriving,*
*In the day, in the night, to all, to each,*
*Sooner or later delicate death.*

*Prais'd be the fathomless universe,*
*For life and joy, and for objects and knowledge curious,*    140
*And for love, sweet love—but praise! praise! praise!*
*For the sure-enwinding arms of cool-enfolding death.*

*Dark mother always gliding near with soft feet,*
*Have none chanted for thee a chant of fullest welcome?*
*Then I chant it for thee, I glorify thee above all,*      145
*I bring thee a song that when thou must indeed come, come*
     *unfalteringly.*

*Approach strong deliveress,*
*When it is so, when thou hast taken them I joyously sing the*
     *dead,*
*Lost in the loving floating ocean of thee,*
*Laved in the flood of thy bliss O death.*      150

*From me to thee glad serenades,*
*Dances for thee I propose saluting thee, adornments and*
     *feastings for thee,*
*And the sights of the open landscape and the high-spread sky*
     *are fitting,*
*And life and the fields, and the huge and thoughtful night.*

*The night in silence under many a star,*      155
*The ocean shore and the husky whispering wave whose voice*
     *I know,*
*And the soul turning to thee O vast and well-veil'd death,*
*And the body gratefully nestling close to thee.*

*Over the tree-tops I float thee a song,*
*Over the rising and sinking waves, over the myriad fields and*
     *the prairies wide,*      160

124 *tallied*: matched.

*Over the dense-pack'd cities all and the teeming wharves and
    ways,*
*I float this carol with joy, with joy to thee O death.*

## 15

To the tally of my soul,
Loud and strong kept up the gray-brown bird,
With pure deliberate notes spreading filling the night.    165

Loud in the pines and cedars dim,
Clear in the freshness moist and the swamp-perfume,
And I with my comrades there in the night.

While my sight that was bound in my eyes unclosed,
As to long panoramas of visions.    170

And I saw askant the armies,
I saw as in noiseless dreams hundreds of battle-flags,
Borne through the smoke of the battles and pierc'd with
    missiles I saw them,
And carried hither and yon through the smoke, and torn and
    bloody,
And at last but a few shreds left on the staffs (and all in
    silence),    175
And the staffs all splinter'd and broken.

I saw battle-corpses, myriads of them,
And the white skeletons of young men, I saw them,
I saw the debris and debris of all the slain soldiers of the war,
But I saw they were not as was thought,    180
They themselves were fully at rest, they suffer'd not,
The living remain'd and suffer'd, the mother suffer'd,
And the wife and the child and the musing comrade suffer'd,
And the armies that remain'd suffer'd.

## 16

Passing the visions, passing the night,    185
Passing, unloosing the hold of my comrades' hands,
Passing the song of the hermit bird and the tallying song of
    my soul,
Victorious song, death's outlet song, yet varying ever-altering
    song,

163 *tally:* accord; or matching score. Cf. ll. 134, 187, 200.   171 *askant:*
indirectly, as in the mind's eye. Cf. *as . . . dreams,* l. 172.

As low and wailing, yet clear the notes, rising and falling,
  flooding the night,
Sadly sinking and fainting, as warning and warning, and yet
  again bursting with joy,                                      190
Covering the earth and filling the spread of the heaven,
As that powerful psalm in the night I heard from recesses,
Passing, I leave thee lilac with heart-shaped leaves,
I leave thee there in the door-yard, blooming, returning with
  spring.

I cease from my song for thee,                                   195
From my gaze on thee in the west, fronting the west,
  communing with thee,
O comrade lustrous with silver face in the night.

Yet each to keep and all, retrievements out of the night,
The song, the wondrous chant of the gray-brown bird,
And the tallying chant, the echo arous'd in my soul,            200
With the lustrous and drooping star with the countenance
  full of woe,
With the holders holding my hand nearing the call of the
  bird,
Comrades mine and I in the midst, and their memory ever
  to keep, for the dead I loved so well,
For the sweetest, wisest soul of all my days and lands—and
  this for his dear sake,
Lilac and star and bird twined with the chant of my soul,      205
There in the fragrant pines and the cedars dusk and dim.

198 *retrievements:* things recovered.

# EMILY DICKINSON 1830–1886

### I asked no other thing

I asked no other thing,
No other was denied.
I offered Being for it;
The mighty merchant smiled.

Brazil? He twirled a button.
Without a glance my way:
"But, madam, is there nothing else
That we can show to-day?"

### The soul selects her own society

The soul selects her own society,
Then shuts the door;
On her divine majority
Obtrude no more.

Unmoved, she notes the chariot's pausing          5
At her low gate;
Unmoved, an emperor is kneeling
Upon her mat.

I've known her from an ample nation
Choose one;                                       10
Then close the valves of her attention
Like stone.

### Some things that fly there be

Some things that fly there be,—
Birds, hours, the bumble-bee:
Of these no elegy.

Some things that stay there be,—
Grief, hills, eternity:
Nor this behooveth me.

There are, that resting, rise.
Can I expound the skies?
How still the riddle lies!

## I taste a liquor never brewed

I taste a liquor never brewed,
From tankards scooped in pearl;
Not all the vats upon the Rhine
Yield such an alcohol!

Inebriate of air am I,                                          5
And debauchee of dew,
Reeling, through endless summer days,
From inns of molten blue.

When landlords turn the drunken bee
Out of the foxglove's door,                                    10
When butterflies renounce their drams,
I shall but drink the more!

Till seraphs swing their snowy hats,
And saints to windows run,
To see the little tippler                                       15
Leaning against the sun!

## A bird came down the walk

A bird came down the walk:
He did not know I saw;
He bit an angle-worm in halves
And ate the fellow, raw.

And then he drank a dew                                         5
From a convenient grass,
And then hopped sidewise to the wall
To let a beetle pass.

I TASTE A LIQUOR. 11 *drams:* small drinks.  13 *seraphs:* angels of the
highest order.

He glanced with rapid eyes
That hurried all abroad,—
They looked like frightened beads, I thought
He stirred his velvet head

Like one in danger; cautious,
I offered him a crumb,
And he unrolled his feathers
And rowed him softer home

Than oars divide the ocean,
Too silver for a seam,
Or butterflies, off banks of noon,
Leap, plashless, as they swim.

10

15

20

### The gentian weaves her fringes

The gentian weaves her fringes,
The maple's loom is red.
My departing blossoms
Obviate parade.

A brief, but patient illness,
An hour to prepare;
And one, below this morning,
Is where the angels are.

5

It was a short procession,—
The bobolink was there,
An aged bee addressed us,
And then we knelt in prayer.

10

We trust that she was willing,—
We ask that we may be.
Summer, sister, seraph,
Let us go with thee!

15

In the name of the bee
And of the butterfly
And of the breeze, amen!

THE GENTIAN WEAVES. 4 *Obviate parade:* Make any ceremonial unnecessary. Cf. *procession,* l. 9.    15 *seraph:* see p. 424, l. 13.

### Of all the souls that stand create

Of all the souls that stand create
I have elected one.
When sense from spirit flies away,
And subterfuge is done;

When that which is and that which was          5
Apart, intrinsic, stand,
And this brief tragedy of flesh
Is shifted like a sand;

When figures show their royal front
And mists are carved away,—          10
Behold the atom I preferred
To all the lists of clay!

### Departed to the judgment

Departed to the judgment,
A mighty afternoon;
Great crowds like ushers leaning,
Creation looking on.

The flesh surrendered, cancelled,
The bodiless begun;
Two worlds, like audiences, disperse
And leave the soul alone.

### How many times these low feet staggered

How many times these low feet staggered,
Only the soldered mouth can tell;
Try! can you stir the awful rivet?
Try! can you lift the hasps of steel?

OF ALL THE SOULS. 1 *create*[*d*]. 6 *intrinsic:* in their essential natures. 12 *all . . . clay:* all living mortals.
HOW MANY TIMES. 2 *soldered mouth:* as if soldered shut.

Stroke the cool forehead, hot so often,               5
Lift, if you can, the listless hair;
Handle the adamantine fingers
Never a thimble more shall wear.

Buzz the dull flies on the chamber window;
Brave shines the sun through the freckled pane;       10
Fearless the cobweb swings from the ceiling—
Indolent housewife, in daisies lain!

### The bustle in a house

The bustle in a house
The morning after death
Is solemnest of industries
Enacted upon earth,—

The sweeping up the heart,
And putting love away
We shall not want to use again
Until eternity.

### Because I could not stop for Death

Because I could not stop for Death,
He kindly stopped for me;
The carriage held but just ourselves
And Immortality.

We slowly drove, he knew no haste,                    5
And I had put away
My labor, and my leisure too,
For his civility.

We passed the school where children played
At wrestling in a ring;                               10
We passed the fields of gazing grain,
We passed the setting sun.

7 *adamantine* : immovable, rigid.

We paused before a house that seemed
A swelling of the ground;
The roof was scarcely visible,                    15
The cornice but a mound.

Since then 'tis centuries; but each
Feels shorter than the day
I first surmised the horses' heads
Were toward eternity.                             20

## No rack can torture me

No rack can torture me,
My soul's at liberty.
Behind this mortal bone
There knits a bolder one

You cannot prick with saw,                         5
Nor rend with scimitar.
Two bodies therefore be;
Bind one, and one will flee.

The eagle of his nest
No easier divest                                  10
And gain the sky,
Than mayest thou,

Except thyself may be
Thine enemy;
Captivity is consciousness,                        15
So's liberty.

## It was not death, for I stood up

It was not death, for I stood up,
And all the dead lie down;
It was not night, for all the bells
Put out their tongues, for noon.

It was not frost, for on my flesh                    5
I felt siroccos crawl,—
Nor fire, for just my marble feet
Could keep a chancel cool.

And yet it tasted like them all;
The figures I have seen                              10
Set orderly, for burial,
Reminded me of mine,

As if my life were shaven
And fitted to a frame,
And could not breathe without a key;               15
And 'twas like midnight, some,

When everything that ticked has stopped,
And space stares, all around,
Or grisly frosts, first autumn morns,
Repeal the beating ground.                          20

But most like chaos,—stopless, cool,—
Without a chance or spar,
Or even a report of land
To justify despair.


*This world is not conclusion*

This world is not conclusion;
    A sequel stands beyond,
Invisible, as music,
    But positive, as sound.
It beckons and it baffles;                           5
    Philosophies don't know,

And through a riddle, at the last,
    Sagacity must go.
To guess it puzzles scholars;
    To gain it, men have shown                      10
Contempt of generations,
    And crucifixion known.

IT WAS NOT DEATH. 8 *chancel:* sanctuary of a church.  20 *Repeal . . . ground:* Stop the beating heart of the earth, as if it had been alive.

### A clock stopped—not the mantel's

A clock stopped—not the mantel's;
  Geneva's farthest skill
Can't put the puppet bowing
  That just now dangled still.

An awe came on the trinket!      5
  The figures hunched with pain,
Then quivered out of decimals
  Into degreeless noon.

It will not stir for doctors,
  This pendulum of snow;      10
The shopman importunes it,
  While cool, concernless No

Nods from the gilded pointers,
  Nods from the seconds slim,
Decades of arrogance between      15
  The dial life and him.

### After great pain a formal feeling comes

After great pain a formal feeling comes—
The nerves sit ceremonious like tombs;
The stiff Heart questions—was it He that bore?
And yesterday—or centuries before?

The feet mechanical      5
Go round a wooden way
Of ground or air of Ought, regardless grown,
A quartz contentment like a stone.

This is the hour of lead
Remembered if outlived,      10
As freezing persons recollect the snow—
First chill, then stupor, then the letting go.

### *Tell all the truth but tell it slant*

Tell all the truth but tell it slant,
Success in circuit lies,
Too bright for our infirm delight
The truth's superb surprise;

As lightning to the children eased
With explanation kind,
The truth must dazzle gradually
Or every man be blind.

### *There is a strength in knowing that it can be borne*

There is a strength in knowing that it can be borne
Although it tear.
What are the sinews of such cordage for
Except to bear?
The ship might be of satin had it not to fight.
To walk on tides requires cedar feet.

### *Until the desert knows*

Until the desert knows
That water grows
His sands suffice;
But let him once suspect
That Caspian fact,                                    5
Sahara dies.

Utmost is relative,
Have not or have
Adjacent sums;
Enough, the first abode                               10
On the familiar road
Galloped in dreams.

UNTIL THE DESERT. 10 *Enough. Enough* [in only].

# GERARD MANLEY HOPKINS 1844–1889

## God's Grandeur

The world is charged with the grandeur of God.
  It will flame out, like shining from shook foil;
  It gathers to a greatness, like the ooze of oil
Crushed. Why do men then now not reck his rod?
Generations have trod, have trod, have trod;      5
  And all is seared with trade; bleared, smeared with toil;
  And wears man's smudge and shares man's smell: the soil
Is bare now, nor can foot feel, being shod.

And for all this, nature is never spent;
  There lives the dearest freshness deep down things;   10
And though the last lights off the black West went
  Oh, morning, at the brown brink eastward, springs—
Because the Holy Ghost over the bent
  World broods with warm breast and with ah! bright wings.

## Spring

Nothing is so beautiful as spring—
  When weeds, in wheels, shoot long and lovely and lush;
  Thrush's eggs look little low heavens, and thrush
Through the echoing timber does so rinse and wring
The ear, it strikes like lightnings to hear him sing;     5
  The glassy peartree leaves and blooms, they brush
  The descending blue; that blue is all in a rush
With richness; the racing lambs too have fair their fling.

What is all this juice and all this joy?
  A strain of the earth's sweet being in the beginning   10
In Eden garden.—Have, get, before it cloy,
  Before it cloud, Christ, lord, and sour with sinning,
Innocent mind and Mayday in girl and boy,
  Most, O maid's child, thy choice and worthy the winning.

GOD'S GRANDEUR. 2 *shook foil:* shaken tinsel. 4 *reck . . . rod:* heed
God's authority. 5-8 *Generations . . . shod:* cf. "The world is too
much with us," p. 257.
   SPRING. 2 *wheels:* possibly whorls, or arching stems. 6 *glassy:* i.e.,
glistening bark. 9 ff. Again, cf. *ibid.* 14 *child:* Christ.

## The Windhover

#### TO CHRIST OUR LORD

I caught this morning morning's minion, king-
    dom of daylight's dauphin, dapple-dawn-drawn Falcon, in
    his riding
Of the rolling level underneath him steady air, and striding
High there, how he rung upon the rein of a wimpling wing
In his ecstasy! then off, off forth on swing,        5
    As a skate's heel sweeps smooth on a bow-bend: the hurl
    and gliding
Rebuffed the big wind. My heart in hiding
Stirred for a bird,—the achieve of, the mastery of the thing!

Brute beauty and valour and act, oh, air, pride, plume, here
    Buckle! AND the fire that breaks from thee then, a billion
Times told lovelier, more dangerous, O my chevalier!    11

No wonder of it: shéer plód makes plough down sillion
Shine, and blue-bleak embers, ah my dear,
    Fall, gall themselves, and gash gold-vermilion.

## Pied Beauty

Glory be to God for dappled things—
    For skies of couple-colour as a brinded cow;
      For rose-moles all in stipple upon trout that swim;
Fresh-firecoal chestnut-falls; finches' wings;
    Landscape plotted and pieced—fold, fallow, and plough;   5
    And áll trádes, their gear and tackle and trim.

THE WINDHOVER. *Windhover:* A small European falcon, the kestrel,
noted for its habit of hovering in the air against the wind.
  1 *minion:* favorite.  2 *dauphin:* prince, eldest son and heir of the king.
4 *rung . . . rein:* from horsemanship: the horse circling "at the end of
a long rein, about its trainer."—*3d ed.,* p. *228. wimpling:* rippling.
6 *bow-bend.* wide turn. 8 *achieve*[*ment*]. 10 *Buckle:* engage, grapple
(?). 11 *told.* counted. *chevalier:* knight; Christ. Cf. *minion, dauphin,*
ll. 1, 2. 12 *plod*[*ding*]. *sillion:* furrow. 14 *gall:* wound. *gash . . .
vermilion:* the wound exposes the glowing red blood.
  PIED BEAUTY. *Pied:* Parti-colored. Cf. *dappled* (l. 1), *couple-colour,
brind*(*l*)*ed,* l. 2, etc.  2 *brinded:* streaked.  3 *in stipple:* as if painted in
spots.  4 *chestnut-falls:* chestnuts fallen from husks.  6 *trim:* equipment.

434

All things counter, original, spare, strange;
  Whatever is fickle, freckled (who knows how?)
    With swift, slow; sweet, sour; adazzle, dim;
He fathers-forth whose beauty is past change:                10
            Praise him.


## Duns Scotus's Oxford

Towery city and branchy between towers;
Cuckoo-echoing, bell-swarmèd, lark-charmèd, rook-racked,
    river-rounded;
The dapple-eared lily below thee; that country and town did
Once encounter in, here coped and poisèd powers;

Thou hast a base and brickish skirt there, sours            5
That neighbour-nature thy grey beauty is grounded
Best in; graceless growth, thou hast confounded
Rural rural keeping—folk, flocks, and flowers.

Yet ah! this air I gather and I release
He lived on; these weeds and waters, these walls are what   10
He haunted who of all men most sways my spirits to peace;

Of realty the rarest-veinèd unraveller; a not
Rivalled insight, be rival Italy or Greece;
Who fired France for Mary without spot.


## Felix Randal

Felix Randal the farrier, O he is dead then? my duty all
    ended,
Who have watched his mould of man, big-boned and
    hardy-handsome

7 *counter:* contrary. *spare:* rare.
  DUNS SCOTUS. (Joannes) *Duns Scotus* (1266 or 1274-1308): A
scholastic philosopher, once at Merton College, Oxford, and a Professor
in the University. His works were a primary influence upon Hopkins.
  3 [city] *that.* 4 *encounter:* meet (in). *coped:* contending. *poisèd:*
matched, balanced. *powers:* the rival philosophies of Scotus and
Aquinas; and, of "country and town." 5 [which] *sours. skirt:* border,
suburb. 6 *-nature* [which]. 7-8 *graceless . . . keeping:* the ugly
growth (i.e., Oxford) has spoiled the rural beauty once in its care
(*keeping*). 12 *realty:* reality, which Scotus (*rarest-veinèd unraveller*)
found in the individual thing. 14 *Who . . . spot:* Scotus was called
to Paris, where he successfully defended (against the Thomists) his belief in the Immaculate Conception of the Virgin Mary.
  FELIX RANDAL. 1 *farrier:* blacksmith.

Pining, pining, till time when reason rambled in it and some
Fatal four disorders, fleshed there, all contended?                    4

Sickness broke him. Impatient he cursed at first, but mended
Being anointed and all; though a heavenlier heart began some
Months earlier, since I had our sweet reprieve and ransom
Tendered to him. Ah well, God rest him all road ever he
        offended!

This seeing the sick endears them to us, us too it endears.
My tongue had taught thee comfort, touch had quenched thy
        tears,                                                          10
Thy tears that touched my heart, child, Félix, poor Félix
        Randal;

How far from then forethought of, all thy more boisterous
        years,
When thou at the random grim forge, powerful amidst peers,
Didst fettle for the great grey drayhorse his bright and
        battering sandal!


## Spelt from Sibyl's Leaves

Earnest, earthless, equal, attuneable, | vaulty, voluminous, . . .
        stupendous
Evening strains to be tíme's vást, | womb-of-all, home-of-all,
        hearse-of-all night.
Her fond yellow hornlight wound to the west, | her wild
        hollow hoarlight hung to the height
Waste; her earliest stars, earl-stars, | stárs principal, overbend
        us,
Fíre-féaturing heaven. For earth | her being has unbound, her
        dapple is at an end, as-                                       5
tray or aswarm, all throughther, in throngs; | self ín self
        steepèd and páshed—qúite

4 *fleshed there:* took hold of his flesh.  6 *Being . . . all:* Received the
sacrament of Extreme Unction.   7 *sweet . . . ransom:* the Holy
Eucharist.  8 *rest . . . offended:* "pardon and deliver" him from his
sins, in whatever ways he offended.  13 *random:* built of odd stones.
14 *fettle:* make ready.

  SPELT FROM SIBYL'S. *Spelt . . . Leaves:* Interpreted from the leaves
upon which the Sibyl or oracle writes the names and fates of persons.
  3 *fond:* tender.  *hornlight:* light of the horned (crescent) moon.
*wound:* turned (as it sets).  *hoarlight:* cold, hard starlight.  4 *earl:*
chief; cf. *stars principal.*  5 *her dapple:* earth's varied beauty.  6
*throughther:* throughout her (?); cf. *through* [each] *other,* an old
speech form.  *pashed:* beaten.

Disremembering, dísmémbering | áll now. Heart, you round
  me right
With: Óur évening is over us; óur night | whélms, whélms,
  ánd will end us.
Only the beak-leaved boughs dragonish | damask the tool-
  smooth bleak light; black,
Ever so black on it. Óur tale, O óur oracle! | Lét life, wáned,
  ah lét life wind                                                    10
Off hér once skéined stained véined varíety | upon, áll on twó
  spools; párt, pen, páck
Now her áll in twó flocks, twó folds—black, white; | right,
  wrong; reckon but, reck but, mind
But thése two; wáre of a wórld where bút these | twó tell,
  each off the óther; of a rack
Where, selfwrung, selfstrung, sheathe-and shelterless, |
  thóughts agaínst thoughts ín groans grínd.


## (*Carrion Comfort*)

Not, I'll not, carrion comfort, Despair, not feast on thee;
Not untwist—slack they may be—these last strands of man
In me ór, most weary, cry *I can no more*. I can;
Can something, hope, wish day come, not choose not to be.
But ah, but O thou terrible, why wouldst thou rude on me   5
Thy wring-world right foot rock? lay a lionlimb against me?
  scan
With darksome devouring eyes my bruisèd bones? and fan,
O in turns of tempest, me heaped there; me frantic to avoid
  thee and flee?

Why? That my chaff might fly; my grain lie, sheer and
  clear.                                                               9
Nay in all that toil, that coil, since (seems) I kissed the rod,
Hand rather, my heart lo! lapped strength, stole joy, would
  laugh, chéer.

7 *Disremembering:* Forgetting.  *you . . . me:* whisper to me.   9
*damask:* weave into patterns, like those on damask steel.  11 *part . . .
pack:* imperative verbs.  12 *reck:* heed.  13 *ware:* be aware, beware.
*tell:* count, intransitive.  14 *sheathe-:* sheathless.

CARRION COMFORT. 1 *carrion comfort:* flesh(cf. mortal man)-devour-
ing comfort: Despair.  5-6 *rude . . . rock?:* rudely torture (*rock*)
me with your foot which tortures (*wrings*) the whole world? *lionlimb:*
a torturing claw (?).  7 *devouring:* cf. carrion, l. 1.  10 *toil:* strife.
*coil:* turmoil.  10-11 *kissed . . . rather:* accepted God's authority, His
service, rather.

Cheer whom though? the hero whose heaven-handling flung
    me, fóot tród
Me? or me that fought him? O which one? is it each one?
    That night, that year
Of now done darkness I wretch lay wrestling with
    (my God!) my God.

## No worst, there is none

No worst, there is none. Pitched past pitch of grief,
More pangs will, schooled at forepangs, wilder wring.
Comforter, where, where is your comforting?
Mary, mother of us, where is your relief?

My cries heave, herds-long; huddle in a main, a chief    5
Woe, world-sorrow; on an age-old anvil wince and sing—
Then lull, then leave off. Fury had shrieked 'No ling-
ering! Let me be fell: force I must be brief.'

  O the mind, mind has mountains; cliffs of fall
Frightful, sheer, no-man-fathomed. Hold them cheap    10
May who ne'er hung there. Nor does long our small
Durance deal with that steep or deep. Here! creep,
Wretch, under a comfort serves in a whirlwind: all
Life death does end and each day dies with sleep.

## I wake and feel the fell of dark, not day

I wake and feel the fell of dark, not day.
What hours, O what black hoúrs we have spent
This night! what sights you, heart, saw; ways you went!
And more must, in yet longer light's delay.

  With witness I speak this. But where I say    5
Hours I mean years, mean life. And my lament
Is cries countless, cries like dead letters sent
To dearest him that lives alas! away.

12 *hero . . . -handling:* God, whose heaven-ruling. *flung me:* as he
flung the rebel angels from Heaven. Cf. Heb. 1216 8; Donne, XIV, p
124; Herbert, p. 135.

No worst. 2 *forepangs:* pangs already suffered. 5 *herds-long:* like
the "cries" of whole herds. 8 *fell:* cruel. *force:* perforce. 13 *comfort
serves:* such comfort as avails.

  I wake and feel. 1 *fell:* cruelty.

I am gall, I am heartburn. God's most deep decree
Bitter would have me taste: my taste was me;     10
Bones built in me, flesh filled, blood brimmed the curse.
  Selfyeast of spirit a dull dough sours. I see
The lost are like this, and their scourge to be
As I am mine, their sweating selves; but worse.


## That Nature Is a Heraclitean Fire and of the Comfort
## of the Resurrection

Cloud-puffball, torn tufts, tossed pillows | flaunt forth, then
    chevy on an air-
built thoroughfare: heaven-roysterers, in gay-gangs | they
    throng; they glitter in marches.
Down roughcast, down dazzling whitewash, wherever an elm
    arches,
Shivelights and shadowtackle in long | lashes lace, lance, and
    pair.
Delightfully the bright wind boisterous | ropes, wrestles, beats
    earth bare     5
Of yestertempest's creases; | in pool and rut peel parches
Squandering ooze to squeezed | dough, crust, dust; stanches,
    starches
Squadroned masks and manmarks | treadmire toil there
Footfretted in it. Million-fuelèd, | nature's bonfire burns on.
But quench her bonniest, dearest | to her, her clearest-selvèd
    spark     10
Man, how fast his firedint, | his mark on mind, is gone!
Both are in an unfathomable, all is in an enormous dark

14 *but worse:* but the condition of the lost is worse [least likely read-
ing]; I am my own scourge, but I am worse off than the lost; or, but
worse is to come.
  THAT NATURE IS. *Heraclitean Fire:* Heraclitus (*c.* 535-*c.* 475 B.C.)
taught that the universe is in a state of ceaseless change, and that its
basic principle is fire (sometimes, *vapor, breath*), which is being transformed into water, earth, and then back to fire again, in endless process.
  1 *chevy:* scamper. 4 *Shivelights:* Strips of light. *shadowtackle:*
like the shadows of interlacing ropes of a ship's tackle. 6 *creases:*
wrinkles. 6-7 *in . . . ooze:* (the wind) dries up the ooze spreading
(*Squandering*) in the pools and upon the rutty surface (peel) of the
earth. 7 *stanches, starches:* stops (as the movement of the blood) and
stiffens into. 8 *Squadroned masks:* Fixed, arranged expressions (the
faces of men). *manmarks* [of his, or which his]. 9 *Footfretted:* Foot-
marked. *it:* earth.

Drowned. O pity and indig⎮nation! Manshape, that shone
Sheer off, disseveral, a star, ⎮ death blots black out; nor mark
              Is any of him at all so stark       15
But vastness blurs and time ⎮ beats level. Enough! the
    Resurrection,
A heart's clarion! Away grief's grasping, ⎮ joyless days,
    dejection.
             Across my foundering deck shone
A beacon, an eternal beam. ⎮ Flesh fade, and mortal trash   19
Fall to the residuary worm; ⎮ world's wildfire, leave but ash:
         In a flash, at a trumpet's crash,
I am all at once what Christ is, ⎮ since he was what I am, and
This Jack, joke, poor potsherd, ⎮ patch, matchwood, immortal
    diamond,
        Is immortal diamond.

14 *disseveral:* separate and aloof.   20 *residuary worm:* the worm which
is heir to what remains of man, the "mortal trash."   23 *Jack:* any
common fellow.   *joke:* fool.   *potsherd:* fragment of a broken earthen
pot.

# THOMAS HARDY   1840–1928

## *Neutral Tones*

We stood by a pond that winter day,
And the sun was white, as though chidden of God,
And a few leaves lay on the starving sod;
    —They had fallen from an ash, and were gray.


Your eyes on me were as eyes that rove            5
Over tedious riddles of years ago;
And some words played between us to and fro
    On which lost the more by our love.


The smile on your mouth was the deadest thing
Alive enough to have strength to die;            10
And a grin of bitterness swept thereby
    Like an ominous bird a-wing. . . .


Since then, keen lessons that love deceives,
And wrings with wrong, have shaped to me
Your face, and the God-curst sun, and a tree,    15
    And a pond edged with grayish leaves.


## *Friends Beyond*

William Dewy, Tranter Reuben, Farmer Ledlow late at
    plough,
    Robert's kin, and John's, and Ned's,
And the Squire, and Lady Susan, lie in Melstock churchyard
    now!


"Gone," I call them, gone for good, that group of local hearts
    and heads;
    Yet at mothy curfew-tide,                    5
And at midnight when the noon-heat breathes it back from
    walls and leads,

FRIENDS BEYOND. 6 *leads:* lead roof.

They've a way of whispering to me—fellow-wight who yet
 abide—
   In the muted, measured note
Of a ripple under archways, or a lone cave's stillicide:

"We have triumphed: this achievement turns the bane to
 antidote,                                                10
   Unsuccesses to success,
Many thought-worn eves and morrows to a morrow free of
 thought.

"No more need we corn and clothing, feel of old terrestial
 stress;
   Chill detraction stirs no sigh;
Fear of death has even bygone us: death gave all that we
 possess."                                                15

W. D.—"Ye mid burn the old bass-viol that I set such value
 by."
Squire.—"You may hold the manse in fee,
   You may wed my spouse, may let my children's memory
 of me die."

Lady S.—"You may have my rich brocades, my laces; take
 each household key;
   Ransack coffer, desk, bureau;                          20
   Quiz the few poor treasures hid there, con the letters kept
 by me."

Far.—"Ye mid zell my favourite heifer, ye mid let the
 charlock grow,
   Foul the grinterns, give up thrift."
Far. Wife.—"If ye break my best blue china, children, I
 shan't care or ho."

All.—"We've no wish to hear the tidings, how the people's
 fortunes shift;                                          25
   What your daily doings are;
   Who are wedded, born, divided; if your lives beat slow or
 swift.

7 -wight: -mortal.   9 stillicide: water dripping.   10 bane: poison.   13
terrest[r]ial.   16 mid: might.   21 con: read.   22 zell: sell.   charlock:
weeds.   23 grinterns: grain bins.   24 ho: be anxious.

"Curious not the least are we if our intents you make or mar,
    If you quire to our old tune,
If the City stage still passes, if the weirs still roar afar."   30

—Thus, with very gods' composure, freed those crosses late
    and soon
    Which, in life, the Trine allow
(Why, none witteth), and ignoring all that haps beneath the
    moon,

William Dewy, Tranter Reuben, Farmer Ledlow late at
    plough,
    Robert's kin, and John's, and Ned's,     35
And the Squire, and Lady Susan, murmur mildly to me now.

## The Impercipient

### AT A CATHEDRAL SERVICE

That with this bright believing band
    I have no claim to be,
That faiths by which my comrades stand
    Seem fantasies to me,
And mirage-mists their Shining Land,     5
    Is a strange destiny.

Why thus my soul should be consigned
    To infelicity,
Why always I must feel as blind
    To sights my brethren see,     10
Why joys they've found I cannot find,
    Abides a mystery.

Since heart of mine knows not that ease
    Which they know; since it be
That He who breathes All's Well to these     15
    Breathes no All's-Well to me,
My lack might move their sympathies
    And Christian charity!

29 *quire:* sing.   30 *weirs:* dams.   31 *freed those crosses:* freed from
those trials.   32 *Trine:* Fates (?). Cf. p. 50, ll. 148, 149 and notes.
33 *witteth:* knows.
    THE IMPERCIPIENT. Cf. Eliot, p. 501.

I am like a gazer who should mark
    An inland company                                            20
Standing upfingered, with, "Hark! hark!
    The glorious distant sea!"
And feel, "Alas, 'tis but yon dark
    And wind-swept pine to me!"

Yet I would bear my shortcomings                                   25
    With meet tranquillity,
But for the charge that blessed things
    I'd liefer not have be,
O, doth a bird deprived of wings
    Go earth-bound wilfully!                                       30

\*     \*     \*

**Enough.** As yet disquiet clings
    About us. Rest shall we.

## The Subalterns

### I

"Poor wanderer," said the leaden sky,
    "I fain would lighten thee,
But there are laws in force on high
    Which say it must not be."

### II

—"I would not freeze thee, shorn one," cried          5
    The North, "knew I but how
To warm my breath, to slack my stride;
    But I am ruled as thou."

### III

—"To-morrow I attack thee, wight,"
    Said Sickness. "Yet I swear                                   10
I bear thy little ark no spite
    But am bid enter there."

26 *meet*: proper.  28 *liefer*: rather.
THE SUBALTERNS. *The Subalterns*: The Subordinates.
2 *fain*: gladly.  9 *wight*: fellow.

444

IV

—"Come hither, Son," I heard Death say;
"I did not will a grave
Should end thy pilgrimage to-day,                    15
But I, too, am a slave!"

V

We smiled upon each other then,
And life to me had less
Of that fell look it wore ere when
They owned their passiveness.                         20

## The Ruined Maid

"O 'Melia, my dear, this does everything crown!
Who could have supposed I should meet you in Town?
And whence such fair garments, such prosperi-ty?"—
"O didn't you know I'd been ruined?" said she.

—"You left us in tatters, without shoes or socks,      5
Tired of digging potatoes, and spudding up docks;
And now you've gay bracelets and bright feathers three!"—
"Yes: that's how we dress when we're ruined," said she.

—"At home in the barton you said 'thee' and 'thou,'
And 'thik oon,' and 'theäs oon,' and 't'other'; but now  10
Your talking quite fits 'ee for high compa-ny!"—
"Some polish is gained with one's ruin," said she.

—"Your hands were like paws then, your face blue and bleak
But now I'm bewitched by your delicate cheek,
And your little gloves fit as on any la-dy!"—            15
"We never do work when we're ruined," said she.

—"You used to call home-life a hag-ridden dream,
And you'd sigh, and you'd sock; but at present you seem
To know not of megrims or melancho-ly!"
"True. One's pretty lively when ruined," said she.       20

19 *fell:* cruel.
THE RUINED MAID. 9 *barton:* farmstead. 10 *thik oon, theäs oon:*
that one, this one. 11 *'ee:* thee. 18 *sock:* sigh loudly. 19 *megrims:*
low spirits, "blues." Cf. Pope, p. 227, l. 24.

—"I wish I had feathers, a fine sweeping gown,
And a delicate face, and could strut about Town!"—
"My dear—a raw country girl, such as you be,
Cannot quite expect that. You ain't ruined," said she.


## Channel Firing

That night your great guns, unawares,
Shook all our coffins as we lay,
And broke the chancel window-squares,
We thought it was the Judgment-day

And sat upright. While drearisome                    5
Arose the howl of wakened hounds:
The mouse let fall the altar-crumb,
The worms drew back into the mounds,

The glebe cow drooled. Till God called, "No;
It's gunnery practice out at sea                    10
Just as before you went below;
The world is as it used to be:

"All nations striving strong to make
Red war yet redder. Mad as hatters
They do no more for Christés sake                   15
Than you who are helpless in such matters.

"That this is not the judgment-hour
For some of them's a blessed thing,
For if it were they'd have to scour
Hell's floor for so much threatening. . . .         20

"Ha, ha. It will be warmer when
I blow the trumpet (if indeed
I ever do; for you are men,
And rest eternal sorely need)."

CHANNEL FIRING. 3 *chancel*: eastern part of a church.  8 *mounds*:
graves.  9 *glebe*: adj.; land assigned to a cleric as part of his benefice.
22 *blow the trumpet*: as in Donne, VII, p. 122.

So down we lay again. "I wonder,     **25**
Will the world ever saner be,"
Said one, "than when He sent us under
In our indifferent century!"

And many a skeleton shook his head.
"Instead of preaching forty year,"     **30**
My neighbour Parson Thirdly said,
"I wish I had stuck to pipes and beer."

Again the guns disturbed the hour,
Roaring their readiness to avenge,
As far inland as Stourton Tower,     **35**
And Camelot, and starlit Stonehenge.

## The Convergence of the Twain

### LINES ON THE LOSS OF THE "TITANIC"

#### I

In a solitude of the sea
Deep from human vanity,
And the Pride of Life that planned her, stilly couches she.

#### II

Steel chambers, late the pyres
Of her salamandrine fires,     5
Cold currents thrid, and turn to rhythmic tidal lyres.

#### III

Over the mirrors meant
To glass the opulent
The sea-worm crawls—grotesque, slimed, dumb, indifferent.

THE CONVERGENCE. *Titanic:* The White Star liner *Titanic* on her westward maiden voyage sank after hitting an iceberg in the North Atlantic on the night of April 14-15, 1912. There were 1517 casualties, including members of several of the most eminent American and British families.

4 *Steel chambers:* Coal furnaces.   5 *salamandrine:* harmless (fires), as the salamander was supposed to live uninjured in flames. Cf. Donne, p. 119, l. 23 and note.   6 *thrid:* thread.

### IV

Jewels in joy designed               10
To ravish the sensuous mind
Lie lightless, all their sparkles bleared and black and blind.

### V

Dim moon-eyed fishes near
Gaze at the gilded gear
And query: "What does this vaingloriousness down
    here?"                          15

### VI

Well: while was fashioning
This creature of cleaving wing,
The Immanent Will that stirs and urges everything

### VII

Prepared a sinister mate
For her—so gaily great—            20
A Shape of Ice, for the time far and dissociate.

### VIII

And as the smart ship grew
In stature, grace, and hue,
In shadowy silent distance grew the Iceberg too.

### IX

Alien they seemed to be:            25
No mortal eye could see
The intimate welding of their later history.

### X

Or sign that they were bent
By paths coincident
On being anon twin halves of one august event,   30

### XI

Till the Spinner of the Years
Said "Now!" And each one hears,
And consummation comes, and jars two hemispheres.

# The Going

*Veteris vestigia flammae*

Why did you give no hint that night
That quickly after the morrow's dawn,
And calmly, as if indifferent quite,
You would close your term here, up and be gone
  Where I could not follow     5
  With wing of swallow
To gain one glimpse of you ever anon!

  Never to bid good-bye,
    · Or lip me the softest call,
Or utter a wish for a word, while I     10
Saw morning harden upon the wall,
  Unmoved, unknowing
  That your great going
Had place that moment, and altered all.

Why do you make me leave the house    15
And think for a breath it is you I see
At the end of the alley of bending boughs
Where so often at dusk you used to be;
  Till in darkening dankness
  The yawning blankness     20
Of the perspective sickens me!

  You were she who abode
  By those red-veined rocks far West,
You were the swan-necked one who rode
Along the beetling Beeny Crest,     25
  And, reining nigh me,
  Would muse and eye me,
While Life unrolled us its very best.

Why, then, latterly did we not speak,
Did we not think of those days long dead,   30
And ere your vanishing strive to seek
That time's renewal? We might have said,
  "In this bright spring weather
  We'll visit together
Those places that once we visited."     35

THE GOING. *Veteris vestigia flammae:* Embers of an old fire.
7 *ever anon:* every now and then. 14 *Had place:* Was foremost. 25 *beetling:* overhanging, projecting.

Well, well! All's past amend,
    Unchangeable. It must go.
I seem but a dead man held on end
To sink down soon. . . . O you could not know
        That such swift fleeing                    40
        No soul foreseeing—
Not even I—would undo me so!


## The Oxen

Christmas Eve, and twelve of the clock.
    "Now they are all on their knees,"
An elder said as we sat in a flock
    By the embers in hearthside ease.

We pictured the meek mild creatures where        5
    They dwelt in their strawy pen,
Nor did it occur to one of us there
    To doubt they were kneeling then.

So fair a fancy few would weave
    In these years! Yet, I feel,                  10
If someone said on Christmas Eve,
    "Come; see the oxen kneel,

"In the lonely barton by yonder coomb
    Our childhood used to know,"
I should go with him in the gloom,               15
    Hoping it might be so.


## Haunting Fingers

A PHANTASY IN A MUSEUM OF MUSICAL INSTRUMENTS

"Are you awake,
    Comrades, this silent night?
Well 'twere if all of our glossy gluey make
    Lay in the damp without, and fell to fragments quite!"

THE OXEN. 2 *Now . . . knees:* Reference to the legend that the
beasts in the stable knelt in worship before the new-born Saviour. 13
*barton:* farmyard. *coomb:* valley, closed at one end.

"O viol, my friend,                                                    5
I watch, though Phosphor nears,
And I fain would drowse away to its utter end
This dumb dark stowage after our loud melodious years!"

And they felt past handlers clutch them,
Though none was in the room,                                          10
Old players' dead fingers touch them,
Shrunk in the tomb.

" 'Cello, good mate,
You speak my mind as yours:
Doomed to this voiceless, crippled, corpselike state,               15
Who, dear to famed Amphion, trapped here, long endures?"

"Once I could thrill
The populace through and through,
Wake them to passioned pulsings past their will." . . .
(A contra-basso spake so, and the rest sighed anew.)               20

And they felt old muscles travel
Over their tense contours,
And with long skill unravel
Cunningest scores.

"The tender pat                                                     25
Of her aery finger-tips
Upon me daily—I rejoiced thereat!"
(Thuswise a harpsicord, as 'twere from dampered lips.)

"My keys' white shine,
Now sallow, met a hand                                              30
Even whiter. . . . Tones of hers fell forth with mine
In sowings of sound so sweet no lover could withstand!"

And its clavier was filmed with fingers
Like tapering flames—wan, cold—
Or the nebulous light that lingers                                  35
In charnel mould.

HAUNTING FINGERS. 6 *Phosphor:* the Morning Star.   7 *fain:* gladly.
16 *Amphion:* by the magic of whose lyre the stones assembled of their
own accord to build the walls of Thebes.   20 *contra-basso:* double-bass
viol.   28 *dampered:* muted.   32 *sowings:* murmurings.   33 *clavier:*
keyboard.   36 *charnel mould:* dust of the grave.

"Gayer than most
Was I," reverbed a drum;
"The regiments, marchings, throngs, hurrahs! What a host
I stirred—even when crape mufflings gagged me well-nigh
    dumb!"                  40

Trilled an aged viol:
"Much tune have I set free
To spur the dance, since my first timid trial
Where I had birth—far hence, in sun-swept Italy!"

And he feels apt touches on him      45
From those that pressed him then;
Who seem with their glance to con him,
    Saying, "Not again!"

"A holy calm,"
Mourned a shawm's voice subdued,    50
"Steeped my Cecilian rhythms when hymn and psalm
Poured from devout souls met in Sabbath sanctitude."

"I faced the sock
Nightly," twanged a sick lyre,
"Over ranked lights! O charm of life in mock,    55
O scenes that fed love, hope, wit, rapture, mirth, desire!"

Thus they, till each past player
Stroked thinner and more thin,
And the morning sky grew grayer
    And day crawled in.      60


### "I was the midmost"

I was the midmost of my world
    When first I frisked me free,
For though within its circuit gleamed
    But a small company,
And I was immature, they seemed    5
    To bend their looks on me.

---

38 *reverb[erat]ed.*   47 *con:* study.   50 *shawm('s):* a double-reed instrument, resembling the oboe.   51 *Cecilian:* sacred. Cf. Dryden, pp. 202-04.   53 *sock:* comedy stage. Cf. Jonson, p. 103, l. 37 and note.   55 *ranked lights:* footlights.

    I WAS. 2 *frisked . . . free:* lived without care.

She was the midmost of my world
   When I went further forth,
And hence it was that, whether I turned
   To south, east, west, or north,        10
Beams of an all-day Polestar burned
   From that new axe of earth.

Where now is midmost in my world?
   I trace it not at all:
No midmost shows it here, or there,      15
   When wistful voices call
"We are fain! We are fain!" from everywhere
   On Earth's bewildering ball!

## Intra Sepulchrum

What curious things we said,
   What curious things we did
Up there in the world we walked till dead,
   Our kith and kin amid!

How we played at love,      5
   And its wildness, weakness, woe;
Yes, played thereat far more than enough
   As it turned out, I trow!

Played at believing in gods
   And observing the ordinances,     10
I for your sake in impossible codes
   Right ready to acquiesce.

Thinking our lives unique,
   Quite quainter than usual kinds,
We held that we could not abide a week    15
   The tether of typic minds.

—Yet people who day by day
   Pass by and look at us
From over the wall in a casual way
   Are of this unconscious.     20

12 *axe:* axis.   17 *fain:* well-pleased.
   INTRA. *Intra Sepulchrum:* Within the Tomb.
   8 *trow:* trust.   11 *codes:* of laws, ordinances.   16 *typic:* true to type,
typically human. Cf. Tennyson, p. 368, l. 127.

And feel, if anything,
That none can be buried here
Removed from commonest fashioning,
Or lending note to a bier:

No twain who in heart-heaves proved          25
Themselves at all adept,
Who more than many laughed and loved
Who more than many wept,

Or were as sprites or elves
Into blind matter hurled,                          30
Or ever could have been to themselves
The centre of the world.


## The Missed Train

How I was caught
Hieing home, after days of allure,
And forced to an inn—small, obscure—
At the junction, gloom-fraught.

How civil my face                                      5
To get them to chamber me there—
A roof I had scorned, scarce aware
That it stood at the place.

And how all the night
I had dreams of the unwitting cause          10
Of my lodgment. How lonely I was
How consoled by her sprite!

Thus onetime to me . . .
Dim wastes of dead years bar away
Then from now. But such happenings to-day    15
Fall to lovers, may be!

Years, years as shoaled seas,
Truly, stretch now between! Less and less
Shrink the visions then vast in me.—Yes,
Then in me: Now in these.                          20

24 *note*: distinction.
THE MISSED TRAIN. 12 *sprite*: spirit.   14 *bar away*: separate.   17
*shoaled*: shallow.

# A. E. HOUSMAN  1859–1936

## To an Athlete Dying Young

The time you won your town the race
We chaired you through the market-place;
Man and boy stood cheering by,
And home we brought you shoulder-high.

To-day, the road all runners come,                    5
Shoulder-high we bring you home,
And set you at your threshold down,
Townsman of a stiller town.

Smart lad, to slip betimes away
From fields where glory does not stay                  10
And early though the laurel grows
It withers quicker than the rose.

Eyes the shady night has shut
Cannot see the record cut,
And silence sounds no worse than cheers                15
After earth has stopped the ears:

Now you will not swell the rout
Of lads that wore their honours out,
Runners whom renown outran
And the name died before the man.                      20

So set, before its echoes fade,
The fleet foot on the sill of shade,
And hold to the low lintel up
The still-defended challenge-cup.

And round that early-laurelled head                    25
Will flock to gaze the strengthless dead,
And find unwithered on its curls
The garland briefer than a girl's.

To an Athlete. 2 *chaired*: carried.

### *Is my team ploughing*

'Is my team ploughing,
    That I was used to drive
And hear the harness jingle
    When I was man alive?'

Ay, the horses trample,                                    5
    The harness jingles now;
No change though you lie under
    The land you used to plough.

'Is football playing
    Along the river shore,                                10
With lads to chase the leather,
    Now I stand up no more?'

Ay, the ball is flying,
    The lads play heart and soul;
The goal stands up, the keeper                            15
    Stands up to keep the goal.

'Is my girl happy,
    That I thought hard to leave,
And has she tired of weeping
    As she lies down at eve?'                             20

Ay, she lies down lightly,
    She lies not down to weep:
Your girl is well contented.
    Be still, my lad, and sleep.

'Is my friend hearty,                                     25
    Now I am thin and pine,
And has he found to sleep in
    A better bed than mine?'

Yes, lad, I lie easy,
    I lie as lads would choose;                           30
I cheer a dead man's sweetheart,
    Never ask me whose.

IS MY TEAM. 26 *pine*: waste away—or, an adjective?

## *On Wenlock Edge the wood's in trouble*

On Wenlock Edge the wood's in trouble;
    His forest fleece the Wrekin heaves;
The gale, it plies the saplings double,
    And thick on Severn snow the leaves.

'Twould blow like this through holt and hanger    5
    When Uricon the city stood:
'Tis the old wind in the old anger,
    But then it threshed another wood.

Then, 'twas before my time, the Roman
    At yonder heaving hill would stare:    10
The blood that warms an English yeoman,
    The thoughts that hurt him, they were there.

There, like the wind through woods in riot,
    Through him the gale of life blew high;
The tree of man was never quiet:    15
    Then 'twas the Roman, now 'tis I.

The gale, it plies the saplings double,
    It blows so hard, 'twill soon be gone:
To-day the Roman and his trouble
    Are ashes under Uricon.    20

## *Terence, this is stupid stuff*

'Terence, this is stupid stuff:
You eat your victuals fast enough;
There can't be much amiss, 'tis clear,
To see the rate you drink your beer.
But oh, good Lord, the verse you make,    5
It gives a chap the belly-ache.
The cow, the old cow, she is dead;
It sleeps well, the horned head:
We poor lads, 'tis our turn now

ON WENLOCK EDGE. 1, 2 *Wenlock, Wrekin:* Shropshire mountains.
4 *Severn:* a Shropshire river. 5 *holt and hanger:* wood and slope. 6 *Uricon[ium]:* Town in Roman Britain, near the present Shrewsbury, in Shropshire.

To hear such tunes as killed the cow.                    10
Pretty friendship 'tis to rhyme
Your friends to death before their time
Moping melancholy mad:
Come, pipe a tune to dance to, lad.'

    Why, if 'tis dancing you would be,           15
There's brisker pipes than poetry.
Say, for what were hop-yards meant,
Or why was Burton built on Trent?
Oh many a peer of England brews
Livelier liquor than the Muse,                           20
And malt does more than Milton can
To justify God's ways to man.
Ale, man, ale's the stuff to drink
For fellows whom it hurts to think:
Look into the pewter pot                                 25
To see the world as the world's not.
And faith, 'tis pleasant till 'tis past:
The mischief is that 'twill not last.
Oh I have been to Ludlow fair
And left my necktie God knows where,                     30
And carried half-way home, or near,
Pints and quarts of Ludlow beer:
Then the world seemed none so bad,
And I myself a sterling lad;
And down in lovely muck I've lain,                       35
Happy till I woke again.
Then I saw the morning sky:
Heighho, the tale was all a lie;
The world, it was the old world yet,
I was I, my things were wet,                             40
And nothing now remained to do
But begin the game anew.

    Therefore, since the world has still
Much good, but much less good than ill,
And while the sun and moon endure                        45
Luck's a chance, but trouble's sure,
I'd face it as a wise man would,
And train for ill and not for good.

TERENCE. 17 *hop-yards:* hop fields.   18 *Burton:* a town famous for
waters used in brewing ale and beer.   22 *To . . . man:* Adapted from
*Paradise Lost,* I, 26.

'Tis true, the stuff I bring for sale
Is not so brisk a brew as ale:                          50
Out of a stem that scored the hand
I wrung it in a weary land.
But take it: if the smack is sour,
The better for the embittered hour;
It should do good to heart and head          55
When your soul is in my soul's stead;
And I will friend you, if I may,
In the dark and cloudy day.


There was a king reigned in the East:
There, when kings will sit to feast,          60
They get their fill before they think
With poisoned meat and poisoned drink.
He gathered all that springs to birth
From the many-venomed earth;
First a little, thence to more,          65
He sampled all her killing store;
And easy, smiling, seasoned sound,
Sate the king when healths went round.
They put arsenic in his meat
And stared aghast to watch him eat;          70
They poured strychnine in his cup
And shook to see him drink it up:
They shook, they stared as white's their shirt:
Them it was their poison hurt.
—I tell the tale that I heard told.          75
Mithridates, he died old.


*Tell me not here, it needs not saying*

Tell me not here, it needs not saying,
   What tune the enchantress plays
In aftermaths of soft September
   Or under blanching mays,
For she and I were long acquainted          5
   And I knew all her ways.

51 *stem:* stock of a plant; source.  *scored:* scratched.  68 *Sate:* Sat.
76 *Mithridates:* King of Pontus (132 B.C.-63 B.C.), who was reportedly
put to death at his own request by a Celtic soldier after he had vainly
tried to kill himself by poison.
   TELL ME NOT. 4 *blanching mays:* whitening hawthorns. See Herrick,
p. 126, l. 14 and note.

On russet floors, by waters idle,
  The pine lets fall its cone;
The cuckoo shouts all day at nothing
  In leafy dells alone;                           10
And traveller's joy beguiles in autumn
  Hearts that have lost their own.


On acres of the seeded grasses
  The changing burnish heaves;
Or marshalled under moons of harvest            15
  Stand still all night the sheaves;
Or beeches strip in storms for winter
  And stain the wind with leaves.


Possess, as I possessed a season,
  The countries I resign,                         20
Where over elmy plains the highway
  Would mount the hills and shine,
And full of shade the pillared forest
  Would murmur and be mine.


For nature, heartless, witless nature,          25
  Will neither care nor know
What stranger's feet may find the meadow
  And trespass there and go,
Nor ask amid the dews of morning
  If they are mine or no.                         30


### Stars, I have seen them fall

Stars, I have seen them fall,
  But when they drop and die
No star is lost at all
  From all the star-sown sky.
The toil of all that be
  Helps not the primal fault;
It rains into the sea
  And still the sea is salt.

### *The farms of home lie lost in even*

The farms of home lie lost in even,
  I see far off the steeple stand;
West and away from here to heaven
  Still is the land.

There if I go no girl will greet me,      5
  No comrade hollo from the hill,
No dog run down the yard to meet me:
  The land is still.

The land is still by farm and steeple,
  And still for me the land may stay:      10
There I was friends with perished people,
  And there lie they.

### *How clear, how lovely bright*

How clear, how lovely bright
How beautiful to sight
    Those beams of morning play;
How heaven laughs out with glee
Where, like a bird set free,      5
Up from the eastern sea
    Soars the delightful day.

To-day I shall be strong,
No more shall yield to wrong,
    Shall squander life no more;      10
Days lost, I know not how,
I shall retrieve them now;
Now I shall keep the vow
    I never kept before.

Ensanguining the skies      15
How heavily it dies
    Into the west away;
Past touch and sight and sound
Not further to be found
How hopeless underground      20
    Falls the remorseful day.

## I did not lose my heart in summer's even

I did not lose my heart in summer's even,
   When roses to the moonrise burst apart:
When plumes were under heel and lead was flying,
   In blood and smoke and flame I lost my heart.

I lost it to a soldier and a foeman,
   A chap that did not kill me, but he tried;
That took the sabre straight and took it striking,
   And laughed and kissed his hand to me and died.

## Smooth between sea and land

Smooth between sea and land
Is laid the yellow sand,
And here through summer days
The seed of Adam plays.

Here the child comes to found                    5
His unremaining mound,
And the grown lad to score
Two names upon the shore.

Here, on the level sand,
Between the sea and land,                         10
What shall I build or write
Against the fall of night?

Tell me of runes to grave
That hold the bursting wave,
Or bastions to design                             15
For longer date than mine.

Shall it be Troy or Rome
I fence against the foam,
Or my own name, to stay
When I depart for aye?                            20

Nothing: too near at hand,
Planing the figured sand,
Effacing clean and fast

SMOOTH. 13 *runes:* literally, ancient Germanic alphabetical characters, usually cut in wood; here, generally, words. See *write,* l. 11.

Cities not built to last
And charms devised in vain,                                25
Pours the confounding main.


### Oh is it the jar of nations

'Oh is it the jar of nations,
    The noise of a world run mad,
The fleeing of earth's foundations?'
    Yes, yes; lie quiet, my lad.

'Oh is it my country calling?                              5
    And whom will my country find
To shore up the sky from falling?'
    My business; never you mind.

'Oh is it the newsboys crying
    Lost battle, retreat, despair,                         10
And honour and England dying?'
    Well, fighting-cock, what if it were?

The devil this side of the darnels
    Is having a dance with man,
And quarrelsome chaps in charnels                          15
    Must bear it as best they can.


### The Olive

The olive in its orchard
    Should now be rooted sure,
To cast abroad its branches
    And flourish and endure.

Aloft amid the trenches                                    5
    Its dressers dug and died;
The olive in its orchard
    Should prosper and abide.

Close should the fruit be clustered
    And light the leaf should wave,                        10
So deep the root is planted
    In the corrupting grave.

OH IS IT. 13 *this . . . darnels:* this side of the grave (?).
THE OLIVE. 6 *dressers:* pruners.

# EDWIN ARLINGTON ROBINSON
1869–1935

## Charles Carville's Eyes

A melancholy face Charles Carville had,
But not so melancholy as it seemed,
When once you knew him, for his mouth redeemed
His insufficient eyes, forever sad:
In them there was no life glimpse, good or bad,          5
Nor joy nor passion in them ever gleamed;
His mouth was all of him that ever beamed,
His eyes were sorry, but his mouth was glad.

He never was a fellow that said much,
And half of what he did say was not heard          10
By many of us: we were out of touch
With all his whims and all his theories
Till he was dead, so those blank eyes of his
Might speak them. Then we heard them, every word.

## Reuben Bright

Because he was a butcher and thereby
Did earn an honest living (and did right),
I would not have you think that Reuben Bright
Was any more a brute than you or I;
For when they told him that his wife must die,          5
He stared at them, and shook with grief and fright,
And cried like a great baby half that night,
And made the women cry to see him cry.

And after she was dead, and he had paid
The singers and the sexton and the rest,          10
He packed a lot of things that she had made
Most mournfully away in an old chest
Of hers, and put some chopped-up cedar boughs
In with them, and tore down the slaughter-house.

REUBEN BRIGHT. 13 *cedar boughs:* i.e., as a preservative.

## The Torrent

I found a torrent falling in a glen
Where the sun's light shone silvered and leaf-split;
The boom, the foam, and the mad flash of it
All made a magic symphony; but when
I thought upon the coming of hard men                    5
To cut those patriarchal trees away,
And turn to gold the silver of that spray,
I shuddered. Yet a gladness now and then
Did wake me to myself till I was glad
In earnest, and was welcoming the time                   10
For screaming saws to sound above the chime
Of idle waters, and for me to know
The jealous visionings that I had had
Were steps to the great place where trees and torrents go.

## Uncle Ananias

His words were magic and his heart was true,
     And everywhere he wandered he was blessed.
Out of all ancient men my childhood knew
     I choose him and I mark him for the best.
Of all authoritative liars, too,                         5
     I crown him loveliest.

How fondly I remember the delight
     That always glorified him in the spring;
The joyous courage and the benedight
     Profusion of his faith in everything!               10
He was a good old man, and it was right
     That he should have his fling.

And often, underneath the apple-trees,
     When we surprised him in the summer time,
With what superb magnificence and ease                   15
     He sinned enough to make the day sublime!
And if he liked us there about his knees,
     Truly it was no crime.

UNCLE ANANIAS. 5 *liars:* cf. Acts 5:1-10. Ananias, lied, not "unto
men, but unto God." 9 *benedight:* blessed.

All summer long we loved him for the same
    Perennial inspiration of his lies;        20
And when the russet wealth of autumn came,
    There flew but fairer visions to our eyes—
Multiple, tropical, winged with a feathery flame
    Like birds of paradise.

So to the sheltered end of many a year        25
    He charmed the seasons out with pageantry
Wearing upon his forehead, with no fear,
    The laurel of approved iniquity.
And every child who knew him, far or near,
    Did love him faithfully.        30

## Leonora

They have made for Leonora this low dwelling in the ground,
And with cedar they have woven the four walls round.
Like a little dryad hiding she'll be wrapped all in green,
Better kept and longer valued than by ways that would have
    been.

They will come with many roses in the early afternoon,    5
They will come with pinks and lilies and with Leonora soon;
And as long as beauty's garments over beauty's limbs are
    thrown,
There'll be lilies that are liars, and the rose will have its own.

There will be a wondrous quiet in the house that they have
    made,
And to-night will be a darkness in the place where she'll be
    laid;    10
But the builders, looking forward into time, could only see
Darker nights for Leonora than to-night shall ever be.

## Miniver Cheevy

Miniver Cheevy, child of scorn,
    Grew lean while he assailed the seasons;
He wept that he was ever born,
    And he had reasons.

LEONORA. 3 *dryad:* a wood nymph. Cf. Keats, p. 344, l. 7.

Miniver loved the days of old 5
  When swords were bright and steeds were
    prancing;
The vision of a warrior bold
  Would set him dancing.

Miniver sighed for what was not,
  And dreamed, and rested from his labors; 10
He dreamed of Thebes and Camelot,
  And Priam's neighbors.

Miniver mourned the ripe renown
  That made so many a name so fragrant;
He mourned Romance, now on the town, 15
  And Art, a vagrant.

Miniver loved the Medici,
  Albeit he had never seen one;
He would have sinned incessantly
  Could he have been one. 20

Miniver cursed the commonplace
  And eyed a khaki suit with loathing;
He missed the mediæval grace
  Of iron clothing.

Miniver scorned the gold he sought, 25
  But sore annoyed was he without it;
Miniver thought, and thought, and thought,
  And thought about it.

Miniver Cheevy, born too late,
  Scratched his head and kept on thinking; 30
Miniver coughed, and called it fate,
  And kept on drinking.

MINIVER CHEEVY. 11 *Thebes:* Ancient city of Boeotia, Greece; enemy
of Athens. Their wars were the frequent subject of poetry and drama.
*Camelot:* King Arthur's seat; the Round Table was there. 12
*Priam('s):* King of Troy. *neighbors:* the "unfriendly" Greeks. 17
*the Medici:* a ruling family of Florence, especially in the sixteenth century, famous as patrons of arts and letters, and for excessive worldliness.

## Cassandra

I heard one who said: "Verily,
    What word have I for children here?
Your Dollar is your only Word,
    The wrath of it your only fear.

"You built it altars tall enough        5
    To make you see, but you are blind;
You cannot leave it long enough
    To look before you or behind.

"When Reason beckons you to pause,
    You laugh and say that you know best;    10
But what it is you know, you keep
    As dark as ingots in a chest.

"You laugh and answer, 'We are young;
    O leave us now, and let us grow.'—
Not asking how much more of this    15
    Will Time endure or Fate bestow.

"Because a few complacent years
    Have made your peril of your pride,
Think you that you are to go on
    Forever pampered and untried?    20

"What lost eclipse of history,
    What bivouac of the marching stars,
Has given the sign for you to see
    Millenniums and last great wars?

"What unrecorded overthrow    25
    Of all the world has ever known,
Or ever been, has made itself
    So plain to you, and you alone?

"Your Dollar, Dove and Eagle make
    A Trinity that even you    30
Rate higher than you rate yourselves;
    It pays, it flatters, and it's new.

CASSANDRA. 1 one: Cassandra, the daughter of Priam of Troy, was loved by Apollo, who gave her the gift of prophecy, but because she spurned his suit, he ordered that her prophecies should not be believed. 29 Dollar, Dove, Eagle: Wealth, Gentleness, Power.

"And though your very flesh and blood
    Be what your Eagle eats and drinks,
You'll praise him for the best of birds,    35
    Not knowing what the Eagle thinks.

"The power is yours, but not the sight;
    You see not upon what you tread;
You have the ages for your guide,
    But not the wisdom to be led.    40

"Think you to tread forever down
    The merciless old verities?
And are you never to have eyes
    To see the world for what it is?

"Are you to pay for what you have    45
    With all you are?"—No other word
We caught, but with a laughing crowd
    Moved on. None heeded, and few heard.

## The Mill

The miller's wife had waited long,
    The tea was cold, the fire was dead;
And there might yet be nothing wrong
    In how he went and what he said:
"There are no millers any more,"    5
    Was all that she had heard him say;
And he had lingered at the door
    So long that it seemed yesterday.

Sick with a fear that had no form
    She knew that she was there at last;    10
And in the mill there was a warm
    And mealy fragrance of the past.
What else there was would only seem
    To say again what he had meant;
And what was hanging from a beam    15
    Would not have heeded where she went.

And if she thought it followed her,
    She may have reasoned in the dark
That one way of the few there were

Would hide her and would leave no mark:    20
Black water, smooth above the weir
    Like starry velvet in the night,
Though ruffled once, would soon appear
    The same as ever to the sight.

## Mr. Flood's Party

Old Eben Flood, climbing alone one night
Over the hill between the town below
And the forsaken upland hermitage
That held as much as he should ever know
On earth again of home, paused warily.    5
The road was his with not a native near;
And Eben, having leisure, said aloud,
For no man else in Tilbury Town to hear:

"Well, Mr. Flood, we have the harvest moon
Again, and we may not have many more;    10
The bird is on the wing, the poet says,
And you and I have said it here before.
Drink to the bird." He raised up to the light
The jug that he had gone so far to fill,
And answered huskily: "Well, Mr. Flood,    15
Since you propose it, I believe I will."

Alone, as if enduring to the end
A valiant armor of scarred hopes outworn,
He stood there in the middle of the road
Like Roland's ghost winding a silent horn.    20
Below him, in the town among the trees,
Where friends of other days had honored him,
A phantom salutation of the dead
Rang thinly till old Eben's eyes were dim.

Then, as a mother lays her sleeping child    25
Down tenderly, fearing it may awake,
He set the jug down slowly at his feet
With trembling care, knowing that most things
    break,

MR. FLOOD'S. 20 *Roland's . . . horn:* Roland, the most famous of
Charlemagne's knights, was slain at Roncesvalles (778), when his
famous horn vainly sounded a call for help. See Chaucer, p. 16, l. 407
and note.

And only when assured that on firm earth
It stood, as the uncertain lives of men     30
Assuredly did not, he paced away,
And with his hand extended paused again:

"Well, Mr. Flood, we have not met like this
In a long time; and many a change has come
To both of us, I fear, since last it was     35
We had a drop together. Welcome home!"
Convivially returning with himself,
Again he raised the jug up to the light;
And with an acquiescent quaver said:
"Well, Mr. Flood, if you insist, I might.     40

"Only a very little, Mr. Flood—
For auld lang syne. No more, sir; that will do."
So, for the time, apparently it did,
And Eben evidently thought so too;
For soon amid the silver loneliness     45
Of night he lifted up his voice and sang,
Secure, with only two moons listening,
Until the whole harmonious landscape rang—

"For auld lang syne." The weary throat gave out,
The last word wavered, and the song was done.     50
He raised again the jug regretfully
And shook his head, and was again alone.
There was not much that was ahead of him,
And there was nothing in the town below—
Where strangers would have shut the many doors   55
That many friends had opened long ago.

## Vain Gratuities

Never was there a man much uglier
In eyes of other women, or more grim:
"The Lord has filled her chalice to the brim,
So let us pray she's a philosopher,"
They said; and there was more they said of her—     5
Deeming it, after twenty years with him,
No wonder that she kept her figure slim
And always made you think of lavender.

But she, demure as ever, and as fair,
Almost, as they remembered her before                    10
She found him, would have laughed had she been there;
And all they said would have been heard no more
Than foam that washes on an island shore
Where there are none to listen or to care.

## The Sheaves

Where long the shadows of the wind had rolled,
Green wheat was yielding to the change assigned,
And as by some vast magic undivined
The world was turning slowly into gold.
Like nothing that was ever bought or sold                5
It waited there, the body and the mind;
And with a mighty meaning of a kind
That tells the more the more it is not told.

So in a land where all days are not fair,
Fair days went on till on another day                    10
A thousand golden sheaves were lying there,
Shining and still, but not for long to stay—
As if a thousand girls with golden hair
Might rise from where they slept and go away.

## As It Looked Then

In a sick shade of spruce, moss-webbed, rock-fed,
Where, long unfollowed by sagacious man,
A scrub that once had been a pathway ran
Blindly from nowhere and to nowhere led,
One might as well have been among the dead              5
As half way there alive; so I began
Like a malingering pioneer to plan
A vain return—with one last look ahead.

And it was then that like a spoken word
Where there was none to speak, insensibly               10
A flash of blue that might have been a bird
Grew soon to the calm wonder of the sea—
Calm as a quiet sky that looked to be
Arching a world where nothing had occurred.

AS IT LOOKED. 3 *scrub*: a tract of stunted trees or bushes.

# WILLIAM BUTLER YEATS 1865–1939

## *The Lake Isle of Innisfree*

I will arise and go now, and go to Innisfree,
And a small cabin build there, of clay and wattles made:
Nine bean-rows will I have there, a hive for the honeybee,
And live alone in the bee-loud glade.

And I shall have some peace there, for peace comes dropping
    slow,          5
Dropping from the veils of the morning to where the cricket
    sings;
There midnight's all a glimmer, and noon a purple glow,
And evening full of the linnet's wings.

I will arise and go now, for always night and day
I hear lake water lapping with low sounds by the shore;   10
While I stand on the roadway, or on the pavements grey,
I hear it in the deep heart's core.

## *The Lamentation of the Old Pensioner*

Although I shelter from the rain
Under a broken tree,
My chair was nearest to the fire
In every company
That talked of love or politics,         5
Ere Time transfigured me.

Though lads are making pikes again
For some conspiracy,
And crazy rascals rage their fill
At human tyranny,         10
My contemplations are of Time
That has transfigured me.

There's not a woman turns her face
Upon a broken tree,

INNISFREE. 2 *wattles:* interwoven twigs.
THE OLD PENSIONER. 7 *pikes:* weapons; long wooden shafts with
pointed steel heads.

And yet the beauties that I loved                    15
Are in my memory;
I spit into the face of Time
That has transfigured me.


## The Two Trees

Beloved, gaze in thine own heart,
The holy tree is growing there;
From joy the holy branches start,
And all the trembling flowers they bear.
The changing colours of its fruit                    5
Have dowered the stars with merry light;
The surety of its hidden root
Has planted quiet in the night;
The shaking of its leafy head
Has given the waves their melody,                   10
And made my lips and music wed,
Murmuring a wizard song for thee.
There the Loves a circle go,
The flaming circle of our days,
Gyring, spiring to and fro                          15
In those great ignorant leafy ways;
Remembering all that shaken hair
And how the wingèd sandals dart,
Thine eyes grow full of tender care:
Beloved, gaze in thine own heart.                   20


Gaze no more in the bitter glass
The demons, with their subtle guile,
Lift up before us when they pass,
Or only gaze a little while;
For there a fatal image grows                       25
That the stormy night receives,
Roots half hidden under snows,
Broken boughs and blackened leaves.
For all things turn to barrenness
In the dim glass the demons hold,                   30

THE TWO TREES. 6 *dowered:* endowed.   13 *Loves:* Cupids.   15
*Gyring:* Conical spiraling. See p. 477, l. 1 and note; p. 478, l. 19.

The glass of outer weariness,
Made when God slept in times of old.
There, through the broken branches, go
The ravens of unresting thought;
Flying, crying, to and fro, 35
Cruel claw and hungry throat,
Or else they stand and sniff the wind,
And shake their ragged wings; alas!
Thy tender eyes grow all unkind:
Gaze no more in the bitter glass. 40


## The Song of Wandering Aengus

I went out to the hazel wood,
Because a fire was in my head,
And cut and peeled a hazel wand,
And hooked a berry to a thread;
And when white moths were on the wing, 5
And moth-like stars were flickering out,
I dropped the berry in a stream
And caught a little silver trout.


When I had laid it on the floor
I went to blow the fire aflame, 10
But something rustled on the floor,
And some one called me by my name:
It had become a glimmering girl
With apple blossom in her hair
Who called me by my name and ran 15
And faded through the brightening air.


Though I am old with wandering
Through hollow lands and hilly lands,
I will find out where she has gone,
And kiss her lips and take her hands; 20
And walk among long dappled grass,
And pluck till time and times are done
The silver apples of the moon,
The golden apples of the sun.


WANDERING AENGUS. 1 *I:* Aengus, Angus, a Celtic god of love.

## No Second Troy

Why should I blame her that she filled my days
With misery, or that she would of late
Have taught to ignorant men most violent ways,
Or hurled the little streets upon the great,
Had they but courage equal to desire?                    5
What could have made her peaceful with a mind
That nobleness made simple as a fire,
With beauty like a tightened bow, a kind
That is not natural in an age like this,
Being high and solitary and most stern?                  10
Why, what could she have done, being what she is?
Was there another Troy for her to burn?

## Paudeen

Indignant at the fumbling wits, the obscure spite
Of our old Paudeen in his shop, I stumbled blind
Among the stones and thorn-trees, under morning light;
Until a curlew cried and in the luminous wind
A curlew answered; and suddenly thereupon I thought    5
That on the lonely height where all are in God's eye,
There cannot be, confusion of our sound forgot,
A single soul that lacks a sweet crystalline cry.

## The Magi

Now as at all times I can see in the mind's eye,
In their stiff, painted clothes, the pale unsatisfied ones
Appear and disappear in the blue depth of the sky
With all their ancient faces like rain-beaten stones,
And all their helms of silver hovering side by side,    5
And all their eyes still fixed, hoping to find once more,
Being by Calvary's turbulence unsatisfied,
The uncontrollable mystery on the bestial floor.

No Second Troy, 12 *Was . . . burn:* Helen "burned" the first Troy.
The Magi, *The Magi:* members of the learned and priestly caste of
ancient Persia. Specifically, the three "wise men" who came to Jerusalem
to do homage to Christ. Cf. Eliot, p. 504.
   7 *Being . . . unsatisfied:* Not being sufficiently assured by the Cruci-
fixion and the Resurrection, etc.   8 *The uncontrollable . . . floor:* The
mystery of Christ's birth in the stable. Cf. p. 477.

## The Wild Swans at Coole

The trees are in their autumn beauty,
The woodland paths are dry,
Under the October twilight the water
Mirrors a still sky;
Upon the brimming water among the stones          5
Are nine-and-fifty swans.

The nineteenth autumn has come upon me
Since I first made my count;
I saw, before I had well finished,
All suddenly mount                                10
And scatter wheeling in great broken rings
Upon their clamorous wings.

I have looked upon those brilliant creatures,
And now my heart is sore.
All's changed since I, hearing at twilight,       15
The first time on this shore,
The bell-beat of their wings above my head,
Trod with a lighter tread.

Unwearied still, lover by lover,
They paddle in the cold                           20
Companionable streams or climb the air;
Their hearts have not grown old;
Passion or conquest, wander where they will,
Attend upon them still.

But now they drift on the still water,            25
Mysterious, beautiful;
Among what rushes will they build,
By what lake's edge or pool
Delight men's eyes when I awake some day
To find they have flown away?                      30


## The Dawn

I would be ignorant as the dawn
That has looked down
On that old queen measuring a town

THE DAWN. 3-4 *On that . . . brooch:* The arms of the city of

With the pin of a brooch,
Or on the withered men that saw                                    5
From their pedantic Babylon
The careless planets in their courses,
The stars fade out where the moon comes,
And took their tablets and did sums;
I would be ignorant as the dawn                                    10
That merely stood, rocking the glittering coach
Above the cloudy shoulders of the horses;
I would be—for no knowledge is worth a straw—
Ignorant and wanton as the dawn.


## The Second Coming

Turning and turning in the widening gyre
The falcon cannot hear the falconer;
Things fall apart; the centre cannot hold;
Mere anarchy is loosed upon the world,
The blood-dimmed tide is loosed, and everywhere          5
The ceremony of innocence is drowned;
The best lack all conviction, while the worst
Are full of passionate intensity.


Surely some revelation is at hand;
Surely the Second Coming is at hand.                               10
The Second Coming! Hardly are those words out
When a vast image out of *Spiritus Mundi*
Troubles my sight: somewhere in sands of the desert
A shape with lion body and the head of a man,
A gaze blank and pitiless as the sun,                              15
Is moving its slow thighs, while all about it
Reel shadows of the indignant desert birds.
The darkness drops again; but now I know

Armagh (Ireland) are said to depict the brooch and breast pin of one
of the "deities" of Celtic folklore.  6 *pedantic Babylon*: see Dan. 2:12,
4:6-7 on Babylon as a seat of learning.   11-12 *coach . . . horses*: probable reference to the chariot of the sun god, Apollo.

   THE SECOND COMING. 1 *Turning      gyre*: The expanding spiral of
the falcon's flight; but also a critical instant—here, ominous—in the
spiralling course of history. See p. 478, l. 19.   12 *Spiritus Mundi*:
World Spirit, the creating spirit; and World Memory.   14 *A . . . man*:
A sphinx-like creature, suggestive of evil. Cf. ll. 15, 17, and *beast*, l. 21.
16 *moving . . . thighs*: as it is coming to life, in the poet's vision.

That twenty centuries of stony sleep
Were vexed to nightmare by a rocking cradle,          20
And what rough beast, its hour come round at last,
Slouches towards Bethlehem to be born?

## Sailing to Byzantium

### I

That is no country for old men. The young
In one another's arms, birds in the trees
—Those dying generations—at their song,
The salmon-falls, the mackerel-crowded seas,
Fish, flesh, or fowl, commend all summer long          5
Whatever is begotten, born, and dies.
Caught in that sensual music all neglect
Monuments of unageing intellect.

### II

An aged man is but a paltry thing,
A tattered coat upon a stick, unless          10
Soul clap its hands and sing, and louder sing
For every tatter in its mortal dress,
Nor is there singing school but studying
Monuments of its own magnificence;
And therefore I have sailed the seas and come          15
To the holy city of Byzantium.

### III

O sages standing in God's holy fire
As in the gold mosaic of a wall,
Come from the holy fire, perne in a gyre,
And be the singing-masters of my soul.          20

21 *beast:* something evil, symbolic of the period of history about to begin. Cf. p. 475, l. 8, *bestial floor;* the *beast* was present at the First Coming, but helpless before the "uncontrollable mystery."

SAILING TO BYZANTIUM. *Byzantium:* Ancient capital of Eastern Christendom, but symbolic of an ideal and eternal world in which all aspects of life are unified. There, the artist "spoke to the multitude and the few alike."—Yeats.

1 *That:* The ordinary, natural world; here. 8 *Monuments . . . intellect:* The objects (*images*) of permanence and beauty, which art makes. See ll. 14, 24, 27-28; cf. p. 481, ll. 53-55; pp. 482-83, ll. 5-8, 9, 17-18. 13 *but:* except. 17-18 *O . . . mosaic:* The sages, holy men purified by God's fire, are like the figures in the mosaic, or are the figures themselves, which being the artist's work are holy. 19 *perne . . . gyre:* turn like the hawk in spiralling flight. Cf. p. 477, l. 1 and note.

Consume my heart away; sick with desire
And fastened to a dying animal
It knows not what it is; and gather me
Into the artifice of eternity.

IV

Once out of nature I shall never take                          25
My bodily form from any natural thing,
But such a form as Grecian goldsmiths make
Of hammered gold and gold enamelling
To keep a drowsy Emperor awake;
Or set upon a golden bough to sing                            30
To lords and ladies of Byzantium
Of what is past, or passing, or to come.

## Leda and the Swan

A sudden blow: the great wings beating still
Above the staggering girl, her thighs caressed
By the dark webs, her nape caught in his bill,
He holds her helpless breast upon his breast.

How can those terrified vague fingers push              5
The feathered glory from her loosening thighs?
And how can body, laid in that white rush,
But feel the strange heart beating where it lies?

A shudder in the loins engenders there
The broken wall, the burning roof and tower         10
And Agamemnon dead.
                              Being so caught up,
So mastered by the brute blood of the air,
Did she put on his knowledge with his power
Before the indifferent beak could let her drop?

24 *artifice of eternity*: the artist-sage's immortal image. See l. 8 and note.
25 *out of nature*: out of the world of sense, in the transcendent state
where he is "gathered" into the *artifice of eternity;* in Byzantium. Cf.
p. 179, ll. 47-48 and note. 27 *such . . . make*: such an image as the
Byzantine artist makes according to the pattern given by the imagination, and not in imitation of a *natural thing* (l. 26); and possibly a
suggestion of Yeats's belief in the reincarnation of souls in new and
different forms.

LEDA AND THE SWAN. *Leda*: A mortal beloved by Zeus (Jupiter), who
visited her in the form of a swan. Among their progeny was Helen,
who was carried off to Troy by Paris and thus became the cause of the
Trojan War. Cf. ll. 10-11; p. 475, l. 12.

11 *Agamemnon dead*: The commander-in-chief of the Greeks at Troy,
who upon his return home was murdered by his wife Clytemnestra aided
by Aegisthus, her lover.

# Among School Children

### I

I walk through the long schoolroom questioning;
A kind old nun in a white hood replies;
The children learn to cipher and to sing,
To study reading-books and histories,
To cut and sew, be neat in everything                    5
In the best modern way—the children's eyes
In momentary wonder stare upon
A sixty-year-old smiling public man.

### II

I dream of a Ledaean body, bent
Above a sinking fire, a tale that she                     10
Told of a harsh reproof, or trivial event
That changed some childish day to tragedy—
Told, and it seemed that our two natures blent
Into a sphere from youthful sympathy,
Or else, to alter Plato's parable,                        15
Into the yolk and white of the one shell.

### III

And thinking of that fit of grief or rage
I look upon one child or t'other there
And wonder if she stood so at that age—
For even daughters of the swan can share                  20
Something of every paddler's heritage—
And had that colour upon cheek or hair,
And thereupon my heart is driven wild:
She stands before me as a living child.

### IV

Her present image floats into the mind—                   25
Did Quattrocento finger fashion it
Hollow of cheek as though it drank the wind
And took a mess of shadows for its meat?

AMONG SCHOOL CHILDREN. 9 *dream:* recollect. *Ledaean:* like Leda's.
Cf. l. 20. No doubt a recollection of Maud Gonne (*she,* l. 10), whom
Yeats loved and lost. 15 *Plato's parable:* i.e., of love; in the *Sym-
posium:* the division into the sexes and the subsequent striving for
union. 19, 24 *she:* cf. *she,* l. 10. 26 *Quattrocento:* the fifteenth century, when such great painters as Andrea del Sarto, Raphael, Michaelangelo were born.

And I though never of Ledaean kind
Had pretty plumage once—enough of that,                    30
Better to smile on all that smile, and show
There is a comfortable kind of old scarecrow.

V

What youthful mother, a shape upon her lap
Honey of generation had betrayed,
And that must sleep, shriek, struggle to escape          35
As recollection or the drug decide,
Would think her son, did she but see that shape
With sixty or more winters on its head,
A compensation for the pang of his birth,
Or the uncertainty of his setting forth?                  40

VI

Plato thought nature but a spume that plays
Upon a ghostly paradigm of things;
Solider Aristotle played the taws
Upon the bottom of a king of kings;
World-famous golden-thighed Pythagoras                    45
Fingered upon a fiddle-stick or strings
What a star sang and careless Muses heard:
Old clothes upon old sticks to scare a bird.

VII

Both nuns and mothers worship images,
But those the candles light are not as those             50
That animate a mother's reveries,
But keep a marble or a bronze repose.
And yet they too break hearts—O Presences
That passion, piety or affection knows,
And that all heavenly glory symbolise—                    55
O self-born mockers of man's enterprise;

41-42 *Plato . . . things:* The material world is an impermanent and
changing reflection (like *spume:* froth) of the ideal world. *ghostly
paradigm:* spirit-like model. 43-44 *Aristotle . . . kings:* Aristotle did
not spare the rod (*taws*) upon his pupil Alexander the Great. 45-47
*Pythagoras . . . heard:* For Pythagoras the universe was essentially
harmony and proportion, and the movement of the planets made a heavenly music. Cf. Dryden, pp. 202-03, ll. 1-15. 49 *Both . . . images:*
A mother worships her son just as a nun worships an image of God.
53 *Presences:* Idealisms, images, born of themselves (*self-born,* l. 56).
Cf. p. 478, l. 8 and note.

## VIII

Labour is blossoming or dancing where
The body is not bruised to pleasure soul,
Nor beauty born out of its own despair,
Nor blear-eyed wisdom out of midnight oil.      60
O chestnut-tree, great-rooted blossomer,
Are you the leaf, the blossom or the bole?
O body swayed to music, O brightening glance,
How can we know the dancer from the dance?

## Byzantium

The unpurged images of day recede;
The Emperor's drunken soldiery are abed;
Night resonance recedes, night-walkers' song
After great cathedral gong;
A starlit or a moonlit dome disdains      5
All that man is,
All mere complexities,
The fury and the mire of human veins.

Before me floats an image, man or shade,
Shade more than man, more image than a shade;      10
For Hades' bobbin bound in mummy-cloth
May unwind the winding path;
A mouth that has no moisture and no breath
Breathless mouths may summon;
I hail the superhuman;      15
I call it death-in-life and life-in-death.

57 *Labour:* The ideal activity of body and soul united in effort, in contrast to *man's enterprise,* l. 56.

BYZANTIUM. 1 *unpurged . . . day:* objects in the world of ordinary experience (cf. *complexities, fury, mire, blood,* ll. 7-8, 24, 29, 33), which are unpurified by the fires of the imagination. Cf. *flames,* ll. 26, 27; *smithies,* l. 35. 5 *starlit . . . dome:* "pure" images, the presentation of which signals a transition from the ordinary world (*day*) to Byzantium (*eternity*). Cf. p. 479, ll. 23-28. 9 *image:* another "pure" image, as it exists, however, solely in the poet's imagination, and not yet realized in art, as the *bird,* l. 17. *shade:* suggesting that the image has the quality of something once earthly. 11-12 *For . . . path:* Analogous to the process creating the image is the experience of the soul divesting itself of mortality in the afterlife. There, earthly experience (*the winding path*) which bound the soul (*bobbin*) like a "mummy-cloth" in a kind of death-in-life is unwound. 13 *A . . . breath:* The immortal, lifeless image (l. 9) "summoned" by the imagination. 14 *Breathless mouths:* i.e., of the poets, in the intense, creative moments. Cf. *Dying,* l. 30.

Miracle, bird or golden handiwork,
More miracle than bird or handiwork,
Planted on the star-lit golden bough,
Can like the cocks of Hades crow,                          20
Or, by the moon embittered, scorn aloud
In glory of changeless metal
Common bird or petal
And all complexities of mire or blood.


At midnight on the Emperor's pavement flit              25
Flames that no faggot feeds, nor steel has lit,
Nor storm disturbs, flames begotten of flame,
Where blood-begotten spirits come
And all complexities of fury leave,
Dying into a dance,                                        30
An agony of trance,
An agony of flame that cannot singe a sleeve.


17 *bird:* the "pure" image now realized in the work of art. Cf. p. 479,
l. 24 and note.   19 *golden bough:* this further associates the *bird* with
the supernatural (*superhuman*), as it recalls the magic bough plucked
by Virgil, at the direction of the Sibyl, which entitled him to visit the
other world.  20 *cocks of Hades:* heralds of rebirth.   21-24 *scorn . . .
blood:* cf. *disdains . . . veins,* ll. 5-8.   26 *Flames:* that is, of the
"smithies of the Emperor," l. 35; fires of the imagination in which the
"images" are wrought.   28 *blood- . . . spirits:* the artists, or the
imaginative faculties of the artists. The artists transcend ordinary life
when they create ("all complexities of fury leave," l. 29). Cf. Donne,
p. 115, ll. 61-62.   30-31 *Dying . . . trance:* the ecstasy of creation.
32 *flame . . . sleeve:* the imagination, which is spiritual, in making the
image out of the world of ordinary experience, does not work the
slightest effect in the world of ordinary experience. This irony marks
the poet's "recession" into the world of the "unpurged images."   33-34
*Astraddle . . . spirit:* In the "unpurged" world, the poet, though a
"spirit," is *blood-begotten* (l. 28) and his very activity as poet necessarily
exposes him to its fury and complexity. The dolphin, traditionally a
friendly agent to such poets as Apollo and Arion (see Dryden, p. 196,
l. 43 and note) and *Lycidas* (see p. 160, l. 164), carries him violently
through the blood and mire. The dolphin (see ll. 38-40), while agent, is
still part of the world of ordinary experience, "mire and blood."   34
*smithies . . . flood:* the fires of the imagination (only) can destroy
(*break*) the sea of ordinary experience, i.e., refine the "unpurged images."

Astraddle on the dolphin's mire and blood,
Spirit after spirit! The smithies break the flood,
The golden smithies of the Emperor!                    35
Marbles of the dancing floor
Break bitter furies of complexity,
Those images that yet
Fresh images beget,
That dolphin-torn, that gong-tormented sea.            40


### Stream and Sun at Glendalough

Through intricate motions ran
Stream and gliding sun
And all my heart seemed gay:
Some stupid thing that I had done
Made my attention stray.                               5

Repentance keeps my heart impure;
But what am I that dare
Fancy that I can
Better conduct myself or have more
Sense than a common man?                               10

What motion of the sun or stream
Or eyelid shot the gleam
That pierced my body through?
What made me live like these that seem
Self-born, born anew?                                  15

36-37 *dancing . . . complexity:* in the ecstasy of creation (cf. 1. 30),
the "bitter furies, etc." are broken (destroyed).    38-39 *images . . .
beget:* the *fresh* (immortal) images, though out of the world of ordinary
experience, paradoxically are begotten upon the "unpurged images of
day," insistently remarked, ll. 33, 40.

# ROBERT FROST 1875—

## The Vantage Point

If tired of trees I seek again mankind,
    Well I know where to hie me—in the dawn,
    To a slope where the cattle keep the lawn.
There amid lolling juniper reclined,
Myself unseen, I see in white defined          5
    Far off the homes of men, and farther still,
    The graves of men on an opposing hill,
Living or dead, whichever are to mind.

And if by noon I have too much of these,
    I have but to turn on my arm, and lo,        10
    The sun-burned hillside sets my face aglow,
My breathing shakes the bluet like a breeze,
    I smell the earth, I smell the bruisèd plant,
    I look into the crater of the ant.

## October

O hushed October morning mild,
Thy leaves have ripened to the fall;
Tomorrow's wind, if it be wild,
Should waste them all.
The crows above the forest call;          5
Tomorrow they may form and go.
O hushed October morning mild,
Begin the hours of this day slow.
Make the day seem to us less brief.
Hearts not averse to being beguiled,        10
Beguile us in the way you know.
Release one leaf at break of day;
At noon release another leaf;
One from our trees, one far away.
Retard the sun with gentle mist;          15
Enchant the land with amethyst.
Slow, slow!
For the grapes' sake, if they were all,
Whose leaves already are burnt with frost,
Whose clustered fruit must else be lost—     20
For the grapes' sake along the wall.

## Home Burial

He saw her from the bottom of the stairs
Before she saw him. She was starting down,
Looking back over her shoulder at some fear.
She took a doubtful step and then undid it
To raise herself and look again. He spoke                    5
Advancing toward her: 'What is it you see
From up there always—for I want to know.'
She turned and sank upon her skirts at that,
And her face changed from terrified to dull.
He said to gain time: 'What is it you see,'                  10
Mounting until she cowered under him.
'I will find out now—you must tell me, dear.'
She, in her place, refused him any help
With the least stiffening of her neck and silence.
She let him look, sure that he wouldn't see,                 15
Blind creature; and awhile he didn't see.
But at last he murmured, 'Oh,' and again, 'Oh.'

'What is it—what?' she said.

                              'Just that I see.'

'You don't,' she challenged. 'Tell me what it is.'

'The wonder is I didn't see at once.                         20
I never noticed it from here before.
I must be wonted to it—that's the reason.
The little graveyard where my people are!
So small the window frames the whole of it.
Not so much larger than a bedroom, is it?                    25
There are three stones of slate and one of marble,
Broad-shouldered little slabs there in the sunlight
On the sidehill. We haven't to mind *those*.
But I understand: it is not the stones,
But the child's mound—'

                      'Don't, don't, don't, don't,' she cried.   30

She withdrew shrinking from beneath his arm
That rested on the bannister, and slid downstairs;
And turned on him with such a daunting look,
He said twice over before he knew himself:
'Can't a man speak of his own child he's lost?'             35

'Not you! Oh, where's my hat? Oh, I don't need it!
I must get out of here. I must get air.
I don't know rightly whether any man can.'

'Amy! Don't go to someone else this time.
Listen to me. I won't come down the stairs.'                    40
He sat and fixed his chin between his fists.
'There's something I should like to ask you, dear.'

'You don't know how to ask it.'

                              'Help me, then.'

Her fingers moved the latch for all reply.

'My words are nearly always an offense.                         45
I don't know how to speak of anything
So as to please you. But I might be taught
I should suppose. I can't say I see how.
A man must partly give up being a man
With women-folk. We could have some arrangement    50
By which I'd bind myself to keep hands off
Anything special you're a-mind to name.
Though I don't like such things 'twixt those that love.
Two that don't love can't live together without them.
But two that do can't live together with them.'                 55
She moved the latch a little. 'Don't—don't go.
Don't carry it to someone else this time.
Tell me about it if it's something human.
Let me into your grief. I'm not so much
Unlike other folks as your standing there                       60
Apart would make me out. Give me my chance.
I do think, though, you overdo it a little.
What was it brought you up to think it the thing
To take your mother-loss of a first child
So inconsolably—in the face of love.                            65
You'd think his memory might be satisfied—'

'There you go sneering now!'

                              'I'm not, I'm not!
You make me angry. I'll come down to you.
God, what a woman! And it's come to this,
A man can't speak of his own child that's dead'                 70

'You can't because you don't know how to speak.
If you had any feelings, you that dug
With your own hand—how could you?—his little grave;
I saw you from that very window there,
Making the gravel leap and leap in air,                    75
Leap up, like that, like that, and land so lightly
And roll back down the mound beside the hole.
I thought, Who is that man? I didn't know you.
And I crept down the stairs and up the stairs
To look again, and still your spade kept lifting.          80
Then you came in. I heard your rumbling voice
Out in the kitchen, and I don't know why,
But I went near to see with my own eyes.
You could sit there with the stains on your shoes
Of the fresh earth from your own baby's grave             85
And talk about your everyday concerns.
You had stood the spade up against the wall
Outside there in the entry, for I saw it.'

'I shall laugh the worst laugh I ever laughed.
I'm cursed. God, if I don't believe I'm cursed.'          90

'I can repeat the very words you were saying.
"Three foggy mornings and one rainy day
Will rot the best birch fence a man can build."
Think of it, talk like that at such a time!
What had how long it takes a birch to rot                 95
To do with what was in the darkened parlor.
You *couldn't* care! The nearest friends can go
With anyone to death, comes so far short
They might as well not try to go at all.
No, from the time when one is sick to death,             100
One is alone, and he dies more alone.
Friends make pretense of following to the grave,
But before one is in it, their minds are turned
And making the best of their way back to life
And living people, and things they understand.           105
But the world's evil. I won't have grief so
If I can change it. Oh, I won't, I won't!'

'There, you have said it all and you feel better.
You won't go now. You're crying. Close the door.
The heart's gone out of it: why keep it up.              110
Amy! There's someone coming down the road!'

'*You*—oh, you think the talk is all. I must go—
Somewhere out of this house. How can I make you—'

'If—you—do!' She was opening the door wider.
'Where do you mean to go? First tell me that.                    115
I'll follow and bring you back by force. I *will!*—'

## Meeting and Passing

As I went down the hill along the wall
There was a gate I had leaned at for the view
And had just turned from when I first saw you
As you came up the hill. We met. But all
We did that day was mingle great and small                    5
Footprints in summer dust as if we drew
The figure of our being less than two
But more than one as yet. Your parasol
Pointed the decimal off with one deep thrust.
And all the time we talked you seemed to see                  10
Something down there to smile at in the dust.
(Oh, it was without prejudice to me!)
Afterward I went past what you had passed
Before we met and you what I had passed.

## The Oven Bird

There is a singer everyone has heard,
Loud, a mid-summer and a mid-wood bird,
Who makes the solid tree trunks sound again.
He says that leaves are old and that for flowers
Mid-summer is to spring as one to ten.                        5
He says the early petal-fall is past
When pear and cherry bloom went down in showers
On sunny days a moment overcast;
And comes that other fall we name the fall.
He says the highway dust is over all.                         10
The bird would cease and be as other birds
But that he knows in singing not to sing.
The question that he frames in all but words
Is what to make of a diminished thing.

## Range-Finding

The battle rent a cobweb diamond-strung
And cut a flower beside a ground bird's nest
Before it stained a single human breast.
The stricken flower bent double and so hung.
And still the bird revisited her young.                    5
A butterfly its fall had dispossessed
A moment sought in air his flower of rest,
Then lightly stooped to it and fluttering clung.
On the bare upland pasture there had spread
O'ernight 'twixt mullein stalks a wheel of thread    10
And straining cables wet with silver dew.
A sudden passing bullet shook it dry.
The indwelling spider ran to greet the fly,
But finding nothing, sullenly withdrew.

## Stopping by Woods on a Snowy Evening

Whose woods these are I think I know.
His house is in the village though;
He will not see me stopping here
To watch his woods fill up with snow.

My little horse must think it queer                    5
To stop without a farmhouse near
Between the woods and frozen lake
The darkest evening of the year.

He gives his harness bells a shake
To ask if there is some mistake.                       10
The only other sound's the sweep
Of easy wind and downy flake.

The woods are lovely, dark and deep,
But I have promises to keep,
And miles to go before I sleep,                        15
And miles to go before I sleep.

## Acquainted with the Night

I have been one acquainted with the night.
I have walked out in rain—and back in rain.
I have outwalked the furthest city light.

I have looked down the saddest city lane.
I have passed by the watchman on his beat          5
And dropped my eyes, unwilling to explain.

I have stood still and stopped the sound of feet
When far away an interrupted cry
Came over houses from another street,

But not to call me back or say good-by;          10
And further still at an unearthly height,
One luminary clock against the sky

Proclaimed the time was neither wrong nor right.
I have been one acquainted with the night.

## Come In

As I came to the edge of the woods,
Thrush music—hark!
Now if it was dusk outside,
Inside it was dark.

Too dark in the woods for a bird          5
By sleight of wing
To better its perch for the night,
Though it still could sing.

The last of the light of the sun
That had died in the west          10
Still lived for one song more
In a thrush's breast.

Far in the pillared dark
Thrush music went—
Almost like a call to come in          15
To the dark and lament.

But no, I was out for stars:
I would not come in.
I meant not even if asked,
And I hadn't been.          20

## The Most of It

He thought he kept the universe alone;
For all the voice in answer he could wake
Was but the mocking echo of his own
From some tree-hidden cliff across the lake.
Some morning from the boulder-broken beach          5
He would cry out on life, that what it wants
Is not its own love back in copy speech,
But counter-love, original response.
And nothing ever came of what he cried
Unless it was the embodiment that crashed          10
In the cliff's talus on the other side,
And then in the far distant water splashed,
But after a time allowed for it to swim,
Instead of proving human when it neared
And someone else additional to him,          15
As a great buck it powerfully appeared,
Pushing the crumpled water up ahead,
And landed pouring like a waterfall,
And stumbled through the rocks with horny tread,
And forced the underbrush—and that was all.          20

## The Gift Outright

The land was ours before we were the land's.
She was our land more than a hundred years
Before we were her people. She was ours
In Massachusetts, in Virginia,
But we were England's, still colonials,          5
Possessing what we still were unpossessed by,
Possessed by what we now no more possessed.
Something we were withholding made us weak
Until we found out that it was ourselves
We were withholding from our land of living,          10
And forthwith found salvation in surrender.
Such as we were we gave ourselves outright
(The deed of gift was many deeds of war)
To the land vaguely realizing westward,
But still unstoried, artless, unenhanced,          15
Such as she was, such as she would become.

THE MOST OF IT. 11 *talus:* rock debris at the cliff's base.

## Directive

Back out of all this now too much for us,
Back in a time made simple by the loss
Of detail, burned, dissolved, and broken off
Like graveyard marble sculpture in the weather,
There is a house that is no more a house          5
Upon a farm that is no more a farm
And in a town that is no more a town.
The road there, if you'll let a guide direct you
Who only has at heart your getting lost,
May seem as if it should have been a quarry—       10
Great monolithic knees the former town
Long since gave up pretense of keeping covered.
And there's a story in a book about it:
Besides the wear of iron wagon wheels
The ledges show lines ruled southeast northwest,    15
The chisel work of an enormous Glacier
That braced his feet against the Arctic Pole.
You must not mind a certain coolness from him
Still said to haunt this side of Panther Mountain.
Nor need you mind the serial ordeal               20
Of being watched from forty cellar holes
As if by eye pairs out of forty firkins,
As for the woods' excitement over you
That sends light rustle rushes to their leaves,
Charge that to upstart inexperience.              25
Where were they all not twenty years ago?
They think too much of having shaded out
A few old pecker-fretted apple trees.
Make yourself up a cheering song of how
Someone's road home from work this once was,      30
Who may be just ahead of you on foot
Or creaking with a buggy load of grain.
The height of the adventure is the height
Of country where two village cultures faded
Into each other. Both of them are lost.           35
And if you're lost enough to find yourself
By now, pull in your ladder road behind you
And put a sign up CLOSED to all but me.
Then make yourself at home. The only field

DIRECTIVE. *22 firkins:* small wooden casks.

Now left's no bigger than a harness gall.                                40
First there's the children's house of make believe,
Some shattered dishes underneath a pine,
The playthings in the playhouse of the children.
Weep for what little things could make them glad.
Then for the house that is no more a house,                              45
But only a belilaced cellar hole,
Now slowly closing like a dent in dough.
This was no playhouse but a house in earnest.
Your destination and your destiny's
A brook that was the water of the house,                                 50
Cold as a spring as yet so near its source,
Too lofty and original to rage.
(We know the valley streams that when aroused
Will leave their tatters hung on barb and thorn.)
I have kept hidden in the instep arch                                    55
Of an old cedar at the waterside
A broken drinking goblet like the Grail
Under a spell so the wrong ones can't find it,
So can't get saved, as Saint Mark says they mustn't.
(I stole the goblet from the children's playhouse.)                      60
Here are your waters and your watering place.
Drink and be whole again beyond confusion.

40 *harness gall:* a sore spot on a horse, caused by the rubbing of the
harness.    57 *Grail:* The Holy Grail, the cup from which Christ drank
at the Last Supper. In the Arthurian story, most knights who searched
for it were the *wrong ones;* only Sir Percival, Galahad, and Bors were
worthy of the quest.    59 *So . . . mustn't:* see Mark 4:11-12 (?).

# T. S. ELIOT  1888—

## The Love Song of J. Alfred Prufrock

*S'io credesse che mia risposta fosse*
*A persona che mai tornasse al mondo,*
*Questa fiamma staria senza piu scosse.*
*Ma perciocche giammai di questo fondo*
*Non torno vivo alcun, s'i'odo il vero,*
*Senza tema d'infamia ti rispondo.*

Let us go then, you and I,
When the evening is spread out against the sky
Like a patient etherised upon a table;
Let us go, through certain half-deserted streets,
The muttering retreats                                              5
Of restless nights in one-night cheap hotels
And sawdust restaurants with oyster-shells:
Streets that follow like a tedious argument
Of insidious intent
To lead you to an overwhelming question . . .                      10
Oh, do not ask, "What is it?"
Let us go and make our visit.

In the room the women come and go
Talking of Michelangelo.                                           14

The yellow fog that rubs its back upon the window-panes,
The yellow smoke that rubs its muzzle on the window-panes
Licked its tongue into the corners of the evening,
Lingered upon the pools that stand in drains,
Let fall upon its back the soot that falls from chimneys,
Slipped by the terrace, made a sudden leap,                        20
And seeing that it was a soft October night,
Curled once about the house, and fell asleep.

And indeed there will be time
For the yellow smoke that slides along the street,
Rubbing its back upon the window-panes;                            25
There will be time, there will be time

THE LOVE SONG, *S'io credesse,* etc.: From Dante, *Divine Comedy:*
*Inferno,* XXVII, 61-66: "If I thought my answer were to one who ever
/ could return to the world, this flame should / shake no more; / But
since none ever did return alive from this / depth, if what I hear be
true, without fear of / infamy I answer thee."

To prepare a face to meet the faces that you meet;
There will be time to murder and create,
And time for all the works and days of hands
That lift and drop a question on your plate;                   30
Time for you and time for me,
And time yet for a hundred indecisions,
And for a hundred visions and revisions,
Before the taking of a toast and tea.

    In the room the women come and go                    35
Talking of Michelangelo.

    And indeed there will be time
To wonder, "Do I dare?" and, "Do I dare?"
Time to turn back and descend the stair,
With a bald spot in the middle of my hair—                     40
[They will say: "How his hair is growing thin!"]
My morning coat, my collar mounting firmly to the chin,
My necktie rich and modest, but asserted by a simple pin—
[They will say: "But how his arms and legs are thin!"]
Do I dare                                                       45
Disturb the universe?
In a minute there is time
For decisions and revisions which a minute will reverse.

    For I have known them all already, known them all:—
Have known the evenings, mornings, afternoons,                 50
I have measured out my life with coffee spoons;
I know the voices dying with a dying fall
Beneath the music from a farther room.
    So how should I presume?

    And I have known the eyes already, known them all—      55
The eyes that fix you in a formulated phrase,
And when I am formulated, sprawling on a pin,
When I am pinned and wriggling on the wall,
Then how should I begin
To spit out all the butt-ends of my days and ways?            60
    And how should I presume?

    And I have known the arms already, known them all—
Arms that are braceleted and white and bare
[But in the lamplight, downed with light brown hair!]
Is it perfume from a dress                                     65
That makes me so digress?

Arms that lie along a table, or wrap about a shawl.
    And should I then presume?
    And how should I begin?

.    .    .    .    .

Shall I say, I have gone at dusk through narrow streets    70
And watched the smoke that rises from the pipes
Of lonely men in shirt-sleeves, leaning out of windows? . . .

    I should have been a pair of ragged claws
Scuttling across the floors of silent seas.

.    .    .    .    .

And the afternoon, the evening, sleeps so peacefully!    75
Smoothed by long fingers,
Asleep . . . tired . . . or it malingers,
Stretched on the floor, here beside you and me.
Should I, after tea and cakes and ices,
Have the strength to force the moment to its crisis?    80
But though I have wept and fasted, wept and prayed,
Though I have seen my head [grown slightly bald] brought
        in upon a platter,
I am no prophet—and here's no great matter;
I have seen the moment of my greatness flicker,
And I have seen the eternal Footman hold my coat, and
        snicker,    85
And in short, I was afraid.

    And would it have been worth it, after all,
After the cups, the marmalade, the tea,
Among the porcelain, among some talk of you and me,
Would it have been worth while,    90
To have bitten off the matter with a smile,
To have squeezed the universe into a ball
To roll it toward some overwhelming question,
To say: "I am Lazarus, come from the dead,
Come back to tell you all, I shall tell you all"—    95
If one, settling a pillow by her head,
    Should say: "That is not what I meant at all,
    That is not it, at all."

    82 *my head . . . platter*: like the head of John the Baptist. See Matt.
14:8.    92 *To have . . . ball*: cf. Marvell, p. 176, ll. 41-42.    94 *Lazarus*
*. . . dead*: see John 11:23 ff.

And would it have been worth it, after all,
Would it have been worth while,                              100
After the sunsets and the dooryards and the sprinkled streets,
After the novels, after the teacups, after the skirts that trail
    along the floor—
And this, and so much more?—
It is impossible to say just what I mean!
But as if a magic lantern threw the nerves in patterns on a
    screen:                                                  105
Would it have been worth while
If one, settling a pillow or throwing off a shawl,
And turning toward the window, should say:
    "That is not it at all,
    That is not what I meant, at all."                       110

.    .    .    .    .

No! I am not Prince Hamlet, nor was meant to be;
Am an attendant lord, one that will do
To swell a progress, start a scene or two,
Advise the prince; no doubt, an easy tool,
Deferential, glad to be of use,                              115
Politic, cautious, and meticulous;
Full of high sentence, but a bit obtuse;
At times, indeed, almost ridiculous—
Almost, at times, the Fool.

I grow old. . . . I grow old . . .                           120
I shall wear the bottoms of my trousers rolled.

Shall I part my hair behind? Do I dare to eat a peach?
I shall wear white flannel trousers, and walk upon the beach.
I have heard the mermaids singing, each to each.

I do not think that they will sing to me.                    125

I have seen them riding seaward on the waves
Combing the white hair of the waves blown back
When the wind blows the water white and black.

113 *swell a progress:* add to the company attending the prince on a
journey, like Polonius in *Hamlet.*  117 *sentence:* significance. Cf. ll.
117-19 with Polonius.

We have lingered in the chambers of the sea
By sea-girls wreathed with seaweed red and brown        130
Till human voices wake us, and we drown.


## Gerontion

*Thou hast nor youth nor age
But as it were an after dinner sleep
Dreaming of both.*

                    [MEASURE FOR MEASURE, III, I]

Here I am, an old man in a dry month,
Being read to by a boy, waiting for rain.
I was neither at the hot gates
Nor fought in the warm rain
Nor knee deep in the salt marsh, heaving a cutlass,        5
Bitten by flies, fought.
My house is a decayed house,
And the jew squats on the window sill, the owner,
Spawned in some estaminet of Antwerp,
Blistered in Brussels, patched and peeled in London.        10
The goat coughs at night in the field overhead;
Rocks, moss, stonecrop, iron, merds.
The woman keeps the kitchen, makes tea,
Sneezes at evening, poking the peevish gutter,
                    I an old man,        15
A dull head among windy spaces.


Signs are taken for wonders. "We would see a sign!"
The word within a word, unable to speak a word,
Swaddled with darkness. In the juvescence of the year
Came Christ the tiger        20

---

GERONTION. *Gerontion:* means a little old man.  *Thou hast nor youth,
etc.:* From the Duke's speech to Claudio ("Be absolute for death, etc."),
*Measure for Measure,* III, i.
    9 *estaminet:* café.  12 *merds:* dung.  18-19 *The . . . darkness:* cf.
". . . Verbum infans, the Word without a word; the eternal Word not
able to speak a word; a wonder sure. And . . . swaddled, a wonder
too."—Lancelot Andrewes.  19 *juvescence:* springtime.  20 *Christ the
tiger:* cf. "I came not to send peace, but a sword."—Matt. 10:34.

In depraved May, dogwood and chestnut, flowering judas,
To be eaten, to be divided, to be drunk
Among whispers; by Mr. Silvero
With caressing hands, at Limoges
Who walked all night in the next room;                     25

By Hakagawa, bowing among the Titians;
By Madame de Tornquist, in the dark room
Shifting the candles; Fräulein von Kulp
Who turned in the hall, one hand on the door.
        Vacant shuttles                          30
Weave the wind. I have no ghosts,
An old man in a draughty house
Under a windy knob.

After such knowledge, what forgiveness? Think now
History has many cunning passages, contrived corridors    35
And issues, deceives with whispering ambitions,
Guides us by vanities. Think now
She gives when our attention is distracted
And what she gives, gives with such supple confusions
That the giving famishes the craving. Gives too late      40
What's not believed in, or if still believed,
In memory only, reconsidered passion. Gives too soon
Into weak hands, what's thought can be dispensed with
Till the refusal propagates a fear. Think
Neither fear nor courage saves us. Unnatural vices        45
Are fathered by our heroism. Virtues
Are forced upon us by our impudent crimes.
These tears are shaken from the wrath-bearing tree.

The tiger springs in the new year. Us he devours. Think
       at last
We have not reached conclusion, when I                    50
Stiffen in a rented house. Think at last
I have not made this show purposelessly

21 *depraved May:* seemingly springtime as depraved originally by pagan
fertility rituals, then by the suffering mankind brought upon Christ.
22-23 *to . . . whispers:* the Holy Communion Service, the "breaking"
and eating of the bread (Christ's body), and the drinking of the wine
(His blood). 23-29 *by . . . door: perversions* of the Sacrament: Silvero, thinking of his china; Hakagawa, *bowing,* not to the Cross, but to
the Titians; de Tornquist, practicing her spiritualism; and von Kulp,
possibly her timid victim. 48 *tree:* i.e., of the knowledge of good and
evil. 49 *tiger:* see l. 20 and note.

And it is not by any concitation
Of the backward devils.
I would meet you upon this honestly.                          55
I that was near your heart was removed therefrom
To lose beauty in terror, terror in inquisition.
I have lost my passion: why should I need to keep it
Since what is kept must be adulterated?
I have lost my sight, smell, hearing, taste and touch:       60
How should I use them for your closer contact?

   These with a thousand small deliberations
Protract the profit of their chilled delirium,
Excite the membrane, when the sense has cooled,
With pungent sauces, multiply variety                        65
In a wilderness of mirrors. What will the spider do,
Suspend its operations, will the weevil
Delay? De Bailhache, Fresca, Mrs. Cammel, whirled
Beyond the circuit of the shuddering Bear
In fractured atoms. Gull against the wind, in the windy
     straits                                         70
Of Belle Isle, or running on the Horn,
White feathers in the snow, the Gulf claims,
And an old man driven by the Trades
To a sleepy corner.

                  Tenants of the house,         75
Thoughts of a dry brain in a dry season.

## Mr. Eliot's Sunday Morning Service

*Look, look, master, here comes two religious caterpillars.*

                      [THE JEW OF MALTA]

    Polyphiloprogenitive
    The sapient sutlers of the Lord
    Drift across the window-panes.
    In the beginning was the Word.

**53** *concitation:* stirring up.   **54** *backward devils:* false religions preceding Christianity.   **55** *you:* Christ.   **68** *De Bailhache . . . Cammel:* random acquaintances.   **68-70** *whirled . . . atoms:* cf. *Measure for Measure,* III, i, ll. 19-21, 118, 124-26.   **69** *Bear:* the constellation, Ursa Major.

   MR. ELIOT'S SUNDAY. 1 *Polyphiloprogenitive:* Excessively prolific. **2** *sutlers:* literally, camp-followers; here presbyters preparing to take up the offering. Cf. ll. 17-18.   **4** *In . . . Word:* see John 1:1. Cf. Thomas, p. 530.

In the beginning was the Word.                5
Superfetation of τὸ ἕν,
And at the mensual turn of time
Produced enervate Origen.


A painter of the Umbrian school
Designed upon a gesso ground              10
The nimbus of the Baptized God.
The wilderness is cracked and browned


But through the water pale and thin
Still shine the unoffending feet
And there above the painter set            15
The Father and the Paraclete.


.    .    .    .    .


The sable presbyters approach
The avenue of penitence;
The young are red and pustular
Clutching piaculative pence.               20


Under the penitential gates
Sustained by staring Seraphim
Where the souls of the devout
Burn invisible and dim.


Along the garden-wall the bees             25
With hairy bellies pass between

6 *Superfetation of* τὸ ἕν: Overfertilization of the One (the Word), by contamination with Greek philosophy, especially Neoplatonism, resulting in hybrid doctrines of the "oneness" of the Trinity. 7 *mensual . . . time:* "conceiving" time. 8 *enervate Origen* (*c.* 185-*c.* 254) : Origen is weak (like the offspring of the modern church) because, although a very great theologian, he held, according to his Neoplatonism, that the Word was only another of God's "spiritual creatures." 9 *Umbrian school:* A school of Italian painters of the fifteenth century, including Perugino, Raphael's master. 10 *gesso ground:* the plaster-like material spread upon the surface to prepare it for the paint. 11 *nimbus:* halo, aureole. 16 *Paraclete:* the Holy Spirit, the third person of the Trinity; Intercessor, Advocate, and Comforter. 18 *avenue of penitence:* the aisle from which the presbyters take up the offering, as if making an offering were penance. 19 *The young:* The numerous offspring of the *sutlers,* ll. 1-2. 20 *piaculative:* expiatory. 22 *Seraphim:* Angels of the highest order. 25 *the bees:* a common ecclesiastical symbol, representing the *Blest office of the epicene* (Christ, the "neutral" intercessor). Some see the presbyters (*bees / With hairy bellies*) as "go-betweens" between the congregation and the gates of penitence as spiritually sterile functionaries usurping the office of the rightful Intercessor.

The staminate and pistilate,
Blest office of the epicene.

Sweeney shifts from ham to ham
Stirring the water in his bath.                    30
The masters of the subtle schools
Are controversial, polymath.


### Sweeney Among the Nightingales

ὤμοι, πέπληγμαι καιρίαν πληγὴν ἔσω.


Apeneck Sweeney spreads his knees
Letting his arms hang down to laugh,
The zebra stripes along his jaw
Swelling to maculate giraffe.

The circles of the stormy moon                     5
Slide westward toward the River Plate,
Death and the Raven drift above
And Sweeney guards the hornèd gate.

Gloomy Orion and the Dog
Are veiled; and hushed the shrunken seas;          10
The person in the Spanish cape
Tries to sit on Sweeney's knees

Slips and pulls the table cloth
Overturns a coffee-cup,
Reorganized upon the floor                         15
She yawns and draws a stocking up;

29-30 *Sweeney . . . bath:* The degradation of the church service
is expressed in the implied comparison with Sweeney's Sunday morning.
31 *subtle:* cf. *sutlers,* l. 2.   32 *polymath:* diversely learned, eclectic.
   SWEENEY. ὤμοι, πέπληγμαι, *etc.:* "Ay me! I am smitten with a mortal blow."—Aeschylus, *Agamemnon.* See ll. 37-38. See Yeats, p. 479,
l. 11 and note.
   1 *Sweeney:* the "primitive man." Cf. *Apeneck, zebra, giraffe.*   4
*maculate:* spotted, striped.   6 *Plate:* La Plata.   7 *Raven:* Corvus, a
southern constellation; suggestive of the bird of death circling above
its prey.   8 *hornèd gate:* one of the twin gates of Sleep; the gate from
which in dreams issue the true shades of the Dead; hence, gate of death.
9 *Orion, Dog (Canis Major,* or *Minor):* Constellations. Orion, in love
with Merope, attempted to win her by violence when her father Oenopion
refused his consent. Slain by the father, he was restored by the sun god
and again slain, mistakenly, by Diana, the chaste moon goddess, who
set him in the heavens as a constellation. Jealous of his happiness there,
however, Diana kills him daily with her darts. Agamemnon (l. 38) also
is associated with Diana (*Artemis*), who once took revenge upon him
for killing one of her hinds.

The silent man in mocha brown
Sprawls at the window-sill and gapes;
The waiter brings in oranges
Bananas figs and hothouse grapes;    20

The silent vertebrate in brown
Contracts and concentrates, withdraws;
Rachel *née* Rabinovitch
Tears at the grapes with murderous paws;

She and the lady in the cape    25
Are suspect, thought to be in league;
Therefore the man with heavy eyes
Declines the gambit, shows fatigue,

Leaves the room and reappears
Outside the window, leaning in,    30
Branches of wistaria
Circumscribe a golden grin;

The host with someone indistinct
Converses at the door apart,
The nightingales are singing near    35
The Convent of the Sacred Heart,

And sang within the bloody wood
When Agamemnon cried aloud,
And let their liquid siftings fall
To stain the stiff dishonoured shroud.    40

## Journey of the Magi

'A cold coming we had of it,
Just the worst time of the year
For a journey, and such a long journey:
The ways deep and the weather sharp,
The very dead of winter.'    5
And the camels galled, sore-footed, refractory,
Lying down in the melting snow.
There were times we regretted

28 *gambit:* pawn; lead.  37 *sang . . . wood:* cf. Sidney, p. 40;
"Philomela," p. 394.  40 *shroud:* Agamemnon's.

The summer palaces on slopes, the terraces,
And the silken girls bringing sherbet.                          10
Then the camel men cursing and grumbling
And running away, and wanting their liquor and women,
And the night-fires going out, and the lack of shelters,
And the cities hostile and the towns unfriendly
And the villages dirty and charging high prices:               15
A hard time we had of it.
At the end we preferred to travel all night,
Sleeping in snatches,
With the voices singing in our ears, saying
That this was all folly.                                        20


Then at dawn we came down to a temperate valley,
Wet, below the snow line, smelling of vegetation;
With a running stream and a water-mill beating the
          darkness,
And three trees on the low sky,
And an old white horse galloped away in the meadow.   25
Then we came to a tavern with vine-leaves over the lintel,
Six hands at an open door dicing for pieces of silver,
And feet kicking the empty wine-skins.
But there was no information, and so we continued
And arrived at evening, not a moment too soon           30
Finding the place; it was (you may say) satisfactory.


All this was a long time ago, I remember,
And I would do it again, but set down
This set down
This: were we led all that way for                        35
Birth or Death? There was a Birth, certainly,
We had evidence and no doubt. I had seen birth and death,
But had thought they were different; this Birth was
Hard and bitter agony for us, like Death, our death.
We returned to our places, these Kingdoms,                40
But no longer at ease here, in the old dispensation,
With an alien people clutching their gods.
I should be glad of another death.

JOURNEY. 10 *sherbet :* a cooling fruit drink.   24, 25 *three trees, white
horse :* recalling the three crosses on Calvary, and the white horse of
Rev. 6:2, 19:11.   41 *old dispensation :* old order ; before the coming
of Christ.

*from* FOUR QUARTETS

## The Dry Salvages

### I

I do not know much about gods; but I think that the river
Is a strong brown god—sullen, untamed and intractable,
Patient to some degree, at first recognised as a frontier;
Useful, untrustworthy, as a conveyor of commerce;
Then only a problem confronting the builder of bridges.        5
The problem once solved, the brown god is almost forgotten
By the dwellers in cities—ever, however, implacable,
Keeping his seasons and rages, destroyer, reminder
Of what men choose to forget. Unhonoured, unpropitiated
By worshippers of the machine, but waiting, watching and
        waiting.        10
His rhythm was present in the nursery bedroom,
In the rank ailanthus of the April dooryard,
In the smell of grapes on the autumn table,
And the evening circle in the winter gaslight.

The river is within us, the sea is all about us;        15
The sea is the land's edge also, the granite
Into which it reaches, the beaches where it tosses
Its hints of earlier and other creation:
The starfish, the hermit crab, the whale's backbone;
The pools where it offers to our curiosity        20
The more delicate algae and the sea anemone.
It tosses up our losses, the torn seine,
The shattered lobsterpot, the broken oar
And the gear of foreign dead men. The sea has many voices,
Many gods and many voices.        25
                    The salt is on the briar rose,
The fog is in the fir trees.

THE DRY SALVAGES. *The Dry Salvages:* ". . . presumably *les trois
sauvages*—a small group of rocks, with a beacon, off the N.E. coast of
Cape Ann, Massachusetts. *Salvages* is pronounced to rhyme with *as-
suages*."—Eliot.
    1 *river:* the Mississippi; but a symbol of the life of man, the course
of his personal history, from birth through experience (likened to
seasonal change) to death (ll. 11-14). See *sea,* into which the river
flows, l. 15.    12 *ailanthus:* a common plant, "tree of heaven," which once
established, is hard to root out (cf. *rank*).    15 *sea:* i.e., of time; the
flux of world history, "all about us."

The sea howl
And the sea yelp, are different voices
Often together heard; the whine in the rigging,                          30
The menace and caress of wave that breaks on water,
The distant rote in the granite teeth,
And the wailing warning from the approaching headland
Are all sea voices, and the heaving groaner
Rounded homewards, and the seagull:                                      35
And under the oppression of the silent fog
The tolling bell
Measures time not our time, rung by the unhurried
Ground swell, a time
Older than the time of chronometers, older                              40
Than time counted by anxious worried women
Lying awake, calculating the future,
Trying to unweave, unwind, unravel
And piece together the past and the future,
Between midnight and dawn, when the past is all deception, 45
The future futureless, before the morning watch
When time stops and time is never ending;
And the ground swell, that is and was from the beginning,
Clangs
The bell.                                                               50

## II

Where is there an end of it, the soundless wailing,
The silent withering of autumn flowers
Dropping their petals and remaining motionless;
Where is there an end to the drifting wreckage,
The prayer of the bone on the beach, the unprayable             55
Prayer at the calamitous annunciation?

There is no end, but addition: the trailing
Consequence of further days and hours,
While emotion takes to itself the emotionless

32 *rote:* noise of the surf dashing upon the shore.   34 *groaner:* "a
whistling buoy"—Eliot.  35 *Rounded:* i.e., by the ship.  37 *tolling bell:*
of a buoy; also the sound of the sea—and of time—which strikes a
deeper note of meaning.  38 *time . . . time:* all time, not simply of
man's life.  46-47 *morning . . . ending:* The bell clanging at the
"morning watch" gives "a sudden illumination" (l. 94) of the fuller,
deeper meaning of time. See Vaughan, p. 185.  55-56 *unprayable . . .
annunciation:* the one whose bone is on the beach was unable to pray
when disaster overtook him; or, prayer is impossible in the critical in-
stants (*annunciations*) in time. Cf. *annunciation*, ll. 68, 86.

Years of living among the breakage                                    60
Of what was believed in as the most reliable—
And therefore the fittest for renunciation.


There is the final addition, the failing
Pride or resentment at failing powers,
The unattached devotion which might pass for devotionless,
In a drifting boat with a slow leakage,                               66
The silent listening to the undeniable
Clamour of the bell of the last annunciation.


Where is the end of them, the fishermen sailing
Into the wind's tail, where the fog cowers?                           70
We cannot think of a time that is oceanless
Or of an ocean not littered with wastage
Or of a future that is not liable
Like the past, to have no destination.


We have to think of them as forever bailing,                          75
Setting and hauling, while the North East lowers
Over shallow banks unchanging and erosionless
Or drawing their money, drying sails at dockage;
Not as making a trip that will be unpayable
For a haul that will not bear examination.                            80


There is no end of it, the voiceless wailing,
No end to the withering of withered flowers,
To the movement of pain that is painless and motionless,
To the drift of the sea and the drifting wreckage,
The bone's prayer to Death its God. Only the hardly, barely
          prayable                                                    85
Prayer of the one Annunciation.


It seems, as one becomes older,
That the past has another pattern, and ceases to be a mere
          sequence—
Or even development: the latter a partial fallacy,
Encouraged by superficial notions of evolution,                      90
Which becomes, in the popular mind, a means of disowning
          the past.

68 *last annunciation:* death.   78 *at dockage:* when tied up.   85-86
*barely . . . Annunciation:* "Be it unto me according to thy word," the
prayer made by the Virgin Mary when the angel "announced" that she
was to become the Mother of Christ. See Luke 1 :30-38.   89 *even development:* uniform progress.

The moments of happiness—not the sense of well-being,
Fruition, fulfilment, security or affection,
Or even a very good dinner, but the sudden illumination—
We had the experience but missed the meaning,                    95
And approach to the meaning restores the experience
In a different form, beyond any meaning
We can assign to happiness. I have said before
That the past experience revived in the meaning
Is not the experience of one life only                          100
But of many generations—not forgetting
Something that is probably quite ineffable:
The backward look behind the assurance
Of recorded history, the backward half-look
Over the shoulder, towards the primitive terror.                 105
Now, we come to discover that the moments of agony
(Whether, or not, due to misunderstanding,
Having hoped for the wrong things or dreaded the wrong
        things,
Is not in question) are likewise permanent                       109
With such permanence as time has. We appreciate this better
In the agony of others, nearly experienced,
Involving ourselves, than in our own.
For our own past is covered by the currents of action,
But the torment of others remains an experience
Unqualified, unworn by subsequent attrition.                     115
People change, and smile: but the agony abides.
Time the destroyer is time the preserver,
Like the river with its cargo of dead Negroes, cows and
        chicken coops,
The bitter apple and the bite in the apple.
And the ragged rock in the restless waters,                      120
Waves wash over it, fogs conceal it;
On a halcyon day it is merely a monument,
In navigable weather it is always a seamark
To lay a course by: but in the sombre season
Or the sudden fury, is what it always was.                       125

94 *sudden illumination:* moment of insight or revelation, into our connection with the past. See ll. 99-101.   98 *said before:* in l. 96.   102
*ineffable:* indescribable.   105 *primitive terror:* cf. "hints of earlier and
other creation," l. 18; Tennyson, p. 360, l. 162.   113 *covered . . . action:* action obscures our sense of involvement in history because it
prevents the disinterestedness that man should cultivate. See l. 169 and
note.   119 *apple . . . apple:* of Eden; the effect of Adam's "bite" time
preserves as the legacy of Original Sin.   122 *halcyon:* calm.   125 *it
. . . was:* viz., *the ragged rock,* l. 120.

### III

I sometimes wonder if that is what Krishna meant—
Among other things—or one way of putting the same thing:
That the future is a faded song, a Royal Rose or a lavender
      spray
Of wistful regret for those who are not yet here to regret,
Pressed between yellow leaves of a book that has never been
      opened.       130
And the way up is the way down, the way forward is the way
      back.
You cannot face it steadily, but this thing is sure,
That time is no healer: the patient is no longer here.
When the train starts, and the passengers are settled
To fruit, periodicals and business letters       135
(And those who saw them off have left the platform)
Their faces relax from grief into relief,
To the sleepy rhythm of a hundred hours.
Fare forward, travellers! not escaping from the past
Into different lives, or into any future;       140
You are not the same people who left that station
Or who will arrive at any terminus,
While the narrowing rails slide together behind you;
And on the deck of the drumming liner
Watching the furrow that widens behind you,       145
You shall not think "the past is finished"
Or "the future is before us."
At nightfall, in the rigging and the aerial,
Is a voice descanting (though not to the ear,
The murmuring shell of time, and not in any language)       150
"Fare forward, you who think that you are voyaging;
You are not those who saw the harbour
Receding, or those who will disembark.
Here between the hither and the farther shore
While time is withdrawn, consider the future       155
And the past with an equal mind.

126 *that: That*, etc., ll. 128-30. *Krishna:* One of the most widely worshipped of the Hindu deities. 128-30 *future . . . opened:* as if there
were no future, or that it is something already past though never experienced. 133 *patient . . . here:* all things change in time, and every
moment he becomes something different from what he was. See ll. 141,
152-53. 149 *descanting:* singing. 150 *murmuring . . . time:* a shell
in which one can hear the sound of the sea, i.e., of time. 154 *Here:*
Now. in the present. 156 *equal:* disinterested, objective.

At the moment which is not of action or inaction
You can receive this: 'on whatever sphere of being
The mind of a man may be intent
At the time of death'—that is the one action                    160
(And the time of death is every moment)
Which shall fructify in the lives of others:
And do not think of the fruit of action.
Fare forward.

        O voyagers, O seamen,                    165
You who come to port, and you whose bodies
Will suffer the trial and judgement of the sea,
Or whatever event, this is your real destination."
So Krishna, as when he admonished Arjuna
On the field of battle.                    170
        Not fare well,
But fare forward, voyagers.


IV

Lady, whose shrine stands on the promontory,
Pray for all those who are in ships, those
Whose business has to do with fish, and                    175
Those concerned with every lawful traffic
And those who conduct them.


   Repeat a prayer also on behalf of
Women who have seen their sons or husbands
Setting forth, and not returning:                    180
Figlia del tuo figlio,
Queen of Heaven.


   Also pray for those who were in ships, and
Ended their voyage on the sand, in the sea's lips
Or in the dark throat which will not reject them                    185
Or wherever cannot reach them the sound of the sea bell's
Perpetual angelus.

---

157 *the moment:* of "sudden illumination" (l. 94). Cf. ll. 46-47 and note.
160 *one action:* death. Cf. *this,* l. 168.    162 *fructify:* bear fruit.    169
*admonished Arjuna:* to cultivate the habit of disinterestedness (cf.
*equal mind,* l. 156), and not to expect action to bear fruit. Cf. Matt.
6:34.    173 *Lady . . . promontory:* The Virgin Mary as *Stella Maris,* to
whom the fishermen and their wives pray.    181 *Figlia . . . figlio:* The
Virgin as "Handmaid of the Lord."    183 *pray:* to the Virgin as *Mater
Dolorosa,* "Mother of Sorrows," for those who have lost their lives at
sea.    185 *reject:* spew out, cast back.    187 *angelus:* a devotion com-
memorating the Incarnation.

V

To communicate with Mars, converse with spirits,
To report the behaviour of the sea monster,
Describe the horoscope, haruspicate or scry,      190
Observe disease in signatures, evoke
Biography from the wrinkles of the palm
And tragedy from fingers; release omens
By sortilege, or tea leaves, riddle the inevitable
With playing cards, fiddle with pentagrams      195
Or barbituric acids, or dissect
The recurrent image into pre-conscious terrors—
To explore the womb, or tomb, or dreams; all these are usual
Pastimes and drugs, and features of the press:
And always will be, some of them especially      200
When there is distress of nations and perplexity
Whether on the shores of Asia, or in the Edgware Road.
Men's curiosity searches past and future
And clings to that dimension. But to apprehend
The point of intersection of the timeless      205
With time, is an occupation for the saint—
No occupation either, but something given
And taken, in a lifetime's death in love,
Ardour and selflessness and self-surrender.
For most of us, there is only the unattended      210
Moment, the moment in and out of time,
The distraction fit, lost in a shaft of sunlight,
The wild thyme unseen, or the winter lightning
Or the waterfall, or music heard so deeply
That it is not heard at all, but you are the music      215
While the music lasts. These are only hints and guesses,
Hints followed by guesses; and the rest
Is prayer, observance, discipline, thought and action.

188-98 *To . . . dreams:* The "Pastimes, etc." (l. 199) by which men
delude themselves about knowing the past, foreseeing the future (cf.
ll. 203-04), or escaping time altogether. 190 *haruspicate:* perform divination by inspection of the entrails of sacrificial victims. *scry:* practice
crystal gazing. 194 *sortilege:* divination, enchantment. 195 *pentagrams:* five-pointed stars used as magical symbols. 196 *barbituric acids:*
"sleeping pills." 196-97 *dissect . . . terrors:* as in psychoanalysis. See
also l. 198. 202 *Edgware Road:* in London. 206 *occupation . . . saint:*
in contrast to the "occupations" noted ll. 188-98. 209 *self-surrender:*
e.g., as expressed in the Virgin's prayer, ll. 85-86 and note. 211 *moment . . . out:* birth, death. 212 *distraction fit:* fit of distraction (?).

The hint half guessed, the gift half understood, is Incarnation.
Here the impossible union.                                    220
Of spheres of existence is actual,
Here the past and future
Are conquered, and reconciled,
Where action were otherwise movement
Of that which is only moved                                   225
And has in it no source of movement—
Driven by daemonic, chthonic
Powers. And right action is freedom
From past and future also.
For most of us, this is the aim                               230
Never here to be realised;
Who are only undefeated
Because we have gone on trying;
We, content at the last
If our temporal reversion nourish                             235
(Not too far from the yew-tree)
The life of significant soil.

219 *Incarnation*: The great "point of intersection of the timeless / With time" (ll. 205-06), and the Incident which gives point to time.    220 *impossible*: to reason. Cf. Yeats, "uncontrollable mystery," p. 475, l. 8. 227 *chthonic*: underworld.    235 *reversion*: residue, the body.

# W. H. AUDEN  1907—

## Musée des Beaux Arts

About suffering they were never wrong,
The Old Masters: how well they understood
Its human position; how it takes place
While someone else is eating or opening a window or just
        walking dully along;
How, when the aged are reverently, passionately waiting   5
For the miraculous birth, there always must be
Children who did not specially want it to happen, skating
On a pond at the edge of the wood:
They never forgot
That even the dreadful martyrdom must run its course   10
Anyhow in a corner, some untidy spot
Where the dogs go on with their doggy life and the torturer's
        horse
Scratches its innocent behind on a tree.

In Brueghel's *Icarus*, for instance: how everything turns away
Quite leisurely from the disaster; the ploughman may   15
Have heard the splash, the forsaken cry,
But for him it was not an important failure; the sun shone
As it had to on the white legs disappearing into the green
Water; and the expensive delicate ship that must have seen
Something amazing, a boy falling out of the sky,   20
Had somewhere to get to and sailed calmly on.


## The Cultural Presupposition

Happy the hare at morning, for she cannot read
The Hunter's waking thoughts, lucky the leaf
Unable to predict the fall, lucky indeed
The rampant suffering suffocating jelly
Burgeoning in pools, lapping the grits of the desert,   5

Musée des Beaux Arts. 14 *Icarus:* A picture in the Royal Museum,
Brussels, by Pieter Breughel (1564?-1638). See Shelley, p. 318, l. 86
and note.

The Cultural Presupposition. 4 *jelly:* slimy animalculous matter.
5 *grits:* sands.

But what shall man do, who can whistle tunes by heart,
Knows to the bar when death shall cut him short like the cry
    of the shearwater,
What can he do but defend himself from his knowledge?


How comely are his places of refuge and the tabernacles of
    his peace,
The new books upon the morning table, the lawns and the
    afternoon terraces!          10
Here are the playing-fields where he may forget his ignorance
To operate within a gentleman's agreement: twenty-two sins
    have here a certain licence.
Here are the thickets where accosted lovers combatant
May warm each other with their wicked hands,
Here are the avenues for incantation and workshops for the
    cunning engravers.          15
The galleries are full of music, the pianist is storming the keys,
    the great cellist is crucified over his instrument,
That none may hear the ejaculations of the sentinels
Nor the sigh of the most numerous and the most poor, the
    thud of their falling bodies
Who with their lives have banished hence the serpent and the
    faceless insect.


### In Memory of W. B. Yeats

(D. JAN. 1939)


I

He disappeared in the dead of winter:
The brooks were frozen, the airports almost deserted,
And snow disfigured the public statues;
The mercury sank in the mouth of the dying day.
O all the instruments agree          5
The day of his death was a dark cold day.

7 *shearwater:* a sea bird.  9 *How . . . peace:* cf. Ps. 84:1; Isa. 52:7.
12 *twenty-two sins:* the specific "rules of the game" in the *gentleman's
agreement.*  13 *avenues . . . engravers:* streets with their places of
entertainment and fascinating wares—to divert man from knowledge of
himself. Cf. l. 8.  17 *sentinels:* guardian patrons of the arts.  19 *serpent:* perhaps, consciousness of evil.  *faceless insect:* anonymity of sub-
human nature. Cf. *jelly,* l. 4.

Far from his illness
The wolves ran on through the evergreen forests,
The peasant river was untempted by the fashionable quays;
By mourning tongues                                               10
The death of the poet was kept from his poems.

But for him it was his last afternoon as himself,
An afternoon of nurses and rumours;
The provinces of his body revolted,
The squares of his mind were empty,                              15
Silence invaded the suburbs,
The current of his feeling failed: he became his admirers.

Now he is scattered among a hundred cities
And wholly given over to unfamiliar affections;
To find his happiness in another kind of wood                    20
And be punished under a foreign code of conscience.
The words of a dead man
Are modified in the guts of the living.

But in the importance and noise of tomorrow
When the brokers are roaring like beasts on the floor of the
        Bourse,                                                  25
And the poor have the sufferings to which they are fairly
        accustomed,
And each in the cell of himself is almost convinced of his
        freedom;
A few thousand will think of this day
As one thinks of a day when one did something slightly
        unusual.

O all the instruments agree                                      30
The day of his death was a dark cold day.

2

You were silly like us: your gift survived it all;
The parish of rich women, physical decay,
Yourself; mad Ireland hurt you into poetry.
Now Ireland has her madness and her weather still,               35

IN MEMORY OF W. B. YEATS. 10-11 *By . . . tongues:* The poet died,
but his poems live through those who mourn his loss (*his admirers,* l.
17). 17 *became his admirers:* dead, he lived only in his admirers.  25
*Bourse:* Stock Exchange (Paris).

For poetry makes nothing happen: it survives
In the valley of its saying where executives
Would never want to tamper; it flows south
From ranches of isolation and the busy griefs,
Raw towns that we believe and die in; it survives,      40
A way of happening, a mouth.


3

    Earth, receive an honoured guest;
    William Yeats is laid to rest:
    Let the Irish vessel lie
    Emptied of its poetry.      45

    Time that is intolerant
    Of the brave and innocent,
    And indifferent in a week
    To a beautiful physique,

    Worships language and forgives      50
    Everyone by whom it lives;
    Pardons cowardice, conceit,
    Lays its honours at their feet.

    Time that with this strange excuse
    Pardoned Kipling and his views,      55
    And will pardon Paul Claudel,
    Pardons him for writing well.

    In the nightmare of the dark
    All the dogs of Europe bark,
    And the living nations wait,      60
    Each sequestered in its hate;

    Intellectual disgrace
    Stares from every human face,
    And the seas of pity lie
    Locked and frozen in each eye.      65

    Follow, poet, follow right
    To the bottom of the night,
    With your unconstraining voice
    Still persuade us to rejoice;

55 *Kipling . . . views:* cf. p. 519, ll. 43-44.   56 *Paul Claudel* (b.
1868) : a distinguished French Catholic writer.

With the farming of a verse    70
Make a vineyard of the curse,
Sing of human unsuccess
In a rapture of distress;

In the deserts of the heart
Let the healing fountain start,    75
In the prison of his days
Teach the free man how to praise.


## September 1, 1939

I sit in one of the dives
On Fifty-second Street
Uncertain and afraid
As the clever hopes expire
Of a low dishonest decade:    5
Waves of anger and fear
Circulate over the bright
And darkened lands of the earth,
Obsessing our private lives;
The unmentionable odour of death    10
Offends the September night.

Accurate scholarship can
Unearth the whole offence
From Luther until now
That has driven a culture mad,    15
Find what occurred at Linz,
What huge imago made
A psychopathic god:
I and the public know
What all schoolchildren learn,    20
Those to whom evil is done
Do evil in return.

---

70 *farming:* cf. Milton, p. 157, l. 65, for another pastoral locution.    71
*Make . . . curse:* Turn evil into good. Cf. Milton, p. 173, ll. 9-10.
SEPTEMBER. *September 1, 1939:* The date on which Hitler ordered
the invasion of Poland and World War II began.
16 *Linz:* an Austrian town where Hitler spent part of his boyhood.
17-18 *What . . . god:* What conception of the parent retained in his
unconscious produced Hitler.

Exiled Thucydides knew
All that a speech can say
About Democracy,                              25
And what dictators do,
The elderly rubbish they talk
To an apathetic grave;
Analysed all in his book,
The enlightenment driven away,               30
The habit-forming pain,
Mismanagement and grief:
We must suffer them all again.


Into this neutral air
Where blind skyscrapers use                   35
Their full height to proclaim
The strength of Collective Man,
Each language pours its vain
Competitive excuse:
But who can live for long                     40
In an euphoric dream;
Out of the mirror they stare,
Imperialism's face
And the international wrong.


Faces along the bar                           45
Cling to their average day:
The lights must never go out,
The music must always play,
All the conventions conspire
To make this fort assume                      50
The furniture of home;
Lest we should see where we are,
Lost in a haunted wood,
Children afraid of the night
Who have never been happy or good.            55


The windiest militant trash
Important Persons shout
Is not so crude as our wish:

23 *Thucydides* (fifth cent. B.C.) : the Greek historian, exiled because of
the failure of his expedition against the Spartan general, Brasidas.
24 *speech:* e.g., the speeches of Pericles reported by Thucydides.   41
*euphoric:* pleasant.

What mad Nijinsky wrote
About Diaghilev                                      60
Is true of the normal heart;
For the error bred in the bone
Of each woman and each man
Craves what it cannot have,
Not universal love                                  65
But to be loved alone.

From the conservative dark
Into the ethical life
The dense commuters come,
Repeating their morning vow;                         70
"I *will* be true to the wife,
I'll concentrate more on my work,"
And helpless governors wake
To resume their compulsory game:
Who can release them now,                            75
Who can reach the deaf,
Who can speak for the dumb?

Defenceless under the night
Our world in stupor lies;
Yet, dotted everywhere,                              80
Ironic points of light
Flash out wherever the Just
Exchange their messages:
May I, composed like them
Or Eros and of dust,                                 85
Beleaguered by the same
Negation and despair,
Show an affirming flame.


*Fish in the unruffled lakes*

Fish in the unruffled lakes
The swarming colours wear,
Swans in the winter air
A white perfection have,

59-60 *What . . . Diaghilev:* Precisely quoted, ll. 65-66 (*Diary*).
Vaslav Nijinsky (1890-1950) was the genius of the Russian ballet;
Sergei Diaghilev, its impresario, who wanted to dominate the dancer's
life. After Nijinsky's marriage their relations were finally broken.  85
*Eros:* Erotic love.

And the great lion walks                    5
Through his innocent grove;
Lion, fish, and swan
Act, and are gone
Upon Time's toppling wave.


We till shadowed days are done,             10
We must weep and sing
Duty's conscious wrong,
The Devil in the clock,
The Goodness carefully worn
For atonement or for luck;                   15
We must lose our loves,
On each beast and bird that moves
Turn an envious look.


Sighs for folly said and done
Twist our narrow days;                       20
But I must bless, I must praise
That you, my swan, who have
All gifts that to the swan
Impulsive Nature gave,
The majesty and pride,                       25
Last night should add
Your voluntary love.


*Lay your sleeping head, my love*

Lay your sleeping head, my love,
Human on my faithless arm;
Time and fevers burn away
Individual beauty from
Thoughtful children, and the grave           5
Proves the child ephemeral:
But in my arms till break of day
Let the living creature lie,
Mortal, guilty, but to me
The entirely beautiful.                       10


FISH IN THE UNRUFFLED LAKES. 13 *The . . . clock:* cf. l. 9.   17-18
*On . . . look:* cf. p. 514, ll. 1-5.

Soul and body have no bounds:
To lovers as they lie upon
Her tolerant enchanted slope
In their ordinary swoon,
Grave the vision Venus sends                        15
Of supernatural sympathy,
Universal love and hope;
While an abstract insight wakes
Among the glaciers and the rocks
The hermit's sensual ecstasy.                        20

Certainty, fidelity
On the stroke of midnight pass
Like vibrations of a bell,
And fashionable madmen raise
Their pedantic boring cry:                           25
Every farthing of the cost,
All the dreaded cards foretell,
Shall be paid, but from this night
Not a whisper, not a thought,
Not a kiss nor look be lost.                         30

Beauty, midnight, vision dies:
Let the winds of dawn that blow
Softly round your dreaming head
Such a day of sweetness show
Eye and knocking heart may bless,                    35
Find the mortal world enough;
Noons of dryness see you fed
By the involuntary powers,
Nights of insult let you pass
Watched by every human love.                         40

## Look, stranger, on this island now

Look, stranger, on this island now
The leaping light for your delight discovers,
Stand stable here
And silent be,
That through the channels of the ear                 5
May wander like a river
The swaying sound of the sea.

LAY YOUR SLEEPING HEAD. 13 *Her:* Venus's, love's.

Here at the small field's ending pause
When the chalk wall falls to the foam and its tall
   ledges
Oppose the pluck                                                      10
And knock of the tide,
And the shingle scrambles after the suck-
   ing surf,
And the gull lodges
A moment on its sheer side.

Far off like floating seeds the ships                                15
Diverge on urgent voluntary errands,
And the full view
Indeed may enter
And move in memory as now these clouds do,
That pass the harbour mirror                                         20
And all the summer through the water saunter.


## In Praise of Limestone

If it form the one landscape that we the inconstant ones
   Are consistently homesick for, this is chiefly
Because it dissolves in water. Mark these rounded slopes
   With their surface fragrance of thyme and beneath
A secret system of caves and conduits; hear these springs    5
   That spurt out everywhere with a chuckle
Each filling a private pool for its fish and carving
   Its own little ravine whose cliffs entertain
The butterfly and the lizard; examine this region
   Of short distances and definite places:                    10
What could be more like Mother or a fitter background
   For her son, for the nude young male who lounges
Against a rock displaying his dildo, never doubting
   That for all his faults he is loved, whose works are but
Extensions of his power to charm? From weathered outcrop
   To hill-top temple, from appearing waters to               16
Conspicuous fountains, from a wild to a formal vineyard,
   Are ingenious but short steps that a child's wish
To receive more attention than his brothers, whether
   By pleasing or teasing, can easily take.                   20

Look, stranger. 12 *shingle :* stones and gravel.
In Praise. *In Praise of Limestone :* cf. Wordsworth, pp. 252-56 ; pp.
267-70.

Watch, then, the band of rivals as they climb up and down
   Their steep stone gennels in twos and threes, sometimes
Arm in arm, but never, thank God, in step; or engaged
   On the shady side of a square at midday in
Voluble discourse, knowing each other too well to think   25
   There are any important secrets, unable
To conceive a god whose temper-tantrums are moral
   And not to be pacified by a clever line
Or a good lay: for, accustomed to a stone that responds,
   They have never had to veil their faces in awe   30
Of a crater whose blazing fury could not be fixed;
   Adjusted to the local needs of valleys
Where everything can be touched or reached by walking,
   Their eyes have never looked into infinite space
Through the lattice-work of a nomad's comb; born lucky, 35
   Their legs have never encountered the fungi
And insects of the jungle, the monstrous forms and lives
   With which we have nothing, we like to hope, in common.
So, when one of them goes to the bad, the way his mind works
   Remains comprehensible: to become a pimp   40
Or deal in fake jewelry or ruin a fine tenor voice
   For effects that bring down the house could happen to all
But the best and the worst of us . . .

                     That is why, I suppose,
   The best and worst never stayed here long but sought   45
Immoderate soils where the beauty was not so external,
   The light less public and the meaning of life
Something more than a mad camp. "Come!" cried the granite
     wastes,
   "How evasive is your humor, how accidental
Your kindest kiss, how permanent is death." (Saints-to-be   50
   Slipped away sighing.) "Come!" purred the clays and
     gravels.
"On our plains there is room for armies to drill; rivers
   Wait to be tamed and slaves to construct you a tomb
In the grand manner: soft as the earth is mankind and both
   Need to be altered." (Intendant Caesars rose and   55
Left, slamming the door.) But the really reckless were fetched
   By an older colder voice, the oceanic whisper:
"I am the solitude that asks and promises nothing;
   That is how I shall set you free. There is no love;
There are only the various envies, all of them sad."   60

    *22 gennels:* narrow passageways—among the rocks.   36-38 *fungi . . .
common:* cf. p. 514, ll. 4-5.   55 *Intendant:* Prospective. Cf. l. 50.

They were right, my dear, all those voices were right
And still are; this land is not the sweet home that it looks,
    Nor its peace the historical calm of a site
Where something was settled once and for all: A backward
    And delapidated province, connected                        65
To the big busy world by a tunnel, with a certain
    Seedy appeal, is that all it is now? Not quite:
It has a worldly duty which in spite of itself
    It does not neglect, but calls into question
All the Great Powers assume; it disturbs our rights. The poet,
    Admired for his earnest habit of calling                   71
The sun the sun, his mind Puzzle, is made uneasy
    By these solid statues which so obviously doubt
His antimythological myth; and these gamins,
    Pursuing the scientist down the tiled colonnade            75
With such lively offers, rebuke his concern for Nature's
    Remotest aspects: I, too, am reproached, for what
And how much you know. Not to lose time, not to get caught,
    Not to be left behind, not, please! to resemble
The beasts who repeat themselves, or a thing like water        80
    Or stone whose conduct can be predicted, these
Are our Common Prayer, whose greatest comfort is music
    Which can be made anywhere, is invisible,
And does not smell. In so far as we have to look forward
    To death as a fact, no doubt we are right: But if          85
Sins can be forgiven, if bodies rise from the dead,
    These modifications of matter into
Innocent athletes and gesticulating fountains,
    Made solely for pleasure, make a further point:
The blessed will not care what angle they are regarded from,
    Having nothing to hide. Dear, I know nothing of            91
Either, but when I try to imagine a faultless love
    Or the life to come, what I hear is the murmur
Of underground streams, what I see is a limestone landscape.


## In Schrafft's

    Having finished the Blue-plate Special
    And reached the coffee stage,
    Stirring her cup she sat,
    A somewhat shapeless figure
    Of indeterminate age                    5
    In an undistinguished hat.

74 *gamins*: cf. *band of rivals*, l. 21.   88 *fountains*: cf. l. 17.

When she lifted her eyes it was plain
That our globular furore,
Our international rout
Of sin and apparatus                                    10
And dying men galore,
Was not being bothered about.

Which of the seven heavens
Was responsible her smile
Wouldn't be sure but attested                           15
That, whoever it was, a god
Worth kneeling-to for a while
Had tabernacled and rested.


## A Walk after Dark

A cloudless night like this
Can set the spirit soaring;
After a tiring day
The clockwork spectacle is
Impressive in a slightly boring                         5
Eighteenth-century way.

It soothed adolescence a lot
To meet so shameless a stare;
The things I did could not
Be as shocking as they said                             10
If that would still be there
After the shocked were dead.

Now, unready to die
But already at the stage
When one starts to dislike the young,                   15
I am glad those points in the sky
May also be counted among
The creatures of middle-age.

IN SCHRAFFT'S. 8 *globular:* global.  10 *apparatus:* a group, or cell,
particularly within the Communist underground, organized to carry out
subversive activities.  18 *tabernacled:* taken up residence.

A WALK AFTER DARK. 4-6 *The clockwork . . . way:* Allusion to the
"proof" of the existence of God by analogy of the world to a watch,
which, it was argued, could not exist without a watchmaker.

It's cosier thinking of night
As more an Old People's Home                    20
Than a shed for a faultless machine,
That the red pre-Cambrian light
Is gone like Imperial Rome
Or myself at seventeen.

Yet however much we may like                     25
The stoic manner in which
The classical authors wrote,
Only the young and the rich
Have the nerve or the figure to strike
The lacrimae rerum note.                          30

For the present stalks abroad
Like the past and its wronged again
Whimper and are ignored,
And the truth cannot be hid;
Somebody chose their pain,                        35
What needn't have happened did.

Occurring this very night
By no established rule,
Some event may already have hurled
Its first little No at the right                  40
Of the laws we accept to school
Our post-diluvian world:

But the stars burn on overhead,
Unconscious of final ends,
As I walk home to bed,                            45
Asking what judgment waits
My person, all my friends,
And these United States.

---

22 *pre-Cambrian:* the earliest division of geological history.   30 *lacrimae rerum:* pathetic (tearful).   36 *What . . . did:* As Auden elsewhere defines "Christian tragedy."   42 *post-diluvian:* after the Flood.

# DYLAN THOMAS 1914–1953

## *The force that through the green fuse drives the flower*

The force that through the green fuse drives the flower
Drives my green age; that blasts the roots of trees
Is my destroyer.
And I am dumb to tell the crooked rose
My youth is bent by the same wintry fever.                    5

The force that drives the water through the rocks
Drives my red blood; that dries the mouthing streams
Turns mine to wax.
And I am dumb to mouth unto my veins
How at the mountain spring the same mouth sucks.              10

The hand that whirls the water in the pool
Stirs the quicksand; that ropes the blowing wind
Hauls my shroud sail.
And I am dumb to tell the hanging man
How of my clay is made the hangman's lime.                    15

The lips of time leech to the fountain head;
Love drips and gathers, but the fallen blood
Shall calm her sores.
And I am dumb to tell a weather's wind
How time has ticked a heaven round the stars.                20

And I am dumb to tell the lover's tomb
How at my sheet goes the same crooked worm.

---

THE FORCE THAT. 1 *fuse:* stem. 7 *mouthing:* gushing out at the
mouth. 12 *ropes . . . wind:* hauls a sail (?). 13 *shroud sail:* the
poet's *sail*—which *drives* him—is like the winding sheet of the dead.
Cf. *sheet,* l. 22; Eliot, "the time of death is every moment," p. 511, l.
161. 16 *leech to:* cling to and suck at.

### Especially when the October wind

Especially when the October wind
With frosty fingers punishes my hair,
Caught by the crabbing sun I walk on fire
And cast a shadow crab upon the land,
By the sea's side, hearing the noise of birds,          5
Hearing the raven cough in winter sticks,
My busy heart who shudders as she talks
Sheds the syllabic blood and drains her words.

Shut, too, in a tower of words, I mark
On the horizon walking like the trees          10
The wordy shapes of women, and the rows
Of the star-gestured children in the park.
Some let me make you of the vowelled beeches,
Some of the oaken voices, from the roots
Of many a thorny shire tell you notes,          15
Some let me make you of the water's speeches.

Behind a pot of ferns the wagging clock
Tells me the hour's word, the neural meaning
Flies on the shafted disk, declaims the morning
And tells the windy weather in the cock.          20
Some let me make you of the meadow's signs;
The signal grass that tells me all I know
Breaks with the wormy winter through the eye.
Some let me tell you of the raven's sins.

Especially when the October wind          25
(Some let me make you of autumnal spells,
The spider-tongued, and the loud hill of Wales)
With fists of turnips punishes the land,
Some let me make you of the heartless words.
The heart is drained that, spelling in the scurry          30
Of chemic blood, warned of the coming fury.
By the sea's side hear the dark-vowelled birds.

ESPECIALLY WHEN. 7 *she:* heart.   8 *Sheds . . . blood:* Pours out
passionate words, exhausting her store.   11 *wordy shapes:* shapes which
move him to words.   12 *star . . . children:* whose movements and
bright expression make them seem like stars.   13 *Some[thing]:* Some
verses.   *make:* compose. See "To John Donne," p. 97, l. 3 and note.   15
*tell:* name or sing.   18 *neural:* "felt on the pulse."   30 *spelling:* naming; cf. *make, tell* (ll. 13, 15).

## In the beginning

In the beginning was the three-pointed star,
One smile of light across the empty face;
One bough of bone across the rooting air,
The substance forked that marrowed the first sun;
And, burning ciphers on the round of space,     5
Heaven and hell mixed as they spun.

In the beginning was the pale signature,
Three-syllabled and starry as the smile;
And after came the imprints on the water,
Stamp of the minted face upon the moon;     10
The blood that touched the crosstree and the grail
Touched the first cloud and left a sign.

In the beginning was the mounting fire
That set alight the weathers from a spark,
A three-eyed, red-eyed spark, blunt as a flower;     15
Life rose and spouted from the rolling seas,
Burst in the roots, pumped from the earth and rock
The secret oils that drive the grass.

IN THE BEGINNING. 1 *three-* . . . *star:* the Divine Creator as a Three-Personed God, in whom are potentially the Light (l. *2*) and the Matter (ll. 3, 4) which achieve realization in the act of creation. 3 *One . . . bone:* The common stock (*bough*) or matter out of which all things are made. *rooting:* conducive to growth; *mis*applied to *air* to emphasize the pervasive operation of the creative force. 4 *substance forked:* as if creation were a process of division, or the splitting off of forms (e.g., *first sun*) from the one original substance. Cf. l. *27*. 5 *burning ciphers:* "lights in the firmament." Gen. 1:14. 6 *Heaven . . . mixed:* No distinction yet exists, as was made after the revolt of the angels; all is one. 7 *signature:* mark of the Creator upon His creation; first, the "pale" light only. 8 *Three-syllabled:* Like ELOHIM, perhaps, the plural name of God in Genesis, signifying His triune nature. Cf. *three-pointed,* l. 1 and note. 9 *after:* after the creation of light, when the firmament was made, the waters were "divided" and "gathered." See Gen. 1:6-8. *imprints:* reflections of the *light* upon the water, probably suggested by Christ's "walking" upon the water, Matt. 14:25-26. 10 *minted . . . moon:* probably a folk interpretation of the "man in the moon"; the *face* is *minted* from the moon's silver. 11 *blood:* of Christ. *crosstree:* the Cross. *grail:* see Frost, p. 494, l. 57 and note. 12 *Touched:* i.e., with the blood's color. 13 *fire:* "breath of life," animating all Nature. 15 *three-eyed:* signifying the trinitarian character. *red-eyed:* cf. pale, l. 7. *blunt:* cf. *pointed,* l. 1. *flower:* suggestive of beauty and growth in Nature, as distinct from the "light-producing" action of the *star.*

In the beginning was the word, the word
That from the solid bases of the light 20
Abstracted all the letters of the void;
And from the cloudy bases of the breath
The word flowed up, translating to the heart
First characters of birth and death.

In the beginning was the secret brain. 25
The brain was celled and soldered in the thought
Before the pitch was forking to a sun;
Before the veins were shaking in their sieve,
Blood shot and scattered to the winds of light
The ribbed original of love. 30

## Why east wind chills

Why east wind chills and south wind cools
Shall not be known till windwell dries
And west's no longer drowned
In winds that bring the fruit and rind
Of many a hundred falls; 5
Why silk is soft and the stone wounds
The child shall question all his days,
Why night-time rain and the breast's blood
Both quench his thirst he'll have a black reply.

When cometh Jack Frost? the children ask. 10
Shall they clasp a comet in their fists?
Not till, from high and low, their dust
Sprinkles in children's eyes a long-last sleep
And dusk is crowded with the children's ghosts,
Shall a white answer echo from the rooftops. 15

19 *the word:* God as the Creator of Man: "In him was life; and the life was the light of men."—John 1:4. See Eliot, p. 499, ll. 18-19 and note. 21 *Abstracted . . . letters:* Drew off the letters to make man in the image of the Word. 22-23 *breath . . . up:* see Gen. 2:6-7. 24 *characters:* letters, which spelled out the meaning of birth and death, i.e., of life. 25 *secret brain:* Divine Intelligence. 26 *brain . . . thought:* the Divine Intelligence was inextricably one with the Divine purpose. 27 *pitch:* original substance. Cf. l. 4. 29 *Blood:* God's blood, symbolic of Divine Love, inseparably from the Intelligence. 30 *ribbed . . . love:* love was a very part of God's body, as Adam's rib, given for Eve, was a very part of him.

WHY EAST WIND CHILLS. 2 *windwell:* probably a well from which the water is drawn by a wind-driven pump.

All things are known: the stars' advice
Calls some content to travel with the winds,
Though what the stars ask as they round
Time upon time the towers of the skies
Is heard but little till the stars go out.                    20
I hear content, and 'Be content'
Ring like a handbell through the corridors,
And 'Know no answer,' and I know
No answer to the children's cry
Of echo's answer and the man of frost           25
And ghostly comets over the raised fists.


## And death shall have no dominion

And death shall have no dominion.
Dead men naked they shall be one
With the man in the wind and the west moon;
When their bones are picked clean and the clean bones gone,
They shall have stars at elbow and foot;               5
Though they go mad they shall be sane,
Though they sink through the sea they shall rise again;
Though lovers be lost love shall not;
And death shall have no dominion.

And death shall have no dominion.                         10
Under the windings of the sea
They lying long shall not die windily;
Twisting on racks when sinews give way,
Strapped to a wheel, yet they shall not break;
Faith in their hands shall snap in two,                   15
And the unicorn evils run them through;
Split all ends up they shan't crack;
And death shall have no dominion.

And death shall have no dominion.
No more may gulls cry at their ears                       20
Or waves break loud on the seashores;
Where blew a flower may a flower no more
Lift its head to the blows of the rain;

AND DEATH SHALL HAVE. 16 *unicorn evils:* one-horned monsters.

Though they be mad and dead as nails,
Heads of the characters hammer through daisies;        25
Break in the sun till the sun breaks down,
And death shall have no dominion.


## When all my five and country senses see

When all my five and country senses see,
The fingers will forget green thumbs and mark
How, through the halfmoon's vegetable eye,
Husk of young stars and handfull zodiac,
Love in the frost is pared and wintered by,        5
The whispering ears will watch love drummed away
Down breeze and shell to a discordant beach,
And, lashed to syllables, the lynx tongue cry
That her fond wounds are mended bitterly.
My nostrils see her breath burn like a bush.        10


My one and noble heart has witnesses
In all love's countries, that will grope awake;
And when blind sleep drops on the spying senses,
The heart is sensual, though five eyes break.


## After the funeral

### IN MEMORY OF ANN JONES

After the funeral, mule praises, brays,
Windshake of sailshaped ears, muffle-toed tap
Tap happily of one peg in the thick
Grave's foot, blinds down the lids, the teeth in black,
The spittled eyes, the salt ponds in the sleeves,        5

25 *Heads . . . daisies:* The dead—represented as characters—will rise
(see l. 7) and drive through the daisies, like the "force" in p. 528,
ll. 1-2.

WHEN ALL MY FIVE. 7 *shell:* perhaps love reduced to a shell of itself.
12 *love's countries:* the senses, in which love lives as well as in the
heart.  14 *is sensual:* feels, passionately.  *eyes:* senses.  *break:* fail.

AFTER THE FUNERAL. 1 *mule praises, etc.:* the pretentious mourning
for Ann.  2-4 *muffle- . . . foot:* nailing shut the coffin (*grave's foot*).
4 *blinds . . . lids:* the nailing fastens the lids of the coffin.  4-5 *teeth
. . . sleeves:* the teeth are black, the watery eyes blinded are in the
"dark of the coffin" along with the tears (*salt ponds*) which Ann shed
and wiped away on her *sleeves* (i.e., Ann and all her sorrows).

534

Morning smack of the spade that wakes up sleep,
Shakes a desolate boy who slits his throat
In the dark of the coffin and sheds dry leaves,
That breaks one bone to light with a judgment clout,
After the feast of tear-stuffed time and thistles          10
In a room with a stuffed fox and a stale fern,
I stand, for this memorial's sake, alone
In the snivelling hours with dead, humped Ann
Whose hooded, fountain heart once fell in puddles          14
Round the parched worlds of Wales and drowned each sun
(Though this for her is a monstrous image blindly
Magnified out of praise; her death was a still drop;
She would not have me sinking in the holy
Flood of her heart's fame; she would lie dumb and deep
And need no druid of her broken body).                     20
But I, Ann's bard on a raised hearth, call all
The seas to service that her wood-tongued virtue
Babble like a bellbuoy over the hymning heads,
Bow down the walls of the ferned and foxy woods
That her love sing and swing through a brown chapel,       25
Bless her bent spirit with four, crossing birds.
Her flesh was meek as milk, but this skyward statue
With the wild breast and blessed and giant skull
Is carved from her in a room with a wet window
In a fiercely mourning house in a crooked year.            30
I know her scrubbed and sour humble hands
Lie with religion in their cramp, her threadbare
Whisper in a damp word, her wits drilled hollow,
Her fist of a face died clenched on a round pain;
And sculptured Ann is seventy years of stone.             35
These cloud-sopped, marble hands, this monumental
Argument of the hewn voice, gesture and psalm,
Storm me forever over her grave until
The stuffed lung of the fox twitch and cry Love
And the strutting fern lay seeds on the black sill.        40

7 *boy:* the poet.   8 *sheds . . . leaves:* he cannot weep.   9 *That:* The
spade. *one bone:* Ann. [in] *to . . . clout:* the stroke (*clout*) of the
spade is like the judgment which announces Ann's resurrection. Cf. p.
532, l. 8; p. 533, l. 25 and note.   14 *hooded:* concealed, humble; cf. *meek,*
l. 27; *humble,* l. 31.   20 *druid:* see Milton, p. 157, ll. 53-55 and note.   21
*But . . . all:* cf. this with invocations in Spenser, p. 47, ll. 55-;
Milton, p. 156, ll. 15-17; Pope, p. 214, ll. 7-12.   26 *crossing birds:* flying in the form of a cross.   27 *skyward statue:* this "elegy"; cf. *monumental / Argument of the hewn voice* (ll. 36-37).   39, 40 *stuffed . . .
fox, fern:* cf. l. 11.   40 *sill:* the sill of the grave.

## A Refusal to Mourn the Death, by Fire, of a Child in London

Never until the mankind making
Bird beast and flower
Fathering and all humbling darkness
Tells with silence the last light breaking
And the still hour                                             5
Is come of the sea tumbling in harness

And I must enter again the round
Zion of the water bead
And the synagogue of the ear of corn
Shall I let pray the shadow of a sound                         10
Or sow my salt seed
In the least valley of sackcloth to mourn

The majesty and burning of the child's death.
I shall not murder
The mankind of her going with a grave truth                   15
Nor blaspheme down the stations of the breath
With any further
Elegy of innocence and youth.

Deep with the first dead lies London's daughter,
Robed in the long friends,                                     20
The grains beyond age, the dark veins of her mother,
Secret by the unmourning water
Of the riding Thames.
After the first death, there is no other.

A REFUSAL TO MOURN. 4 *last light:* death, or the end of the world.
7-9 *enter . . . corn:* return to or be transmuted into the elements,
symbolized as a water drop, or an ear of corn, a state likened to the
Heavenly City (*Zion*) or some holy place (*synagogue*). 11 *salt seed:*
tears. 15 *mankind . . . going:* her death was representative of the
common fate of humanity. 16 *down . . . breath:* down the full scale
(of the voice), strike all the notes (of elegy). Cf. "the tender stops of
various Quills," p. 161, l. 188. 20 *long friends:* those long dead, her
friends in their common humanity. See l. 15.

## Poem in October

It was my thirtieth year to heaven
Woke to my hearing from harbour and neighbour wood
   And the mussel pooled and the heron
      Priested shore
        The morning beckon           5
With water praying and call of sea gull and rook
And the knock of sailing boats on the net webbed wall
     Myself to set foot
       That second
In the still sleeping town and set forth.          10

My birthday began with the water—
Birds and the birds of the winged trees flying my name
    Above the farms and the white horses
       And I rose
        In rainy autumn           15
And walked abroad in a shower of all my days.
High tide and the heron dived when I took the road
      Over the border
        And the gates
Of the town closed as the town awoke.        20

A springful of larks in a rolling
Cloud and the roadside bushes brimming with whistling
    Blackbirds and the sun of October
       Summery
        On the hill's shoulder,        25
Here were fond climates and sweet singers suddenly
Come in the morning where I wandered and listened
      To the rain wringing
        Wind blow cold
In the wood faraway under me.          30

Pale rain over the dwindling harbour
And over the sea wet church the size of a snail
    With its horns through mist and the castle
       Brown as owls
        But all the gardens        35

POEM IN OCTOBER. 6 *water :* of mythological significance, as the poet's name *Dylan* is the Welsh for *sea* and the name of a Welsh god of the waves.

Of spring and summer were blooming in the tall tales
Beyond the border and under the lark full cloud.
       There could I marvel
        My birthday
   Away but the weather turned around.          40


      It turned away from the blithe country
And down the other air and the blue altered sky
    Streamed again a wonder of summer
        With apples
       Pears and red currants         45
And I saw in the turning so clearly a child's
Forgotten mornings when he walked with his mother
    Through the parables
      Of sun light
  And the legends of the green chapels      50


    And the twice told fields of infancy
That his tears burned my cheeks and his heart moved in mine.
    These were the woods the river and sea
      Where a boy
      In the listening         55
Summertime of the dead whispered the truth of his joy
To the trees and the stones and the fish in the tide.
     And the mystery
      Sang alive
  Still in the water and singingbirds.      60


    And there could I marvel my birthday
Away but the weather turned around. And the true
    Joy of the long dead child sang burning
      In the sun.
      It was my thirtieth        65
Year to heaven stood there then in the summer noon
Though the town below lay leaved with October blood.
    O may my heart's truth
      Still be sung
  On this high hill in a year's turning.      70

---

41 ff. *It turned away, etc.:* cf. Wordsworth, pp. 261-66; Vaughan, pp. 184-85.

# Fern Hill

Now as I was young and easy under the apple boughs
About the lilting house and happy as the grass was green,
　　　The night above the dingle starry,
　　　　　Time let me hail and climb
　　　　Golden in the heydays of his eyes,　　　　　　5
And honoured among wagons I was prince of the apple towns
And once below a time I lordly had the trees and leaves
　　　　Trail with daisies and barley
　　　Down the rivers of the windfall light.


And as I was green and carefree, famous among the barns　10
About the happy yard and singing as the farm was home,
　　　　In the sun that is young once only,
　　　　　Time let me play and be
　　　　Golden in the mercy of his means,
And green and golden I was huntsman and herdsman, the
　　　calves　　　　　　　　　　　　　　　　　15
Sang to my horn, the foxes on the hills barked clear and cold,
　　　　　And the sabbath rang slowly
　　　In the pebbles of the holy streams.


All the sun long it was running, it was lovely, the hay
Fields high as the house, the tunes from the chimneys, it was
　　　air　　　　　　　　　　　　　　　　　　20
　　　　　And playing, lovely and watery
　　　　　　And fire green as grass.
　　　　And nightly under the simple stars
As I rode to sleep the owls were bearing the farm away,
All the moon long I heard, blessed among stables, the
　　　night-jars　　　　　　　　　　　　　　　25
　　　　　Flying with the ricks, and the horses
　　　　　　Flashing into the dark.


And then to awake, and the farm, like a wanderer white
With the dew, come back, the cock on his shoulder: it was all
　　　　　Shining, it was Adam and maiden,　　　30
　　　　　　The sky gathered again
　　　　And the sun grew round that very day.

FERN HILL. Cf. Wordsworth, pp. 252-256 ; Vaughan, pp. 184-185.
　3 *dingle :* small secluded valley. 　25 *night-jars :* night birds. 　26 *ricks :*
haystacks.

So it must have been after the birth of the simple light
In the first, spinning place, the spellbound horses walking
    warm
        Out of the whinnying green stable        35
          On to the fields of praise.

And honoured among foxes and pheasants by the gay house
Under the new made clouds and happy as the heart was long,
        In the sun born over and over,
          I ran my heedless ways,        40
        My wishes raced through the house high hay
And nothing I cared, at my sky blue trades, that time allows
In all his tuneful turning so few and such morning songs
        Before the children green and golden
          Follow him out of grace,        45

Nothing I cared, in the lamb white days, that time would
    take me
Up to the swallow thronged loft by the shadow of my hand,
        In the moon that is always rising,
        Nor that riding to sleep
          I should hear him fly with the high fields    50
And wake to the farm forever fled from the childless land.
Oh as I was young and easy in the mercy of his means,
        Time held me green and dying
        Though I sang in my chains like the sea.

# PRINCIPAL TEXT SOURCES

GEOFFREY CHAUCER  "Truth": This poem and "Gentilesse" are reprinted from *The Complete Works of Geoffrey Chaucer*, ed. F. N. Robinson, published by Houghton Mifflin Company, Boston (Student's Cambridge Edition).

*The Canterbury Tales:* The text is based on that of various editions. (See also To the Reader, pages xviii-xix.)

SIR THOMAS WYATT  The text of the first eight poems is adapted from the transcript of The Egerton Manuscript 2711 (British Museum) prepared by E. Flugel, *Anglia*, XVIII (1896), XIX (1897). The text of the last two, "Is it possible?" and "Forget not yet the tried intent" (in The Devonshire Manuscript—Additional MSS. 17492, British Museum) is based on that given in the *Collected Poems of Sir Thomas Wyatt* (ed. Kenneth Muir, London, 1949; Cambridge, Mass., Harvard University Press, 1950). Throughout, the editorial work of Mr. Muir as well as that of A. K. Foxwell (*The Poems of Sir Thomas Wiat*, London, 1913) has been taken into account.

SIR PHILIP SIDNEY  *Astrophel and Stella:* First published, London, 1591. The text of the selection given here is based on that published in 1598 with the *Arcadia* and other pieces.

"Leave me, O Love . . .": This and the three poems following are selected from *Certaine Sonets . . . Never before printed* included with the *Arcadia*, 1598.

*Arcadia: The Countesse of Pembrokes* [Sidney's sister's] *Arcadia*, a prose "romance," first published, London, 1590, and later, from another manuscript source. The Songs given here are from Book Three of the later version, as published in the third edition, 1598.

EDMUND SPENSER  *The Shepheardes Calender: Conteyning twelve AEclogues proportionable to the twelve monethes:* First published anonymously, London, 1579. The text of "November" reproduces that of the quarto of 1579, and much of the gloss of "E.K.," the original editor. The "Johns Hopkins Spenser," referred to as *Variorum*, is frequently consulted.

*The Faerie Queene: Disposed into twelve books, Fashioning XII. Morall vertues*, London, 1590. The text of the selection given here is based on that of the edition of 1596.

*Prothalamion: Or A Spousall Verse:* The text is that of the first edition, London, 1596.

WILLIAM SHAKESPEARE  *Sonnets:* From *Shake-Speares Sonnets. Never before Imprinted.* London, 1609.

"The Phoenix and Turtle": The text given here is essentially that of the first edition in *Diverse Poeticall Essaies on . . . The Turtle and Phoenix* included in *Loves Martyr: Or, Rosalins Complaint, Etc.*, London, 1601.

*Songs:* The text of the Songs is based on that of the Folio of 1623.

BEN JONSON  *Epigrams:* The text is that of the first edition, in *The Workes of Benjamin Jonson*, London, 1616.

"Song: To Celia": The text is based on that from *The Forest*, included with Epigrams in the *Workes*, 1616.

"Her Triumph": This selection from *A Celebration of Charis*, from *Underwoods*, is based on that first published in the "second volume" of the *Workes*, London, 1640.

*Songs:* As published in *The Workes of Benjamin Jonson*, London, 1616.

*To the Memory of My Beloved, the Author Mr. William Shakespeare: And What He Hath Left Us:* First published in the First Folio of Shakespeare's plays, 1623, from which the text is taken.

JOHN DONNE  With the exception of the first of the Holy Sonnets ("Thou hast made me . . .") and "Hymn to God My God, in My Sickness," first published 1635, all of the other poems appeared first in *Poems by J. D. With Elegies on the Authors Death*, London, 1633. The text here is based on all of the early printed editions.

ROBERT HERRICK  The text of the first eight poems is that given in *Hesperides, etc.*, London, 1648.
    "His Litany, to the Holy Spirit": The text of this and the poem following is that given in *His Noble Numbers, Etc.*, first published, London, 1647[8], in the same volume with *Hesperides*.

GEORGE HERBERT  The text of the selections given here is based on that of *The Temple . . . By Mr. George Herbert*, Cambridge, 1633.

JOHN MILTON  The text of "On Time," *L'Allegro* and *Il Penseroso*, and *Lycidas* is principally that in *Poems, &c.*, 1673 (2nd ed.).
    *Sonnets:* The dates as generally agreed upon are parenthetically noted at the end of each poem. The text given here of all but the two published in 1694 is based on that in the edition of 1673. The text of the "1694 sonnets" is that found in the Cambridge Manuscript (*Facsimile of the Manuscript, etc.*, ed. William Aldis Wright, Cambridge, 1899).
    *Paradise Lost:* First published, London, 1667. The text of the selections given here is principally that of the second edition, 1674.

ANDREW MARVELL  The text is based on *Miscellaneous Poems. By Andrew Marvell, Esq. etc.*, London, 1681.

HENRY VAUGHAN  All selections except "The Revival" are from *Silex Scintillans: Or, Sacred Poems and Private Ejaculations:* the first three from the first edition, London, 1650; the others from the second edition, 1655.
    "The Revival": From *Thalia Rediviva*, where first published, London, 1678.

JOHN DRYDEN  *Mac Flecknoe* (first published 1682): The text given here and that of "The Tears of Amynta" is from *Miscellany Poems*, London, 1684.
    "A Song for St. Cecilia's Day, 1687," "Song to a Fair, Young Lady . . . ," "Rondelay": The text is found in *Examen Poeticum* (*The Third Part of Miscellany Poems*), London, 1693.
    "The Secular Masque": The source of the text given here is *The Pilgrim*, London, 1700.
    *Songs:* In order, respectively, from *The Indian Emperor* (1667), *Secret Love* (1668), *Tyrannick Love* (1670), *An Evening's Love* (1671), *The Conquest of Granada, I* (1672).

ALEXANDER POPE  *The Rape of the Lock:* The text is based on that in William Warburton's edition of the *Works*, 1751.
    *Of Taste:* In the half-title only; *An Epistle to the Earl of Burlington. Occasion'd by his Publishing Palladio's Designs of the Baths, Arches, Theatres, &c. of Ancient Rome* (London, 1731). The text (ll. 99-168) is essentially that of the first edition.
    *Of . . . Riches: An Epistle to the Right Honorable Allen Lord Bathurst* (London, 1732). The text (ll. 338-402) is that of the first edition incorporating important changes which Pope made later.
    *An Essay, etc.: To H. St. John, Lord Bolingbroke,* in four "epistles," which were published separately between February 20, 1733 and January 24, 1734; and, together, in 1734. The text of the selection (Epistle II, ll. 1-30) is from Warburton's edition of the *Works*, 1751.
    *An Epistle to Dr. Arbuthnot:* The text of the selections (ll. 193-214, 305-33) is that of the first edition, incorporating important revisions made for the later editions of 1735, 1739, and 1751.

WILLIAM BLAKE   The text of "How sweet I roam'd from field to field" is from *Poetical Sketches,* London, 1783. The text of poems from *Songs of Innocence* (1789) and from *Songs of Experience* (1794) is based on the original editions.

WILLIAM WORDSWORTH   The text used for all the selections except those from *The Prelude* is that in *The Poetical Works,* London, 1849-50. A New Edition.
   *The Prelude:* Written 1799-1805, and after much revision published 1850, some parts having already appeared as independent poems. The text is that of the first edition, 1850.

SAMUEL TAYLOR COLERIDGE   *The Rime of the Ancient Mariner:* First published in *Lyrical Ballads,* 1798; later revised (1800); and the marginal gloss added (1817). The text given here of both this poem and "Dejection: An Ode" is that in Coleridge's own copy of *The Poetical Works,* London, 1834.

LORD BYRON (George Noel Gordon)   The text of all selections given here is based on that in *The Works of Lord Byron: With His Letters and Journals, and His Life.* By Thomas Moore, Esq. London (John Murray), 1832.
   *Childe Harold's Pilgrimage:* The first two cantos were published in 1812. Cantos III, IV, from which the selections given here are drawn, were published, respectively, 1816 and 1818.
   *Don Juan:* The first two cantos were published anonymously July 15, 1819, and without indication of the publisher; the remaining fourteen, during the next five years.

PERCY BYSSHE SHELLEY   The text of all the selections except *Adonais* is based upon the *Poetical Works,* ed. Mrs. Shelley, London, 1839.
   *Adonais:* The text is that of the Pisa edition, 1821. Some later readings are admitted.

JOHN KEATS   *Sonnets:* The text of the first two sonnets is that of *Poems* (1817); of the others, that of the *Remains* as given in *The Poetical Works,* ed. H. W. Garrod (Oxford, 1939).
   *Odes:* The text of selections given here is from *Lamia, etc.,* 1820.

ALFRED, LORD TENNYSON   "Mariana," "The Lotos-Eaters," "Ulysses": The text for these poems is based on that in *Poems,* London, 1853. The eighth edition.
   *The Princess: A Medley:* The text of the selections here is based on the fourth edition, 1851.
   *In Memoriam:* First published, 1850. The text is based on the fourth edition, 1851.

ROBERT BROWNING   The basic text is that of *The Poetical Works,* London, 1870.

MATTHEW ARNOLD   "To Marguerite": The text of this poem as well as of "Philomela" is based on the 1853 edition.
   "The Scholar Gipsy": The text given here is substantially that of the first edition, *Poems,* 1853.
   "Dover Beach": The text is from *New Poems,* London, 1867.

WALT WHITMAN   The text of all the selections is principally that of the *Complete Poems & Prose of Walt Whitman, 1855 . . . 1888. Authenticated & Personal Book (handled by W. W.).*

EMILY DICKINSON   All but the last three titles are reprinted from *Poems by Emily Dickinson,* edited by Martha Dickinson Bianchi and Alfred Leete

Hampson. First published February, 1937; copyright, 1938, by Little, Brown and Company.

"Tell all the truth but tell it slant" and the two poems following are from *Bolts of Melody, New Poems of Emily Dickinson,* edited by Mabel Loomis Todd and Millicent Todd Bingham, and published by Harper and Brothers. Copyright, 1945.

GERARD MANLEY HOPKINS   The text of all the selections is from the Third Edition of *Poems of Gerard Manley Hopkins. The First Edition with Preface and Notes by Robert Bridges Enlarged and Edited with Notes and a Biographical Introduction by W. H. Gardener.* Published by Oxford University Press, London. Copyright, 1948.

THOMAS HARDY   The poems here are reprinted from *Collected Poems* by Thomas Hardy, published by The Macmillan Company, New York, and The Macmillan Company of Canada, Ltd. Copyright, 1926.

A. E. HOUSMAN   All poems but "Oh is it the jar of nations" are reprinted from *The Collected Poems of A. E. Housman,* published by Henry Holt and Company, Inc., copyright 1922, 1940 by Henry Holt and Company; 1936, 1950 by Barclays Bank, Ltd.

"Oh is it the jar of nations" is reprinted from *My Brother, A. E. Housman,* by Laurence Housman. Copyright 1937, 1938. Published by Charles Scribner's Sons. Both books are published in England by Jonathan Cape, Ltd.

EDWIN ARLINGTON ROBINSON   "Charles Carville's Eyes," "Reuben Bright," "The Torrent" reprinted from *The Children of the Night* (1890-1897) by Edwin Arlington Robinson. Published by Charles Scribner's Sons.

"Uncle Ananias," "Leonora," "Miniver Cheevy," reprinted from *The Town Down the River* by Edwin Arlington Robinson, published by Charles Scribner's Sons. Copyright, 1910, by Scribner; 1938 by Ruth Nivison.

"Cassandra," "The Mill," "Mr. Flood's Party," "Vain Gratuities," "The Sheaves," "As It Looked Then" reprinted from *Collected Poems* by Edwin Arlington Robinson, copyright, 1929, by The Macmillan Company.

WILLIAM BUTLER YEATS   The selections here are reprinted from *Collected Poems* by W. B. Yeats, copyright, 1951. Published by The Macmillan Company and The Macmillan Company of Canada, Ltd.

ROBERT FROST   The poems are reprinted from *Complete Poems of Robert Frost,* published by Henry Holt and Company, Inc. Copyright 1930, 1947, 1949, by Henry Holt; 1936, 1942 by Robert Frost.

T. S. ELIOT   The first five poems are reprinted from T. S. Eliot, *Collected Poems 1909-1935,* copyright 1936.

"The Dry Salvages" is from *Four Quartets,* copyright 1943 by T. S. Eliot. Both books are published by Harcourt, Brace and Company, Inc., and in England, by Faber and Faber, Ltd.

W. H. AUDEN   "Musée des Beaux Arts," "In Memory of W. B. Yeats," "September 1, 1939," "Lay your sleeping head, my love," are reprinted from *Another Time,* copyright 1940 by Auden. "The Cultural Presupposition," "Fish in the unruffled lakes," "Look, stranger on this island now" are from *The Collected Poetry of W. H. Auden,* copyright, 1945, by W. H. Auden. "In Praise of Limestone," "In Schrafft's," "A Walk after Dark" are from *Nones.* All are published by Random House, Inc.; in England, Faber and Faber, Ltd., publish *Collected Shorter Poems* and *Nones.*

DYLAN THOMAS   These poems are reprinted from *The Collected Poems of Dylan Thomas,* copyright, 1952, 1953, by Dylan Thomas; published by New Directions.

# Index of Authors, Titles, and First Lines *

* Where title and first line are identical, only the first line (marked *) is given. Titles beginning with *A, An,* or *The* are listed according to the word which the article modifies.

546

547

# In the Shelter of His Wings

## Resting in God's Tender Care

PAINTINGS BY *Carolyn Shores Wright*